THE MUGHALS AND THE SUFIS

MUZAFFAR ALAM

The Mughals and the Sufis

Islam and Political Imagination
in India, 1500–1750

The Mughals and the Sufis: Islam and Political Imagination in India 1500–1750 by Muzaffar Alam was first published by Permanent Black D-28 Oxford Apts, 11 IP Extension, Delhi 110092 INDIA, for the territory of SOUTH ASIA. First SUNY Press edition 2021.

Not for sale in South Asia

Cover design by Anuradha Roy.

Published by State University of New York Press, Albany

© 2021 Muzaffar Alam

All rights reserved

Printed in the United States of America

No part of this book may be used or reproduced in any manner whatsoever without written permission. No part of this book may be stored in a retrieval system or transmitted in any form or by any means including electronic, electrostatic, magnetic tape, mechanical, photocopying, recording, or otherwise without the prior permission in writing of the publisher.

For information, contact State University of New York Press, Albany, NY www.sunypress.edu

Library of Congress Cataloging-in-Publication Data

Names: Alam, Muzaffar, 1947- author.
Title: The Mughals and the Sufis : Islam and political imagination in India, 1500-1750 / Muzaffar Alam.
Description: First SUNY Press edition. | Albany : State University of New York Press, 2021. | "First published by Permanent Black D-28." | Includes bibliographical references and index.
Identifiers: LCCN 2021006831 | ISBN 9781438484891 (hardcover) | ISBN 9781438484907 (ebook) | ISBN 9781438484884 (paperback)
Subjects: LCSH: Sufism--India--History. | Islam and politics--India. | Islam and state--India. | Mogul Empire--Religion. | Mogul Empire--Politics and government. | India--Politics and government--997-1765.
Classification: LCC BP188.8.I4 A76 2021 | DDC 297.4--dc23
LC record available at https://lccn.loc.gov/2021006831

10 9 8 7 6 5 4 3 2 1

for
RIZWANA
and
our family and friends

Contents

	Preface and Acknowledgements	ix
1	Introduction: A Long View of Sufism and Political Culture in India	1
2	The Mughals, the Sufi Shaikhs, and the Formation of the Akbari Dispensation	48
3	A Sufi Critique of Religious Law, *Tasawwuf*, and Politics in Mughal India	94
4	Shah Madar, Sufi Religion, and a View of "True Islam" in a Mughal Chishti *Tazkira*	128
5	Strategy and Imagination in a Mughal Sufi Story of Creation	164
6	In Search of a Sacred King: Dara Shukoh and the *Yogavasisthas* of Mughal India	217
7	Piety, Poetry, and the Contested Loyalties of Mughal Princesses, *c.* 1635–1700	259
8	The Naqshbandi Shaikhs of Sirhind in Aurangzeb's Empire and Its Aftermath	331
	Conclusion	389
	Bibliography	397
	Index	431

Preface and Acknowledgements

LIKE IMPERIAL dispensations in many places and times, Mughal India involved a complex nexus between political elites and religious divines. They had mutual sympathies as well as differences – sometimes apparently irreconcilable – regarding the management of politics and the social order. In this book I have tried to show the trajectory of these differences, historical and political, as well as the efforts on each side to accommodate and adjust with the other.

Amongst both political and religious elites, there were varieties of voices and positions. If one group of religious leaders made a plea to implement the injunctions of the *shari'a* – with little consideration for prevailing social realities – there was also a powerful counter-impulse to maintain local tradition and be amenable to the demands of a different time. In the process of contestation and negotiation, then, there was a regular effort to invoke past practices and ideologies. The chapters of this book examine the fine grain of these efforts and debates.

In preparing this volume I have received help from many friends and colleagues. Sanjay Subrahmanyam, with whom I have had the privilege of publishing many things over the past quarter-century and more, made sure I include here not simply my finished research but also complete versions of several scattered and half-done reflections. These I have rethought, completed, and fused with my overarching theme in order that the book be read and understood as a single entity with a unifying thread and purpose. Over the course of revision, refinement, and unification Sanjay offered valuable suggestions for which I am most grateful.

I recall with affection and a deep sense of gratitude many extended discussions with my friend the late Simon Digby around questions relating to the part played by Sufis in politics, and their support and opposition to various medieval and early-modern Indian rulers. Having earlier learnt much about this significant aspect of Sufi life in matters mundane from my teachers in Aligarh, the late Professors S. Nurul Hasan and K.A. Nizami, I found Simon Digby's unconventional views rather stimulating and thought-provoking. As this book went to press, the distressing news came from Delhi of the sudden passing away of Sunil Kumar in January 2021. Sunil was a warm and generous friend of long standing, as well as a close colleague with whom I enjoyed discussing different aspects of medieval Indian and Islamic history. His own work not only dealt with the political history of the Sultanate, but with questions of Sufism in the pre-Mughal period, where he provided us with many subtle and important insights.

I have also benefited from several conversations with Francis Robinson, in particular during the year 2018–19 when he was in Chicago as a visiting professor of South Asian Islam.

I am grateful to my friend Ishtiaq Ahmad Zilli for his constant encouragement and help with some important references available, in particular, in old issues of *Ma'arif*, the prestigious Urdu journal of the Shibli Academy (in Azamgarh) which he edits. I appreciate his generous help, and recall his friendship and unfailing courtesy going back to our days as young students of Mughal history in Aligarh.

I have benefited from conversations with Dipesh Chakrabarty, Whitney Cox, Thibaut d'Hubert, Rochona Majumdar, and C.M. Naim at the University of Chicago's School of South Asian Languages and Civilizations (SALC), and with Cornell Fleischer, Frank Lewis, Tahera Qutbuddin, and John Woods at its school of Near Eastern Languages and Civilizations (NELC).

I would also like to thank Manan Ahmed, Sajjad Alam, Seema Alavi, Shahid Amin, Razi Aquil, Gautam Bhadra, Rajeev Bhargava, Neeladri Bhattacharya, Evrim Binbaş, Kunal and Shubhra

Chakrabarti, Stephen Dale, Jennifer Dubrow, Richard Eaton, Carl Ernst, Munis Faruqi, Shamsur Rahman Faruqi, Roy Fischel, Michael Fisher, Yohanan Friedmann, Rajarshi Ghose, Rebecca Gould, Abhishek Kaicker, Sudipta Kaviraj, Scott Kugle, Bruce Lawrence, Anubhuti Maurya, Harbans Mukhia, Polly O'Hanlon, Francesca Orsini, Parimal Patil, Margrit Pernau, Velcheru Narayana Rao, Kumkum Roy, Maryam Sabbaghi, Ziauddin Shakeb, Sunil Sharma, Samira Sheikh, Chander Shekhar, David Shulman, Romila Thapar, my late friend Kirti Trivedi, Madhu Trivedi, and Neha Virmani for their support and encouragement, for providing references, books, and copies of manuscripts relevant to my research, and several other forms of assistance.

My greatest debt is to my young friends, my past and present students, amongst whom are Ananya Chakravarti, Andrew Halladay, Sonam Kachru, Shariq Khan, Rajeev Kinra, Hajnalka Kovacs, Jane Mikkelson, Daniel Morgan, Sanjukta Poddar, and Hasan Siddiqui. All my past students now hold teaching or postdoctoral positions in various universities. They have all assisted me over the years in writing the chapters of this book. Shariq Khan was always available, facilitating access to books online, in particular in the chaotic circumstances of covid-19, when I missed Chicago's fabulous library collections and its helpful library staff. I benefited from the questions, sometimes really difficult ones, that some of my undergraduate students often asked about Sufi responses to the demands of early-modern and modern times.

I am also grateful to Khwaja Piri, Director of the Noor Microfilm Centre; the Iran Cultural House, New Delhi; the staff of the Khuda Bakhsh Oriental Library, Patna; the Asiatic Society Library and National Library, Kolkata; the Maulana Azad Library; the Department of History Seminar Library; the Nawwab Muzzammilullah Collection, Aligarh; the British Library, the Royal Asiatic Library, and the SOAS Library, London; the Bodleian Library, Oxford; the Bibliothèque nationale de France, Paris; and the Staatsbibliothek zu Berlin – for their help in providing me access to their valuable collections of manuscripts and rare books.

I have no words adequate for my gratitude to Rukun Advani for our conversations and email exchanges while he was editing this book. He is an old and great friend, he has been for me much more than my publisher.

My family – Rizwana, Adnan and Sahba, and Asiya – have been a source of sustenance all these years. My grandson Omar is a source of delight and joy over the months that we annually live together. I have no words adequate for the expression of my debt to them.

In transliterating Perso-Arabic words I have generally followed the system adopted by F. Steingass in his *Comprehensive Persian–English Dictionary*. But I have retained only two diacritical marks, the raised comma for *hamza* and the inverted comma for *'ain*. In transliterating word combinations, too, I have preferred to put a hyphen (-) between the first word and the letter 'i', indicating its combination with the second word, while in Arabic combinations the Arabic definite article has been consistently written as 'al'. I have thus written *sulh-i kull* and Nizam al-Din, while Steingass would have had them as *sulhi kull* and Nizamu'd din.

Earlier versions of some of these chapters were published as follows:

"The Mughals, the Sufi Shaikhs, and the Formation of the Akbari Dispensation", *Modern Asian Studies*, Vol. 43, No. 1, 2009, pp. 135–74.

"The Debate Within: A Sufi Critique of Religious Law, *Tasawwuf* and Politics in Mughal India", *South Asian History and Culture*, Vol. 2, No. 2, 2011, pp. 138–59.

"Strategy and Imagination in a Mughal Sufi Story of Creation", *Indian Economic and Social History Review*, Vol. 49, No. 2, 2012, pp. 151–95.

"In Search of a Sacred King: Dara Shukoh and the *Yogavasisthas* of Mughal India", *History of Religions*, Vol. 55, No. 4, 2016, pp. 429–9.

A shorter version of one of these chapters, entitled "Shah Madar, Sufi Religion, and a View of True Islam in a Mughal Chishti *Tazkira*" will appear in Francesca Orsini, ed., *Objects, Images, Stories: Simon Digby's Historical Method*, Delhi: Oxford University Press.

1

Introduction
A Long View of Sufism and Political Culture in India

During its three centuries of rule over India, the Mughal dynasty encountered a series of challenges and successfully overcame a number of them. These included armed resistance from several ethnic groups, such as Rajputs, Afghans, Marathas, etc. There was also periodic dissatisfaction, sometimes expressed even as open rebellion, by the same military and political elites – the so-called "Turanis" – that had accompanied the founding families from Central Asia into northern India. The chief challenge that the Mughals faced was similar to that which confronted a number of other empires of the time from China to Europe: how to manage a diverse and varied subject population spread out across a vast territory.[1] Compounding the difficulty was the fact that the bulk of their subjects did not share the same religion as the Mughals, i.e. they were non-Muslims. Preceding Muslim dynasties had encountered this challenge too. With the establishment of the Delhi Sultanate had come a demand from the *'ulama* for non-Muslims to be given the option of either accepting Islam or facing extermination. The sultan of his day had resolved this question by suggesting that since Muslims did not have the required strength and resources – the Muslim state

---

[1] Faroqhi, *The Ottoman and Mughal Empires*, pp. 107–37.

having just been founded – it was difficult to implement such a drastic injunction. The ruler was supported in his stance by the powerful – and indeed virtually uncontested – Sufis of the time.[2]

The Mughals, however, had to deal with a more complex situation, having to walk a tightrope to placate, accommodate, and negotiate with divergent interest groups and ideologies. Unlike the "self-made" sultan of the thirteenth century, who came from an obscure and humble background, the Mughals had their own significant cultural and religious heritage to contend with. They were the direct descendants of Timur, a highly significant figure in the cultural and political history of Sunni Muslim dynasties. Their ancestors in Central Asia had also had their own religious masters, who were virtually royal *pirs*. With the Mughals, the rule established had not merely been familial and dynastic but included the rule of their spiritual masters. So the traditions that Indo-Muslim rulers had relied on before the Mughals were not uncontested any more; as a matter of fact this had grown into a contest that persisted throughout the Mughal period.

My book, *The Languages of Political Islam* (2004), had focused on this problem, but I have since been impelled to look at this large issue of Mughal governance in related other directions and with greater attention. The shape this interest has taken over the past years has meant several short studies on Mughal politics and Muslim religious thought – in particular Sufism. Some – but not all – of that research having been published, this book now brings together my existing reflections on the subject as a coherent set of chapters.

I should also clarify that these chapters are interconnected in terms of the questions and issues raised, though the individual actors dealt with vary; and that in ordering them I have kept chronology and logical sequence in mind to the extent desirable. The central and overarching questions I have posed are these:

---

[2] This is at the broadest level my argument in an earlier work: see Alam, *The Languages of Political Islam in India*.

What was the position of the various Sufi orders in the context of Mughal politics? Did their discourses contain arguments and discussions, explicit or implicit, that had been conceived to resolve the political and social issues of the time? Were such writings hortatory and persuasive in intent? Did these writings convey guidance to followers in an effort to reach accommodative or palliative or conciliatory or non-combative positions in the prevalent circumstances of the applicability of Islamic laws and tenets on non-Muslim subject populations?

There is no dearth of literature on Mughal Indian Sufism. But the perspective from which I have tried to see the connection between prevailing politics and Sufism is not at the heart of this literature. I would argue that my attempt here is to read some important Mughal Indian Sufi texts in a fresh light, which is to say in terms of the relationship of Sufism and the Sufi orders with the Mughal political order, as well as the interrelationships among Sufi orders – particularly the Naqshbandis and the Chishtis, and to a lesser extent the Qadiris. Viewed from this perspective of Mughal history, it will become apparent that the texts I examine have not received the attention they deserve in relation to the complexity of the Mughal political order. Moreover, from the perspective of religious studies the interrelationship of the various Sufi orders – whether that relationship was one of appreciation and give-and-take or rivalry and hostility – has not been thoroughly analysed.[3] Therefore I believe a significant advantage of the approach adopted here is that it brings to light new and crucially important dimensions of previously known historical actors from Mughal India, dimensions that have been occluded from

---

[3] See, for instance, on the Naqshbandi Sufis, Rizvi, *A History of Sufism in India*, 2 vols; Nizami, "Naqshbandi Influence on Mughal Rulers", pp. 41–52; Friedmann, *Shaykh Ahmad Sirhindi*; Rahman, *Islam*; and ter Haar, *Follower and Heir of the Prophet*. For the Chishtis, see Ernst and Lawrence, *Sufi Martyrs of Love*; Nizami, *Tarikh-i Masha'ikh-i Chisht*. Important recent reconsiderations include Amin, *Conquest and Community*; Moin, "The Millennial and Saintly Sovereignty of Emperor Shahjahan", pp. 205–17.

the vantage points both of religious studies and Mughal political history.[4]

In the Introduction, my purpose is also more extensive. As someone who has had a long teaching career in both India and abroad – where many of my students have been of South Asian origin – it has become clear to me that very few people now approach the Mughals and their history directly. By this I mean that their readings are often informed by a set of perceptions that have been handed down from the post-Mughal period, including by some major political and intellectual figures of nineteenth- and twentieth-century South Asia. These later figures had their own agendas and were responding to the politics of their own time, which had in turn been shaped by colonialism, anti-colonialism, pan-Islamism, and other ideologies and movements that for the most part did not exist before 1750. Therefore, I have thought it useful to provide a *longue durée* view of writings on Sufism and politics, going well beyond the Mughal period, because of the profound impact some of these later writings continue to have on both historians and the general public today.

Tasawwuf in Mughal Society

In Mughal India of the seventeenth century, *tasawwuf* – or what is usually termed Sufism – had a pre-eminent position with all its manifestations: doctrinally, *wahdat al-wujud* (Unity of Being) and *wahdat al-shuhud* (Unity of Perception); in practice, the ties between *pir* and *murid* (master and disciple), as well as visits to shrines, audition parties (*sama'*), etc. In the time of Shah Jahan

[4] For instance, when Mughal emperors and nobles met with Sufis, it is interesting to examine the questions they sought clarifications on. For instance, the *wazir* Sa'd-Allah Khan was chosen to serve as a *hakim* (judge) by both the advocates and the opponents of the practice of *sama'*; Shah Jahan met Sufis and asked them for their help in understanding matters of beliefs and religious practices, such as the question of the differences between 'Ali and Mu'awiya. Earlier, Jahangir also met a Chishti Sufi and expressed his inability to give up drinking and be regular in his daily prayers.

(r. 1628–58) this finds fitting expression in the words of his daughter, Princess Jahanara, in the preface to her text *Munis al-Arwah*, examined in some detail later in this volume. It is her view there that every Muslim needs to be associated with one or the other of the Sufi orders. She writes that stability and strength in the human world are due to the felicitous presence of and blessings from the dust of the feet of saints:

> All blessings descend from the sky to the earth by virtue of the blessed souls of this majestic group. Fortunate is the one who associates with them with sincerity and devotion, and thereby secures the full share of their blessings and absolute benefit. It is the source of the Muslim's salvation, and elevates his status in the life hereafter. Almighty God made association and devotion with this noble group a means and source of salvation for believers, protecting them from the fire-pits of Hell and elevating them to high places in Paradise. The master–disciple practice (*piri–muridi*) is an essential part of pious Islamic life and a manifestation of absolute benefit for believers. It is manifested solely from God's perfect and eternal grace. The fates and fortunes of believers are interwoven with the path (*tariqa*) of *piri–muridi* and principles (*qa'ida*) of *silsila*. Thus, all Muslims, men and women, are integrated or organised into groups of one or the other Sufi order.

Thereafter she adds that "on the day when all will be fearful and terrified for their own selves, rows of disciples will rise under the banners of their masters (*safha-i muridan dar saya-i 'alam-i piran-i khud khwahand istad*). And on account of the blessings of these masters, they will remain safe from that day's terror."[5] In this conception of the world and the afterlife, therefore, the very fabric of social life is held together by Sufis and their networks.

At the same time, we need to be careful when characterising the nature and consequences of competition between different groups of Sufis. Jahanara had connections with both the Chishti

---

[5] Jahanara, *Munis al-Arwah*, Preface. All translations from non-English sources are mine, unless otherwise specified by the source citation in the bibliography.

and the Qadiri orders, but the Naqshbandis too flourished during this period. Subsequently, during Aurangzeb's reign, because of the emperor's close relationship with the Naqshbandi–Mujaddidis, they came to be especially prominent in later-seventeenth- and early-eighteenth-century Delhi. Thereafter, in the eighteenth century, we see the growing importance of figures such as Shaikh Muhammad Zubair, the fourth Naqshbandi *qaiyum*, as well as Mirza Mazhar Jan-i Janan, Khwaja Muhammad Nasir 'Andalib and his son Mir Dard, and finally Shaikh Ghulam 'Ali (d. 1824). But this did not imply that other *silsilas* – the Chishtis in particular – had faded away. Indeed, under the leadership of Shah Kalim-Allah Shahjahanabadi, Shaikh Fakhr al-Din Dehlavi, and his succesors the Chishtis regained popularity amongst the Delhi elites, including the royal court, after a relative eclipse in their fortune when the Mujaddidis were gaining ascendancy, especially via their presence at the royal court.[6]

During the sixteenth and seventeenth centuries there seems therefore to have been a kind of spiritual competitiveness and rivalry among the Sufis, in particular between the Chishtis and the Naqshbandis. At the time the Mughals established their power in India, the Chishtis still enjoyed a supreme position in the country, with even the dethroned sultan and nobles from whom the Mughals wrested power having been associated with the Chishti order. With the Naqshbandi shaikhs, who also began to settle in north India, there seem to have emerged conditions for debate and dispute regarding the spiritual authority of various figures. It was a situation of competitive spirituality in which the master of one or the other order could be projected as imperfect and lacking in accomplishment, or even as having strayed from the path of true Islam. There is evidence of this, of which some examples are notable. One such example took shape as the report that in Lahore a Chishti saint, Saiyid Ilah Bakhsh, was known

---

[6] Nizami, *Tarikh-e Masha'ikh-i Chisht*, Vol. 5, pp. 222–49; Sahir, *Mihrab-e Tahqiq*, pp.77–91.

to be God-seeing (*khuda-bin*) and God-showing (*khuda-numa*). When Shaikh Adam Binori (d. 1643), a prominent disciple of Shaikh Ahmad Sirhindi, heard of this, he sent a message to Saiyid Ilah Bakhsh through one of his servitors: "I have heard that people call you *khuda-bin-o-khuda-numa*. Do you endorse it? If you do, then you must repent from this condemnable belief (*'aqida-i bad*), for any person who believes he can see God in this world is a heretic (*mulhid-o-zindiq*)." The report adds that when the servitor delivered his letter the Chishti shaikh graced him with the same bliss by showing him God. As a result the bearer of the letter, being intoxicated with the experience, vowed upon recovering consciousness to stay with the shaikh and not return to Binori, his erstwhile master. Yet Shaikh Ilah Bakhsh told him to go and report his experience to Binori. Thereupon, Adam Binori too desired to be similarly blessed, but there was an intractable problem: Ilah Bakhsh wanted Binori to first become his disciple, which of course Binori could not possibly accept, being himself an eminent shaikh of his own order.[7] In other words, amongst the Sufis were some practices and beliefs not approved of by others, to the extent that these practices could be projected as heresy. As a result, we encounter radically opposed portrayals of the same individual – as with Akbar and Dara Shukoh – in two sets of Sufi texts. Such differences, it can be presumed, would have had implications for the laity seeking association with one or the other Sufi. Doubts proliferated on the best way of attaining not just exemplary piety and virtue but even one's basic Muslim identity.

It is therefore important to historically contextualise incidents suggesting conflict and rivalry between the Chishtis and the Naqshbandis. Most such instances of competitive spirituality come from the Sufi *tazkiras*, texts compiled during the second half of the seventeenth century by the Chishti–Sabiris, who appear at the

---

[7] 'Ali, *Sawati' al-Anwar,* British Library, India Office MSS, Ethé 654 (I.O. Islamic 2705), fl. 405: "*qaid-i mashikhat-i u paiband-i way shud, wa u ra az ni'mat-i 'uzma ki ru'yat bashad mahrum sakht.*" Needless to add, the author is himself a Chishti.

time to have been projecting their doctrinal positions and ritual practices rather aggressively. Of two such incidents, the first relates to certain anti-Sunna *bid'a* acts that a noted Chishti shaikh from Gangoh, Shaikh Muhammad Da'ud (d. 1683–4), who frequented Delhi in Aurangzeb's time, practised in the city. When the emperor came to know of these acts, he appointed Mulla 'Abd al-Qawi to find out the truth and stop them. The shaikh tried initially to make the mulla see reason by explaining his acts in the light of *hadith* and jurisprudence. But when the mulla was not persuaded, the shaikh apparently recited a Hindi couplet (*doha*) and, in a state of trance, proclaimed that since he himself was a maker of the injunctions of the *shari'a* (*bani-yi ahkam* and *sahib-i shar'*), the mulla had no basis on which to ask for any proof of validity for his acts. The result of the shaikh's rage was that Mulla 'Abd al-Qawi lost all knowledge of the *shari'a*, which he regained only after the shaikh forgave him. The mulla then advised the emperor to refrain from interfering in the shaikh's acts.[8]

The second incident consists in the report that at a *sama'* session at the *'urs* (annual death commemorative celebrations) of Shaikh Sufi Badhani in the *qasba* of Kaithal, a certain Shaikh 'Abd al-Qadir, *pir* of the above-mentioned Ilah Bakhsh of Lahore, declared in a state of trance: "Look here! Khwaja Mu'in al-Din, the Prophet of India (*nabi-i Hind*) has arrived." Alarmed by this, the *qazi* of the *qasba*, who was present there, said this was blasphemous; he accused the shaikh of having become a *kafir* for calling a mere Sufi a prophet, and declared he deserved to be executed. In defence of the shaikh, the plea was made that since he had made his statement in a state of trance (*wajd*), he could not be punished. It was also maintained that his use of the word *nabi* had not implied prophethood as such; rather, he had meant by it a person "who tells us about the Essence and Attributes of God (*mukhbir-i zat-o-sifat-i Haqq*)." The *qazi*, however, refused to budge. After

---

[8] Ibid., fls 439 b-440a. For Mulla 'Abd al-Qawi, see Sheikh, "Aurangzeb as Seen from Gujarat", pp. 557–81.

which, so the report goes, a special sort of Sabiriya–Chishtiya wrath became manifest, and the shaikh declared: "O Qazi! Since you have vowed to shed the blood of a dervish unjustly, you will die yelping like a dog." Whereupon the *qazi* was seized with pain and fell ill. He appealed for the shaikh's forgiveness but it was too late: the *qazi* consequently died.[9]

It would, all the same, be stretching the point from these examples of conflict to generalise the notion that the Chishti and the Naqshbandi shaikhs, whom we often see competing with each other during the seventeenth century, were always trying to outdo their rivals and hell-bent on establishing their own supremacy over the other. One counter-example suggesting the opposite of contention is of a prominent Naqshbandi–Mujaddidi shaikh in Delhi, Shah Ghulam 'Ali, who lived in the later-eighteenth and early-nineteenth century (d. 1824), and who writes: "I gained so much from the splendid Chishtiya *silsila* that I fear people [if they come to know] will think I had no sincere devotion to the Naqshbandiya, and that I have developed the habit of eating the bread of one person and thanking another."[10] Later in the nineteenth century, as we will see below, there is clear evidence of close interactions between the two orders, as well as of the borrowing of ideas and practices from each other, to the extent that towards the end of the century it became increasingly difficult to distinguish between the practices of the two orders as they came together.

Eighteenth-Century Delhi

Conscious efforts were certainly made in the eighteenth century to efface or at least attenuate the earlier rivalry. A major illustration of this direction is to be found in the century's greatest religious scholar and Sufi, Shah Wali-Allah, noted for his attempt to

---

[9] 'Ali, *Sawati' al-Anwar*, British Library, India Office manuscripts, Ethé 654 (I.O. Islamic 2705), fls 453b-454a.
[10] Dehlavi, *Makatib-i Sharifa*, , Letter 101, p. 424.

reconcile the doctrinal basis of the Mujaddidi–Naqshbandis on the one hand and the Chishtis on the other.[11] Shah Wali-Allah (d. 1762) is perhaps best known as a scholar who tried to reconcile the different schools of jurisprudence in works such as *al-Insaf fi al-Bayan Sabab al-Ikhtilaf* and '*Iqd al-Jid fi al-Ijtihad wa al-Taqlid*, as well as for reconciling the Sunni–Shi'i division more generally in his text entitled *Izalat al-Khafa 'an Khilafat al-Khulafa'*. But a factor in his attempt at harmonising varying Sufi doctrines could also have been his uncle Shaikh Abu al-Riza's (d. 1690) strong positions on *wahdat al-wujud*. Shaikh Abu al-Riza was a disciple of Khwaja Khwurd, son of Khwaja Baqi Billah, who was well known for a strong *wujudi* position.[12] Also, Shah Wali-Allah's father, Shaikh 'Abd al-Rahim (d. 1719), who was initiated into the Naqshbandi order by a disciple of Shaikh Adam Binori, was a great admirer of Ibn 'Arabi and a believer in *wahdat al-wujud*. According to a report, he expressed this belief in one of his vernacular *dohas*:

> The Beloved existed before Creation;
> Now there is Creation, but the Beloved cannot be found.
> Rahim wishes to join the Beloved,
> In the manner raindrops join the ocean.[13]

Shaikh 'Abd al-Rahim is well known as a great scholar who founded the Madrasa Rahimiya, and his claims in terms of *tasawwuf* were also very high; and in parallel with Shaikh Muhammad Ma'sum's claim to *qaiyumiyat*, he too claimed to be a *qaiyum*. Shah Wali-Allah records several miracles (*kashf-o-karamat*) of his father

---

[11] The reconciliation, Shah Wali-Allah writes, follows a vision in which the Prophet himself assigned him this task. See *Fuyuz al-Haramain*, pp. 53–7 and 197–202, cited in Rizvi, *Shah Wali-Allah and His Times*, p. 217.

[12] For his account, see Wali-Allah, *Anfas al-'Arifin*, pp. 87–158. Shah Wali-Allah also reproduces his correspondence with Shaikh 'Abd al-Ahad Wahdat, pp. 123–58, on the question of *wujud* and some other issues of *tasawwuf*. He also writes that the Mughal army, initially in trouble against the Satnami rebels, finally overcame them with his prayers (p. 90).

[13] Rizvi, *Shah Wali-Allah*, pp. 206–12. Rizvi cites the *doha* from Shah Wali-Allah, *Anfas al-'Arifin*, p. 81.

and his own prime focus, when discussing *tasawwuf*, is in terms of the concept of *ihsan*. He writes that Islam has two principal dimensions: one relates to a Muslim's everyday life, including his prayers and dealings with others, and the responsibility for protecting and promoting this dimension lies with jurists and traditionalists (*fuqaha wa muhaddisun*); the other dimension concerns the purification of hearts, which belongs to the domain of Sufis and the friends of God (*auliya'*). The core of this second aspect is *ihsan*, which the Prophet has interpreted as "worshipping God as if you are watching Him and if you are unable to watch Him, the belief should be that you are being watched by Him."[14] In his book *Hama'at* (Teardrops) he elaborates jointly on this idea of *tasawwuf* as *ihsan* with a brief discussion of its historical development. He says his book is based on his personal vision of the truth, and that it was completed "solely from inspiration, and without mixing it with [Hellenistic] philosophy". He intends it to provide a guideline for the direct path (*sirat-i mustaqim*), both for his own self and for those who follow him.[15] The first phase in the historical development of *tasawwuf*, he writes, was the time of the Prophet and his companions, followed by a period when the term *tasawwuf* began to be used more commonly. Those who engaged with *tasawwuf* were known as Sufis; they are to be found listening to *sama'*, intoxicated, dancing, and ripping at their clothes; many such have forsaken worldliness and become ascetic. They recognised the Essence of Divinity (*zat*) and realised that everything in this world is derived from Him (*tanazzulat*, i.e. stages of descent). There was no discussion then, let alone any distinction, at this point in time between the *shuhudi* and *wujudi wahdat*. Also, there were no distinct groupings as yet, though among individuals there appeared to be differences; despite this, all were acceptable to God, and the world was graced with

---

[14] "*Al-Ihsan an ta'buda Allah ka'annaka tara-hu, fa-in lam tara-hu fa-innahu yaraka*".

[15] Wali-Allah, *Hama'at*, pp. 60–7.

their blessings. In view of subsequent differences that split and divided the Sufis, the conclusion of this section deserves special notice. Shah Wali-Allah argues that "when we discuss the Sufis, we should take care that the states (*ahwal*) and sayings (*aqwal*) of the members of a given group should be judged according to [the] taste of the times when they lived. Likewise, it is not appropriate to compare, collate, and judge the states and sayings of one era of Sufis by another."[16]

Then follows a chapter wherein Shah Wali-Allah discusses the first stage of a *salik* (or devotee), which is *ta'at* or worship. He says that nearly all *tariqas* or paths to reality (*haqiqa*), though different, begin with Junaid Baghdadi, except those who claim to have direct connection to the Prophet, and those are called Uwaisis. Significantly, he mentions in particular the figure of Shah Badi' al-Din Madar among followers of the latter path. It is particularly noteworthy that, in relation to nearly all the *tariqas* that he discusses in this book, Shah Wali-Allah mentions his own connection with them. In this specific chapter he avers that the *salik* should not get involved in discussion over the stages of descent (*tanazzulat*) from the Divine Essence (*zat-i ahad*), through Oneness (*wahdaniyat*), souls (*arwah*), and the world beyond ('*alam-i misal*), to this world ('*alam-i ajsam*). Another important piece of advice he provides the *salik* here is to the effect that after he has made some progress, and if on his own he is capable of appreciating the traditions of the Prophet, the Prophet's companions, and their immediate successors (*ahadis* and *asar*), he should act along those traditions. Alternatively, he may follow any one of the four schools of jurisprudence.[17] He then discusses the litanies and prayers (*aurad, azkar,* and *waza'if*) of the different *tariqas*.[18] Thereafter, he expatiates for about eighty pages on the forms of relation (*nisbat*), and states that once a person reaches the climax

[16] *Hama'at,* pp. 73–6, and 77.
[17] Ibid., pp. 78–81.
[18] Ibid., pp. 82–7.

of a *nisbat*, he becomes a *qutb*. Shah Wali-Allah then has an entire chapter on miracles performed by Sufis (*karamat* and *khawariq*), which he explains in terms of the ability of Sufis to discern what is lying in store in the world beyond (*'alam-i misal*) for the future of this world: "This *faqir* has been told that *karamat* and *khawariq*, which are usually considered unnatural acts are, in themselves and within their limits, very much according to nature."[19]

As has been noted briefly above, an important part of Shah Wali-Allah's discourse on *tasawwuf* relates to the possibility of harmony and reconciliation between the doctrines of *wahdat al-wujud* and *wahdat al-shuhud*. He builds the argument in his long letter to the noted Medina-based scholar Shaikh Abu Tahir al-Kurdi al-Madani, the text of which is incorporated in his *Al-Tafhimat al-Ilahiya* and reproduced there entitled *Faisla-i Wahdat al-Wujud wa Wahdat al-Shuhud*. In it he says that the common Sufi objective is spiritual attainment, and that they all see the reality of *wujud* in the Being of God. The difference is only that one group considers and calls the created world a manifestation (*mazhar*) and the other a reflection (*zill*); therefore, the distinction between them lies only in matters of interpretation and synthesis.[20] However, Shah Wali-Allah's intervention was not wholly welcomed in Mujaddidi Sufi circles. A certain Ghulam Yahya, at Mirza Mazhar Jan-i Janan's instance, compiled a treatise entitled *Kalimat al-Haqq* (The True Word) in refutation of his position. Later, in reply Shah Wali-Allah's son Shah Rafi' al-Din (d. 1833) wrote another treatise entitled *Damgh al-Batil* (Piercing the False).[21] Shah Wali-Allah's grandson Shah Isma'il Shahid (d. 1831) too commented in depth on these doctrinal questions in his book *'Abaqat* (Perfumes), reiterating and reaffirming his position, albeit in a more nuanced way. With a view to mollifying the Mujaddidis

---

[19] Ibid., p. 258.
[20] Wali-Allah, *Al-Tafhimat al-Ilahiya*, Vol. 2, *tafhim* 243, pp. 261–83. For a discussion of this text, see Faruqi, *The Mujaddid's Conception of Tauhid*, pp. 95–100; Baljon, *Religion and Thought of Shah Wali-Allah Dihlawi*, pp. 56–63.
[21] Shah Rafi' al-Din Dehlavi, *Majmu'a-i Rasa'il; Ma'arif*, October 2020.

perhaps, he added, clarified, and elaborated the point that Shah Wali-Allah accepted Shaikh Ahmad Sirhindi as a *mujaddid* (*irhas*), and that he had actually completed the work that Sirhindi had started.[22] Later, however, Isma'il Shahid seems to have changed his position and inclined more toward the truth of *wahdat al-shuhud*. This was after he joined the Tariqa-i Muhammadiya, which was a much more radical reformulation of the Mujaddidi order under Saiyid Ahmad Shahid. A statement of his changed stance is given in *Sirat al-Mustaqim*, a *malfuz* collection of Saiyid Ahmad Shahid, the first textual expression of the new order.

The *'Abaqat* begins with a statement by Shah Isma'il to the effect that he does not know much about the abstruse discourses of *tasawwuf*, but was lucky enough to have learnt about them from the treatises of his grandfather Shah Wali-Allah, works such as *Sat'at* (Radiance) and *Lamhat* (Glances), and felt that the ideas discussed there needed detailed elaboration, in particular as many people did not read and interpret them correctly. The *'Abaqat* thus presents itself as a defence and elaboration in profounder idiom of what Shah Wali-Allah had already said. Shah Isma'il also asserts that were he to get the chance, he would write specific commentaries on these *risalas*.[23] Besides an introduction (*muqaddima*) and conclusion (*khatimat al-kitab*), he divides his book into four parts, each following after what he terms an *al-ishara* (lit. indication; signal). In the first part, which is the most comprehensive, we find forty-three sections (termed *'abaqas*), in which he discusses stages of existence (*maratib-i tanazzul al-wujud al-haqiqi*) or descents (*tanazzulat*).[24] The remaining three parts are, respectively, on visions and manifestations (*tajalliyat*); on affirmation (*ijab*) and choice (*ikhtiyar*); and on the stages of souls (*maratib al-nafs*). In the conclusion he deals with the important idea of requital (*misal*) to be found in Shah Wali-Allah.

[22] Shah Isma'il Shahid Dehlavi, *'Abaqat*.
[23] Ibid., pp. 2–4.
[24] Ibid., pp. 4–9, *muqaddima*, and pp. 10–78, Part One.

In the first nineteen sections (*'abaqas*) of Part 1, the discussion is focused on monotheism (or *tauhid*). Later, in Sections 20 and 21, Shah Isma'il asserts that there are two major groups among believers in *wujud* and *tauhid*. One comprises those who believe in what he terms *wujud-i 'ainiya*, in which many have included Ibn 'Arabi, though without providing appropriate justification. The other group coheres around *wujud-i wara'iyya*, their leader having been Shaikh Ahmad Sirhindi (the Imam al-Mujaddid). There was also a third group, which was the best, and the most important leader of this group was his grandfather, the finest of seekers after truth (*afzal al-muhaqqaqin*). In the twenty-first *'abaqa* he says the difference between the first two lay in words alone (*niza'-i lafzi*), as had been explained by his grandfather. But some of the later Sufis – meaning the Mujaddidis of Shah Wali-Allah's time – thought this conflict went beyond words and was real (*al-muta'akhkhirun min al-mutasawwifa tawahhamu al-ikhtilaf al-waqi'*), which, he claims, showed they had read neither Ibn 'Arabi nor Sirhindi closely. He therefore invites the reader to read these original thinkers as well as their interpreters – such as 'Abd al-Rahman Jami and Sadr al-Din Qunawi in the case of Ibn 'Arabi, and in Sirhindi's case his hagiographer Badr al-Din Sirhindi and Sirhindi's *maktubat*, themselves.[25] Shah Isma'il also claims that the concept of *shuhudiyat* as employed by Abu al-Hasan Simnani is not the same as that of Shaikh Sirhindi.[26] The later *'abaqas* then contain the details of the same arguments. There is also an *'abaqa* on the variety of relationships of *al-Qaiyum*, i.e. God the Creator, with the created.

In sum, Shah Isma'il seems to take very seriously the objections raised against Shah Wali-Allah's ideas by other Mujaddidis of his time, and replies to them in his own very philosophically charged language.

---

[25] Ibid., pp. 39–41, *'abaqa* 20, Urdu translation, pp. 83–9, and 41–3, *'abaqa* 21, Urdu translation, pp. 89–93.

[26] Ibid., p. 43, Urdu translation, pp. 93–4.

Sufis in Nineteenth-Century North India

However, as we know, Shah Isma'il changed his position in course of time, his new position being manifest in his texts: namely, *Sirat-i Mustaqim*,[27] and *Radd-i Ishrak* – written in Arabic, which he later translated into Urdu as *Taqwiyat al-Iman*, and which was also elaborated upon as *Tazkir al-Ikhwan* in 1834–5, after his death, by one of his disciples.[28] Shah Isma'il was above all a scholar and seems right from the start to have been – as Syed Ahmad Khan says of him – interested in reform and an insistence on Sunnat and Shari'at. Later, he became a disciple of Saiyid Ahmad Shahid, a member of the family of Shah 'Alam-Allah (d. 1684) of Rae Bareli (in Awadh), and a disciple and successor (*khalifa*) of Shaikh Adam Binori. Saiyid Ahmad had come to Delhi for his education as a young student, where he met Shah Wali-Allah's son Shah 'Abd al-'Aziz (d. 1824) and, according to one report, became his spiritual disciple. Soon after, he left Delhi and joined the military bands of Nawab Amir Ali Khan of Tonk (d. 1834), the so-called Pindaris. On his second visit to Delhi, he had already earned repute as a great Sufi master. At this point Shah Isma'il met

---

[27] See Shah Isma'il Shahid Dehlavi's *Sirat-i Mustaqim*. Originally written in Persian, this is a *malfuz* of Saiyid Ahmad Shahid divided into four chapters and an epilogue, besides an introduction and conclusion. Shah Isma'il, who is generally described as the author-compiler, wrote the introduction, and perhaps also the epilogue, and only two chapters, while the other two chapters (the second and third) were compiled by Shah 'Abd al-Hayy Phulati, son-in-law of Shah 'Abd al-'Aziz. The book focuses on defining *tasawwuf*, Saiyid Ahmad's high spiritual stature in the context of all the major Sufi orders, including the guidance and instruction he received directly from God, and also the notion of *bid'a* in contemporary Sufi traditions and practices. For an analysis of the text, see Gaborieau, "Sufism in the First Wahhabi Manifesto", pp. 149–64.

[28] Shah Isma'il Shahid Dehlavi, *Taqwiyat al-Iman*, a treatise exclusively on the refutation of *shirk* (idolatry) of different natures, discussed in five chapters (*fasl*), beginning with a general introductory chapter on monotheism (*tauhid*). In the *Tazkir al-Ikhwan*, divided into seven chapters on (*fasl*), the primary discussion is on prevailing customs and rituals.

him and asked, in order to test his spiritual accomplishments, if he, Saiyid Ahmad, could teach him how to say prayers (*namaz*) with *huzur-i qalb* (total devotion). Saiyid Ahmad did so, and as a result Shah Isma'il became his disciple.[29] Saiyid Ahmad, even though he had begun as a Mujaddidi, then reformulated the order and called it Tariqa-i Muhammadiya.[30]

Shah Isma'il thus became attached to the endeavours of Saiyid Ahmad Shahid and travelled with him to Arabia for the hajj, and also through several parts of India. He compiled his master's utterances in the form of the *Sirat-i Mustaqim*. A brief review of the contents of this work shows his departure from his earlier positions on *tasawwuf* – those that we saw in his *'Abaqat*. The contents include rejection and damnation of what are termed "the innovations of deviant Sufis", "idolaters who behave as Sufis", "heretical interpretations of Ontological Monism", "excessive reverence for the *murshid*", and "vows and gifts offered to the tombs of the saints". The contemplation of the image of one's shaikh (*tasawwur-i shaikh*) is absolutely prohibited and treated as a form of idolatry. Harsher in fact are his stances on *sunnat* and *shari'a* in his *Taqwiyat al-Iman*. The Tariqa-i Muhammadiya was therefore different from all the Sufi orders of the time, including the Naqshbandi–Mujaddidi. In fact Saiyid Ahmad, though originally a Mujaddidi, claimed that his initiation was Uwaisi, directly from the Prophet, Fatima, 'Ali, and ultimately God himself. The result was that, at the time, even the Delhi Naqshbandis of the school of Mirza Mazhar Jan-i Janan considered him and his followers adversaries. In their assessment Saiyid Ahmad, Isma'il Shahid, and their followers had in effect acted like Wahhabis.[31] From a certain standpoint, then, this is an important turn in the history

---

[29] Khan, *Asar al-Sanadid*, Vol. 2, pp. 80–4. A similar incident is also reported about Shah 'Abd al-Hayy's relationship with Saiyid Ahmad.

[30] For a discussion of the history and context of this new order, see Gaborieau, "Criticising the Sufis", pp. 45–67; Nizami, *Reform and Renewal in South Asian Islam*, pp. 167–85. See also Haroon, "Reformism and Orthodox Practice", pp. 177–98.

[31] Ibid., p. 458.

of Sufism in India – certainly from what it was in the seventeenth century; and it was moreover a direction not in accord with Shah Wali-Allah's Sufism. Shah Wali-Allah, as we saw, showed reverence for nearly all the Sufi traditions, going so far as to claim that Sufis continue to be spiritually sublime even after death. His was a catholic perspective whereby the qualities of the stage a Sufi had attained persisted in the afterlife, legitimising visits to Sufi graves and seeking their intercession in prayer (*du'a*). For his part, Saiyid Ahmad Shahid did not reject *tasawwuf* as such, continuing with the existing practice of the master–disciple (*pir-o-murid*) relationship, and claiming for himself the highest stage of spirituality.³² But Shah Isma'il and he did seek to put a distance between themselves and certain aspects of the received understanding of *tasawwuf*.

Among the Sufis who lived in the nineteenth century, Haji Imdad-Allah (1815–1898), a noted disciple of the Chishti–Sabiri Shaikh Nur Muhammad Jhanjhanvi (d. 1843), played a critical role in reconciling the different groups of the Sufis, an endeavour similar to Shah Wali-Allah's earlier. Haji Imdad-Allah, though a leading Chishti–Sabiri Sufi of his time, was also wholly familiar with the nuanced doctrinal and practical features of the Naqshbandi–Mujaddidi order, having been first initiated into and receiving a *khilafat* in that *silsila*.³³ With Imdad-Allah and his masters is associated a significant change in nineteenth-century Chishti–Sabiri Sufism, apparently following a detailed meeting with Saiyid Ahmad Shahid. It is reported that when in the course of his missionary tour in the Saharanpur–Muzaffarnagar region,

---

³² Since his body was lost in the battle of Balakot where he died fighting against the Sikhs under Ranjit Singh, many of his followers believed he was still alive and in hiding, and would return to lead them to triumph. See Gaborieau, *Le Mahdi incompris*. See also Meerathi, *Tazkirat al-Rashid*, Vol. 2, pp. 270–2.

³³ Imdad-Allah writes that the Prophet himself guided him for both these initiations. Thanawi, *Karamat-e Imdadiya*, p. 50; and Rahman, *Tazkira-e Masha'ikh-e Deoband*, p. 71, cited in Kamal, *Masha'ikh-e Chishtiya Sabiriya*, pp. 197–8.

north of Delhi, Saiyid Ahmad arrived in Nanauta, the birthplace of Imdad-Allah, the infant Imdad-Allah was placed in his lap. Saiyid Ahmad blessed the child by accepting him via the practice of *bai'at al-tabarruk* (pledging allegiance to a shaikh for his blessing). Then, in Saharanpur, Saiyid Ahmad met Shah 'Abd al-Rahim Wilayati (d. 1830), a Chishti–Sabiri shaikh who pledged allegiance to him and ordered his disciples to do the same. Amongst these was Miyanji Nur Muhammad (d. 1843), the future teacher of Imdad-Allah, who had been especially summoned for this purpose to Saharanpur from Lohari, a nearby village. Later, Saiyid Ahmad and Wilayati again met in private, and, as the two emerged from the meeting room, both were apparently mutually inspired by the other's *nisba*. Saiyid Ahmad was overcome with weeping (a sign among the Chishti Sufis), while Wilayati was calm (a sign of the Naqshbandi shaikhs).[34] Thereafter, Wilayati remained with Saiyid Ahmad until his death in the battle of Mayar in October 1830. His main successor, Miyanji Nur Muhammad, also accompanied Saiyid Ahmad to the north-west frontier region but was later sent back to help with logistics.[35] Thus, Haji Imdad-Allah, who emerged as the *pir* of all the notable late-nineteenth- and early-twentieth-century Deobandi scholars and Sufis, was connected to Saiyid Ahmad's movement. Imdad-Allah also advocated and actually participated in *jihad* against the East India Company and its power,[36] this at a time when some who had accompanied

---

[34] Husaini, *Saiyid Ahmad Shahid se Haji Imdad-Allah ke Ruhani Rishte*, p. 59. For a slightly different version, see Thanawi, *Hikayat-i Auliya*, pp. 149–50. Interestingly, Thanawi says the spiritual level that Wilayati possessed before was greatly enhanced after he pledged allegiance to Saiyid Ahmad. I owe these references to Aamir Bashir (University of Chicago): see his "*Shari'at* and *Tariqat*". Also see the discussion in Nizami, *Reform and Renewal in South Asian Islam*, pp. 153–95, where he traces the sources of such changes to the earlier connection between the Delhi-based Wali-Allahi scholars and the Chishti–Sabiris of Amroha.

[35] Husaini, *Saiyid Ahmad Shahid se Haji Imdad-Allah ke Ruhani Rishte*, p. 91.

[36] Alavi, *Muslim Cosmopolitanism*, pp. 222–66. This has been an integral

Saiyid Ahmad in Balakot were prepared for a kind of reconciliation with the British.[37]

We must also note Imdad-Allah's attempt to bring the *'ulama* of the time closer to Sufism. *Tasawwuf*, of course, continued with its primary concern with purification of the soul (*tazkiya-i nafs*), with revelation and miracles (*kashf-o-karamat*) as salient features. This is visible in both Thanawi, who advocated struggle against what he considered a regime of *kafirs*, and in Husain Ahmad Madani, who was in favour of fighting shoulder to shoulder with Hindus against the British. Among Imdad-Allah's *'ulama* disciples were some notable in their own right, influenced by Saiyid Ahmad Shahid and Shah Isma'il Shahid's somewhat uncompromising attitude to certain basic tenets of Sufism, while several others held different views; in short, his disciples were not in unison in relation to certain religious matters in Sunni Islam. We have on the one hand Deobandi *'ulama* – such as Muhammad Qasim Nanautwi, Rashid Ahmad Gangohi, Khalil Ahmad Saharanpuri, and Ashraf 'Ali Thanawi – flatly disputing the validity of practices and ceremonies such as *fatiha, 'urs,* and *sama'*. On the other are Imdad-Allah's equally dear disciples – such as Maulana Lutfullah of Aligarh, Maulana Ahmad Husain of Kanpur, and Maulana 'Abdus Sami' of Rampur – who continue strongly advocating these very practices. These differences among them could have been owing to the impact of larger reform movements in the world of Islam. In order to resolve the differences, Haji Imdad-Allah was, in his own words, forced to write a treatise entitled *Faisla-i Haft Mas'ala* (Judgment on Seven Questions), which in some measure follows the footsteps of Shah Wali-Allah. Of the seven issues in-

---

part of history and memory among the *'ulama*: see, for instance, Madani, *Naqsh-e Hayat*, Vol. 2, pp. 52–67. Some scholars question the validity of this claim: see Haq, *Muslim Politics in Modern India*, pp. 6–12; and Kamal, *Masha'ikh-e Chishtiya Sabiriya*, pp. 202–7, for a rejoinder.

[37] For Karamat Ali Jaunpuri, for instance, see Ghose, "Politics of Faith", Chapter 2, pp. 81–135.

cluded in the *risala* were the celebration of the Prophet's birthday, i.e. *maulud*, in particular during the third lunar month, Rabi'i, and *qiyam*, that is, standing up to recite and offering *salam* to the Prophet before concluding the *maulud*; celebrations of the death anniversary of a saint (*'urs*); the performance of music (*sama'*); *fatiha*, i.e. prayers and distribution of food and sweetmeats to seek blessings for the dead; and asking for help from any power other than God (*nida-i ghair Allah*). Imdad-Allah's advice and principal position were in favour of harmony and compromise. He had a special fascination for Rumi's *Masnawi*, and so his position may also have been inspired by Rumi's oft-cited conciliatory stance.[38] While Imdad-Allah cites several *hadiths* in support of his position, he explained and legitimated the question of *nida-i ghair Allah* via Rumi's portrayal of a feature of the legendary Majnun's expression of love for Layli:

> Somebody saw Majnun in the desert,
> Recording his sorrow on [the sands of] it,
> The sands were his paper, and his fingers were his pen,
> It looked as if he was writing a letter to someone.
> He was asked: O crazy Majnun what is this!
> To whom are you writing this letter?
> Majnun replied: I am practising writing Layli's name,
> And I'm consoling my heart in this way.

Unfortunately for Imdad-Allah, his position was not acceptable to all his disciples, and in particular not to the Deobandi *'ulama*. Some of them pleaded that they had pledged themselves to him in terms of *tariqa*, not in terms of *shari'a*, and that Imdad-Allah did not know enough about Islamic law. The differences thus continued. On the one hand 'Abdus Sami' of Rampur wrote a treatise entitled *Anwar-i Sati'a* (Bright Lights) in support of observing the *maulud*, for instance, while another disciple, Khalil Ahmad of Saharanpur, wrote a treatise, *Al-Barahin Qati'at al-*

---

[38] Simnani, *Chihl Majlis*. Shibli Nu'mani also cites this story in his *Sawanih-i Maulana Rum*, see below, fn. 65.

Zalam al-Anwar al-Sati'a (Definitive Proofs on the Darkness of Bright Lights) to refute its argument.[39] The group around Khalil Ahmad, mostly associated with the Deoband School, were later condemned as Wahhabis, in the manner that Isma'il Shahid and Saiyid Ahmad Shahid had been. The issues taken up in *Faisala-i Haft Mas'ala* in fact remained the core points of conflict among the Sunni Muslims of South Asia in the twentieth century.[40]

Deoband Shaikhs and the Chishti–Sabiri Tradition

Among Imdad-Allah's disciples, Ashraf 'Ali Thanawi, a Deoband-trained scholar, was among the most representative Sufis of the tradition developed by his master. He revived Imdad-Allah's own *khanqah*, the Imdadiya in Thana Bhawan (Muzaffarnagar District); like his master, he had been initiated into several orders but identified himself primarily as a Chishti–Sabiri. This was despite the fact that in his doctrines and practices are to be found similarities with the Naqshbandi–Mujaddidi tradition. Thanawi also differed in relation to several issues from those his own master had espoused. Thus, Thanawi did not accept the resolution of even a single issue raised and discussed in *Faisala-i Haft Mas'ala*. He projected them as misguided innovations (*bid'at aur zalalat*) which could lead to idolatry and unbelief (*shirk* and *kufr*). He also seems to have broken off contact with several of Imdad-Allah's

---

[39] For an excellent discussion around Imdad-Allah's plea and his Deoband-oriented disciples' position on some of the issues discussed by him, see Ingram, *Revival from Below*, pp. 55–110. See also Meerathi, *Tazkirat al-Rashid*, Vol. 1, pp. 114–36, correspondence between Ashraf 'Ali Thanawi and Rashid Ahmad Gangohi for Gangohi's plea for adhering strictly to shari'a and *sunna*, even if it implies disregard of one's *pir*'s position, for instance. Gangohi, and for that matter the Deobandi *'ulama*, developed their own way of *maulud*: idem, Vol. 2, p. 284; idem, *Tazkirat al-Khalil*, pp. 131–51 for a *munazara* (against) the *bid'atis* in Bhawalpur.

[40] See Sanyal, *Devotional Islam and Politics in British India*; and more recently, Tareen, *Defending Muhammad in Modernity*.

disciples who endorsed their master's judgments.[41] For instance, the disciple differed from the master in his views of *sama'* – a significant practice of the Chishti–Sabiri order, as well as on the writings of Ibn 'Arabi, the first to propound and elaborate the idea of *wahdat al-wujud* (Unity of Being), the effective doctrinal basis of the order. In his treatise on *sama'*, titled *Haqq al-Sama'* (The Truth about *Sama'*), he focuses almost solely – in nearly all the ten sections – on questions of jurisprudence. He begins with the statement that *sama'* was prohibited by the imams of all schools of jurisprudence, followed by a section on Hanafi jurisprudence with textual citations in support of its prohibition. For instance, he cites 'Abd-Allah ibn Mas'ud saying that "the voice of song creates hypocrisy in the heart in the same way as water sets grass in the earth." Strangely, he also approvingly cites a *fatwa* of Shah 'Abd al-'Aziz Dehlavi, undoubtedly a great Hanafi scholar but not identified as a Chishti saint.[42] He does cite the sayings of past Chishti Sufis, but only to highlight conditions and restrictions that they had suggested or recommended for convening a *sama'* audition, while maintaining total silence over their regular indulgence in it.[43]

The second instance of his departure from earlier Chishti tradition is illustrated by his views on Ibn 'Arabi, the first to propound the doctrine of *wahdat al-wujud*, long the core of the ideological framework of the Chishtis. Here it would be pertinent to note the discussion in the preface of a book, *al-Tanbih al-Tarabi fi Tanzih Ibn al-'Arabi* (Pleasing Admonition to Absolve Ibn al-'Arabi) that Thanawi composed concerning Ibn al-'Arabi's writings. Here are some passages from his discussion:

> Shaikh Ibn al-'Arabi is amongst the most disputed Sufis of Islam because of some statements attributed to him whose apparent meaning (*zahir*) is in contradiction to the *shari'a*. Some scholars

---

[41] Thanawi, *Imdad al-Fatawa*, pp. 274–84.
[42] Thanawi, *Haqq al-Sama'*, pp. 3–4.
[43] Ibid., pp. 23–6.

have condemned him while some others regard him as a saint (*wali*) and in consideration of the historical context in which he lived, they denied the attribution of these statements to him, or else interpreted them in terms acceptable to the *shari'a*. Still others asserted that his statements did not concern the *shari'a*. All these statements relate to the sciences concerning miracles and visionary insights (*'ulum-i mukashafa*),[44] there is nothing reported from him relating to the *'ulum-i mu'amala* (sciences regarding human relationships).

Since the time that I have been in the company of the people of God – thanks to God I have been endowed with this blessing since my childhood – I have been interested in *tasawwuf*, but only in the [aspect of] *'ulum-i mu'amala*, since matters relating to doing and not doing (*amr-o-nahy*) concern the *'ulum-i mu'amala*, and in order to get close to God, it is only by acting upon these that this is achieved. And even if I had temperamentally relished the *'ulum-i mukashafa*, I was never rationally attracted (*'aqli raghbat*) to them, since these are hardly helpful in getting access (*qurb*) to God. [Instead] the danger in them is so strong, that a few errors in them could even destroy the faith. May Allah protect us. Thus, I never paid attention to Ibn al-'Arabi's famous books, nor did I ever intend to have a look at them. This was of course notwithstanding occasional and miscellaneous browsing of some of these books. But since I had always seen my own elders very devoted to him as they were devoted to other great figures in *tasawwuf*, I had respect and admiration for him in my heart . . .

It was in 1338 [1919 CE] that I started reading him regularly when I began to write a *sharh* (commentary) on his *Fusus al-Hikam* (Bezels of Wisdom) entitled *Khusus al-Kilam* (Special Words). I mentioned the reason for this in the introduction to that work. [But] having commented only on some parts, I gave up this work. I would never forget how terrible and suffocated I felt while reading the themes that he wrote on. While reading some portions I felt extremely pained, which I have also mentioned in my remarks on them. This was also a

---

[44] Rashid Ahmad Gangohi however defines it as an integral part of a Sufi's gnosis / knowledge, defining it as journey into the Zat, a definitive knowledge of observation (of Truth), and it has little concern with miracles *(murad az 'ilm al-mukashafa sair fi-Allah ast ki 'ilm al-yaqin wa shuhud hasil shawad warna kashf-o–karamat chize nist)*. Meerathi, *Tazkirat al-Rashid*, Vol. 1, p. 252.

reason for giving up this commentary. About seven years have passed since, and during these years I did not go back to it, according to my original position. But in these days, it has occurred again to my heart that the commentary should have been written so that people were neither misguided by his writings nor would they dare to have been disrespectful to him. This purpose could have been obtained fully by completing the originally planned *sharh*. But in essence, the same purpose could be achieved by a different method too, i.e. by collecting from Ibn al-'Arabi's own writings those lines which contradict his ambiguous and misleading statements. A single speaker (especially when he is of sound mind, and also learned, religious and accomplished) cannot logically make contradictory statements.

There could be only two possibilities of reconciliation then. Either the statements which are sound and correct (*zahirat al-dalala wa maqtu' al-sihha*) are read with the statements that are unclear and unsound (*muhtamalat al-dalala wa muhimat al-butlan*) or vice versa. It is also obvious that the latter should be rejected, so that the former is chosen. In fact, this method, of reading his unsound statements with reference to his own sound statements, is the best and most profitable for exonerating the Shaikh [Ibn al-'Arabi] from the objections levelled against him, as it is said that the person living in the house knows best what is inside of it. Thus, disrespect (*tazlil*) for the shaikh – which is born because of taking his words only in their outward sense – will disappear. Ibn al-'Arabi's own statements will generate doubts regarding the validity of the others. One set of statements is not corroborated by the other.

Even if this is not done (*agar ek ko dusre ki taraf raje' na bhi kiya jaye*), the *reductio ad absurdum* is only a state of doubt, since we have no exact chronology of Ibn al-'Arabi's statements. When one is unsure about something, it is appropriate to be careful, more obviously in the case of Ibn al-'Arabi [whom our elders have held in great esteem]. He should not be maligned for statements that are only outwardly problematic. His clearly correct statements (*zahir al-sawab*) should be taken as the essence (*asl*) and the obviously wrong ones be declared subordinate to this essence . . . When an imam's speech is contradictory, [only] the one which corresponds to the obvious [*shar'i*] position is acceptable (*iza ikhtalfa kalamu imam, yukhazu bima yuwafiqu al-adillat al-zahira*). This will be beneficial to both sides, and will safeguard both the truth of the *shari'a* as well as the rights of the saints (*auliya*).[45]

We should note here that, despite his obvious reticence, Thanawi could not dissociate himself from Ibn al-'Arabi, while noting the problem that he had experienced when he began his commentary on the *Fusus al-Hikam*. Presumably, he kept mulling over Ibn al-'Arabi's ideas and writings for nearly a decade. Finally, as he himself tells us, he arrived at the idea of how best to continue his relationship with Ibn al-'Arabi as one associated with the tradition of *wujudi* Sufis. Interestingly, Thanawi states that his interest in *tasawwuf* was not primarily through *'ilm al-mukashafa* but through *'ilm al-mu'amala*. This sounds contrary to how Shah Wali-Allah had defined *tasawwuf*, as noted above. The concept of *mu'amala*, Shah Wali-Allah had suggested, belonged to the domain of jurists. In the tradition from which Thanawi hailed, words like *wajd* (ecstasy) – and its derivatives *wijdan*, *zauq* (delight), and *jazba* (passion) – would imply a spiritual trance and an inexplicable sublime experience akin to drunkenness. But in the way Thanawi modified the tradition, these words did not have the same meanings. We should not however forget the fact that among the Deoband *'ulama* Thanawi wrote most prolifically on *tasawwuf* and Persian Sufi poetry.[46]

The 'Other' in Indian *Tasawwuf*

Notwithstanding the presence of those who, while claiming to be Sufis, instrumentalised the implications of *wahdat al-wujud*, the doctrine did overall promote an atmosphere of social harmony and community coexistence in Mughal India. A manifestation of this was also the nourishment it provided the Mughal policy of *sulh-i kull* (Peace towards All), discussed in several of the following

---

[45] Thanawi, *al-Tanbih al-Tarabi fi Tanzih Ibn al-'Arabi*, pp. 1–3.
[46] He wrote, for instance, extensive commentaries on Rumi's *Masnawi* (*Kalid-i Masnawi*) and Hafiz Shirazi's *Diwan* (*'Irfan-i Hafiz*).

chapters. In addition to Dara Shukoh's translation of the *Yogavasistha* (discussed in Chapter 6), the same prince had several similar works to his credit, such as the *Majma' al-Bahrain* and the translations of *shlokas* from the Upanishads inspired by the doctrine. This spirit is further illustrated in the early-eighteenth century in the Awadhi Qadiri Sufi Shah 'Abd al-Razzaq's proclamation (as well as the belief of his followers) that he was a close "friend" of Lord Krishna.[47] Closer to our own time in the twentieth century, these ideas found echoes in the poetry of Hasrat Mohani.[48] Amongst the Chishtis, much before 'Abd al-Rahman Chishti, Mir 'Abd al-Wahid Bilgrami's *Haqa'iq-i Hindi* was charged with the same spirit.[49] In the early-nineteenth century the idea continued to retain its legitimacy amongst Muslim Sufis. While at one level we have in these incidents a sense of legitimacy being lent to the Other's beliefs, on the other hand these are obviously contradictions of orthodox Islamic law.

The seventeenth-century Naqshbandi tradition, however, did not support these attitudes and practices. In one of Shaikh Ahmad Sirhindi's letters in *Maktubat-i Imam-i Rabbani*, written in response to a letter of a Hindu named Hriday Ram, we see a scathing critique of the accommodative approach. Hriday Ram had shown interest in being initiated into the Naqshbandi order without, however, committing to Islam. Sirhindi was aghast at his audacity. For a Hindu even to ask to join the order and speculate on possible affinities between Muslim and Hindu divinities struck him dumb – though not for long, as it soon struck him into pithy eloquence. Forcefully rejecting non-dualism, Sirhindi says "It is extreme folly to think of Ram and Rahman as one. Creation and the Creator cannot be the same."[50] Even so, in the

---

[47] Alam, *Languages of Political Islam*, pp. 108–11.
[48] Rizvi, "Hasrat ki bhi Qabul ho Mathura mein Haziri", pp. 78–88; Naim, "The Maulana Who Loved Krishna", pp. 37–44.
[49] Bilgrami, *Haqa'iq-i Hindi*.
[50] Sirhindi, *Maktubat-i Imam-i Rabbani*, Vol. 1, Letter 167, pp. 170–1. Sirhindi however does not deny the advent of the prophets in India.

eighteenth century the major Mujaddidi–Naqshbandi luminary Mirza Mazhar Jan-i Janan (d. 1784) took a more generous line on Hindu deities, equating the Vedas and the Dharmashastras with Muslim scriptures and law codes. He cited the well-known Qur'anic verse: "In each community there had been a prophet", and therefrom argued that India cannot have been left without prophets. Once, in the presence of his disciple, he snubbed his *pir-bha'i* (with whom he had shared a master) when the latter was critical of a visitor who had been relating his dream about Krishna and Rama, in which he had seen one of them in the middle of a fire and the other sitting at its edge.[51] Of greater significance for our purposes is that in the line of a major eighteenth-century Naqshbandi–Mujaddidi shaikh, Naʿim-Allah Bahraichi (d. 1803; he was himself a *khalifa* of Mirza Mazhar Jan-i Janan), there is evidence of two Hindu Sufis who, despite their intentions, were stopped from converting to Islam.[52] An equally important piece of evidence which needs to be considered is the regular use by another nineteenth-century Naqshbandi–Mujaddidi Sufi, Shah Fazle Rahman Ganj Muradabadi (1793–1895), of terms like "Manmohan" (a common name for Lord Krishna) and "Parmeshar" in his Awadhi Hindi translation of parts of the Holy Qur'an, published with the title of *Manmohan ki Batein*.[53]

Modern Muslim Intellectuals and *Tasawwuf*

The reform and reformulations of Sufi traditions and practices – in particular within the Naqshbandi–Mujaddidi order over the nine-

---

[51] Alam, *Languages of Political Islam*, pp. 173–6.

[52] Dahnhardt, *Changes and Continuity in Indian Sufism*, pp. 79–106 for Ramchandraji Fatehgarhi (d. 1913) and Brij Mohan Lal Kanpuri (d. 1955), sixth and seventh in line from Mirza Jan-i Janan; and pp. 195–334, for a discussion of their doctrine and methodology. Significant also is Gian Giuseppe Filippi's foreword to this book for the view that he cites of Shah Abu'l Hasan Zaid Faruqi, a direct descendant of Sirhindi, and a major Mujaddidi Shaikh in twentieth-century Delhi.

[53] Muradabadi, *Manmohan ki Batein*.

teenth century that we saw above – have also been explained in terms of the challenges that the coming of "modernity" posed to South Asian Islam.[54] Challenges from the West certainly led to radical changes in the approaches of modern Muslim intellectuals to Sufism. These changes could variously be categorised as reformism, revivalism, and modernism or Westernisation. In all three categories we notice the emergence of a kind of indifference and apathy, or even opposition, towards Sufism. We may begin by considering a major figure in this respect, namely Sir Syed Ahmad Khan (d. 1896). In the second volume of his first major book, *Asar al-Sanadid* (1845–6), Syed Ahmad wrote a section on Sufis (*masha'ikh*), physicians (*hukama'*), scholars (*'ulama*), those who had memorised the Qur'an (*huffaz*), poets, calligraphers, and prominent musicians of Delhi. These were all his contemporaries at some point or the other. He begins this section with an account of one of the major eighteenth-century Naqshbandi–Mujaddidi shaikhs, Shah Ghulam 'Ali (d. 1824). He says his father, elder brother, and even mother were all disciples of Shah Ghulam Ali. He also emphasises his own connection with the same master and says that as a young boy he called him Grandfather (*dada hazrat*). Syed Ahmad was only seven years old when Shah Ghulam 'Ali passed away. Although he takes due note of his *karamat*, he focuses more on his ethics and piety (*akhlaq, taqwa*). Syed Ahmad also writes about Saiyid Ahmad Shahid in this section, whom he praises extravagantly for his spiritual attainments, noting that even a Sufi scholar as renowned as Shah 'Abd al-'Aziz, the eldest son of Shah Wali-Allah (d. 1762), was hesitant – on account of his piety and spiritual attainments even at a young age – about taking him on as his disciple. In sum, Syed Ahmad seems very impressed by him, including with his struggle for establishing an Islamic *imamat* in north-western India, his struggle against the Sikhs, and his eventual martyrdom. To be noted also are the terms Syed Ahmad

[54] Metcalf, *Islamic Revival in British India*; Weismann, *The Naqshbandiyya*, Chapters 6, 7, and 8, pp. 85–146; Robinson, "Islamic Reform and Modernities in South Asia", pp. 26–50; Lawrence, ed., *The Rose and the Rock*, pp. 66–103.

uses for Isma'il Shahid, such as *qami' al-bid'at* (destroyer of innovation), besides praising his intelligence and understanding of convoluted theological texts, as well as his association with Saiyid Ahmad Shahid. Thus, at least at this stage, in his accounts of Sufis and Sufism Syed Ahmad Khan shows a distinct appreciation for its social, political, and theological aspects.[55]

A few years later, however, in 1849 to be precise, Syed Ahmad wrote a treatise, *Kalimat al-Haqq* (Word of Truth) to critique prevalent practices around *pir–murid* relationships. Around the same time he published a treatise called *Namiqa dar bayan mas'ala-i tasawwur-i shaikh*, which was on the Sufi practice of imagining the Sufi master. Slightly later, in 1859, he wrote a treatise entitled *Rah-i sunnat dar radd-i bid'at* (The Path of Sunna and the Refutation of Innovation), which in a measure echoes his views as expressed in *Kalimat al-Haqq*, albeit in stronger terms, unequivocally condemning *bid'at* and extolling *sunnat* (the tradition of the Prophet).[56] In *Kalimat al-Haqq*, citing from the Qur'an, *hadith*, and Shah Wali-Allah's writings (such as *al-Qaul al-Jamil*), he says Islam as religion was already perfected in the time of the Prophet; what was added later was mere deception (*dhoka*) and rubbish (*zatall*). He also disapproves of the idea of initiation (*bai'at*), and the notion of a spiritual lineage (*silsila*), mentioning in particular the Qadiriyya, Naqshbandiyya, and Chishtiyya, and the related belief that *pirs* rescue their *murids* in the hereafter. "In the Hereafter, God will himself be the judge. Without God's grace, neither the *pir* nor any *faqir* will be able to intercede. It will be a time such that no one will pay attention to anyone else. Everybody will be worried about themselves. The *pir* will have no clue about his *murid* and the *murid* will have no idea about his *pir*. No one there will ask 'Are you a *murid* in the Qadiriyya, or the Naqshbandiyya, or the

---

[55] Khan, *Asar al-Sanadid*, Vol. 2, pp. 15–20, 33–5, and 80–4.

[56] These two *risalas* were reproduced in 1883 when Sir Syed published in Volume 1, Part 1, a collection of his writings titled *Tasanif-i Ahmadiya*. Later, Muhammad Isma'il Panipati, reproduced them in Volume 5 of his edited 16-volume work, *Maqalat-i Sir Sayyid*, pp. 267–90 and 354–429.

Chishtiyya?'"⁵⁷ Syed Ahmad subsequently wrote a review of his *Rah-i sunnat dar radd-i bid'at* in which he admits the work was composed under the influence of Ahl-i Hadith and Wahhabis. He reiterates, however, that what he said earlier was with reference to religious beliefs and prayers (*'aqa'id-o-'ibadat*), and that he has indubitably revised his position with reference to matters pertaining to everyday secular life, such as people's taste for mangoes, which were obviously available neither to the Prophet nor to any of his close companions. He sums up this *risala* as follows: "O Muslim brothers! Know that you cannot attain salvation with the practices that some *pir* has come up with. It is only with the tradition and acts (*sunnat*) of the Prophet of God (Peace be upon Him) and by following the way of his close companions that you will find salvation."⁵⁸

Syed Ahmad also expresses very harsh views on *tasawwuf* in several pieces he wrote later, reproduced in the *Maqalat-i Sir Sayyid*. One of these is entitled *Mukashafa*. In it he describes the five categories of *kashf* (the mystic's mysterious knowledge and miracles), as given in the writings of the Sufis: *nazari, nuri, sirri* or *ilahi, ruhani* (by which stage the seeker begins to have visions of divinity), *sifati,* and *zati.* Interesting to note is that for each category after the first stage he has a paragraph, each of which opens satirically: "And he [the Sufi] cooks this thought more and more (*aur wo is khayal ko aur ziyada pakata hai*)"; and he ends by saying: "which is nothing other than his [the Sufi's] own thoughts (*jo bajuz us ke khayal ke ko'i aur dusri chiz nahi hai*)". He concludes the essay with a quotation in Arabic that begins:

---

⁵⁷ *Maqalat-i Sir Sayyid*, Vol. 5, pp. 267–90: "*Qiyamat mein Allah ap insaf karega. Phir jab tak Allah hi fazl na kare, wahan na pir ki himayat chalegi na faqir ki. Wo aisa bura waqt hoga, ke ko'i kisi ki sudh na lega. Apni apni nafsi mein giriftar honge. Na pir ko murid ki khabar hogi aur na murid ko pir ki. Wahan ye na puchha ja'ega ki tu Qadiriya khandan mein murid hai, ya Naqshbandiya mein, ya Chishtiya mein.*"

⁵⁸ Ibid., pp. 427–9.

By God, this is a pearl, whoever has said it (*wa-Allahi durr man qala*): that *tasawwuf* is the turning of the human soul (*nafs*) towards imaginary matters, and it stays there, until he believes that what is in his imagination is actually existent, while the reality is that it is existent only in his imagination (*khayal*), and nothing else. Similarly, he moves from one [figment of the] imagination to another [figment of the] imagination, and believes it to be something else, while it is not something else, except that it is also his imagination. And as this imagination grows, he thinks that this is God, together with his Attributes. At this stage, he thinks that his self has risen to a high stage, and he has recognised God as He deserves to be recognised. But [in fact] God is above and beyond all this. In truth, there is nothing like Him. He is the only Hearer, and the Knower.[59]

In the same vein, he wrote three other pieces: *Waqi'at 'Ammat al-Wurud* (Everyday Happenings), *'Ajaibat ka Zuhul aur 'Ajaibat ka Qubul* (Forgetting and Believing in Wonders), and *Karamat aur Mu'jiza* (Miracles of the Saints and the Prophets). In the *Waqi'at* he writes that when an incident is unusual and occurs among ordinary people, it is called a coincidence (*ittifaq*); but when such a thing happens with a holy person, people think of it as a miracle (*karishma*).[60] In the *'Ajaibat* article Syed Ahmad says it was over

[59] Khan, *Maqalat-i Sir Sayyid*, Vol. 1, pp. 110–13: "altasawwuf huwa irja' alnafs 'ila umur khayaliya, wa al-mudawamat 'alaiha ila zaman hatta tatakhaiyyal al-umur bi–khayalihi, kana haza al-umur maujuda fi nafsihi lakinna al-maujud fi khayal, huwa khayaluhu, la shai'a ghairih. Wa hakaza yataraqqi min khayal ila khayal akhar wa yatasawwar shai'a akhar. Wa lakinna laisa shai'a akhar illa khayal nafsihi, fa'iza taraqqa haza al-khayal, yatakhayyal huwa Allah, lao sha'n min shuyunihi. Wa al-an yatakhayyal innahu rafa'a nafsahu ila a'la al-darjat, wa 'arafa Allah haqqa ma'rifatihi. Wa Allah bari 'an haza, wa al-haqq inna-hu laisa ka-mislihi shai'a, wa huwa al-Sami' al-Basir." At the end of this essay, the editor Muhammad Isma'il Panipati expresses his opinion that this idea of Syed Ahmad, which he also elaborates in the other three articles, is incorrect and precludes belief in any Prophet whatsoever. While this and the following two articles are reproduced from an earlier collection of Syed Ahmad's articles "*Sir Syed ke akhri mazamin*", the last one, *Karamat and Mu'jiza*, was published in 1888 in Aligarh's *Tahzib al-Akhlaq*.

[60] Ibid., pp. 114–17.

the course of history that Islam acquired wondrous stories which, thus, have nothing to do with Islam (*Islam mein 'ajaibat nahi hain*). He concludes the article with a sarcastic plea: "May God save us from these wonder-worshippers."⁶¹ In the third, *Karamat aur Mu'jiza*, he provides details of false beliefs and superstitions and ridicules them, one such being the notion of being healed by the prayers of a Sufi. He concludes the essay thus: "... in all illiterate, uncivilised, and uncultivated countries and peoples, belief in miracles is always present. But when the light of knowledge spreads, these kinds of things are erased ... Such beliefs are a major and strong obstacle for Muslims to civilise themselves. It is also completely opposed to the fundamentals of Islam ... Thus, until the belief in miracles disappears from [among] the Muslims, it is impossible for them to be fully civilised."⁶²

In short, despite the fact that Syed Ahmad's father, mother, and elder brother had close devotional connections with the Naqshbandi–Mujaddidi order, he himself grew increasingly sceptical about, or at least indifferent to, the spiritual aspects of *tasawwuf*. Later, in his post-1857 writings, he did not even consider *tasawwuf* a part of Islam, seeing it instead as the principal reason for the backwardness of the Muslim community.

Shibli Nu'mani (d. 1914)

The other major figure among Muslim "modernist" intellectuals of late-nineteenth- and early-twentieth-century India who wrote extensively on Islam and its history was Shibli Nu'mani. In fact, it turns out that though Shibli wrote nothing on *tasawwuf* in particular, one of his major works is a biography of Maulana Jalal al-Din Muhammad Rumi (d. 1273), author of the greatly noted six-volume *Masnawi*.⁶³ Rumi's position as a major Sufi has never

---

⁶¹ Ibid., pp. 118–22.
⁶² Ibid., pp. 123–7.
⁶³ Shibli Nu'mani, *Sawanih-i Maulana Rum*. There are several editions of this book, and the latest are some from Azamagarh: reprint, Darul Musannefin

been seriously in doubt, and his poetry, including his *Masnawi*, is regarded as one of the best expositions of Sufism. Ironically, Shibli's fascination for Rumi was not because of his *tasawwuf*, rather it was because he considered Rumi an extraordinary theologian, at par with the likes of Abu al-Hasan al-Ash'ari (d. 936) and Abu Hamid al-Ghazali (d. 1111). Shibli's biography of Rumi is the fourth in a chain of his writings on Islamic theology, *'Ilm al-Kalam, al-Kalam*, and *al-Ghazali* being its predecessors.[64] Shibli was in fact aware of the anomaly involved in claiming Rumi for Islami theology sans his Sufism, and therefore says: "to classify him [Rumi] in the category of theologians and write a biography of him as such will surprise readers. But in my understanding true theology is precisely this: the interpretation and explanation of Islamic beliefs (*Islam ke 'aqa'id*), and the elaboration of their realities and truths (*haqa'iq wa ma'arif*) such that they may be completely internalised (*khud ba khud dil nashin*). Rumi is so skilled in this respect that there is scarcely a writer as good. Which is why to exclude him from any grouping of theologians would be a gross injustice."[65]

However, he has three chapters relating to *tasawwuf* in this book: "*Tasawwuf*", "*Tauhid-i Wahdat al-Wujud*", and "*Maqamat-i Suluk-o-Fana*".[66] He also integrates within his discussion of Rumi's biographical details some of his spiritual experiences, such as the "spiritual chain (*silsila-i batini*)" and "ecstasy and trance (*wajd-o-istighraq*)". He provides material showing Rumi entranced for days on end, and how if on the street he happened to hear a good voice he would remain there in order to start dancing ecstatically. Under the *silsila-i batini* he mentions Rumi's *silsila-i jalaliya* and his practice of dance and *sama'*. Shibli also writes of Rumi's meetings with other Sufis of his time, such as Sadr al-Din al-Qunawi,

---

Shibli Academy. The references here are from a very early printing, published from Daftar-i Urdu-i Mu'alla, Shahjahani Press, Delhi, n.d.

[65] Shibli Nu'mani, *'Ilm al-Kalam*; idem, *al-Kalam*.
[65] *Sawanih-i Maulana Rum*, pp. 9–10.
[66] Ibid., pp. 124–36.

Najm al-Din Razi, Muhyi al-Din ibn al-ʿArabi, Saʿd al-Din Hamawi, and Auhad al-Din Kirmani. But he is not interested in the details of exchanges between Rumi and these Sufis. He also mentions the great India-based Sufi Bu ʿAli Qalandar (d. 1324) and his meeting with Rumi, and takes relish in describing a famous incident with a bearing on Rumi's universal conciliation. This relates to Rumi saying he agreed with all seventy-two sects of Muslims. A contemporary of his attempted to confirm if this was actually Rumi's position, and if true take him to task for it. When it was indeed confirmed as Rumi's position, the interrogator began foul-mouthing Rumi. In response, Rumi smiled and said: "Whatever you say – I agree with that as well." The embarrassed contemporary thereupon departed.[67] The incident also contains echoes of the attitude of a seventeenth-century figure such as ʿAbd al-Rahman Chishti and his narrative of Shah Badiʿ al-Din Madar.

Such discussions remain rather nominal and brief in Shibli's writings, but his book has several detailed chapters on how Rumi dealt with important questions such as the essence and attributes of God, prophethood, revelation, the vision of angels, miracles, the soul and spirit, resurrection and predestination.[68] He was also fascinated by the quality and reputation of Rumi's poetry, characterising the *Masnawi* amongst the four most popular and most read Persian works (the other three being the *Shahnama* of Firdausi, the *Gulistan* of Saʿdi, and the *Diwan-i Hafiz*). Shibli had a particular fascination for Persian poetry. He acknowledges that *tasawwuf* was already a poetic subject before Rumi's *Masnawi* but stresses that none of the earlier poems on the theme became as famous, not even one as popular as *Hadiqa-i Sanaʾi*. This, according to Shibli, was because none of the others were works of theology: the *Masnawi* for him is in the main a book of Muslim theology.[69] Like Syed Ahmad Khan, Shibli had no affiliations with

---

[67] Ibid., pp. 23–34.
[68] Ibid., pp. 104–72.
[69] Ibid., pp. 50 and 76–7.

any of the Sufi *silsilas* of his time, nor did he write anything on Sufism in India or the Islamic world.[70] His interest above all was Muslim theology, which he wanted to discuss and discourse upon. The Shibli Academy, which he established, and which was promoted by his noted disciples after his death, as well as its famous magazine *Ma'arif*, only began to include essays on Sufic themes by fellows of the Academy much later, a trend which seems to have been inspired by his disciple Saiyid Sulaiman Nadwi (d. 1953). These later essays, for instance those written by Saiyid Sabahuddin 'Abdur Rahman, were later also published with revisions and additions in a volume entitled *Bazm-i Sufiya*.[71]

A similar attitude is observable in yet another major Muslim writer and poet of the time, Altaf Hussain Hali (d. 1914). His magnum opus, *Musaddas-i Hali*, glorifies the Islamic past and laments the fate of his own time. Yet, even though he glorifies the memory of past Muslim philosophers, rulers, and conquerors, nowhere does he hint at any past Sufis adding, let alone bringing glory, to Islam. Rather, when he comes to his own times, he notices mainly the decadent and fraudulent descendants of members of Sufi centres tricking common Muslims of the day.[72]

---

[70] In a recent issue of *Ma'arif*, July 2020, pp. 34–43, Muhammad Ilyas al-A'zmi has published (with introductory comments) an account of a lecture on *tasawwuf* that Shibli gave at Khwaja Husain Nizami's invitation in Delhi in 1908. (I am grateful to Professor I.A. Zilli for this reference.) In this piece, there is a brief discussion of the time of the Prophet and his companions, and some citations from Rumi as well as some Indian scholars such as Qazi Sana'-Allah Panipati. Interestingly Shibli, here following Shah Wali-Allah and very much against Sir Syed, suggests that *tasawwuf* is a proper part of Islam by drawing from the teachings of the Prophet and the practice of his companions. Unfortunately, what has been published is a summarised version of his lecture, which first appeared in Hasan Nizami's journal *Nizam al-Masha'ikh* in January 1910. Incidentally this is the only independent piece on the subject we have from Shibli. The full original version of the lecture is still untraceable.

[71] Rahman, *Bazm-i Sufiya*.

[72] Hali, *Hali's Musaddas*. This edition by Shackle and Majeed includes the Urdu text, Hali's *dibachas*, and notes to the first editions of 1879 and 1886.

Muhammad Iqbal (d. 1938)

Amongst the major modern Muslim thinkers of South Asia, Iqbal takes a particularly complicated position on *tasawwuf*. It is reported that, following in the footsteps of his father, he was initiated into the Qadiri Sufi *silsila*. Iqbal himself tells us he was highly influenced by the Sufic doctrines of 'Abd al-Karim al-Jili (or Jilani), a noted disciple of Shaikh Ibn al-'Arabi.[73] Iqbal also extols the sublimity and passion of (Sufi) love in several of his verses, as in the following:

'Ishq dam-i Jibrail, 'ishq dil-i Mustafa
'Ishq khuda ka Rasul, 'ishq khuda ka kalam.[74]

Love is the breath of Gabriel, Love is the heart of Mustafa.
Love is the Prophet of God, Love is the Word of God.

Elsewhere he says:

Biya ba majlis-i Iqbal yak do saghar kash,
Agarche sar na tarashad qalandari danad.[75]

Come to the assembly of Iqbal and drink a cup or two.
Even though he doesn't shave his head, he knows the ways of the *qalandar*.

The question whether he simply possessed knowledge of it (*danad*) or believed in and practised it too is clarified in many of his verses, as in the following in which he confesses to have experienced the pangs of (spiritual Sufi) love:

Is kashmakash mein guzri meri zindagi ki raten.
Kabhi soz-o-saz-i Rumi, kabhi pech-o-tab-i Razi.[76]

---

[73] Farman, *Iqbal aur Tasawwuf*, p. 98, citing from Iqbal's article, "The Doctrine of Absolute Unity as Expounded by Abdul Karim al-Jilani", pp. 237–46.
[74] *Kulliyat-i Iqbal*, p. 386.
[75] Iqbal, *Payam-i Mashriq*, p. 308.
[76] Ibid., p. 309.

The nights of my life have been spent in this dilemma.
At times, the passion of Rumi; at others, the convolutions of Razi.

He expresses his debt to several Sufis, including Rumi, whom he passionately affirms as his master and mentor (*murshid*), stating moreover that he learnt from him as a disciple (*murid*) an entire philosophy of life in his living presence.[77] We also have Iqbal's strongly critical views of *wahdat al-wujud*. He believed that in this doctrine there was a kind of belittling of the human will or force (*khudi*), a thesis which he develops powerfully in his *Asrar-i Khudi*, where he also takes issue with the great Persian poet Hafiz Shirazi. This caused a furore among the Muslim notables around him, including the likes of the Urdu poet Akbar Ilahabadi and Khwaja Hasan Nizami. They accused him of taking an anti-*tasawwuf* stand, against which Iqbal defended his position forcefully though also apologetically.[78] He supported and admired the doctrine of *wahdat al-shuhud* and was highly impressed by Shaikh Ahmad Sirhindi, as demonstrated in the following lines of his poem entitled "*Mujaddid-i Alf-i Sani*":

> *Gardan na jhuki jis ki Jahangir ke age,*
> *Jis ke nafas-i garm se hai garmi-yi ahrar,*
> *Wo Hind mein sarmaya-i millat ka nigahban,*
> *Allah ne bar waqt kiya jisko khabardar.*[79]

> He who did not bow his head before Jahangir,
> He whose vital breath sustains the passion of free souls,
> He who protects the precious spirit of the community in India,
> Whom God alerted at just the right time.

---

[77] Ibid., p. 426. I owe this point to Shariq Khan, who is developing it in his forthcoming detailed study of the afterlife of Rumi's *Masnawi* in India. According to Annemarie Schimmel, Iqbal's idea of *khudi* was in fact inspired by Rumi's *Fihi ma Fihi*. See Schimmel, *Gabriel's Wing*, p. 13: "Rumi had [already] used the term *khudi* in the sense of the spiritual, unperishable Self of the human being."

[78] Farman, *Iqbal aur Tasawwuf*, pp. 116–17. In the second edition, Iqbal removed Hafiz's verses from *Asrar-i Khudi*.

[79] Iqbal, *Payam-i Mashriq*, p. 450.

Iqbal thus brackets the Mujaddid-i Alf-i Sani, Aurangzeb, and Shah Isma'il Shahid, calling them *ahrar* (literally free men, i.e. heroes), and says they revived an Islamic way of living (*Islami sirat*); whereas the abundant presence of Sufis and their centuries-old accretion of power had not brought them success. It is thus that he clarifies his position and redefines *tasawwuf*.

Iqbal also believes that in the struggle between reason (*'aql*) and love (*'ishq*), love triumphs; but his conception of reason and love are not those of the earlier Sufis. His is a new perspective, and the result that he arrives at varies from that of his predecessors. In this context the word *faqr* (originally, poverty) too acquires a new meaning in Iqbal – namely, disinterestedness.[80] He says "foreign influences, Platonic philosophy, and Vedantic philosophy have distorted the soul of Islamic philosophy and changed the strand (*rang*) of *tasawwuf* that became a part of Muslim life. The fundamental principle of Islam is *tauhid*, while *tasawwuf* is based on the principle of *hama ust* (All is He). *Tauhid* is positive, *hama ust* negative."[81] In a letter to Saiyid Sulaiman Nadwi he writes: "There is no doubt that the existence of *taswwuf* in the land of Islam is an alien plant, which was nourished in the intellectual environment of 'Ajamis." In another letter, to Siraj al-Din Pal, he writes:

> The first poet of *tasawwuf* is 'Iraqi, and the last poet is Hafiz. It is surprising that all the poetry of *tasawwuf* was produced during the political decline of the Muslims. And this was inevitable. Look at the Muslims of India themselves – the climax of literary perfection was *marsiya-gu'i* in Lucknow . . . All of these have distorted and refuted the signs of Islam in a strange and heart-warming way. Everything despicable in Islam has been portrayed as praiseworthy.[82]

---

[80] *Faqr* is an extremely important factor in strengthening the self because without it a person lives in a state of servitude. Diagne, *Islam and Open Society*, pp. 28–31; Dar, *A Study in Iqbal's Philosophy*.

[81] Bijnori, *Sirat-i Iqbal*, p. 138, cited in Farman, *Iqbal aur Tasawwuf*, p. 118.

[82] Farman, *Iqbal aur Tasawwuf*, p. 112.

Iqbal also comes to the same conclusion regarding the development of Islamic culture in his *Reconstruction of Religious Thought in Islam*.[83] Inevitably, there are bound to be disagreements among historians regarding the correct interpretation of the complex thought of Iqbal on the place of *tasawwuf* in Islam. But there is no gainsaying his own profound ambivalence on the question.

Conclusion

We have seen above how, since the beginning of the eighteenth century, efforts have been made to reconcile the two major doctrinal bases of Sufi practices. Shah Wali-Allah led the effort in the eighteenth century, later augmented in part by a noted member of his family, Shah Isma'il Shahid, at least in the earlier stages of his career. The effort was reignited in the nineteenth century, most notably by Haji Imdad-Allah. However, he also waged *jihad* against the British, as a result of which he had to leave the country. In fact his masters, 'Abd al-Rahim Wilayati and Nur Muhammad Jhanjhanvi, actually left their homes and, instead of spending time on meditation and *muraqaba*, decided to join Saiyid Ahmad Shahid's struggle against the "enemies of Islam". This is an important illustration of the overlap and interconnection between various Sufi ideologies and practices. In my understanding even Thanawi, in whose *tasawwuf* we saw a combination of the conventional Chishti–Sabiri and the Naqshbandi–Mujaddidi, represents a measure of the same conciliation.

Around the same time, two other Deoband shaikhs, Mahmud Hasan and Husain Ahmad Madani, reinforced the Mughal Indian Chishti–Sabiri tradition of amity and social harmony between the different communities. We also noted changes, some very radical, in the approach of Muslim intellectuals to *tasawwuf* and its relationship with everyday life following South Asia's deeper contact with the West in the colonial period. Here we have a fascinating effort at conciliation in the form of Iqbal's philosophy.

[83] Siddiqui, "A Historical View of Iqbal's Ideas on *Tasawwuf*", pp. 411–27.

Because of his concern with action, he showed an appreciation for the doctrine of *wahdat al-shuhud*, but also bowed his head in reverence to Rumi, a most noted exponent of *wahdat al-wujud*. Ritualised or ethical *tasawwuf* continued in some measure as an integral part of the Muslim social order in South Asia – as it had been under the Mughals. But it is important for us to recognise the existence of profound elements of discontinuity as well as threads of continuity in how the Sufis were located in society and politics after the end of Mughal rule. The reticence, and even outright hostility, shown by some major Muslim intellectuals and leaders of the modern period to medieval and early-modern Sufism has therefore informed the way in which they and their followers read Mughal history. It has meant that the heroes for some have become the villains for others, and vice-versa. These effects can be seen as much in India as in Pakistan, as well as in the South Asian diaspora. An awareness of the impact of these later trends on today's perspectives can help us approach the materials of the Mughal period with a more informed longer-term understanding, thereby avoiding anachronistic readings of texts and historical situations.

The chapters that follow begin with a consideration of the Mughal–Sufi relationship within a larger sixteenth-century context, focusing on the strategies that the early Mughals adopted to build up their power in India. I review the positions of the two most important Sufi groups, namely the Indian Chishtis and the Central Asian Naqshbandis, juxtaposing the political benefits or losses that the Mughals saw in their association with them. While the Naqshbandi worldview and the legacy of the legendary 'Ubaid-Allah Ahrar (d. 1490) clashed, to an extent, with the Mughal vision of power, in the Chishti ideology they found strong support for themselves; consequently the Chishtis held the edge at the time of Akbar. Yet the Naqshbandis under Khwaja Baqi Billah (d. 1603) continued in their endeavour to establish their place in Mughal

India and regain the status they had enjoyed in Central Asia. These considerations are also necessary in order to re-evaluate the debate on the ideology and politics of Shaikh Ahmad Sirhindi.

The next three chapters are centrally devoted to the Chishti view of *tasawwuf* and politics. The question of Mughal Indian religious thought and *tasawwuf* has generally been discussed with reference to the Naqshbandi order, with particular attention given to Shaikh Ahmad Sirhindi, founder of the Mujaddidi branch of that order in India, as well as his disciples and ideology. Discussions have revolved around the nature and extent of their influence on seventeenth-century Mughal Indian religious culture and politics. Indeed, the memory of Sirhindi's achievements has been so integral to the history of South Asian Islam that when we recall seventeenth-century Muslim religious culture in India, his name comes immediately to mind. Sirhindi and Shaikh 'Abd al-Haq Muhaddis Dehlavi (d. 1643), and of course Shah Wali-Allah, are regarded the progenitors of the destiny of South Asian Muslims, the principal sources of all religious ideas and movements that subsequently shaped Islam in South Asia. There lived in Mughal times, however, an important Chishti Sufi, 'Abd al-Rahman Chishti Sabiri (d. 1683), who too rearticulated Sufi ideology in significant ways, defining in his discourse the problem of the Sufi's relationship to *shari'a*, in particular concerning specific religious jurisprudential schools (*mazhab, fiqh*) as well as the politics of the time. We find him rereading and redefining the Islamic past and Muslim religious traditions. And yet this strain of seventeenth-century thought is practically untouched in modern South Asian scholarship. Indeed, one of our best authorities projects the Chishtis during the high Mughal era as virtually inactive, reviving only later in the eighteenth century.[84] Some other major historians of Indian Sufism, such as Saiyid Athar Abbas Rizvi, for instance, discuss Shaikh 'Abd al-Rahman's

---

[84] There are, however, discussions of the Chishtis of the Mughal period in Nizami, *Tarikh-i Masha'ikh-i-Chisht*, pp. 224, 231; Rizvi, *History of Sufism*, Vol. 2; Ernst and Lawrence, *Sufi Martyrs of Love*; and Farooqi, *Medieval India*, pp. 125–51 and 165–211.

Sufism and employ his treatises as a resource for the history of Mughal Indian Sufism. Notwithstanding their work, I believe there are many significant features of Chishti's thought that get little attention, let alone the discourses and the debates in which Chishti engaged his contemporaries.

Shaikh 'Abd al-Rahman Chishti wrote extensively. He produced a huge *tazkira* of Sufis entitled *Mir'at al-Asrar*, beginning with early Islamic history and coming down to his own time. This work has a long introduction with a comprehensive discussion on some basic features of Islam, such as the definition and meaning of *sunna*, obedience to the Prophet's teachings and traditions, and the distinction between *nubuwwat* (prophethood) and *wilayat* (sainthood). In one of the chapters that follow I attempt to understand the position he took in *Mir'at al-Asrar* by reading this *tazkira* together with his other writings, focusing in particular on the long preface to this work, wherein he elaborates on his definition of *tasawwuf* and asks what the real religion of the Sufi should be. 'Abd al-Rahman also undertakes a far-reaching reassessment of key elements in the wider traditions of Indian Islam. Drawing on a range of Indian and Middle Eastern influences, he rejects the narrow legality-centred formulation of the Naqshbandis and offers a distinctive vision of Chishti spiritual support at the heart of the Mughal political order. This discussion, we will see, was not new to Mughal India and formed part of a longer debate regarding *tasawwuf* and *fiqh* (jurisprudence) or *shari'a* in the Islamic tradition.

An illustration of the significance of the debate in Mughal India was a full-fledged treatise on the theme titled *Maraj al-Bahrain* (Meeting of the Two Oceans) by Shaikh 'Abd al-Haq Muhaddis Dehlavi. Dehlavi in turn refers back to an important fifteenth-century treatise on the same theme, *Qawa'id al-Tasawwuf* by Ahmad Zarruq, a noted Moroccan scholar and Sufi who pleaded for what has been described as "juridical Sufism".[85]

---

[85] For Zarruq and his impact on 'Ali Muttaqi, see Kugle, "Usuli Sufis: Ahmad Zarruq and His South Asian Followers", pp. 181–204. Also see Kugle, *Rebel Between Spirit and Law*.

A subsequent chapter turns to the intriguing figure of Shah Madar, focusing in particular on his portrayal by 'Abd al-Rahman Chishti in his *Mir'at-i Madariya*. Shah Madar, apparently born and raised in Syria in a Jewish family, moved to North India during the fifteenth century and is generally regarded as a highly heterodox (*bi-shar'a*) Sufi. Even today the Madari order is generally thought of as deeply antinomian, with popular representations showing its adherents gathering on the occasion of the saint's death ('*urs*) like a group of Muslim *yogis*, some of them even practising extreme mortification, smoking hashish, and intoning their saint's name with each puff. Chishti for his part portrayed him as an exemplary representative of classical Islam, as the Prophet's envoy who after having been specially trained and tutored under the supervision of the Prophet's cousin and the first Shi'i Imam 'Ali, was entrusted with propagating and strengthening the Muslim faith in India. Still, Madar encountered serious challenges to his way of Islamic proselytising, at the level of both ideology and practice. In course of his portrayal Chishti also discusses how and why such an apologetic portrayal of a deviant Sufi was made in the Mughal Indian religious milieu.

Another chapter consists of a close reading of a seventeenth-century text, *Mir'at al-Makhluqat* (Mirror of Creation), also written by Shaikh 'Abd al-Rahman Chishti. This work, purportedly a translation of a Sanskrit text, attempts to reconcile Hindu and Muslim accounts of human genesis and cosmogony. Chishti adopts rhetorical strategies and mythological elements of the Purana tradition in order to argue that evidence of the Muslim prophets was available in ancient Hindu scriptures. He accepts the reality of ancient Hindu gods and sages and notes the truth inherent in their message. In doing so Chishti adopts elements of an older argument within the Islamic tradition that posits thousands of cycles of creation and multiple instances of Adam, the father of the human race. He argues however that the Hindu gods and sages belonged to a different order of creation and time and were not in fact human. The text bears some generic resemblance to *Bhavishyottarapurana* materials that we know from the nineteenth century, but is their precursor by two centuries. Chishti combines aspects of polemics with a deft use of politics. He addresses Hindu intellectuals who claimed the prestige of an older religion, while also engaging with Muslim theologians and even Sufis such as the Naqshbandi–Mujaddidis. This chapter also illustrates a significant feature of Mughal Indian culture, i.e. the interest Muslims showed in India's Hindu religious traditions. The period saw translations into Persian of several major Hindu texts, at the Mughal court and elsewhere. With the appearance of these translations, they had access to "Hindu" pasts and legends that stretched the limits of their imagination.

The sixth chapter therefore discusses one such text from the Mughal court, namely the Persian translation of the *Yogavasistha* done or commissioned by the Mughal prince Dara Shukoh. Dara Shukoh has often been projected as the beacon of Mughal non-sectarian political culture, as a champion of Akbar's policy of *sulh-i kull*. On the other hand some historians, juxtaposing his politics and leadership capabilities with those of Aurangzeb, have condemned him for his deficiencies as a military and political commander. He has also been portrayed as a saintly scholar interested both in Sufi traditions as well as ancient Hindu religious scriptures. My own purpose, in this chapter, is not to take a position with regard to these various approaches. Rather, I am concerned with the prince's approach to the translation of the *Yogavasistha*. To bring his engagement with this text into view as deserving historical attention, I ask the following questions: Why did Dara Shukoh commission a new translation of the *Yogavasistha* in 1656, when over half a century earlier Nizam Panipati had already published a translation of the "complete" text, and besides which three other versions of the text were available to him? Did he see in the *Yogavasistha* something that was missing in the existing Persian versions? With these questions in mind I revisit several translations and recensions of the *Yogavasistha*, giving in brief the reasons why various Mughal scholars and their patrons chose this text and how they sought to embody their visions of it into Persian. Thereafter I discuss in particular Dara Shukoh's translation and try to understand both the prince's personality and his politics in the larger context of Mughal history, which I do in order to understand how his political vision reconciled the demands of spiritual truth and temporal power.

Dara Shukoh had a close relationship with the noted Chishti–Sabiri saint Shah Muhibb-Allah of Allahabad (d. 1648). The Sufi order with which he was principally affiliated was neither Chishti nor Naqshbandi: rather, he was a Qadiri, an order which also had access to the Mughal court. This is further illustrated in a chapter dealing with Princess Jahanara's writings and career, which ran parallel to that of her brother Dara Shukoh. The chapter also includes details about another of Shah Jahan's daughters, Roshan Rai, better known as Roshanara, which show the Naqshbandi–Mujaddidis' access to the imperial household in its feminine aspect. In addition, this chapter juxtaposes the case of Jahanara with the literary – and in a measure also spiritual – career of Zeb-un-nisa', the noted daughter of Aurangzeb. Orientalist accounts of these princesses depict them employing the usual tropes of lasciviousness and illicit love. I focus here instead, among other sources, on the letters written either by them or to them, as well as their own writings, and try to reconstruct their religious and literary lives, showing that these princesses had considerable political autonomy, and that, like their male counterparts, they enjoyed close and often devotional proximity to Sufi shaikhs.

The last chapter then returns to take an in-depth look at the Naqshbandi–Mujaddidi shaikhs of Sirhind and the period of their ascendancy in the Mughal court around Aurangzeb's reign. I focus in particular on their relationships with the emperor himself, and the implications thereof. Finally, I follow this up with a look at their position in the early-eighteenth century, after the death of Aurangzeb, when the focus shifts from Sirhind to Delhi, and from the court to late-Mughal society at large. This chapter makes particular use of the writings of the Naqshbandis, including extensive collections of their letters which provide details of their engagement with the court and a variety of significant political actors.

Taken together, the chapters of this book provide a varied and complex reading of the relationship between various groups of Sufis and Mughal political culture over the course of some three centuries. By focusing on certain lesser-known and under-studied figures and their writings, I also hope to reorient our understanding of the cultural history of the Mughal period and its actors. The next generation of scholars will, I believe, take this subject of study even further into new and exciting areas.

2

The Mughals, the Sufi Shaikhs, and the Formation of the Akbari Dispensation

Introduction

THE AUTHORITY EXERCISED by the Mughal dynasty over much of northern India in the sixteenth, seventeenth, and eighteenth centuries depended in part on various forms of legitimacy that were provided to it from outside the narrow sphere of elite politics. To be sure, the Mughals were also able to rule for so long and with such success because they successfully managed a composite political elite made up of elements both from northern India and from the Deccan (as well as other "peripheral" regions), and migrants from Central and West Asia. However, as with a number of dynasties of the Muslim world in the period, a crucial element in the strategies of rule that they adopted were their relations with religious figures of various sorts. My attempt in this chapter is to understand the changing relationship between the Mughal rulers and the Sufi shaikhs, focusing on the early days of the formation and consolidation of the Mughal state in India. The question of the Mughal–Sufi equation, as we know, has generally been discussed with reference to the Naqshbandi order. Scholars have devoted particular attention to Shaikh Ahmad Sirhindi (d. 1624), the founder of the Mujaddidi branch of that order, his disciples, and his ideology. Their questions have revolved around the extent and nature of the influence of this group on seventeenth-century Mughal Indian politics.¹ There is no denying the importance of this debate, and as a matter of fact in writing as I do here I was initially motivated by the desire to contribute to it. In the course of my study of the relevant materials, however, I realised that I would be in a better position to re-evaluate this subject if I placed Mughal–Sufi relationships within a larger sixteenth-century context and not limit the discussion to the Naqshbandi shaikhs.²

My attempt now is to examine the career, politics, and ideology of Sufis who occupied a central position in the social and cultural life of Indian Muslims in the early-sixteenth century, the time when the Mughals conquered India and began to build up their power. I describe in brief the political and doctrinal life of Shaikh 'Abd al-Quddus Gangohi (d. 1537), a leading Chishti shaikh of the time. Gangohi was the *pir* (preceptor), and very nearly the royal *pir*, of the Afghans, the arch-rivals of the Mughals. How then did the Mughals deal with him? How did he reconcile himself with the new situation? Was there any change in his position, or later, after his death, in the position of other people and institutions

---

[1] This is true of almost all modern historians, regardless of whether they have highlighted evidence to support, qualify, or reject the validity of this proposition; the contours of the proposition itself have not shifted. See for example Habib, "The Political Role of Shaikh Ahmad Sirhindi", pp. 36–55; Ahmad, *Studies in Islamic Culture*, pp. 182–90; Nizami, "Naqshbandi Influence", pp. 41–52; Friedmann, *Shaykh Ahmad Sirhindi*; Rahman, *Islam*, p. 148; ter Haar, *Follower and Heir*; Damrel, "The 'Naqshbandi Reaction'", pp. 176–98.

[2] Rizvi, "Sixteenth Century Naqshbandiyya Leadership", pp. 153–65; Dale, "The Legacy of the Timurids", pp. 43–58; and Buehler, "The Naqshbandiyya in Timurid India", pp. 209–28 – all these provide useful details on the Naqshbandis' relations with the early Mughals. However, they do not discuss the complexities of Mughal encounters with Indian Sufis. Damrel's discussion of some Chishti Sufi rites and practices with reference to Sirhindi is essentially meant to show his connections with the Chishtis and the similarities in their "politics" and Sufi practices. Cf. Damrel, "The 'Naqshbandi Reaction' Reconsidered".

related to the Chishti order? Can we explain the changes that did occur in terms of evolving conditions in the wake of the establishment and consolidation of the Mughal empire? What was the response of the Mughals and why did it take the form it did? I also discuss the visits of Central Asian Naqshbandi shaikhs to the Mughal court. Besides details of their relations with the early Indian Mughals, I draw attention to the nature of their relations with the Timurid rulers in Central Asia. This I do to understand problems that arose in the wake of their visits. I thus ask if, with the Mughal conquest of India, these Naqshbandi shaikhs also saw the prospect of an extension of the domain of their power, and if the legacy of the ideology and practice of Central Asian Naqshbandi *tasawwuf* hindered progress in building the Mughal state in India, thereby creating difficulties for the Mughals. In particular, the connections between Akbar's new administrative measures on the one hand, and the views of the Sufi shaikhs (whether Chishtis or Naqshbandis) on the other, seem to me to deserve analysis.

Finally, I examine in this chapter whether, in the new conditions of Akbar's India, the Naqshbandis rearticulated their *tasawwuf* in a bid to renegotiate their relationship with the Mughals. Several details critical to my argument have been developed earlier, in particular by scholars of Central Asia. However, I reinterpret these same elements in the perspective of the development of Mughal Indian politics and religious culture in order to provide a more useful context for questions often asked by historians of Mughal India.

The Chishti Shaikhs, the Afghans, and the Mughals

In the mid-1520s, when Zahir al-Din Muhammad Babur entered northern India with a plan to establish Mughal power in the subcontinent, Shaikh 'Abd al-Quddus Gangohi, a member of the Sabiri branch of the Chishti order, was probably the most noted Sufi shaikh around, with his deputies (*khalifas*), disciples (*murids*), and ordinary associates (*mutawassils*) spread over almost the entire upper northern Indian plain. They belonged to diverse groups, ranging from lowly weavers and peasants to very high members of the political class, including the reigning monarch and many of his courtiers, nobles, and commanders.[3] Gangohi's early career was in Rudauli, in Awadh, where he was initiated into the Sabiri line of the Chishti order by Shaikh Muhammad, a grandson of the eminent Chishti Sabiri saint Shaikh Ahmad 'Abd al-Haqq of Rudauli (d. 1434). He moved to the Punjab in the wake of Rajput uprisings in Awadh following the death of Bahlol Lodi (r. 1451–88) and settled in the Afghan-dominated town of Shahabad, near Karnal, north of the Yamuna river. In Shahabad, Gangohi spent the most important portion of his life, living there for over thirty-eight years, building an intimate affinity with the ruling Afghan king of the Lodi dynasty and his nobility. He had close relations with, and a special appreciation of, Sultan Sikandar Lodi (r. 1488–1517), for this sultan – at least according to Sufi accounts – was generous to the '*ulama* and the pious, so that in his reign, "in fear of his dreadful and dazzling sword, and because of the grandeur of his exalted kingly power, sinners and mischief mongers were totally annihilated [literally: disappeared into the darkness of night and inexistence.]"[4] Worth noting also is that Sikandar Lodi, as the later chronicler Muhammad Qasim Firishta reports, was the first Muslim king to create facilities for Hindus to learn Persian, and thus be trained to take charge of several offices under the Persianate Muslim government.[5]

Gangohi, like many Afghan nobles of the time, was however

---

[3] For the weavers (*ha'ikan* and *safed-baf*) of Saharanpur and Thanesar as Gangohi's disciples, see 'Ali, *Sawati' al-Anwar*, British Library, India Office Library MS, Ethe 654, fols 370a and 385b.

[4] Ibn Rukn, *alias* Miyan Khan ibn Qiwam al-Mulk Jaunpuri, *Maktubat-i Quddusiya*, p. 45.

[5] Firishta, *Tarikh-i Firishta*, Vol. I, p. 344; Urdu transl. by 'Abdul Hay Khwaja, p. 552.

unhappy with Ibrahim Lodi (r. 1517–26), though unlike them he did not welcome the Mughals, whom he saw as a divine scourge, set loose as divine retribution in the world of sinful Afghans. Indeed, the flourishing Afghan town where he lived with his family turned desolate with news of the feared Mughal invasion of the region. He left Shahabad, moved farther to settle in Gangoh on the eastern bank of the Yamuna river, this move being intended to remove him from the route of the invaders. But as he was nearly the sole royal *pir* of the Afghans, he was persuaded by his disciples to join them in the Afghan camp in order to bless them and pray for them in their imminent fight against the Mughals under Babur.

Gangohi anticipated the Afghan defeat, thought of fleeing, but eventually managed only to send his family away to Gangoh. He was constrained to stay back with Ibrahim Lodi's army together with his eldest son Shaikh Hamid, and his servitor (*khadim*) Sayyid Raja. With the Lodi Sultan's defeat and death, the Sufi fell into the hands of the Mughals, who first forced him to undo his turban, which they then threw around the necks of his son and *khadim*. This elderly *pir* of the Afghans was then forced to walk on foot from Panipat to Delhi, a distance of some forty miles, while his son and *khadim* were tied to the saddle of a horse by the shaikh's long turban.[6] Soon after, he was released, and spent the last eleven years of his life in Gangoh, where he died in 1537.

In 1530, when Babur died, the Afghan struggle to regain lost power was still unabated. According to the *Lata'if-i Quddusi*, the most detailed and reliable *tazkira* of the shaikh, throughout the years of the Afghan fight against Babur's son and successor Humayun, Gangohi remained opposed to the Mughals. He even allegedly gave support to and admired Sultan Bahadur Shah of Gujarat, the arch-enemy of Humayun on the western frontiers of his domain. In this context the details of two visions of one Dattu Sarwani, a noted Afghan disciple of Gangohi, are interest-

---

[6] Shaikh Rukn al-Din, *Lata'if-i Quddusi*, p. 64.

ing. One of these visions pertains to Humayun's campaigns in Gujarat. According to the *Lata'if-i Quddusi*, one night, when Sultan Bahadur Shah was in the port of Diu, and at a time when Humayun had gone to Gujarat and threatened to capture that kingdom, the shaikh appeared in Dattu's dream, commanding him to go to Gujarat, convey his greetings to the *pirs* there, and give them the following message:

> Humayun Padishah is destroying Islam. He makes no distinction between infidelity and Islam, plunders it all. I have come to the aid of Islam, and to your aid, and if you agree, I shall come there, join you, and drive Humayun out of the country of Gujarat; and if it pleases you I shall go to the country of Mandu to drive him out from there and you may drive him out from Gujarat, so that Islam may have peace and rest.

Accordingly, Dattu reached Gujarat and delivered the shaikh's message first to Hazrat Shah Manjhan and then to Shaikh Ahmad Khattu, the two major Sufi divines of the region. They both welcomed and endorsed the shaikh's mission, promised their support, and requested him to come to them "so that we may together drive away Humayun from both the country of Mandu and the country of Gujarat, in order that Islam may grow strong and there may be stability in the land."[7]

The other vision concerns Sher Shah's battle against Humayun, in which the Afghans defeated the Mughals and made them flee India in 1540. The text of the *Lata'if-i* reports, through the voice of Dattu:

> When Sher Shah Sur and Humayun Padishah opposed each other on the banks of the Ganges, Humayun Padishah was on the side of the *qasba* of Bhojpur and Sher Shah was on the other side. In a general gathering, Humayun Padishah said, "If this time I am victorious and

---

[7] Ibid., pp. 79–80. For an English translation, see Digby, "Dreams and Reminiscences", pp. 71–2. My translation of some of the words and phrases is different.

the Afghans are defeated, I will not leave a single Afghan alive, even though he be a child." When I heard this story I was very worried. After this Humayun Padishah had a bridge of boats bound together, crossed the Ganges, and encamped on a bank of the river. I continued worrying. Suddenly, in a dream my *pir* and helper Hazrat-i Qutb-i 'Alam appeared and said, "Dattu, look at the way the royal tent of Sher Shah is now standing." I saw it was standing very high, but that the pegs of the tent ropes were undone in the camp of Humayun Padishah, and that the royal tent of Humayun Padishah had fallen down, so that the Mughals were scattering and fleeing. Humayun Padishah was rallying them, saying, "Don't leave me alone." He was lamenting, wandering around in a distressed and stunned state. "Have you seen the state of the Padishah?" Hazrat-i Qutb-i 'Alam asked. "I have seen it," I submitted. He then said, "Victory is Sher Shah's, defeat is Humayun's. The support of the *pirs* is on the side of Sher Shah."[8]

These visions reflect a kind of consciousness – the consciousness of opportunities to upset the Mughal position in Gujarat, Malwa, or eastern India, these being opportunities which the most persistent of their Afghan opponents, including the dreamer Dattu, were very likely observing with interest.[9] However, the fact that they were incorporated into Gangohi's *tazkira* and remained an integral part of it shows the image of the shaikh that Gangohi's descendants and disciples preferred to keep, even when, as we shall later see, they vied with their rivals, the Naqshbandis, to exert influence in Mughal official circles.

Gangohi also, however, seems periodically to have tried to develop good relations with the Mughal conquerors. There are letters written by him to Babur, Humayun, and to a Mughal noble, Tardi Beg. Besides the routine contents that such letters transmit, namely exhortations for pious acts and generous care for the learned and the saintly, in his letter to Babur Gangohi projects himself as an orthodox Sunni advocate of a rather narrow and bigoted juristic

[8] Shaikh Rukn al-Din, *Lata'if-i Quddusi*, p. 83; Digby, "Dreams and Reminiscences", pp. 180–1.

[9] Cf. Digby, "Dreams and Reminiscences", p. 80n.

version of the *shari'a*.¹⁰ To an extent he contradicts here an earlier position elaborated in his *Rushdnama*.¹¹ Not much though can really be made of his apparently changed position, especially if we take into account the fluid and ambiguous political conditions in which these letters were written. Features of indigenous devotional religion in fact continued to be part of his *tasawwuf*. He also never gave up teaching the *Rushdnama* to his disciples.¹²

As one recovering from the trauma and humiliation of Mughal captivity, Gangohi's uncompromisingly bigoted position in his letter to Babur could have been intended to reinstate himself as a pious *pir*, the unstated assertion being that his closeness to the erstwhile rulers had been for a purely religious objective, unrelated to anything profane or this-worldly. Whether he succeeded in his effort or not is a moot point. There is not much evidence in the existing contemporary sources, either from courtly circles or Sufi fraternities, to show his – and for that matter of any other Chishti shaikh's – regular and sustained connections with the early Mughals. The position of *pir* to Babur and Humayun was still a preserve of the Naqshbandis of Mawarannahr (Transoxiana).¹³ Humayun showed interest in some Indian saints, but they, as we shall see, were not Chishtis. Much later, in Akbar's reign, the emperor's ideologue and historian Abu al-Fazl says Humayun, with some of his companions, used at times to visit the shaikh for companionship in his divinely inspired and animated assembly

---

[10] Ibn Rukun, *Maktubat-i Quddusiya*, pp. 224–5 and 335–9.

[11] Digby, "'Abd al-Quddus Gangohi", pp. 1–66, in particular pp. 34–66; Rizvi, *A History of Sufism in India*, Vol. I, pp. 339–49.

[12] Digby, "'Abd al-Quddus Gangohi"; see also Khan, "Shaikh Abdul Quddus Gangohi's Relations", pp. 73–90.

[13] Babur however did pay homage to the tombs of Qutb al-Din Bakhtiyar Kaki and Nizam al-Din Auliya in Delhi. Cf. Khan, *Tabaqat-i Baburi*, p. 92; Dale, *The Garden of the Eight Paradises*, pp. 199 and 331. Babur also visited the shrines of some other saints, like the one of Shaikh Sharaf al-Din Yahya Maneri in Bihar (ibid., p. 444). Yahya was however a Firdausi Suhrawardi and not a Chishti saint, as Dale suggests. For his life, see Rizvi, *A History of Sufism in India*, Vol. 1, pp. 228–40.

for the experience of truth and gnosis.¹⁴ This fleeting mention was then copied with obvious additions and hyperbolic effects in almost all the later Chishti *tazkiras* and some Mughal chronicles. Among the principal Sufi *tazkira* writers who so copied was the noted seventeenth-century scholar 'Abd al-Rahman Chishti, author of the *Mir'at al-Asrar*.¹⁵ Like Gangohi, he was a Sabiri and hailed from Rudauli. Interestingly, the authority that 'Abd al-Rahman cites for this report is Abu al-Fazl's *Tazkirat al-Auliya*, an obvious reference to the chapter entitled "Auliya-i Hind" (Saints of India) in the *A'in-i Akbari*. How and why were these images of Mughal–Chishti connections formulated in the course of the consolidation of Mughal imperial power under Akbar? For an understanding of the Mughals' rather late appreciation of the need to build close contacts with India-specific Sufis, it will be useful to first consider the trajectory of their relations with their erstwhile Mawarannahri *pirs* in Transoxiana, and in India as well.

Naqshbandi Shaikhs and Timurids in Mawarannahr

In the late-fourteenth century the Mughals' great ancestor Amir Timur is reported to have maintained close relations with Amir Kulal, the *pir* and preceptor of Shaikh Baha al-Din Naqshband, after whom the Sufi *silsila* came to be subsequently known.¹⁶ This was principally a routine spiritual relationship of a *murid* (seeker, disciple) with a *murshid* (guide, preceptor). In the fifteenth

---

¹⁴ al-Fazl, *A'in-i Akbari*, p. 214.

¹⁵ Cf. 'Abd al-Rahman Chishti, *Mir'at al-Asrar*, British Library, Ms. Or. 216, fol. 483; 'Ali, *Sawati' al-Anwar*, fol. 381a. For an analysis of *Mir'at al-Asrar*, see Lawrence, "An Indo-Persian Perspective", pp. 19–32; Ernst and Lawrence, *Sufi Martyrs of Love*, pp. 58–64. For 'Abd al-Rahman Chishti see also Amin, "On Retelling".

¹⁶ Algar, "A Brief History of the Naqshbandi Order", and idem, "Political Aspects of Naqshbandi History", pp. 3–44 and 123–52.

century, however, things changed with the emergence of Khwaja 'Ubaid-Allah Ahrar (d. 1490), the second great figure in the *silsila* after Baha al-Din, with whom the Naqshbandis expanded the frontiers of their influence far beyond Mawarannahr into Iran and Ottoman territory. Now, the relationship between a Naqshbandi master and his disciples, in particular pertaining to people associated with power, also acquired a special social and political significance. Khwaja Ahrar was not only a spiritual preceptor (*pir*), but also a kind of paramount political patron for his disciples, amongst whom were a large number of Timurid rulers and their nobles in Central Asia. He and several of his descendants and disciples claimed they were not simply spiritual masters but also the source of strength and help in politics and power struggles.

Mulla Fakhr al-Din ibn Husain Wa'iz al-Kashifi, the author of *Rashhat 'Ain al-Hayat*, the renowned *tazkira* of the khwaja and his associates, devotes a full chapter to describe the khwaja's interventions in politics with the objective of setting the record straight, as he thought it ought to be. A chapter entitled "An account of the miracles of Hazrat-i Ishan that pertain to his bestowal of conquering power to the kings, rulers and the others of his time" (*zikr-i tasarrufat-i ki hazrat-i Ishan betaslit-i quwwat-i qahira nisbat besalatin wa hukkam waghair i ishan az ahl-i zaman pish burda and*) contains numerous anecdotes of his support or opposition to one or the other ruler of his time.[17] Let me quote here an anecdote that also shows in some detail the khwaja's avowed mission and method:

> Hazrat-i Ishan had a vision (*dar waqi'a dida budand*) that it was with his help that the *shari'a* would acquire strength, which in turn, he thought, was to be achieved through the support of rulers. He then came to Samarqand to meet Mirza 'Abd-Allah bin Mirza Ibrahim bin Shahrukh, the sultan of the city. I [the author] had also accompanied the Hazrat. On arriving in Samarqand, the Hazrat told one of the

---

[17] Kashifi, *Rashhat 'Ain al-Hayat*, pp. 516–69, for stories about Ahrar's relations with Sultans 'Abd-Allah, Abu Sa'id, Mahmud, and Babur, for instance.

nobles who had come to meet him, that the purpose of his visit to the city was to meet with the sultan and that it would be very good if he helped him in this matter. In a rude way the noble said: "Our Mirza (ruler) is young and carefree. It is difficult to have an audience with him. And what do dervishes have to do with such tasks?" The Hazrat lost his temper and said: "We have not come here on our own. We have been commanded [by God and the Prophet] to be in touch with the rulers (*beikhtilat-i salatin amr karda and*). [We] will bring another [ruler], if your Mirza is unconcerned." When the noble left, the Hazrat wrote his [the sultan's] name on the wall, then erased it with his saliva and said: "Our mission cannot be carried out by this ruler and his nobles." The Hazrat left for Tashkent the same day. The noble then died after a week, and a month later Sultan Abu Sa'id Mirza marched from Eastern Turkestan against Mirza 'Abd-Allah and slaughtered him.[18]

Ahrar thus saw himself as having been divinely ordained to protect Muslims from the evil of oppressors (*Musalmanan ra azsharr-i zalama nigah darim*) and help them achieve their purpose (*maqsud-i Muslimin bar-awurdan*).[19] This he thought he could achieve by "trafficking with kings and conquering their souls" (*ba padshahan bayast ikhtilat kardan wa nufus-i ishan ra musakhkhar kardan*). There was thus in him clear awareness of a political role that he believed he had been assigned. As a matter of fact, in the prevailing conditions he believed it would be inappropriate for him to be just sitting on a street corner, devoting time to routine prayer and the spiritual training of disciples – as a regular shaikh would normally do.[20] The chronicler Khwandamir thus reports that Sultan Abu Sa'id and his son, Sultan Ahmad, sought Ahrar's advice in important state matters.[21] Whether this meant the elevation of political activity to the level of a kind of

---

[18] Ibid., pp. 518–19.

[19] Ibid., p. 295.

[20] Ibid., p. 329. See also Gross, "Multiple Roles and Perceptions", pp. 109–21.

[21] Khwandamir, *Habib al-Siyar*, Vol. 4, pp. 87 and 109.

principle of the Naqshbandi *silsila* is not as important as the fact that all this was with a view to ensuring the implementation of the cause of the *shari'a*. This was something new and different from the mere loyalty to the *shari'a* which, earlier, Shaikh Baha al-Din had insisted upon.²²

Ahrar's power and triumph are to be explained perhaps more in terms of his enormous wealth and organising skill than his spiritual and Sufi qualities, howsoever unusual and unprecedented such wealth and skill might have been. He was probably the biggest single landowner of Central Asia in his time. He possessed thousands of acres of the best irrigated lands in Tashkent, Samarqand, Bukhara, Kashkadaria, and other places. He also owned 64 villages surrounded by irrigating canals, 30 out-of-town orchards, 11 town estates, scores of commercial establishments and artisanal workshops, numerous arcades of shops and commercial stalls, town baths, and water mills.²³ These properties were critical for the system of protection and patronage that Ahrar developed; they included a considerable financial network made up of these holdings and his other trading activities, both regional and international. A large number of people and officials were involved in this network, working with Ahrar himself at the central *khanqah*, and spread out in various places all over Turkestan, Mawarannahr, and Khurasan, to maintain and administer these properties. Many such were not formally his spiritual disciples. With this organised wealth Ahrar was able to help both commoners and rulers in times of financial difficulty.²⁴ It was in this way that he rearranged the

---

²² I intend to maintain a distance here from scholars who think that all through their history the Naqshbandi Sufis have been involved in one or the other sort of political activity. I have therefore emphasised the words "new" and "different". See also Algar, "Aspects of Naqshbandi History", pp. 123–52; and Gross, "Multiple Roles of a Sufi Shaikh", pp. 109–21.

²³ Cf. Chekhovich, *Samarqand Documents*, pp. 67, 72, 125, 244, and 247; Kashifi, *Rashhat*, pp. 227, 228, 246, and 328. See also Gross, "Economic Status of a Timurid Sufi Shaikh", pp. 84–104. For Ahrar's estates in Kabul, see also Dale and Payind, "The Ahrari Waqf in Kabul", pp. 218–33.

²⁴ Cf. Paul, "Forming a Faction", pp. 533–48.

forces of the Naqshbandi *silsila* to an unprecedented degree, building and consolidating his overriding position and uncontested power in the region.

The nature of Ahrar's unusual relations with the rulers of the region is illustrated by the behaviour of Sultan Ahmad Mirza who, along with some of his nobles, was initiated by him into the Naqshbandi order. The sultan was not simply extraordinarily respectful and overawed in the presence of Khwaja Ahrar. He thought it best never to position one knee over the other in the Khwaja's presence, and on occasion was reported to tremble and sweat out of fear in his presence (*az haibat wa dahshat-i majlis-i Hazrat-i Ishan gosht-i shana-i wai mi larzid wa qatrat-i arq az jabin-i wai mi chakid*).[25] In return, he received the khwaja's full support and, according to Babur's own testimony, even if he was a man of ordinary intelligence he was successful only because "his, highness, the khwaja, was there accompanying him step by step."[26]

Babur's own father, 'Umar Shaikh Mirza, was also a disciple of the khwaja, who often visited the mirza and treated him as his son.[27] According to Abu al-Fazl, "the king [Umar Shaikh] was always of a dervish mind and inclined to the society of religious persons and asked for wisdom at the doors of the hearts of the God knowing, especially the holy Nasir al-Din Khwaja Ubaid-Allah, known by the name Khwaja Ahrar."[28] The khwaja is also reported to have given substantial amounts of money to the mirza, once 250,000 dinars and on another occasion 70,000 dinars, to relieve the tax burden of the Muslims of Tashkent.[29]

---

[25] Babur, *Baburnama*, English translation by A.S. Beveridge, p. 33. Also see Wheeler M. Thackston's translation, p. 53; Kashifi, *Rashhat*, p. 531.

[26] Babur, *Baburnama*, Beveridge transl., pp. 33 and 34; Thackston transl., pp. 53–4.

[27] Ibid., Beveridge transl., p. 15; Thackston transl., p. 41.

[28] Abu al-Fazl, *Akbarnama*, Vol. I, ed. Agha Ahmad 'Ali and Rahim, p. 84; English transl. H. Beveridge, p. 219. See also Babur, *Baburnama*, Beveridge transl., p. 15, Thackston transl., p. 9.

[29] Rizvi, *A History of Sufism in India*, Vol. II, p. 177. Rizvi cites *Samarqand Documents* and a Tashkent MS. of a *tazkira* of Ahrar, *Maqamat-i Khwaja Ahrar*.

A measure of the khwaja's intimacy with the mirza was the fact that at Babur's birth, he, his father-in-law Yunus Khan (the ruler of Moghulistan), and Maulana Munir Marghinani (one of the major theologians of the time, who had composed the chronogram of the birth of the prince), "begged his Holiness" – writes Mirza Haidar Dughlat – "to choose a name for the child and he blessed him with the name of Zahir al-Din Muhammad. [But] that time the Chaghatai were very rude and uncultured . . . and not refined . . . as they are now; thus they found Zahir al-Din Muhammad difficult to pronounce, and for this reason gave him the name of Babur."[30] In the words of Abu al-Fazl, the "weighty appellation with its majesty and sublimity, was not readily pronounceable or current on the tongues of the Turks, the name Babur was [thus] also given to him."[31] In Farghana, the khwaja also had close links with the important families of nobles and high officials. One such was the family of 'Abd-Allah, who made use of the joint name of Khwaja-Maulana-Qazi, because he combined in his house the positions of *muqtada* (religious guide), *shaikh al-Islam and qazi*.[32]

The Mawarannahri Shaikhs and the Early Mughals

Although associated with the moment of his birth, Khwaja Ahrar had died by the time Babur rose to power. But the prince nevertheless attributes several of his achievements to the khwaja's blessings. Shortly before he took Samarqand in 1501, he had seen the khwaja in a dream. He writes:

> His Highness Khwaja 'Ubaid-Allah seemed to come; I seemed to go out to give him honourable meeting; he came in and seated himself; people seemed to lay a table-cloth before him, apparently without sufficient care and, on account of this, something seemed to come to his Highness Khwaja's mind. Mullah Baba (? Pashagari) made me

---

[30] Dughlat, *A History of the Moghuls*, p. 173.
[31] Abu al-Fazl, *Akbarnama*, Vol. I, p. 87, Beveridge transl., p. 225.
[32] Babur, *Baburnama*, Beveridge transl., pp. 89–90; Thackston transl., p. 65.

a sign; I signed back, "Not through me the table-layer is in fault." The Khwaja understood and accepted the excuse. When he rose I escorted him out. In the hall of that house he took hold of my right or left arm and lifted me up till one of my feet was off the ground, saying in Turki, "Shaikh Maslahat has given (Samarkand)." I really took Samarkand a few days later.[33]

As a matter of fact, in that town the followers of the khwaja held a considerable position at the turn of the century. They paid no levies to the government under the khwaja's principle of *himayat* and they sometimes even dictated who should have supreme power in the town. For only a brief while, in 1494, did they have some difficulty when Sultan Mahmud Mirza, who was for a few months in possession of the town, made new regulations and treated them with harshness and oppression.[34] Khwaja Ahrar's son, Khwaja 'Abd-Allah (better known as Khwajagi Khwaja), and Khwaja Muhammad Yahya were their leaders. Earlier, in 1499, when Babur intended to capture the town, he was told by the *begs* to approach Khwaja Yahya with whose consent, they thought, "the town may be had easily without fighting and disturbance." In Babur's own understanding, too, the matter was to be resolved when Khwaja Yahya would decide to "admit us to the town".[35] The issue thus was not simply one of spiritual power; Khwaja Yahya was clearly involved in the politics of the town. Earlier, the same year that the Tarkhanis of the town had revolted against Baisunghar Mirza and raised his half-brother Sultan 'Ali Mirza to supreme power, Khwaja Yahya blessed the latter and became his *pir*. But, interestingly enough, the rebels could not lay hands on Baisunghar as he had taken refuge in the house of Khwaja 'Abd-Allah.[36] Babur noted and appreciated this political involvement: "Through these occurrences, the sons of His Highness Khwaja

---

[33] Ibid., Beveridge transl., p. 132; Thackston transl., pp. 98–9.
[34] Ibid., Beveridge transl., p. 41, Thackston transl., p. 28.
[35] Ibid., Beveridge transl., p. 124, Thackston transl., p. 93.
[36] Ibid., Beveridge trans, pp. 61–3, Thackston transl., p. 45.

'Ubaid-Allah became settled partisans, the elder [Muhammad 'Ubaid-Allah, Khwajagi Khwaja] becoming the spiritual guide of the elder prince, the younger [Yahya] of the younger."[37] Later, when the Uzbek ruler Shaibani Khan conquered Samarqand, he had apprehensions about Khwaja Yahya and therefore dismissed him, with his two sons, Khwaja Muhammad Zakariya and Khwaja Baqi, towards Khurasan. Some Uzbeks followed them, and near Khwaja Kardzan killed both the khwaja and his two young sons. Babur expressed strong resentment at this incident.[38] As a ruler of Mawarannahr, all the same, Shaibani Khan could not afford to be indifferent to the great Naqshbandi lineages. While he treated the descendants of Khwaja Ahrar harshly, he offered prayers at the shrines of Khwaja 'Abd al-Khaliq Ghijduwani (d. 1220) and Shaikh Baha al-Din Naqshband (d. 1389), along with a large number of his nobles, the *'ulama* and Sufis, who included several noted Naqshbandis of the time.[39] Later, Shaibani Khan's nephew, 'Ubaid-Allah Khan, restored the major part of the Ahrar family lands. Still later, the descendants of Khwaja Yahya became the *shaikh al-Islam* of the city of Samarqand, combining with it the trusteeship of rich endowments settled on the tomb of Khwaja Ahrar.[40]

It is well known that between 1500 and his conquest of India, Babur came into contact with Shah Isma'il Safavi and with his help avenged himself upon the Uzbeks for the devastation they had wreaked on the Timurids and their associates in Central Asia. Because of his close relations with the Safavid Shah, who was not an orthodox Shi'a but a zealous propagator of heterodox Shi'ism, Babur is also alleged to have temporarily developed Shi'a leanings. It is also reported that a Naqshbandi shaikh of the time, Ahmad

---

[37] Ibid.
[38] Ibid., Beveridge transl., p. 128, Thackston transl., p. 96.
[39] Isfahani, *Mihman-nama-i Bukhara*, pp. 43 and 61. See also Schimmel, "Some Notes", pp. 149–66. Ghijduwani was separated by five links in the *silsila* before its crystallisation under the auspices of Baha al-Din Naqshband.
[40] Algar, "A Brief History of the Naqshbandi Order", pp. 15–16.

ibn Jalal al-Din Khwajagi, admonished him for seeking help from the shah of Iran and asked him instead to accept Shaibani Khan as a *khalifa*.[41] Be that as it may, Babur remained a lifelong devotee of Khwaja Ahrar. Of interest here is an anecdote pertaining to Babur's victory over Ibrahim Lodi in the battle of Panipat in 1526. The anecdote is reported by a seventeenth-century historian, Muhammad Sadiq. Sadiq writes that as Babur's army was too small, as against the huge and near-countless Afghan brigade, he felt overwhelmed and feared he might lose the battle. He then contemplated the image of Khwaja Ahrar as he had heard it described. All at once there appeared a horseman dressed in white, fighting against the Afghans, who were thereafter completely routed. Later, after the fight, he narrated the incident to one of his nobles. The noble told Babur that his description of the horseman in white was of Maulana Ahmad Khwajagi. The same day, Babur sent one of his close courtiers to Khwajagi with gifts, together with a portrait drawn on a piece of paper. Babur, according to Sadiq, included the following verses too in the letter he wrote to the saint:

Dar hawa-i nafs gumrah umr zayi' karda-im
pish-i ahl-i faqr az atwar-i khud sharminda-im
Yak nazar bar mukhlisan-i khasta dilfarma ki ma
Khwajagi ra manda aknun Khwajagi ra banda-im.

[41] See Fazl-Allah ibn Ruzbihani Isfahani, *Suluk al-Muluk*, British Library, London Ms. Or. 253, Preface, fol. 3a. Isfahani writes that with Babur's help, heresy, which is to say Shi'ism, spread in Mawarannahr and that he, like the Iranian Shi'i leaders, played a detestable role in bringing mosques and other religious centres of the region beyond the River Jihun under the control of the heretic Shi'as. The region was thus afire with their mischief (*fitna*). All this happened because he invited the red-capped Safavid *qizilbash* to come to his help in his fight against the Uzbeks to recover Samarqand and Bukhara. But for 'Ubaid-Allah Khan's gallant struggle (*jihad*), the rites and symbols of the true faith would have been completely routed in the region. See also the printed edition of this text of Isfahani edited by Muhammad Ali Muvahhid, p. 50. For an English translation of this work, see Aslam, *Muslim Conduct of State*, pp. 31–3.

> I have wasted my life in pursuit of what my misguided soul desired
> I am ashamed of my conduct before the ascetics
> Please spare a glance for your infirm devotees
> I am now a slave of Khwajagi, who[se directives] I had neglected.[42]

The saint seems to be the same Ahmad Khwajagi who had earlier thought poorly of Babur's seeking help from the Safavid shah. The letter sounds like penitence for his earlier comportment and a reaffirmation of his devotion to Khwajagi Ahmad in particular, and to Naqshbandi saints in general.

Although Babur does not mention this incident himself, his continuing faith in and loyalty to the Naqshbandi order is pretty clear. On 6 November 1528, when he fell ill in India, he decided to render into poetry a treatise of Khwaja Ahrar entitled *Risala-i Walidiya*, believing he would be able to cure himself of the disease:

> I laid it to heart that if I, going to the soul of His Reverence for protection were freed from this disease, it would be a sign that my poem was accepted ... To this end I began to versify the tract ... Thirteen couplets were made in the same night. I tasked myself not to make fewer than ten a day; in the end one day had been omitted. While last year every time such illness had happened, it had persisted at least a month or forty days, this year by God's grace and His Reverence's favour, I was free, except for a little depression, on Thursday the 29th of the month (November 12). The end of versifying the contents of the tract was reached on Saturday the 8th of the first Rabi (November 20th). One day, 52 couplets had been made.[43]

From Samarqand, where the khwaja's family were normally resident, Babur invited to Hindustan the khwaja's grandsons – Khwaja

---

[42] Sadiq, *Tabaqat-i Shahjahani*, British Library, India Office Library Ms, Ethe 705, fols 192b–193a. Khwajagi Ahmad, a disciple of Maulana Muhammad Qazi, who was a disciple of Khwaja Ahrar, died in 949 AH. He is buried in Dehbid.

[43] Babur, *Baburnama*, transl. Beveridge, pp. 619–20, Thackston transl., p. 420; Dale, *The Garden of the Eight Paradises*, pp. 176–7.

Khawand Mahmud (also known as Khwaja Nura) and Khwaja 'Abd al-Shahid (the second son of Khwajagi Khwaja), and his great-grandson Khwaja Kalan (a grandson of Khwaja Yahya). The last two were guests of honour at a feast Babur gave in Agra on 18 December 1528. On this occasion, they sat to his right and received rich presents.[44] However, they chose not to stay in India. Khwaja Khawand Mahmud, the third invitee, set out for India only in the spring of 1530, but before he arrived, says Mirza Haidar Dughlat, Babur had died. The khwaja was nevertheless received in Agra with great honour by the new ruler, Humayun.[45] Soon, however, "for some [unspecified] reasons" he left for Kabul, where he passed away.[46] In Dughlat's account lies a vague clue for why he did not tarry at Humayun's court. Khwaja Khawand had apparently come with the intention of occupying exclusive position as the emperor's royal spiritual master. But while Humayun welcomed him and showed him respect, he was, says Dughlat, devoted to a Shattari Sufi saint, Shaikh Phul.

> At that period there had arisen in Hindustan a man named Shaikh Phul. Humayun was anxious to become his disciple, for he had a great passion for the occult sciences – for magic and conjuration. Shaikh Phul, having assumed the garb of a Shaikh, came to the Emperor and taught him that incantation and sorcery were the surest means to the true attainment of an object. Since doctrines such as these suited his disposition, he became at once the Shaikh's disciple. Besides this person there was Maulana Muhammad Parghari who, though a Mulla, was a very [irreligious] and unprincipled man, and who always worked hard to gain his ends, even when they were of an evil nature. The Shaikh asked the aid of Mulla Muhammad and,

---

[44] Babur, *Baburnama*, transl. Beveridge, pp. 632 and 641–2, Thackston transl., pp. 426 and 432; Dale, *The Garden of the Eight Paradises*, pp. 427–8. Dale also mentions one unidentified Khwaja Chishti.

[45] Dughlat, *A History of the Moghuls*, p. 398; Abu al-Fazl, *Akbarnama*, Vol. II, p. 194, English transl., p. 301.

[46] Dughlat, *A History of the Moghuls*, p. 398; Khan, *Ma'asir al-Umara*, Vol. II, p. 575.

in common, by means of flattery, they wrought upon the Emperor for their own purposes, and gained his favour.

Not long after, I went to visit the Emperor . . . but I could never gather that he had learned anything from his *pir*, Shaikh Phul, except magic and incantation. But God knows best. The influence of Shaikh Phul thus confirmed, Maulana Muhammad, or rather the Emperor and all his following, neglected and slighted Khwaja Nura, who had a hereditary claim to their veneration. This naturally caused the Khwaja great inward vexation.[47]

The sorcery and magic Dughlat mentions were Sufi prayers and litanies known as *da'wat-i-asma-i hasana*, in vogue among the Shattaris in India. The practice involved the observation and study of stars and other heavenly bodies. Humayun's fascination with the Shattari saints, we may guess, could have been because of his own interest in the astronomical sciences. Later in the century, the chronicler 'Abd al-Qadir Bada'uni tells us Humayun harboured a great devotion for and trust in Shaikh Phul (or Bahlul) and his younger brother, Shaikh Ghaus of Gwalior, and had learned from them the method of *asma'*. In 1540, when during his campaigns in eastern India against Sher Khan Humayun heard the disturbing news of his brother Mirza Hindal's plan to rebel, he sent Shaikh Bahlul to try talking his brother out of the idea and seek reconciliation instead. Hindal and the other nobles in his retinue, however, suspected the shaikh was acting in collusion with the Afghans. The shaikh was thus killed by one of Hindal's associates.[48]

[47] Dughlat, *A History of the Moghuls*, pp. 398–9. See also Thackston, ed., *Tarikh-i Rashidi*, pp. 345–7.

[48] Bada'uni, *Muntakhab al-Tawarikh*, Vol. III, pp. 4–5; Khan, *Ma'asir al-Umara*, Vol. II, pp. 575–6. Humayun remained close to Shaikh Muhammad Ghaus until he lost his empire to the Afghans and fled to Iran. The shaikh then left for Gujarat. When Humayun regained power he returned to Delhi. The emperor, however, died soon afterwards and the saint was disappointed at his reception by Bairam Khan, the regent of the young Emperor Akbar. He then retired to Gwalior where he died in 970 AH. See also Nizami, "Shattari Saints", pp. 56–70.

As for Khwaja Khawand, he seems to have left for Lahore at the invitation of another of Humayun's brothers, Mirza Kamran. By this time, Mirza Dughlat had also arrived in Lahore for the honour of "kissing his feet". While they were in Lahore, the Safavid ruler Shah Tahmasp invaded Qandahar and captured it. This obviously caused Kamran "immense grief", and when Dughlat at his request told the khwaja about his misfortune, the latter is reported to have said to him:

> I have seen His Holiness [Khwaja Ahrar] in a vision. He asked me, "Why are you sad?" I replied: "On account of Kamran Mirza, for the Turkomans have taken Kandahar. What will come of it?" Then His Holiness advanced towards me and taking me by the hand said: "Do not grieve; he will soon recover it." And thus, indeed, it came to pass, for Kamran Mirza marched against Kandahar, and the troops of Tahmasp Shah gave up the city to him in peace.

Dughlat's account shows not simply his anguish over Humayun's treatment of the Khwaja. It reiterates the Timurids' continuing faith in and devotion to the family of Khwaja Ahrar. Humayun was therefore also perturbed by the khwaja's decision to depart from his court and begged him to stay, but the latter would not listen to his entreaties. He then sent Maulana Muhammad Parghari to Lahore to persuade the khwaja to return, and upon his continued refusal the maulana begged that his sins be forgiven and beseeched that he write a reply to the letter from Humayun. In response the khwaja reportedly wrote only the following verse:

Humai gu mafigan saya-i sharaf hargiz
daran dayar ki tuti kam az zaghan bashad

Say, O Huma [bird], never cast thy noble shadow
In a land where the parrot is less accounted than the kite.

Dughlat says in this response there was a curious pun, for Humayun Padishah did not eventually come to throw his shadow in the country (India) where the parrot was rarer than the kite.

Dughlat also notes that in those days he often heard the khwaja say: "I have seen in a vision, a great sea which overwhelmed all who remained behind us in Agra and Hindustan; while we only escaped after a hundred risks"; and Humayun's defeat at the hands of Sher Shah eventually came about three years later, just as the khwaja had predicted.[49]

The unfortunate Humayun thus missed the blessings of both the Naqshbandi khwaja of his ancestral homeland, Mawarannahr, and the great Chishti shaikh of Hindustan. Later, his relations with Khwaja Khawand appear to have been restored somewhat. In 1546, during an illness of the emperor in Kabul, the khwaja and his son Khwaja Mu'in were the only people, besides his personal attendant, who were allowed to visit him.[50] Humayun also had some contact in Kabul with Maulana Zain al-Din, an eminent Naqshbandi of his time, and with Khwaja 'Abd al-Bari, a great-great-grandson of Khwaja Ahrar.

It is also worth noting that the Mughals were matrimonially connected with some of the great Naqshbandi lineages. A daughter of Babur was married to Nur al-Din Muhammad, a descendant of Khwaja 'Ala al-Din 'Attar, who was the first *khalifa* (disciple) of Khwaja Baha al-Din Naqshband. Their daughter, Salima Begum, as we will see, was later married to the powerful Mughal noble Bairam Khan. Humayun's younger son, Mirza Muhammad Hakim, the ruler of Kabul, gave his sister, Fakhr al-Nisa, in marriage to Khwaja Hasan Naqshbandi, a descendant of Baha al-Din Naqshband, after the death of her first husband, Abu al-Ma'ali. Khwaja Hasan thus became very powerful in Kabul for a time in the later-sixteenth century.[51]

[49] Dughlat, *A History of the Moghuls*, pp. 399–400; Khan, *Ma'asir al-Umara*, Vol. II, p. 575. Ross' translation of the phrase "*wa sargardan raft*" here is confusing. He adds the name of Maulana Muhammad in square brackets and translates the phrase as "[Maulana Muhammad] returned stupefied".

[50] Abu al-Fazl, *Akbarnama*, Vol. I, p. 253, English transl., pp. 493–4.

[51] Bada'uni, *Muntakhab al-Tawarikh*, Vol. II, p. 72. Commenting on Khwaja Hasan's absolute power, some of the wits of the period used to say:

In the early phase of Mughal settlement in Hindustan, the presence of certain Naqshbandi saints as *pirs* (but not necessarily as the royal *pir*) and as important members of the Mughal elite, is unmistakable. The second phase of Timurid contact with the subcontinent begins with Humayun's return from his exile in Iran. Humayun, as we know, died soon after his return and resumption of power in Delhi. The process of recovery of the lost territory, its consolidation, and further expansion only took place in Akbar's time. It is thus necessary to turn to how the Naqshbandi khwajas figured at this critical juncture in the shaping of Mughal power.

Akbar Encounters the Naqshbandis

At the beginning of Akbar's reign (1556–1605) Khwaja 'Abd al-Shahid, who had earlier visited Babur's court, arrived anew from Samarqand. Akbar received him "with respect and kindness" and granted him the *pargana* of Chamari in Punjab. There the khwaja lived for about two decades, "with piety and severe austerities, striving much in the path of holiness as a compendium of all such perfection as man can attain to." He was widely respected and people from all walks of life visited him, acquiring grace from his "precious utterances", "being directed thereby in the path of righteousness and godly living." The khwaja, according to the chronicler Bada'uni, was a "symbol" based on the earlier model of Khwaja Ahrar. In 1561, when the Mughal commander Husain Quli Khan chasing the rebel mirzas (who had risen up against Akbar) arrived at Chamari, he received from the khwaja an assurance of his own victory, and the holy man's dress as a present. Bada'uni concludes: "The result of this prayer was that having arrived by forced marches in Tulambah he [Husain Quli]

"If our Master be Master Hasan / We shall have neither sack nor rope left." For his position and other Naqshbandi positions at Mirza Hakim's court in Kabul, see Subrahmanyam, "A Note on the Kabul Kingdom", pp. 89–101; Faruqui, "The Forgotten Prince", pp. 487–523.

gained a glorious victory."⁵² In 1574, however, the khwaja left India, also according to Bada'uni, following a premonition of his fast approaching death. "The time of my departure is drawn nigh," the khwaja is reported to have said, "and I have been commanded to convey this handful of bones, of which I am composed, to the burying place of my ancestors in Samarqand." He died shortly after his arrival in Samarqand.⁵³ However, the real reason and occasion for the khwaja's departure seems to have been the rapid decline of the Naqshbandis from the favour of the emperor. To gain a clearer sense of this decline, we may examine the career of another noted Naqshbandi, Sharaf al-Din Husain, who also visited Akbar's court early in his reign.

Sharaf al-Din Husain was the son of Khwaja Mu'in and a grandson of Khwaja Khawand Mahmud. He had lived with his father in Kashghar, where the latter had made a fortune as a merchant dealing in precious stones.⁵⁴ He was sent by the ruler of Kashghar to offer condolences on the death of Humayun in 1556 and to congratulate Akbar on his accession.⁵⁵ Sharaf al-Din came on this mission accompanied by Khwaja 'Abd al-Bari, who had earlier been sent by Humayun to Kashghar at the time of his expedition to reconquer India. Khwaja 'Abd al-Bari also belonged to "the noble line of the Naqshbandi Khwajas", and we learn that he was the "son of Khwaja 'Abd al-Khafi, son of Khwaja 'Abd al-Hadi, son of Khwajagan Khwaja, son of Khwaja Ahrar – may his grave be holy."⁵⁶

---

⁵² Bada'uni, *Muntakhab al-Tawarikh*, Vol. III, p. 40; Khan, *Ma'asir al-Umara*, Vol. II, p. 379; al-Fazl, *Akbarnama*, Vol. II, p. 127, English transl., p. 195.

⁵³ Bada'uni, *Muntakhab al-Tawarikh*, Vol. III, p. 40.

⁵⁴ Abu al-Fazl, *Akbarnama*, Vol. II, pp. 194–5, English transl., pp. 301–2; Khan, *Ma'asir al-Umara*, Vol. III, p. 234. Khwaja Mu'in had the monopoly of jade trade with China.

⁵⁵ Abu al-Fazl, *Akbarnama*, Vol. II, p. 195, English transl., pp. 302–3; Khan, *Ma'asir al-Umara*, Vol. III, p. 234.

⁵⁶ Abu al-Fazl, *Akbarnama*, Vol. II, p. 21, English transl., p. 37.

Now, Sharaf al-Din soon rose in eminence in the Mughal court through the influence of Maham Anaga and Adham Khan, important figures of the early years of Akbar's reign. He received the high rank of "amir", and was given *jagirs* in Ajmer and Nagor. During the fifth year of his reign, the emperor gave him his half-sister Bakhshi Banu Begum in marriage. In the seventh year he was deputed to capture the fort of Mertha. Abu al-Fazl notes that he was assigned a high mansab of 5000.[57] In the eighth year, his father Khwaja Mu'in, "hearing of his son's exaltation and grandeur", also arrived from Kashghar. The emperor received him with respect, gave him "honourable quarters and treated him with favours such as kings show to dervishes."[58] The Naqshbandis at this stage were obviously held "in great esteem", to the extent that Mulla Mubarak, whom Bada'uni portrays as a man opportunistically inclined to doing what was most rewarding at a given moment, "adapted himself to their rule".[59] It has been noted that Bairam Khan's wife, Salima Sultan Begum, also came from a Naqshbandi family. She was a

> daughter of Nur al-Din Muhammad, Nur al-Din was the son of 'Ala al Din Muhammad, who was the son of Khwaja Hasan, commonly known as Khwajazada Chaghaniyan. This Khwajazada was grandson of Khwaja Hasan 'Attar, who again was a direct descendant of Khwaja 'Ala al Din, the first *khalifa* of Khwaja Baha al-Din Naqshband. We should also keep in mind that Khwajazada Chaghaniyan was the son-in-law of Sultan Mahmud, son of Sultan Abu Sa'id Mirza.[60]

[57] Abu al-Fazl, *Akbarnama*, Vol. II, p. 128, English transl., p. 197; Khan, *Ma'asir al-Umara*, Vol. III, pp. 234–5.

[58] Abu al-Fazl, *Akbarnama*, Vol. II, p. 195, English transl., p. 303; Khan, *Ma'asir al-Umara*, Vol. III, pp. 235–6.

[59] Bada'uni writes that he followed "many and various rules of life". For a time, during the reigns of the Afghan emperors, he used to keep company with Shaikh 'Ala'i, and in the beginning of the Emperor's [Akbar's] reign, when the Naqshbandi order was held in great esteem, he adapted himself to their rule, and for some time he was attached to the Hamadani Shaikhs, and at last when the Iraqis were in great favour at the Court he spoke as "one of their religion": *Muntakhab al-Tawarikh*, English transl., Vol. III, p. 74.

[60] Abu al-Fazl, *Akbarnama*, Vol. II, p. 64, English transl., p. 97; Khan, *Ma'asir al-Umara*, Vol. I, p. 375.

Soon after, however, the Naqshbandis' position seems to have declined, even though some of them held a couple of offices until about the end of the 1570s. One 'Abd al-'Azim, better known as Sultan Khwaja, the son of a disciple of Khwaja 'Abd al-Shahid, was selected to be the *amir-i hajj* in 1576. He returned from Mecca in 1578 and then held the office of the *sadr* until his death in 1584.[61] In 1578 another Naqshbandi, Khwaja Muhammad Yahya, a direct descendant of Khwaja Ahrar, was appointed *amir-i hajj*.[62] After the 1570s, however, we have only Sultan Khwaja with a position of some eminence at Akbar's court, as his daughter was married to Prince Daniyal in 1588. But Sultan Khwaja's seems to be an altogether peculiar case. His position, according to a report, owed to his "conversion" in support of Akbar's religious innovations of the time, which meant unquestioned obeisance to the emperor and a nearly total deviation from the Naqshbandi Ahrari tradition.[64]

A major factor behind the turn in the emperor's attitude could have been the revolt of Sharaf al-Din Husain in the 1560s. Akbar decided to tackle this with uncompromising firmness. He refused to listen even to Khwaja 'Abd al-Shahid's recommendation on the matter, which must have disappointed the khwaja and forced him to leave for Samarqand.[65] This appears to be a major reason for what happened – and not simply a wish to die in Samarqand, as Bada'uni would have us believe of his departure in 1574. In fact, Bada'uni gives this hagiographical explanation while writing the biographical notices of the saint in the third volume of his history.

[61] Khan, *Ma'asir al-Umara*, Vol. II, p. 380.
[62] Bada'uni, *Muntakhab al-Tawarikh*, Vol. II, p. 267.
[63] Khan, *Ma'asir al-Umara*, Vol. II, p. 381.
[64] Bada'uni, *Muntakhab al-Tawarikh*, Vol. II, pp. 340–1. According to Bada'uni, Sultan Khwaja requested the emperor at the time of his death to interr him in a grave with a special lamp and to fix a grill facing the sun so that the light thereof might obliterate his sins. He willed so to please the emperor and because he was a follower of the new faith, *Din-i Ilahi*, in which light and the sun had a special sacred place. The author of the *Ma'asir al-Umara* (Vol. II, pp. 381–2) dismisses this story as an instance of Bada'uni's bigotry.
[65] Bada'uni, *Muntakhab al-Tawarikh*, Vol. II, p. 171; Abu al-Fazl, *Akbarnama*, Vol. II, p. 195, English transl., p. 303, for Sharaf al-Din's revolt.

In the context of his description of the incident in the second volume, however, he himself provides a clue to the real reason for the saint's departure. He says that the saint "felt much grief at the refusal [to accept his advice] and left much saddened, even though the Emperor did not neglect any marks of due honour and respect, and publicly even read the *fatiha*."[66]

The Sufi Shaikhs and the Formation of the Akbari Dispensation

The seemingly disproportionate grief of the khwaja reported by Bada'uni, might have been a consequence of the new developments at Akbar's court, where, he realised, there would be little place left for the Mawarannahri–Naqshbandis to live in their erstwhile style. In several modern writings on Mughal India, we have excellent accounts of the details of these developments.[67] I need not repeat them all, except to briefly mention some. The most momentous of these was the emperor's marriage with a Rajput princess early in his reign, and together with it a number of administrative measures, such as the abolition of pilgrimage taxes and the hated *jizya*, and the giving up of the practice of forcibly converting prisoners of war to Islam. By the mid-1560s there had also evolved a new pattern of emperor–noble relationship which suited the needs of a new Mughal state, to be defended now by a nobility of diverse ethnic and religious groups, amongst whom the Hindus and the Shi'as came to occupy a significant position. The

---

[66] Bada'uni, *Muntakhab al-Tawarikh*, Vol. II, p. 171. Bada'uni also reports that the Khwaja commanded immense respect among the rulers of Kabul and Central Asia. On his way to Samarqand, when he arrived at Kabul "it happened that Mirza Shah Rukh had just taken the people of Kabul captive, and was returning with them to Badakhshan. By means of the intercession of the Khwaja nearly 10,000 persons obtained deliverance . . ." Cf. Bada'uni, *Muntakhab al-Tawarikh*, Vol. III, p. 40.

[67] Cf., for instance, Richards, "The Formulation of Imperial Authority", pp. 126–67; Khan, "The Nobility under Akbar"; idem, *The Political Biography of a Mughal Noble*, Introduction, pp. ix–xx.

Mughals were originally Hanafi Sunnis, and Akbar too, until the 1570s at least, remained faithful to this tradition. On the other hand, the new non-Muslim and non-Sunni recruits into Mughal state service were not asked to abandon their old customs and beliefs. On the contrary, several non-Muslim rituals began to be integrated into an evolving Akbari political culture of governance. All this was evidently not compatible with the Naqshbandi khwajas' perception of a Muslim state. A major task of the ruler, with whom they had contact – as is illustrated by Khwaja Ahrar's relations with the rulers of his time – was not simply to ensure the comfort (*asa'ish*) and welfare (*rifahiyat, khair*) of Muslims, but also to discourage and abolish the customs of strangers (*rusum-i biganagan*). In their view, Muslim society was to be totally free from the evil (*sharr*) of non-Muslim social practices.[68] Earlier, Shaikh Baha al-Din Naqshband (d. 1389) had proclaimed that the distinctive feature of his *silsila* was total conformity and obedience to the traditions of the Prophet and his venerable companions (*chang dar zail-i mutaba'at-i sunnat-i Mustafa zada im wa iqtida ba asar-i sahaba-i kiram-i u namuda*), and that his followers formed a community of the perfect (*kamilan-i mukammal*), having attained high status because of their adherence to the path of the Prophet, and that the best and the quickest way to the Truth was to provide relief to the heart of the Muslim.[69]

Although it is difficult to accept the understanding of some historians regarding the so-called "highly centralised absolutism" or "highly systematised administration" under Akbar, there is no denying the fact that the years between 1560 and 1575 saw a rapid change in the position of the Chaghatai nobles and that this was in the main intended by the emperor to buttress the power around

---

[68] Cf. Urunbaev, *The Letters of Khwaja 'Ubayd Allah Ahrar*, pp. 114, 128, 143, 145, 146, 166 and 169, letter nos 49 (50), 59 (62), 282 (286), 284 (288), 304 (308) and 306 (310). See also Paul, "Forming a Faction", pp. 540–1. *Biganagan* means strangers, foreigners, which in the context implied the customs and practices introduced and established by the Mongols.

[69] Cf. Parsa, *Qudsiyya*, p. 61 (text), p. 51 (Introduction); Jami, *Tariqa-i Khwajagan*, p. 89.

his person. Revolts by the old guard – the Mirzas, the Qaqshals, and the Atka Khail, for instance – which followed, and which precipitated measures aimed at weakening their strength, showed the intensity of their disapproval and resistance to this change. Those *jagirs* that they had hitherto held concentrated within a region were dispersed, while nearly all the civil and financial offices were now staffed by non-Chaghatai groups.[70] The fortunes of the Naqshbandis, who had an established affinity with the Chaghatais, were ensured according to one report because of the high and unmatched strength of the latter in the early years of Akbar's reign.[71] Their pre-eminence then would very likely suffer a serious setback in the wake of increasing corrosion in the power of the Chaghatai nobles.

From the mid-1570s we see unmistakable signs of Akbar moving away from the pattern of Islamic rulership of the erstwhile Timurids, and that the change is shared on occasion and in some measure with members of the nobility and the Naqshbandi Sufi lineage. Akbar favoured now a kind of universal kingship, emphasising an undisputed and all-encompassing power for the ruler. He now had a new capital for his empire, Fatehpur Sikri, built in large measure in deference to the association of the location with a saint, but it was he, the emperor, not the place or the saint, who was to be lauded as the centre of authority in the new Timurid polity in India.[72] Critical as it was, this feature of the evolving Akbari dispensation of power clashed with Naqshbandi ideas regarding authority and kingship.

I have already summarised some key features regarding the position of Khwaja Ahrar. After him, too, were saints of the lineage who combined wealth with spiritual accomplishments to strengthen their intervention in the political domain. Khwaja Ju'ibari and Khwaja Mushtari, two members of the same family of Naqshbandi shaikhs in Uzbek-ruled Mawarannahr, were celebrated

[70] Khan, *The Political Biography of a Mughal Noble*, Introduction.
[71] Khan, *Ma'asir al-Umara*, Vol. II, pp. 584–5.
[72] Richards, "The Formulation of Imperial Authority".

for their legendary wealth; and, according to one report, from Turkestan to Khurasan there was not a city, desert, or place where these khwajas had not built a canal. One of them enjoyed a yearly income equal to the entire revenue collected by the Uzbeks from Samarqand, the other held over 2000 properties administered by his expert personal employees. They dominated the grain market, owned over a hundred shops in Bukhara alone, and their joint property is said to have surpassed even that of Khwaja Ahrar.[73] In another case, Makhdum-i A'zam (d. 1543), a disciple of Maulana Muhammad Qazi (d. 1516), a noted *khalifa* of Khwaja Ahrar, established an ascendancy over the ruler of Kashghar in the same way as had Khwaja Ahrar over Sultan Abu Sa'id, and the power in his family remained for decades, until in 1678 one of his descendants, Khwaja Afaq, managed to dislodge the ruler in Yarkand and became the ruler himself.[74] The power to terminate and appropriate the authority of a king was thus within the realm of a Naqshbandi shaikh's political activity. We have already seen how disobedience to Khwaja Ahrar led to the elimination of Mirza 'Abd-Allah, the ruler of Samarqand. A statement attributed to him by the author of *Rashhat 'Ain al-Hayat* is also significant:

> If we acted only as a shaikh in this age, no other shaikh would find a disciple. But another task has been assigned to us, to protect the Muslims from the evil of oppressors, and for the sake of this we must traffic with kings and conquer their souls, thus achieving the purpose of the Muslims. *God Almighty in His grace has bestowed on me such power that if I wish I can, with a single letter, cause the Chinese emperor who claims divinity to abandon his monarchy and come running over thorns to my threshold.* But with all this power I await God's command: whenever He wills, His command reaches me and is executed.[75]

---

[73] Cf. Damrel, "Forgotten Grace", pp. 80–1. Damrel cites Haider, "Agrarian System in Uzbek Khanates", pp. 157–78, and Haider, "Urban Classes in the Uzbek Khanates"; Foltz, *Mughal India*, pp. 97–9.

[74] Cf. Shaw, "The History of Khwajas", and Rene Grousset, *Empire of the Steppe*, cited in Algar, "Political Aspects", p. 128.

[75] Cited in Algar, "The Naqshbandi Order", pp. 123–52. Emphasis mine.

Later Naqshbandi–Ahrari shaikhs, who had keen remembrances of a share in power, would then have found it difficult to adjust to a political environment where the king did far more than assert his sole authority. Akbar, for example, had the audacity to throw overboard the shaikh's recommendation, and moreover when it came from a scion of the great Naqshbandi lineage. Quite noticeably, therefore, Akbar moved away from the Naqshbandis. The emperor had begun to see the seeds of a formidable challenge to his plan for power and political pre-eminence in the activities of several supporters of the Naqshbandi lineage at the court of his half-brother, Mirza Hakim, in Kabul. A glimmering of these sentiments is evident from events in the 1580s. While his nobles and deputies were assigned the task of suppressing serious rebellions in Gujarat and the east, Akbar himself commanded the expedition to deal with Mirza Hakim in the Punjab.[76] As we will see later, Kabul served as the centre for relaunching the Naqshbandi order in India, even after the termination of Mirza Hakim's regime.

In the late 1570s Akbar favoured the Chishti order. This is not to suggest that the Chishti saints' concerns were purely spiritual, with no taste whatsoever for power and politics. Their past too shows cases of their conflict with rulers.[77] A significant feature of their politics had, however, been their support to rulers in the endeavour to adjust the nature of Muslim power to the Indian environment.[78] Again, no Chishti shaikh ever amassed wealth comparable to that of Khwaja Ahrar alongside a mission to reform a political regime, rewarding those who listened to his exhortations and became submissive, and punishing those that dared act independently. As against this, the Chishtis had generally pleaded for

[76] Subrahmanyam, "A Note on the Kabul Kingdom"; Faruqui, "The Forgotten Prince".

[77] Digby, "The Sufi Shaykh and the Sultan", pp. 71–81; Kumar, "Assertions of Authority", pp. 37–65.

[78] For a discussion around this question, see Alam, *The Languages of Political Islam*, pp. 81–114.

THE MUGHALS, THE SUFI SHAIKHS 79

a kind of asceticism and preferred to advise and bless the political authorities from a distance. Indeed, their *tasawwuf* had been based on a doctrine, *wahdat al-wujud*, which had hitherto facilitated religious synthesis and cultural amalgam. In some Chishti treatises of Akbar's time, the doctrine was expressed and elaborated in a much more forceful tone, even including a plea to recognise the illegitimacy of belief in Islam as superior to every other religion. "The whole world is a manifestation of love (*'ishq*)", to quote from one such treatise, "and we see everything as perfect ... As you begin *iradat* (become a *murid* and join the order) you stop quarrelling over *kufr* and *iman*. There is no precedence of one religion over the other ... After you experience the limitlessness of unbounded Beauty you can see His Grace present both in a *kafir* and a Muslim."[79] Nothing could have provided stronger support to "Akbar's dream".

Akbar's visits to the shrine of Khwaja Mu'in al-Din, the founder of the Chishti *silsila* in India, best illustrates his fascination with the order. The circumstances in which the emperor was, according to Abu al-Fazl, drawn towards the khwaja are interesting. One night, while on a hunting expedition, Abu al-Fazl writes, the emperor heard people in a village near Agra singing Hindi verses in praise of the khwaja. The emperor was impressed by the saint's popularity, often discussed his "perfections and miracles", and developed a "strong inclination" to visit the shrine.[80] He undertook several journeys to Ajmer, one of which was on foot – all the way from Fathpur to the holy city of the saint. He also constructed several buildings around the shrine, arranged for its management, and provided grants for the care and comfort of pilgrims. Then, in 1564 in Delhi, he visited the tomb of Nizam al-Din Auliya,

---

[79] Cf. Bilgrami, *Sab' Sanabil*, pp. 330–1. Bilgrami wrote the treatise in Persian – of which the original is still unpublished – in 969 AH/1562. Later, in 974/1567, he compiled the better known *Haqa'iq-i Hindi*, in which he gave Islamic meanings to the words and expressions explicitly "Hindu".

[80] Abu al-Fazl, *Akbarnama*, Vol. II, p. 154, English transl., p. 237; Currie, *The Shrine and Cult*, p. 100; Nizami, *Akbar and Religion*, p. 104.

while in 1569 he began the construction of palaces in Fathpur Sikri – selected as the site of his new capital, a token of respect for a living Chishti saint, Shaikh Salim Chishti, through whose prayers he believed he was blessed with a son (who was named after the shaikh).[81]

By the 1570s Akbar thus appeared as an exclusive devotee of the Chishti saints, both dead and alive. In 1581, on his way to the Punjab, he visited the *khanqah* of another major Chishti saint of the period, Shaikh Jalal al-Din, in Thanesar. This visit is of special importance for our purposes since the grand old shaikh was a noted *khalifa* of Shaikh 'Abd al-Quddus Gangohi. Akbar was accompanied by the two brothers Abu al-Fazl and Faizi. They had a long conversation with the shaikh and discussed with him the secrets of divine realities and mystical sensibilities (*haqa'iq wa ma'arif*). The emperor, as the recorded memory in later Chishti *tazkiras* has it, was so impressed with the shaikh's response that he even expressed a desire to give up kingship. The shaikh, however, dissuaded him from precipitate action by saying:

> First you find a person who can match you and sit [on the throne] in your place, and then come for this work ... Your justice for an hour is better than the prayers of a thousand saints. Piety and sainthood for you lies in your being just to God's people (*khalq-i Khuda*) and in conferring benefits upon them. Remember God. Kingship does not prevent you from remembering Him.[82]

Did Akbar then recognise the Chishtis as royal *pirs*? Nothing in our sources suggests that he did. What did Akbar expect a Sufi to be? Which Sufis did he like to be close to? We are provided an answer to these questions in a remark by Abu al-Fazl on Mirza

---

[81] Richards, "Formulation of Imperial Authority"; Currie, *The Shrine and Cult*, pp. 99–102 and 152–4; Nizami, *Akbar and Religion*, pp. 104–5, 111, and 117.

[82] 'Ali, *Sawati' al-Anwar*, British Library, India Office Ms. Ethe 652 (I.O. Islamic 2705), fols 389b–390b; 'Abd al-Rahman Chishti, *Mir'at al-Asrar*, British Library, Ms. Or. 216.

Sharaf al-Din's revolt. The remark also supports and in a measure reiterates the reasons that were given above for the decline of the fortunes of Naqshbandis:

> It is an old custom for the divinely great and for acute rulers to attach to themselves the hearts of dervishes and the sons of dervishes. And they have exhibited this tendency, which is both an intoxicant which destroys men, and sometimes as a means of testing their real nature. If the matter be looked into with the eye of justice, it will be evident to the prudent and awakened-hearts, that the favour shown by the Shahinshah to this father and son exhibited both motives. Accordingly the concomitants of His Majesty's fortune withdrew in a short time the veil from the face of Mirza Sharaf al Din Husain's actions, and his real worthlessness and insubstantiality became manifest to mankind. When God, the world-protector, wills to cleanse the site of the eternal dominion from the evil and black-hearted, and to deck it with the sincere and loyal, a state of things spontaneously arises which could not be produced by a thousand planning. The hypocrites depart from the threshold of fortune by the efforts of their own feet and fall into destruction. Such was the evil-ending case of Mirza Sharaf al-Din Husain, who by influence of the man-throwing wine of the world did not remain firm of foot, but left his place, and into whose head there entered thoughts of madness and melancholy.[83]

It is time to return to the question posed at the end of the first section of this chapter. We know that Abu al-Fazl wrote his history – in which he included a brief three-line description of 'Abd al-Quddus Gangohi – in the 1590s, by when the Akbari dispensation had in a sense been fully formed. While he does not neglect regard for the truth, the basic duty of a historian, his portrayal of the developments of the earlier years is in several cases influenced by the particular ideology and concerns of this late phase of Akbar's rule. We also know that he was not a mere chronicler. He had his own philosophy of life and social order, and propounded, promoted, and defended the ideology of this

---

[83] Abu al-Fazl, *Akbarnama*, Vol. II, p. 195, English transl., p. 303.

dispensation. He wrote history with a mission. So to appreciate the significance of this particular case we may also note the following points. Firstly, the description of the shaikh as noted above is very brief indeed. Secondly, one line of this brief notice, which comprises the information about Humayun's visit and his meeting with the shaikh, begins with the word *guyand*, i.e. "they say" or "it is said", which in a measure implies it is based on a kind of hearsay or on something remembered and constructed by the associates of the shaikh himself.[84] This also means that while Abu al-Fazl wants his audience and posterity to take note of what is recounted, he is not particularly concerned with its truth. Again, we know that Gangohi was the royal *pir* of the enemies of the Mughals, that he had supported them, and on that count suffered humiliation at the hands of the Mughals. The memory of these details, already recorded, and incorporated in the *tazkira* of the shaikh written by his son, repeatedly read in the circle of the shaikh's associates and followers, threatened to adversely affect the good relations that Akbar had developed with the Chishtis and which Abu al-Fazl applauded. There was however also the memory of the shaikh's efforts to restore his own relations with the Mughals, as we can guess from the letters he wrote to Babur, Humayun, and Tardi Beg. The shaikh also seems to have visited Agra in 1537 for a brief stay, just before his death.[85] And it is not unlikely that the efforts in this direction continued in the changed political atmosphere to create conditions of friendship with the new rulers, and that in the

---

[84] "*Guyand Jannat Ashyani ba barkhi az kar agahan bezaviya-i u dar shudi wa anjuman-i agahi garmi pizirafiti*". Abu al-Fazl generally seems to be very meticulous in his choice of words to indicate the evidence and degree of authenticity of what he describes. While describing a person's descent and family line, for instance, if he is certain about it he prefers the simple "*ast*" or "*and*", that is to say: is or are. In cases where he wants to remain noncommittal, he uses expressions like "*khud ra az (. . .) nazhad bar shamurd*", i.e. "he counted himself Saiyid-born". Cf. *Ai'n-i Akbari*, pp. 211 and 214, for example.

[85] Cf. Digby, "Shaikh Abd al-Quddus Gangohi".

process there also emerged stories of the emperor's meeting with the shaikh. Since the Mughal court's contact with the Chishtis was in practice an endorsement of Abu al-Fazl's own ideology, he promotes the memory of this anecdote bearing on an intimate contact between the two. Pointedly, he does not allude to the shaikh's life over the time of Afghan rule: he wants his readers to forget everything that might recall the Mughals' distance from him. His aim is to emphasise the necessity and significance of the Mughal court's good relations with the Chishtis. If at all a king needed – which in Abu al-Fazl's view he did indeed – to "attach to himself the hearts of dervishes", such dervishes in India should be the Chishtis, certainly not the Mawarannahri–Naqshbandis.

Interestingly, Abu al-Fazl is the sole authority cited for this anecdote in the later Chishti *tazkiras*, as if his was a piece of contemporary evidence by an eyewitness to the event. Obviously, in these *tazkiras* were added words and phrases implying that Humayun had regular meetings with the shaikh – as the earlier Afghan rulers had had.[86] A seventeenth-century non-Chishti account, however, mentions the anecdote without referring to Abu al-Fazl.[87] Relevant here is also the oft-cited Mughal–Sufi *tazkira* written by Shaikh 'Abd al-Haqq Dehlavi (d. 1642), about the same time that Abu al-Fazl wrote his history, wherein this anecdote finds no place, even though Dehlavi's account of Gangohi is pretty detailed, comprising over 1400 words.[88] This may be because Dehlavi did not share Abu al-Fazl's concern, and also because his primary connection was with the Qadiri *silsila*.

Akbar for his part retained his faith in Khwaja Mu'in al-Din, and thereby remained in contact with the Chishtis, even after what Bada'uni and some Naqshbandis projected as the emperor's rejection of Islam.[89] In return the emperor too received notice-

[86] Chishti, *Mir'at al-Asrar*, fol. 427; 'Ali, *Sawati' al-Anwar*, fol. 381a.
[87] Sadiq, *Tabaqat-i Shahjahani*, British Library, India Office Ms., Ethe 705, fol. 195b.
[88] Dehlavi, *Akhbar al-Akhyar*, pp. 227–30.
[89] Bada'uni, *Muntakhab al-Tawarikh*, Vol. II, pp. 272–3.

able appreciation from Chishti circles. If Abu al-Fazl is to be believed, on the occasion of one of his visits to Ajmer the people connected with the shrine told the emperor that they saw the khwaja in a dream saying: "If he [Akbar] knew the amount of his own spirituality, he would not bestow a glance on me, the sitter in the dust of the path of studentship."[90] At the time of his visit to Shaikh Jalal al-Din in Thanesar, the old shaikh, who because of his advanced age generally lay in bed in a half-conscious state, asked his attendants to give him support to stand up and welcome the emperor, "the Caliph of the age". In the seventeenth-century Chishti *tazkiras*, Akbar is remembered and mentioned as a just and pious king, devoted to Khwaja Mu'in al-Din, and also on occasion with Arabic phrases such as *rahima-hu Allah* (may God bless him) and *anar Allahu burhana-hu* (may God illumine his proof), which are generally used for saints.[91]

The Return of the Naqshbandi Shaikhs

The Naqshbandis, as outlined earlier, came to India along with the Mughals. But far from being royal *pirs*, as they had been in Central Asia, here they did not manage to maintain good relations with the Mughal rulers. In the society outside the charmed circle of the ruling class, too, they made not much of a mark as notable Sufi shaikhs. In Indian conditions they noticed that other shaikhs, the Chishtis most prominently, exercised a greater appeal, and that the Naqshbandi heritage of explicitly combining power (or *wilayat*) with rulership had to an extent come in the way of their achieving the high position they wanted and aspired to. The competition was stiff. They had to reckon with the existing

[90] Abu al-Fazl, *Akbarnama*, Vol. II, p. 324, English transl., p. 477. This incident, characterised by Nizami as sycophancy (*Akbar and Religion*, p. 104), could also be taken as an illustration of how Akbar gradually grew antithetical to Sufism. For a discussion around this dimension of Akbar's politics, see Lawrence, "Veiled Opposition to Sufis", pp. 436–51.

[91] Chishti, *Mir'at al-Asrar*, fol. 236a; 'Ali, *Sawati' al-Anwar*, fol. 389b.

popular Sufi orders, assert and establish the supremacy of their own order, argue outhow it was the best, and how even in matters relating to the principle and practice of poverty and asceticism (*faqr, tark-i dunya*) they were really far ahead of the Chishtis. They always remained within the limits of the traditions of the Prophet and stated that their primary task was to achieve "the purpose of the Muslims", even as they engaged with worldly politics and trafficked with kings.

Two further major Naqshbandi saints, Khwaja Khawand Mahmud 'Alavi Husaini (d. 1652) and Khwaja Baqi-Billah (d. 1603), came to India and established their *khanqahs* during Akbar's reign. Khawand Mahmud was perhaps the first to be directed by his *pir*, Shaikh Muhammad Ishaq Dehbidi (d. 1599), to come to India to propagate the Naqshbandi mission. Thereupon he joined a caravan and set out for Lahore. When he arrived in the town of Gujrat in the Punjab, where the road bifurcated – one path leading to Kashmir, the other to Lahore – he fell into a mystic trance and his horse took the route towards Kashmir. After he regained consciousness, he decided to continue his journey in the direction of Kashmir, believing this was what God and his master would have wanted. He settled in Kashmir, and, though he had some initial difficulty, succeeded in establishing the order on a firm footing in the Valley. His son and successor, Khwaja Mu'in al-Din (d. 1674) was also a prominent saint in the Valley. Khawand Mahmud's influence, despite his efforts to come close to some nobles in Delhi and Agra, did not really extend beyond the Valley.[92]

It was Khwaja Muhammad Baqi-Billah – a member of the family of Khwaja Ahrar from his mother's side – who took up the challenge of reinstating the Naqshbandi order in the heartland of Mughal Hindustan. He came to settle in Delhi from Kabul in

---

[92] Rizvi, *A History of Sufism*, Vol. II, pp. 181–5. For a comprehensive discussion of Khawand Mahmud's career, see Damrel, "Forgotten Grace". See also Ahmad, *Hazrat Khwaja Naqshband*, pp. 358–407.

1599, inspired and perfected in the order by Khwaja Muhammad Muqtada Amkinagi (d. 1600). He had earlier been to India, and had lived and wandered in Sambhal, Lahore, and Kashmir. He lived very briefly in Delhi, for slightly over four years, but before his premature death in 1603 he had virtually reinstated the Naqshbandi order.[93] He left behind four major *khalifas*: Shaikh Ilahdad (d. 1640), Shaikh Husam al-Din (d. 1633), Shaikh Taj al-Din Sambhali (d. 1642), and Shaikh Ahmad Sirhindi (d. 1624). Of these, the last two occupied prominent positions in strengthening and propagating the teachings of the order in India and abroad in the Islamic lands in the seventeenth century. Sirhindi, we know, also founded a new branch, the Mujaddidi, of the order.[94]

There is plenty of information about the nature of Baqi-Billah's *tasawwuf* and *karamat* in the contemporary and near-contemporary writings of his disciples and *khalifas*, and also in the *tazkiras* compiled during the seventeenth and early-eighteenth centuries. For the following discussion, however, I have drawn in the main on his own writings, i.e. *malfuzat* (table talk) and *maktubat* (letters), and poetry, edited and published together with his poems in one volume by two leading twentieth-century Naqshbandi–Mujaddidi scholars.[95] I here select a few issues which were in his view the distinctive features of the order and which also in some measure illustrate a rather combative overtone. He compares the features of his order with those of the other orders, the Chishti in particular, pointing succinctly to flaws in the latter. He emphasises and stresses the dimensions of mystical sensitivity (*wajd, zauq*), without losing contact with mundane power. Regarding the *pir*, for instance, he observes that according to the Naqshbandi order there can be more than one *pir*. For the *pir*, as the Chishti and Suhrawardi shaikhs understood it, was not simply one from

---

[93] Rizvi, *A History of Sufism*, Vol. II, pp. 185–93; Rizvi, "Sixteenth Century Naqshbandiyya Leadership", pp. 153–65.

[94] Rizvi, *A History of Sufism*, Vol. II, pp. 195–263 and 336–8.

[95] Baqi-Billah, *Kulliyat-i Baqi-Billah*.

whom the seeker received the *khirqa* (robe). There were two other categories of *pir* as well, which he characterised as the *pir-i talim* who gives training in litanics, and the *pir-i suhbat* whose company resulted in general benefit and in enabling the seeker to appreciate the diverse avenues of spiritual progress.[96] Baqi-Billah thus was keen to initiate into his *silsila* even those who already had their *pirs* – of the Chishti, Suhrawardi, or any other lineage – in India. This amounted to making a bid to extend the domain of his own order, even if it meant a violation of generally accepted Sufi practice. In this connection the following passage helps explain why he did this:

> Someone reported in the presence of Hazrat-i Ishan (Baqi-Billah) that a certain person [the author hints at Nizam al-Din Thanesari, a leading Chishti shaikh, but does not mention his name] says that Hazrat-i Ishan emancipates seekers from having faith in former *pirs* and insists that they receive teaching only from him. He (Baqi-Billah) said this was not the case. "But if I find some of the seekers in two minds, I advise them to concentrate on one path . . ." Then he said that the faith that he had in the shaikhs of the other *silsilas* is hardly found among them. In particular, the people of India's beliefs about their *pirs* verge on idolatory.[97]

But while for him, and for that matter for any other shaikh of his order, it was legitimate to lure the followers of other *silsilas*, he did not allow the *murid* of a Naqshbandi to seek guidance from any other *pir* in India. Elaborating on the relationship between the seeker and the preceptor, he wrote to his *khalifa*, Shaikh Taj al-Din:

> And similarly in the moral conduct (*adab*) of the Naqshbandi Ahrari path you should be firm like a mountain, never mixing it with the path of the other . . . Whoever is your murid is *your* murid *only*. Train and teach him according to Naqshbandi path only . . . Of what interest is the person who receives the light from you and then attends upon a Shattari [shaikh]?[98]

[96] Ibid., Section *Malfuzat*, pp. 31–2.
[97] Ibid., p. 35.
[98] Baqi-Billah, *Kulliyat-i Baqi-Billah*, Section *Ruq'at*, p. 77.

With reference to the discourse on *tauhid* and *wujud*, we are aware that the Chishtis in India followed Ibn al-'Arabi (d. 1240) and maintained that the position of 'Ala al-Daula Simnani (d. 1336), who contested Ibn al-'Arabi's stand and propounded a contrary view, was not correct. Baqi-Billah for his part took a different stand. He proposed that both Ibn al-'Arabi and Simnani were right. Still, while he tried to reconcile the two views and suggested that the difference between them was only in words rather than in deeper substance, he argued that Simnani was closer to the truth:

> His (Simnani's) *shuhud* (perception) is the most perfect *shuhud*. The difference is that a group of the *'ulama* [read: Indian Sufis] believe that things do not exist objectively and that their external appearance is only like the appearance of the reflections in a mirror. In sum, they recognise only one existence. The shaikh [Simnani] with his power of perception (*shuhud*) and its pre-eminence recognised the objective existence of things too.[99]

Further, Baqi-Billah firmly rejected the Chishtis' understanding of *tauhid*. He openly challenged Shaikh Nizam al-Din Thanesari –nephew and son-in-law of Jalal-al-Din Thanesari, who after the latter's death was virtually the sole spokesman of the Sabiri branch of the Chishti order – to debate him about the matter and prove his position if he was right in an assembly of *'ulama* and Sufis. In the circle of his associates, the belief was that Thanesari, even if he was considered to be the most perfect Indian dervish, did not possess adequate knowledge and mystical sensitivity to appreciate Simnani's observations on Reality, and that his understanding was based on wrong and misleading translations and interpretations. Baqi-Billah was aware of the intensity of such offensive opinion (*gustakhi*). But he asserted that he was constrained to express himself thus with the sole objective of disseminating and protecting the position of the true sect and bringing forth the correct meanings of the utterances of the great shaikhs. He

---

[99] Ibid., p. 123.

wanted, or so he claimed, to save people from being misled and thus sinking into the whirlpool of mistaken belief. He wrote also that often the illumination experienced by a Sufi in an early stage of his mystical journey was taken as the real epiphany (*tajalli*). This was an error and was just a reflection of, and not the real light of, *tajalli*.[100] This assumes a special import, considering that the Mawarannahri–Naqshbandis, including the great Ahrar and Shaikh 'Abd al-Rahman Jami, were mostly *wujudis*.[101]

Baqi-Billah's competitive attitude towards his contemporary Chishti shaikhs is also illustrated by his observations on *sama'* or Sufi music. *Sama'* had come to be an integral part of Chishti Sufi life and was regarded as a means to experience and achieve the spiritually sublime; in this, the order drew support from the life and teachings of the early great saints whose Sufi accomplishments the Naqshbandis also recognised. Baqi-Billah however contested their reading and interpretation of their predecessors. He took up the case of Shaikh Nizam al-Din Auliya, whose practice was the most oft-cited evidence in support of musical practices, and remarked that in his *malfuzat*, where Nizam al-Din discussed the legality of *sama'*, he appended the condition that the listener be a true lover of God. This evidently meant, Baqi-Billah added, that he disapproved of its practice. True love of God, Baqi-Billah added, required total and unqualified submission to the path (*sunna*) of the Prophet. A true follower of his path would never indulge in an act for which there was no precedent in the life

---

[100] Ibid., p. 118.

[101] Algar, "A Brief History", and ter Haar, "The Naqshbandi Tradition in the eyes of Ahmad Sirhindi", pp. 21 and 89–90 for references to the *wahdat al-wujudi* leanings of Khwaja Baha al Din Naqshband's disciple, Khwaja Muhammad Parsa, Ubaid-Allah Ahrar and his disciple Abd al-Rahman Jami (d. 1492). The majority of Jami's writings involve either commentaries on Ibn al-'Arabi or elaborations in prose or poetry of his ideas of *wujud*. See, for instance, Jami's *Naqd al-Nususfi Sharh Naqsh al-Fusus*, Editor's Introduction. See also Morris, "Ibn 'Arabi and His Intrepreters, Part II", pp. 101–19; Addas, *The Quest for the Red Sulphur*, p. 291.

of the Prophet. The Prophet never listened to music, nor did he ever permit its performance.[102] Indian Sufis had failed to get the correct meaning of the discourses in the texts composed in India, too, as they misunderstood and misinterpreted Ibn al-'Arabi and Simnani. Islam in India was to be as Baqi-Billah saw it, whatever its practice in the past.

In all this obviously lay a critique of the very basis of the prevailing understanding of *tasawwuf*. "Our *tariqa*", Baqi-Billah noted, "is based on three things: an unswerving faith (*rusukh*) in the truth of the beliefs of the Sunni community (*ahl-i sunnat wa jama'at*), knowledge, gnosis (*agahi*) and prayer ('*ibadat*). Laxity in any one of these throws one out of our *tariqa*."[103] The principal duty of a seeker, he said, was to follow the *shari'a*. "Correct beliefs," he reiterated, "regard for *shari'a* and sincere attention to God are the greatest wealth. No mysticism (*zauq, wijdan*) is comparable with this."[104] Indeed, the ultimate aim for him was to achieve what the earlier shaikhs of his lineage characterised as *musalmani*. When a seeker asked him about its implications, he said: "*Musalmani* is the *murad* [the desired goal, but it] is difficult." It is achieved only with divine grace, and is beyond the circle of human effort. To become a *musalman* is the very reality (*haqiqa*) of mysticism (*ma'rifa*).[105] In one of his letters, he elaborates on the question saying that beauty (*jamal*) and perfection (*kamal*) in a seeker follow from his submission (*bandagi*), which means prayer, fasting, alms-giving, *hajj*, war with infidels, regard for the rights of parents and others, and justice.[106]

Furthermore, Baqi-Billah pleaded for the need to insist on maintaining the distinction between infidelity (*kufr*) and faith (*iman*). He dismissed as heretic (*zandaqa*) and extremely stupid (*ablahi, safahat*) ideas that encouraged words which implied aban-

---

[102] Baqi-Billah, *Kulliyat-i Baqi-Billah*, Section *Malfuzat*, pp. 42–3.
[103] Ibid., p. 25.
[104] Ibid., p. 36.
[105] Ibid., p. 29, and Section *Ruq'at*, p. 137.
[106] Baqi-Billah, *Kulliyat-i Baqi-Billah*, Section *Ruq'at*, p. 139.

doning of the *shari'a*, the admiration of unbelief, and an emphasis on the basic similarity of a believer and an infidel.[107] A measure of the intensity in his attitude on the matter was reflected in his resistance to the idea of treatment by a Hindu physician during his illness. He relented when told that this had been arranged at his mother's wish. All the same, he did not like the presence of the Hindu physician and turned his face away from him when he visited.[108]

It is, however, significant that together with these statements – addressed to Indian shaikhs in the main, and in a rather uncompromising and aggressive tone – he also disapproved of a Sufi's direct involvement in power and money-making. He thus discouraged a feature of Ahrari *wilayat* which had hitherto legitimated the drive of a Naqshbandi shaikh to aspire to a position alongside the ruler, if not above him. As already noticed, this was one of the factors that alienated Akbar. To Baqi-Billah, *musalmani* or the highest stage in *tasawwuf* was to be accomplished with poverty (*faqr*) and negation of self (*nisti*), and not with power and wealth.[109] He showed no direct concern for power politics but was in close contact with people at the helm of affairs and spared no pains recommending the cases of his associates and disciples.

Among others, he recommended the case of Shaikh Ahmad Sirhindi for an adequate cash grant.[110] Of the eighty-six of his available letters, no less than thirteen were addressed to people engaged in state service and trade. His addressees included Shaikh Farid Bukhari, who, according to a report, bore all the expenses of his *khanqah*.[111] Mirza 'Aziz Koka; and the *sadr al-sudur* Miran Sadr-i Jahan Pihani. Some of these recipients have been mentioned by the compiler as his sincere devotees (*az umara i mukhlis*), but it is unclear whether they really became his *murids*.

---

[107] Ibid., pp. 122–3.
[108] Baqi-Billah, *Kulliyat-i Baqi-Billah*, Section *Malfuzat*, pp. 49–50.
[109] Ibid., pp. 130–1.
[110] Ibid., pp. 91, 93, 98, 105, 107, 118, 120, 130, 133, 134, and 135.
[111] Ibid., p. 36.

Baqi-Billah used all his strength and accomplishments to reinstall the Naqshbandi *silsila* as a great, if not the greatest, mystic order in Mughal India. He joined issue with the contemporary saints of the other orders and tried to demonstrate the supremacy of his order. He disapproved of several features of prevailing Sufi culture that lent strength to some important features of the Akbari dispensation. He also hinted that it was the purification of things Indian, and their redefinition, that were the essence of his mission in coming to Hindustan. Nowhere, however, did he actually comment on their legality or illegality, let alone pronounce a verdict on the faith of the emperor. On this question his approach seems to have been different from the one we generally associate with his noted disciple, Shaikh Ahmad Sirhindi. Can we assume that this was because he died prematurely, leaving his mission incomplete while he was still mobilising strength? We are discouraged from following this line of speculation by the fact that Sirhindi, howsoever powerful he may have been, was not the sole spokesman of the Naqshbandi order after his death. But this is a major question which still demands careful examination, and which should be dealt with separately.

Conclusion

This chapter has traced the relationship between the Mughal dynasty in India and various groups of Sufi shaikhs over the course of the sixteenth century. Rather than focusing exclusively, or even largely, on the Naqshbandi–Mujaddidi tradition of the early-seventeenth century, I have attempted to look at the competition between various orders of Sufis for influence over the Mughals. In this, the central role is played by the competitive axis between the Chishtis and the Naqshbandis, the former having exercised considerable influence over the Afghans while the latter were, in a manner of speaking, the "ancestral" saints of the Central Asian Timurids. We have seen how the mainstream of the Ahrari Naqshbandi tradition from Transoxiana failed in the end, for a number of reasons, to consolidate its hold in India during the reign of Humayun, leading to the brief ascendancy of the Shattari order. Eventually, after a phase of Chishti reassertion that characterises the early years of Akbar's rule (and his relations with both Ajmer, and the more proximate figure of Shaikh Salim Chishti), the Naqshbandis were able to rally themselves. This is in no small measure because of the key role played by Khwaja Baqi-Billah, master of the celebrated Shaikh Ahmad Sirhindi, in reinventing both an aspect of their theology and their concrete functioning as an order.

A fuller consideration of Mughal–Sufi relations would naturally take us to a full examination of events and processes of the seventeenth century. That would also require a careful investigation of the role played by members of the Chishti order in the seventeenth century, including the key personage of 'Abd al-Rahman Chishti (mentioned only in passing here). Only by examining the full range of materials produced by different orders about themselves, and about each other, while keeping in view the political compulsions that shaped the choices of the Mughal emperors and their elites, may we grasp the intricacies and complexities of this field.

3

A Sufi Critique of Religious Law, *Tasawwuf*, and Politics in Mughal India

> If a prophet had been sent to this community [of Muslims], he would have practised the Hanafi law. – **Shaikh Ahmad Sirhindi,** *Maktubat*

> The Sufi has no *mazhab*. – **'Abd al-Rahman Chishti,** *Mir'at al-Asrar*

IN THE DEVELOPMENT of Indian Muslim religious learning and Sufi thought, seventeenth-century Mughal India occupies a special position. As noted in the previous chapter, several important Sufi orders flourished: the Naqshbandi, Suhrawardi, Qadiri, and Chishti. Arriving from Central Asia alongside the Mughal regime, the Naqshbandis established an especially important branch in India, known as the Mujadiddi, the originator being one of the best-known Indian Sufi and religious thinkers, Shaikh Ahmad Sirhindi (d. 1624). This Indian branch eventually spread far beyond the subcontinent to cover more or less the entire Islamic East. The period also witnessed the rise of another well-known religious thinker, Shaikh 'Abd al-Haqq Muhaddis Dehlavi (d. 1642), one of the few Indian Muslim scholars to visit Hijaz and receive training in advanced religious learning. Upon his return to India, Dehlavi established his own institutions to disseminate what he had acquired, to which his own particular contribution was his rejuvenation of the science of *hadith*. A member of the Qadiri order, Dehlavi's *Akhbar al-Akhyar*, a *tazkira* of South Asian Sufis, is amongst the oft-cited Sufi texts.[1] These two figures dominate the history of seventeenth-century Muslim religious culture in India.

This chapter, however, will take as its starting point an oft-overlooked religious discourse initiated by a Chishti shaikh. Much as Sirhindi revitalised the Naqshbandi order in the seventeenth century, the Chishtis also rearticulated their ideology in significant new ways, partly in reaction to the formulations of the Naqshbandi order. Integral to this discourse is the problem of the Sufi's relationship to a specific religious jurisprudential school (*mazhab*). In this debate, the Chishtis not only reacted to their political and religious environment but also re-read and redefined the Islamic past and Muslim religious traditions. Yet, this train of seventeenth-century thought is practically untouched by modern South Asian scholarship. Indeed, one of our best authorities projects the Chishtis during the Mughal era as virtually inactive, reviving only later in the eighteenth century.[2] Even for the Naqshbandis, scholarship has been largely confined to the Naqshbandi reaction to Akbar (d. 1605).

My primary source for the Chishti view of this period comes from the writings of Shaikh 'Abd al-Rahman (d. 1683). Hailing from Awadh, 'Abd al-Rahman was a major shaikh of the Sabiri branch of the Chishti *silsila* with close family connections to two eminent saints of the Chishti Sabiri order, Shaikh Ahmad 'Abd al-Haqq of Rudauli (d. 1434) and Shaikh 'Abd al-Quddus Gangohi (d. 1537).[3] 'Abd al-Rahman was thus a prime spokesman for his order and presents a lucid view of the Chishti position.

---

[1] For Sirhindi, see Friedmann, *Shaykh Ahmad Sirhindi*; Rizvi, *The Muslim Revivalist Movements*; ter Haar, *Follower and Heir of the Prophet*; for Dehlavi, see Nizami, *Hayat-i Shaikh 'Abd al-Haqq Muhaddis Dehlavi*; Lawrence, "Biography and the 17th Century Qadiriya of North India"; Kugle, "'Abd al-Haqq Dihlawi"; and Alim Ashraf Khan, *Shaikh 'Abd al-Haqq Muhaddis Dehlavi*.

[2] There are, however, discussions of the Chishtis of the Mughal period in Nizami, *Tarikh-i Masha'ikh-i-Chisht*, pp. 224 and 231; Rizvi, *History of Sufism*, Vol. 2; Ernst and Lawrence, *Sufi Martyrs of Love*; and Faruqi, *Medieval India*.

[3] For Chishti, see Rizvi, *History of Sufism*, Vol. 2, pp. 27, 289, 368–9,

Shaikh 'Abd al-Rahman Chishti's *Mir'at al-Asrar*

'Abd al-Rahman wrote prolifically, with five of his books bearing the word *Mir'at* in their titles.[4] Here, I discuss primarily his *Mir'at al-Asrar*, one of the most comprehensive biographical dictionaries of the Sufis. It was written during the seventeenth century and covered about a thousand years, from the time of the Prophet down to the date of its compilation (AH 1065/AD 1654), and it cost the author about twenty years' of labour from start to finish (AH 1045/AD 1635 to AH 1065/AD 1654). Bruce Lawrence has analysed this text by focusing on its Indo-Persian flavour.[5] The book reads like a definitive statement of the legitimacy of Chishti ideology and practice, including the doctrines of *wahdat al-wujud* (unity of being) and *sama'* (music).

Besides an introduction, the book is divided into twenty-three chapters (*tabaqas*). The first is devoted to the life of the Prophet Muhammad and his ten select companions (*'ashra-i mubashshara*), including the Four Pious Caliphs, followed by an independent chapter on the Fourth Pious Caliph and the Prophet's cousin and son-in-law, 'Ali, and his prominent descendants, Hasan, Husain, Muhammad Baqir, Ja'far Sadiq, Musa Kazim, Musa Riza, Abu

---

and 396; Ernst and Lawrence, *Sufi Martyrs of Love*; Digby, "'Mas'udi'", pp. 783–4; Amin, "On Re-telling the Muslim Conquest", pp. 24–43; and Amin, "Un Saint Guerrier", pp. 265–93.

[4] These are *Mir'at al-Asrar, Mir'at-i Madariya, Mir'at al-Haqa'iq, Mir'at-i Mas'udi,* and *Mir'at al-Makhluqat*. All are still unpublished. Several are available in different oriental holdings. There are Urdu translations of *Mir'at al-Asrar* by Wahid Baksh Sayyal Chishti Sabri and of *Mir'at-i Mas'udi* by Muhammad Abd al-Ghani Shah Qadiri as *Saulat-i Mas'udi*. There are also other Urdu recensions of *Mir'at-i Mas'udi*: Amin, "On Re-telling the Muslim Conquest", pp. 36–7n. 'Abd al-Rahman also intended to write yet another book titled *Mir'at al-Wilayat*, on the life of Shaikh 'Abd al-Jalil Uwaisi. See *Mir'at al-Asrar*, f. 225b.

[5] Lawrence, "An Indo-Persian Perspective", pp. 19–32.

Ja'far Muhammad, 'Ali Naqi, Abu Muhammad, and Abu al-Qasim Muhammad – the noted imams according to the *Isna 'Ashari* (the Shi'i creed). Chapter 3 mentions several other early Sufi luminaries, with Khwaja Hasan Basari as their leader. These chapters provide the origins and sources of the Chishti *silsila*. The earlier chapters are arranged chronologically, though in chapters 17 and 18 the mould is broken and saints of two generations are rather anachronistically discussed. The intention here seems to be to place other saints separately under the leadership of two major Indian Chishti saints, namely Khwaja Mu'in al-Din (d. 1236) and Qutb al-Din Bakhtiyar Kaki (d. 1235). In the later chapters the focus is primarily on Indian Sufis, in particular on the Chishtis. But here too Chishti mentions some eminent non-Indian saints, such as Khwaja Baha al-Din Naqshband (d. 1390) and Khwaja Muhammad Parsa (d. 1421), whose career and teachings had a close bearing on the Naqshbandi saints of his own time. These saints include Khwaja Baqi-Billah and Shaikh Ahmad Sirhindi, whose views are discussed below.

Of particular interest is the arrangement of the last twelve chapters. These chapters – with the sole exception of chapter 15, perhaps – begin with descriptions of saints with the attribution "Chishti", implying their leadership (*qutb*) in the group of the saints mentioned therein. The author, as noted, belonged to the Sabiri branch of the Chishti order, beginning with 'Ali Sabir. But, Sabir's history being disputed, the author's focus in these later chapters remain largely on the Nizami branch of the order.[6] He does not mention Sabir in any of these chapters as the leader of the saintly groups, although three saints of the Sabiri branch, namely Shams al-Din Turk Panipati (d. after 1318), Jalal-al-Din Panipati (d. 1371), and Ahmad 'Abd al-Haqq (d. 1483) occupy distinct positions in the concluding three chapters. 'Abd al-Rahman thus

---

[6] The doubts were first raised by Shaikh 'Abd al-Haqq Muhaddis Dehlavi in his *Akhbar al-Akhyar*, regarded as a most authentic *tazkira* from Mughal India. See Nizami, *Tarikh-i Masha'ikh-i-Chisht*, p. 215; and Rizvi, *History of Sufism*, Vol. 1, p. 154.

presents himself as the spokesman of the entire Chishti *silsila*, irrespective of the particular branch to which he belonged.

He also gives due attention to less-known Sufis of northern India and Awadh, the region to which he himself belongs, in order to highlight the local connections of the Chishti order and, in the words of Carl Ernst, "to create a local, sacred geography for Indian Islam."[7] The aim of 'Abd al-Rahman in writing this *tazkira* is to establish the significance of Chishti saints in the Sufi lineage.

Of special importance is the long introduction, which discusses *tasawwuf, wilayat*, and questions pertaining to the Sufi shaikh's religion or juridical position (*mazhab*), as well as his relations with rulers of his day, and which includes elaborate praise of 'Ali. At the very outset when praising Allah, he puts it thus: "He is the Lord of The East and of The West, and that He exists in every direction that you turn your face . . .", affirming the inviolability of the Sufi doctrine of *wahdat al-wujud*. He then delineates the distinction between *nubuwwat* (prophethood) and *wilayat* (sainthood) and claims both of these were perfectly embodied in Prophet Muhammad. Muhammad as *nabi* (Prophet) communicated the messages that he received from Allah, mediated through Jibril (Gabriel); whereas as a *wali* (saint, friend of Allah), Muhammad received instructions direct from Allah, with no mediation, and the author maintains that *wilayat* is superior to *nubuwwat*.

Furthermore, he elaborates the view that complete obedience to the Prophet is not restricted to following the teachings he disseminated as a *nabi*; rather, there is the additional requirement of obedience to the Prophet's instructions, which he gave as a *wali* and which are known to the select of the *umma* through the Prophet's cousin 'Ali. This complete obedience is much beyond the purview of what people of the externalia (*ahl-i zahir*) take as the entirety. The author adduces the support of Khwaja 'Ubaid-Allah Ahrar (d. 1490), who, as noted in the previous chapter, was a leading saint of the Naqshbandi order – Chishti's choice thus serving a polemical purpose.

---

[7] The phrase is from Ernst, "The Khuldabad–Burhanpur Axis", pp. 169–83.

The author invokes several traditions of the Prophet to highlight the superiority of 'Ali over the other companions. When Nimrod threw Abraham into the fire, Jibril came to him and asked if he needed his help, to which Abraham replied "Yes, but from Allah." In appreciation, Allah transformed the fire into a flower bed, leaving Abraham unharmed. On this occasion Abraham also received a black blanket (*gilim-i siyah*), eventually inherited by Muhammad after various other Biblical prophets. This *gilim* the Prophet transferred to 'Ali, saying "O 'Ali, I made you my deputy in both life and after my death." The author cites further examples regarding the question of deputyship (*khilafat*) following the Prophet's death, citing the oft-repeated tradition amongst the Shi'is: "Whosoever's master I am, 'Ali is also his master. O God, befriend him who befriends 'Ali, and make an enemy of him who is an enemy of 'Ali, and abandon him who leaves 'Ali."[8]

Chishti's position on 'Ali is rather exaggerated, even if it does not fall outside the purview of the Sunni tradition. The position, and the attempt it represents to find common ground with the Shi'i tradition, indicates some political anxiety regarding the difference between the Sunni and Shi'i communities. As we will see, Shah Jahan himself appeared to be concerned with the same question and Chishti's view presents a solution to this political knot.

The "Religion" (*Mazhab*) of the Sufi

Chishti's Introduction also includes a brief review of the different religions (*milal wa nihal*), and the seventy-two sects of Islam, followed by a discussion of the 73rd sect, that is the creed of the *ahl-i sunna wa jama'a*. Obedience to the tradition of the Prophet, his family members (*ahl-i bait*) and his companions was among the essential features of this creed and represented the true path (*sirat-i mustaqim*), based on a balanced (*i'tidal*) approach to Islam, far from excess and paucity (*ifrat wa tafrit*). Integral to Chishti's understanding of this creed was obedience to 'Ali and his family.

[8] *Mir'at al-Asrar*, f. 18a.

The prime duty of a *salik* (traveller of the Sufi path) was to follow the path of his preceptor (*pir wa shaikh*):

> The *salik* should know with all sincerity (*sidq*) of his heart that following the venerable sufis is the same, with regard to its form and meaning (*suratan wa ma'nan*) as following the Refuge of the Prophethood [i.e. the Prophet]. Thus it is necessary for the seeker (*talib*) on the path to God (*rah-i Haqq*) to understand truly the states (*ahwal*), sayings (*aqwal*), and beliefs (*'aqa'id*) of the Sufis and to complete his journey on the Straight Path (*sirat-i mustaqim*) in their footsteps.[9]

To Chishti, the model for a *salik* is his *pir*, without much regard for schools of jurisprudence (*fiqh*) or dogmatics and scholasticism (*kalam*). He illustrates this point from the example of Shaikh Nizam al-Din Auliya', the great Chishti shaikh who enjoyed an authoritative position beyond his own order and who, despite being a Hanafite, supported and indulged in *sama'* and kissing of the ground (*zamin bosi*) before the shaikh, which were unlawful in Hanafite jurisprudence. Questioned about his practices, the shaikh replied saying he did what he had seen his *pirs* do.[10]

Still, to Chishti the *salik*'s greatest master was Ibn al-'Arabi. He cites extensively from *Fusus al-Hikam*, which includes a discussion of the issue of *wahdat al-wujud* (unity of being) and showed its connections to the three related ideas of oneness, that is, *ahadiyat*, *wahdat*, and *wahidiyat*.[11] Ibn al-'Arabi, we know, was

---

[9] *Mir'at*, f. 4b.

[10] Ibid., f. 9a. On the other hand, Shaikh Ahmad Sirhindi says that the Sufi's practice does not decide the legality or illegality of an act. In matters of *sama'* what is reckonable is the opinion of Abu Hanifa, Abu Yusuf or Imam Muhammad and not the act of Abu Bakr Shibli and Abu Hasan Nuri. "The false Sufis of this age having taken their own *pirs* as models justify song and dance as part of Faith." See Sirhindi's long letter to Khwaja Baqi-Billah's sons, Khwaja 'Ubaid-Allah and Khwaja 'Abd-Allah, in Rahman, *Selected Letters of Shaikh Ahmad Sirhindi*, p. 102. Muhaddis Dehlavi's position, however, is flexible. Cf. Dehlavi's letters published on the margins of his *Akhbar al-Akhyar*, pp. 57–81.

[11] In Sufi cosmology, the first three levels of existence (*wujud*) are explained

the greatest master of the doctrine. Importantly, amongst the best interpretations of Ibn al-'Arabi, Chishti identifies the writings of 'Ala al-Daula Simnani (d. 1336), who was a model for Baqi-Billah and Sirhindi and in whose doctrine of *wahdat al-shuhud* (unity of perception) they found the real truth.[12] Chishti writes: "Shaikh Muhyi al-Din ibn 'Arabi in his *Futuhat al-Makkiya* described the Straight Path (*sirat-i mustaqim*) in detail, and Shaikh 'Ala al-Daula Simnani described the same thing, without subtracting or adding, in the sixth chapter of his book *'Urwat al-Wusqa*, in the most excellent manner."[13] Chishti explains that Simnani held a different view initially, but eventually realised the validity of Ibn al-'Arabi's position when he scaled the highest pinnacle of *tasawwuf*.[14] In support of this, Chishti refers to a long discourse in Simnani's notable treatise, *'Urwat al-Wusqa*, where the latter describes his encounter with the devil. The devil whispered doubts to him about the validity of his beliefs and faith by pointing to the proliferation of prophets and sects and asking how Simnani could know that only Muhammad represented the real truth.[15] Chishti summarises the whole discourse in his own words (*maqsad*

---

as (1) *Ahadiyat* (Unicity), which implies the *Zat-i Mutlaq* (Absolute Essence); (2) *Wahdat* (Unity), also called the *Ta'ayyun-i Awwal* (First Differentiation), *Barzakh-i Kubra* (Great Isthmus), and *Haqiqat-i Muhammadi*; (3) *Wahidiyat* (Oneness), which is *'Alam-i Kaun wa Makan* (World of Being and Space).

[12] Cf. Khwaja Baqi-Billah, *Kulliyat-i Baqi-Billah*, Section *Ruq'at*, p. 123; Friedmann, *Shaykh Ahmad Sirhindi*, pp. 24 and 26; ter Haar, *Follower and Heir of the Prophet*, pp. 34 and 42; Rizvi, *History of Sufism*, Vol. 2, pp. 208–10. For Simnani, see Elias, *The Throne Carrier of God*.

[13] *Mir'at*, f. 4b.

[14] For Chishti's citation of Simnani, see *Mir'at*, f.4b. Chishti invokes Jami too in his support. See the editor's introduction in Simnani, *Al-'Urwa li ahl al-Khalwa wa al-Jalwa*, p. 37. But for a different opinion, see 'Ala al-Daula's *Chihl Majlis*, pp. 35, 49, 137, and 140.

[15] Cf. Simnani, *Al-'Urwa li ahl al-Khalwa wa al-Jalwa*, pp. 304–12. During this period, Muhaddis Dehlavi also had serious reservations about reading Ibn al-'Arabi's *Fusus al-Hikam* and *Futuhat-i Makkiya*. Cf. Dehlavi's letters published on the margins of his *Akhbar al-Akhyar*, pp. 28–9 and 92–3.

mukhtasar kard), concluding with the definition of a Sufi's true and final religion.

Despite rebutting the devil's arguments, Simnani, Chishti continues, was still troubled because he observed that many adherents of the *sunna* themselves quarrelled over petty juridical questions. He therefore decided that it was better to be alone than to be in bad company (*al-wahdat khairun min jalis al-su'*). Soon, however, he received a vision (*batariq-i waqi'a*) of a group of the people of purity (*ahl-i safa*). They explained that they were God's servants and carried out, with heart and soul, the task of regulating governance (*siyasat*), worship (*'ibadat*), and purity (*taharat*), both in form (*surat*) and content (*ma'na*). They followed Muhammad's religion and the monotheistic faith (*millat-i hanifi*, i.e. Abraham's creed). In their way and course of life (*tariq wa mazhab*), extremities (*ghulu wa taqsir*) had no place. They took the utmost caution in matters of *mazhab* and presented and practised it in the most excellent manner (*ba-wajh-i ahsan*). They added: "We do not call anyone unbeliever (*kafir*) who says the *kalima* (the word of the faith), so long as he turns his face toward our direction of prayer (*qibla*)."[16] Simnani, Chishti reports, was delighted by this and regarded their *mazhab* as the best, and these people as the most perfect. They told him: "Our group is known as the Sufis."[17]

To Chishti, only this group could rightly be called adherents of *Ahl-i Sunna wa Jama'at*. This group was on the path of moderation (*i'tidal*), the straight path (*sirat-i mustaqim*), avoiding both excess and shortcoming. Chishti sums up his argument with verses from the *Masnawi* of Maulana Rumi, which was widely read in Mughal India.[18]

---

[16] *Mir'at*, ff. 6a–8a.

[17] Ibid., f. 8b.

[18] Rumi's *Masnawi* was regularly read to Akbar: Abu al-Fazl, *Akbarnama*, Vol. 1, p. 271. 'Abd al-Haqq Muhaddis Dehlavi prepared a recension of it: Nizami, *Hayat-i Shaikh 'Abd al-Haqq Muhaddis Dehlavi*, p. 84. 'Abd al-Latif 'Abbasi Gujarati, a Mughal Indian bureaucrat and scholar, prepared a critical edition of the *Masnawi*: Ansari, "Lata'if al-Lughat", pp. 33–45; Khatoon,

Stay away from imitation (*taqlid*) and bigotry (*ta'assub*),
erase the thought of both from the tablet of the heart.
Bigotry arises from the temptation of the carnal soul (*nafs*);
imitation disgraces the people.
Bigotry obstructs the way of the travellers,
the way of imitation is also a way to destruction.
O God, subdue the rebel carnal soul,
root out bigotry from our soul.
Show me the way of realisation to God's Unity,
release me from the prison of imitation.[19]

Chishti's arguments here were not simply in the service of a "shapeless mysticism".[20] Rather, he proposes a nuanced theoretical argument to redefine the everyday life of a Muslim and even stakes his claim to the essential definition of the *sunna* as opposed to the content of later innovations (*bid'a*). This argument is best understood perhaps in the context of the better-studied views of Sirhindi on *sunna* and *bid'a*.[21]

Chishti augments his position with further anecdotes, from Farid al-Din 'Attar's (d. 1220) *Tazkirat al-Auliya*. Khwaja Abu al-Hasan Hasri, an eminent disciple of Abu Bakr Shibli, was asked by the Caliph (during his stay in Baghdad) to which school of jurisprudence he belonged. Hasri answered that he had earlier followed Abu Hanifa's school, then, Imam Shafi'i's school. His present concern, however, made him totally oblivious to *mazhab*. The Caliph asked what this concern was. Hasri replied that it was *tasawwuf*. He explained: "Sufism is that [experience] without which nothing in both the worlds [i.e. this world and the life

---

"'Abd al-Latif 'Abbasi Gujarati aur Masnavi-i Maulana-i Rum". See also Alam, "Rumi's Masnawi".

[19] *Mir'at*, f. 8a. See also Vikor, "The Shaykh as *Mujtahid*", p. 360; Radtke, "Ijtihad and neo-Sufism", pp. 909–21.

[20] Rosenthal, *The Technique and Approach of Muslim Scholarship*, p. 3. For the Sufi's social role, see Kugle, *Rebel Between Spirit and Law*, pp. 7–41.

[21] See Ansari, *Sufism and Shari'ah*.

hereafter] can find neither rest nor peace."[22] Chishti then further bolsters this argument by quoting the Persian poet Hafiz Shirazi (d. 1389), again a very popular poet in Mughal India, and whose language of wine and goblet contained religious truths:

> Set aside the quarrels of the seventy-two sects:
> since they did not see reality, they adopted the path of illusion.[23]

Chishti also invokes the eminent fourteenth-century Firdausi scholar and Sufi, Shaikh Sharaf al-Din Yahya Maneri (d. 1381), particularly his *Sharh-i Adab al-Muridin*, to assert that it was not necessary for the Sufi to follow the *mazhab* of Abu Hanifa, or any other imam's school.[24]

Chishti then elaborates on the content of the Sufi's *mazhab*. He contends that the principles (*qawa'id*) of this *mazhab* are the strongest. Other schools' followers can take recourse either to transmission and tradition (*naql wa asar*) or to reason and speculation (*'aql wa fikr*). Sufis, however, have gone beyond this. Whatever is unseen (*gha'ib*) for others is manifest (*zahir*) to them. The truth is unveiled (*kashf*) to the Sufi when others reach it only through argumentation (*istidlal*). The Sufi is always in states and stages of truthfulness (*sidq*) and, inwardly, constantly keeps company with God Most High. However, the Sufi's *mazhab* too has an outer dimension, related to proper conduct (*adab*), and this is their law (*shari'a*). Their interaction with God's creatures (*ba-khalq mu'amalat*) has precedence over the quest to fulfil their own desires (*nik amad khalq ra na justan-i murad-i khwud ra*).[25]

---

[22] *Mir'at*, f. 8b. See also Nishapuri, *Tazkirat al-Auliya*, p. 759.

[23] Ibid. Hafiz, like Rumi, was also widely read in Mughal India. See Abidi, "Diwan-i Hafiz: Nuskha-i Shahan-i Mughaliya", pp. 3–26; Qasemi, "Sharh-ha'i-i Diwan-i Hafiz dar Hind", pp. 119–27; Azmi, "Hikayat-i az Hafiz-i Shiraz dar Sahna-i Razm wa Bazm-i Timuriyan", pp. 18–24; Rahman, "Falgiri-i Padshahan-i Timuri-i Hind az Diwan-i Hafiz", pp. 127–35.

[24] *Mir'at*.

[25] Ibid.

For saints of all orders, their prime concern is to follow in the footsteps of their own shaikh and to avoid contravening the practice of their masters. Chishti here draws upon the prominent Chishti Shaikh Saiyid Ashraf Jahangir Simnani (d. after 1437), citing the following lines:

> Know that in the world everyone, according to his own wisdom (*'irfan*)
> chose a pious legal school (*mazhab*).
> They all, through the discovery of their wisdom (*wijdan-i 'irfan*), boast to each other about their particular stature (*mansab*).
> If they knew how different is our practice (*mashrab*) [from the *mazhab*]
> they would leave *mazhab* and embrace *mashrab*.[26]

Chishti illustrates his position with anecdotes of the earlier Chishti masters, including Nizam al-Din Auliya' (cited above), Shaikh Farid al-Din Ganj-i Shakar Mas'ud, and Qutb al-Din Bakhtiyar Kaki (d. 1235).[27] The goal here is not only to follow the individual shaikh but to gain, through his intercession, access to the ultimate reality, regardless of what particular laws prescribe:

> *Chu bad-i saba dar ba dar ku ba ku*
> *talabgar-i u yam, talabgar-i u*
>
> Like the morning breeze, from door to door, from alley to alley
> Him I seek, [only] Him I seek.[28]

The *salik* therefore needed authentic details of the lives of the perfect masters of the past. There was a moment in Simnani's discourse when, according to Chishti, he awoke, longing to see these noble souls he had encountered in his vision. As his desire increased, Chishti says Simnani prayed to God to enable him to be in their company and service. As Simnani could not see them

---

[26] Ibid., f. 9b.

[27] Ibid. Chishti here cites Ashraf Simnani's epistles, *Lata'if-i Ashrafi* and *Maktubat-i Ashrafi*, and Mir Saiyid Muhammad Kirmani's *Siyar al-Auliya*.

[28] *Mir'at*, f. 35a.

in the manifest world, he resorted to reading books about their lives and principles. Moreover, he found that reading such biographies enabled him to separate the authentic Sufi from the fraud who merely donned his garb.[29] Chishti thus writes an extensive *tazkira* or biographical dictionary of the Sufis, beginning from the first Masters, the Prophet himself and 'Ali. The result was the *Mir'at al-Asrar*.

The Debate on Religious Law and *Tasawwuf*

'Abd al-Rahman Chishti's views in the Introduction were articulated in a new way, serving as a model for some of the later Chishti *tazkiras*.[30] They form part of a longer debate regarding *tasawwuf* and *fiqh* (jurisprudence) or *shari'a* in the Islamic tradition. From the beginning, the proponents of these categories of Islamic social thought and practice strove to evaluate the legitimacy of one another according only to their own criteria. Sufism was certainly taken as an integral part or even as the core of religious truth. However, social conditions in the middle ages of Islamic history led to the visible empowerment of jurists and theologians, broadly identified as the *'ulama*. Consequently, it was Sufism whose validity came to be subject to evaluation by the yardstick of theology and jurisprudence.[31] By the eleventh century, with the publication of Abu al-Qasim al-Qushairi's (d. 1072) *Risala* and the *Kashf al-Mahjub* of 'Usman 'Ali Hujwiri (d. after 1089), a kind of compromise had emerged. A true Sufi, according to these two texts, was one who always acted in accordance with the *shari'a* (*wali an buwad ki af'al-i u muwafiq-i-shari'a buwad paiwasta*).[32] Al-Ghazali's (d. 1111) writings are also a turning point in this process.

[29] Ibid., ff. 8a and 12b.

[30] See, for instance, Barasawi, *Iqtibas al-Anwar*, compiled in 1130 AH/1717–18. I thank Shah Nadim for bringing this translation to my notice.

[31] Cf. Karamustafa, *Sufism, the Formative Period*, pp. 96–113.

[32] *Risala al-Qushairi* (Persian translation by Abu 'Ali Hasan ibn Ahmad 'Usmani, Shagird-i Ab al-Qasim Qushairi), p. 42; see also Chapter 29,

However, the underlying conflict between Sufi and jurist continued unresolved, re-emerging vividly in the thirteenth century in the writings of Ibn al-'Arabi (d. 1240) and the poet Jalal al-Din Rumi (d. 1273). Ibn al-'Arabi represented jurists (*fuqaha*) as fanatics and adversaries of religious truth, comparing their treatment of the Sufis to the pharaohs' treatment of the prophets.[33] Their desire to please their royal patrons had distorted their interpretation of the law.[34] Replying to an allegation that he followed the Zahiri *mazhab*, Ibn al-'Arabi asserted that he did not follow any particular school.[35]

Most significantly, Ibn al-'Arabi held that an average Muslim was not to adhere to any particular school of thought: "Instead he can seek the most accommodating judgments in the law (*shar'*) and follow them as this entails greater mercy for him . . . [Ibn al-'Arabi's] school of law (*madhhab*) is one that makes it easier for the community."[36]

Jalal al-Din Rumi went even further. He is reported to have said once that he was one with all seventy-three sects of Islam (*man ba haftad wa sih mazhab yaki am*). Abused by the follower of a particular school for this statement, Rumi smiled and replied, "I am also in agreement with whatever you say (*ba in ki tu miguyi ham yaki am*)."[37]

We see echoes of this debate elsewhere in the Islamic world. The Egyptian scholar 'Abd al-Wahhab al-Sha'rani (d. 1565) took up

---

pp. 426–35, Chapter 42, pp. 467–76 and Chapter 52, pp. 591–621; 'Ali ibn 'Usman Hujwiri *alias* Data Ganj-Bakhsh, *Kashf al-Mahjub*, in particular pp. 13–14, 432–4.

[33] Corbin, *Creative Imagination*, pp. 68, 71, 86.

[34] Chodkiewicz, *An Ocean Without Shore,* p. 21.

[35] Cited in Ghorab, "Muhyiddin Ibn al-'Arabi", p. 200. Ibn Hazm al-Zahiri al-Andalusi or Abu Muhammad 'Ali ibn Ahmad ibn Sa' id ibn Hazm (d. 1064) was a philosopher, historian, and theologian-founder of a school of jurisprudence. He emphasised the letter of the law and thus he and his school came to be known as *al-zahiri*.

[36] Ghorab, "Muhyiddin Ibn al-'Arabi", p. 201.

[37] Simnani, *Chihil Majlis,* 124.

this issue in several treatises.[38] He writes that all schools of jurisprudence were correct and it was altogether another matter that only four – Malikite, Hanafite, Shafi'ite, Hanbalite – flourished. In his opinion, all were connected to the same core of religious truth. Of greater importance was his oft-repeated sentiment:

> O brother, try to acquire knowledge in all sincerity and also to act on it so that you can traverse the path quickly and are in a position to glimpse the stature of the *mujtahids*. You thus also become aware of the source (*al-'ayn al-'ula*) from which your imam received his knowledge. Having drunk your fill from the source, you will be together with your imam in drinking from the same source.[39]

Sha'rani states forcefully that a perfect Sufi (*wali*) has already reached the source, standing side by side with the imam and therefore has his own school (*mazhab*).[40]

He then turns to the average person approaching a perfect Sufi for spiritual guidance. Should he give up the religion he customarily follows and, like the perfect Sufi, believe in the correctness of all schools without experiencing it himself? Sha'rani advises that the novice should continue to tread on the same path, and thus approach the source.[41] Drawing on the teachings of Shaikh 'Ali Khawass, however, he asserts that the novice cannot achieve perfection in the practice of *shari'a* so long as he adheres to only one school (*mazhab-i-mu'ayyan*). This perfection is achieved when all the *hadith* of the Prophet and all the schools are harmoniously blended in one:

> Thus perfect *Shari'a* is in reality another name for all the schools of religion and the traditions of the Prophet blended together – but for only those with understanding. O brother, you should blend

---

[38] For Sha'rani, see Winter, *Society and Religion in Early Ottoman Egypt*; Johnson, "The Unerring Balance"; and Pagani, "The Meaning of the *Ikhtilaf al-Madhahib*", pp. 177–212.

[39] 'al-Sha'rani, *Al-Mizan al-Kubra*, Vol. 1, p. 38.

[40] Ibid., pp. 28–9.

[41] Ibid., pp. 29–30.

all the *hadith*, the sayings of the *'ulama* and the traditions together and then it will become evident to you how great is the *Shari'a,* and what is its true weight.[42]

More surprisingly and importantly, Sha'rani seems to go even further in implying the unity of all religions and not merely the schools of religion within Islam: "I have heard my Shaikh 'Ali Khawass saying that when a seeker of the Sufi path reaches his destination he does not simply cease to give preference to one *mujtahid* over the other but also is enlightened with the truth of the divine verse, 'We do not discriminate between God's apostles' (*la nufarriqu baina ahadin min rusulihi*)."[43]

We must note here, however, that when Sha'rani elaborates, he returns to the question of the difference or the unity of the *schools* of religion. Finally, he also states that the entire tradition and history from the Prophet's time, down to that of the *salik* who achieves perfection, will be encompassed in the *salik*'s vision as being correct.[44] Significantly, he eventually places the Sufi above the imam of a school, referring to Ahmad bin Hanbal's (d. 855) relationship with a contemporary Sufi, Abu Hamza of Baghdad. Ahmad bin Hanbal used to visit Abu Hamza to seek solutions for difficult theological issues and was also reported to urge his sons to visit Sufis regularly for "they [the Sufis] have achieved a stage in faith (*ikhlas*) that we have not reached yet."[45]

In Chishti's views we find reverberations of this larger debate within Islam. We see much evidence of how Chishti sought direct support from the views of Ibn al-'Arabi and echoed those of Sha'rani. Perhaps Chishti benefited also from the transregional travels of Sufis and religious scholars from India to other parts of the Islamic world. Sha'rani, as an Egyptian, belonged to the

---

[42] Ibid., pp. 35–6.
[43] Ibid., pp. 39–40.
[44] Ibid., p. 44.
[45] al-Sha'rani, *Al-Tabaqat al-Kubra*, p. 10. See also Surur, *Al-Tasawwuf al-Islami wa al-Imam al-Sha'rani*, p. 72.

Ottoman world, and his ideas may have resonated within Mughal India too.⁴⁶ Chishti's intervention was not, therefore, merely a ripple "upon the limitless ocean" of Islamic history, which "remains transparent and dissolves as it arose".⁴⁷ We see here how ripples originating in the turbulence of Islam's early centuries continued to trouble the religious and, as I will argue below, political waters in seventeenth-century India.

But why was the debate revived in this fashion in seventeenth-century north India? Significantly, Chishti's *Mir'at al-Asrar* comes after most Naqshbandi views have been represented in a mature and aggressive form in Shaikh Ahmad Sirhindi's letters and treatises.⁴⁸ 'Abd al-Haqq Muhaddis Dehlavi's writings, although not identical with Sirhindi's views, also contributed to a certain religious milieu that emphasised the "orthodox" view of religious ideology and practice.⁴⁹ *Mir'at al-Asrar* was thus an effort to engage with the Naqshbandi saints' criticisms of their ideology and practice and lay out an alternative Chishti position.

---

⁴⁶ Some later scholars were certainly familiar with Sha'rani's writings. Shah Wali-Allah Dehlavi cites a passage from Sha'rani's *al-Yawaqit wa al-Jawahir* in the concluding section (*tatimma*) of Book (*qism*) One in his *Hujjat al-Allah al-Baligha*. Cf. Wali-Allah, *Hujjat al-Allah al-Baligha*, pp. 157–8. As we know, this debate was raging in the Islamic world from at least the fifteenth century. See Fleischer, "Ancient Wisdom and New Sciences", pp. 232–43; Binbaş, "Sharaf al-Din 'Ali Yazdi". For an earlier period, see Berkey, *Popular Preaching and Religious Authority*, in particular pp. 88–96.

⁴⁷ The metaphor is from Rosenthal, *The Technique and Approach of Muslim Scholarship*, pp. 2–3.

⁴⁸ Sirhindi wrote *Risala-i Radd-i Rawafiz*, also known as *Risala-i Radd-i Mazhab-i Shi'a* before 1600, *Mabda' wa Ma'ad* around 1600–10; whereas his *Maktubat* (letters) were compiled in *South Asian History and Culture* 155, making three volumes during the years 1616 and 1622. Friedmann, *Shaykh Ahmad Sirhindi*, pp. 1–7; ter Haar, *Follower and Heir of the Prophet*, pp. 5–6 and 10–21.

⁴⁹ Dehlavi, *Maraj al-Bahrain*, pp. 64–90, summarises at the end of this treatise, the Maghribi jurist-Sufi Ahmad Zarruq's *Qawa'id al-Tariqa fi al-Jama' bain al-Shari'a wa al-Haqiqa*, pp. 64–90, transl. pp. 183–216. See Kugle, "'Abd al-Haqq Dihlawi" for a discussion on Dehlavi's training in Hijaz and Zarruq's influence on his thought.

The Naqshbandi View of *Tasawwuf*

The Naqshbandis, we know, came to India along with the Mughals.[50] We also saw in the preceding chapter that, despite their history as royal *pirs* in Central Asia, they struggled to maintain good relations with the early Mughal rulers. Outside the charmed circle of the ruling class too, they made little mark as notable Sufi shaikhs. In the late-sixteenth and early-seventeenth centuries, however, an important member of the order, Khwaja Baqi-Billah (d. 1603), succeeded in restoring their ascendancy. He developed a ruthless critique of the prevailing Chishti understanding of *tasawwuf*. He rejected outright the Chishtis' understanding of *tauhid* and their observance of *sama'* and dismissed as heretic (*zandaqa*) and stupid (*ablahi, safahat*) the admiration of unbelief (*kufr*) and emphasis on the underlying unity between a believer and an infidel. The principal duty of the traveller of the Sufi path (*salik*) was to follow the *shari'a*, which was the very reality (*haqiqa*) of gnosis (*ma'rifa*).[51]

In the writings of his most eminent disciple, Shaikh Ahmad Sirhindi, these criticisms became sharper and more elaborate. The *salik's* efforts will turn to naught if his vision (*kashf*) digresses even a hair's breadth from the Qur'an and *sunna* (the tradition of the Prophet).[52] There can be no evading the rulings of the law (*ahkam-i fiqhiya*) in all matters, obligatory (*fara'iz*) or desirable (*mustahabbat*).[53] He who observes the law without fail (*multazim-i shari'a*) possesses real knowledge (*ma'rifa*) and he who does not (*mudahin-i shari'a*) is deprived of it (*az ma'rifat bi-nasib ast*). The more one observes the law the greater is one's share in gnosis

---

[50] Algar, "A Brief History of the Naqshbandi Order", pp. 3–44, and idem, "Political Aspects of Naqshbandi History", pp. 123–52; Rizvi, *History of Sufism*, Vol. 2, pp. 174–93; Damrel, "Forgotten Grace", Chapter 3, pp. 92–171; Dale, *The Garden of the Eight Paradises*.

[51] See Chapter 2, Alam, "The Mughals, the Sufi Shaikhs and the Formation of the Akbari Dispensation".

[52] Sirhindi, *Risala-i Mabda' wa Ma'ad*, Persian text, p. 21.

[53] Sirhindi, *Maktubat-i Imam Rabbani*, Vol. 2, p. 91.

(*harchand iltizam bish, ma'rifat bish*).⁵⁴ In a letter to his disciple, Sirhindi insists that for a person choosing the Sufi path, the first and foremost requirement is a correct creed in total compliance with one of the *Ahl-i Sunna wa Jama'a*; and secondly, a regard for the *shari'a* obligations as given "in our jurisprudence (*fiqh*)". Sufi knowledge comes third. He continues:

> If without fulfilling the requirements of the first two stages you experience Sufic elation, this experience would be your undoing and you must seek refuge with Allah . . . Even the Brahmins, the Hindu Jogis, and the Greek philosophers come across different discoveries and epiphanies as they pretend to know or to have the divine knowledge. Experiencing Sufic elation without the two requirements is similar to these pretenders. They did not gain anything except their humiliation and disaster from such claims. Instead of coming close to divinity, they have been thrown far from it and have totally been deprived of divine grace.⁵⁵

"Our jurisprudence" is then defined as Hanafi jurisprudence. Sirhindi prescribes the school of Abu Hanifa as the ideal *mazhab*.⁵⁶ He exaggerates his position inordinately in relation to the imams of the other schools.⁵⁷ In *kalam* (theology, scholasticism, dogmatics) too, Sirhindi seems to give preference to the Maturides over all other schools.⁵⁸

Furthermore, Sirhindi highlights Shi'is as the promoters of false religion and notes that even in India, on their account, Muslims were greatly troubled. In this regard the Preface he wrote to his treatise *Radd-i Rawafiz* is interesting. After quoting several verses from Amir Khusrau, emphasising that in Hindustan the Islamic faith operated in full grace, he says:

---

⁵⁴ Ibid., Vol. 2, pp. 55, 109.
⁵⁵ Ibid., Vol. 1, pp. 227, 258–9.
⁵⁶ Sirhindi, *Risala-i Mabda' wa Ma'ad*, p. 21.
⁵⁷ Ibid., p. 54.
⁵⁸ Ibid., p. 71.

Shari'a had respect, dignity, and glory. Islam was triumphant, infidelity was vanquished and humiliated in the entire land from Ghazni in the north-west, to the eastern seashore of the subcontinent. Nowhere was to be found a Jew or a Christian, a fire-worshipper or a Mu'tazilite, Kharijite or a Rafizi. For about five hundred years this situation remained until the time of [the Central Asian king,] 'Abd Allah Khan. Shi'ism was then dominant in Khorasan. 'Abd Allah Khan invaded Khorasan. As a result many Shi'is were killed while many others fled to and sought refuge in Hindustan, where they became close to the rulers and misguided the people with their deceptive and wrong creed. Thus, even if the land and Muslims of Khorasan were rescued from the Shi'i's mischief, the land of India (*diyar-i Hind*) was plagued by the advent of these irreligious people . . .[59]

Shi'is, for Sirhindi, were not only a plague in India but "the cause of schism and depravity in the whole world". Being a direct descendant of 'Umar Faruq, the Second Pious Caliph, he found mere oral disputation with them to be insufficient. His zeal for Islam and Faruqi blood flew him into a rage, the result of which was the writing of this treatise.[60]

Sirhindi is known as the renovator of Islam (*Mujaddid-i Alf-i Sani*), the person who reinstated the *shari'a* to its rightful place

---

[59] Sirhindi, *Risala-i Radd-i Rawafiz*, pp. 119–20. This treatise also has a second version, equally harsh and polemical in tone, published under a different title. The preface in this version does not include the account of this imagined dominance of Islam in the subcontinent, nor does it cite Amir Khusrau's verses. Cf. Sirhindi, *Risala dar Kawa'if-i Shi'a*. In yet another unpublished version, this account figures inside the text. Cf. Sirhindi, *Risala Radd-i Shi'a*, Aligarh Muslim University MS., ff.16a–17a. This passage may have been interpolated some time in the eighteenth century, in the wake of the increasing Shi'a–Sunni divide, to project the image of Sirhindi as the frontline defender of Sunni Islam in India. The value of the treatise may thus have been intended to be greater than even the big tomes on this theme written during that century by Shah Wali-Allah (d. 1762) and Shah 'Abd al-Aziz (d. 1823). I thank Professor I.A. Zilli for the Aligarh MS. reference.

[60] Sirhindi, *Risala-i Radd-i Rawafiz*, pp. 119–20.

against the measures taken by Akbar.⁶¹ In the dominant South Asian Muslim view, this is considered Sirhindi's major role, regardless of *tasawwuf*. Several modern serious historians, however, project Sirhindi as only a Sufi. "Sirhindi was a Sufi and must be assessed as such."⁶² My purpose here is not to engage with these modern interpretations; rather, I am considering the tradition handed down by Baqi-Billah and Sirhindi in order to show its antagonistic relationship with the views of ʿAbd al-Rahman Chishti. This difference reflected a debate that had raged since the early days of Islamic history (as we saw above).

ʿAbd al-Rahman not only endeavoured to rearticulate the Chishti position in this debate, he specifically addresses the issues of *samaʿ*, the concept of *tauhid*, and the relationship between *tasawwuf* and *shariʿa*. But he was also careful to invoke, as we saw, the very figure that the Naqshbandis took as the prime source for their understanding of *tauhid* and *tasawwuf*, namely ʿAla al-Daula Simnani. By doing so, Chishti reminds his readers of the Naqshbandi shaikhs' disregard of the past, implying that Baqi-Billah and Sirhindi invoked Simnani only selectively for their own purposes.

In *Mirʾat al-Asrar* Chishti also attempted to show the ancient relationship of his order with the land of Hindustan. In reacting to the Naqshbandis' claims, he was in a sense invoking the old Persian adage, *Kai Amadi wa kai pir shudi?* – meaning "When did you come and when did you become the *pir* (old and wise)?" In fact, he suggested, only Chishtis deserved to be designated the

---

⁶¹ For modern Urdu writings on Sirhindi, see Alam, *Mujaddid-i Alf-i Sani ki Ihya-i Tahrik-i Islam aur Salatin-i Mughaliya*, and Faruqi, *Hazrat Mujaddid aur unke Naqidin*.

⁶² Friedmann, *Shaykh Ahmad Sirhindi*, pp. 111 and 41–8. Friedmann reasserts it in the conclusion: "Sirhindi was first and foremost a Sufi and must be seen in this light." He concludes that Sirhindi's demand for strict implementation of the *shariʿa* is only in "the few letters [of his] to Mughal officials": p. 114. Friedmann also suggests that this demand was only with reference to the state; he does not explain why Sirhindi reiterates this position even in his letters to his own sons and ordinary disciples.

true religious leaders of the land. By their grace and blessings, Islam came and flourished in India. Shaikh Abu Muhammad Chishti blessed and fought, even if only spiritually, with the army of Mahmud of Ghazni, the first, according to the author, to bring the power of Islam to India. Subsequently, the triumph of Sultan Shihab al-Din Ghuri (d. 1206) over the Rajput ruler Rai Pithora, and the establishment of "Muslim" power in northern India, also owed to the blessings of a Chishti saint, Khwaja Mu'in al-Din Chishti of Ajmer:

> Thus it may be noted that the first and the last conquest of Hind owed to the blessings of the Chishti saints. Mahmud of Ghazni and Shihab al-Din Ghuri were able to rule over Hindustan because the Chishti saints' control over the entire country. And so long as this world exists, this control (*tasarruf*) will continue. Thus, all the saints agree on this the country of Hindustan is the heritage of the Chishtis and that the country is spiritually in their control.[63]

Mu'in al-Din, Chishti writes, was not an ordinary saint (*wali*); he was like a prophet (*nabi*), as India did not have a proper prophet. He provided leadership and guidance to prominent religious or military leaders, such as Salar Mas'ud Ghazi and Khwaja Badi' al-Din Madar, whose endeavours, as Chishti highlights in his *Mir'at-i Mas'udi* and *Mir'at-i Madariya*, strengthened the spread and consolidation of Islam in India.[64]

[63] *Mir'at*, f.221b. Elsewhere Chishti writes that the khwaja was specially instructed by the Prophet, during a visit to Medina, to come to India and settle in Ajmer, for "God has entrusted to him the country of Hind . . . and in that land Islam will be in ascendancy because of his power (*tasarrufat*) and he will have there a large number of his disciples." Cf. Chishti, *Mir'at-i Mas'udi*, ff.94.

[64] Chishti, *Mir'at-i Mas'udi*, ff.13a, 17b–18a, 23b–25b, and 38a for references to Salar Mas'ud's birth, his early education and training in Ajmer, and Khwaja Abu Muhammad Chishti's help to Sultan Mahmud Ghaznavi in his fight in India; idem, *Mir'at-i Madariya*, f.12a, for references to the Prophet's instructions to Madar to go to Hindustan, and visit first the shrine of Khwaja Mu'in al-Din Chishti at Ajmer to receive from him guidance for his (Madar's) mission in Hindustan. See also Chapter 4.

Chishti and the Mughal Rulers

It would be incomplete, however, to read this discourse only in the context of religious disputation.[65] Through these discussions Chishti lends support to the Mughal politics of *Sulh-i Kull* (peace with all) as well. Sirhindi's portrayal of Akbar as a heretic and a serious threat to Islam is familiar.[66] The millenarianism (*tajdid-i alf-i sani*) in Sirhindi's and his disciples' writings may have revolved around Akbar's aspirations as a millenarian leader and his "anti-Islamic politics".[67] 'Abd al-Rahman Chishti not only demonstrated his appreciation of Mughal politics, he also had special praise for the Mughal rulers.

Alongside details of the saints in *Mir'at al-Asrar*, we have the author's notices of contemporary rulers. Chishti sees the Sufis as the principal co-ordinators of balance in the temporal world. Although they are the first receivers of divine epiphanies, they reach commoners through the intercession of rulers of the day. The rulers are leaders of the people (*muqtada-i 'alam*) who transmit

---

[65] For a recent discussion on *sulh-i kull*, see Kinra, "Revisiting the History and Historiography of Mughal Pluralism".

[66] Nizami, "Naqshbandi Influence", pp. 41–52; Qureshi, *The Muslim Community*, pp. 166–82; Ahmad, *Studies in Islamic Culture*, pp. 182–90; Rizvi, *The Muslim Revivalist Movements*, pp. 223, 225, and 246–7. See also Sirhindi's letter to Shaikh Farid in Rahman, *Selected Letters of Shaikh Ahmad Sirhindi*, pp. 182–6. "... the infidels forcibly enforced the ordinances of infidelity in public, [while] the Muslims were too weak to openly practice the injunctions of Islam, and if they did it they faced execution. What a suffering for them! Alas, alas (*wa musibata wa hasrata wa huzna*)!" Shaikh 'Abd al-Haqq Muhaddis Dehlavi has also been portrayed as taking the same position. A major – in fact the only – evidence in support of this understanding is a letter of the shaikh to Shaikh Farid at the death of the emperor Akbar. Cf. Nizami, *Hayat-i Shaikh 'Abd al-Haqq Muhaddis Dehlavi*, pp. 378–85; Khan, *Shaikh 'Abd al-Haqq Muhaddis Dehlavi*, p. 49, and also the Foreword to this book by Ziya al-Haqq Haqqi Dehlavi, a noted descendant of the shaikh.

[67] Tattavi and Qazwini, *Tarikh-i Alfi*, Vol. 1, pp. 241–3. I thank Dr Azfar Moin for this reference. But I think this passage seems to have been superimposed without any context.

the divine bounty (*faiz*) they have received through their contact with Sufis. This discussion is integrated into his general discussion on the *wahdat* of divinity. Here too Chishti draws on his forebears:

> Shaikh 'Ala al-Daula [Simnani] and Mir Saiyid Ashraf Jahangir [Simnani] wrote that, regardless of what kind the rulers may be, proper manners (*adab*) should be observed with regard to them. Shaikh Sharaf al-Din Maneri [also] writes in his commentary on the *Adab al-Muridin* to the effect that Khwaja Muhammad ibn Sirin said if God commands me from heaven saying whatever you pray for today will be granted, then in all my prayers I would pray for the ruler (*sultan*) of the time, for the whole creation (*khalq*) would benefit from my prayer for the ruler. And further he writes . . . once, Nizam al-Din Auliya' showed much humility in front of Sultan 'Ala al-Din Khalji. His disciples (*muridin*) were astonished, wondering what this meant. He said that through [the sultan's] sovereignty, his *wilayat* [sainthood] is evident and transmitted [to the common folk], while mine is veiled.[68]

The king is thus a manifestation of God and performs a critical part of divine work in the visible world, as the Sufi does in the unseen. In fact, the king occupies an even greater position: "the king would be an *abdal* [a category of Sufi saint] if he is tyrannical (*zalim*), and a *qutb* [lit. pole, the highest category of saint] if he is just (*'adil*)."[69]

Thus, Chishti's narrative of the Mughal rulers in the *Mir'at al-Asrar* is highly significant, showing the closeness of their relationship with Sufis in general and with the Chishtis in particular. He writes that when the 14-year-old Akbar ascended the throne in 1556, he became sole ruler of the entire country with the spiritual blessings of the great Khwaja Mu'in al-Din Chishti. The khwaja bestowed upon him and his descendants the rule of the country. Akbar returned his debt through sincere devotion to the khwaja, visiting his shrine in Ajmer, building a grand mosque there, helping to settle the town, arranging for the safety and convenience of

[68] *Mir'at*, ff. 12.
[69] Ibid.

its residents, and building a city wall and royal palace within its confines. He also granted appropriate allowances (*waza'if-i naqd wa zamin-i madad-i mu'ash*) to the descendants of the khwaja and the caretakers of the shrine. He earmarked villages for food and other expenses for pilgrims and the poor visiting the shrine. He appointed a functionary (*mutawalli*) to take care of those visiting the shrine, arrangements that Chishti says continued into his day.[70]

Chishti notes that Akbar's son, Nur al-Din Jahangir, exceeded even his father in his devotion and sincerity to the khwaja, augmenting the grants and regularly visiting the shrine with great humility. After his death, Shah Jahan visited the shrine in the very first year of his reign, in 1627, and showered on it a similarly laudable munificence.[71]

For both Akbar and Jahangir, Chishti uses the epithet *rahima-hu-Allah*, routinely used for a saint and meaning "May God bless him". This is noteworthy in relation to Akbar in particular, known in other significant Sufi literature – notably that of the Naqshbandi–Mujaddidi, which has percolated into the memory of South Asian Muslims – as the defiler of Islam. Chishti also emphasises Jahangir's intimacy with contemporary saints and, by extension, his connection with the author himself. Chishti notes that he was himself in the company of the emperor, having on several occasions the opportunity to confer with him. Around the same time, the saints Saiyid Ni'mat-Allah Qadiri (who later became the Qutb of Bengal), Saiyid Muhammad Gujarati (who was a *khalifa* of Shah Mahbub-i 'Alam), and Shaikh 'Usman (a resident of Bayana), were also present in Akbarabad. For about a year, Chishti and Saiyid Ni'mat-Allah would regularly meet Shaikh 'Usman to obtain his grace.

One day, Saiyid Ni'mat-Allah reported to Shaikh 'Usman that Jahangir had summoned Saiyid Muhammad to speak to him alone. The emperor reportedly said that his heart recognised Saiyid Muhammad was a man of gnosis, and therefore he would

---

[70] Ibid., f. 230b.
[71] Ibid., f. 507a.

confide in him. He affirmed that he and his ancestors were Muslims, worshippers of truth (*haqq parast*). He then said that the litanies he repeated morning and evening were not meant to worship the sun but rather to control it (*taskhir-i aftab*), so that it remained in his service to help him. Jahangir then said that, in the past, rulers as well as philosophers and saints had resorted to the practice of controlling the stars, a fact referred to in Sufic texts (*musannafat-i Sufya-i shuma*).[72] He affirmed his commitment to seeking the Truth, even placing his rulership at the command of Saiyid Muhammad. However, he said he was unable to give up drink, to which he had become habituated since childhood, nor could he perform the five daily prayers with absolute regularity. With this frank statement, the emperor sought Saiyid Muhammad's guidance (*hisbatan lillah mara rah-i Khuda benumayed*). The saint replied:

> According to our saints, prayer is the principal part of religion and so is abstaining from drinking. Because of your good intention, however, you have entered already into the circle of the Friends of Truth (*dustdaran-i haqq*). God has created everyone for a particular task. You have been given the *khilafat* and the country to rule. Your job is to protect this God-given country and fulfil the needs of the people with justice. Do keep remembering God all the time and regard Him as ever present and watchful. This is your duty (*haqq shinasi*) and that is sufficient.[73]

Chishti recounts that when Shaikh 'Usman heard about this incident, he was delighted and blessed the emperor. Here again it

---

[72] Jahangir alludes here to the Shattari practice of *da'wat-i asma*, perhaps. We know Humayun's fascination for the Shattaris: Badayuni, *Muntakhab al-Tawarikh*, Vol. 3, pp. 4–5; Khan, *Ma'asir al-Umara'*, Vol. 2, pp. 575–6; and Jahangir too had close connections with Shaikh 'Abd-Allah, son of Shaikh Wajih al-Din of Gujarat: Jahangir, *Tuzuk-i Jahangeeree*, pp. 209 and 213. For the Shattaris, see Nizami, "Shattari Saints and Their Attitude Towards the State", pp. 56–70; Kugle, "Heaven's Witness", pp. 1–36. I thank Hasan Siddiqui for this reference.

[73] Ibid., f. 507b.

is worth noting that the circle Chishti describes gathered around the emperor included Qadiri Sufis, not Naqshbandis.

The connections Chishti describes sometimes had a more practical bent, namely an association with management of the state. He notes that although the state was under the care of Shaikh Pir Shattari, the king's person was to be taken care of by his own *murshid*, Shaikh Hamid Chishti, who died in 1622.[74] As nobody was appointed in his place, the king, who fell ill upon his return from Kashmir, took a turn for the worse, leading eventually to his death. The role of Sufis in this vital task is highlighted in a more personal way when Chishti recounts the penultimate days of Shah Jahan's rule. This was when illness prevented the emperor's Chishti servants from taking care of him. Chishti draws a direct connection between the unfortunate and unavoidable slackening of Chishti vigilance and the consequent chaos that led to the war of succession and the ascension of Aurangzeb, with, as Chishti puts it, "the consensus of the *'ulama* of the time."[75]

As for Shah Jahan, because he was trained by a Sufi, he was not only a true follower of *ahl-i sunna wa jama'a* as understood in general by Sufis, but reached a very high level of *tasawwuf* in his own right. While in Akbarabad, Chishti reports seeing Prince

---

[74] Ibid., f. 508a. For his role in initiating 'Abd al-Rahman into the Chishti Sabiri order, see Rizvi, *History of Sufism*, Vol. 2, p. 289.

[75] *Mir'at*, ff. 508a–10a. Chishti says he was in the service of the Mughal emperor before Shah Jahan's time. At Jahangir's command he visited the northern hills, where he met Acharya Muni Bhadra, agent of the Hill Raja and an expert on Indian history, from whom, he claims, he got some details about his book on Salar Mas'ud. Cf. Chishti, *Mir'at-i Mas'udi*, f.92a. He reports in *Mir'at al-Asrar* (f.508a) that he left for his village to live in seclusion (*gushai inziwa*) in 1618, when Jahangir left for Kashmir. He returned to the court apparently after Shah Jahan came to power. See also Rizvi, *History of Sufism*, Vol. 2, pp. 288–9, 368–9, and 369–70 for the Naqshbandi saints' appreciation of Aurangzeb, who, according to the author of *Khazinat al-Asfiya'*, was a disciple (*murid*) of Sirhindi's son, Khwaja Muhammad Ma'sum Sirhindi: *Khazinat al-Asfiya'*, Vol. 1, p. 640, citing *Tazkira-i Adamiya*. See Chapter 8.

Shah Jahan visiting a Sufi shaikh every day to learn about Sufic texts and to read the *Tabaqat-i Nasiri*, a historical text by Minhaj al-Din al-Siraj.[76] Amongst the valuable sciences the Sufi taught him was the exegesis of the Qur'an, *hadith*, and various Sufi texts.[77] Chishti believed that the emperor was destined to spend his last years as an ascetic (*tarikin*), interpreting his incarceration as a God-given spiritual opportunity to perfect his soul. Shah Jahan spent these days worshipping Allah, reciting the Qur'an and studying the books of exegesis of the Qur'an and *hadith*. For Shah Jahan, too, Chishti uses the epithet *Rahima-hu-Allah*.[78] He also traces the emperor's genealogy to the mythical Alanqua, following Abu al-Fazl, and describes Timur both as a powerful king and as a *wali*.[79]

More significantly, however, Chishti brings to our notice the emperor's belief and policy with reference to Shi'is and non-Muslims. In Chishti's eyes, Shah Jahan was unusually well equipped by God to maintain and follow the *mazhab* of the *ahl-i sunna wa jama'a*, without nurturing any prejudice (*bila ta'assub*). When the emperor enquired as to the correct theological position regarding the Shi'is and the right to succession of Abu Bakr, the First Pious Caliph, he was told it was wisest to maintain silence on such matters. On another occasion, referring to the dispute surrounding the *khilafat* between 'Ali and Mu'awiya, he was told that 'Ali deserved to be the caliph. On both occasions, Shah Jahan delightedly agreed. Chishti notes that, in fact, the emperor merely received the response he desired and concludes that Shah Jahan was not prejudiced against any particular sect. As a matter of fact, he was, as Chishti portrayed him, a follower of the *mashrab* of *sulh-i kull*,

---

[76] Shaikh Sufi was a disciple of Shaikh Nizam al-Din of Amethi, an eminent Chishti saint of Awadh in the sixteenth century. See Rizvi, *History of Sufism*, Vol. 2, pp. 288–9.

[77] *Mir'at*, f. 508a.

[78] Ibid., f. 510a.

[79] Ibid., ff. 12. For Abu al-Fazl's account of the genealogy of the Mughals, see Abu al-Fazl, *Akbarnama*, trans. Beveridge, Vol. 1, pp. 34–40.

the path of peace with all. To illustrate his point further, Chishti contrasted the vengeful attitude of the Uzbek ruler of Turan and the Shah of Iran after their conquests of Iran and Turan, with the generosity Shah Jahan showed to defeated enemies. Thus, Shah Jahan did not stray from the path of balance (*i'tidal*), avoiding divine wrath and staying firmly with the injunctions of the Qur'an and *hadith*.[80] This same policy in India had led to the triumph of Islam. As word of the justice of Shah Jahan spread, people of all communities came to his lands. Even Hindus and fire-worshippers became so obedient in relation to Islam that in each street and bazaar a cow, when slaughtered, would cause no objection to be raised and Hindus even gave their daughters willingly in marriage to the emperor and his nobles. No one challenged the sovereignty of the Mughal ruler.[81]

Thus, in Chishti's words, the Mughal emperors are ideal rulers under whom not only Islam and Muslims but also a variety of other ethnic and religious groups thrived. This is, in significant measure, on account of their close association with Sufis who, with the exception of Naqshbandi Sufis, underpin the health of the state. This subterranean nature of benign Chishti Sufi influence, which worked through the subtle processes of divine and temporal intercession, contrasts with the relationship between ruler and Sufi in the Naqshbandi tradition, where the Sufi's power extended even to the point of challenging the ruler's authority.[82]

Most tellingly, in his brief mention of Aurangzeb, Chishti notes that the emperor came to power with the support of the *'ulama* and not through the divine intercession of Sufis. Indeed, in Chishti's view, the ideal state was one in which subjects were free to follow their own customs and social practices, as had been the case in his portrayal under Shah Jahan. Moreover, he believed this was the true path of Islam.

---

[80] *Mir'at*, f. 509a.
[81] Ibid.
[82] For more on this subject, see Chapter 2, above.

Towards a Redefinition of Tradition

Through his discussion of the Sufism of the past masters in *Mir'at al-Asrar*, Chishti also attempts to re-read the Islamic past and give a new definition of Islam in the prevailing social and religious climate. Chishti's project of legitimising Mughal power acquires particular resonance precisely because of the presence of an opposing viewpoint – that is, Sirhindi's – which, in Chishti's view, threatened to destabilise Muslim authority in the land. He cites the earlier texts to illustrate and buttress his understanding of a given doctrine – that is, Sufism – and thus legitimate his position. This is further illustrated in his account of the dispute between the fifteenth-century Indian saint Shah Badi' al-Din Madar and the *'ulama* of the time. Madar, as we know, was a Malamati Sufi, whose sayings and actions, from the orthodox viewpoint, could at best be a *sanad* for himself. Chishti, however, portrays him (as I will show in the next chapter) as a great saint and scholar, tutored directly by the Prophet and his descendants before he moved to India, and by Khwaja Mu'in al-Din Chishti in India. His actions and sayings represent the authentic or classical Islam, Chishti says:

> As a matter of fact, there was little difference or variation in Islam in the time of the Prophet and after him for thirty years during the regimes of the pious caliphs, when the Prophet's tradition was followed in full. Subsequently, under the Umayyads and Abbasids, when power came into the hands of some conceited rulers, the *'ulama* were constrained to act on [the rulers'] wishes . . . It is in this milieu that religious differences surfaced and religious matters began to be decided according to the opinions of the jurists (*mujtahid*). Everywhere and in every stage, there appeared a new religion and the person who deviated from the path of a given sect was declared to be a *kafir*. The Prophet had foreseen this and had foreboded the emergence of over seventy sects. He had, however, also predicted that only one of these would be on the right path. Each of these sects then pretended to be the right one.
>
> For ages, the *'ulama* of each sect followed and acted upon the opinions of their own masters and thus they became used to it. It

was because of their prejudices for this practice that they turned hostile to Shah Madar, who after a gap of over seven centuries, tried to revive and propagate what in actuality was the practice of the first Muslims, the companions of the Prophet. Shah Madar wanted the people to adhere to the religion of the straight path.[83]

The struggle between *sunna* and *bid'a* was an integral part of the dynamics of Islamic history and tradition. In seventeenth-century India, this struggle is dramatised by the differences between Baqi-Billah and Sirhindi on the one hand, and Chishti on the other. However, what is important here is the lack of consensus on what constitutes the *sunna*. Madar was accused of indulging in what could be termed as *bid'a*, but it is precisely these controversial actions that Chishti sees as the real content of *sunna*. Similarly, Naqshbandi thinkers saw the Mughal politico-religious system as heretical, a view that still dominates in the Muslim imagination of South Asia. This same system was legitimised by Chishti through his reading of *sunna*.

The relationship between Muslim authority and Sufis is of old provenance in the history of India.[84] Even when they opposed the rulers, they supported them in their endeavour to buttress their power. In the thirteenth century, when the rulers found themselves in a fix in the face of orthodox cries for the implementation of *shari'a* – requiring the forced conversion or annihilation (*imma al-Islam, imma al-qatl*) of non-Muslims – the Sufis and the Chishti Sufis in particular provided an ideological rationale for a pragmatic politics to the sultans. In Mughal India too, when Akbar and Jahangir developed the policy of *sulh-i kull*, another Chishti Sufi attempted to provide the same ideological underpinnings. 'Abd al-Rahman was not of the same stature as Nizam al-Din Auliya'.

---

[83] Chishti, *Mir'at-i Madariya*, ff. 25a–27a. Significantly, a similar discussion in a more learned style figures in the eighteenth century in Wali-Allah, *Hujjat al-Allah al-Baligha*, Vol. 1, pp. 152–4.

[84] Cf. Digby, "The Sufi Shaikh and the Sultan", pp. 71–81; Kumar, "Assertion of Authority", pp. 37–65; Aquil, *Sufism, Culture and Politics*, pp. 172–99.

But as a noted scholar he was conversant with this history and drew upon it to buttress his views, and thereby lend support to the politics of the Mughal rulers. Here, again, he appears to have also been inspired by 'Ala al-Daula Simnani, to whom is attributed the saying, "*al-Sufi ibn al-waqt*, the Sufi is the man of the moment."[85]

Conclusion

In exploring these debates, I have in this chapter attempted to show not only the variety of views at play but also the vigour of the contestation within, and its polemical nature. What emerges from the writings of Shaikh 'Abd al-Rahman Chishti is the radical difference between the Chishti view and that of the Naqshbandis – and, indeed, of the "orthodox" Sunni view more generally. Through the dialectical discourse that 'Abd al-Rahman creates to validate the Chishti position, one can reconstruct the well-known opposing ideology of Shaikh Ahmad Sirhindi and the Naqshbandi order. This makes apparent the tension between *tasawwuf* and the formal Islam of jurisprudence. For the Chishtis, a Sufi's overt adherence to a given school of jurisprudence amounts to an undesirable narrowness of approach, even bigotry. But adherence to a particular jurisprudential school is integral to Sufi practice in Sirhindi, who asserts the primacy of the Hanafi school and its propounder Abu Hanifa over all other schools and imams. 'Abd al-Rahman Chishti, too, is a follower of the Hanafi school. But nowhere in this discourse does he reveal his personal adherence to it. Instead, he appeals to a range of religious figures from the Islamic tradition broadly acceptable to the entire religious community, in particular to his interlocutors, the Naqshbandis.

However, the difference between them does not end here. It is clearly present in their definition and practice of the overall Sunni tradition. 'Abd al-Rahman is a Sunni, and for him Islamic truth reaches its apogee in the concept of *ahl-i sunna wa jama'a*. For

---

[85] Simnani, "Mala budda minh fi al-Din", p. 117.

him, this concept is open and accommodating. In the Chishti tradition, moreover, 'Ali is cast in a prominent role. Although it is not true that in Sirhindi's tradition 'Ali has no place, it is nonetheless worth noting that 'Abd al-Rahman never wrote a repudiation of the Shi'i tradition, and in fact begins his discourse with a laudatory description of 'Ali. But in Sirhindi's writings a distinct process of "othering" the Shi'i tradition is clearly discernible. Chishti self-consciously advocates a path that does not depend on the vilification of others.

Furthermore, in the period when 'Abd al-Rahman Chishti was active, Delhi and Agra had developed significant ties to the larger Islamic world, in particular to Mecca and Medina. This is illustrated in previous writings by Delhi's connections with Hijaz in the revival of the science of *hadith* in India. This connection, as I have suggested, is also manifest through several other important channels, as shown by the echoes of 'Abd al-Wahhab al-Sha'rani's ideas in Chishti's writings. Thus, India was connected not only to the orthodox trends in the wider Islamic world but also to its more open and radical ideas.

Finally, Chishti's discourse sheds light on the political culture of Mughal India. The policy of *sulh-i kull* was not confined to the Mughal court; rather, its inclusive politics shaped the thought and practice of a wider range of actors in Mughal India.[86] The acceptance of this policy among the popular Chishti order indicates a constituency for this policy that extended well beyond the Mughal political elites. In this context, 'Abd al-Rahman Chishti's portrayal of the Mughal rulers is deeply revealing. Sirhindi's condemnation of Akbar was not shared by all Muslims, nor even by the other Sufi shaikhs.

The Sunni Muslim view of religion and politics is thus not represented solely by Shaikh Ahmad Sirhindi, nor, for that matter, by Shaikh 'Abd al-Haqq Muhaddis Dehlavi. Rather, as the Chishti

---

[86] For an excellent recent discussion on *sulh-i kull*, see, Kinra, "Revisiting the History and Historiography of Mughal Pluralism".

position demonstrates, this view must be complicated if we are to understand the full range of Muslim political and religious positions in Mughal India. Chishti's view was surely more than a politically astute affirmation of Mughal policy. The evidence examined here suggests that it was, rather, part of the wider political and religious climate that precipitated the consolidation of this policy. We might ask, too, as I have done in the Introduction above, why this view has found no place in South Asian Muslim history and memory. The other kind of Sufi, as we know from Chishti, was not removed from the currents of his day, but rather, as "a man of the moment", also shaped and reacted to the various pressing debates of his time.

4

Shah Madar, Sufi Religion, and a View of "True Islam" in a Mughal Chishti *Tazkira*

SHAH BADIʿ AL-DIN MADAR (1315–1436) – whose chief shrine (*dargah*) can be found in Kanpur District – though regarded as an unorthodox (*bi-sharʿ*) Sufi, nevertheless occupies an important place in nearly all modern works on Indian Sufism.[1] Nevertheless, some significant aspects of his life and mystical practices (*tasawwuf*) made available to us by pre-modern texts deserve closer attention. The purpose of this chapter is twofold: to analyse the various portraits of Shah Madar that emerge from several different Mughal histories and biographical compendia (*tazkiras*), and to examine and contextualise one of these in particular, the *Mirʾat-i Madariya*, compiled by Shaikh ʿAbd al-Rahman Chishti (d. 1683) around 1643–54.[2]

Shah Madar in Mughal Indian *Tazkiras*

Not much information about Shah Madar can be gleaned from sources dating back to his own time, with the exception of some

---

[1] See, for instance, Rizvi, *A History of Sufism in India*, Vol. 1, pp. 318–20. For a series of recent excellent articles, Falasch, "Islamic Mystic Tradition in India", pp. 254–72; idem, "Badiʿ al-Din Shah Madar to Qazi Shihab al-Din Daulatabadi", pp. 53–81; idem, "Badiʿ al-Din", pp. 144–7. I have not been able to consult the broader work in German by Falasch, *Heiligkeit und Mobilität*.

[2] Chishti, *Mirʾat-i Madariya*. I have collated the Aligarh MS with the

references in works by the fifteenth-century saint Saiyid Jahangir Ashraf Simnani, primarily *Lata'if-i Ashrafi*, and a few references in the context of Shah Mina (d. 1479), the noted fifteenth-century Chishti shaikh of Lucknow. But in Mughal India, Madar was already much noted as a major Sufi; there are accounts of him – mostly short notices – in 'Abd al-Qadir Bada'uni's (d. 1605) *Muntakhab al-Tawarikh* and *Najat al-Rashid*; Abu al-Fazl's (d. 1602) *A'in-i Akbari*; and also in the major Sufi *tazkiras*: Shaikh 'Abd al-Haqq Muhaddis Dehlavi's (d. 1642) *Akhbar al-Akhyar*; Muhammad Ghausi Shattari's (d. 1617) *Gulzar-i Abrar*; Muhammad Sadiq's *Tabaqat-i Shahjahani*; and Dara Shukoh's (d. 1656) *Safinat al-Auliya'*. The author of the mid-seventeenth-century *Dabistan-i Mazahib* also relates interesting stories about him and his disciple, a certain Shaikh Jumman.

Bada'uni

It is interesting that Bada'uni, the famous historian of Akbar's time who was very sensitive to as well as much concerned with the orthodox Sunni tradition, uses very reverent and respectful adjectives for Shah Madar. He refers to him as "*badi' al-haqq wa al-milla wa al-din, qutb al-masha'ikh al-kibar, manhaj al-islam*". In the context of the discussion in *Najat al-Rashid* concerning *sajda* (prostration) and whether it can be considered legitimate only when directed towards God, or whether prostration before mortal men is also permissible, he invokes Shah Madar. The reason for this was reports of Madar's visage being unusually luminous, as though illumined by a light, to the extent that wherever he went he covered his face of necessity, for, if he uncovered it, those who saw him were awestruck and would fall at his feet and prostrate themselves before him.[3] Elsewhere, in a discussion on religious

---

British Library MS., Addn. 16,858. References here are however all from the Aligarh MS.

[3] Bada'uni, *Najat al-Rashid*, pp. 146–8.

knowledge (*'ilm-i din*), Bada'uni briefly mentions the correspondence between Shah Madar and Qazi Shihab al-Din Daulatabadi (d. 1445), one of the most famous theologians of his time who was associated with the Sharqi court in Jaunpur; in this way, Bada'uni demonstrates Shah Madar's high stature even in the spheres of normal, orthodox religious learning. In an aside, Bada'uni says that knowledge (*'ilm*) is that which one imparts to others and which benefits them, and only if one is asked should one explain and share such knowledge. In this context, Bada'uni again refers to Madar, saying that for the average person Madar's level of knowledge was unattainable; however, if Madar were asked something specific he would, howsoever difficult the subject, respond and explain it. So Madar's high stature is portrayed by Bada'uni as consisting not just in Sufi gnostic knowledge (*ma'rifat*), but in general knowledge too.[4] It is worth noting that Bada'uni himself went to visit Shah Madar's shrine (*ziyarat-i mazar-i fa'iz al-anwar-i Shaikh-i Kibar*) in Makanpur during the time of his appointment as *sadr* in Kant and Gola in Awadh.[5]

Shaikh 'Abd al-Haqq Muhaddis Dehlavi, *Akhbar al-Akhyar*

In his *Akhbar al-Akhyar*, Shaikh 'Abd al-Haqq Muhaddis Dehlavi (d. 1642) alludes to nearly all the uncommonly miraculous features of Shah Madar. He begins by recapitulating the reports of others ("*Gharib ahwal wa 'aja'b-i atwar az wai naql mikunand*"), narrating the strange and wondrous legends attributed to Madar's mystical practices. For instance, Madar is said to have refrained from eating; his clothes, though never washed, remained perpetually clean; he veiled his face because his beauty compelled prostration in the beholder; and it was said by some that he had close

---

[4] Ibid., pp. 172–4. For Daulatabadi, see Ahmad, *The Contribution of India to Arabic Literature.*

[5] Bada'uni, *Muntakhab al-Tawarikh*, Vol. 2, p. 93.

contact with the Prophet Muhammad mediated by only five or six links, whereas others claimed he had direct and unmediated contact with the Prophet. Interestingly, Dehlavi adds explanatory expressions such as "due to his long life, or for some other reason" ("*be sabab-i kibr-i sann ya jihat-i digar*"). He also mentions Qazi Shihab al-Din Daulatabadi's (d. 1445) correspondence with Madar. "Some attribute other things to him that have no basis in truth (*asle nadarad*) and that fall outside of the domain of the *shari'a* and *tariqa*. He sounds sceptical when narrating the story of Madar's encounter with the ruler of Kalpi, who had visited him while Madar was there. Madar had declined to meet the ruler because at the time he was busy conversing with a saint. Affronted, the ruler had commanded Madar to leave Kalpi. This command had then resulted in a curse upon the ruler: blisters developed all over his body, and when his *pir*, Shaikh Siraj al-Din Sukhta, intervened to cure him, he too suffered and died. Dehlavi writes: "He heard about it from some scholars of Kalpi, who said this story (*in qissa*) was famous in our region. It has no proper authority, God knows best (*maqtu' bi-hi wa-Allahu a'lam*)." The tone of Dehlavi's narrative of Madar thus sounds rather negative and dismissive, even though he does report that "people say (*guyand*) that Madar had attained a [very high and uncommon] stage of spirituality (*samadiyat*)."[6]

Muhammad Ghausi Shattari's
Gulzar-i Abrar

On the other hand Muhammad Ghausi Shattari (d. 1617), whose *Gulzar-i Abrar* records more such details, is quite positive, recounting and explaining even some of the anti-*shari'a* acts that were in vogue in his time in Shah Madar's *silsila*. He first gives a basic factual account of Madar – his name, his title (*laqab*), his shrine, etc. – after which he says there are stories about the saint

---

[6] Dehlavi, *Akhbar al-Akhyar*, p. 170.

which are difficult to comprehend by reason (*'aql*) alone: people say Madar was in the company of Jesus, that he was granted eternal life by God, and that he met the Prophet and conveyed Jesus' greetings to him. Shattari then moves on to the stranger features (*'aja'ib*) of his life, such as his meeting with the prophet Khizr (Elias), their conversation regarding the Prophet's eternal life, and his extreme generosity. In the year that he met Khizr, it is said that Madar decided to die. Shattari also describes the extreme measures taken by some of Madar's followers – such as shunning all clothing and going around naked. Yet he also says this was an extreme form of devotion, one which arose from a false interpretation of Madar's emphasis on *wahdat al-wujud*. He then narrates the history of how this particular memory came into being: since Madar had attained the highest stage of Oneness with God, celibacy, and asceticism (*wahdat* and *tajrid*), so that nothing was left except him and God, anecdotes pertaining to his asceticism and other "strange" acts (*'aja'ib*), Shattari says, became exaggerated, leading to a false image of the saint, and thus entered popular memory. People believed that by the end he wore only a tiny cloth, and that he had roamed around in the cold climate of Kashmir wearing nothing – a story to which many colourful details were later added, as we will see, in the *Dabistan-i Mazahib*. Shattari also mentions several *khalifas* of Shah Madar, in addition to Saiyid Jumman, some of whom are also mentioned in the *Dabistan*.[7]

Muhammad Sadiq, *Tabaqat-i Shahjahani*

In another Mughal *tazkira*, *Tabaqat-i Shahjahani*, compiled in the time of Shah Jahan (r. 1628–58), which comprises accounts of the saints and scholars who flourished during the reigns of various Mughal rulers, Madar figures as a contemporary of Timur (d. 1405). The author, Muhammad Sadiq (d. 1642?), draws heavily

[7] Shattari, *Gulzar-i Abrar*, pp. 74–8.

on Dehlavi's *Akhbar al-Akhyar* for his account of the saint. However, Sadiq does not follow Dehlavi in the latter's evaluation of the saint, and holds the saint in high esteem while trying to paper over the more extreme and uncommon legends (*'ajib-o-gharib*) associated with him. Sadiq interprets the saint's illumined face, which compelled general prostration, as evidence on him of the divine light (*nur-i ilahi*), so that many people came to him with their difficulties, which he always miraculously resolved. Sadiq adds the word "outward" (*zahir*) when he mentions cases of violation of the *shari'a* by Madar and his followers, and writes that Madar and his reverent *khalifas* would have been averse (*bizar*) to the more recent practices of many of his followers – those who walk around naked and behave imprudently (*barahnagi wa bibaki ki dar muntasiban-i in khanwada dar in nazdiki hadis shuda*).[8] Sadiq's portrait of Shah Madar and of his order is thus quite close to the one we saw in Shattari's *Tazkira*.

Shah Madar, the Saint of the Commoners: Dara Shukoh's *Safinat al-Auliya'*

In the prince Dara Shukoh's *Safinat al-Auliya'*, which borrows almost all of its information from the *Akhbar al-Akhyar*, mention is made in particular of Madar's *'urs* in Makanpur, where, Dara Shukoh writes,

> nearly five to six hundred thousand pilgrims come from all directions and regions of India, carrying many flags. They bring presents and offerings for the shrine, and report that they observe the saint's strange and unusual miracles even today. And, of the four parts of the plebeian and elite (*wazi'-o-sharif*) people of India, the two of them who predominantly are those of noble birth (*ashraf*) are the *murids* of Shah Muhyi al-Din 'Abd al-Qadir Jili [the eponymous founder of the *silsila* to which the prince belonged], while of the remaining three parts, one comprises the *murids* of Shah Madar, who are mostly the

[8] Sadiq, *Tabaqat-i Shahjahani*.

low-born (*ajlaf*), and the last part, divided into two equal halves, is shared by Khwaja Muʿin al-Din Chishti and Baha al-Din Zakariya of Multan.⁹

Thus, in Dara Shukoh's view, the Madari order was primarily popular with lowly and oppressed groups. This image is also upheld by the author of the *Dabistan-i Mazahib*, who confirms the picture and embellishes it with wondrous tales and legends about Shah Madar.

The *Dabistan-i Mazahib* (compiled around 1650)

Dara Shukoh's account, though reflecting shades of elite prejudice, is endorsed with much more detail in the *Dabistan-i Mazahib*. Shah Madar and the Madaris figure in this book in a section titled "On the various beliefs and customs of the people of India" ("*Dar ʿaqaʾid-i mukhtalifa-i ahl-i Hind*"), which is, strangely, the last part of a chapter of the book (*taʿlim*) describing the beliefs and customs of Hindus (*aqaʾid-i Hinduʾan*). I quote here the passages where Shah Madar and his followers are mentioned:

> Let it be noted that there is a group among the Hindus who call themselves Musalman-Sufis, and they share several beliefs and customs with the Sufis . . . They are in large numbers in India, and the foremost and best known among them are the Madaris, who, like the *awadhut* ascetics (*sanyasiyan*) have matted hair, smear their bodies with ashes (*bhabhut*), wear chains around their necks and heads, and carry black standards with them and wear black turbans. They don't recognise [the value of] *namaz* and *roza* (prayer and fasting). They sit in front of the fire, and drink copious amounts of *bhang* [an intoxicating drink made from hemp leaves] all the time. The most extreme among them don't wear anything, [even] in the winter in Kabul and Kashmir and other similarly cold places . . . When they are together, they recount [the story] that at the time when the

⁹ Dara Shukoh, *Safinat al-Auliyaʾ*, pp. 187–8.

Prophet went on his *mi'raj* (ascension), God commanded him to walk around the heavens; when he came to the entrance of paradise, he found it very narrow, narrower than the eye of a needle; Rizwan [the custodian of paradise] invited him in. The Prophet said: "How can I enter with this body through this passage?" [Thereupon] Jibril told him to say, "*Dam Madar*". The prophet said this and passed through the needle-hole passage and entered paradise.

It is said that when Badi' al-Din Madar arrived in India, there lived a *jogi* who was worshipped by many Indians and had many disciples. When Madar became settled in a certain area, he sent a young boy, named Jumman, to fetch some dry cowdung to light up a fire. It so happened that Jumman fell in with the assembly of the *jogis*, who, sensing him to be Muslim, killed him, cut him into pieces and devoured him. Sometime later, since Madar did not receive anything with which to kindle a fire, he went in search of Jumman, and saw the assembly of the *jogis*. He asked them, "What have you done with my pupil (*chela*)?" They replied that they hadn't seen him. Madar then called Jumman's name, and parts of him responded from within the bellies of the *jogis*: "*Dam Madar*". Madar then said to the *jogis*, "Should I bring forth Jumman from all of you, or only from one of you?" They replied, "Only from one." Madar then focused his attention and the scattered limbs of the body of Jumman became united in the belly of the principal *jogi*, such that none of the *jogis* could see anything, and the boy's body emerged from the *jogi*'s nose in such a way that neither the nostril of the *jogi* expanded, nor were the limbs of Jumman diminished. The *jogis* then fled, and Madar continued settling down in that region, which is known today as Makanpur.

Many Madaris from all parts of the world gather once a year on a certain day in Makanpur. They claim that the blind and lame can be cured there. They also say that once Chitapa, the wife of Bahram Kul, came to their assembly with the intention of testing both Hindu and Muslim sages (*darvishan-o-kamilan*). She said, "Whoever unties my *samran* [a bracelet of beads tied around the arm] and does not get seized with lust – he is a perfect saint." All the Hindu and Muslim saints who were present came forth, but when they saw Chitapa's face, they all became enamoured of her. At the very end, it was Jumman's turn. He came close to Chitapa, placed the *samran* on his penis (*zakar*), and yet was still completely free from lust. It is said that the erection of Jumman's penis was not due to any lustful desire; it was the [special] strength of the saints that [enabled them to] disperse sexual power throughout the limbs of the body. There is no doubt that Jumman occupied a place higher than all the [other] Hindu and Muslim saints. They [the Madaris] have many such tales.[10]

Conclusion of the Preliminary Survey of Sources

In the six-decade interval from the time of Bada'uni's account to the composition of the *Dabistan*, various accounts of Shah Madar proliferated in Mughal Indian hagiographical texts. In the process the saint's image underwent a radical transformation. One major feature of his Sufism that came to be emphasised was his close contact with the Prophet, mediated only by a few links; some Madaris claimed that he met the Prophet, and had had the honour of having been the Prophet's direct disciple. In the *Dabistan*, on the other hand, the Prophet himself is shown to be the one who benefited from Madar's spiritual power, since it was only by uttering the phrase "*Dam madar*" that he was able to enter paradise on his *mi'raj* night. A great number of Madaris subsequently began to dress and behave like *jogis*, consuming *bhang*, which was believed to enable access to and appreciation of the deepest and most divine secrets. Interestingly, in one narrative the Prophet too was blessed to learn and be able to teach his people the secrets of the angelic world (*'alam-i Malak wa malakut*) in return for his offer of a turban to the *jogis* to clean, strain, and prepare *bhang*.[11] Mughal India was, therefore, teeming with

---

[10] Malik, ed., *Dabistan-i Mazahib*, Vol. 1, pp. 188, 189–91. See also the English translation: Shea and Troyer, *Dabistan*, Vol. 2, pp. 216, 220–6.

[11] Cf. Malik, ed., *Dabistan-i Mazahib*, pp. 189–90. The story figures in the section where we find the account of Shah Madar and the Madaris, though these *jogis* do not seem to be associated with Shah Madar. The story runs as follows: One day the Prophet, while travelling across the universe, guided by Jibril, arrived at a place where he saw forty naked people sitting

these many contradictory legends at the time when a prominent Chishti–Sabiri scholar and saint, Shaikh 'Abd al-Rahman Chishti (d. 1683), compiled his *Mir'at-i Madariya*, the only independent, pre-modern (although very short) *tazkira*, or hagiographical account, of Shah Madar's life.[12]

'Abd al-Rahman Chishti's Account of Shah Madar

Chishti states that there exist many different reports of the events related to Shah Madar's life (*ahwal-i an hazrat*), and that for a long time he himself tried to find out what was true about him from various works of history, hagiography, and notable collections of *malfuzat* that were compiled and written by scholars from different regions; however, none of the accounts satisfied him. Finally, after searching for a long time, he came across a treatise called the *Risala-i Iman-i Mahmudi* by one Qazi Mahmud Kanturi, which he read first in 1053 H/1643 while he was on pilgrimage to Ajmer. Qazi Kanturi, 'Abd al-Rahman Chishti writes, was a highly respected *khalifa* of Shah Madar, and had described in his treatise everything that he had witnessed of Madar with his own eyes. Chishti used this as a source for his book, supplementing what he had gleaned from what Saiyid Ashraf Jahangir Simnani, a contemporary of Shah Madar, had written about him, and also making use of some details that had been successively reported

---

around, busy doing something. The Prophet asked them if he could be of any service to them; they declined. They were preparing *bhang*, and as they had no cloth with them, they needed a piece to finally clean and strain it. They then happily accepted (*khushdil shudand*) the Prophet's offer of his turban to finish the preparations. The turban turned green with the *bhang*'s colour (*rang-i bang ba 'amama mand*), and it is because of this that the emblematic colour of the Prophet's family is green. In return the *jogis* also offered him the *bhang*, and as he took a sip he was enlightened with all the secrets of the world of the angels. The secrets that the people learnt from him were all due to their grace.

[12] See the previous chapters in this volume.

from the saint's time by people of piety and integrity. He confirmed and cross-referenced (*mukarrar tahqiq namuda*) the reliability of what he selected from these resources, also adding some information from a few other books that he accessed in the meantime. Nevertheless, Chishti refrained from writing the final draft and putting out the book, for, as Chishti writes, Madar did things that were contrary to customary practices. Chishti therefore did not have courage to write the book, fearing that he might become "the target of the arrows of reproach (*nishan-i tir-i malamat*)" from people who know and see only the outward appearances of religion (*arbab-i zahir*). So, for many years he wavered (*mutaraddid*), and even sought spiritual guidance from Shah Madar through esoteric channels.

At long last, after about eleven years, on a Friday night in the month of Zu'l-Qa'da in the year 1064 H/September 1654, the right time finally came. Chishti was accompanying a noted Madari Sufi of Sandila, Shaikh Aman-Allah, who was on his way to pay homage to the shrine of Shah Madar in Makanpur. There, Chishti was blessed, and acquired permission from Madar himself to write this book. "Write it," Madar commanded him, and added, "it is an auspicious [project]; and wherever there might be any discrepancy, I will inform you directly of what exactly happened (*har ja ki khilaf numa khwahad bud, man az qarari-waqi'a tura agah khwaham sakht*)."[13] In this way, Chishti was able to enhance the authenticity of his account with this esoteric imprimatur from Madar and his direct spiritual command to him (*be-hukm-i batin*), which, being in full conformity with Sufi practices and beliefs of the time, made the project acceptable to his audience.

Shah Madar's Early Years and First Exposure to Islam

A notable and unique feature of Chishti's account is his description of Shah Madar's Jewish ancestry and early education. Citing Qazi Kanturi, he writes:

[13] *Mir'at-i Madariya*, fls 72a–73.

His [Madar's] ancestors were the noble descendants of the Bani Isra'il prophets; his father, a man of high status, was Abu Ishaq Shami [from Syria] . . . He [Abu Ishaq] followed the religion (*millat*) of Moses, was a direct descendant of Aaron, was always busy, and was blessed with righteousness, piety, and a love of truth (*salah, taqwa, haqq-parasti*). He was, however, unlucky in that none of his children survived past infancy. Madar's birth followed a long period of his father's fervent prayers and supplications to Moses and Aaron, after a blissful dream in which Madar's father saw Moses, who prophesied his birth. "O Abu Ishaq, give up your worries, for God will bless you with a unique (*badi'*) son, in whom my *wilayat* will be manifest."

Chishti then discusses in brief the importance of *wilayat-i Musawi* and indicates that some other Sufis too, such as Najm al-Din Kubra of Khwarazm (d. 1221), had possessed it.[14] But the fact that Shah Madar's *wilayat-i Musawi* was prophesied by Moses himself – and moreover in a dream experienced by a non-Muslim – deserves attention here. A striking feature of this account is that Chishti uses such terms as *taqwa* and *haqq-parasti* to describe the piety and religious inclinations of Madar's Jewish father. In other words, Chishti is open enough to recognise these virtues and qualities in a non-Muslim.

Madar's first teacher, Huzaifa, was a peerless Jewish scholar (*kahin*) from Syria, with whom Madar apparently read the *Torah* (Old Testament), the *Injil* (New Testament), and other divine books. Here too it is worth noting that Chishti projects Huzaifa as a saintly man (*mard-i haqqani*) to whom many miracles were attributed (*bisyar khariq-i 'adat az u zahir mishudi*). Madar had a taste for divine learning ('*ilm-i ladunni*), so he learned the holy books by heart within a few years and became famous (as a Jewish scholar) in Syria. However, he remained curious, and longed to experience the real truth. He had heard from Huzaifa about one Ahmad, whose advent, as his teacher had taught him, was prophesied in the *Injil* and through whose mediation (*wasila*) one

---

[14] Ibid., fls 74–75a. For Najm al-Din Kubra, see Rizvi, *A History of Sufism*, Vol. 1, pp. 93–5 and 126–7.

could access Divinity (*yaft-i zat-i hazrat-i uluhiyat*); this man was to come after Moses and Christ. Madar became impatient (*talab-i haqq bi-ikhtiyar ghalib gasht; qarar wa aram az wai beraft*) to know who this Ahmad was and where he lived. In response to his query, his teacher told him that he (Ahmad) was no longer in this world, but that "his followers are there in Mecca and Medina". After some time had passed, and Madar had lost both his parents, he relinquished all the worldly wealth and goods that he had inherited and set off for Mecca.[15] Chishti's respectful expressions to refer to the pious acts and virtues of Madar's father and first master are worth noting. Even more noteworthy is that Madar's initial forays into Islam and mysticism are portrayed as based on intimations about Islam that he received from a Jewish scholar, who taught him non-Jewish books as well. Selections from Kanturi's book may have been his starting point, but Chishti here seems to have added elements and inserted his own discourses and opinions.

In Mecca, Madar read the Qur'an and studied the *hadith* and the books of the founders of Muslim jurisprudence (*mujtahids*) such as Abu Hanifa and Abu 'Abd-Allah al-Shafi'i. However, he was disappointed in the great number of varied opinions (*aqwal-i mukhtalifa*) in these sciences, so he decided to discontinue his studies there and return home. Madar was not to be forsaken by Divinity, however; a divine voice told him that he should depart for Medina, and when he arrived there and approached the Prophet's shrine, he was greeted by the Prophet himself with these words: "Welcome, O Badi' al-Din Qutb al-Madar! God willing, you will soon attain the goal." Nowhere does Chishti mention Madar's formal conversion to Islam; nevertheless, he portrays Madar as having had full access to the sacred spiritual presence (*ruhaniyat*) of the Prophet, from whom he acquired his knowledge of true Islam (*talqin-i islam-i haqiqi*).

The Prophet then turned Madar over to the charge of 'Ali. Madar departed for Najaf, where 'Ali, having guided him in the

[15] *Mir'at-i Madariya*, fls 75b–76b.

principles of the straight path (*sirat-i mustaqim*), the essence of truth (*haqq al-haqq*), and all the stages of true gnosis (*'irfan-i haqiqi*), entrusted him to the care of his great-grandson, Imam Muhammad Mahdi bin Hasan 'Askari. Significantly, Madar's education with Mahdi included the study of eight other divine books, different from the four known and revealed to the prophets of mankind. Chishti describes the four of them as *Ragori, Jajari, Sattari,* and *Athan*, which were revealed to the religious leaders of the *jinn*.[16]

Two Tangential Discussions: Religious Differences and Sectarianism

At this point, Chishti interrupts the narrative flow of the *Mir'at-i Madariya* in order to discourse on two important subjects: the first is the issue of the diversity of religious ideas and beliefs, and the second concerns the differences between Sunnis and Shi'is within the Muslim community. Chishti's position on both issues is markedly different from the typical Sunni-Islamic scholarly understanding of these matters, and, as we will see, this position taken by Chishti may form part of a religious strategy that had great significance and resonance for the period in which he was writing.

Chishti here reiterates what he had said earlier in his *Mir'at al-Makhluqat*, and the evidence he invokes – the Qur'an, *Rauzat al-Safa*, Tabari's *Ta'rikh*, and *Jawahar al-Tafsir* – are the same sources he used in the earlier text. We may also speculate that by the four *jinn* books that he mentions here, namely *Ragori, Jajari, Sattari,* and *Athan*, he might have meant the *Rg Veda, Yajur Veda, Sama Veda,* and *Atharva Veda*.

However, in this text, Chishti also mentions four additional books, namely *Mir'at, 'Ayn al-Rabb, Sarmajan,* and *Mazhar-i Alf,* which he identifies as having been revealed to the sacred leaders

---

[16] Ibid., fls 76b and 77.

of the angels, for which he produces as evidence the vision of the famous Sufi saint Shah Niʻmat-Allah Wali Kermani (d. 1431). Niʻmat-Allah Wali recounts how once, while he was meditating, he travelled to the sky where he saw a great angel sitting on a decorated chair, with about 70,000 angels standing around him respectfully (*ba-adab istada*). He was surprised and asked who he was. They said he was God's *khalifa*.

> I said who is this God's *khalifa*, other than our father, Adam? Thereupon that angel called me and said your father [Adam] was the *khalifa* on earth and [I am] the *khalifa* on the fourth sky . . . Perhaps you have not read in the Qur'an that "I make him [Adam] *khalifa* on the earth (*inni jaʻilun fi l-arzi khalifa*)." I then bowed my head and realised that we cannot comprehend how mysterious the divine creation is; in the face of divine knowledge, we are all ignorant. Beyond each knowledgeable person there is another man more knowledgeable still. There has been a *khalifa* on every [level of the] sky (*falak*) and earth (*zamin*) to inhabit it.[17]

Chishti then cites Ibn al-ʻArabi from his *Fusus al-Hikam*:

> Shaikh Muhyi al-Din writes that all the prophets' paths are one, even though their religions (*din*) and religious laws (*shariʻa*) might be different due to the diversity of the peoples who follow them. Peoples of each era have their own particular character and set of abilities which correspond to that era, and the prophet of each group brought the divine message in such a form that it was in tune with the abilities of that people (*bi hasb-i qabiliyat-i an qaum*). This is the reason that the religions and religious laws of the prophets sometimes vary one to the other. And this does not violate the oneness of the source (*asl*) of the [various] paths, [all of which are] a call to God and to true religion. God is the One Absolute. The Great name of the Guide (*hadi*) never ceased in the [task of] guiding mortal creatures, nor will it ever cease.[18]

Chishti also cites a few verses from the Qur'an in support of this, notably the one which says that God sent prophets to the

---

[17] *Mir'at-i Madariya*, fls 77b and 80.
[18] Ibid., fl. 81.

various communities with books in their own languages (*wa ma arsal-na min rusulin illa bi-lisani qaumi-hi*),[19] and that there was not a single community which did not receive a prophet who warned them of the consequences of their evil deeds (*im min ummatin illa khala fiha nazir*).[20] In the course of this discussion, Chishti asserts that

> the scholars who are concerned only with appearances (*'ulama'-i zahir*) do not agree that prophets were also sent to the *jinn* and the angels. Prophethood, according to them, is unique to human communities; other communities were not deserving of it. And they believed this despite the fact that their own divine book contains the verse, "I have created the *jinn* and humans so that only they worship me (*ma khalaqtu l-jinna wa'l-insa illa li-ya 'buduni*)."[21]

The *Mir'at-i Madariya* then is not just a descriptive history, nor is it a typical hagiographical account of Shah Madar. Chishti weaves many different polemical discourses into the narrative, many of which were relevant, as we shall see below, to the political situation of the time during which he was writing. In addition to the discussion that the coming of the prophets and divine books was not peculiar to the history of mankind, Chishti introduces a brief discussion on the concept of the *mahdi*. Was Muhammad Mahdi, who mentored and taught Madar, the same promised Mahdi who in Islam is said to arrive in order to rescue humanity as the End-Time draws near? He writes:

> Since the matter is disputed, it is appropriate here to mention the opinions of every sect, so that there should be no misunderstandings about the position of God's friends due to any prejudice. A majority of the Sunni *'ulama'* (*ahl al-sunnat wa' l-jama'at*), however, deny the fact that Muhammad Mahdi (who taught Madar) is the promised Mahdi, while at the same time they accept that the promised Mahdi, who the Prophet said will appear close to the Day of Judgment, will be born in the family of Fatima. The promised Mahdi has not yet

[19] Qur'an, 14.4.
[20] Ibid., 35.23.
[21] *Mir'at-i Madariya*, fls 79b–80a. For the verse, see Qur'an, 51.56.

been born. [On the contrary,] all the Twelver Shi'i *'ulama'* report that, according to the *hadith* of the Prophet and the sayings of the *imams* of the family of the Prophet, the promised Mahdi is the same as Muhammad bin Hasan 'Askari. He is the twelfth *imam*, the master of the time (*sahib-i zaman*), the seal of *wilayat-i Muhammadiya*, who disappeared at God's command from the sight of the people. He will reappear when the Divine Will shall ordain it, close to the Day of Judgment. It is a sin to deny this true *imam*. They [the Shi'i *'ulama'*] cite the *hadith*, reported in the *Mishkat*, that he who does not recognise the *imam* of his time and dies had died the death of an ignorant person (*man lam ya'rif imama zamani-hi wa mata, mata maitatan jahiliyatan*).[22]

Chishti then adds that the question of the Mahdi has been discussed in detail in Shi'i books, whose contents, he laments, "cannot be encompassed in his short treatise". But what is interesting is the fact that Chishti thereafter cites the opinions of three noted Sunni scholars, all in support of what we saw above was the unanimous position of the Shi'i *'ulama*:

> The author of *Nusus al-mulhama fi madh al-a'imma*, who followed the jurisprudential school (*mazhab*) of Imam Malik, a leader and *imam* of the people of the *sunnat wa jama'at*, reports that the promised Mahdi and Imam Muhammad bin Hasan 'Askari is the same person, while Shaikh Muhyi al-Din Ibn al-'Arabi writes in chapter three hundred and seventy-six of his book, *Futuhat-i Makkiya*, that "be it noted that the advent of Imam Mahdi, whose father is Imam Taqi son of Imam Naqi, and so on [up to 'Ali] is inevitable. Most fortunate with him are the people of Kufa; he will invite the people to God with his sword. He will slaughter those who will reject [his invitation], and whoever will oppose him will be doomed."

The *Shawahid al-Nubuwwa* of 'Abd al-Rahman Jami, the noted scholar, poet, and Sufi, is the third Sunni book which Chishti cites in support of the Shi'i scholars' position. "Hazrat Maulana 'Abd al-Rahman Jami, an experienced and established Sufi who

---

[22] Ibid., fl. 78.

followed the Shafi'i school, has described in detail the life and achievements (*ahwal-o-kamalat*) of Imam Muhammad bin 'Askari, including the account of his birth and his disappearance, in his *Shawahid al-Nubuwwa*, using the accounts of the compilers of the biographies (*siyar*) to excellent effect."

There is yet another Sunni text, titled *Maqsad-i Aqsa*, by a certain Shaikh 'Aziz Nasafi, that Chishti cites. Nasafi writes that Shaikh Sa'ad al-Din Hamawi, the noted disciple of Najm al-Din Kubra, had compiled a full-length book on Imam Mahdi, in which he stated that Imam Mahdi had unmatched spiritual powers. It also says that the Mahdi will appear endowed with absolute *wilayat*, and with him all the differences between religions, evil, and tyranny will come to an end. The Prophet has prophesied his good qualities, and with his advent the entire inhabited earth will be freed from tyranny and there will be only one true religion. In short, if the wicked Antichrist has already been born in the time of Prophet Muhammad, and is still alive and hidden, and if Christ is also hidden and alive, then it cannot come as a surprise if Imam Muhammad bin Hasan 'Askari is also believed to have been born and hidden, to return like Christ and Antichrist at a divinely determined time. It serves no purpose to deny "the opinions of these sages and the words of the imams who hailed from the family of the Prophet" because of narrow sectarian prejudice (*az rah-i ta'assub*).[23]

Shah Madar is Sent to Hindustan

'Abd al-Rahman Chishti then returns to his narrative of Shah Madar. Once Madar had attained perfection in all the branches of knowledge, Mahdi took Madar back to 'Ali, who was pleased with his accomplishments and himself accompanied Madar back to Medina to visit the Prophet. Having seen that Madar had mastered all the hidden divine secrets (*asrar-i makhfi*), the Prophet

---

[23] Ibid., fls 78b–79b.

commanded him to go to Mecca to give thanks to God for all the blessings with which he had been endowed. The Prophet also told Madar that from Mecca he should leave for Hindustan and, based on whichever place Khwaja Muʿin al-Din of Ajmer would guide him to settle, to "show the misguided people there the right path (*gum-gashtagan-i badiya-i zalalat ra be-tariq-i sirat-i mustaqim hidayat*)".[24] In a different context, ʿAbd al-Rahman also mentions another Chishti saint, Abu al-Fath Chishti of Awadh, predicting Madar's future greatness. The author thus obviously attempts to establish a connection between Shah Madar and the Chishti *silsila*.[25]

Chishti narrates in great detail in the style of a *dastan* the circumstances of Madar's arrival in India: he travelled for a few days by land and then took a ship. The ship, when it was not even halfway in, was trapped in a storm; it dashed against a rock and was wrecked (*jahaz . . . para para gasht*), the travellers and their goods were all drowned (*mardum maʿ asbab ghariq-i bahr-i fana gashtand*), barring a few, eleven persons in all, who managed to reach the shore on a broken wooden board. Madar was one of them, but the other ten died of hunger and thirst so that Madar was the only one who eventually survived. He was however horrorstruck, having seen their sufferings and death, and prayed to God that he never have the need to eat and drink (*chun an deh tan ra dida ki az gursnagi-o-bitabi-o-bi-istiqlali be-hal-i bad murdand . . . tabiʿat-i u az akl-o-shurb mutlaq ramida gasht wa az Haqq taʿla wa subhanahu imdad-i in maʿni khwast*). He then walked up to a mountain, where he saw a magnificent residence, and as he entered it he saw a beautiful garden full of multicoloured flowers, in the middle of which stood a decorated house where an extraordinarily handsome and majestically attired man was seated on a ruby throne. The man was so luminous that Madar could not even look at him. The garden and the house

[24] Ibid., fl. 81b.
[25] Ibid., fls 101–102a.

all around were lit up (*munawwar az anwar-i u*) because of that illumined person (*mard-i nurani*). He invited Madar to dine with him. Madar was hungry but told him he had asked God to give him strength against ever desiring to eat. The man said he had with God's command (*be-farman-i Ilahi*) arranged for him to share the same food (*haman ta'am*). Madar then had the honour of sitting on the throne beside him, and he fed him with his own hand nine morsels, with each of which he saw each of the heavens and finally the entire universe was fully illumined before him. The man thereafter gave him a turban (*dastar*), a shirt (*pirahan*), and a pair of trousers (*izar*), and said that these clothes too would remain neat and clean for him for his entire remaining life. He then said to Madar:

> I leave you now to God's care. You will not meet with worldly accidents any longer, you will cross these hills and jungles without any difficulty, and reach Hindustan where you will stay . . . You will be called both in this world (*'alam-i nasut*) and in the world of angels (*'alam-i malakut*) with the title of Shah Madar, a title which none will obtain after you.

Then the man disappeared, and with him the mansion and garden too disappeared. Madar stood stunned and bowed his head in meditation. He heard a divine voice say that "the man was the leader of the *unsuri* angels, who had control over the entire inhabited world. His name was Shekhisa. Remember his name and seek his help whenever in future you are in need."[26]

The miraculous power that Shah Madar acquired here was a part of *samadiyat* – a term which figures in several other Mughal *tazkiras* in the context of his *tasawwuf*. Now graced with this unique spiritual power, Madar entered Hindustan through Gujarat, and, guided by this angelic individual, finally arrived in Ajmer as the Prophet had instructed him. In Ajmer, Madar stayed for some time at a place in a mountain, which Chishti says was

---

[26] Ibid., fls 83b–86a.

still remembered as a sacred place, with the dervishes visiting in order to light a lamp there. Khwaja Muʿin al-Din Chishti then told him to go to the region surrounding Awadh and Jaunpur and settle there. Madar first reached Kalpi, and then Jaunpur, and finally travelled through Awadh.[27] The details that Chishti gives hereafter are noted in the existing secondary literature and need not be repeated here.[28]

Shah Madar in Hindustan: Discourse on *Samadiyat*, Religious Knowledge, and Sufism

What is of interest to us are some important discussions that Chishti introduces here: first, relating to the Uwaisi *silsila*;[29] second, the definition of knowledge; and third, on Sufism. Chishti writes that Madar was the first Uwaisi saint in India and adds that since this was a time far before anyone in India was aware of the importance of the Uwaisis, a major Awadhi figure, Shaikh Saʿad-Allah of Kantur, wrote to Shaikh Jahangir Ashraf Simnani (d. 1436) and asked him about it.[30] Simnani confirmed the validity of the order and wrote that Shaikh Farid al-Din ʿAttar (d. 1220), the noted saint-poet and author of *Mantiq al-Tair* (Conference of the Birds), regarded the Uwaisis as the most notable saints.[31] They needed no *pir* and received direct training from the Prophet like

[27] Ibid., fl. 86a.
[28] Cf. Rizvi, *A History of Sufism in India*, Vol. 1, pp. 318–20; Falasch, article "Badiʿ al-Din".
[29] The *silsila* in which the *pir* or spiritual master, and *murid* or disciple could belong to at different times. The attribution is to Uwais Qarani, who accepted Islam at the time of the Prophet and earned a very high status, virtually the same as of his companions (*sahabi*), even though he never met him. The Prophet allowed him to stay and serve his old and ailing mother.
[30] For Simnani, see Rizvi, *A History of Sufism*, Vol. 1, pp. 266–70.
[31] For a brief discussion around ʿAttar and his *Mantiq al-Tair*, see Green, *Sufism*, pp. 108–15. See also Lewisohn and Shackle, eds, *ʿAttar and the Persian Sufi Tradition*.

the legendary Uwais Qarani. Chishti adds that Madar also was linked to 'Ali and thus to the Prophet through another Uwaisi saint, Shaikh 'Abd-Allah Makki, who had lived 200 years before his time. In this way, Chishti establishes a high spiritual position for Madar, even though he was not a disciple of any of the known Sufi masters of his time; however, it is due to his double Uwaisi status that he was able to commune with 'Ali and the Prophet, regardless of their separation in time and space.[32]

Perhaps here Chishti also joins issue with Shaikh 'Abd al-Haqq Muhaddis Dehlavi, who had explained Madar's meeting with the Prophet in terms of his "long life or some other reason (*be-jihat-i digar*)". In the process, Chishti cites 'Ala al-Daula Simnani, who writes that a Sufi after he scales the high position of *samadiyat*, does not remain in need of food and drink. He also makes Madar himself explain the significance of his *samadiyat*. Chishti writes that Shaikh 'Abd al-Rahman Qidwa'i,[33] a senior Shaikh of his time, who was also a *khalifa* in the Madariya order, reported – albeit through a reliable and unbroken (*mutawatar*) chain of reporters – the following:

> One day, in response to a query by one of his disciples as to how Madar survived without eating, Madar stated: "Whosoever comes into existence cannot remain alive without food; however, some people have human food (*ta'am-i nasut*), while some others have angelic food (*ta'am-i malakut*); it is for this reason that the Prophet prohibited his companions from continuous fasting, and he explained his own practice as follows: 'I am not like you, I live with my God, who gives me food and drink.'"[34]

---

[32] *Mir'at-i Madariya*, fls 82–83a. Chishti here copies verbatim from Jahangir Ashraf Simnani's *Lata'if-i Ashrafi*, compiled by his disciple Nizam Yamani. See the Urdu translation by 'Abd-ul-Haqq and 'Abd-us-Sattar, Vol. 3, pp. 234–5. Interestingly both Simnani and Chishti count the poets Nizami Ganjawi and Hafiz Shirazi among the Uwaisi saints.

[33] For Shaikh 'Abd al-Rahman Qidwa'i, see Chishti, *Mir'at al-Asrar*, p.1164.

[34] *Mir'at-i Madariya*, fl. 87a.

Chishti then says that, such being the case, it is possible that Madar, because of his special connections with the Prophet, could have acquired the special ability (*niʿmat-i khas*) from the Prophet. After all the Prophet ʿIsa had remained in that position throughout his whole life, alive without food or water, sustained only by angelic food. The Prophet Adam also remained in heaven for all of five hundred years, surviving on this sort of sustenance (*niʿmat*). Chishti says that it should come as no surprise that God bestowed similar capacities upon one of Adam's descendants.[35] Similarly, it is recounted by Chishti (echoing previous hagiographical accounts) that Madar remained impeccably clean while wearing the same clothes throughout his life.

Among the people with whom Madar corresponded in Awadh and Jaunpur was the famous Qazi Shihab al-Din Daulatabadi, known as *malik al-ʿulama* (chief of the scholars). Chishti reproduces Madar's response to Daulatabadi's letter.[36] Without going into the details of the correspondence, what is important for our purposes is that through Madar's letters Chishti does not simply define what real knowledge is, but rather tries to show the depth of Madar's knowledge. There is a brief discussion of the concept of *ʿalam-i misal* and the eternity of the soul, which is meant perhaps to explain Madar's meeting with the Prophet and his direct contact with him through his Uwaisi position.[37] It is also significant that Madar is not simply shown as debating with Daulatabadi, but with other scholars of the time too, amongst them Qazi Mahmud Kanturi, whose book on Madar, as we saw above, was the main source of Chishti's account, and who having been convinced of Madar's greatness became his disciple. There is also an exchange with Qazi Mutahhar, with whom Madar

---

[35] Ibid., fl. 87.

[36] Ibid., fls 94a–96b. Ute Falasch has an essay on this subject: "Badiʿ al-Din Shah Madar to Qazi Shihab al-Din Daulatabadi", pp. 53–81.

[37] "The world of archetypal images, the world of Forms"; a world beyond this world of average human beings, accessible only to some high-statured Sufis.

had a long debate lasting for seven days, on the question of the unity of being (*wahdat-i wujud*). Chishti mentions Qazi Mutahhar as a scholar with comprehensive learning (*jam'-i 'ulum*) who had especially come to test (*imtihan*) Madar's level of knowledge.[38]

Notable in this context is the anecdote that Chishti recounts about one Shaikh Husain Balkhi, who was being trained in *'Awarif al-Ma'arif*, a famous Sufi text, by the noted Firdausi Sufi from Bihar, Shaikh Sharaf al-Din Yahya Maneri. When he was only halfway through this text, Manyari was on the brink of death, and, seeing that Balkhi was very disturbed and anxious about his further training after his teacher's death, Manyari told him that soon there would be a unique saint named Shah Madar in Jaunpur; he should visit him and read the rest of the text with him.[39] Here Chishti also takes issue with Dara Shukoh, who projects Madar, we saw above, primarily as the *pir* of the poor and lowly (*ajlaf*). In Chishti's narrative, however, Madar comes across as a highly literate scholar with a command over many features of true knowledge in Islam, even from an orthodox theological perspective.

That Chishti mixes polemic with his narrative and takes a definitive position on certain key issues is illustrated also by his point about Madar's encounter with the ruler of Kalpi, Qadir Shah (r. 1410–30). Chishti says it is reported that during his first stay in India, while in Kalpi, Shah Madar refused to meet Qadir Shah, the ruler, because he was busy conversing with a non-Muslim *yogi* at the time. But, Chishti writes, this is something that Madar's enemies (*ahl-i nifaq*) have said to tarnish his reputation as a "liberal" Sufi, for though Madar was in fact busy in conversation with a dervish, he had not been informed by his *khadims* of the ruler's visit. The ruler, however, believed the misreport and commanded them to ask Madar to leave Kalpi. Enraged, Shah Madar in turn cursed him, whereupon the ruler's body was covered in blisters.

---

[38] *Mir'at-i Madariya*, fl. 99.
[39] Ibid., fl. 93.

Chishti says that, soon after, Qadir Shah lost his territory to Sultan Hoshang Shah of Malwa.[40]

Chishti perhaps also intends here to critique both those who misreported and the ruler's prejudice against non-Muslim dervishes. In an endeavour to project Shah Madar's miraculous power, he mentions a similar incident in the context of his visit to Lucknow, where a major Sufi of the city, Shaikh Qiyam al-Din, did not welcome him and also questioned why Qazi Shihab al-Din Qidwa'i (to whom we will turn below) was in Madar's service. Shaikh Qiyam too, like Qadir Shah, bore the brunt of Madar's displeasure.[41]

Shah Madar, Sufism, and the Bani Isra'il in Awadh

In the course of his account of Madar's sojourn in Awadh, Chishti mentions a certain Qazi Shihab al-Din, identified as a member the Bani Isra'il (*ki az qaum-i bani isra'il bud*). Qazi Shihab al-Din rose to become one of the closest disciples of Madar; in fact, in the context of the details regarding Qazi Shihab al-Din's close relationship with Madar, Chishti presents some critical comments on what a Sufi's role in society should be. It is reported that a very serious epidemic raged in the region (perhaps of Makanpur), and people appealed to Madar to deliver them from it. Madar assigned responsibility for rescuing the people – irrespective of their religion – to Qazi Shihab al-Din, since he was Madar's closest (*mahbub-tarin*) disciple. He instructed the Qazi to go to an elevated place and engage in prayers; the Qazi did so and in the process, after three days, a severe dust storm arose from which appeared a strong flame, as powerful as lightning. The Qazi, who was himself aflame (*shihab*, a luminous meteor), opened his mouth

---

[40] Ibid., fls 88a–89a. See also Rizvi, *A History of Sufism*, Vol. 1, p. 318.

[41] *Mir'at-i Madariya*, fl. 90a. Shaikh Qiyam died within a few days of their encounter.

and swallowed it. As a result, the plague epidemic disappeared; but he began to suffer from severe stomach pain. This was reported to Shah Madar, who came to his disciple, put his hand on his stomach, and cured him.[42] Since then, this anecdote has entered popular memory, and even modern accounts of this Bani Isra'il family preserve the memory of this anecdote, calling Shihab al-Din "the flame-eater (*shu'la-khor*)".[43]

Chishti here touches on two points. First, the nature of Sufism, and second, the relationship between Shah Madar and Qazi Shihab al-Din. What is Sufism? The implication is that it does not just involve writing books and debating terms such as *wahdat* and *wujud* and *shuhud*, which formed part of the seventeenth-century Mujaddidi–Naqshbandi discourse on gnosis and divinity. Here, Chishti takes issue with this discourse and suggests that a critical component of Sufism is to serve people, irrespective of their religious affiliations. And in Madar's case this aspect of Sufism was embodied in Qazi Shihab al-Din, a member of the Bani Isra'il, and identified as his dearest disciple. Chishti also tells us that Qazi Shihab al-Din was given the authority to decide to whom the spiritual Sufi authority (*wilayat*) over Lucknow should go, and it was he who gave it to Shah Mina, the major Chishti Sufi of the period.[44] Here again 'Abd al-Rahman Chishti highlights Madar's connection with the Chishti *silsila*.

We could speculate on whether Madar's closeness to Qazi Shihab al-Din was on account of their shared Bani Isra'il connection. Madar was also in contact with other Sufis in the region, such as a certain Qazi Akhi Jamshid, and four or five others, all of whom seem to have been from the Bani Isra'il community. Madar also personally met some of them.[45] Chishti lists among Shah Madar's special prayers one *fatiha-i kitab-i injil*, which he

---

[42] Ibid., fl. 89b, for mention of Qazi Shihab al-Din, and fls 100–101a for the particular incident of the epidemic.

[43] Kidwai, *Biographical Sketch of Kidwais of Avadh*.

[44] *Mir'at-i Madariya*, fl. 98.

[45] Ibid., fl. 89a.

also calls *du'a-i bishmakh*, and says that in Shah Madar's circle it was read and repeated twelve times after the morning prayer. This prayer closely resembles a short formula in Hebrew, "*bismakh ani 'ose*" ("by your name I act"), which some scholars claim was an exordium prefacing various incantations and prayers.[46] Chishti also mentions another prayer called *'azimat-i kabira*, which Shah Madar and his disciples recited three times after the evening prayer. This prayer originated in the "earlier sacred scriptures" (*suhuf-i adam*, perhaps meaning the Qur'anic expression *suhuf-i ula*).[47] In addition to several prayers directly inherited from 'Ali, Chishti mentions that he himself learned these special prayers from Shaikh 'Abd al-Rahman Qidwa'i, who in turn learned them from Abu al-Fath Qidwa'i, and so on and so forth, in a chain that went via Qazi Mahmud Kanturi back to Shah Madar. It is significant that these special prayers in 'Abd al-Rahman Chishti's time remained in the families of these Bani Isra'il shaikhs and not just among the followers of Shah Madar.[48] We should note however that in Shah

---

[46] See Shaked, "Some Iranian Themes in Islamic Literature", pp. 143–58, esp. p. 152. Also Montgomery, *Aramaic Incantation Texts from Nippur*.

[47] The reference is to the Qur'anic verse: "*inna haza la-fi's suhufi'l-ula, suhuf-i ibrahima wa musa* (verily this is in the earlier scriptures, the scriptures of Abraham and Moses)". Qur'an, 87: 18 & 19.

[48] *Mir'at-i Madariya*, fls 104a and 105. It is worth recalling here Minkowski's discussion of the *Sulaimanacaritra*, a fifteenth-century Sanskrit account of David and Solomon drawn from the Old Testament. He mentions the Qidwa'is as a possible source for this text and as carriers of the Jewish tradition in the region. But he also doubts that they could have been the sources for this particular text since they did not have any connections with the Lodi court. Minkowski, "King David in Oudh". Unfortunately we do not possess many sources on the Bani Isra'il in north India. There are however individual references to several members of the Bani Isra'il, including the Qidwa'i community of Awadh, many of whom served as *qazis* in the region. Some of them also lived in Delhi and had close connections with the ruling elites of the time, such as Qazi 'Abd al-Karim and Qazi Qiwam al-Din, who were associated with Nizam al-Din Auliya'. Cf. Chishti, *Mir'at al-Asrar*, pp. 906–7, also 1097–1102 for Shaikh Akhi Jamshed Qidwa'i, and 1118–19 for Shaikh Muhammad Abkash; in a modern account, a member of the

Madar's order there were many other prayers and litanies, which Chishti mentions in some detail and some of which, he writes, he has also included in his treatise, *Aurad-i Chishti*.[49]

The Sufi's Religion and the Question of "True Islam"

An important discourse that Chishti introduces in connection with Madar's encounters with the *'ulama* of the region where he settled is his explanation for their opposition to him. He writes that when Madar arrived in Jaunpur, Sultan Ibrahim Sharqi (r. 1402–40), who was familiar with his encounter with the ruler of Kalpi and the subsequent problems, welcomed him, and thus the sultan and all his nobles (*jami' a'yan*) and the people of the city (*ahl-i shahr*) earned his blessings. The most noted *'alim* of the time, the chief of the scholars (*malik al-'ulama*), Qazi Shihab al-Din, and his followers (*mutabi'an*), however, declined to meet him. Out of hostility to Madar, the Qazi would also mention and associate him with several unpleasant things in the meetings and discussions at his own house and at the court. But the sultan paid little attention to his canards.[50] As a matter of fact, none of Madar's enemies

---

Qidwa'i community also notes several members associated with the politics and administration of pre-modern Awadh: Kidwai, *Biographical Sketch of Kidwais of Awadh*, passim. As for the fact that Madar is mentioned as a Saiyid in the other hagiographical accounts, including that of Dara Shukoh, some Bani Isra'il in the region also claimed Saiyid status, and we can surmise from this what the term meant to them – chief, leader, descendant of a prophet, not necessarily the Prophet of Islam, Muhammad, but of Musa (Moses) and Harun (Aaron). Kidwai also mentions how a Bani Isra'il acquired the Saiyid status; see idem, *Biographical Sketch of Kidwais*.

[49] *Mir'at-i Madariya*, fls 103b–106b.

[50] Finally, following a correspondence with Madar on some theological questions, and on the advice of Jahangir Ashraf Simnani, Qazi Shihab accepted Madar's greatness (*dar zumra-i mu'taqidan-o-mukhlisan dakhil gashta wa sa'adat-i darain hasil namud*): *Mir'at-i Madariya*, fl. 97.

could harm him anywhere due to his unusually miraculous powers. Madar too ignored them, because of his unshaken belief (*nihayat-i istighraq*) in *wahdat al-wujud* and the path (*mashrab*) of *sulh-i kull*. Thereafter, citing Qazi Kanturi, 'Abd al-Rahman Chishti takes a historical angle to argue that such diversity of opinion and practice did not exist when Islam first began:

> The reason of the *'ulama'-i zahiri*'s opposition to Shah Madar was that he had learnt religion (*'ilm-i dini*) and acquired the gnosis of truth (*ma'arif-i yaqini*) from the sublime souls (*ruhaniyat-i pak*) of the Prophet and 'Ali. He had [also] read the divine books (*kutub-i asmani*) with Imam Muhammad Mahdi ibn Muhammad 'Askari, had transcended the differences between the various schools of jurisprudence (*mazahib*), and attained the true path (*mashrab-i haqq*). Before him, all *'ulama'* were like schoolchildren (*tifl-i maktab*). Madar followed exactly the path of the Prophet and of the imams of the Prophet's family. The *'ulama'* did not appreciate those acts and practices of his that did not correspond to the opinion and the analogies (*qiyas*) of the leaders of jurisprudence (*mujtahids*) and thus disputed with him.
>
> Their dispute apart, the whole world knows that the time of the Prophet witnessed none of the [later] differences of *mazahib*; and also, during the thirty years of the Pious Caliphate following the Prophet's death . . . there was little difference [in understanding] the Prophet's sayings and doings. After the first caliphate was over and power came to the Umayyads, and after them to the 'Abbasids, the rulers wanted the *'ulama'* to abide by them. Some of them, like Abu Hanifa and Ibn Hanbal [the founders of the Hanafite and Hanbalite schools], because of their integrity did not follow the wills of these rulers; they were therefore put in prison. Some scholars also died because of the rulers' tyranny.[51] Thus began the inevitable differences in many religious matters (*umur-i din*), and cases were decided according to the opinion and effort (*ra'i wa ijtihad*) of the leaders of jurisprudence (*mujtahids*). Subsequently in every place and at every age a new *mazhab* arose, and the *'ulama'* decided that whoever

---

[51] The text apparently suggests that Abu Hanifa and Ibn Hanbal themselves died of the rulers' tyranny, which is an exaggeration, and incorrect.

denied or deviated from the *mazhab* of his *mujtahid* was an infidel (*kafir*).⁵²

It is this historical tendency with roots in human disputation, Chishti contends, that explains the *'ulama*'s distrust of Shah Madar and his followers' unorthodox practices – which were noted in seventeenth-century accounts. Chishti continues:

> This matter [that differences would emerge among Muslims] was already known to the Prophet, and he had taken his companions in confidence and had told them that "my *umma* will be divided into seventy-two different sects, with only one of them being the true one." Thus, every group thought itself to be the true group, and [now] over seven hundred years have passed, with the *'ulama'* of each *mazhab* acting on the opinions of the *mujtahid*s of their schools. They thus have become hardened in such practices.
>
> Shah Madar pursued the practice (*suluk*) of the very first Islamic community, of the companions and the followers of the Prophet, and because of his own extreme concern for truth he wanted the people [of his time] to follow the *mashrab* of the straight path (*sirat-i mustaqim*). This is why the *'ulama'-i zahir* were prejudiced against him and turned against him everywhere. Some accused him of being a renegade, some said he was a Shi'i (*rafizi*), others said he followed Mahdism [of Saiyid 'Abd-Allah of Jaunpur], still others declared him an infidel (*kafir*). Everyone, depending on their affiliations, had their own reaction to him, and hurled stones at him. Eventually they all became ashamed of their acts. In the same way as they opposed Madar, at the time of the appearance of Imam Mahdi the *'ulama'* of each *mazhab* will oppose him.⁵³

Chishti here redefines the history of Islam, and since he is aware of the importance (and disputability) of the position he takes, he also adds part of the Islamic messianic tradition to his discourse, and in that context he brings in the names of the major scholars and saints with a view to lending support to his understanding.

⁵² *Mir'at-i Madariya*, fls 90b–91b.
⁵³ Ibid., fls 90b–92a.

Chishti writes then, drawing on Ibn al-'Arabi's *Futuhat-i Makkiya*, that after the coming of Imam Mahdi, religion will revert to what it was in the beginning, in the classical period of Islam, before the emergence of sectarian differences and squabbles:

> After the coming of Muhammad Mahdi, religion will be on the same path as it was when the Prophet himself was alive. Religion will be such that even were the Prophet alive, he would not command anything else. Thus, when the Imam comes, nothing will remain except this pure religion, pure in the opinion of the analogists (*ahl-i qiyas*, i.e. the jurists). Then, too, the *'ulama'* of each school (*mazhab*) will engage in debates with the Imam.[54]

As a conclusion, Chishti states that the religion of the Sufis is the religion of the time of the Prophet. In that period, because of the revelation and the grace of the rays of prophethood, the souls of the community were free from evil desire, and their beliefs were free from the tinge of difference: they were all of one heart, one opinion, one language (*hama yak dil wa yak ra'i wa yak zaban*). The hearts of the Sufis, when they are entranced by the sweetness of divine love, are completely indifferent to this world. In them the strains of all differences are annihilated and destroyed (*mustasil*). They see everyone with the eyes of grace and affection and are free from enmity and hostility (*'adawat wa mukhalafat*). They form the *firqa-i najiya*, i.e. the theologically correct sect that alone will receive salvation. And this is their unique religion, inherited from the Sufis of the early years of Islam. This is the religion that Shah Madar followed and propagated.[55]

Shah Madar's Unique Death

According to 'Abd al-Rahman Chishti, Shah Madar died in Makanpur on the last Thursday, Jumada I, 840 H/November 1436, during the reign of Sultan Ibrahim Sharqi. If indeed he was

[54] Ibid., fl. 92b.
[55] Ibid., fls 90b–93a.

born in 715 H/1315 in Syria, he lived for all of 120 years, having spent about 35 years in Syria, 40 years in Mecca and Medina, and the rest in Hindustan. The final moments of Madar's life are also presented by Chishti in an unusual, even unique way, recorded perhaps only for Madar, who had attained the high stage of *samadiyat*. He writes that when Madar realised his death was imminent, he asked his disciples to bring several pitchers of water from the river, then told them to keep them in his room and leave, for the angels (*mardan-i ghaib*) would come, wash him, and put him in a shroud. Then he closed the door and became busy with God (*mashghul be haqq*), while his disciples waited outside the door. After a while a voice came, announcing his death, and the door opened by itself. The disciples went into the room and saw Madar's body washed and shrouded and laid out to rest on a bench. They went to pray, for the angels had left and Sultan Ibrahim Sharqi built a tomb on his grave.[56] Thus ended Madar's long and unique life in 'Abd al-Rahman Chishti's recounting. The Prophet Moses called him Badi' (unique) and endowed him with his *wilayat*; the Prophet Muhammad and 'Ali taught him lessons in true Islam and bestowed upon him the position of *Qutb al-Madar* (axis of the orbit), confirmed later by the chief of the angelic world. Madar's prayers and Sufi rituals included one he called *badi' al-'aja'ib bi'l khair*, and he died too in a *badi'* (or unique) way.

Concluding Remarks

Why did Chishti compose this text? And how can we explain why he chose to highlight certain aspects of his narrative? Was he sanctifying the region that he himself came from by this association? Madar's chief Indian activities and engagements were in Makanpur, Jaunpur, and Awadh; and Chishti, as we know, came from the same region. Did he want to connect Madar, a Sufi from the fifteenth century who was important in common

---

[56] Ibid., fls 108 and 110.

memory, with the Chishti saints? In his narrative, Madar first visits the founder of the Indian Chishti *silsila* in Ajmer; he is projected to have taken guidance there for further missionary activities in Hindustan. Within that region Shaikh Abu al-Fath Chishti predicts Madar's coming when Qazi Mahmud Kanturi's father, Qazi Hamid 'Usmani, takes his son to Abul al-Fath and predicts that his son will be Madar's disciple. Also, a major saint of the region, Shah Mina of Lucknow, who was still young at the time of Madar, was blessed and predicted to be the Shah of the *wilayat* of Lucknow.[57] But most important is the need to consider how Chishti portrays Madar as obtaining his training in "true Islam" (*talqin-i islam-i haqiqi*); does this have a bearing on developments of the time when Chishti was compiling his text? Here it is interesting to note that, besides Islam, Chishti explains Madar's position as *mashrab-i sulh-i kull* – and, in fact, this is how he redefines Islam – for in his rereading of the Islamic past he defines (early) Islam through the concept of *mashrab-i sulh-i kull*. Can we connect Chishti's account here in this text with his accounts of Sufism and Sufis in his other writings, namely, *Mir'at al-Makhluqat*, and *Mir'at-i Mas'udi*?

'Abd al-Rahman Chishti was writing in seventeenth-century Mughal India, when the Mughal state promoted a set of policies with an aim to reduce the threat of conflict and confrontation between Sunnis and Shi'is, and also between Muslims and non-Muslims. In order to build this policy, Akbar took several measures which were not approved of by theologians and the *'ulama*, nor even by the newly arrived Sufi shaikhs – the Naqshbandis from Central Asia. The Naqshbandis' assertion of their disapproval of the new broad policy of tolerance resulted in their estrangement from the Mughal court. They could not tolerate the new ethos since they still harboured vivid memories of having been spiritual masters at the time of the Timurids in Central Asia, and they had come to India with their own ideas about the correct

---

[57] *Mir'at-i Madariya*, fls 101–103a.

form of Islam. Part of the Naqshbandis' political agenda, then, was to criticise the Mughals, and especially all of Akbar's policies, as trying to create an ethos antithetical to the spirit of true Islam. So the Naqshbandis, with Shaikh Ahmad Sirhindi in the lead, declared Akbar a heretic, and this remained the memory of Akbar in orthodox Sunni writings and in Naqshbandi–Mujaddidi circles.

This notional threat did not have much of an impact on the Mughal state under Akbar (d. 1605) and Jahangir (d. 1627). The Mughal ruling elites' effort continued to be to achieve proximity with local ruling elites; they had to compromise with them using whatever means were available – including entering into matrimonial alliances with non-Muslims. Akbar himself had taken non-Muslim women as wives; and Jahangir, during whose reign Chishti lived in the Mughal capital and began to advocate his view of Islam, approved of this, and in general adhered to Akbar's vision. Another important aspect of the social background in the seventeenth century was that the Mughals also depended very heavily on Iranian support. There was a long history of Iranians supporting the Mughals' ancestors: they had helped Babur when he was forced out of Khojand and Farghana by the Uzbek Shaybanids. Culturally, Iran was very much a force to be reckoned with, since Persian had spread far beyond Safavid borders and was a prestige language in all the "gunpowder empires", and beyond. The Mughals' ancestral lands too had been Persianised for a long time. A good many of the Iranians were Shi'is, and it was in the best interest of the Mughals not to do anything that might exacerbate sectarian differences.

The Chishtis, as we saw earlier in this book, had exercised a dominant influence over much of northern India at the time when Babur launched his victorious campaign against Ibrahim Lodi (d. 1526). Ibrahim Lodi's own personal master was a Chishti saint, whom he commanded to remain on the battlefield even during intense clashes so that he could confer blessings continuously. The Lodis' defeat was thus a blow to them. The second great blow to the Chishtis came when, due to the arrival of the Naqshbandis, they were no longer close to the royal family, since the Mughals and Naqshbandis were all Central Asian, and their spiritual master was 'Ubaid-Allah Ahrar (d. 1490). The Chishtis, then, found themselves ejected from the privileged circles of power. However, they had their own understanding of the social situation in India. Their doctrinal foundation was the concept of *wahdat al-wujud*, and their practices were very different from those of the newly arrived Central Asian Sufis, who typically thought that all non-Islamic customs must be avoided. The Chishtis had incorporated Braj and Awadhi *doha*s into their rituals, and in general embraced many practices considered "non-Muslim". We may take, by way of examples, the *Chandayan* by Mulla Da'ud, a Chishti Sufi; or Malik Muhammad Jayasi's *Padmavat*, where the story is Hindu in form but Muslim in spirit. Several features of Chishti tradition and practice were borrowed from local Hindu practices (e.g., *habs-i dam*). The Chishtis were, then, also eager to reclaim their place of prominence in the political world and would have been all too ready to advertise themselves as masters of such forms of adjustment, which the Mughals were open to in order to secure their power.

All of this is the social and political background that needs to be borne in mind when we consider the context in which 'Abd al-Rahman Chishti was writing his account of Shah Madar. It is of immense significance that he projects a story of one being sent from Medina with special instructions to go not to India, but first specifically to Ajmer, to learn what he needed in order to best spread the teachings of Islam in the subcontinent. It is also important to note that Madar is portrayed as an extreme and unorthodox figure. This, then, was also part of the Chishti vision of Islam in India. Chishti was able to appropriate the legend of Madar, which had lived on in the popular imagination, and adapt it for his own purposes, to present a viable theological and ideological alternative to the Naqshbandi political and religious creed. Indeed, the Chishtis had every reason to claim superiority over the Naqshbandis: they had been in India since the eleventh century and had been rooted in the countryside for many generations. Chishti, then, among other things, was also trying to sanctify the region from which he had emerged.

This was not insignificant, since many a Mughal ruler sought out stories of saints by sending people to collect those accounts from the countryside. They did this because they realised that such accounts were integral to the popular conception of Indian Islam. Jahangir even sent someone to a remote local ruler in a poorly accessible mountain area just to get a local report on the life of Salar Ma'sud Ghazi. We thus return in this instance to themes and threads that I have discussed earlier. Besides the esoteric aspects, rituals, and pious religious practices, Sufis were not indifferent to the politics of their time; their doctrines and hagiographical accounts were fairly clearly and frequently directed towards political ends.

5

Strategy and Imagination in a Mughal Sufi Story of Creation

Introduction

A SIGNIFICANT FEATURE OF Mughal Indian culture was the interest of its rulers in India's Hindu religious traditions and its "Hindu past". They commissioned translations into Persian of several major Hindu texts, including the *Mahabharata*.[1] With the appearance of these translations, Muslim scholars and divines were given access to pasts and legends that would have stretched their imagination. Muslims of the time traced the origins of the world, for instance, to the birth of Adam, who in their estimate lived around 7000 years earlier, while they now learned that according to the Hindu tradition the world and its inhabitants had existed for hundreds of thousands of years. Many of them must have dismissed these new discoveries as mere myth, but many others struggled to make sense of them, faced as they were with the need to develop effective strategies for survival in a heterogeneous religious environment. Shaikh Abu al-Fazl's (d. 1602) attempt to provide an account of Hindu cosmogony, and later in the seventeenth century Prince Dara Shukoh's (d. 1659) attempt to project the similarities between Islam and Hindu religious

---

[1] It was notably described by Abu al-Fazl as "the most honoured, most sacred and most comprehensive book" of the Hindus. See Abu al-Fazl, *A'in-i Akbari*, pp. 18–19. Also see *Mahabharat*, Persian translation.

traditions, were manifestations of such a struggle.² In the following pages, I discuss a similiar venture, in this instance an account of human genesis, as a story told by the eminent seventeenth-century Mughal Sufi whom we have repeatedly encountered in the earlier chapters, none other than Shaikh 'Abd al-Rahman Chishti (d. 1683).³

Stories and anecdotes had long been integral to Sufi discourses. A large number of *malfuz* texts comprised mostly anecdotes, while even in those where the discussion was predominantly doctrinal the exposition was interspersed with stories. Nizam al-Din Auliya', as Mir Hasan Sijzi reports in the *Fawa'id al-Fu'ad*, related stories from Baghdad, Bukhara, and other cities of the Islamic East in almost every *majlis* with his disciples and devotees. We have in some Sufi texts, such as in Khwaja Nasir 'Ali 'Andalib's *Nala-i 'Andalib* (compiled in eighteenth-century Delhi), the delineation of the entire *tariqa* code cloaked in tales.⁴ The story that I am concerned with here, found in Chishti's treatise *Mir'at al-Makhluqat*,⁵ has no roots in the Islamic world. It comes almost exclusively from

---

² Abu al-Fazl, *A'in-i Akbari*, ed. Syed Ahmad Khan, see the chapter titled *Ahwal-i Hindustan*, pp. 360–556; English transl., vol. III, pp. 1–358; Dara Shukoh, *Majma 'al-Bahrain*, pp. 1–82. See also Hasrat, *Dara Shikuh*, Part Two, pp. 174–292. For a dismissive treatment of this knowledge, see Bada'uni, *Muntakhab al-Tawarikh*, Vol. 2, pp. 178, 223, 235, 279; Firishta, *Tarikh-i Firishta*, Vol. I, pp. 11–29.

³ For biographical details and some descriptions of his writings, see Rizvi, *A History of Sufism in India*, Vol. 2, pp. 27, 289, 368–9, 396; Ernst and Lawrence, *Sufi Martyrs of Love*; Digby, "Mas'udi", pp. 783–4; Amin, "On Retelling", pp. 24–43; Amin, "Un saint guerrier", pp. 265–93. See also Faruqui, *Medieval India*, pp. 52, 54, 62, 126n.

⁴ Cf. Islam, *Sufism in South Asia*, pp. 1–67, for a discussion on stories and parables in Sufi texts. See also for examples, Dehlavi, *Fawa'id al-Fu'ad*; 'Andalib, *Nala-i 'Andalib*.

⁵ The text, still unpublished, is one of five major works by 'Abd al-Rahman Chishti. Several manuscripts are available in India and elsewhere. I have read and collated three of them: (*a*) Aligarh MS. (Maulana Azad Library, Aligarh Muslim University, Aligarh, Habibganj Collections, *Farsiya Tasawwuf*,

the world of the Hindus, evoking a time when Islam had yet to appear on the world stage.

I first read about the *Mir'at al-Makhluqat* in S.A.A. Rizvi's *History of Sufism in India*. Rizvi noted that he employed Chishti's writings, including *Mir'at al-Makhluqat*, as a major source for his history, and he was perhaps the first modern historian to do so. K.A. Nizami, another noted historian of Sufism in India, who wrote extensively both in English and Urdu, nowhere mentions this text. Though Bruce Lawrence and Carl Ernst used and discussed another very important work by Chishti, namely the *Mir'at al-Asrar*, they did not refer to the *Mir'at al-Makhluqat*.[6] On the other hand the text has not been ignored altogether, as a comprehensive study of it is expected soon.[7] The treatment of it by Rizvi was, however, somewhat problematic. Identifying it with the text entitled *Yoga-Vashista*, Rizvi writes:

> Shaikh 'Abdu'r-Rahman Chishti, a descendant of Shaikh Ahmed 'Abdu'l-Haqq of Rudauli, who succeeded to the leadership of the Chishti order in 1032/1622 was an interesting personality. A scholar of Sanskrit, he gave new explanations to the *Bhagavad-Gita* in the light of Islam, most notably in his work, the *Mir'atu'l Makhluqat*, which associated the Hindu cosmogony of *Yogavasistha* philosophy with Muslim Beliefs.[8]

21/343); (*b*) Chishti Khanqah, Sarkhej, Ahmadabad MS. (microfilm, Noor Microfilms Centre, Iran Cultural House, Embassy of Iran, New Delhi); and (*c*) British Library, London MS. (India Office Library Or. 1883). All references here (unless specifically cited) are from the British Library MS., which is bound and paginated continuously with several other manuscripts, including 'Abd al-Rahman Chishti's rendering of the *Gita*, titled *Mir'at al-Haqa'iq*.

[6] Ernst and Lawrence, *Sufi Martyrs of Love*.

[7] Svevo D'Onofrio and M. Karimi Zanjani-Asl are preparing a critical edition and translation of the text, to be published soon. Earlier, Mohammad Zaki had published a brief note, "*Mir'atul Makhluqat* of Abdur Rehman Chishti", pp. 352–4.

[8] Rizvi, *History of Sufism*, Vol. I, p. 14. Rizvi briefly describes the contents of *Mir'at al-Makhluqat* elsewhere as well: Rizvi, *History of Sufism*, Vol. 2,

Nowhere in the text, however, as we will see below, is there any reference to the *Yogavasistha*, even though the narrator in the text is none other than Vashista Muni himself. This confusion may have arisen because Chishti identifies the source of his story as '*Malfuz-i Bashist*' (The Utterances of Bashist). This could well be mistaken for a translation of the *Yogavasistha*, particularly in light of the fact that a couple of actual Persian translations of the *Yogavasistha* were also titled by their translators as *Farmuda-i Bashist* (The Sayings of Bashist) or *Kalimat-i-Bashist* (The Words of Bashist).[9]

The *Mir'at-al-Makhluqat*, which Chishti claims is a Persian translation of the Sanskrit original by the sage Vasistha, is centred on the figures of Mahadeva and Krishna. It effectively makes use of the concept of *yugas* in order to present a relativist argument that places the Prophets Adam and Muhammad (and the latter's grandson Husain) in a narrative connecting them with events from the time of the early-Hindu tradition. It is currently unclear what the Sanskrit work was that Chishti used, or whether it even existed. It seems to bear some generic resemblance to *Bhavishya Purana* materials. I shall show how the *Mir'at* and its author combined rhetorical and political strategies to provide a reconciliation between Hindu and Muslim traditions without surrendering the key ideas that gave a superior position to the Muslim tradition. I will contrast this work with similar stories and narratives presented by Chishti and other Muslim scholars elsewhere.

The Story

'Abd al-Rahman Chishti begins his *Mir'at al-Makhluqat* with the claim that he has read several well-known Indian history books and

---

p. 396. He seems influenced here by the description of this text in Rieu's catalogue: Rieu, *Catalogue of the Persian Manuscripts*, Vol. III, p. 1034a.

[9] Cf. Panipati, *Jug Bashist*, p. 9; the Bibliotheque nationale de France, Paris, MS. Supplement Persan 16, f. 5b. Panipati also termed his translation "*sakhunan-i haqa'iq bayan*" of Bashist. For the phrase "*kalimat-i Bashist*",

scriptures, written in antiquity, in search of an account of Adam, the father of humankind (Abu al-Bashar). Initially, he failed in his search, but "after a great effort" he then "discovered a book written by Bashist Muni in which the births of Adam and Muhammad along with their descendants were given in detail." Chishti calls this text *Malfuz-i Bashist*, invoking the well-known Sufi genre of "table-talk", even though, as we will see below, it is written in the *purana* style and is purportedly borrowed from the *Uttarakhanda*.[10] He alleges that the leaders of the Hindu community, because of their prejudices (*ta'assub*), had bowdlerised their books and kept this narrative in them secret (*makhfi midashtand*).[11] Chishti thus implied that they did so because it contained information in support of Islam and the beliefs of Muslims. His tone is polemical, but interestingly in the succeeding passages he also invokes a close relationship between the traditions of the two communities:

> Bashist was an accomplished member of the community of the *jinns* and had a position of *muni*. Muni in their terminology is used for prophet. Bashist communicated the knowledge to that community, having received it from Mahadeva. Mahadeva was Abu al-Jinn [father of the jinns] and he was the [principal] prophet (*rasul-i mursal*) of the jinns. Tabari and other historians agree on the fact that there were prophets amongst the jinns for their guidance and education.[12] The

---

see Qutb-i Jahani, *Atwar fi Hall al-Asrar*. See also the published version of Qutbjahani's translation, *Majmu'a-i Rasa'il*, p. 47.

[10] *Mir'at al-Makhluqat*, f. 238a. Sarkhej Ahmadabad MS. (p. 1) has *Malfuz*, only, Aligarh MS. (f. 1a) calls it *Kitabi-i Bashist*.

[11] Chishti, *Mir'at al-Makhluqat*, f. 239a. It is difficult to say what exactly this treatise was. Chishti generally mentions unknown books as sources for his writings elsewhere too. See his *Mir'at-i Madari*, British Museum MS., f. 2b, where he mentions *Iman-i Mahmudi*, a biographical account of Shah Madar by one Qazi Kanturi as his source. See also Shahid Amin's writings for the *Mir'at-i Mas'udi*. Chishti's story in *Mir'at al-Makhluqat* seems to have been drawn on several *puranas* that he may have read or the *kathas* based on *puranas* that he may have heard.

[12] Tabari (d. 922) mentions the jinn in his *tarikh* in the context of his

Qur'an says "and the *jinns*, we had created before, from the fire of a scorching wind . . ."[13] The author of *Rauzat al-Safa'* reports from Ibn 'Abbas [a companion and cousin of the Prophet] that the name of Abu al-Jinn was Soma with the title of Jann and that in the Book of Adam it is written that Jann's name was Tamus . . . In sum the author, Tabari, and *Rauzat al-Safa'*,[14] have mentioned the four ages (*zamana*) as four cycles (*daura*) of the stars (*sawabit*).[15]

---

discussion of the angels, Iblis' position in their midst, and also where he (Tabari) discusses the creation of Adam. Cf. Tabari, *Tarikh al-Rusul wa al-Muluk*, Vol. I, pp. 81–90. In his *tafsir* (commentary), however, interpreting the verses, "O you assembly of jinns and humans! Did you not receive messengers from among you, who told you of My signs, and warned you about the meeting of this day?' (Qur'an, 6:130), he mentions several *hadiths* and early-Muslim scholars' views to show if there were prophets from among the jinns themselves. Cf. Tabari, *Jami 'al-Bayan*, Vol. 9, pp. 559–62. See also Vol. 14 for his comments on the verse, "I did not create the jinns and the humans except to worship Me alone" (Qur'an, 51: 56). It is significant that in some *tafsirs* written in India in the later Mughal period, Hindu deities are identified as some such jinn prophets. Qazi Sana-Allah (d. 1810), *Tafsir-i Mazhari*, Vol. 4, pp. 217–18. For Qazi Sana-Allah (Qadi Thana'-Allah Panipati), see Rizvi, *Shah 'Abd al 'Aziz*, pp. 558–73.

[13] "*wa'l janna khalaqna-hu min qablu min nar is-sumun*". This verse follows the verse, "We created man from sounding clay, from mud moulded into shape'. Qur'an, 15: 26 and 15: 27.

[14] Here the text which has signs of deletion following the words "Tabari" and "*awurda*" (has mentioned) has to be read with some care. Since Chishti earlier mentions Tabari and *Rauzat al-Safa'*, when he sums up, the scribe first wrote both names and then deleted Tabari. He deletes the verb "*awurda*" too, which is an obvious error, for the verb for this sentence "*qarar dada and*" comes later. We know that the discussion of time (*zaman*) in Tabari's *Tarikh* is totally different. Cf. Tabari, *Tarikh al-Rusul wa al-Muluk*, Vol. 1, pp. 9–80. But *Rauzat al-Safa'* does mention cycles (*dauras*) of time, and also cycles of "recompense", an echo of which we will notice below in Chishti's description in jinns' time of a sequence – from their glory to their dishonour and decline. Cf. Mir Khwand, *Tarikh-i Rauzat al-Safa'*, Vol. I, pp. 20–1, English transl., Vol. I, pp. 36–8.

[15] Chishti, *Mir'at al-Makhluqat*, f. 239b; for cycles of time, *Rauzat al-Safa'*, pp. 36–8. Mahadeva in the Hindu tradition is the god Shiva, and Bashist

Chishti then describes the four eras (or *yugas*) according to the Hindu calculation of time:

> The first of four ages was *Satjug*, comprising over seventeen lakhs twenty-eight thousand years (1,728,000), the second was *Treta*, comprising twelve lakh ninety-six thousand years (1,296,000), the third is known as *Dwapar* which comprised over eight lakh sixty-four thousand years (864,000), and the fourth is *Kaljug*, comprising over four lakhs and thirty-two thousand years (432,000). Today, which is the one thousand and forty-first year (1141 AH) from the *hijrat* of our Prophet, there have passed four thousand seven hundred and thirty years (4730) from the Kaljug... In two of these four ages, the jinns reigned supreme in the inhabited portion of the earth (*rubʿ-i maskun*). They had a law (*shariʿat*), given by God, and acted according to it. During the third era most of them became too involved in this world (*ghalba-i kasrat-i dunya*), and began to turn their faces from and revolted against the Divine Commands. [Subsequently] God commanded the angels to chastise them until they were annihilated.[16]

Chishti seems comfortable with this calculation of time, for in some earlier Islamic literature too the time before Adam was divided into four ages, even though the duration of each of the four ages was much less than a Hindu *yuga*.[17] Further, in the Sufi tradition, as we will see below, the world had existed much before the traditional figure of Adam. Chishti thus begins with a language of universalism, a plea for the possibility of some kind of intellectual exchange with Hinduism. However, he continues to maintain important differences. Hindu gods, he says, lived

---

(Vasistha) is the noted sage (*rishi*) whose speech comprises the well-known text, *Yogavasistha*. Cf. Mani, *Puranic Encyclopaedia*, pp. 723–31, 834–7.

[16] Chishti, *Mirʾat al-Makhluqat*, f. 240a.

[17] Cf. Mir Khwand, *Rauzat al-Safaʾ*, pp. 20–1. According to Ibn ʿArabi, the jinns had lived and been in control of this world for 60,000 years before the creation of humankind. There were twelve principal groups, and they fought among themselves. Cf. Ibn ʿArabi, *Al-Futuhat al-Makkiya*, Vol. 2, pp. 276–86.

before Adam. Rama, Krishna, and Arjuna had no connection with Adam. He writes that it is incorrect to think,

> ... as some people do, that they were the descendants of Abu al-Bashr (Adam). Ramchand lived during Treta and Bashist has written that he was a descendant of Brahma, who lived in Satjug. Mahadeva also lived in Satjug and both these two persons were created by absolute God, without mother and father. Brahma was created out of light (*nur*) and fire (*nar*) and Mahadeva from fire and air (*bad*), while Adam was created towards the end of the Dwapar age. Although Kishan and Arjun were contemporaries of the descendants of Adam, Biyas [Vyasa] has traced their genealogy to Raja Jada. Raja Jada also lived in the Tratya [Treta] age and because of this connection Kishan is known as *Jada bansi*, that is, from the family (*nasl*) of Raja Jada. In fact, until the time of Kishan and Arjun, Adam's descendants had not come to the country of Hind and there the jinns and '*unsuri*, i.e. non-*nur*, angels,[18] were still in command. Biyas writes that the coming of Kishan was for the annihilation of Kans and for the killing of the entire community of the jinns in the battle of Mahabharat. The purpose was to vacate Hind so that Adam's descendants would take it over. Thus the time of the jinns ended.[19]

Having said this, Chishti hastens to add that in the exterminated past, too, the world was graced with the Divine Truth, brought from Heaven by Hindu gods and sages, and this is what he projects to be a true Sufi's religion (*mashrab*):

> Mahadeva jinn was made of fire but in his own community he was matchless, both in physical and spiritual perfection. He would come out with the message of oneness of God (*tauhid*) and would divulge

---

[18] Earlier in the introductory note in the *Mir'at*, Chishti mentions two categories of angels (*mala'ik*), one *nurani*, that is, made of light, and another '*unsuri*, made of elements, and he says that these angels are the same as those identified as *nari*, that is, made of fire. Chishti, *Mir'at al-Makhluqat*, f. 238b.

[19] Chishti, *Mir'at al-Makhluqat*, f. 240b. For Kans (Kamsa) the notorious demon-king of Mathura, who was killed by Krishna, and Kishan (Krishna) and Ram (Rama), the Hindu gods, see Mani, *Puranic Encyclopaedia*, pp. 382–83, 420–9, 631–40.

the secrets. The Qur'anic verse, "I did not create the jinns and the humans except to worship Me alone",[20] is proof of the (divine) gnosis of the jinns. It is written in the *Tafsir-i Zahidi* that before the coming of our Prophet, the Devs and the jinns would rise high to the sky and listen to the conversation of the angels. After the advent of the Prophet, however, their way to the sky has been closed . . . In believing this there is no harm. The religion of the Sufis is that we should appropriate the good thing and good word (*sukhan-i nik*) from each community. This is the message in the *hadith* of the Prophet, "take what is good and pure, reject what is dirty and impure".[21]

Thereafter 'Abd al-Rahman Chishti returns to the story by providing details of what necessitated the creation of Adam and the laying of the foundation of "Islamic time" at the beginning of Kaljug. For the principal part of his story, as we will see, Chishti – or else the person who wrote the original Sanskrit – adopts the *Purana* and *Kathasaritasagara* style, apparently to make it sound like a genuine tale told by Mahadeva in response to his wife Parvati's queries – the *Kathasaritasagara* and some *Puranas* were available in Persian in Mughal India at this time.[22]

---

[20] "*ma khalaqtu'l jinna wa'l insa illa liya' budun.*" Qur'an, 51: 56.

[21] Chishti, *Mir'at al-Makhluqat*, f. 241a. This *hadith*, "*khuz ma safa, da' ma kadir*", is oft-cited in Sufi texts: see Kashani, *Misbah al-Hidaya*, p. 281; Sadriniya, *Farhang-i Masurat-i Mutun-i 'Irfani*, p. 230. Amongst the important Sufi commentaries on the Qur'an, *Tafsir-i Zahidi* by Abu Nasr al-Raruhaki, is still unpublished. An important manuscript is available in the Khuda Bakhsh Oriental Public Library in Patna: see Muqtadir, ed., *Catalogue of Arabic & Persian Manuscripts*. Unfortunately, I did not have access to any of the manuscripts and could therefore not verify Chishti's statement. For a summary of Qur'an commentaries, see Godlas, "Sufism", pp. 350–61.

[22] For a useful discussion of *puranas* as a genre constructed around the central principle of "revealing mysteries", see Rocher, *The Puranas*; idem, "Reflections on One Hundred and Fifty Years", pp. 64–76; Bonazzoli, "Remarks on the nature of the *Puranas*", pp. 77–113; idem, "Composition of the *Puranas*", pp. 254–80. For the *kathasaritasagara* style, Somadeva, *Tales from the Kathasaritasagara*, Introduction and esp. p. 2. For reference to the text in English translation, see Somadeva, *The Ocean of Story*, Vol. 1, pp. 4–6, 10.

Since during the time of Satjug (*zaman-i satjug*), that is the first age, the '*unsuri* angels and the jinns led their lives in comfort and luxury, with no problem, they grew haughty. During the entire period of Treta, the second age, they did things contrary to divine commands. At this time, Mahadeva said to them that if they wish for their welfare, they should not give up the path of the divine law (*shari'a*). They did not listen to his advice because of their arrogance. They were too attached to the world [their own]. Mahadeva was ashamed [at his advice being turned down by his own community]. He told these rebels, "Beware, God willing, during the time of Dwapar, God will create a person who will not leave a trace of you in the inhabited part of the earth." Having said this, he set out for Kailash.[23]

Mahadeva's wife, Parvati, heard all this in astonishment. She followed her husband. One day, when Mahadeva was well settled in his appointed place in Kailash mountain and was resting, Parvati considered it opportune to ask a question: "Since the day when you said that in the Dwapar age God would create one who will annihilate the entire community of the *devatas* (gods) and *daits* (*daityas*, demons), and so on and will take over the inhabited part of the earth, I have continued in amazement. Now, please tell me the nature of this person." Since Mahadeva had immense love for his wife, he started telling her the true story (*bayan-i waqi'*).[24]

Here, 'Abd al-Rahman Chishti breaks his narrative, inserting a parenthesis to clarify how this Mahadeva–Parvati conversation came into this world through Vasistha Muni, and why he translated

---

The text was also available in Persian in Mughal India. We may speculate that Chishti may have had access to this version, known as *Darya-i Asmar*, translated by Mustafa ibn Khaliqdad 'Abbasi. See 'Abbasi, *Darya-i Asmar*, pp. 9–11, 13–14. Some elements of the puranic stories were also to be found in Abu al-Fazl, *A'in-i Akbari*, ed. Syed Ahmad Khan, p. 532; English transl., pp. 318–19.

[23] Mount Mahameru, with the golden-coloured peak of Himavan (Himalaya), the seat of Shiva, according to the *Puranas*. See Mani, *Puranic Encyclopaedia*, pp. 364–5, 462–3.

[24] Chishti, *Mir'at al-Makhluqat*, f. 241.

it from Sanskrit, "the language of God", into Persian. He says that at the time Mahadeva started telling the story,

> Bashisht Muni, busy with prayers at the base of the Kailash mountain, overheard it. Since he was immensely devoted to Mahadeva, he wrote (*dar qalam awurd*) all the details. From Bashist, Sut and Saunak, who were great scholars in Namikhar, report these details (*dar qaum-i khwud mujahid-i kamil budand wa 'abid wa zahid, anha az Bashist Mun naql mikunand*),[25] the *ashloks* of which are translated here. Initially, I had intended to communicate and copy these *ashloks* verbatim but since not everybody can understand them, I have given here only one of the [original] *ashloks* as evidence. The rest are in translation so that all understand them without difficulty (*bitakalluf*).[26]

Chishti then picks up the thread to continue with what Mahadeva said in response to Parvati's question:

---

[25] Sut (Suta) and Saunaka: Suta was the disciple of Vyasa, who learnt the *Puranas* and *Mahabharata* from him and recounted them to Saunaka and the other *rishis* assembled at Naimisaranya (Nimasar, in the modern district of Sultanpur, Uttar Pradesh). Saunaka was the one who organised the assembly. Mani, *Puranic Encyclopaedia*, pp. 517, 774; see also Rocher, *The Puranas*, pp. 53–9, 161. Abu al-Fazl writes Nimasar as Nimakhar, which he describes as a "shrine of great resort", with numerous temples and a tank called Brahmawaratkund, and also the springhead of a stream about which the Brahmans say that "its sand shapes itself into the form of *Mahadeo* which quickly disappears again and of whatever is thrown in, as rice and the like, no trace remains", *A'in-i Akbari*, ed. Syed Ahmad Khan, p. 327, English transl., p. 183.

[26] Chishti, *Mir'at al-Makhluqat*, f. 240b. Chishti here cites a *shloka*: "*aado manya pra'it bodha ait mahesha nilakanthi hast maha kotaha tarkand hadiya*", which appears to contain some Sanskrit words but is totally unintelligible. I approached several Sanskrit specialists to read and make sense of this *shloka*, but to no avail. The *shloka* may have been distorted because of the Persian copyists' ignorance of the language, as Chishti himself seems to know Sanskrit, and we know that he translated the *Gita* as *Mir'at al-Haqa'iq*. Cf. Vassie, "Persian Interpretations of the Bhagavadgita". We will see below his unusual familiarity with Sanskrit philosophical texts.

O Parvati, he will have a long life and will be the best of all creatures. His eyes will be bulging like lotus (*nilufar*) flowers; his face will be illumined like thousands of full moons. O Parvati, when Brahma manifests that world-adoring and matchless person in the being of Adam, the people shall be helpless all around and fall in prostration before him. It is about this situation that Shaikh Farid al-Din ʿAttar [d. c. 1230] writes:

> *Gar nabude zat-i haq andar wujud.*
> *Ab-o-gil ra kai malak karde sujud.*

> If God Himself were not manifest in his person, how then would the angels have prostrated before a person made of mud and water.[27]

O Parvati, at that time God will command all the creatures to prostrate themselves before Adam, all *devtas*, *rishis*, *daits*, *rakshas*, et cetera, will then fall down and be prostrate. God has said, "and when we said to the angels, fall prostrate before Adam, they fell prostrate, except Iblis; he refused, and was arrogant and a disbeliever."[28] O Parvati, when all the creatures have fallen prostrate, a *devata* named Hanwant, that is, ʿAzazil, will refuse to prostrate himself, and out of jealousy he will utter words in contempt, and say that this is the worst creature, created out of the dirty earth, while my creation is from a delicate fire. He will then address the other *devatas* and say: "O dear ones, please do justice, how can I be prostrate before him?" The Word of God that he [Iblis] said – "I am better than he; You created

---

[27] There are several verses by Farid al-Din ʿAttar with strong affinities to this verse, besides being in the same metre. Cf. ʿAttar, *Musibat-nama*, pp. 58, 242; idem, *Ushtur-nama*, pp. 30, 302–3, under *hikayat-i adam*. In the *Asrar-nama* ʿAttar gives the same verse in a different order: "*dar adam bud nuri az wujudash/wagarna kai malak karde sujudash*" (there existed a light of His Being in Adam / otherwise how could the angels have prostrated before him): idem, *Asrar-nama*, p. 47. Interestingly, another poet, Amir Husaini Haravi, cites the same verse with a difference in the second part of the first line of the verse. Instead of ʿAttar's "*zat-i haq andar wujud*", Amir Hasan writes "*partav-i haq dar wujud*": Haravi, *Masnawi-ha-i ʿIrfani*, p. 44.

[28] "*wa iz qulna lil malaʾikati usjudu fasajadu illa iblis aba wa istakbara wa kana min al-kafirin*", Qurʾan, 2: 34.

me from fire, and You created him from clay"[29] – carries the same sense. O Parvati, Hanwant *devata* shall turn disobedient knowingly because all *devatas* will see that God made Adam with His own hands and that He instilled His own light into him. Hanwant humiliated himself because of his arrogance and ignorance. He will be neither in heaven nor in any other place where Brahma lives, nor in my place, nor in the place of any other *devatas* or *gandharb* [heavenly beings]. He will be nowhere near any *rishi* nor the rajas, nor even in the company of the *jogis*. No one will give him a place and he will become a vagabond (*sargardan*), roaming between the earth and the sky. O Parvati, arrogance is the worst vice, a real *'arif* [man of gnosis] is one who regards God as present and watchful everywhere and remains humble and obedient. Since he looked at Adam with contempt, he was thrown into Hell. O Parvati, God has given Adam the kingdom of the seven climes (*badshahi-ye haft iqlim*), endowing him with full strength, bravery, and all kinds of sciences of the people of ancient times. God says, "and He taught Adam all the names".[30] O Parvati, all beings created of fire will fear Adam, he will dominate over all others, will make the residence of his descendants the entire earth and thus bring the world under his control.[31]

Chishti then shows how, with the birth of Adam, began the history of the human beings who inhabit the world of the time in which he and others, both Muslims and Hindus, live. Parvati then asked Mahadeva how a woman could be created for him, made of clay and possessing such beauty, bravery, and gnosis. Mahadeva is said to have replied:

> O Parvati, his woman will be created out of his left side, she will be like the full moon, her body will be dazzling like pure gold, she will be born as a sixteen-year-old girl. And from that very moment, the life will be joyous (*ba'aish*). She will be the most perfectly beautiful woman ... And people having seen his world-adoring beauty will say she is Parvati and that he is Mahadeva, while as a matter of

---

[29] "*ana khairun minhu khalaqatani min narin wa khalaqtahu min tin*", Qur'an, 38: 76.
[30] "*wa 'allama adam al asma'a kullaha*", Qur'an, 2: 31.
[31] Chishti, *Mir'at al-Makhluqat*, f. 242.

fact you and I will be sitting over the mountain of Kailash, living a joyous life there.

Mahadeva then continues in the same vein:

O Parvati, the first son that will be born of them will be called Badila, he will be very strong and will perform several miracles. Then there will be a daughter who will be married to him. Badila then, accompanied by his wife, will leave Adam to settle [in other parts of] the earth. Within a little time there will be many sons and daughters, steadily taking control of the world. A second son of Adam will be named Hansila, he will be so brave and strong that all the jinns and *daits* will fall obedient to him. Whoever refuses to obey him will be killed (*halak*). And then there will be another daughter who will be handed over in marriage to Hansila. The third son of Adam will be named Dahanki and will be fearless, will not accept Brahma and Bishan and will contemptuously annul all the rituals and prayers of their faith. Wherever their places of worship will be, he will urinate over them. And thus our faith will encounter evils. He will do everything, religious or worldly, opposed to our *devatas*. Adam's fourth son will be named Badhal. Five *iqlims* (claims, countries) will be under his control, some of these he will forcefully wrest from the *devatas* and *daits*. He will also collect *kharaj* (tributes, revenues) from them forcibly. He will do the thing which should never have taken place, all rulers will be obedient to him and he will bring in a new *shari'at*. O Parvati, in the same manner, each son of Adam will be married to the daughter who will follow. In all, there will be twenty-one sons and twenty-one daughters, and of them two sons will clash with each other over one daughter as a result of which one of the sons will be killed. The survivor, taking that girl with him, will set out for the country of Koshal where he will grow in power and strength, accumulate piles of gold and silver, extracting them from the mines as well as the mountains and will distribute them to the people. Many thus will go to his country and according to their own desire will get the gold and silver. He will be a great king and will repent for the sin he committed, and will do excessive prayers, dressed all the time in blue. O Parvati, from the sons of Adam there will be countless people born. From one son there will be one thousand, from one thousand there will be one lakh, and from the one lakh there will be one crore, and so on. I cannot in fact give you the exact figure of the descendants of Adam.[32]

The names of Adam's sons and daughters are strange here and, even though some of the details remind us of the Biblico-Islamic story of the clash between Habil and Qabil (or Abel and Cain), the survivor takes the girl with him to Koshal, a country with an evidently Indian name. An Islamic story thus acquires an Indic colour. 'Abd al-Rahman Chishti's claim apart, his text is much more than a mere translation of Vashista's story. While he tries to register the voices of his dramatis personae in the way that a *pauranika* would have done, he makes his own presence noticed all through as central narrator. As a matter of fact, a large portion of the details here are from familiar Islamic literature. This becomes clearer as we move to the remaining parts of the story. Chishti supplies first the deep prehistory and then, as an astute narrator, brings it up to recognisable contemporary times. Here he narrates the significance of the birth of the Prophet Muhammad, his mission, the Qur'an, and Islam for people in the age of Kali:

> [Mahadeva said: After] six thousand years, (when "Adam's descendants will have adopted strange ways of living and the earth will be fed up with their sinfulness") the Almighty (God) will create a wonderful person from among the children of Adam in the country of Mundali, which is located between the seas, a land which will be appropriate for [God] Bishan. Upon this Parvati asked Mahadeva: "Tell me the truth, whether the person who will be created by God in such a blessed place, will be born in the house of a *devata* or a *rishi*." In response Mahadeva said, "O Parvati, he will be from the loin of Kant Bunjh, who will be in wisdom and gnosis like an ocean so that from him [what] will emerge [will be] a pearl. And the name of his wife will be 'Sak Rekha' [Sagarika]. He will have read three *Beds* – *Siyam Bed, Rig Bed*, and *Jajar Bed* – and the fourth *Bed, Atharban Bed* he would leave after having read up to the letters, '*alif, lam*' alone."[33]

[32] Ibid., f. 243.

[33] A version of this part is also available on a website, www.ezsoftech/akram/orpohetprophecies.asp, which shows the nineteenth-century milieu of

Clearly, this part has special value for 'Abd al-Rahman Chishti. He thus buttresses it with a statement by the sage Vyasa,[34] the master narrator of the *Mahabharata* and the *Puranas*, as well as with Vasistha Muni's emphasis on the significance of his telling, when replying to a question and doubts expressed by his pupils, Sut and Saunak, regarding the truth of the story. Chishti writes:

> Sut and Saunak asked Bashist that as he [Kant Bunjh] was to be like the ocean in gnosis, why then would he refuse to go ahead in the fourth *Bed* beyond *alif lam*. Bashist replied: "Brahma created the four *Beds* [for the use in the four different ages], which were all taught to some of the '*unsuri devatas* who were really able and were advised to work according to the *Siyam* in Satjug, *Rig* in Tratya [Treta], and *Jajar* in Dwapar. The Almighty would then create people from the globe (*kura*) of the earth who would practise according to the *Atharban Bed*. There are four *charns* (sections) in the *Atharban Bed*. Three of these will be read by Adam and his other descendants. The fourth one, which will combine in itself the purpose and substance (*maqsud*) of all the *Beds* will be practised by none other but Mahamat. If anyone will read the fourth *charn* without the permission of Mahamat he will get no benefit. Kant Bunjh will not read this fourth *charn* of *Atharban Bed* so that it remains intact as if held in trust (*amanat*)." Up to this point was the speech of Bashist.

Chishti's language of universalism here assumes added strength. The prophets before Adam, to whom even though the Divine Truth had been revealed, were still jinns, genealogically different from Adam and the other prophets of humankind. But the books of both worlds, as Vasistha here affirms in Chishti's words, have

---

religious disputations in India. It cites and translates from the introduction (*muqaddima*) of a commentary on the Qur'an entitled *Anwar al-Qur'an* by one Maulana Sayyid Rahat Husain Gopalpuri. Gopalpuri apparently read this part as drawn from "Baran Uttar khand" (Brahmottarakhand). He also gives the meanings of the words "Kant Bunjh" and "Sank Rakhiya" – mentioned by Mahadeva as the names of Muhammad's father and mother – as "Abdullah" and "Amina", which were their actual names in Arabic.

[34] Mani, *Puranic Encyclopaedia*, pp. 885–8.

the same lineage; they are what the Hindus of his time identified as the Vedas. The first three of these were guides for the jinns' eras, whereas the last expressed itself in the four major Divine Books – Zabur, Taurah, Injil, and Qur'an – for mankind at different stages of their history. Chishti inserts all this as a parenthesis. He then continues with the story of Muhammad, now endorsed by Vyasa too, attributing to the Prophet Muhammad nearly all the virtues and miraculous qualities that were then popular within Indian Sufi Islam. According to Chishti, Mahadeva tells Parvati that Kant Bhunj will have three sons and the name of the third son, who will survive, will be Mahamat, that is Muhammad, who will be endowed with excellent etiquette (*auza'*), will come circumcised, will have no hair anywhere on his body except on his head and beard, and will not worship the gods that the people of his tribe worship.

> Biyas has also written in his book, *Bhabikh (Bhavishya) Uttarpuran*, that in the future, that is Kaljug, Mahamat will be born, whom the Muslims will call Muhammad. He will always have the shade of a cloud over his head and he will not cast a shadow. On his body no flies will ever sit. And for him the earth will get shrunk (*ura tayy-i zamin khwahad bud*) and he will have enormous virility, he will struggle only for the *din* (faith, religion), will have no concern for *dunya* (this world), and whatever he will gain he will spend in the name of God. He will eat little; the king of the time will be his enemy but he will be the friend of the people. The Almighty will send to him a *Puran* of thirty *adhyay* (divisions), that is the *siparas* of the Qur'an will be revealed to him, and everyone acting according to this book will reach God. At that time there will be no path left to reach God except his.
> And, Mahamat, Mahadeva reports, will not simply set aside ... all the prayers and *shari'ats* of previous ages, he will impart teachings of his own *shari'at* to the people of his time. He will struggle to make the world like his own self and ... in the manner that we write the *sankh*, that is an era, in our books, in the same way will they have their *sanat* (era) of Mahamat until the end of the Kaljug age in their books.[35]

[35] Chishti, *Mir'at al-Makhluqat*, ff. 244a–b.

Time, Chishti implies, will then be measured according to a new calendar, and nothing will be left outside it.

The martyrdom of Husain, the Prophet's grandson, forms the third important part of the story, wherein we also note a significant feature of Chishti Sufi ideology, namely the high stature of 'Ali and his scion.[36] The Prophet Muhammad, Chishti writes, reporting of course from Mahadeva – all mediated in turn through the words of Vasistha – will have a daughter, better than a thousand sons, very beautiful, peerless, and extremely devoted to the worship of God, never lying and free from all minor and major sins. She will be close to God through the intercession of her father. God then will bestow two auspicious sons on her. Both will be men of gnosis, brave, courageous, generous, and matchless in all good works. God will not create any others as perfect, physically or spiritually. These sons of hers will be successors of the Prophet. Here too Chishti adds his own voice by citing a *hadith* in the narrative, giving the impression that it originates in Mahadeva.[37] He then continues, stating that the descendants of the Prophet's grandsons will be many and through them Islam will grow day by day. The Prophet will love his grandsons. All of their deeds will be in keeping with Divine Will. They will always endeavour to perform Divine Duty; they will attend to the plight of the poor and seek to ameliorate it. After the death of the Prophet, some unlawfully born miscreants (*haramzadas*) will kill them unjustly and thus the entire earth will be rendered leaderless. Their killers will be renegades (*malechh, murtadd*), dishonoured and rejected

---

[36] See Chapter 3.
[37] The *hadith* is *"inallaha ja'ala zurriyata kulli nabi fi sulbihi wa ja'ala zuriyati fi sulbi 'ali ibn abi talib"* (God placed the descendants of every prophet in his loins, but He placed my descendants in the loins of 'Ali ibn Abi Talib). The *hadith* is reported in several collections, *manaqib*, *tazkira*, and history books. Cf. Sakhawi, *Al-Ajwibat al-Murdiyya*, Vol. 2, pp. 424–5; Muttaqi, *Kanz al-'Ummal*, Vol. 11, p. 600. Chishti mentions this *hadith* as copied from *Mishkat* (*kama fi al-Mishkat*). I could not locate these very words in the *Mishkat al-Masabih*, he may have been referring to the *Mishkat al-Anwar*.

in both faith (*din*) and worldly matters (*dunya*). In their hearts they will have little devotion to the Prophet, even if in appearance they claim it. Gradually, many people will join them and will act in opposition to the illumined path that the Prophet and his descendants had shown.[38] Clearly, Chishti here states his own position about the martyrdom of Husain and his killers, that is the Umayyid Caliph Yazid, his commander Ibn Ziyad, and their army, and is thus in a measure also in dialogue broadly polemically with his own community. The polemical overtones become louder as he nears the end of the story and asserts the triumph of his faith *vis-à-vis* the Hindus:

> Towards the end of Kaljug, the strength of the miscreants will increase, with the entire world facing turbulence (*fasad*). O Parvati, at that time God will send a perfect man (*mard-i kamil*) to support the faith of Mahamat, he will bring the entire inhabited part of earth under his control, putting in shame the hypocrites (*munafiq*). All will then be on the right path, the illumined path that Mahamat and his descendants would have bequeathed. The [true] faith will again be triumphant, from the east to the west, and no one will remain opposed to it. Nowhere will one see a Hindu or a hypocrite. Mahamat's faith will triumph everywhere in perfect form in the last phase of the Kaljug. All people will act upon the *shari'at* of Mahamat that the incomparable God (*bichun*) had laid down in *Atharaban Bed*, that is, the fourth book.[39]

The situation, however, will not remain the same for long, Mahadeva adds. As the rule is that everything that rises up eventually declines, the power of that perfect man after his death too will eventually be dismantled. The world will acquire a different colour and chaos and disturbance will dominate. People will start living like animals; they will not discriminate between mother and sister. Fearing lest it be totally destroyed because of the excessive sin of its people, the earth itself will then appeal to God for

[38] Chishti, *Mir'at al-Makhluqat*, f. 245.
[39] Ibid., f. 245b.

deliverance. What then follow is a very significant part of the story. Mahadeva continues:

> O Parvati, God will accept the earth's prayer, and subsequently He will appear in Sambhal in the house of a Brahmin, in the form of the powerful (*qahhar*) Kalki. The sky and the earth will then be shaken, a forceful storm will blow, and the Day of Judgment (*qiyamat*) will descend upon the people of the earth. Everything will be annihilated, darkness will prevail over the world, and it will remain in the same state of ruin and desolation for some time. At that moment, God will re-create Adam, along with all his descendants. He will then address Mahamat's daughter, asking her to appeal for justice on behalf of her sons. God will command: "Go there, to Heaven to meet your sons." God will again command her to request anything she would want. Mahamat's daughter will then raise her hand, saying: "O God, be kind and award deliverance to those who recited the word (*kalima*) of Mahamat." In kindness God will then say, "I have forgiven the community of Muslims." Mahamat's daughter will then lie in prostration together with her sons and then take the entire community of Muslims with her to Sarg, that is Bihisht. Their time (*daura*) will thus end; the Kaljug will be over. These are the words (*kalimat*) that Mahadeva communicated to Parvati. God knows best what is right.[40]

Here Chishti appears to have literally borrowed part of a late-medieval Vaishnava text, the *Kalki-Purana*, a continuation of the *Bhagavata-Purana* which deals with future events, describing the deeds of Vishnu to be performed at the close of the Kali-yuga, when he will be born as Kalki, son of Visnuyasas and Sumati of Sambhalanagarama. Chishti apparently also conflates the other parts of this text where it mentions Adharma's creation, the degradation of people, and Vishnu's approach (along with the earth) to Brahma for redress.[41] The coming of Kalki in Chishti's

---

[40] Ibid., f. 246a.
[41] Cf. Hazra, *Studies in the Upapuranas*, pp. 303–8. Hazra considers it a very late (but no later than the eighteenth century) Vaishnava work, as there

story, however, is not to free the earth from the influence of Kali and establish the *varnashrama-dharma*, a perfect version of which to him was obviously in the teachings of Muhammad. What is notable is that he has, as earlier, integrated into it his own Islamic voice to maintain that the human time that began with the birth of Adam is not cyclical; it is linear, which will terminate with *qiyamat* when everyone will get the results of her or his deeds. But another feature of this part of the story is also that while Chishti disputes and refutes the Hindu notion of time, he joins issue with his own community when he projects the killing of Husain as the gravest sin committed in Kaljug. Among the first things that God will do on the Day of Judgment is award justice to Fatima, who then is portrayed as a most compassionate intercessor for Muslims. Chishti breaks the story here with a polemical discourse, saying: "In sum the speech (*kalam*) of Mahadeva clearly repudiates [the idea of] the transmigration of the human soul which implies continuity of time, whereas it terminates eventually."[42]

The story is now about to end, but with a view to enhancing the prospects of its acceptability Chishti makes Vasistha reaffirm what Mahadeva has said. Here, he uses the popular Hindu belief about the sage Vasistha, who is eternal. Just as he was present and overheard Mahadeva converse with Parvati and recorded their conversation, he lived millions of years later in Chishti's time. In response to a query from Sut and Saunak, he asserts rather angrily and says it is not only that he recorded Mahadeva's conversation with Parvati about the world of Adam, he was also a witness to the truth and actual occurrence of what he has narrated:

> Sut and Saunak asked Bashist: "You knew what Mahadev said about the world of Adam; later his birth and the birth of his descendants

---

is no reference in it to Shankaracharya's achievements, while it is also not mentioned by any known Smriti-writers. For a brief description of Kalki Avatara, see also Abu al-Fazl, *A'in-i Akbari*, ed. Syed Ahmad Khan, p. 532; English transl., pp. 318–19.

[42] Chishti, *Mir'at al-Makhluqat*, f. 245a.

also took place in your presence. Was all that happened later as Mahadeva had forecast, or was there any discrepancy?" Bashist replied: "You and I have lived all through this world, and yet you have not gained full knowledge (*'irfan-i kamil*). They all were born in our presence (*huzur-i ma wa shuma*). What difference (*tafawut*) did you see that you dared ask this question and doubted the truth of what Mahadeva said?"[43]

Here too Chishti apparently adds his own Islamic voice. For he has Vasistha add: "O my dear ones, what Mahadeva said was not from himself; he reported what was written there in the Surg, i.e. heavens (*aflak*). Where can the discrepancy then be?"[44] Vasistha then elaborates his response to further convince Sut and Saunak of the truth of the story. He retells it in brief, and this time adds how the fascinating character of Narad Muni had a role in facilitating the world for Adam and his descendants. Vasistha continues and says that after all the creatures at God's command had prostrated themselves before Adam, He proclaimed that He had given the entire inhabited part of the earth to Adam, and that the community of jinns should all move to the forests, mountains, and islands. Having heard this, some *devatas* left for Heaven, while Mahadeva, accompanied by Parvati, left for the Kailash mountain, "where they are still living luxuriously". Most *rishis* who were sensible left the earth and set out for the mountains. But some rulers of the community and a few others did not vacate the earth immediately. As the number of Adam's descendants increased, and as they pushed ahead, these rulers and people who were gradually dislodged from the earth decided to resist their advance, and also gained an upper hand in the scuffle that ensued. At that time, some of the descendants of Adam who were close to God complained to Him about the existing situation. God accepted their supplication

[43] Ibid., f. 246.
[44] Ibid., f. 246b. *Surg*, that is, *svarga* or the heavens (*aflak*) probably means here *Lauh-i Mahfuz* which, according to Muslim belief, are the preserved tables in Heaven on which the transactions of mankind have been written by God from eternity.

and commanded Narad to go down to earth to tell the jinns that all the three Vedas which contained their *shari'at* had been annulled; their *shlokas* and prayers were no longer of any use. While in their *shari'at* the cow was worshipped, it was to be slaughtered and eaten in the new world. He also offered them a fresh compromise: besides moving to mountainous terrain, they had the option of giving up the worldly life and going up to Heaven to live in the world of spirits. Narad in particular was instructed to warn them of dire consequences in case they refused to act upon the divine command. Narad was initially hesitant about descending to earth. He feared for his own purity as the country of the jinns had turned into a "breeding ground of sins". On an assurance of protection from God, however, he came down and communicated God's message to the leaders of the jinns. For twenty years, Narad stayed on the earth, persuading them to follow the divine command. Thereafter, many *devatas* also set out for Kailash, met Mahadeva there, and reported to him about Narad's visit with God's orders. On their asking where they should reside in the mountains, Mahadeva said: "I live in one branch (*shakh*) of Kailash, there are still two more branches vacant, and you should go and settle there." They then retired to these branches and began to live there, "where from the power of God there is also available to them the elixir of life (*ab-i hayat*)." The story in Vasistha's words (*sukhan-i Bashist*) closes here, followed by what Vyasa said in addition.[45]

Of the disastrous consequences that Narad warned the jinns of, the following is of special interest for us, as it has a bearing on a significant feature of Chishti's narrative. Narad said:

> If you disobey the Divine Command out of your arrogance, you will be ruined. It is to your benefit that you leave this land, otherwise God will create in your own community a person named Kishan who will be endowed with His attributes. He will annihilate you so completely that no trace of your existence will ever be found.[46]

---

[45] Ibid., f. 247.
[46] Ibid., ff. 247a–248a.

In Vasistha's story it was Mahadeva, Lord Shiva, who was shown as having predicted the birth of Adam, the beginning of human time, and its triumph. Chishti now shows Lord Krishna too as one who fights demons in order to facilitate the settlement of Adam's descendants in India. Mahadeva, Krishna, Adam, Muhammad, and Husain all fought against evil and struggled to establish truth on earth, but they belonged to different sets of time. Among the legends and strong memories in both Hindus and Muslims around 'Abd al-Rahman Chishti were details of the battle of the Mahabharata – the Pandavas, the Kauravas, Arjuna, Lord Krishna – and also of the forces of evil such as Kansa and Jarasandha and their annihilation at Lord Krishna's hands. Their stories, all from the Hindu past, must have remained alive with the new converts to Islam, circulating among Muslim "foreigners" through Persian translations of the Hindu texts and their retellings in the vernacular. The battle of the Mahabharata and the rule of the descendants of the Pandavas was in fact now also integrated as part of the current period of human history.[47] The question then would be whether the truth for which Lord Krishna and the Pandavas fought was part of the human time that continued into the period when Adam was born, or whether it too belonged to the eras of the jinns, and whether Lord Krishna also foresaw and forecast the termination of his time, as did Mahadeva and Narad. Chishti brings in these details, as given by Vyasa, the principal reporter of the Mahabharata. But Vasistha and his disciples Sut and Saunak are first shown as advisers and helpers to the jinns in vacating the earth for Adam's descendants. It is difficult to speculate if, by invoking the authority of Vyasa here, Chishti once again is hinting at the Hindu pandits having hidden this critical portion of the text, the accusation with which he started his narrative. Indeed, Chishti says that when the jinns heard the story from Vasistha, they were astonished and shocked. They then all collected at Sut and Saunak's residence in Nimkhar and requested

---

[47] Alam and Subrahmanyam, *Writing the Mughal World*, pp. 396–428, for some seventeenth- and eighteenth-century works that include their histories.

their advice, with a pledge to follow it – considering their elevated stature, knowledge of the Vedas, and Divine Will. Sut and Saunak suggested the same as Mahadeva. They also said, "as the Kaljug will descend, we will also give up this transient life". Many of the jinns then apparently followed their example.[48] Some *daits* (*daityas*, demons), such as Kans, Saspal (Sisupala), and Jarasandh, and others who were considerable kings, did not on account of their arrogance and haughtiness follow them out. Most of these tyrants lived in India (Hindustan), and for this reason Adam's descendants, who were by then in control of several countries, could not enter the land. Narad, having observed this situation, returned to Heaven and reported it to God. Vasistha accompanied him. It was at this juncture that God created Krishna. Vyasa is thereafter mentioned as having summed up his account as follows:

> [Krishna] was born from the womb of Devaki, the sister of Kans *Dait*. Basdev, an '*unsuri devata*, was Kishan's father. This Kans was a cruel king and lived in Mathura. He had a huge army and power, had subjugated all the Rajas of Hind, and was a source of a variety of mischief and turbulence. The people, tired of his tyranny, approached the pious people of their own community. They consoled them and assured them that Kishan, born from the womb of Devaki, would kill Kans. Some of the astrologers had also forewarned Kans of this. Kans thus would get every child born of Devaki killed – this story is well known – and he made big plans to destroy Kishan. God however kept Kishan safe and after a while he destroyed Kans and brought the country under his control. After that Jarasandh, the father-in-law of Kans, mobilised another army together with several other Rajas and invaded Mathura. Kishan defeated him too.[49]

Chishti thus portrays Krishna as the destroyer of all evil forces in power on the eve of Kali-yuga. Even after his retreat from Mathura to Dwarka, following his triumph over Kans and Jarasandha (the king of Magadha), he returned to combat Sisupala, the king of Chedi and commander-in-chief of Jarasandha's armies, and other

---

[48] Chishti, *Mir'at al-Makhluqat*, f. 248a.
[49] Ibid.

demon kings.⁵⁰ He failed nowhere as "the all-knowing God, using His absolute power, manifested Himself in the guise (*kiswat*) of Kishan; no one therefore could overpower him." Chishti concludes the narrative part of *Mir'at al-Makhluqat* with a description of the battle of the Mahabharata, the return of the descendants of the Pandavas to rule, and their contact with Adam's descendants. This sounds like a kind of explanation of why, even during the centuries after Adam, the religion of the jinns continued in a certain form. He writes:

> Thereafter took place the battle of Mahabharat, between the Kauravas and Pandavs. They [the Kauravas] were a hundred brothers and there were several million people in their retinue. Kishan subjugated them all in one swoop (*ba yak qalam*). He then advised the Pandavs to perform *jag-asmed* [Ashvamedha]. They together with their armies made a round of the whole earth. And wherever [the old] Rajas were left, they killed them. When no haughty person was left on this earth, Kishan wanted to depart and go in hiding. At that time he summoned Arjun, Udhav, and Ankod and told them that "since Kaljug has arrived, I will go into hiding, and you too taking all the Pandavs together, should move to the snow-clad mountains. Give up your transient existence as there is no time left any more for you to live on this earth." He told Udhav to go to Badri Kedar mountain and be engaged in worshipping God. Ankod was advised to go to Mansarovar and stay there. Kishan then went into hiding. He lived in this world for a hundred and eight years. After him the Pandavs climbed the snow-clad hills and sacrificed their lives. About a thousand years later, it was seen that some of the Rajas from their (the Pandavas') generation had stayed back on earth; and around that same time several of Adam's descendants who had settled there, gained in strength. Their power grew day by day. Some descendants of the son who had killed his brother, and had run away and become rulers in India, married the daughters of the jinns and built and settled in [the city of] Qanauj, named after their father, Qabil (Cain). Deprived of the book of Adam they embraced the religion of the jinns, and

⁵⁰ Ibid. For such figures as Jarasandha, Sisupala, Chanura (Chanura II) and Vajranabha, see Mani, *Puranic Encyclopaedia*, pp. 177, 349–50, 719–20, 821.

read the *Beds*. After some time, as the time of the advent of Mahamat drew closer and the succession of lineages of the jinns began to be discontinued, they were constrained to adopt the descendants of Adam as their sons and settled them in their place instead. They themselves disappeared and [then] the entire inhabited quarter of the world came under the control of Adam's descendants. Whatever God desired became manifest. This is the meaning of what God said, "Allah does what He wants, and He commands what He intends."⁵¹

The Story Retold in the *Mir'at al-Asrar*

In his other better-known work entitled *Mir'at al-Asrar*, Chishti repeats a version of this narrative in the context of a discussion of Hindu cosmogony. But the retelling here reads like a more detached and "learned" account, without the flow and story-like quality of the *Mir'at al-Makhluqat*; the latter contains a number of different voices and the narrative sweeps along, while the *Mir'at al-Asrar* contains fewer "dialogic" elements and reads like a more sober summary of knowledge about other people. The narrative here runs as follows:

> The Indian philosophers hold the view that the first creature that came to existence after the creation of the heavens and the elements was Brahma [the text has *Brenha* throughout]. At the time when God Most High manifested the sphere of land on the sphere of water, the land appeared in the middle of the water like a lotus flower, and some of the heavens and the elements brought forth from the land Brahma, who then became busy with praising God. Brahma's natural life span (*'umr-i tab'i*) is equal to a hundred years of that world, and he is the cause behind the creation of all creatures. In his lifetime, the land is drowned in water several thousand times and the world becomes annihilated. By God's command, earth appears again. All

⁵¹ "*yaf'al-ullahu ma yasha-u*", and "*wa yahkamu ma yurid*", Qur'an, 14: 27 and 5: 1. Chishti, *Mir'at al-Makhluqat*, ff. 249–250a. Arjuna, one of the Pandava brothers, was one of the central protagonists in the battle of the Mahabharata; Udhav (Uddhava), a Yadava, was an intimate friend of Krishna: Mani, *Puranic Encyclopaedia*, pp. 803–4.

Indian philosophers agree on the point that the way the cycle of the days, weeks, months, and years goes on and one follows each other, in the same way the four periods, which they call the four *jugs*, follow each other in a continuous cycle, without interruption. The duration of each *jug* is 12,000 years of the year of that world; according to the year of this world, it is equal to 4,320,000 years. Consequently, the duration of the first period, which is called *sat jug* is 1,728,000 years of the year of this world. The life-span of the people of that period was 100,000 years. The duration of the second period, which is called *treta jug* is 1,296,000 years, of the year of this world. The life-span of the people of that period was 10,000 years. The third period is called *dwapar jug*; its duration is 864,000 years of the year of this world. The life-span of the people of that period was 1000 years. The duration of the fourth period which is called *kaljug* is 432,000 years, of the year of this world. The life-span of the people of that period is 100 years. These four *jugs* are called one *chaukari* or four periods (*chahar zamana*) or four cycles (*chahar daura*). The duration of one day of Brahma is equal to thousand *chaukari jug*; Brahma's nights likewise.

When Brahma's day, the duration of which is one thousand *chaukari jug*, reaches its end, all land becomes drowned in water. This is called *parlay*, and Brahma becomes immersed in sleep in the World of Similitudes (*'alam-i misal*). He stays in sleep for the same duration as the duration of his day. When his morning arrives, the water dries out, Brahma wakes up from his sleep and begins to create the creatures. In this manner when 360 days and nights pass, one year of his life-span is completed; his life-span consists of one hundred such years. When he becomes a hundred years old, he dies; after this no trace remains of the world and whatever lies in it. This is called *mahaparlay*. Then God Most High, with His wisdom and power, creates another Brahma, and all creatures come into existence the way it had happened before. Their [the Indian philosophers'] belief is that in this way 1000 Brahmas had been created. The life-span of this Brahma is 50 years and half a day. The Indian philosophers wrote voluminous books about this matter, but only the authentic parts written in them have been summarised here. [52]

---

[52] Chishti, *Mir'at al-Asrar*, British Library MS. Or., 216, f. 244a.

Chishti goes on to mention the "Hindu" account of Adam without repeating the charge against the pandits that they had concealed it. He also mentions the text that contains the account and describes cyclical time, without any polemical note which – as we noticed above and will observe again below – he brings into the story in his *Mir'at al-Makhluqat*:

> Further, some philosophers of that community who are free from prejudice narrate without prejudice from their heavenly book *Bed* (*Veda*) that when 3000 years are left from the *dwapar jug*, the Omnipotent, by infusing moonlight into the mixture of the elements, from the sphere of land creates a man called Dubja [*Dvija*], i.e. Adam. He has a great knowledge of God (*khuda-shinas*), embodies all branches of knowledge (*jami'-i 'ulum*), is beautiful, of graceful stature, intelligent (*'aqil*) and protects his honour (*ghayur*). His wife comes from one of the ribs on his left-hand side, and from her countless children will be born, and until the time of the *kaljug* the whole earth will be gradually filled with them.
>
> In every period, from amongst the children of Adam a few special servants will be honoured with the proximity of God (*qurb-i ilahi*), will provide guidance to others, and, with the power given by that God, they will subject the species of jinns. Some of them will attain the rank of king (*saltanat*) or chief train (*riyasat*). Among them the best will be Mahamat, that is Muhammad, who will be born in the period of *kaljug* and will be close and beloved to God the Most High. He will reach the [highest] level of perfection. Gradually all creatures will follow him, to such a degree that even some angels and the majority from the species of the jinns will obey his commands. In the *kaljug* his followers will acquire such dominance that they will demolish and obliterate the Indians' places of worship and pilgrimage centres. The water of the river Ganges will also disappear and no Hindu will be seen from East to West. At last, that religion (*din*) will reach its perfection, and, in the last part of the *kaljug*, the deeds of people will gradually become bad and human beings will live like animals. In that time no rain will fall from the sky, the vegetation will dry out and the land will become like a human finger. No water will remain in the springs and rivers and all living beings will perish. For some time the world will be dark and devoid of light until the

end of the time of *kaljug*. At that time a black cloud will appear with awe and gravity (*mahabat wa wiqar*) and will cause rain to fall, in the form of procreating matter (*ba-surat-i mani*), on the whole surface of the earth. From this the whole world will suddenly become green and fresh, and all living beings of the past will appear in their archetypical forms (*misali ajsad*). To each of them the Omnipotent will mete out punishment or reward (*'itab wa khitab*), in accordance with their [past] deeds, and will give place to some of them in Paradise, to some others in Hell, and to some of them in the place in between (*a'raf*, a kind of purgatory). With this, the cycle of *kaljug* ends and Brahma, on the command of God the Most High, begins to bring forth creatures the way he had done before.

Thus, in this way *parlay*, by which *qiyamat* is meant, is of three kinds: the first is the major *parlay* (*parlay-i kabir*), which is when Brahma dies; the second is the minor *parlay* (*parlay-i saghir*), which is when Brahma's cycle ends; the third is the micro-*parlay* (*parlay-i asghar*), which takes place at the end of each four *jug* cycle, as it has been described above.

In any case, much had been written on this subject, but the intellect (*'aql*) falls short of comprehending it. These secrets will not be unveiled as long as the eyes of insight (*dida-i basirat-i 'arif*) are not filled with Divine light, with the help of spiritual exercises and striving (*safa-i riyazat*) and the Lord's grace (*faiz-i mawahibat-i Ilahi*).[53]

The passage thus ends with a Sufi's state of *hairat* (astonishment, awe) and his desire to acquire the ability to understand it with divine help. While Chishti thus does not entirely accept these Hindu accounts, his approach is not dismissive either. In the *Mir'at al-Asrar*, we will see below, he also brings in a version of "pre-Adamite" time in Sufi terms, invoking the evidence of the vision of the great Shaikh Ibn 'Arabi (d. 1240).

The Reception of the Story

'Abd al-Rahman Chishti was not the first South Asian Sufi to write a text with narrative elements from the Hindu world blended with

---

[53] Ibid., ff. 244a–245b.

details from Islamic literature. These inclusions occur in several Sufi-*yoga* treatises composed in eastern Bengal in the fifteenth and sixteenth centuries. At about the same time, Sayyid Sultan wrote the *Nabivamsa*, in which Krishna finds a place among the thousands of divine envoys between the Biblico-Islamic prophets Ibrahim and Musa. He narrates numerous myths and legends of the Hindu past before describing the advent of Prophet Muhammad, and thus presents his own view of human history. Sayyid Sultan mentions reasons for writing this text. He was unhappy to see Muslims read about the Hindu gods Rama and Krishna, because they did not know Arabic and were virtually ignorant of their own traditions and history. Sultan therefore claims he decided to write the text to reform such sinners.[54] Such writing has been taken as a kind of indigenisation of Islam, or what has been characterised as a "syncretistic tradition".[55] Chishti's story is however radically different from the one given in Sultan's *Nabivamsa*. According to the *Nabivamsa*, all the four Vedas belonged to the world of the Hindus. God (Niranjan)

> . . . sent to earth the four Vedas carried by the four gods, Brahma, Vishnu, Shiva and Hari [*sic*], men followed them and became *dharmik* under the guidance of those who read the Vedas to them: the *dvijavara*. But later on, men stopped paying any attention to these texts. So Niranjan had to admit that the creation of these Vedas had been of no use and he ordered an angel to place them in the ocean.

Similarly Krishna, even if sent by God to guide people towards the right path, himself fell in the trap of Satan (or Iblis) and indulged in sinful acts. Sayyid Sultan's portrayal of Narad too is very negative. He played the role of Iblis, was "quarrelsome and a gossip-monger whose numerous missions as a messenger brought disaster to those he was sent to."[56] Chishti's account of the Hindu

---

[54] Tarafdar, *Husain Shahi Bengal*, pp. 198–225; Bhattacharya, "Hari the Prophet", pp. 192–208.
[55] Roy, *The Islamic Syncretistic Tradition in Bengal*.
[56] Bhattacharya, "Hari the Prophet".

world is not so brazenly negative, even if his tone is often polemical. He does not hint at any shortcoming or failure on the part of the Hindu gods and sages. In his account only the three Vedas belonged to the Hindu world, while part of the fourth Veda was significantly the Qur'an itself.

We have no clear evidence at present of how Chishti's *Mir'at al-Makhluqat* was received. What was the reaction to it amongst either Muslims or Hindus? At the end of the text, Chishti alludes to his intention to communicate to the Hindus (*hinduwan*) of his time through the stories in his text. As we will see below, after having given the story of the jinns, Chishti asserts that the Hindus were, like he himself and other Muslims, descendants of Adam. What is more, if we consider the nature of the *puranas*, on which he models his story, we have further evidence that Chishti had in mind an audience of Hindus, including Brahmans, who could engage with his story. The *puranas* were meant to legitimise evolving religious customs and practices with reference to the Vedas. But within the broad Puranic genre the references to the Vedas would often, in a literal sense, be inaccurate, appearing sometimes as outright inventions by their authors. What is more, a Puranic text was not expected to be the same in each successive iteration. In this connection, it would not be out of place to cite an early-nineteenth-century European experience of Puranic transmission:

> In 1805, Captain Francis Wilford reported on his experiences when he asked a Pandit to copy, for him, some relevant passages from the *Puranas*. The Pandit knew what Wilford wanted, and he gave him exactly what he wanted. The Pandit knew that Wilford was looking for the term *Sveta* to refer to the British Isles; so the Pandit changed a few geographical names to have them read *Sveta*. He even composed, on his own, "two voluminous sections", one supposed to belong to the *Skandapurana*, another to the *Brahmandapurana*, in which he narrated all the Puranic stories which he assumed would help Wilford. The only recognition he got for his labours is that Wilford calls him an impostor, and his composition a forgery.[57]

[57] Rocher, "Reflections on One Hundred and Fifty Years", pp. 71–2; see

Yet this would not have been the response to the "novelties" in Chishti's story, whether he was just a translator of an already composed Sanskrit "*purana*", or whether he himself composed them in Persian.

We should also note a much later Muslim response in a polemical mode, namely a nineteenth-century exegesis of the Qur'an entitled *Anwar al-Qur'an*, whose author, a Maulana Syed Rahat Hussain Gopalpuri, mentions 'Abd al-Rahman Chishti in the Introduction to his work. Gopalpuri used a part of the story that describes the birth of the Prophet Muhammad and the advent of Islam to show that the prophecy for the coming of Muhammad already existed in the ancient Hindu scriptures. The book, published sometime in the 1800s, is rare and I have unfortunately not been able to locate it. An enthusiastic Muslim has luckily provided a translation of this portion on a website entitled "the prophecies for Muhammad". Interestingly, Shaikh 'Abd al-Rahman Chishti, who we know was recognised as an eminent Sufi saint in his own time, is identified on the website as "Molvi", which generally means a not very highly regarded theologian. The language of *Mir'at al-Makhluqat* is also incorrectly called Urdu. The person who uploaded the translation on the website, or Maulana Gopalpuri himself, may have consulted or seen an Urdu translation, of which I am unaware. The website also mixes up the sources that Chishti mentions as his authorities and contains the observation that the story in the *Mir'at* could have been borrowed from an earlier text, *"Alloopnishad"*, compiled at some point during the reign of Akbar, in which Muhammad has been mentioned as a prophet (*rasul*). The noted Hindu reformer and revivalist Dayanand Saraswati's

---

also idem, *The Puranas*, pp. 49–50. Rocher notes that such Puranic texts are found even in earlier times, to which additions continued to be made, accounting among other things later for the East India Company as well, pp. 151–4. One such text is the *Bhavishya Purana* edited in two volumes with Hindi translation by Shri Ram Sharma Acharya. This includes accounts of the Muslim sultans of Delhi and the Mughal emperor Akbar.

Satyartha Prakash is cited as the authority for this reference.[58] The reference to Chishti in the *Anwar al-Qur'an*, it is clear, was already a part of nineteenth-century religious disputations.[59]

We have noticed that the *Mir'at al-Makhluqat* does not simply contain a prophecy for the coming of the Prophet of Islam, but begins with the story of Adam and tries to connect it with the known Hindu cosmogony. I am not in a position to conclude whether this story was devised by Chishti himself or that he borrowed it from somewhere else. We have seen that at least part of the story was borrowed with modifications from the medieval *puranas*. What needs also to be noted is that in the story the Brahmanical cyclical time of *yugas* is filled with Islamic content. Adam is created when, in the Dwapar age, evil and chaos came to reign. The story is a narrative from the eras before Adam to the seventh century, the time of Prophet Muhammad's grandson, Imam Husain. The cycles of decline are followed by the emergence of a saviour who resolves all problems and re-establishes goodness on earth. Krishna, Adam, Muhammad, and Husain are seen as saviours who appeared to resolve the problems of people and did away with sin and evil. True, the past of the Hindus is annihilated as well as appropriated; Hindu gods are sanctified and, in a measure, also exterminated. The Hindu gods are all asked to depart, go away to the mountains, leaving the inhabited world to Adam. There is clear recognition of a time before Adam. The divine power of Mahadeva and Brahma, and the sanctity of Vasishtha and other Hindu sages, are all recognised: Mahadeva tells the story, Brahma creates Adam in clay, and Vasistha records the sacred story of origins. But after the creation of Adam, the past before the time of Adam is dissolved. The continuity in time

---

[58] The website www.ezsoftech/akram/prophetpropheies.asp cites Chapter 14, p. 739, of *Satyartha Prakash*; this reference is possibly to the Urdu translation; in the English translation by Shri Durga Prasad, *Light of Truth*, see pp. 559–60.

[59] For some chap-books in Urdu, see 'Usmani and Tariq, *Agar ab bhi na jage to*; Upadhyaya, *Kalki Avatar aur Muhammad Sahib*.

is ruptured. The time which has human meaning as well as sacred meaning is to be traced to Adam, though his creation is traced back to the divine will of Mahadeva and Brahma. Islamic rituals and practices are legitimated through the divine voice of Mahadeva and a dialogue with the sanctifying symbols of Brahmanism. The Qur'an is the fourth Veda, sanctified as a book of thirty *adhyayas*. The legitimacy of *shari'at* and the Qur'an is derived through a narrative that recognises the need to locate Islamic texts within the world of Hindu scriptures.

'Abd al-Rahman Chishti adduces support for Hindu cosmogony from Islamic traditions as well. He cites from a companion of the Prophet, 'Abd-allah ibn 'Abbas, the noted fifteenth-century historian Mirkhwand, the historian and commentator on the Qur'an Abu Ja'far ibn Jarir Tabari, and the twelfth-century author of a Sufi commentary on the Qur'an, *Tafsir-i Zahidi*. He also inserts in the story, wherever appropriate, Qur'anic verses and *hadith*. He clearly says that Mahadeva also had true divine vision and that Lord Krishna was amongst those who were sent by God to fight against injustice and tyranny. Mahadeva and Lord Krishna both struggled, one using his words and the other his weapons, to create conditions for the settlement of Adam's descendants in India.

We know that Krishna had already figured in Chishti Sufi traditions in Awadh, in particular the area from which our author came. The noted Awadhi poet Malik Muhammad Jayasi of *Padmavat* fame also composed a text entitled *Kanhavat*, the story of Lord Krishna.[60] Vaishnava songs that were recorded and commented upon in the *Haqa'iq-i Hindi* by the sixteenth-century Chishti luminary Mir 'Abd al-Wahid Bilgrami (d. 1569) centred around Lord Krishna. Bilgrami suggested that

> Krishna and other local names used in such verses symbolised the Prophet Muhammad, or "Man", and even sometimes the reality of human being (*haqiqat-i Insan*) in relation to the abstract notion of the oneness (*ahadiyat*) of Divine Essence. *Gopis* sometimes stood for

[60] Jayasi, *Kanhavat*; Orsini, "Inflected Katha", pp. 195–232.

angels, sometimes for the human race, and sometimes in relation to the relative unity (*wahidiyat*) of divine attributes. Braj and Gokul signified Sufi notions of the world (*'alam*) in their different contexts, while the Yamuna and the Ganga rivers stood for the sea of unity (*wahdat*) and the ocean of gnosis (*ma'rifat*); or else for the river of *hads* (origination) and the *imkan* (contingent or potential existence). The *murali* (Krishna's flute) represented the appearance of entity out of non-entity; and so on.[61]

It could be argued that Chishti went a step further, and in this connection it is interesting to note the way that he begins the *Mir'at al-Haqa'iq*, another treatise he prepared as a "translation" of the *Gita*. Both the *hamd* (praise of God) and *na't* (praise of the Prophet) are in characteristic Sufi idiom, inspired by the doctrine of *wahdat al-wujud*. He mentions the *Gita* as a book that reveals the secrets of *tauhid*:

> In the name of God, the compassionate, the merciful. He is the first, He is the last, He is the manifest, He is the unmanifest; and He is the knower of all things. He is the first, meaning: "I was a hidden treasure and I desired to be known, so I created creation to be known." He is the last, meaning: "Everyone that is thereon will pass away, and the countenance of your Lord of glory and kindness will remain." He is the manifest, meaning: "God is the light of the heavens and the earth. So, whichever way you turn there is the countenance of God." He is the unmanifest, meaning: "And in yourselves. Do you not see? In all we saw, we saw nothing but the beloved."
>
> Thus it was known that there is no one except Him. And thus the verse: From all sides without a tune (to carry it) comes the note of *There is no God but He*. Thus it became known that the building, annihilation, manifestation, and concealment of the world are all [from] the note *huw*. The discerning have decided that this same note is the sound *kun*, and some have called it the sound of the letter *h*, again some say that it is the sound of blowing for which David's tunes are famous. God – may He be exalted – has said: *I breathed*

---

[61] Bilgrami, *Haqa'q-i Hindi*; see also Rizvi, *Muslim Revivalist Movements*, pp. 60–2. For 'Abd al-Wahid Bilgrami's biography, see Bilgrami, *Ma'asir al-Kiram*, Vol. 2, pp. 65–6.

into him of my spirit. [However] the proposition intended by all the divines is one [one and the same] because, save the one being, there is no being in existence in either the manifest world or the unmanifest. Hence: *There is nothing but Him in the two regions.* How can anyone describe the note that is without description, and it is indescribable insomuch as it is without parallel. The saying of God – may He be exalted – on this secret is: *There is nothing in His likeness in earth, and He is the knower of all things.* Since whatever is in all the world is me, the like of me cannot be found in either world. So, out of excess of longing for his own belovedness in himself, for the manifesting of his own love [He] began again and again to intone the phrase *kun*. As Hazrat 'Iraqi says [in a] *ghazal:*

> Love plays the instrument in key / Where is the lover to hear the sound?
> With every breath it plays another note / It begins every beat with a plectrum
> Throughout the world is the sound of His note / How can He hold back the sound?
> From every atom his secret / Hear for I am not telling [it].

God – may He be exalted – has said: *Whatever is in the skies or on the earth praises God. Indeed God is the knower of everything.* At every instant out of love, He tells his secret in His own tongue. People, because [you are] loved, hear with your own ears how you were made. I speak with every tongue and listen with every ear. This is all the more wonderful for my ear and tongue are invisible. Like the sun I am visible on the face of every particle. Such is the extent of my visibility that I am invisible. *Through me, he hears, sees and speaks.* Since I became totally beloved, who is the lover?

Favour and boundless praise [be] on that possessor of [divine] knowledge and secrets. Hazrat Muhammad Mustafa – may God's prayers and peace be upon him – whose true nature is oneness. Hence: *I am Ahmad without the 'm'.* His merit cannot be expressed by the pen. God has informed us: *Were it not for you I would not have created the heavens.* Who has the power to describe the possessors of that bliss? That sun of the two worlds is the likeness of the spirit, and each of these four essences is like the four elements. Therefore, the spirit is with the elements and the elements are with the spirit. Beloved, love and lover, all three are one here. Since the union is immeasurable, what role has separation? Hazrat Khwaja Hafiz has informed [us] concerning this state:

> The drinker, the singer, the vintner, all are he,
> the thought of water and roses along the path is pretence.

Next, the servant–sweeper at the threshold of the Khwajas of Chisht, 'Abd al-Rahman 'Abd al-Rasul 'Abbasi al-'Alawi al-Chishti, writes a few words in clarification of the doctrine of *tauhid*. I called this treatise *Mir'at al-Haqa'iq* which is known in Hindawi as the *Gita*, [in] which Krishna explained to Arjuna, by means of examples, the secret of *tauhid*. Byas collected and put together that explanation in order to instruct people. All the learned Hindus agree that Krishna has taken the secrets of the knowledge of the unification of God – may He be praised and exalted – from the four *Beds* and has revealed this explanation in the *Gita*. So, just as the enlightened Shaykh Sufi Qutb-Jahani once wrote a commentary on the *Kashf al-Kunuz*, also known as *Yoga Vasistha*, now for the sake of some true friends, who are as a flaming torch seeking after the sublime goal, the above-mentioned translation has been written out in Persian. Concerning [the doctrine of] *unity of being*, Hazrat Raja spoke thus [in a] verse:

> I saw the being of the pure essence in every place and at all times,
> I saw [it] manifest in every direction, alley and view.

The Prophet's words – on whom be peace – on this secret are: *Take what purifies and eschew what defiles*. What is meant by purity is the knowledge of *tauhid*; what is meant by defilement is polytheism. We look for virtue, wherever it is available (*Bayad mata'-i niku az har dukan ki bashad*).

Whoever has understood has understood. I forbid myself to talk with [other] people, But when the conversation turns to you, I cannot stop talking.[62]

In view of these other examples of Chishti's thoughts and renderings of Hindu cosmogony, the *Mir'at al-Makhluqat* becomes

---

[62] Cited with some modification from Vassie, "Persian Interpretations".

all the more intriguing and important. From the characters mentioned in the *Mir'at*, and the notions of time and historical imaginings they represent, Chishti appears to be making an attempt to reconcile the history of Islam with pre-Islamic and indeed pre-historic India. He chooses to present his position in the form of a *purana* of his own, which perhaps echoes or imitates the *Uttarakhanda* and *Bhavishottarapurana*, which he mentions; and the *Kalk-i Purana*, as we have seen earlier. To my mind, the contents and the literary form both need to be considered carefully because embedded in them are crucial clues regarding the intended audience of the text and the nature of its production. To begin with, we could consider that Chishti may himself have propounded the text – which he wrote in Persian – orally in Hindawi as well, and thereby widened the scope of his audience to include non-Persianate Muslims and Hindus. Given the structure and content of the text and its high degree of intertextuality, I believe this to be highly probable. After all, who would be impressed by the author's usage of *Bhabikhottrapurana*, the oral Awadhi pronunciation of the *Bhavishyottarapurana,* or his careful noting of the names of Sanskrit philosophers, if not people themselves familiar with those names? Could we imagine that there may have been two stages of orality between the Sanskrit and Persian texts? The first would have been one in which the *puranas* (including the *Bhagavata purana*, with details of Krishna's battles and his opponents) and the *Mahabharata*, and perhaps also the arguments of Sanskrit philosophers, were narrated and explained by the pandits and the local *kathavachikas* in the villages and *qasbas*; and the second, one in which Chishti would have reworked that information and woven it together with Islamic traditions to provide a competing narrative.

The Sufi Vision of Time: A Hundred Thousand Adams

Even without using conjecture to imagine the local and perhaps oral audience of Chishti's work, there was another vibrant debate in which his text would have found a ready-made audience. This debate centred on the problem of the origins of the world. This was also a more general question for Muslim thinkers as the religion spread across new regions. It was easier to disqualify the pre-Islamic period in the original Arabic-speaking area; but, just as Christianity had to find some way of valuing pagan times which contained Greek and Roman philosophy, in Persia and elsewhere the issue was what attitude to adopt on the time before Islam.[63] More accommodating thinkers were trying to find a way of valuing that earlier time and finding ways of translating their thoughts about bygone time in Islamic terms. In fact, in his introduction to the Persian translation of the Mahabharata, mentioned at the beginning of this chapter, Abu al-Fazl says one of the objectives in getting translations of the Mahabharata was to let Muslims – who believed that the world was only 7000 years old – know about the ancient character of the earth and the people living therein (*kuhnagi-yi ʿalam wa ʿalamiyan*).[64] Chishti belonged to an intellectual milieu responding to its habitat creatively. The existence of discrepant views on the ancientness of the world was a significant idea in the *Mir'at al-Makhluqat*, but he poses the question again in his *Mir'at al-Asrar*, in the context of his account of Shaikh Saʿd al-Din Hamawi:

> Shaikh Sadr al-Din Qunawi, who had been in his [i.e. Saʿd al-Din Hamawi's] *subhat*, said: "I heard from him that there have been seven covenants (*mawasiq*, pl. of *misaq*) and that it [i.e. the covenant]

---

[63] Tavakoli-Targhi, "Contested Memories of Pre-Islamic Iran", and idem, "Orientalism's Genesis Amnesia". There were also some mentions of Indic temporality in some early Arabic histories, but we are not in a position to assume that these texts were available in Mughal India. See for instance Balkhi, *Kitab al-Badaʾa wa al-Tarikh*, Vol. 2, pp. 146–7. For a discussion of such texts, see Bladel, "The Astrological Current". For a generally accepted Islamic view of the origins of the world, see Razi, *Mirsad al-ʿIbad*, Chapter 2, *dar bayan-i mabdaʾ-i maujudat*, pp. 37–97. According to this text the *Nur-i Muhammadi* was the first to exist, and incidentally the jinns came much later.

[64] *Mahabharat*, Persian translation, Abu al-Fazl's Introduction, pp. 18–19.

was not limited to the covenant when God Most High asked the souls: 'Am I not your Lord?'"[65] I mentioned this to Shaikh Muhyi al-Din ibn 'Arabi, who then said: "He must have meant it in general (*kulliyat*), otherwise the particulars (*juz'iyat*) were more than this." He writes in his commentary to 'Ali's *diwan* that when the Zodiac is at noon, the sphere of the water will encompass the sphere of the land and no living being will remain on earth. Following this, the address (*khitab*) will come: "O earth! swallow your water, and O sky! withhold [your rain]!"[66] And the Zodiac will pass the turning point of the day (*ma'dal al-nahar*), the land will appear, and God Most High will create Adam and his descendants anew, in accordance with the effect of the positions of the heavenly bodies (*auza'-i falakiya*), "the way we created them the first time", as God Most High says, so "that they should be no confused doubt about a new creation?"[67] According to the sayings of the Greek philosophers, this event will take place in 80,000 years (twenty times 4000 years). But it was not specified whether this [year] is meant as God's year (*sal-i Ilahi*) or a temporal year (*sal-i zamani*, "year as a measure of [our] time"). In any case, if in this situation the Day of the Covenant and the Day of the Resurrection take place several times, it is not something that would be outside of the power (*qudrat*) of the Omnipotent (*qadir-i mutlaq*). Mulla Ahmad writes in his *Tarikh-i Hukama'* that many philosophers, if not all, deny that there would be any beginning or any end of creation. Further, they say that the universe is the essence of the Necessary Being (*zat-i wajib al-wujub*), and will subsist from pre-eternity to post-eternity. Although a group [of philosophers] maintains that the universe is other than God (*ghair-i haqq*) and asserts the contingency of the world (*hudus-i'alam*), nevertheless even they cannot determine the beginning and the end of the universe.

The Indian, Chinese and Firangi philosophers put the beginning of the creation at several thousand years ago . . . This belief is supported by Chapter 331 of the *Futuhat al-Makkiya* of the Great Shaikh [Ibn

[65] "*alastu bi-rabbikum?*", Qur'an, 7: 172.

[66] "*ya arzu'bla'i ma'aki wa-ya sama'u'qli'i*", Qur'an, 11: 44.

[67] "*ka-ma ansha'ahum awwala marrah . . . bal hum fi labsin min khalqin jadid*", Qur'an, 50: 15.

'Arabi], in which he narrates a *hadith* of the Prophet: "Verily God created hundred thousand Adams".[68]

In the same chapter the Great Shaikh relates a story: "While circumambulating the Ka'ba, I witnessed a vision in the World of Similitudes (*'alam-i misal*) that a group of pious people were circumambulating the Ka'ba with me, but I did not recognise them. Upon this, they said "some years ago we too were circumambulating the Ka'ba sanctuary, just as you are doing now." Then the Great Shaikh relates: "When I heard this, a thought came to my heart that these must be bodies belonging to the World of Similitudes. As soon as this occurred to me, one of them turned to me and said: 'I am one of your forefathers'. I asked: 'How long has it been since you left this world?' He said: '40,000 years passed since I died.' Astonished, I said: 'But it was only 7000 years ago that Adam died.' He asked: 'Which Adam are you talking about? This Adam was in the beginning of the first cycle of these 7000 years.'"

The Great Shaikh says: "Upon hearing this, I remembered the *hadith* of the Prophet according to which God Most High created a hundred-thousand Adams the way he created the Father of the Mankind (*Abu al-Bashar*)." Following this, the Great Shaikh writes that it is possible that after every cycle of 7000 years the descendants of one Adam become extinct and the descendants of another Adam come into existence, and this chain will go on as long as the world is contingent, until the Resurrection comes (*wa badin waza' ta qiyam-i qiyamat muntahi gardad*), because all prophets have brought us news of this, and on the Day of Resurrection God Most High will bring to life the progeny of all Adams, all at once; this is not difficult for the Omnipotent (*qadir-i mutlaq*). And God knows best.

In short, the essence of what several of the philosophers, verifiers of the Truth, said concerning the past and the present times is that the eternal wisdom of the Absolute, the Wise (God Most High), creator and originator of the whole universe, requires that the higher bodies [the bodies on the sky] exercise their influence on the lower bodies [the bodies on Earth], especially the seven planets, the effect of which on the people of the world and whatever is in it [the world]

---

[68] "*Innallaha khalaqa mi'atah alfin Adama*". Cf. Ibn 'Arabi, *Al-Futuhat al-Makkiya*, Vol. 3, p. 549. See also Chittick, *Imaginal Worlds*, pp. 81–95.

is accepted and ascertained. In the terminology of the philosophers the heavenly bodies are called "fathers" and the four elements are called "mothers", and whatever is produced by the effect of the higher and the lower bodies and by the intermingling of the lower bodies is called the "three kingdoms of nature" (*mawalid-i salasa*), or, vegetation, animals, and minerals. It is said that the influence of each of the seven planets is manifested for the period of thousand years. Because the Father of Mankind (Adam) came into existence in the Cycle of Saturn (*Zuhal*), or, at the end of the third period, his life-span and the life-span of his descendants who were born in this period, was longer. In this way Adam's life-span was a thousand years, or, according to a different tradition, 930 years. Likewise, the life-spans of his sons too were long. Because the appearance of our Prophet is connected with the Cycle of the Moon, or the fourth period, in which the life-spans are in between 60 and 70 years, with some reaching 100 years, for this reason the Prophet said the life-span of the people of my community is within 70 years (*bain al-sab'in*). Therefore, the scholars, verifiers of the Truth, hold the view that when 7000 years are completed, one week of God's days – one of which is equal to a thousand years – is completed. But it should be known that according to them [these scholars], there are two types of days of God, short (*sighar*) and long (*kibar*). The short days are also called temporal days (*ayyam-i zamani*, "days of time") and the long ones [are called] God's days. The duration of the short day is a thousand years, as the venerable verse of Qur'an has it: "Verily a Day of your Lord is like a thousand years of your reckoning",[69] while the long day, that is, from God's days, is equal to about 50,000 years. The venerable verse of the Qur'an – "The angels and the Spirit ascend unto Him in a Day that equals fifty thousand years"[70] – points to this truth. This is the reason why the author of the *Futuhat al-Makkiya* writes that in the hereafter (*akhirat*) one day is equal to 50,000 years, while one day in the World of Similitudes is equal to a thousand years.[71]

---

[69] "*wa-in yauman 'inda rabbika ka-alfi sanatin mimma ta'uddun*", Qur'an, 22: 47.

[70] "*ta'ruju-l-mala'ikatu wa-r-ruhu ilaihi fi yaumin kana miqdaruhu khamsina alfa sanatin*", Qur'an, 70: 4.

[71] Chishti, *Mir'at al-Asrar*, British Library MS., ff. 243a–244a.

In the circle of such Sufis, too, "the world and the people of the world" were much older than the 7000 years ascribed to them in the Islamic tradition. Relevant here are also the *hadith* that describe the ancientness of the world in Islamic tradition. Two of them recount Moses' queries to God regarding the origins of the world, which are traced to a million years ago. God's response mentions ten cycles (*'ashr marrat*) of creation, each lasting for 100,000 years, consisting of 50,000 years of development (*'imarat*) followed by 50,000 years of desolation (*kharab*), until the time of Adam. Twice during these one million years, God created cities, once 70,000 of them, and the second time only 3000, but made of pure gold and silver, wherein 30,000 different Adams and their descendants lived for 900,000 years. All of these Adams lived before Adam the father of mankind. It is reported that after God completed the story of his Creation he asked Moses to count and note the world's ancientness. Moses, according to one report, could not count them. He fainted, and when he recovered he sought the forgiveness of God for his having even dared raise the question. According to another report he counted 8359 years up to Adam the father of mankind, but could go no further. There are also several other *hadiths* reported by 'Abd-allah ibn 'Abbas, the cousin of the Prophet Muhammad and 'Abd-Allah 'Amr ibn al-'As. One such *hadith* recounts the creation of heaven and earth as having happened 6,080,000 years ago, and the place was then initially populated by demons and demigods (*devan*). Such *hadiths* were of questionable authenticity from the point of view of orthodox theologians, but they continued to be cited in Islamic literature, and became part of the Muslim imagination.[72]

We may thus conclude that even if Chishti was confronted by apparently conflicting Indic and Islamic traditions, he had enough support in his own Sufi traditions to enable him to blend the two, at least in an imagination of the origins of the world. The

---

[72] Cf. *Safina-i Bahr al-Muhit*, f. 41; *Sharh-i Masnawi-yi Maulana Rum*, f. 1785; Zarqani, *Mukhtasar al-Maqasid*, p. 706.

Chishti Sufi thus combines different and apparently incompatible traditions: on the one hand Indic historical imaginings of *yugas* populated by gods, *rishis*, and heroic kings; and on the other the Sufi and non-Sufic Islamic imagination. What is interesting is that in Chishti's narrative the originary being is always named Adam. By comparison, we may note here that Shaikh Ahmad Sirhindi considers the 100,000 Adams, even as they appeared in Ibn 'Arabi's vision, to have lived in the World of Similitudes (*'alam-i misal*), and in that world alone.[73]

Polemics and Politics

There is also a political subtext which links Chishti's voluminous textual production to the wider conditions of the time. While Chishti Sufis had spread far and wide in India and established a dense network of their order's houses and disciples, at the beginning of the seventeenth century they had come under attack for both their ideology and practices.[74] In response, 'Abd al-Rahman Chishti demonstrated his knowledge of Indian traditions and endorsed certain Shi'i beliefs indirectly, showing both the *'ulama* and his opponents among the Naqshbandi saints how much more knowledgeable about, rooted in, and at ease he was on Indian soil. Concurrently, he was able to delineate the hollowness of indigenous beliefs and demonstrate their weaknesses through a discussion of Hindu religious philosophy, furnishing evidence from the Hindu tradition itself. It was these features of Chishti practice, and not what was dismissed in the Naqshbandi writings as "deviance" (*bid'a* or *zandaqa*), that legitimated their supreme religious leadership in the land.[75] The Chishtis, with 'Abd al-Rahman as their principal spokesperson, were then able to portray themselves as the real defenders of the Faith. While they appreciated indigenous social and religious practices, they rearticulated

---

[73] Sirhindi, *Maktubat*, Vol. 2, pp. 42–4.
[74] See Chapter 2.
[75] See also Chapter 3.

Islamic beliefs to make them more acceptable in local conditions. Their language of accommodation to the locality is integral to their strategy to strengthen and refurbish the universalism of their tradition. It would be in order to now note the following polemical passages in the *Mir'at al-Makhluqat*, where, after summing up Vasistha's account, Chishti engages in a disputation, refuting the validity of the Hindu belief in the transmigration of the soul (*tanasukh*). The Chishti Sufi writes:

> In sum this conversation of Mahadeva, which closes with [an account] of the end of time, clearly demolishes *tanasukh*. Some of the theologians (*mutakallimin*) of the community, because of their inadequate knowledge and comprehension ('*irfan*), believe in *tanasukh* while Biyas, who is their major religious leader, has furnished several reasons to show its invalidity. Some other *rishis* also agree with him.[76]

Chishti summarises the different relevant positions, showing his close reading and understanding of ancient and medieval Hindu philosophy in nearly the same way as the story in the *Mir'at* demonstrates his familiarity with the variety of medieval *puranas*. The argument in the Brahmanical texts in support of *tanasukh* he presents is as follows:

> In this world there is one who is a king and the other is a poor man, one of them turns blind, the other lame, one of them is helpless, the other possesses power. Such being the case, it becomes clear that whatever one does, one's condition corresponds to one's own deeds in this world. Otherwise, the implication will be that God is arbitrary and tyrannical, [and] that he makes one a king and the other a pauper and hapless without any reason or one's virtue or fault.[77]

The argument for the doctrine of rebirth from inequalities among living beings in terms of their conditions, status, and experiences is an argument of long standing in Indian philosophical

---

[76] Chishti, *Mir'at al-Makhluqat*, f. 246a.
[77] Ibid., f. 246.

literature, associated initially with Jaina and Buddhist attempts to argue for *karma* and reincarnation.[78] Chishti seeks support for his own arguments, invoking perhaps Shankaracharya and Vyasa:

> Shankaracharj taking a cue from the reasoning of Biyas, says that there is no such *avatar*. God is almighty, He is wise, whatever He wants He does. Don't you see the carpenter who makes the throne of the king and the planks of the door from the same wood? [Similarly] the potter makes a bowl for the king and also an alms bowl for the beggar from the same piece of clay. Was there any fault in that piece of wood or clay, by virtue of which they got such returns? He also says that in the beginning no creature could have done good or bad, and yet one of the creatures was a human being, the other an angel, and yet another an animal.[79]

From this, Chishti infers that it is clear the advocates of *tanasukh* are unaware of the implications of their own position. Yet, even though the Chishti Sufi makes an effort to use the ideas of Shankara and Vyasa to refute *tanasukh*, he does so, as we know, by considerably oversimplifying their views. Shankara has a very nuanced account of *karma* and rebirth, one part of which emphasises the function of human actions, and the other the role of the Creator. He uses the link between actions and their results, and the mechanism of rebirth, to justify the fact that it is beings themselves, and not God, who are responsible for these inequalities.[80]

---

[78] The following, for example, is from a Jaina text: "Here in the east, west, north, and south many men have been born according to their merit, as inhabitants of this our world – some as Aryas, some as non-Aryas, some in noble families, some in low families, some as big men, some as small men, some of good complexion, some of bad complexion, some as handsome men, some as ugly men. And of these men one man is king": Jacobi, *Jaina Sutras*, 2.1.13.

[79] Chishti, *Mir'at al-Makhluqat*, f. 246a.

[80] On the complexity of Shankara's position on rebirth in this context, see Clooney, "Evil, Divine Omnipotence", pp. 530–48; Narhari, "Samkara and Vyasa", pp. 20–6; Herman, "Indian Theodicy", pp. 265–81; Matilal, "Samkara's Theodicy".

After this Chishti once again cites from Udayanacharya's *Nyay-akusumanjali* in support of the idea of God's omnipotence and implies thereby a form of support for his own position:

> The second *ashlok* in the treatise *Kusmanjal* (*Nyayakusumanjali*) of Udayancharj (Udayanacharya) refutes the position of Jamin (Jaimini). Jamin says: "I do not accept the argument of creation (*khalq*); the soul is eternal (*azali*), no one created it; it comes into existence and goes off on its own (*khud ba khud*)." Udayancharj refutes this. He says: "You yourself admit of [the existence of] *atman* and *paramatman*. These [are the terms that] mean soul and eternal God." He also says that "in this world whatever exists has come out apparently from one phenomenon. We and you do not have enough power to create our own selves or the world. And, if you say that everything comes out of its own, then this too is wrong. For, if it were so, then nothing would have been subjected to any change; everything would have kept itself fully secured; nothing would have disappeared. Anything that changes also disappears. Thus it is clear that there is a creator who has created everything and he also annihilates it. If you say that the changes in a thing are effected by time then I would say that the person who [does so] create a thing should possess knowledge as well as power. If these two qualities are not there in Time, how can it be a creator (*khaliq*)? And if these qualities are there in Time, then you have not quite understood what I mean. God is the same phenomenon that you consider to be Time."[81]

This passage shows Chishti's extraordinary familiarity with some sections of Hindu scholasticism. Udayanacharya is a major early philosopher; his *Nyayakusumanjali* is regarded as the first systematic account of Nyaya theism. While Udayana does develop arguments against the epistemology of the Mimamsa tradition, the founder of which is said to be Jaimini,[82] the phrase *"khud ba khud"* instead echoes the atheistic Charvaka position which, as described by Udayana in the fifth verse of the first chapter of the *Nyayakusumanjali*, maintains that things are spontaneous or

---

[81] Chishti, *Mir'at al-Makhluqat*, ff. 245b–246a.

[82] On Mimamsa arguments against creation and a creator God in general see, Varma. "Non-Theism in the Mimamsa Philosophy", pp. 179–91.

"accidental" (*akasmikavada* or *akasmat bhavati*). The Charvakas, we know, maintain that an event springs into existence at a particular time not because there is a cause behind it but because it is the nature (*svabhava*) of the event to happen at that time. Udayanacharya refutes their position. "The production of an effect at a particular time and its non-production at a time earlier or later than that," he maintains, "can be explained only by the fact that it has a cause which determines it."[83] In Udayanacharya too, Chishti saw support for his position. He then goes on to demonstrate his knowledge of Vyasa's *Vedanta*:

> The third *ashlok* from Jabal Rishi and Biyas, available in the third chapter (*charn*) in the *Bedant*, which rejects Jamin and Gautam who advocate *tanasukh* and support *avatar*. They say that one earns the returns of both the good and the bad deed in this world itself. It is because of this assumption (*wahm*) that they had adopted the *mazhab* (belief) of *tanasukh*. Jabal and Biyas say, "You have misunderstood it; the returns of good and bad are *surg* and *narg*, that is heaven and hell. And if one gets the result of vice and virtue that one will get, what is the purpose of souls coming back again into different bodies in this world? It is certain that the seeds of vice and virtue bud into flowers in heaven. As they get this return, the seeds are extinguished, and without seeds nothing can grow."[84]

Chishti then gives his own assessment of Vyasa (credited by some as being the author of the *Vedanta-sutras*) and Jabala (a sage often quoted in the *Vedanta-sutras*) as supreme theologians and saints, while he calls Gautam and Jaimini mere philosophers "who had gone astray" (*be-janib-i digar rafta and*).

They were, however, still great. "Plato too was Gautam's pupil," he asserts.[85] Chishti then concludes the *Mir'at al-Makhluqat* with

---

[83] Amma, *Udayana and His Philosophy*, pp. 14–16, 19–35.

[84] Chishti, *Mir'at al-Makhluqat*, f. 246a.

[85] While this remark shows Chishti's close reading of Indian philosophy and his contacts with the Brahman scholars of his own time, it is not fictitious. There is a fragment, preserving a memory that claims that Indian philosophers

an interesting message – that "the Hindus are Adam's descendants, but they have forgotten their ancestors, the religion of their ancestors, and their own selves. Indeed, they are wrong in tracing their genealogy to the community of jinns. They do so unknowingly and out of ignorance."[86]

Conclusion

The seventeenth-century Sufi 'Abd al-Rahman Chishti lived in the Gangetic valley at the height of Mughal rule, a milieu that seems incessantly to have confronted him with conflicting cosmologies and theological principles. It appears that he wanted to carefully craft something that offended no one, sounded plausible, and allowed him to argue and manoeuvre. At the same time, he maintained his inherited identity and traditions within the complex religious and political space of Mughal India. Even as he used the religious concepts of others, he did so by keeping the key concept of his beliefs unimpaired. Brahma creates Adam but is subordinated to *Qadir-i Mutlaq* (Absolute God); God manifests Himself in Krishna, comes down to earth to fight the forces of evil, but Krishna is not God himself.

Central and somewhat startling in *Mir'at al-Makhluqat* is the idea that the beliefs of both Hindus and Muslims are many-stranded and internally plural, and therefore there can be significant similarities between the individual strands. This breaks down the abstract and comprehensive difference between the two religions

---

taught Plato, via Socrates, particularly concerning theology. Lacrosse, "Some Remarks", pp. 247–63. Islamic philosophers also noticed the similarity of Indian and Greek ideas of transmigration, and in some cases sought to show a diffusion of ideas. For example, Suhrawardi in his "Philosophy of Illumination" places the doctrine of the Pythagoreans and Plato on reincarnation in the mouth of the Buddha (*bodasaf*). See Walbridge, *The Wisdom of the Mystic East*, p. 79. Some historians and philosophers traced the Indian ideas on reincarnation to Pythagoras, via his disciples who are said to have visited India. See Walker, "The Doctrine of Metempychosis", pp. 219, n. 11, 222.

[86] Chishti, *Mir'at al-Makhluqat*, f. 249b.

as total systems, completely obstructing mutual curiosity and accommodation. We cannot ignore, however, the polemics inherent in 'Abd al-Rahman Chishti's position, whatever its politics. It was his endeavour to construct a narrative where his own tradition might still emerge paramount, and it is perhaps with this aim that he brought in the different scales of time from the Islamic tradition.

'Abd al-Rahman Chishti's reflection on time was esoteric and included questions about the age of the world, human genesis, and so on. He found that the scales of Hindu time were much vaster than the scales in "orthodox" Islamic thought, and he used this discrepancy not simply to say that Hindus believe in fanciful and false things. He subsumed one time-scale within the other; what is even more remarkable is that the subsumption is of Islamic time within the larger cycles of Hindu cosmogony. Islam had encompassed several aspects of Judaism and Christianity – admitting, for instance, the prophetic status of Moses and Jesus. Early Islamic scholars had discussed the significance of such integration. But this was much easier to accomplish, since the Qur'an itself was full of biblical prophets and Muhammad had proclaimed himself their successor. To describe the Indic gods and sages as prophets was a far more difficult task. None of them had been mentioned in either the Qur'an, *hadith*, or for that matter in any early Islamic texts of the "classical" Islamic period. Again, what Chishti does with reference to his discourse on time is somewhat the opposite of the process of absorbing Biblical prophets within an Islamic ecumene. In the *Mir'at al-Makhluqat*, he subsumes Islamic time into Hindu time, even as he makes the latter the time of the jinns. I would assume that he does so to explain the discrepancy between the two times in Islamic terms and thereby enhance his position's acceptability within his own community. It is also relevant to notice in this context that Chishti seems to make a distinction between core and secondary beliefs in Islam. His intellectual reasoning and manoeuvres relate to what appear as secondary ideas. As a result, without disrupting certain core Islamic sensibilities, he modifies the idea of a clear separation and necessary conflict between the doctrines of the two religious systems, and advocates a curious form of dialogue.

Is there implicit advice here to Muslim theologians, the Naqshbandi shaikhs and their close associates, and members of the royal family and large parts of the nobility? Were they being asked to learn and interact seriously with the central ideas and beliefs of the Other, and not live complacently in ignorance of it? Tempting as it is to answer this question in the affirmative, a fully convincing response must await a clearer sense of the audience of this and other texts of this prolific and adventurous author.

Before I conclude, it may not be out of order to note here that around the seventeenth century, and earlier too, we come across similar discussions in Europe regarding the nature of pre-Adamite time and the world. Such discussions arose in the wake of the new science of the Renaissance and the discovery of the New World. The discussion in Europe was grounded in the Book of Genesis. The efforts of some thinkers were at reconciliation between religious dogma and the new discoveries, while others opted for a wholesale rejection of older religious explanations.[87] There is no doubt that, by comparison, 'Abd al-Rahman Chishti's discourse is solely in the frame of religion and revealed wisdom. But notable in this discourse is the author's attempt at reconciling his own religious beliefs with those of the "Hindi" people who also lived in India. The attempt may have had extrinsic political motivations related to the Mughal context of a multi-religious empire. However, his polemical stances are relatively simple. He did not have a brazen Islamicising agenda that was deviously cloaked in the language of universalism. As he projects the origins of the human world with Adam, he traces the lineage of his religion to a world wherein hundreds and thousands of Adams had passed through. The European quest for the origins of the world, by contrast – particularly in attempts to incorporate the newly discovered

---

[87] Grafton, *New Worlds, Ancient Texts*; Livingstone, *Adam's Ancestors*, pp. 1–79.

"savages" of the New World into a pre-existing knowledge about the world – quickly took a turn towards carefully categorised and hierarchical thinking. This was directed in some measure at least to the problem of justifying the European usurpation of native rights to self-rule and of native enslavement.[88] Moreover, whereas 'Abd al-Rahman Chishti does not in the final analysis deny the common origin of man, including the Hindus of his time whose views he repudiates and whom he accuses of hiding their knowledge of Adam, Europeans even debated the possibility of polygenesis to explain the observed diversity of the world.[89]

It has often been assumed that the principal impetus to rethinking Biblical chronologies and origins came from the discovery of the New World in the aftermath of the Columbian voyages. While there is undoubtedly some truth in this, the conversation between votaries of the Religions of the Book and other traditions in the sixteenth and seventeenth centuries, whether Indic or Chinese, could also throw up important challenges with regard to these same questions. Whether or not Chishti was one of the "new intellectuals" of seventeenth-century India, there can be little doubt that the challenges he faced as well as the solutions he found mark him out as an important voice of the period, one who has yet to find his proper place in general accounts of the intellectual history of Mughal times.

---

[88] Pagden, *The Fall of Natural Man*, pp. 10–14, 27–56; Randles, "'Peuples sauvages'".

[89] Livingstone, *Adam's Ancestors*, pp. 109–200.

6

In Search of a Sacred King
Dara Shukoh and the *Yogavasisthas* of Mughal India

DARA SHUKOH IS A well-studied figure in Mughal Indian history. He has been portrayed as a saintly scholar, the beacon of Mughal non-sectarian political culture, particularly insofar as he was interested in the Muslim Sufi traditions as well as ancient Hindu religious scriptures. He had close connections with some of the most eminent Qadiri Sufis of his time, compiled two Sufi biographical/hagiographical dictionaries (*tazkiras*), wrote three significant treatises on intricate mystical doctrines, studied Indic philosophy and religious scriptures, and, by undertaking to translate into Persian several Hindu texts from the original Sanskrit, initiated a discussion of Islam's close relations with Hindu traditions.[1] Several modern historians, commenting on his politics, intellectual ambitions, and leadership qualities, have also highlighted his deficiencies as a military and political

---

[1] See, e.g., Hasrat, *Dara Shikuh*, pp. 43–157, for his works on Sufis and Sufism; and pp. 174–292, for works on Hindu traditions. For a discussion of Prince Dara Shukoh's individual treatises, see also Crollius, "Reflections on the Majma'-al-Bahrayn of Dara Shukoh", pp. 44–51; Louis Massignon, C.L. Huart, and Jean Filliozat's articles, in English translation, in Waseem, *On Becoming an Indian Muslim*, pp. 95–144. For some admirable recent studies, see Kinra, "Infantilizing Baba Dara", pp. 165–93; idem, *Writing Self, Writing Empire*, pp. 240–85; Faruqui, "Dara Shukoh, *Vedanta*", pp. 30–64.

leader, thus explaining his failure and the triumph of his masterful brother Aurangzeb.² In some Mughal Indian records, too, his portrayal is contrasted with that of Aurangzeb.³ My purpose in this chapter is not to take a position on these various approaches, but something more specific: I consider here an important scholarly work written by Dara Shukoh, namely, his translation of the *Yogavasistha* which, though the subject of earlier scholarly attention, can withstand some more for the purposes of the perspective of this book.⁴

To bring the prince's involvement with this text more clearly into view for my analysis of relationships between the Mughals and the Sufis, and therefrom with a broader Indic ethos of religio-philosophical exchanges, I ask a series of questions: Why did the prince commission a new translation of the text when, over half a century earlier, Nizam Panipati had already published a reasonably "accurate" and "faithful" translation, and when other versions apart from Panipati's were also available to him? Did the prince see in the *Yogavasistha* something that was missing in the available Persian versions? Why did he choose to prepare or commission

---

² For a good recent discussion of this, see Faruqui, *The Princes of the Mughal Empire*, pp. 169–80; see also Qanungo, *Dara Shukoh*, Vol. I, pp. 62–6 and 269–74. For detailed studies of Dara Shukoh's politics and philosophy, see also Gandhi, *The Emperor Who Never Was*; Nair, *Translating Wisdom*; Chanda, *Dara Shukoh*.

³ See, e.g., Bernier, *Travels in the Mogul Empire*, pp. 6–7 and 10–11: "Dara was not deficient in good qualities . . . but he entertained too exalted an opinion of himself . . . spoke disdainfully of those who ventured to advise him, and thus deterred his sincerest friends." But Bernier says of Aurangzeb that he "was devoid of that urbanity and engaging presence, so much admired in Dara: but he possessed a sounder judgment, and was more skilful in selecting for confidantes such persons as were best qualified to serve him with faithfulness and ability."

⁴ Dara Shukoh, *Jugbashist*. For a recent study of Dara Shukoh's interest in Indic traditions and the Persian *Yogavasistha*, see Gandhi, "The Prince and the *Muvahhid*", pp. 65–101: The article draws on her doctoral dissertation, idem, "Mughal Self-Fashioning".

a new translation in 1655, a very late time in his princely career and the very year in which he had not only established his image as a saint but also put into play his designs to claim the Mughal throne? Of course, Dara Shukoh's efforts, including his relationship with Hindu saints like Baba Lal, had precedents in earlier Mughal courts, but he went a step further than his forebears in that he found an element of truth in Indic texts.[5] Nevertheless, it is worth asking whether the significance of his involvement with the *Yogavasistha* may have been bound up with concerns that became increasingly central to Dara Shukoh's politics.

With these questions in mind I seek to revisit the Mughal *Yogavasisthas*, first briefly considering the reasons why Mughal scholars and their patrons chose this text and how they sought to present their visions of it in Persian. Thereafter I consider Dara Shukoh's translation, situating it in the larger context of Mughal political culture.

The *Yogavasistha*

The book of Vasistha and his yoga (*Yogavasistha*), also called *Maha-Ramayana*, or *Vasistha-Ramayana* – to provide two among several of its alternative titles – is a work of philosophical narratives.[6] The word yoga in the title, as the work clarifies, refers to a kind of philosophical knowledge (*jnana*) and not to ascetic praxis.[7] The work is a long dialogue between the sage Vasistha (Vasistha

---

[5] Cf. Kinra, "Infantilizing Baba Dara".

[6] The compound *yogavasistha* is more commonly translated as "Vasistha's Yoga". But the compound is perhaps best resolved, on the precedent of the title of Kalidasa's *Abhijnasakuntala*, as "the book relating to Vasistha and his Yoga". Personal communication with Sonam Kachru, from a conversation with Victor D'Avella and Gary Tubb, South Asia Languages and Civilizations, University of Chicago.

[7] See Slaje, "Liberation from Intentionality", pp. 171–94; Hanneder, *Studies on the Moksopaya*, pp. 57–9; Dasgupta, *A History of Indian Philosophy*, Vol. 2, p. 131.

Muni, transliterated as "Basisht" in Persian translations) and Prince Rama (venerated as Sri-Ramachandra, or "Ram Chand" in Persian translations), and comprises over 32,000 verses.

The *Yogavasistha* has lived many lives, even in the relatively short time between its introduction as an innovative book in Kashmir titled *Moksopaya* (The Means of Freedom) around the tenth century, and its subsequent circulation as the *Yogavasistha*, with variations in the framing stories that introduce the book and certain changes in philosophical vocabulary. The variations amount to the nesting of this work in a frame more suited to a Brahmanical theological tradition and allowing much of the distinctive vocabulary of the text to be replaced by standard Vedantic terms.[8] In between the extensive (*brhad*) texts there was a version of the work in 5000 verses that came to be known as the *Laghu Yogavasistha* (Concise *Yogavasistha*). This version was perhaps once known as *Moksopayasara* (The Essence of the Means to Freedom), a work attributed to Abhinanda of Kashmir, but of which neither the date nor the author are certain. Some of the organisational changes introduced by the *Laghu* have, however, affected later versions of the *Yogavasistha*, including the arrangement of chapters in the two Mughal Persian translations – those of Nizam Panipati and Dara Shukoh. Several other versions further abridged, or re-represented, the core philosophical doctrines of the text.[9]

These works are linked by some important features, of which the first is the fact that the philosophical conversation between Rama and Vasistha Muni is situated as an episode in the Ramayana. The second is the use of philosophical narratives, many of which are unique to these texts (after which they travelled extensively) and uniquely expressive of the philosophical aims of the text. The core of this philosophy concerns the nature of what is most real and

---

[8] Slaje, *Vom Moksopaya-Sastra*.

[9] For the variety of "short" versions of the *Yogavasistha*, see the discussion and references cited in Hanneder, *Studies on the Moksopaya*, pp. 10–13. See also Thomi, "The *Yogavasistha*", pp. 107–16.

the vision of liberation in life (*jivanmukti*), stressing that a non-ascetic freedom in action is not only possible but desirable on the basis of thought, and on the kind of rational inquiry exemplified in the work. It is not spiritual praxis, or ritual, or even meditation that promotes freedom, but thought, which can in principle be engaged in by anyone, irrespective of social status, eligibility, or entitlement to Brahmanical norms. As the *Laghu* puts it, whether one is eligible (*adhikara*) to receive instruction in the text depends solely on the desire to know, which in turn depends on not being one who is either utterly incapable of being taught, or already possessed of knowledge. Social standing, considerations of ritual purity, and membership in a community simply do not serve as criteria for eligibility: this is a significant feature of the book's overall philosophical outlook.[10]

A point that cannot be emphasised enough concerns the way in which this work was self-conscious about its function as a model for knowledge on the part of rulers caught between the conflicting demands of disenchantment and disengagement (*vairagya*) from the values of power and pleasure on the one hand, and the need to seemingly promote such values through their engagement in the world on the other.[11] Notably, the dilemma of rulers caught between conflicting values is presented by the text as being the result of reasoned deliberation (*vicara*) – an achievement, and not a symptom of despondence or mere emotional confusion. The resolution of the dilemma, then, must similarly be rational and must lead kings back into the world through skilful and reasoned activity.

In stressing the role of this text as a model for the thought

---

[10] "Persons qualified to read this work called Vasistha . . . should neither be Ajnanis (the ignorant or the worldy wise), nor those Jivanmuktas (liberated ones), who have reached their Jnana-Atman, freeing themselves from all pain, but only those who, conscious of being under bondage, long after freedom from it, and are in that vacillating position, from which they contemplate attaining Moksha": Aiyar, *Laghu Yogavasishtha*, 1st edn, 42; rpntd edn, p. 1.

[11] Jurgen Hanneder emphasises this aspect of the text. On the use of the

of kings, one can highlight first the framing story of the man who will become the ideal ruler, Rama, who requires the philosophical conversation and narratives of the text to elucidate and confirm his awakening, to make him capable of ruling. But there is also the emphasis on kings in the philosophical narratives of the work to consider.[12] There is also a prophecy included in the book that depicts the work being read on a certain day to King Yasovarman of Kashmir by his ministers, when so efficacious were the philosophical conversations promoted by the work that even overhearing these conversations between ministers and kings induced enlightenment. Or so the stories would have us believe.[13] And it is not the stories alone, for the use of the text in history seems to confirm the prophecy.[14] The subsequent history of the text confirms it was a "mirror for princes", as we might say following the Persian idiom. For example, it is worth noting that the *Moksopaya* is depicted as being used to alleviate the distress of Zain al-'Abidin of Kashmir at the end of that monarch's life.[15]

---

text in instructing those in power (Ksatriyas), see Hanneder, *Studies on the Moksopaya*, p. 194.

[12] For a discussion of kingship as it is thought through in a few exemplary stories of the *Yogavasistha*, see Doniger, *Dreams, Illusions*, pp. 132–4 and 135–43.

[13] For a translation of this story, see Venkatesananda, *Vasistha's Yoga*, p. 169. Liberation through overhearing one's own story is of course a trope found in the framing story of the *Kathasaritsagara*. The *Yogavasistha* clearly intends its own philosophical frames to be a model for, and a model of, future situations of self-realisation. On the use of this trope in the *Yogavasistha* and its reception in Kashmiri historiography I am grateful to Sonam Kachru for pointing out how the *Moksopaya* is said to have been used to reveal to King Zain al-'Abidin his own life story as it might be if the theories of the *Yogavasistha* were true. Kachru, "Of Forgetting".

[14] See Hanneder's discussion of five historical cases from the tenth to the eighteenth century, including the Mughals, wherein the text has actually served this purpose: idem, *Studies on the Moksopaya*, pp. 132–3.

[15] On the *Moksopaya* in the court of Zayn al-'Abidin, see Obrock, "History at the End of History", pp. 221–36.

Dara Shukoh, as we will see, saw this potential of the *Yogavasistha*, a fact which also perhaps explains his dissatisfaction with earlier translations. But before we look at the strategies of reading and translation that the prince encouraged, a few words are required to contextualise the Persian *Yogavasisthas* that enjoyed currency both within and outside the world of the Mughal court.

The Persian *Yogavasisthas*

Three readily available versions existed in Persian before Dara Shukoh's.[16] One was from the age of Akbar (r. 1556–1605), prepared in 1597 under the patronage of his son and successor Prince Salim (better known as Jahangir; r. 1605–28), by one of the prince's associates (*kamtarin-i bandagan-i dargah*), Nizam Panipati.[17] Two other versions were from the reign of Jahangir: one by Sufi Qutb-i Jahani, also known as Shaikh Sufi Sharif,[18] and

---

[16] These three translations are available in print, and there are also numerous manuscripts in several Asian and European libraries. In addition there is an illustrated manuscript of this text, prepared in 1602 and preserved in the Chester Beatty Library, Dublin, from which Wendy Doniger has reproduced fourteen paintings. She says it is the earliest extant manuscript of the *Yogavasistha*, probably produced for Akbar (r. 1556–1605); cf. Doniger, *Dreams, Illusions,* p. 304. Gandhi, "Prince and the *Muvahhid*", cites a 2010 unpublished paper by Heike Franke in support of the manuscript having been prepared for Akbar. Again, when describing the Persian translations, Hasrat mentions one by Pandit Anandan, citing Ethe and Rieu; cf. Hasrat, *Dara Shikuh,* 234. I think Hasrat misreads Abhinandan as Bahanandan and supposes him to be "Anandan". The three works mentioned in the following six lines in the text are copies of Panipati's translation of Abhinandan's *Laghu Yogavasistha*.

[17] Panipati, *Jug Basisht*. I have not come across any reference to the translator. He may have belonged to the noted Chishti-Sabiri Sufi family of Panipat; cf. Rizvi, *A History of Sufism in India*, Vol. 2, pp. 274–5, for this family.

[18] Sufi Qutb-i Jahani, *Risala-i Atwar*. The text is apparently based on *Yogavasistha-sara*, a summarised selection from the *Laghu Yogavasistha* by Qutb-i Jahani, the same text that Dara Shukoh cites in the preface of his translation and which induces the vision he mentions. The colophon of an Aurangzeb-era

another by Abu al-Qasim Findiriski (d. 1050/1640–1), a visiting Iranian philosopher.[19] Panipati's translation was a literal rendering of Abhinanda Kashmiri's *Laghu Yogavasistha*, while Shaikh Sufi Qutb-i Jahani's *Atwar dar Hall-i Asrar* is apparently based on the *Yogavasistha-sara* and was dedicated to the emperor Jahangir; the *Yogavasistha* penned by Abu al-Qasim Findiriski is self-consciously a selection (*muntakhab*) rather than a continuous translation of a Sanskrit text.

---

manuscript, copied in Agra on Rabi 7, 1070 (23 November 1659), refers to the author as Shaikh Sufi Sharif, who dedicates the translation to Jahangir. The emperor is mentioned with high-flying adjectives such as "*haqa'iq wa ma'arif-agah, vaqif-i asrar-i ma'dan-i 'irfan va yaqin*." Sufi Sharif compiled another treatise, *Ghara'ib al-atwar fi kashf al-Anwar*, containing the conversation between Mahadeva and Krishna (*Mukalama-yi Krishn Mahadev*), which, as its preface notes, took place on Mount Kailash, the abode of Mahadeva. Cf. Khuda Bakhsh Library, Patna, MSS 2081/2081 and 2082/2082. This text is also referred to as *Kashf al-Kunuz* and *Tuhfa-yi Majlis*. Cf. India Office MS. 1836, British Library, London; see also Chand and Abidi's introduction to the edition of Dara's translation. Mojtabai mentions an English translation, which unfortunately I could not access, and I am not sure if this is the same *Yogavasistha-sara* that Qutb-i Jahani used.

[19] Mir Abu al-Qasim Findiriski was a noted teacher of philosophy in Isfahan, and men like the famous Sadr al-Din Shirazi and Sarmad Kashani, the poet and a close companion of Dara Shukoh, were among his pupils. Findiriski was not a prolific writer. Among his writings is a small treatise, *Risala-yi Sana'iyya*, on the aims of the arts, crafts, and sciences; a work in Arabic, *Risala fi-l haraka*; a mystico-philosophical *qasidah*; and a number of *ghazals, qit'as*, and *ruba'is*. He visited India several times, first in 1606 and then in 1611, and stayed for a number of years. His connection with the noted Zoroastrian priest and author Azar Kaivan is also reported. He died in Iran; cf. Fathullah Mojtabai's Introduction to his edition of Findiriski, *Muntakhab-i Jug Basisht*, pp. 16–20. This edition is based on Mojtabai, "*Muntakhab-i Jug Basisht*". Both Abidi and an editor of Nizam Panipati's translation, Jalali Naini, think Findiriski added a commentary to the translation but did not have an independent text of his own. This impression is based on the manuscripts they inspected, respectively. Abidi is clearer on this point, whereas Naini seems confused even with respect to determining

The *Yogavasistha* of Nizam Panipati

Panipati's translation begins, after the conventional praise of God and the Prophet, as follows:

> People of understanding and those who seek the correct path are not concerned with [lit. their attention is not directed to] this world (*'alam-i fani*), but rather to the world of eternity (*'alam-i baqa*). Being separate from the earth and water and physical things of this world, their souls wander in the garden of the palace of the hidden. They are the opposite of [those who desire] the transitory pleasures of this world and those ignorant and oblivious to the realities who are consumed by these pleasures of the world and of the body . . . Prince Salim . . . leaving aside carnal desires, is like those pious and God-knowing people and the Sufis; his attention is directed towards mysticism (*tasawwuf*). Even if he is very busy with matters concerning state management (*mulk-dari*), all his remaining hours are spent in attending to spiritual concerns and care for the poor and the knowledgeable. Scholars of Arabic and other sciences, experts in Persian poetry and prose, historians and Hindu pandits all assemble at his evening gatherings. Important books such as Maulana Rumi's *Masnawi*, the *Zafarnamah, Waqi'at-i Baburi, Jami' al-Hikayat*, and other histories and stories comprising exhortations and admonitions are read out to him and discussed in his court. In this same period, he gave instructions that the *Jugbasisht*, which consists of wonderful and valuable exhortations and advice derived from reliable books of the Brahmin philosophers of India, should be translated from Sanskrit into Persian. Accordingly, this ordinary slave of his court, Nizam Panipati, took charge of (*mutasaddi*) its translation. The contents and substance (*mazmun wa ma hasal*) of this book were obtained from Patahan Mishra Jaipuri and Jagannat Mishra Banarasi, without any addition or interpolation. These were then translated into simple Persian.[20]

---

the period in which Findiriski wrote. My reading of this text is based on Mojtabai's critical edition. In his view, Findiriski's work is an independent text.

[20] Panipati, *Jug Basisht*, pp. 1–3.

Panipati projects Prince Salim as one who appreciated and displayed a yearning to learn the truth and was thus interested in scholarship. The work sustains a focus consistent with the prince's image. Given the presence of pandits in his court and his interest in stories, we can surmise that he was told of the *Yogavasistha* in one of the assemblies described above, whence his desire for a translation of the text in Persian. Panipati's portrait of the prince in the work's Preface modifies the received image of Jahangir, who is often projected as a tippler and who, when he ascended the throne, had little interest in management of the kingdom, which he handed over to his queen, Nur Jahan. In Panipati we thus have valuable support for several recent studies of the emperor.[21] We know that Jahangir was interested in *tasawwuf* and cultivated an interest in Indic traditions. We also know that Jahangir continued Akbar's policy of encouraging Hindus and Muslims to try being open to each other's traditions.[22]

The Translator's Preface is followed by a long Introduction entitled "Muqaddama-i kitab-i Jugbasisht" which seems to adapt Abhinanda's Introduction to his *Laghu Yogavasistha*.[23] Abhinanda, as noted above, prepared a shortened version of the extended *Yogavasistha*, considering the latter dauntingly long; he divided his redaction into six chapters, each chapter subdivided into sections. The first section of the first chapter begins with the framing

---

[21] Compare Koch, *Mughal Art and Imperial Ideology*, pp. 12–37; Lefèvre, "Recovering a Missing Voice", pp. 452–89; idem, "Pouvoir et noblesse dans l'Empire moghol", pp. 1287–1312; Alam and Subrahmanyam, *Writing the Mughal World*, pp. 249–310.

[22] For Jahangir and the Sufis, see Jahangir, *Toozuk-i Jahangeeree*, pp. 27, 211, 212, 218, 239, 278, and 281; Lahori, *Majalis-i Jahangiri*, pp. 184–6, 221, and 226; Chishti, *Mir'at al-Asrar*. For Jahangir's relations with Hindu saints, see Jahangir, *Toozuk-i Jahangeeree*, pp. 175–6, 177, 279, and 281 (about Jadrup). For Akbar's interest in religious amity and understanding, see, e.g., Abu al-Fazl's introduction to the *Mahabharata*, Persian translation. For Jahangir's appreciation of and interest in maintaining Akbar's policy, see Jahangir, *Tuzuk-i Jahangiri*, p. 16.

[23] Panipati, *Jug Basisht*, pp. 5–10.

story, which contains a dialogue between the sage Bharadwaja and Valmiki; it begins with Bharadwaja addressing Valmiki, his master, thus:

> O Perfect Master, it is not hidden from you that this world is a trap for animate beings, a place for the imprisonment of those who are oblivious. Be gracious enough to tell me in detail about Ram Chand. He, with all his many spiritual and physical perfections in this world, which is a prison for the ignorant and oblivious – how did he lead his life and in what manner did he live with the people of God and eventually, from this space of nothingness? How did he walk towards the realm of eternity (*'alam-i baqa*)?[24]

The translation, in most of the manuscripts, concludes the sage Vasistha's advice as follows:

> Know it for certain that the fortunate one who mobilises all his strength and surrenders his heart to the remembrance of Truth, sitting in a corner, even if he appears to be destitute, acquires a stature which allows him to see all the things of the world, such as honour, status and wealth, as lower even than blades of grass . . . This world, and whatever is visible in it, all are spectacles of the beauty of the Truth and manifestations of Absolute Being. You have seen the Hidden Light, reflected in so many forms and shapes and you have believed in this [false] knowledge of yours and have tied your heart to it. My last guidance and the substance of well-wishing for you is that so long as you say, "This is me, this is from me," you will remain imprisoned in toil and sorrow. Cross the boundaries of your own self. Consider yourself engrossed in the remembrance of Truth. Do not attribute any act to your own self. Be free from all toils and sorrows. That Hidden Beauty, that Absolute Existence which knows no bounds, that is so terse and without qualities, pure from all names and signs and attributions, and His Person, is above rising and setting, birth and dying, youth and old age, remains always in the same position. The complete and ultimate recognition of Him is that under no circumstance should one see one's own self, and in all circumstances one should surrender oneself to Him, to hide oneself from one's own

[24] Ibid., p. 12.

eyes. After you have surrendered yourself and have given all your acts, speech, hearing, giving, taking – in sum, all your silences, your stillness, and your motion – to Him and know that everything is from Him, make this recognition of Him the achievement of yourself. This is the ultimate goal of those who know God.[25]

Thereafter, the benefits and many blessings that accrue from the reading of the text are listed.

The *Yogavasistha* of Shaikh Qutb-i Jahani

Although Nizam Panipati's translation was produced in the court, it appears to have gained currency outside the court as well. It is

[25] Ibid., p. 483. It should be noted, however, that not all manuscripts of Panipati's work end here. One manuscript in fact continues beyond this point for several pages and ends in the following fashion: "Basisht said, 'O Ram Chand, leave this task, and with full concentration and without any lust and desire, enter the business of the world (*kar o bar-i 'alam*).'" Here the forty-second *sarga* of the *nirvan prakaran* ends. "Balmik said, 'O Bharadwaj, Vasista Rsi [*Vasistha rsi*] narrated to Ram Chand this account of the wonders and miracles, which are like the boats of the ocean of the world, in eighteen days. To hear these stories which give you the recognition of God, so many *devatas, rsis, siddhas, gandharvas*, Brahmins, and great kings assembled. All throughout these days, from the fountain that sprang from the mouth of Vasistha *rsi*, they drank this elixir. Finally, they left for their own places.' Ram Chand, having heard these stories (like the ocean without waves and like flower petals falling from the sky upon the head of Ram Chand, who himself was the form of Visnu that had descended upon him), in this way acquired *jogabhyas* and *jnanrup* [*jnana-rupa*] and became desireless. After that, Ram Chand came to his father, Raja Dasrat [Dasaratha] and to his brothers. He then paid his respects (*namaskar*) to Vasistha *rsi* and said to him, 'O perfect preceptor, because of your attention and kindness, all the doubts that I had in my heart have now disappeared. My heart is now at peace, free from heat or cold, sorrow and happiness, good and evil. With your sunlight, you have removed the evil of the world (*moha*), which is a great darkness (*andhakar*).' Vasistha, hearing this from Ram Chand, was pleased. Then all the *devatas, rsis, gandharvas*, and *siddhas* came and paid their respects to Ram Chand, saying, 'O Ram Chand, with your grace and because of you, we heard this most perfect knowledge; and it is to you masters [i.e. Vasistha and Ram], who are the removers of the sorrows and evils of the world, that we pay our respects and take our leave.'" Ibid., editors' comments; epilogue, pp. 488–9.

noteworthy, then, that Shaikh Qutb-i Jahani, within a short while of Panipati's work being available, set about producing his preferred version of the *Yogavasistha*, based on the *Yogavasistha-sara*. It begins thus: "This is a treatise titled *Atwar dar Hall-i Asrar*, [whose purpose is] to write the accomplishments of Basisht and Ram Chand, who achieved the search of gnosis and brought it out from behind the veil. It was translated into Persian and given another garb."[26] And this is how the first chapter, or "way" (*taur*), begins:

> Basisht says: I prostrate myself respectfully and sincerely to that steady Light which is eternally stable and fixed in one place. Restlessness does not find a path to it. He who is pure and free from any connections with all directions, peripheries, times, and places, about whom we cannot say that he is in the east or that he is in the west, or in the south or the north, whether above or below, in time or in space; there is no beginning or end for him. Instead, he is eternal, steady for all time, the one who is exact knowledge and gnosis, and the path to find him is nothing but the knowledge of one's own self. The *hadith* "*Man 'arafa nafsahu faqad 'arafa rabbahu*" (Verily he who knew his self knew his Lord) points to the same gnosis.
>
> Basisht says: The addressee of these noble words and worthy of these subtle ways and conduct is the seeker of the path of investigation, the one who intends to liberate himself from the prison of this world, who emerges from "*kun wa makun*" (be and not be) and who wants to manifest himself in oneness and colourlessness, freeing himself from whatever else exists.[27]

Qutb-i Jahani then begins the speech of Vasistha Muni: "Basisht says: O Ram Chand, the attachments of the world are a terrible

---

[26] Qutb-i Jahani, *Risala-yi Atwar*, p. 47. The text proceeds to give a summary of its contents: "It comprises over ten *atwar*, or ways, alluding to various practices on the mystical path: the first is the description of *tajrid*, celibacy; the second is the description of the fact that the world is just an illusion (*khayal*); the third deals with liberation; the fourth – the bliss of the heart (*jami 'iyat*); the fifth – the removal of desire; the sixth describes knowledge (*ma'rifat*) of the self; the seventh, knowledge of Truth; the eighth concerns the discovery of the self; the ninth treats knowledge of one's own condition; and the tenth deals with the perfection of the knowledge of Truth."

[27] Ibid., p. 47.

disease and its medicine is nothing but continuous thought: 'Who am I, and what is this world? From where did it emerge?'"[28] Nowhere in the text is there mention of the many stories that abound in the original *Yogavasistha* and that contribute to its distinctive message and meanings. The text thus gives no sense of the framing story of Valmiki and Bharadwaja, nor explains the reason for the discourse being given and recorded, nor for whom it was originally intended. Similarly, the text ends without any reference to what happened to Rama after Vasistha's discourse.[29]

We may perhaps assume that this presentation of the text amounts to a substantial selection of the philosophy contained in the *Yogavasistha* already available in Persian translation by Panipati rather than a continuous translation; however, the author gives the impression that he translated the work, not that he merely abstracted it from another translation. The text's organisation into ten chapters also does not support the notion of it being a selection culled from an earlier translation. Qutb-i Jahani dedicated the translation to Jahangir, but we do not know whether the translation was commissioned by the emperor.

Abu al-Qasim Findiriski (d. 1640–1)

An important example of the circulation of the *Yogavasistha* in Mughal India can be found in Abu al-Qasim Findiriski's

---

[28] Ibid., p. 48.

[29] The text concludes as follows: "O Ram Chand, keep thinking that you are the exact truth. See, find out, and always bear in mind the following: I am that pure and subtle [reality] that has become manifest in several forms. This world is the [manifestation] of the plurality of my appearances (*libas*). I am all in service and also in control. I am pure and detached from everything. When you know this and act upon it, you will attain the exact truth in which there remains no trace of doubt, and it [this truth] will come to light through your actions. Whatever I have expressed to you, Ram Chand, if you regard yourself as one, you will be one. But if you regard yourself as many, you will be many. For one continuously appears to be many, just as the moon, which has only one existence, is seen in many pots [filled with water]. But, when

Muntakhab-i Jug Basisht (Selections from the *Yogavasistha*). The manuscript that Fathullah Mojtabai used as a basis for his edition and translation of Findiriski's *Muntakhab* says on the front page that the text was translated from the original Sanskrit into simple Persian ("*Az zaban-i hindi tarjuma bi farsi-yi sada*"). Then follow four verses in appreciation of the *Yogavasistha*:

Hamchu ab ast in sukhan bi jahan
Pak o danish fazai chun Qur'an
Chun zi Qur'an guzashti o akhbar
Nist kas ra bi-din namat guftar
Jahil-i ku shanid in sukhanan
Ya bi-did in latif sarwistan [var: Ya bi-did in latif sirr o bayan]
Juz bi-surat bi-din na paywandad
Zan ki bar rish-i kh'ish mi-khandad

This book/speech (*sukhan*) is for the world like water,
Pure and wisdom-giving like the Qur'an
When you have passed through the Qur'an and the traditions of the Prophet
From no one else is there a speech of this nature.
The ignoramus who heard this speech
Or saw this fine garden of eucalyptus [var: Or saw this delicate secret and expression]
Sees only the appearance of it
And thus makes a fool of himself.[30]

Findiriski's text is also a summary of sorts. In fact it is not even divided into chapters, as is Qutb-i Jahani's text. It reads rather like a long essay or perhaps a commentary on selected themes of the philosophy of the *Yogavasistha*. The first three pages are prefatory, beginning with the praise of God identified as Brahm (Sanskrit:

---

you see it with the inner eye, you understand, and you find that all are one. There is absolutely no plurality and multiplicity." Ibid., p. 64.

[30] Findiriski, *Muntakhab*, p. 29. My translation is slightly different from Findiriski's; cf. his Introduction in English, p. 33.

Brahman), who is absolute light, pure reason, joy embodied, which descended and thus left its Absolute position to create the world of duality and plurality. It is on the fourth page of the edited text that the discussion begins: "Now I tell you about the Oneness of God and the emergence of plurality (*hala sukhan dar wahdat . . . mi-kunam*), and thereby explain to you the reality of Creation, how that One person (*zat*) with perfect attributes became several persons (*zat-ha*), in what way He expressed himself into so many creatures."[31] In the 120 pages that follow we have two or three more discussions on various subthemes, each indicated by variations of the phrase "Now I tell you".[32]

More notably, unlike in the earlier Persian versions, nowhere is the sage Vasistha shown to be addressing or teaching Ram Chandra. Moreover, while in Qutb-i Jahani's text there are virtually no Sanskrit words, in Findiriski's text, the critical Sanskrit technical terms are provided in their original form with an elaboration. Examples include *Brahm* (brahman), *chidatman* (cidatman), *jiwatman* (jivatman), *pramatman* (paramatman), *jnan* (jnana), *dhyan* (dhyana), *ahankar* (ahamkara), *muja* (moksa), and *kriya* (kriya). This is perhaps the reason why Findiriski has been referred to as the commentator (*sharih*) of the *Yogavasistha*.

The text revolves around a few main themes, told and retold in a variety of metaphors and exhortations: one must, for example, first recognise that the foundation or basis for any reality is One, Brahm, and that all other entities derive from that One reality. Moreover, these forms or entities will themselves be destroyed, but the basis of reality, Brahm, will never perish. Second, one must recognise that mankind's own belief in independent existence is an illusion, and existence is merely a worldly imprisonment. The goal should always be to train the mind on that One from whom existence derives in order to find release from the imprisonment. The text, as can be discerned from these two themes, consistently

---

[31] Ibid., p. 33.
[32] See, e.g., ibid., pp. 87 and 90.

ponders the question of illusion, deception, and the discernment of reality.[33]

One of the most characteristic features of this text is that it is interspersed throughout with Persian verses illustrating the themes mentioned above.[34] Most of these verses are by "Fani", but there are also several verses from Rumi, 'Attar, Ni'mat-Allah Wali, and the like. Perhaps "Fani" here is Findiriski himself, given that he figures so prominently.[35]

Findiriski thus uses both prose and poetry in his version. While distinctive, it is clearly related to the Persian *Yogavasisthas* we have

---

[33] For example, Findiriski insists in a striking passage that it is not the sky that is blue but rather the imperfection of the perceiver who believes it to be blue. This is, of course, the metaphor with which Valmiki's response in the *Laghu Yogavasistha* begins, choosing one often invoked in the *Moksopaya* and counselling its reader that "overlooking" the manifest colour of the sky is an analogue of "overlooking" manifest facts about personal identity. See verse 6 in Panasikara, *Laghuyogavasistha*, p. 6; cf. Kachru, "Of Forgetting". In other instances, Findiriski exhorts the reader to learn how to distinguish a rope from a snake or to recognise that reality is like the water, not the waves, that one perceives. Findiriski, *Muntakhab*, pp. 27 and 105. For these metaphors (and other metaphors in the *Yogavasistha*), see the extended discussion in Doniger, *Dreams, Illusion and Other Realities*, pp. 261–8. Findiriski also describes the characteristics of Brahm: "He is calm, like water undisturbed by the wind." *Muntakhab*, p. 35; "He is visible from everywhere, like the sky", ibid., p. 39; "He is timeless", ibid., p. 83.

[34] On this characteristic of translations of theological works or those considered mystical, see Ernst, "Muslim Studies of Hinduism?", pp. 173–95 and 183–4.

[35] Mojtabai suggests that this Fani is Fani Isfahani (d. 1807), who lived in the eighteenth century, much after Findiriski's death; and these verses apropos Findiriski's prose were interpolated by someone sometime before 1816; cf. Mojtabai, "Introduction", in "*Muntakhab*", p. 44. My educated guess is that this could be Muhsin Fani Kashmiri (d. 1671). Because Fani Kashmiri rose in fame and reputation during Shah Jahan's reign, he may not have been well known at the time that Findiriski was in India. Unfortunately, I was not able to locate the verses that Findiriski cites in Fani Kashmiri's published works; cf. Fani Kashmiri, *Diwan-i Fani*; idem, *Masnawiyat-i Fani*.

considered above: the concluding statement is virtually a verbatim reproduction of the passages with which Panipati closes his translation, although refined and also studded with the following verse of Hafiz:

Ay gada-i khanqah, baz a ki dar dair-i mughan,
Mi-dahand ab-i wa dil-ha ra tawangar mi-kunand

O fakir of the Sufi hospice, come in
Here in the temple of the fire-worshippers
They serve a drink
And make the hearts rich.

And of 'Attar:

Chun hama chizi-at faramush shud
Bar dil o jan-at bi-gushayand rah

When all you possess is lost
The path opens in your heart and soul.[36]

Findiriski was in India at a time when the Mughal policy of commissioning translations (or retranslations) of some major Indian religious and secular texts (like the Mahabharata, the Ramayana, and the Panchatantra) had encouraged a broad trend of comparative philosophical and gnostic investigation.[37] His interest in and translation of the *Yogavasistha* came about in this social and intellectual milieu. There was also room to examine points of commonality between different sects and traditions with an eye towards minimising the threat of conflict in the real world. Given the contemporaneous Safavid emphasis on strict adherence to a particular Shi'a tradition and intolerance, discovering ways towards the dissipation of potential conflict doubtless greatly appealed to

---

[36] Findiriski, *Muntakhab*, 126; my translation.
[37] For studies of translations in Mughal India and their social and cultural impact, see Ernst, "Muslim Studies of Hinduism?"; Nair, "Sufism as Medium and Method", pp. 390–410; Truschke, *Culture of Encounters*.

Findiriski. This seems apparent even in the way he frames and presents the text, which is not as a projection of the Indic past or present but rather as something within the scope of Persian thought and writing. His copious use of Persian poetry to illustrate certain points in his text, as well as the deliberately Persian–Sufi linguistic register, seems to have been an attempt to craft a text that might, without these elements, have been dismissed as alien and purely Indic and not acceptable within the textual horizons of the Persianate elite.

The *Yogavasistha* in Persian as a Sufi Text

The first translation by Nizam Panipati from Akbar's era was literal, while the two from the age of Jahangir – Shaikh Sufi Qutb-i Jahani's *Atwar dar Hall-i Asrar* and Abu al-Qasim Findiriski's *Muntakhab-i Jug Basisht* – are interpretive to greater or lesser degrees. Setting aside these differences, in all the Persian versions of the *Yogavasistha* we see a greater emphasis on the spiritual concerns of the *Yogavasistha* (i.e. an emphasis on the knowledge of Being, rather than on the connection between knowledge and action in the world made possible by knowledge). Indeed, the history of Findiriski's version of the text is both part and proof of the fact that from Jahangir's time onward the text was primarily received as Sufi. Findiriski, a traveller and newcomer to India who had learned Sanskrit, seems to have been so taken with Qutb-i Jahani's version of the text (since it bore clear filial ties to the philosophy of Ibn 'Arabi) that, when it came time to choose a text for his own translation project, he selected not the Upanishads or the Ramayana but the *Yogavasistha*. Moreover, he not only improved and expanded on Qutb-i Jahani's version but seamlessly integrated Persian spiritual poetry into the text, creating a nuanced and deeply personal elucidation of his understanding of Hindu dharma from his Sufi poetic reading of the *Yogavasistha*. As far as preparing the text as a Sufi work goes, Findiriski's version represents in some ways an advance beyond Qutb-i Jahani's work because of its explicit attention to showing how the ideas in the original text are continuous with, and directly comparable to, those in the Persian Sufi tradition.

It also appears from both Qutb-i Jahani's and Findiriski's texts that in the seventeenth century, in certain circles at least, there was a serious effort to engage with the apparent similarities in different religious traditions; this trend, as we know, culminated in Dara Shukoh's *Majma' al-Bahrain* and *Sirr-i Akbar*.[38] In both interpretive versions of the *Yogavasistha* the exclusively spiritual concern is detectable even at the level of linguistic register. In this regard the headings of various chapters in Qutb-i Jahani's text are instructive. Six of the ten chapters in the treatise (1, 6, 7, 8, 9, and 10) have distinctive Sufi overtones: "Tajrid" (Celibacy), "Ma'rifat-i Nafs" (Knowledge of self), "Ma'rifat-i Haqq" (Gnosis/Knowledge of Truth), "Yaft-i Nafs" (Discovery/Experience of self), "Ma'rifat-i Hal-i Khud" (Knowledge of one's own state/condition), and "Kamal-i Ma'rifat-i Haqq" (Perfect Knowledge of Truth). Apart from such a striking emphasis at the outset, there are recurring words in the text, such as *'alam-i fani* (transitory world), *zat-i haqq* (divine essence), and *'arif* (mystic, gnostic), as well as *suluk* (treading the Sufi path), *murshid* (spiritual guide), and *talib* (seeker), all terms appropriate for a Sufi text.[39] This immersion in Sufi registers of thought and speech may be seen best, perhaps, via extended examples.

In chapter 5, Vasistha Muni advises Rama as follows:

Ay Ram Chand, chun dar suhbat-i ahl-i suluk khud ra bi-gumari wa dar mutala'a-i kutub-i 'ilm-i sufiya warzish namai, ma'rifat-i nafs ki

---

[38] This was, of course, not something entirely new. Much earlier, as we know, Shaikh 'Abd al-Quddus Gangohi (d. 1537) compiled the *Alakhbani* or *Rushdnama*; cf. Digby, "'Abd al-Quddus Gangohi", pp. 1–66; Rizvi, *History of Sufism*, Vol. 1, pp. 336–49 and 359–62; Alam, *The Languages of Political Islam*, pp. 91–4; Ernst, "Fayzi's Illuminationist Interpretation of Vedanta", pp. 356–64.

[39] Qutb-i Jahani, *Risala-yi Atwar*, pp. 47, 48, and 49.

asl-i matlab ast zud bi dast ari na ki muddat-ha mihnat namai wa an matlab hargiz bi dast nayayad.

O Ram Chand, when you are in the company of the people of the Sufi path (*suluk*), and struggle to study the books of the science of the Sufiya, that is when you quickly achieve knowledge of the self (*ma'rifat-i nafs*), which is the prime objective, and which you can never achieve through ages of hard work and effort.[40]

In chapter 6 Vasistha says:

Ay Ram Chand paydai wa na-paydai-yi 'alam ki 'ibarat az baqa wa fana ast wa qiyamat wa ba's isharat bar an ast az nadani wa az na-yaft-i tu-st. Chun yaft-i haqq dast dahad 'alam na-padid gardad wa nist-i mutlaq namayad. Pas mansha'-i wujud-i 'alam nadani ast wa fana-yi an samara-i ma'rifat.

O Ram Chand, the survival and annihilation of the world, which means eternity (*baqa*) and transience/mortality (*fana*), and the Day of Judgment (*qiyamat*) and Resurrection (*ba's*), are because of your ignorance. When you discover Truth (*haqq*), the world disappears and you see absolute nothingness. Thus, the source of being/existence (*wujud*) of the world (*'alam*) is ignorance, and its annihilation is the fruit of Gnosis (*ma'rifat*).[41]

Findiriski also contributes to what could be termed the creation of a Sufi register for the reception of the *Yogavasistha*. His variation

---

[40] Ibid., p. 57.

[41] Ibid., 58. One might also cite here the opening lines of chap. 7: *"Ay Ram Chand har sana wa shukr-i ki bi zuhur mi-rasad az hama haqq wa bar haqq ast ghair-i haqq digar-i kist ki tawanad bi-din sifat zuhur namud. Pas hamid wa mahmud wa hamd har sih 'ayn-i 'ilm-i ma'rifat ast wa zuhur-i sifat-i ust balki 'ayn-i u wa khud dar hama wa bi hama balki 'ayn-i hama wa az hama bi niyaz wa az hama juda"* ("O Ram Chand, whatever praise and thanks that emerge, they are all from God [*haqq*] and are all for God [*haqq*]. Except God, who else could possess this quality? Thus, the one who praises, and the one praised, and the praise itself – all three are the exact signs of *ma'rifat* and the manifestations of His quality; that He himself is, in all, without all, exactly all and independent and separate from all."): ibid.

on the *Yogavasistha*, which we have seen interspersed with Persian poetry, can be appropriately thought of as a Sufi commentary on selected passages of the *Yogavasistha*. The following verses of Fani are noteworthy in this respect, elaborating on the idea of Brahm:

> Its nearness and its distance, its union and its separation,
>   where is that?
> He himself is the sign of the universe,
>   where is that sign?
>
> In His light, there is no space even for a small grain of dust.
> Everything is mortal, except His face.
> Know that in His various and countless forms, there is no manifestation (*zuhur*) other than His own light.
> It is the same hidden light which manifests itself in a variety of colours and forms.[42]

Findiriski also quotes the following verse, replete with Sufi tropes:

> We know no-one but God
> We know not ourselves different from Him
> All is He, yet we do not see Him
> We are we, yet we know not.[43]

And another instance:

> The heart came [as] the place of the manifestation of the light of epiphany (*mazhar-i nur-i tajalli*).

[42] Findiriski, *Muntakhab*, p. 33. Later Findiriski, again in the words of Fani, writes: "The essence of this appearance is one Existence / The others exist from this Existence / The multiplicity manifests from the same oneness / It appears one, and it also appears many / The appearance of multiplicity is not different from oneness / For in both the worlds there exists only one God." Ibid., p. 41. A further example of Findiriski's Sufi register can be found in another iteration of his interpretation of Brahm: "The pure person (*zat-i pak*) of Brahm, in all these forms and manifestations (*mazahir*) is nothing but its own manifestation (*zuhur*) / Whatever exists is nothing but the light of His beauty / You say yes (*bala*) and you ask, am I not (*alastu*)?" Ibid., p. 37.

[43] Ibid., p. 43.

The heart came [as] the valley of Sinai for the mount of epiphany (*tur-i tajalli*).[44]

These are but a few examples from a text brimming with Sufi tropes, in particular those offered in proof of the doctrine of the unity of being (*wahdat al-wujud*). Such words as *sufi*, *safa* (piety, purity), *fana*, and *baqa* recur throughout. Vasistha's advice to Rama is to walk the path of *suluk*.[45] Mojtabai also points out that Findiriski's translation is compatible in its style and register with his other works.[46]

It is these works, and this interpretive ambition, that form the background of what I will argue is Dara Shukoh's distinctive translation and the horizon of its relevance and interpretation. For Dara Shukoh did not simply produce yet one more Sufi *Yogavasistha*.

Dara Shukoh's Translation

Dara Shukoh's translation, like Panipati's, follows Abhinanda's *Laghu Yogavasistha*. Dara Shukoh, however, leaves out several verses, abbreviates others, and in a number of cases adds a kind of explanatory note from other relevant texts, including some medieval commentaries on *Yogavasistha*.[47]

The translation before the standard edition of Chand and Abidi was published twice in the nineteenth century. An Urdu translation titled *Minhaj al-Salikin* (Path/Practice of the Sufis) was also published in the nineteenth century.[48] The Urdu title suggests that its translator read Dara's translation as a Sufi text, continuous with the horizons of the Persian *Yogavasisthas* we saw above; arguably, such a reading of Dara Shukoh was intended to relate his *Yogavasistha* seamlessly with his other writings and was meant

[44] Ibid., p. 67.
[45] Ibid., p. 71.
[46] Mojtabai, "Introduction", in "*Muntakhab*".
[47] See Chand and Abidi, "Introduction", in Dara Shukoh, *Jugbashist*, pp. 5 and 13.
[48] Cf. Abu al-Hasan, *Minhaj al-Salikin*.

to be justified by his other works. This is not unusual. Chand and Abidi also emphasise the text's Vedantic overtones and its continuity with Sufi registers of thought.[49] Yet Dara Shukoh does not seem to regard the *Yogavasistha* as an exclusively theological and religious work representative of the Hindu Other, something to be used only for a project of comparative religion. To him such a reading was only a part, albeit a very important part, of his project. Instead, Dara Shukoh saw fit to emphasise the political overtones of the *Yogavasistha*.

He embarked on his translation in 1655–6 (1066 AH). It is important to recall that by this point he had constructed and established his own self-image as an exemplary Sufi. Indeed, in the self-description found in his other works, he appeared to cast himself as almost a spiritual master, beyond even the rhetorical conventions of Sufi literature.[50] His break with the purely Sufi reception of the *Yogavasistha* is, then, significant. To the historical context we must add that, by this time, Dara Shukoh had clearly articulated his political ambition for the Mughal throne and begun various machinations to achieve this aim against the other claimants in the court.[51] It is in this dual context – i.e. a prince whose self-image was that of a Sufi and who now sought to establish his political claims to the throne – that we may best locate the significance of his turning to the *Yogavasistha*.

Several features of Dara Shukoh's scholarly engagement with the text (and not only as a claimant for the throne) reward close attention, from his production of a textual basis for the translation

---

[49] Cf. Chand and Abidi's comments in their "Introduction", in Dara Shukoh, *Jugbashist*. See also Gandhi, "Prince and the *Muvahhid*".

[50] See, e.g., Dara Shukoh, *Sakinat al-Auliya'*, pp. 5–6, and idem, *Hasanat al-'Arifin*, p. 29. See also Qanungo, *Dara Shukoh*, Vol. 1, pp. 113–15.

[51] See Qanungo, *Dara Shukoh*, Vol. 1, pp. 145–64; Faruqui, *Princes of the Mughal Empire*, pp. 169–80, for the circumstances leading to Dara Shukoh's brothers' resentment and preparation for a fight after Dara Shukoh was proclaimed heir apparent (*wali-'ahd*) with the high-sounding title of *Shah-i Buland-Iqbal* (king of high fortune) in 1656.

to the interpretive registers through which he sought to understand the work. For the prince, by his own account, seemed dissatisfied not simply with existing translations or the way the *Yogavasistha* had been interpreted, but even with the textual bases on which earlier translations had been prepared.[52] He therefore laid out new criteria for his translation, commissioning the production of a new source text before the translation was even begun. In this source text itself he brought to bear other texts, including commentaries on the *Gita*, the *Yogasastra*, and even the Puranas.[53]

The translation is not necessarily Dara Shukoh's solitary achievement; indeed, there seem to have been several scholars involved in preparing the text that formed the basis of the translation, including several pandits who dictated the text to others who, in turn, transcribed it.[54] In this context, it should be noted that while the prince is referred to in the third person (as the person who requests or commands the translation to be prepared "under his auspices"), he is careful to emphasise that it is he who will confirm the research of the scholars under his supervision *("Mi-khwaham in kitab-i mustatab ra bihtar az an dar huzur-i ma tarjuma kunand wa sukhanan-i in ta'ifa ra mutabiq-i tahqiq ki dar aksar-i mauza' taqrir kunam")*.[55] However, in what did his supervision consist? Does it imply that he contributed enough to be legitimately called the translator of the text? This is an area of uncertainty, since his reported command for the preparation of the text also includes evidence of his own research and interpretation.[56]

---

[52] Dara Shukoh, *Jugbashist*, p. 3.

[53] Ibid., p. 5.

[54] Chand and Abidi, on the basis of the manuscripts they have used, surmise that the translator may have been Banwali Das Wali, also known as Baba Wali Ram, the Persian translator of *Praboda Chand Uday (Prabodhacandrodaya)*, since in some verses the translator gives his name as Wali. See Chand and Abidi, "Introduction", in Dara Shukoh, *Jugbasisht*.

[55] Dara Shukoh, *Jugbashist*, p. 3.

[56] It may be noted here that Dara Shukoh preferred a similar method in his translation of the Upanishads as well: Dara Shukoh, *Sirr-i Akbar* (*Sirr-*

More generally, Dara tries to internalise the message of the *Yogavasistha* within the Persianate world without constantly marking the source text a cultural Other. The editorial and workmanlike ways in which Dara Shukoh attempts to render the text continuous with the horizons of literary Persian are of interest precisely because here we may see Dara at his most continuous, and yet distinctive, in relation to earlier works on the *Yogavasistha*. We return to the message in the next section, but here we focus on the details and texture of his translation.

From the Preface it is clear that Dara Shukoh wanted to be very lucid in this new translation about the Persian equivalents of the original Sanskrit terms. To avoid confusion, however, he advises that the first time a term occurs it should be translated or interpreted in Persian but in the course of the text, when the term recurs, he wants this interpretation to be repeated, or even the original Sanskrit term used, in order that readers become familiar with the term in both languages. This is in accord with his other translated works to which he appended glossaries, like the *Majma 'al-Bahrain*.

More striking still are the lexical choices made in the story. For instance, when Rama addresses Visvamitra, he calls him not *rikshir* or *rikshir-i kamil*, an awkward borrowing found in Panipati's work, but simply *ustad* (master), *dana-yi buzurg* (the wise elder), *brahman-i hama-dan* (the all-knowing Brahmin), and *buzurg-i hama-dan* (the all-knowing elder).[57] Another example of such felicitous transcreation is in the episode where Visvamitra approaches King Dasaratha with the demand that he allow Rama leave to travel to the forest to destroy the demons. Dara Shukoh

---

ul-Asrar). For a discussion, see D'Onofrio, "A Persian Commentary to the Upanishads", pp. 533–63; see also Hasrat, *Dara Shikuh*, pp. 275–85 and 212–15, for the prince's knowledge of Sanskrit and his contact with Sanskrit scholars; Qanungo, *Dara Shukoh*, 211–12.

[57] Panipati, *Jug Basisht*, pp. 27 and 38; Dara Shukoh, *Jugbashist*, pp. 18, 20, 21, 22, and 28.

translates the source of this evil with the generic Persian term *shayatin* (devils), whereas Panipati faithfully renders this with *rakshas* (demons, after the Sanskrit *raksasa*), even explaining them as followers of Ravana.[58] Clearly, Dara Shukoh's choice of terms was more attuned to the Persian ear.

This does not mean, however, that Dara's text is more Persianised or Arabicised. On the contrary, in Panipati's text we see on occasion such heavily Persianised and Arabicised expressions as "barak-Allah" and "ahsanta, ahsanta", which are absent from Dara Shukoh's version.[59] Dara Shukoh also tried to avoid unnecessary parenthetical interpolations, as exemplified by Panipati's equivalents for the months of *Kunwar* and *Kartik* with Persian *Mihr* or *Aban* or redundant phrases like "as it is written in the reliable texts of the people of Hind" (*dar kutub-i muʿtabar-i ahl-i hind*) and "according to Hindu belief" (*dar iʿtiqad-i hunud*).[60]

Dara Shukoh's attentiveness to the Persian literary palate goes even further. For example, the "Bairag Prakaran" (chapter of disenchantment, or *vairagya-prakarana* in Sanskrit) immediately follows the Preface in Dara Shukoh's text, excising the Preface of Abhinanda found in Panipati's version. Certainly, this excision indicates Dara Shukoh's relatively slighter dependence on Abhinanda's recension and his access to a wider set of Indic texts. However, in removing this Preface certain particularities pertaining to the "Hindu dharma" found in it, such as the meanings of the words *avatara* and *yuga*, are eliminated; it is as if Dara Shukoh found them distractions from what he deemed the central message of the text. This conjecture is supported by Dara Shukoh's tactful avoidance of concepts such as the transmigration of souls, which are reported faithfully in Panipati's version.[61] The prince seems to judge such concepts, which would only serve unnecessarily to

[58] Panipati, *Jug Basisht*, p. 19; Dara Shukoh, *Jugbashist*, p. 12.
[59] Panipati, *Jug Basisht*, p. 55.
[60] Ibid., pp. 29, 35, 41, and 42.
[61] Ibid., pp. 13, 29, and 53.

distance Persian Muslim readers from the text, as subsidiary to the primary message.

Perhaps in these examples we may understand Dara Shukoh's significant claim that earlier translators "could not raise the veil from the bride of nuanced ideas that resides in the book" (*az chihra-i 'arusan-i daqa'iq-i u parda bar-nadashtand*).[62] As part of his effort to unveil this bride, Dara Shukoh significantly and intentionally simplified the text.

A comparison of Panipati's text with Dara Shukoh's can illustrate the extent to which Shukoh accomplished this. Thus, Panipati's version is much longer than Dara Shukoh's, following almost exactly Abhinanda's original text. Dara Shukoh's is significantly shorter in spite of the fact that he brought in illuminating interpolations from other Indic texts. This mechanical comparison aside, we must also ask for what purpose, and how, the prince summarised the text. We have seen that, unlike Findiriski and Qutb-i Jahani, Dara Shukoh attaches importance to the stories themselves, reproducing them, albeit in shortened form, and that he does so selectively. Thus, Dara Shukoh's dissatisfaction with Findiriski's and Qutb-i Jahani's method of redaction was also because of their exclusive focus on philosophy, eliminating valuable lessons that the stories offer. And yet Dara Shukoh's text is precise and lucid. Rather than translating the stories verbatim, he describes them in a clear, uncluttered, and focused manner, avoiding the digressive details in the Sanskrit text. He does so because his intellectual concern in rendering this text into Persian was to keep it accessible and readable for a Persianate audience, without losing the substance of the work, including its deployment of stories.[63]

---

[62] Dara Shukoh, *Jugbashist*, p. 3.

[63] A cursory comparison of one chapter in Dara Shukoh's version of the text with Nizam Panipati's version can show us this. For example, in Panipati's version, before chapter 6 begins there is a four-page preface explaining at length the topic, the number, and the names of the stories, and a summarised account of the philosophy of Yoga. This is totally absent in Dara Shukoh's version. Following this preface, Panipati devotes four pages to a discussion of the philosophy of this chapter before the first story begins. This is reduced

The Political Orientation of Dara Shukoh's Text

We have so far examined Dara Shukoh as a textual editor, facilitating the continuity and reception of the *Yogavasistha* in Persianate literary culture. We may see this as one way in which his efforts sought to go beyond those of his predecessors, even while furthering their aims. But we must now attend to Dara's political interpretation of the text, paying attention to the political context for his interest in the *Yogavasistha*. A point worth noting here is that the prince is mentioned in hyperbolic terms, indicating that he is a king (*shah*), a highly accomplished saintly figure, and the perfect manifestation (*mazhar-i atamm*) of virtuous conduct, with high ethical virtues (*makarim-i akhlaq*).[64]

Let us begin this analysis with a striking example of how Dara Shukoh brings a larger universe of Indic texts into conversation with his translation, an episode in which the reasons for an erstwhile conflict between the sages Vasistha and Visvamitra is given. Significant here is that while Panipati alludes to the conflict between the two sages and the sermon given to them by Brahma after

---

to a mere introductory paragraph in Dara Shukoh's work, which plunges *in medias res* into the first story. Panipati, *Jug Basisht*, pp. 287–90 and 291–4; Dara Shukoh, *Jugbashist*, p. 161. Again, while Panipati's final chapter is an intimidating 197pp., Dara Shukoh renders it in a concise 56pp. This concision is achieved partly by summarising the stories effectively: e.g., the first story of Busunda takes 18 pages in Panipati's and only 9 in Dara Shukoh's translation. Further, Dara Shukoh eliminates certain stories altogether: e.g., after the story of Vasistha's meeting with Mahadev and the discourse on true worship, on which Panipati dilates largely through the lengthy descriptions of Mahadev, Dara Shukoh's version goes straight from the story of Arjuna and Krsna to that of the kings Bhagirath and Sukhdej; Panipati's version has three intervening stories, spread over 8pp. Panipati, *Jug Basisht*, pp. 357–65. Panipati's expansive style is strikingly exemplified by his rendering of the story of Sukhdej, over 68pp., which Dara Shukoh provides in 19pp. Panipati, *Jug Basisht*, pp. 376–444; Dara Shukoh, *Jugbashist*, pp. 227–46.

[64] Dara Shukoh, *Jugbashist*, p. 3.

resolving the conflict, he does not elaborate on this episode.[65] Dara Shukoh, however, ensures that the episode is included and sets out the circumstances of the conflict as depicted in the *Yogavasistha*, including within his translation allusions that an Indic audience could have been expected to know. At the point in the narrative when this conflict is first mentioned, Visvamitra says to Vasistha:

> "Remember the time when there was enmity between us and we were ready to fight against each other. Brahma then came and forged an understanding between us. As a result, we were freed from stabbing reproaches against each other and the haughty nature of our conflict. It so happened that thereafter our enmity turned into friendship and love. Tell Ram Chand the very things that Brahma told us then." When Visvamitra finished his speech, Vyas ["Vyasa"] and Narad ["Narada"], who were among those present in the audience, applauded him. Basisht then said, "O Visvamitra, it is wise on my part to accept your advice. All that Brahma had then said to remove doubts and suspicions, I remember it all completely."

In brief, the story of the enmity between Visvamitra and Vasistha is written here. Visvamitra was the son of Raja Gadi. One day, when out on a hunt, he passed by the place of the worship of Vasistha, who requested him to grace his abode as a guest. Thereupon, Visvamitra laughed and said, "You are a *faqir*, you are a *darvish*, what hospitality can you offer me?" Vasistha said, "Whatever I have with me, I will offer you." Thereupon he made arrangements for his guest, bringing him wonderful and copious amounts of food, sweetmeats, perfumes, and fresh fruit. In fact he brought more even than was necessary for a king's table. Visvamitra, seeing this, was astonished. One of his servants remarked upon the fact that Vasistha kept the Kamdin [i.e. Kamadhenu, the wish-granting cow] in his house, and whatever he asked of her, she gave. Visvamitra, as he was leaving, asked Vasistha to give him this cow. Vasistha said, "If the cow is amenable, then take her." Visvamitra replied saying if Vasistha gave him the cow, he would take it. In the meanwhile Kamdin asked Vasistha, "What fault have I committed that you are throwing me out of your house?" Vasistha said, "I am not making you leave of my own choice. King Visvamitra

---

[65] Panipati, *Jug Basisht*, p. 55.

is taking you forcibly." Kamdin said, "If you are not giving me to him willingly, then I will take care of things myself." When Kamdin left Vasistha's house, from each drop of Kamdin's sweat which fell on the ground on the way because of the hot wind, a brave man was born. These brave men then destroyed the army of Visvamitra in the blink of an eye. Visvamitra then fled alone, and Kamdin returned to Vasistha's house. Visvamitra, in a rage, invaded Vasistha's house several times and, each time, Kamdin destroyed his whole army.

Finally, the defeated Visvamitra said, "Fie on the Chatri [Ksatriya] and fie on his power! The Brahmin is the truly powerful." He then resolved to become a Brahmin. With this determination, he came to be engaged in ascetic mortifications (*riyazat wa mujahada*) for sixty thousand years, during which time Brahma visited him a couple of times and asked him, "What do you want?" Visvamitra replied, "I want to be a Brahmin." Brahma said, "Since you are of the Chatri lineage, become a Raj Rsi [rajarsi]." A Raj Rsi is a king who has the power of rishis – the seers who have knowledge of past and future. Visvamitra did not agree to this, and again immersed himself in ascetic mortifications. Eventually Brahma said, "If this is truly your desire, then become a Brahmin, a Brahm Rsi." Then Visvamitra said, "Only if Vasistha calls me a Brahm Rsi will I accept this status." At Brahma's request, Vasistha agreed.[66]

After this comes another story highlighting the meanings, significance, and demands of power of a Ksatriya and a Brahmin. Why interpolate this story, in particular, and at such length? The full significance of such choices, I believe, cannot be understood unless we allow the political orientation and ramifications of both the stories and Dara Shukoh's sensitivity to this aspect of the text to emerge clearly. The story of Visvamitra and Vasistha is, after all, exemplary of a concern in Hindu mythology to understand and think through the connections between various forms of power – to think through the conditions under which varieties of power can be drawn on in a lifetime and that will then serve as authorities in turn. Dara Shukoh was right, perhaps, to see that

[66] Dara Shukoh, *Jugbashist*, pp. 39–41.

it is no accident that both Visvamitra and Vasistha are present in the framing story of the *Yogavasistha*, a text he recognised as centrally concerned with the connections between royal power (to which he aspired) and spiritual truth (that he claimed to possess). The prince here is a step ahead of his great-grandfather Akbar, who could only aspire to Ksatriya status, to claim his intimacy with the Rajputs of his domain.[67] Dara Shukoh sought a much higher position: a combination of the powers of a "Raj Rsi" and a "Brahm Rsi". Again, a comparison between Panipati and Dara Shukoh in the introductory part of the text illustrates the prince's focus more substantively. In the introductory section of Panipati's text, where the framing story of Bharadwaja and Valmiki is given, we have no explicit reference to Rama's position as a ruler in the question Bharadwaja poses to Valmiki.[68] It should be noted that Qutb-i Jahani and Findiriski do not even allude to this frame story. This contrasts with the way Dara Shukoh presents the opening chapter of the "Bairag Prakaran":

> There was one pupil of Balmik named B[h]ardwaj. One day in solicitude and extreme humility, he asked the all-knowing master, How could Ram Chand, with perfect gnosis and deliverance which implied liberation in life (*jivan-mukt*), manage the task of kingship and authority (*raj* and *saltanat*)? "Please be kind and tell me this story," Balmik said, "O son, I tell you what you ask for. From hearing this, you will be able to remove from yourself the darkness of ignorance. Ram Chand was a great king in India, endowed with perfect justice, bravery, munificence, and gnosis. The real purpose of writing this book is the narration of the divine realities and gnosis which will become clear in the context of the story of Ram Chand."[69]

This brief anecdote reveals that the *Yogavasistha* is intended primarily to resolve the apparent contradiction between spiritual and temporal power. This is the problem at the heart of Bharadwaja's question to Valmiki regarding how Rama could be king despite

---

[67] Cf. Ziegler, "Rajput Loyalties," pp. 242–84.
[68] Panipati, *Jug Basisht*, p. 12.
[69] Dara Shukoh, *Jugbashist*, pp. 6–7.

having achieved the highest stage of spiritual life (*jivanmukti*). Thus, Panipati initially describes Rama's predicament not as one of rulership but simply as living with God's creatures (*ba khalq-i khuda*). The *Laghu Yogavasistha* has often been read as though the main idea it focuses on is the most general one of "being in time as suffering" (*samsara*), and not more specifically political forms of activity. In contrast, Dara Shukoh introduces from the very beginning his interest in seeing the text's ideas on rule and power (*raj* and *saltanat*). However, it is not as if Dara Shukoh is simply projecting his own concerns into those of the *Yogavasistha*. Abhinanda's *Laghu Yogavasistha* also touches not only on how one can continue to engage in *samsara* – the world described theologically – but, to use its own terms, how one can engage in the kind of action constitutive of political life ("*ramo vyavahrto hy asminkarunyad bruhi me guru*"; verse 4). This emphasises not an existential sense of being in time but rather the interaction between beings according to norms of governance. It is more than possible that Dara Shukoh is not so much translating his own concerns into the text as emphasising the salience of this dimension of Bharadwaja's question. After all, he does use both *samsara* (the world conceived of as suffering through rebirth) and *vyavahara* (the social world) to frame his question.[70]

It is therefore not surprising that Dara Shukoh's translation displays a clear focus on the stories in which kings figure prominently, and in which the concern of the story is to elucidate the nature of statecraft, even while keeping in mind the overarching spiritual concerns of the work.[71] Panipati's book, being a complete translation, also abounds in stories of kings, but only as a matter of course. Dara Shukoh renders the many exhortations meant for King Ramachandra into crisp language and with greater stylistic impact than Panipati.

[70] See Panasikara, *Laghuyogavasistha*, p. 5. I owe this reference to Sonam Kachru.
[71] See Dara Shukoh, *Jugbashist*, pp. 130, 198, and 377, for such stories of kings.

An early example of how narratives in Dara Shukoh's *Yogavasistha* emphasise kings and power is the story of King Janaka in which the focus is on how ignorance is the source of all suffering and on how knowledge enables the king to be freed from his ego (*ahamkara*) and rule without being entangled in material concerns. Summarising this tale, Vasistha says:

> O Ram Chand, the Naiyayikas claim that the world and reality are distinct, the Vedantins claim that they are one, the followers of Patanjali claim that the world is in part a reality separate from the great reality of God. However, the essence of all three opinions returns to the same thing, like the waves of the sea, which, even if they appear different, eventually merge with the greater body of water. The root of all these waves is the ocean. O Ram Chand, from these inquiries, it becomes clear that you too should be detached from the world, and also be one with the world. Perform the works of the world in appearance, but don't be polluted. You tell your acquaintances that so-and-so is your son and so-and-so is your brother, but consider them all as one.[72]

This latter point seems to dovetail beautifully with Dara Shukoh's long-standing interest in the unity of different religious traditions, an interest amply expressed in his reading and analysis of other Indic texts too. Indeed, the title of one of his works, as we know, translates as The Meeting of the Oceans (*Majmaʿ al-Bahrain*). We also know that he prepared a long glossary of Sanskrit terms with their equivalents in Persian. This same purpose is manifest in this translation too. In the course of his teachings, Vasistha once notes:

> O Ram Chand, I present before you also the path of gnosis that Mahadev taught me. At the time when I was worshipping on Mount Kailasa, I kept before me academic books and beautiful flowers. It was the twentieth day of the month of Sawan, and four *gharis* of the night had passed when I saw a light emerging from the distance. I saw Mahadev approaching with his hand placed over Parvati's shoulder.

[72] Ibid., p. 168.

Immediately, I picked up the flowers in my hand and moved forward to welcome him. I placed the flowers and some water by his feet, and in all humility and respect I brought them to my hut. He sat for some time and then asked me, "Have you accomplished the level of worship without being distracted (*'ibadat-i tafriqa*)? Has your heart been relieved with Truth? Are you free from fear and apprehension?" I replied, "The person who has been habituated to your memory, in him remains no distraction (*tafriqa*) or fear. Does any objective remain for him that he has not achieved? Since you have illumined this place with your coming, may I dare ask you – What is that worship of god (*dev-puja*) which contains in itself all the perfections and virtues?" Mahadev replied, "Don't regard Visnu, Brahma, Mahadev, and the other bodies and souls as God. *Dev* [*deva*] is that which has no origin and no end, which has no form, no appearance, and no resemblance, is neither born nor bred by anyone. Absolute and pure existence, joy itself, and knowledge itself (*anand swarup wa gyan swarup; anandasvarupa wa jnanasvarupa*). Perform prayer and worship (*puja* and *'ibadat*) for him. Let the others worship the form. What I mean is as follows: Since the people of the world find the form closer and the meaning very far [from their understanding], the perfect masters allowed them to have the form before them initially, so that their heart could remain at peace. After that, step by step, attention is drawn away from the world of form and guided to recognise the real target. Just as to one who has become tired of walking and believes that his destination is very far, someone will say to him that the destination is only one short course away, so that he can imagine the destination is close and thus walking will for him become less burdensome. O Basisht! Water, flowers, rice, sandal, agarwood, and the lamp are all the requisites of worship of the imagined forms.

The requisites of the worship of the real God (*Dev*) are altogether different. The water required for him is knowledge, the flower is monotheism (*tauhid*), the rice is lawful livelihood, the sandal is the purity of the inner soul, and the agarwood is the heat of love, while the lamp is the light in the heart. If by any chance this God has a face, head, hand, or leg, then his form is the entire universe. His head is the pinnacle of the sky (*akasa*), his leg is the abyss of the underworld (*patal*), his hand extends to the furthest point in all directions. All eyes and all ears are his eyes and his ears. The wise man worships such a

God. His worship is this: that he could be believed to be present in seeing, in hearing, in smelling, in tasting, in touching, in exhaling, in wakefulness, and in sleep; that is to say, the worshipper knows he is the seer, the listener, the speaker, the taster, the one who touches, the one who breathes, the wakeful, and the dreamer are all he. A moment of his remembrance results in limitless fruit. If you remember him for a full day, you become the perfect gnostic and arrive at the stage of liberation (*mukt* [*mukti*]). This is what *jog* [*yoga*] is, and this is what *Dev puja* is. The best worship of him is that you look into your own self, you see him in your own self, and you consider him present in joy, grief, relief, in trouble; when you are rich and when you are destitute; and in all these conditions, you keep treading the same path, and in no condition do you forget him. O Basisht, when the guidance of the master sits in the heart of the people, divine gnosis emerges automatically." Having said this, Mahadev left. Basisht then said, "O Ram Chand, even today I worship in the same way that Mahadev guided me. I have no attachment to anything whatsoever."[73]

Mahadev's instruction to Vasistha here demonstrates clearly Dara Shukoh's own Sufic understanding of religious ritual and piety. He also sees here something in the text that he shared with the earlier Persian translations of it and with his own readings of other Hindu texts.[74] However, it is noteworthy that immediately after such a section, Dara Shukoh's text returns to political issues. In response to this speech, Rama expressed delight at his master's teaching and a desire to hear these things again and again. Vasistha then advised him to be free of all desire. Upon hearing this, Rama asked him to tell him something for the further efflorescence of his heart, in response to which Vasistha alluded to the story of Krsna and Arjuna.

Starting with this most famous episode from the Mahabharata, told here in the context of the correct channelling of desire, the *Yogavasistha* presents a fascinating concatenation of stories of kings.[75] In the idiom of the *Yogavasistha*, the narrative runs thus:

---

[73] Ibid., pp. 214–17.
[74] See also *Sirr-i Akbar*, Dara Shukoh's translation of the Upanishads.
[75] It is interesting to note that one of the ways in which desire may be

When Arjuna saw his relatives on the battlefield and baulked at the prospect of killing them, Krsna explained that these were mere forms, illusions. Only the eternal soul, which has no relation to any one person, can never be killed. Death occurs only for the body, not the soul. Krsna explains that since Arjuna has been born as a Ksatriya, it is his duty to act in the battlefield: "To turn your face from the battlefield is the height of cowardice."[76] Of course, this story has deep personal resonance with Dara Shukoh's own political situation: the question of how a spiritually accomplished person, as both Arjuna was and Dara claimed to be, could allow himself to engage in a war of succession against his own brothers haunts both Arjuna and Dara.

Following this conventional redaction of the well-known story of the *Gita*, the *Yogavasistha* continues in a different vein, emphasising the importance of steadiness and firmness in decision making; this point is further illustrated by the story of King Bhagiratha. Vasistha exhorts Rama: "O Ram Chand, steady your own reasoning, so that whatever you encounter, [seemingly] good or bad, you still accomplish [your work]. Like Raja Bhagiratha, be firm in carrying out your duty. This is how the difficult works which others cannot carry out will become easy for you."[77] After relating this exemplary story of King Bhagiratha, Vasistha continues, "O Ram Chand, with a steady heart and in a fully relaxed manner, sit in communion with the *pramatman* [*paratman*], like Raja Sakraduj [Sikradhvaja]."[78] Vasistha then relates the story of this king. In this manner, Dara Shukoh's text unfolds as a series of stories about kings in a more explicit, direct, and precise manner.

---

channelled correctly is by the cultivation of ethical norms in politics, which Dara Shukoh translates tellingly as *tahzib-i akhlaq*. As a device to ensure justice to their subjects, irrespective of their religious identity, the Mughals relied more heavily on *akhlaqi* norms than on the conventional *shari'a*. See Alam, *Languages of Political Islam*, pp. 26–69.

[76] Dara Shukoh, *Jugbashist*, p. 219.
[77] Ibid., p. 222.
[78] Ibid., p. 226.

Dara's Dream Reconsidered

Before we conclude, we must return to the beginning of Dara Shukoh's *Yogavasistha* and note that his immediate inspiration for translating the text came from a dream after reading Qutb-i Jahani's version:

> After I read the translation of a selection from the book [*Yogavasistha*] by Shaikh Sufi, one night [in a dream] I saw (*waqiʿ*) two persons: one elderly in appearance standing on a higher plinth, and another standing slightly lower. I realised that the person standing on the higher plinth was Basisht, and the other was Ram Chand. The difference in the appearance of these two respectable persons was that Basisht's beard and moustache (*mahasin*) had a few gray hairs, while the other had not even a single gray hair. Since I had benefited enormously from this wise book, I could not help but approach Basisht, and paid my respects. Basisht showed me extraordinary kindness; he placed his hand on my back and said to Rama, "O Ram Chand, he is the true extraordinary seeker. Embrace him." Ram Chand embraced me with great love. Then Basisht gave Ram Chand a sweetmeat, and he offered it to me to eat with his own hands. I ate that sweetmeat. After seeing this dream/vision (*waqiʿ*), the yearning to possess a new translation grew.[79]

Here we may pause to note something of importance: this is the reported dream of a prince who not only finds himself in the company of Rama and Vasistha but is recognised by them as of their kind – as a seeker of the Truth. Dreams are, of course, important both in Sufi and Indic traditions. In his own Sufi works as well, the prince claims to have seen unusual dreams.[80] Yet this

---

[79] Ibid., p. 4.

[80] Compare, e.g., *Sakinat al-Auliya'*, in which Dara Shukoh mentions an angel (*hatif*) telling him four times in a dream that God bestowed on him what no other king on earth ever got: Dara Shukoh, *Sakinat al-Auliya'*, p. 5. For dreams in Islamic and Sufi traditions, see Green, "The Religious and Cultural Role of Dreams", pp. 287–313; Felek and Knysh, *Dreams and Visions*, pp. 181–296. We may also note a later Mughal prince's dreams in

dream of being recognised and placed in a genealogy of seekers of truth, fulfilling as it does the twin criteria of royal authority and spiritual virtues based on being a seeker of truth, deserves special attention, not least because of the central function of dreaming (as a vehicle and topic of stories) stressed by the *Yogavasistha* itself.

One way to begin thinking about this striking dream is to recall the function of the framing story. Here Dara Shukoh sees himself not at the inception of the book, which begins with the conversation between Valmiki and Bharadwaja, but in a frame before the time of the book, as it were: he imagines himself a part of the conversations between Rama and Vasistha, which Valmiki recalls for us. Dara Shukoh has thus envisioned himself in the time not of the book but of the events that the book presents to us and from which the book derives. By virtue of this dream, Dara, who ostensibly lives long after the time depicted in the work, not to mention the work itself, has gone to the very source of its knowledge.

That there is a world in which multiple temporalities are possible, such that Rama and Valmiki are still present and enjoying the conversations that Valmiki reports to us as having occurred in the past, is something that the message of the *Yogavasistha* itself might encourage us to believe. Dara's dream then is a continuation, of a kind, of the form and message of the *Yogavasistha*.

But there is a striking convergence with the Sufi tradition as well. There is a well-known practice among Sufis to seek sanction for treating a subject not from a book but from the very person about whom the book is concerned, and this sanction comes in the form of a true vision disclosed by a dream. These visions disclose the always contemporary character of historical exemplars, even if such visions are only the preserve of a few, as Dara Shukoh here presents himself. A more striking way to frame the *Yogavasistha*

---

the eighteenth century, in which this prince also envisions power. Alam and Subrahmanyam, *Writing the Mughal World*, pp. 427–66, esp. pp. 455–64.

as a Persianate work – and to accomplish the rapprochement of Indic and Islamic traditions – is hard to imagine.

Conclusion

Dara Shukoh's translation represents a conscious break from the previous Mughal *Yogavasisthas*: his version was a novel attempt to include an Indic text within the Muslim imagination, not just of mystical matters but of ideal kingship. The *Yogavasistha's* imaginaire, in which Rama is depicted as both a spiritual master and an ideal king, had obvious resonances for Dara Shukoh's own career and ambitions. The text thus also represents an important move on Dara Shukoh's part to prepare for his own ascension to the throne by casting his future kingship on the model of the ideal Rama.

However, we can also see that Dara Shukoh's text was a plea to consider other sources for normative theories of kingship in the Mughal court. The Mughal search for such theories had been dominated by Perso-Islamic *akhlaq* literature, which drew on Graeco-Hellenic traditions as gleaned through Arabic and Persian sources. We have a sort of a European mirror for princes, compiled in Persian by the Jesuit Jeronimo Xavier and presented to Jahangir, in which Xavier discusses norms of governance (*adab-i saltanat*), with illustrations from the stories of Biblical, Roman, and also medieval and early-modern European kings.[81] All this is indicative of the Mughal rulers' quest for political theories and practices outside the boundaries of the *shari'a* and Islam. Akbar's interest in the Mahabharata can be read as a sign of his curiosity about India's political culture, yet within him there was no great urge to imbibe or emulate Indic governance norms.[82]

[81] I have seen two of the Jerome Xavier manuscripts, one available in Rome at the Biblioteca Casanatense, MS. no. 2018, dated Rabi' 23, 1018 (June 1609). It comprises over 267 folios. A second manuscript, no. 7030, very likely copied from the same original, is preserved in the Library of the School of Oriental and African Studies, London. Comprising over 286 folios, it is dated Ramadan 8, 1018 (5 December 1609). For an analysis of this text,

By contrast, Dara Shukoh's reading of the *Yogavasistha* seems a marked departure from Akbar's curiosity and general inclination towards the fulfilment of an inner urge to recognise alternative imaginative understandings of spirituality and their implications for action in the world of politics. He is not merely interested, he becomes deeply immersed in what has aroused his interest. He tries getting to the heart of the matter of a religious narrative and presents it as an Indic source for a normative theory of kingship suited to the Mughal court. As such, this needs to be understood as a step in the direction of the indigenisation of the state in Mughal India. Akbar integrated the local elites, including the Hindu Rajputs, into his government, to the extent that the Mughal–Rajput alliance has sometimes been seen as a Mughal–Rajput state.[83] But neither in Tusi (d. 1274), the premier representative of the *akhlaq* tradition nor in Jeronimo Xavier's iteration of the European tradition, does one find that a saint can also be a king without violating the norms of one or the other.

I am aware of a strand of scholarship which shows how the early Mughals, pursuing their Central Asian ancestors and the Iranian rulers, projected themselves as sacred and saintly kings.[84] What I propose here is that it is only in the *Yogavasistha* that Dara Shukoh found a model for the Indian saint-king, on which presumably he would have gone on to build the moral foundations of his own reign. It is in the dream of Dara where, true to the teachings of the *Yogavasistha* concerning time and narrative, the prince finds himself in the company of a counterfactual genealogy – in

---

see Alam and Subrahmanyam, "Mediterranean Exemplars". See also Sidarus, "A Western Mirror for Princes", pp. 73–98. For Jerome Xavier, his works, and his engagement with the Mughal court, see Alam and Subrahmanyam, *Writing the Mughal World*, pp. 249–310.

[82] Cf. Truschke, *Culture of Encounters*.

[83] Cf. Mayaram, "The Mughal State Formation", pp. 169–97, and idem, *Against History, Against State*, pp. 97–125.

[84] Cf. Moin, *The Millennial Sovereign*.

which Dara is the younger brother of Rama, his elder and contemporary.

Dara Shukoh is thus not merely a Sufi scholar or a Mughal prince; he is also a political theorist in the timeless company – as seen in his dream – of the ideal ruler and seeker of truth, Rama. The *Yogavasistha* is a book of the many worlds that exist alongside our own. Dara Shukoh, perhaps, was alone in seeing the reality of the political dream it was possible to have on the basis of the *Yogavasistha*, in which a Persian prince could find in himself the successor of Rama, with access to the possible reality of the ideal political forms, norms of conduct, and governance associated with Rama. Whether this could have been only a dream – like Dara's dream, with which he began his *Yogavasistha*, a dream of political hope inspired by the *Yogavasistha's* sense of possible worlds that we must narrate into existence – is another story.

7

Piety, Poetry, and the Contested Loyalties of Mughal Princesses, c. 1635–1700

Introduction

WOMEN IN TIMURID ROYAL households regularly occupied high positions in politics and could enjoy a great deal of autonomy in their personal lives. The very fact that Timur is known as "Gurgan" (son-in-law) indicates the position and power he acquired because of his marriage to a woman from a Chinggisid household. Timur's senior wife's status was noted in particular by Ruy González de Clavijo, the Spanish ambassador, whom she entertained at Timur's court in 1404. In the wake of the official festivities at Timur's court in Samarqand, Clavijo reports that there was a separate entertainment by the chief queen with much drinking and eating by both sexes.[1] Following the death of Timur's son Shahrukh Mirza (r. 1405–47), his queen Gauhar Shad Begum is reported to have sent the news

---

[1] "[The] chief wife of the Lord gave her entertainment in an enclosure of very rich tents, to which a great assembly of people came, as well as ambassadors from various countries, as friends of her own, both knights and ladies." There was also a significant presence of the royal women at these festivities. See Markham, ed., *Narrative of the Embassy of Ruy González de Clavijo*, p. 159, and also pp. 155–8 for a description of royal women drinking and eating together with royal men and ambassadors at festivities.

to absent princes and decided many of the initial actions that had to be taken to prevent disorder. She was actively involved in making peace among the princes vying for the throne.[2] Timurid women did not merely have exceptional sway in dynastic politics, they had direct ties with major amirs, would sometimes defy their husbands, and – this is noteworthy – "when such independent behaviour was used for the good of the dynasty, it was considered praiseworthy."[3] Princesses were responsible for a great deal of architectural patronage: palaces were often named after princesses, and they commissioned gardens and shrines. Many were buried in ornate tombs they themselves had commissioned. We also have evidence of relatively high female literacy among the princesses of the Safavids of Iran, another Perso-Turkish dynasty with which the Mughals had close (if at times conflictual) relations. Safavid princesses were highly cultivated and knowledgeable; some of them were known for their skill and intelligence: Bija Munajjimah, an astrologer, "was well known for her science of computing calendars but also as a rival of the noted poet Jami in literary relations." Shah Tahmasp's queen accompanied him on hunting expeditions.[4]

In India the women of the Timurid (Mughal) family inherited and cultivated a similar culture of political and literary accomplishment. Gulbadan Begum, Humayun's sister, for instance, was not simply the author of the *Humayun Nama*, a well-known chronicle of the period, she also virtually led a major delegation of pilgrims to Mecca.[5] Humayun's chief widow, Hamida Bano Begum, decided to stay on in Delhi when the capital shifted to Agra in order to supervise the building of Humayun's tomb. Akbar's Rajput wife Maryam Zamani maintained her own religion and cultural autonomy inside the palace. Nur Jahan was sometimes

---

[2] Manz, "Women in Timurid Dynastic Politics", pp. 121–39.
[3] Ibid., in particular p. 129.
[4] Szuppe, "Status, Knowledge, and Politics", pp. 140–69.
[5] Alam and Subrahmanyam, *Indo-Persian Travels*, p. 299.

portrayed as the virtual ruler of her own time despite the legendary brilliance of Jahangir.[6] In short, the Mughal woman's position was to be reckoned with both politically and culturally. In this chapter I examine the history of three major Mughal princesses of Shah Jahan and Aurangzeb's time, namely Jahanara, Roshanara or Roshan Rai, and Zeb-un-nisa'.

There have been several modern reflections on these princesses. These include various writings by Afshan Bokhari on Jahanara, focusing in particular on the princess as a patron of architecture. There is also a monograph by Nausheen Jaffery on the princess' life and accomplishments. Finally, one of Jahanara's works, *Munis al-Arwah*, edited decades ago in Aligarh, was published in Karachi. The edition has a long introduction by the editor, Qamar Jahan Begum, which includes a discussion of the princess' biography.[7] About Roshanara we have nothing of equal significance except some European accounts with scandalous stories of her illicit sexual relations, her image as a jealous sister of Dara Shukoh and Jahanara, and an "agent" for Aurangzeb.[8] For Zeb-un-nisa' too we have stories of her alleged love affairs even in some serious academic writings, together with a few biographical notices and some comments on her poetry.[9] Therefore, it appears that we still

---

[6] For a recent study of the role of women in early Mughal times, see Lal, *Domesticity and Power*; also, Alam and Subrahmanyam, *Indo-Persian Travels*, pp. 24–44, 299–300, *passim*. For Nur Jahan, see Prasad, *History of Jahangir*, pp. 159–72, *passim*; and the subsequent discussions by Hasan, "The Theory of the Nur Jahan 'Junta'", pp. 324–35, and Habib, "The Family of Nur Jahan", pp. 74–95. Nur Jahan has also been the subject of a popular account: Lal, *Empress*.

[7] Bokhari, "Imperial Transgressions", Vol. 4, pp. 86–108; also Bokhari, "Between Patron and Piety", pp. 120–42, and Bokhari, "Masculine Modes of Female Subjectivity", pp.165–202. Also see Jaffery, *Jahan Ara Begum*. For the princess' writings, see Jahanara, *Munis al-Arwah*, Introduction.

[8] Bernier, *Travels in the Mogul Empire*, pp. 14 and 100; for the original text, see Tinguely, ed., *Un Libertin dans l'Inde Moghole*, pp. 52, 122. Also see Tavernier, *Travels in India*, Vol. 1, pp. 299–300.

[9] Sharma, "Forbidden Love", pp. 767–79. See also Sarkar, "Zeb-un-Nissa's

need to examine the available evidence about these princesses, which is not inconsiderable. I will consider here some aspects of their intellectual and spiritual lives, which in Roshanara's case is also another side of her history.

Jahanara Begum: An Introduction

Jahanara, the eldest surviving daughter of Shah Jahan (d. 1666), was born in Ajmer in 1614. She was trained by some of the most illustrious and literate women of Mughal India. Having grown up as a highly literate member of the royal family, she also had an interest in spreading education. She founded a madrasa attached to the Jama Masjid she built in Agra. In 1631, when Shah Jahan's wife Mumtaz Mahal died, the emperor entrusted to her full responsibility for the management of the royal household. Subsequently, she earned the title of Sahibat al-Zamani (Mistress of the Age) and came to be referred to as Begum Sahib. Jahanara not only had full control over palace affairs, her role in Shah Jahan's time sometimes appears to have been that of a chief secretary of state. For instance, some of the autonomous chiefs of the hill regions of northern India approached her so that she might act as a mediator as they attempted to remedy their relationship with the emperor. She was put in charge of the imperial seal and several important officials directly served her.[10]

The princess was also interested in commercial matters. She held the customs revenues assigned to her from the Surat port, which she continued to hold even after Aurangzeb came to power. Her stake in the port of Surat explains her initial indifference and eventual

---

Love Affairs", pp. 79–90. Sarkar does not accept these stories, nor does he agree, however, with the suggestion that she was a poet with the pen name "Makhfi". Sarkar also mentions the fictional work of the celebrated Bhudev Mukhopadhyay (1827–94), which concerns the princess.

[10] The details given here, and a part of the following information, are summarised from Jaffery, *Jahan Ara Begum*.

hostility to Shivaji, who sacked the city in 1664.[11] She owned a number of ships, some of which took pilgrims for the hajj to Mecca along with her cargo. There is a record of a pilgrim travelling from Mecca on *Sahibi*, one of her ships. European traders too were aware of Jahanara's considerable influence in the Mughal court. Thus, anyone who brought gifts for the emperor was also likely to bear special gifts for her.[12] By all accounts Jahanara carried out the work assigned to her effectively. We get an idea of her extraordinary managerial skills from her supervision of her brothers' costly weddings, including the wedding of Dara Shukoh, on which some 16 lakh rupees were spent. Like her father, she had a passion for building. She commissioned gardens in cities across the empire, including Delhi, Agra, Kabul, Kashmir, Lahore, Ambala, and Surat. These gardens usually had a caravanserai attached. She commissioned another caravanserai in Chandni Chowk in Shahjahanabad in 1650, which European travellers considered second only to Delhi's Jama Masjid.[13] Besides the Jama Masjid of Agra with the madrasa attached, she also built a mosque in Kashmir for her spiritual preceptor, Mulla Shah Badakhshi.[14]

Although she had special affection for Dara Shukoh, she had a reputation for being just and generous, and won the trust of everyone in the family.[15] She thus acted as an honest broker in disputes amongst her brothers. For example, on the occasions when Aurangzeb had a problem with his elder brother Dara Shukoh, he sought Jahanara's mediation. Aurangzeb, we know,

---

[11] Ibid.; Sarkar, *Shivaji and His Times*, pp. 97–108. On Jahanara's connection with Surat, see also Moosvi, *People, Taxation and Trade*, pp. 264–5, 272–4.

[12] Ibid., p. 79, cited from *Badshahnama*; see also Manucci, *Mogul India*, Vol. 1, pp. 65, 208; Tavernier, *Travels in India*, Vol. 1, pp. 113, 115.

[13] See Khan, *Mir'at al-'Alam*, Vol. 1, p. 182 for two gardens, Bagh-i Sahibabad and Bagh-i Si Hazari, built by her.

[14] Bokhari, "Masculine Modes of Female Subjectivity".

[15] For Dara Shukoh's relations with Jahanara, see also the discussion in Gandhi, *The Emperor Who Never Was*.

was not fortunate enough to have a position at the court and also suspected Dara Shukoh's interference in matters important to him, personal as well as administrative and political. But he trusted Jahanara, expected his problems to be resolved and mediated by her – whether they related to the kind of mangoes he should send the emperor, or his suspicions of Dara having interfered in his audience with the emperor, or matters pertaining to emoluments for his armed contingent. Her role as an effective mediator can be seen as she sought to diffuse the conflict between Aurangzeb and Shah Jahan too. After Aurangzeb's victory over Dara Shukoh in the war of succession, Jahanara apparently made a plea to him to have full faith in their father and meet him in person.

Jahanara's Writings

About forty documents and letters written by Jahanara or addressed to her have survived, besides minor administrative orders. Twenty-seven of them are from Aurangzeb and give evidence of her high status.[16] These letters, besides demonstrating her influence, show her extraordinary command over language and confidence in her understanding of the *shari'a*, Muslim religious traditions and ethics, and the politics of her time. Worth serious consideration is a famous letter she wrote to Aurangzeb during the war of succession.[17] Since the aim of the letter was to dissuade Aurangzeb from challenging Dara Shukoh, and thus in effect the emperor Shah Jahan, she begins it in perfect Persianate diplomatic style with praise for Aurangzeb in high-sounding words and phrases – wise, enlightened brother (*biradar-i khiradmand-i bidar-maghz*), adorned with elegant virtues (*siyar-i latifa*), of a generous nature (*akhlaq-i karima*), laudable manners (*adab-i*

---

[16] Khan, *Adab-i 'Alamgiri*, Vol. 2, pp. 800–32; Jaffery, *Jahan Ara Begum*, reproduces them in her book.

[17] Razi, *Waqi'at-i 'Alamgiri*, pp. 46–9; Kamboh, *'Amal-i Salih*, Vol. 3, pp. 219–20, for a summary version. For a translation of the full letter, see Mikkelson, "The Way of Tradition", pp. 240–60.

hamida), and a sound disposition (*tab'i salima*). She writes then that it was thus extremely distressing for her to hear that a brother as noble (*an biradar-i wala-guhar*) had mounted a rebellion (*fasad-o-'inad*) against the emperor, who, besides being his father, was also his true guide (*murshid* and *qibla*) and "endeavouring to please whom is [equal to] striving to please God (*raza-i u raza wa khushnudi-yi Khuda'i 'azza wa jall wa rasul ast*)". Aurangzeb should thus consider, she suggests, securing the happiness of the emperor "as a way of attaining bliss in both this world and the life hereafter" (*khushnudi-yi an hazarat ra husul-i sa'adat-i darain fara girifta*), and must avoid a battle which would spill the blood of Muslims. She cites in the letter two phrases from the Qur'an as illustration of her view of the emperor and the reprehensiveness of any act leading to a clash or to a conflict and thus bloodshed among Muslims.[18] And as she knew it was not the emperor but her favourite brother Dara Shukoh against whom the rebellion was really targeted, she adds a sentence in an effort to make him appreciate the stature of an older brother in Muslim tradition: even if the turmoil were aimed against Dara Shukoh, "this still cannot be condoned by the principles of wisdom; for according to *shari'a* and convention (*shar'an wa 'urfan*) alike, an elder brother has the position of a father (*hukm-i pidar darad*)." In this she demonstrates confidence in her own understanding of *shari'a* and the norms of basic social ethics. She then concludes by emphasising that the meaning of the Qur'an's command of obedience to "those charged

---

[18] One of these two phrases is *"uli'l-amr-i minkum"* which figures in the verse: "O ye who believe! Obey Allah, and obey the Messenger, and those charged with authority among you. If ye differ in anything among yourselves, refer it to Allah and His Messenger, if ye do believe in Allah and the last Day. This is best and most suitable for final determination." Qur'an, 4: 59. Another phrase is *"yasfiku'd-dima"*, and the verse wherein it figures is: "Behold, thy Lord said to the angels: 'I will create a vicegerent on earth.' They said: 'Wilt Thou place therein one who will make mischief therein and shed blood? Whilst we do celebrate Thy praise and glorify Thy holy (name)?' He said: 'I know what ye know not'." Qur'an, 2: 30.

with authority among you (*uli'l-amr-i minkum*)" is obedience to the emperor (*imtisal-i amr-i shahinshah ast*), and that to advance even a step on the path of opposition to him implies opposing the command of God (*takhaluf-i farman-i Malik al-mulk namudan ast*). Jahanara advises Aurangzeb not to march on to Agra and instead to convey his demands so that they may be presented to the emperor, and she herself "will make sincere efforts to satisfy and fulfil his [Aurangzeb's] aims and desires (*maqasid o ma'arib*)." Summing up yet again, she tries to mollify Aurangzeb's apprehensions by calling him "the delight of the eye of the empire and [its] governance (*qurra-i basira-i saltanat o jahanbani*)". Jahanara wrote as an ally of Dara Shukoh. But her language is very delicate and its tone appeasing. She also speaks to Aurangzeb's religious sensibilities. She failed, however, to stop him from indulging in what she calls sedition. Aurangzeb did not heed her request, though his response to Jahanara's letter was polite.[19]

Jahanara also had to her credit two important Sufi texts, *Munis al-Arwah* (Companion of the Souls), and *Risala-i Sahibiya* (A Treatise by the Sahib, i.e. Jahanara herself). She apparently wrote *Munis al-Arwah* in 1639 and added an appendix (*zamima*) to it during her visit to Ajmer in 1643–4.[20] It is a short book,

---

[19] *Waqi'at-i 'Alamgiri*, pp. 50–6; *'Amal-i Salih*, pp. 220–2.

[20] Several manuscripts of *Munis al-Arwah* are available, and a complete listing of them is yet to be prepared. Besides a manuscript in the Abdur Rahman Chughtai Museum, Lahore (apparently dating to 1051 H.), and another from the National Museum of Pakistan, Karachi, these include British Library, London, Additional 16733; Or. 250; and Or. 5637 (the last an autograph copy); and Bodleian Library, Oxford, Fraser 229. Shibli Nu'mani mentions a special manuscript in beautiful *nasta'liq*, prepared by 'Aqil Khan Razi in 1068/1657–8: see his essay in *Al-Nadwa*, April 1911. This manuscript was exhibited at the London Exhibition in May 1911 as a specimen of Persian calligraphy and is today in the collection of the Darul Musannefin Shibli Academy, Azamgarh. Qamar Jahan Begum has edited the Persian text, as noted above. There is also an Urdu translation titled *Mu'in al-Arwah* by Muhammad 'Abdus Samad Kalim Qadiri, published from Matba' Rizvi, Delhi, 1891.

divided into three sections. One of the sections comprises a preface praising God, the Prophet, and the first four Pious Caliphs. Interestingly, she also includes her lineage down till the emperor Akbar. The second section contains accounts of the lives and sayings of the five major Chishti shaikhs, and of the founders and propagating masters of the order in India, namely Khwaja Mu'in al-Din of Ajmer (d. 1236), Shaikh Qutb al-Din Bakhtiyar Kaki of Delhi (d. 1235), Shaikh Farid al-Din Ganj-i Shakar of Pak Pattan (d. 1265), Shaikh Nizam al-Din Auliya' of Delhi (d. 1325), and Shaikh Nasir al-Din Chiragh of Delhi (d. 1356); the section is replete with stories of their miracles. She draws here on Jami's *Nafahat al-Uns* (Fragrances of Love), and a number of other *tazkiras* that she had read on the advice of her brother Dara Shukoh. She also mentions that for this section she read several *tazkiras* compiled in India, including the works of Abu al-Fazl and Shaikh 'Abd al-Haqq Muhaddis Dehlavi. Her second book, *Risala i-Sahibiya*, which she wrote in 1640–1, is an account of a noted Qadiri shaikh of her own time, Mulla Shah Badakhshi, whom she also chose as her spiritual master. The prose in both the texts is studded with choice poetry, including several verses of her own.[21]

In the *Munis al-Arwah* Jahanara restates the widely held belief and social practice of the time that an average Muslim, man or woman, needs to be associated with one or the other Sufi order. Stability and strength in the human world is due to the grace (*barakat*) of the saints (*masha'ikh wa auliya'*). Association with them (*iradat-wa-ikhlas, 'aqidat*) ensures blessings and good fortune (*fuyuzat wa barakat*), is the source of a Muslim's salvation (*wasila-i nijat*), and elevates his or her status in the life hereafter (*darjat-i jinan*). The preceptor–disciple practice (*tariqa-i piri wa muridi*) is, according to her, an essential part of pious Islamic life; it is a manifestation of God's perfect and eternal grace (*kamal-i-karam-i azali*). Muslims thus need to be organised and integrated (*manut wa marbut*) into groups of one or the other Sufi order (*silsila*).

[21] Jahanara, *Risala-i Sahibiya*, pp. 78–110 (henceforth *Sahibiya*).

Following this, Jahanara describes with a sense of pride and satisfaction how she was initiated into the Chishti order as a humble spiritual disciple (*az kamtarin-i muridan*) of Khwaja Mu'in al-Din Chishti when she was only twenty years old.²² However, at the age of twenty-six or twenty-seven, as we will see, she was initiated into the Qadiri order too. Still, and significantly, she continued to regard Khwaja Mu'in al-Din Chishti as her real spiritual master and patron (*pir-i dastgir*). She says she is constantly engaged in reading histories of the saints, in particular the saints of the Chishti order, which she describes as the most famous and widely followed order not simply in Mughal India but throughout the inhabited regions of the world (*tamam-i mamura-i jahan*). When she decided to write an account (*tazkira*) of the Chishti Sufis, she called it *Munis al-Arwah*, intending to play on the title of an older Sufi treatise, *Anis al-Arwah* (Friend of the Souls), which she believed was written by her *murshid* Khwaja Mu'in al-Din.²³

As noted, Jahanara claimed she had been directly initiated into the Chishti order by Khwaja Mu'in al-Din himself, even though he had lived over 400 years earlier, between the 1140s and the 1230s, at the time of the establishment of the Sultanate of Delhi. This initiation came through what may be termed an "Uwaisi" connection, a reference to Uwais al-Qarani (*c.* 594–657), who became a Muslim and was awarded a high status by the Prophet without ever meeting him, though they were contemporaries. To claim such status was not common in Sufi tradition and reflects her heightened sense of spiritual elevation.²⁴ Jahanara also writes that God Himself had planted the seeds of desire for the Path in her heart (*haqq -subhanahu wa ta'ala- mahaz az karam o lutf-i khwish dar dil-i in za'ifa zauq-i talab-i rah-i haqq markuz sakhta*

---

²² *Munis al-Arwah*, pp. 6–7.

²³ Many historians doubt the authenticity of this text. See Habib, "Chishti Mystic Records", pp. 1–42, for a discussion on this and some other Sufi texts of pre-Mughal North India.

²⁴ See the chapter on Shah Madar, Chapter 4, above. See also Rizvi, *A History of Sufism*, Vol. 1, p. 25.

bud).²⁵ Interestingly, at this stage of her life there is no evidence of her association with any living contemporary Chishti Sufi. Two important themes are noticeable: on the one hand her demonstration of devotion towards the Chishtis, which could be perceived as part of the standard Mughal imperial tradition, following Humayun and especially Akbar;²⁶ and on the other her bold claim to individuality, even a superior position within that same tradition, particularly as a woman of high material position and spiritual stature. From her claim of an Uwaisi-style connection with Khwaja Muʿin al-Din Chishti, and also from a close reading of her relations with her Qadiri *murshid* Mulla Shah Badakhshi, we can begin to discern a strategy being deployed towards shaping a self-image.

Jahanara: The Perfect Woman (insan-i kamil)

Jahanara's claim to being a direct *murid* of Khwaja Muʿin al-Din Chishti – a claim to "Uwaisiyat" – placed her above many Sufis of her time, including her brother Dara Shukoh whom, significantly, she also mentions as her guide (*murshid*). The claim was obviously not in tune with dominant Sufi practice. Dara Shukoh thus advised her to seek out a master among contemporary Sufis in order to learn and continue her spiritual progress, which she did. The story of her search, related in her second book, *Risala-i Sahibiya*, needs to be studied afresh. The princess apparently wrote it in 1640–1; it narrates the story of her search for a living spiritual master, and how she finally became the disciple of Mulla Shah Badakhshi (d. 1661), a prominent disciple and *khalifa* of Miyan Mir (d. 1635), himself a Qadiri Sufi of great repute and status from Jahangir and Shah Jahan's reigns who was also Dara Shukoh's spiritual master.²⁷ The *Risala* is in part an account of Shah Badakhshi

---

²⁵ *Sahibiya*, p. 95.
²⁶ See Chapter 1, above.
²⁷ For an account of his life, see Kulabi, *Ahwal-i Shahi*. The manuscript also contains Badakhshi's letters to Jahanara, fls 45a–48a. According to this,

and gives us an insight into Jahanara's spiritual views and practices. Also notable is the fact that in a significant portion of the treatise she highlights her own experience as "an account of this weak and deficient person (*zikr-i ahwal-i in za'ifa*)".[28] Thus in approximately half of *Sahibiya* (pp. 95–110) she provides her own account in fascinating detail, which, she writes, is "an exact testimony without exaggeration or distortion".[29] The princess also states that the real purpose and explicit aim in this work is the desire that her name and work thereafter be always mentioned alongside her master Mulla Shah.[30] But more important, and this deserves our special attention, is the reason she gives for writing her treatise: "I had read in some books that notable Sufis of the past narrated an account of their own reform and guidance. So, I too followed their practice."[31] She thus believed she had acquired a high spiritual status and meritorious position, as had notable Sufis of the past.

She says she went in 1639 to Lahore with her father, Shah Jahan, and there found more time and opportunity to meet her brother Dara and discuss important spiritual matters with him. She grew closer to him, becoming like "one spirit in two bodies", or "one soul that breathes in two forms".[32] He guided her and suggested works of Sufism for her to read and study. Dara Shukoh

---

it was Badakhshi who suggested the title of the princess's treatise, *Sahibiya*. For his, Miyan Mir's, and also Dara Shukoh's Sufism, see Rizvi, *A History of Sufism*, Vol. 2, pp. 126–46.

[28] *Sahibiya*, pp. 95–110.

[29] Ibid., p. 79: *"bayan-i waqi' ast bila ziyad-o-nuqsan."*

[30] Ibid.: *"matlab-i asli az nawishtan-i halat-i khwud in bud ki khwastam ism-i in za'ifa-i pur-gunah wa nama-i siyah ba'd az ism-i sami-yi an-hazrat mazkur- o-mastur shawad."*

[31] Ibid.: *"wa niz dar ba'z-i kutub khwanda budam ki mashai'kh-i salaf qaddas-Allahu asrara-hum hidayat-i ahwal-i khwud ra nawishta-and, man ham bar sunnat-i ishan 'amal namudam."*

[32] Ibid., p. 96: *". . . yak ruh-im ki dar do qalab damida shuda wa yak jan-im ki dar do jism dar amada."*

being soon after deputed to lead the upcoming campaign in the north-west frontier (Kabul), Jahanara was temporarily separated from him. However, they continued their discussions through correspondence, and in one of his letters he suggested that she meet two prominent Sufis: Shaikh Daula in Gujarat and Haji 'Abd-Allah in Tal Jalal Ghakkar. She therefore met both *en route* as she accompanied her father in his preparations for the Kabul campaign. She was, however, not satisfied with either shaikh, and when she met her brother again in Hasan Abdal he advised her to read still more books on Sufism. We see Jahanara thus gradually becoming more religious and spiritual, and more accomplished as a scholar. She frequently cites Qur'anic verses and *hadith* that showcase her extensive knowledge of Islamic traditions. She comments, for instance, on the famous *hadith*, "Die before you die (*mutu qabla an tamutu*)".[33] We see her developing, perfecting, and exerting her own knowledge, aesthetics, and subjectivity.

When the idea of the Kabul campaign was abandoned, a decision that Jahanara ascribes to famine, they returned to Lahore. There she met more scholars and Sufis and became even more anxious and eager to find a master to whom she could apprentice herself formally. Her criteria for selecting such a teacher were as clearly stated as her standards were high: she took a vow that she would be disciple to none until she found a worthy teacher, saw him as worthy with her own eyes, and became familiar with his spiritual state and achievements (*maqamat-o-halat*). The person she finally chose was one well regarded by her brother Dara Shukoh, whom she again describes as her closest confidant (*ham biradar o ham mahram*).[34] These circumstances, as we will see, make an interesting contrast with Roshanara's methods of acquiring

[33] Ibid., p. 98.
[34] Ibid., p. 99: "... *be khwud qarar dadam ki ta murshidi kamili 'arif-billah be-ham narasad, wa u ra na binam, wa halat-o-maqamat-i nik bar man zahir nashawad wa biradar-i 'ali-miqdar ki ham biradar-o- ham mahram-i man-and bar haqiqat-i an buzurgwar waqif nashuda, mara nafarmayand, talqin nashawam.*"

knowledge from Sufi teachers, which was entirely conducted through correspondence and therefore in perfect conformity with *shariʿa* norms of propriety. Though such a process of selection by a woman could be taken as militating against convention, considerations of propriety did not prevent Jahanara from going about finding a master in her chosen way. Indeed, she believed it the best and most appropriate (*bihtar wa munasib-tar*) way of selecting a *murshid*.[35]

Jahanara then describes in some detail her method of finding a spiritual guide. She first sought out a worthy Chishti Sufi. Each time she heard of a likely saint or recluse, she sent off her retainers to investigate. She says many Chishti saints of her time were secretive and reclusive (*mastur al-hal*), and difficult to track down.[36] In Lahore she heard of a certain Qadiri Sufi called Mulla Khwaja Bihari, a disciple of Miyan Mir. She liked him and asked him to initiate her into the order, but he declined. She was by this time twenty-seven, and more anxious and eager than ever to find a master, feeling strangely her own strength to be waning and time running short.[37] At this point the imperial camp moved to Kashmir, where they remained for a time, and where Jahanara undertook several famous projects, including the building of a mosque. She had heard of Mulla Shah Badakhshi as another disciple of Miyan Mir. Dara Shukoh, on account of his own relations with him, told her Mulla Shah was a great saint and worthy teacher, and that she should try to apprentice herself to him. However, the idea of transferring her allegiance from one Sufi order to another gave her pause. She had hitherto always considered herself as belonging to the Chishti order, and was not immediately convinced that she could achieve the kind of enlightenment she so ardently sought in the Qadiri order, or

---

[35] Ibid., p. 99.
[36] Ibid., p. 100.
[37] Ibid., p. 98: "... *quwwat-i khwud ra ruz be-ruz dar tanazzul mi-didam wa aksar-i dardmand-i budam, danistam ki saʿat be-saʿat quwwat-i zahiri dar maʿraz-i zawal ast.*"

in any other order.³⁸ Eventually, having heard Mulla Shah's great fame proclaimed throughout Kashmir, she decided to forgo her own self-imposed conditions.³⁹ She tried to get to know him by whatever means were at her disposal. Before seeing him in person, she was able to behold him by way of a portrait, a likeness of him drawn on paper and given to her by Dara Shukoh, and from that time on she began to meditate upon his likeness in the manner that disciples meditate upon their teachers' likenesses in the typical Sufi initiation practice.⁴⁰ These practices led her to have a vision: the Prophet Muhammad, his Four Companions, and other saints all appeared to her, and she presented to them her own doubts about transferring spiritual allegiance from one order to another.⁴¹ After she had posed these questions, she experienced a heightened state, somewhere between sleep and waking, and saw herself again in the company of Muhammad and his exalted companions. This time, *hazrat-i akhund* (that is, Mulla Shah) was among them too, his head placed at the feet of the Prophet. The Prophet said to him, "Oh Mulla Shah, you have lit the lamp of the house of Timur (*Ay Mulla Shah, tu chiragh-i Timuriya ra roshan kardi*)."⁴² Jahanara says when she came out of this state, her heart blossomed with this good news like gardens within gardens, and she composed some quatrains:

Shaha tu-i an-ki mi-rasanad ze safa
fayz-i nazar-i tu taliban-ra be-khuda

---

³⁸ Ibid., pp. 99–100.
³⁹ Ibid., p. 102: *"shurut-i ki ba khwud karda budam ki ta chunin buzurg-i ra be-chashm-i khwud na binam wa . . . ma'lum nakunam, murshid nakhwaham girift."*
⁴⁰ Ibid., pp. 98, 99, 100–2. For the passage, pp.100–1, describing her visit to Kashmir and encounter with Mulla Shah, see also Sharma, *Mughal Arcadia*, pp. 162–3.
⁴¹ Ibid., p. 103: *"Chun dar khatir khutur mi-guzarad ki man dar silsila-i Chishtiya murid-am wa al-hal ki be-tariqa-i Qadiriya mi-dar-ayam, aya ma-ra kashayish-i ru namayad ya na? wa az-in irshad o talqin-i hazrat-i shahi [Mulla Shah] fayida bakhshad ya na?"*
⁴² Ibid., p. 103.

bar har ki nazar kuni be-maqsud rasad
nur-i nazar-i tu shud magar nur-i khuda[43]

O [Mulla] Shah, it's you with your purity
[and] the grace of your glance, who takes your disciples to God.
Everyone you look at reaches his goal,
the light of your glance has perhaps become the light of God.

An kas ki az ru-i sidq daulat khwah ast
U ra be-su-i daulat rah ast
Daulat ya'ni ma'rifat-i zat-i mutlaq
in daulat dar khana-i Mulla Shah ast[44]

He who sincerely seeks [true] wealth,
Can [surely] find the way to it.
I mean the wealth of the Divine Essence,
that wealth which is in the house of Mulla Shah.

With this remarkable vision Jahanara bypassed her own condition of having Dara Shukoh approve her choice – instead the approval came straight from the Prophet himself! She says none of her ancestors (*az aslaf hich*) had been blessed with such good fortune – of being guided directly by Muhammad in this way. And she projected herself as no less than "the lamp of the house of Timur".

The princess remained in Kashmir for six months and slowly but steadily developed a close relationship with Mulla Shah. She began by cooking food and sending it to him, though he took little notice of this obeisance; she wrote letters to him and he responded, explaining the secrets of the unseen world. But then Shah Jahan decided to leave Kashmir and Jahanara made up her mind to finally try to meet Mulla Shah in person. Meanwhile Mulla Shah had, through intermediaries, provided her with his own shawl, something only given to special disciples. She describes touching it to her eyes and placing it upon her head. Finally, the

[43] Ibid.
[44] Ibid., p. 86.

meeting took place, after she was forthright enough to request it. The custom was that if rulers requested an audience, compliance was inescapable. Worth noticing is the fact that Mulla Shah did not agree to meet her only as his disciple; he saw her as a ruler too. Jahanara drew on this custom and was finally able to see Mulla Shah in person. She says she saw him twice: once with her brother, and the second time without him. This marked the culmination of a gradual but great transformation: at first he would not even respond to requests to initiate her, and now he agreed to meet her in person. He rode up on his horse and dismounted by a tree; she was on an elephant. She describes him as extraordinarily handsome. "The world-decorating beauty of that kind *murshid*, who like the full moon of the sky and the brilliantly shining sun bestowed his grace to the seekers [of truth]."[45] After presenting him with the customary carafe of rosewater and betel-leaf (*paan*), she was officially initiated, experiencing the true recognition (*iman-i haqiqi*) of God, who is perfect (*atamm wa akmal*). She recognised not only knowledge (*ma'rifat*) of the skies, earth, and the whole cosmos, but the superiority of humans over angels. We may again note here one of her *ruba'is*, which shows her vision of Sufism, affirmed after her initiation by Mulla Shah into the Qadiri order:

Ta muddat-i bist sal dar just wa ju
didim ki zahiran be-yabam-ash be-u
Tahqiq shud in dar talab-i khwud budim
Ma'lum shud in ramz ki khwud budim-i u
Andar pay-i an nigar-i shukh-i sarmast
budam ki shawam ze la'l-i u mast-i alast
Nagah yaki be-janib-i khwud didim
dar sina-i khwud yaftamash dast be-dast.[46]

---

[45] Ibid., pp. 106–7: *"jamal-i giti ara-i an murshid-i mihraban ki chun badr-i asman wa khurshid-i taban be taliban faiz rasan bud."*

[46] Ibid., p. 86. For discussions, disputes, and polemics around Shah Badakhshi's view of *tauhid* and Dara Shukoh's support to him, see also *Ahwal–i Shahi*, fls 28a, 31, 34a–37b.

> After searching for twenty long years,
> it appeared I found Him at last.
> I discovered that in reality, I had looked for my own self,
> I came to know the secret that I myself was He.
> Pursuing that coquettish beloved, I had staggered with passion,
> for Him to get drunk on the wine of 'alast'.[47]
> I suddenly saw it all at once inside my own self,
> I found Him very close in my own chest hand in hand.

She also writes later that a person is not even human, but is closer to an animal, if he or she does not attain this level of appreciation of the truth. Life is meaningless without this sort of radical enlightenment; on the other hand, whoever is blessed with this enlightenment is the perfect human, even a woman (*insan-i kamil, agarchi zan-ast*), superior to all other creatures. Here the human being gets lost in the Absolute Being, a drop of water turns into the ocean, a speck of dust becomes the sun, and a part becomes the whole (*hasti-yi u dar hasti-yi mutlaq gum shud, wa qatra bahr gasht wa zarra aftab wa juzw kull*). In this state, the human is liberated from the concerns of death, judgment, punishment, and heaven and hell. Jahanara reiterates that both men and women (*chi zan wa chi mard*) could be graced with this great wealth and proud boon (*daulat-i'uzma wa ni'mat-i kubra*), for God does not discriminate between His friends along gender. If a perfect man is possible, then so is a perfect woman. She quotes here the famous Shaikh 'Attar about a legendary woman saint of early Islam, Rabi'a of Basra, and perhaps thinks of herself as the Rabi'a of her own time.[48]

> *An na yak zan bud bal sad mard bud*
> *pay ta sar jumla gharq-i dard bud*

---

[47] Reference to the Qur'anic verse '*alastu bi-rabikkum*' (Am I not your Lord?), Qur'an 7: 172.

[48] Ibid., p.108: "*har ki be zati mutlaq 'ishq u muhabbat darad insan-i kamil ast, agarchi zan ast.*"

She was not a single woman but was [equal to a] hundred men.
From head to foot she was totally immersed in pain [of love of God].

She then cites eight verses, a few of which I will quote below, and which she claims she herself composed extempore in passionate love (*shauq-o-wajd*) of God and her own master:

Inha hama ra zuhur-i haq mi binam
zatast yaki jumla sifat mi binam
Naqsh-i fana baqast bi-rangi-yi yar
bi-rang beshaw rangaha ra mashumar

I see all this as a manifestation of Truth.
The Essence is one, all I see is His attributes.
The impress of annihilation is itself the eternity of the colourless Beloved.
Be colourless, count not the colours.

Yar amad dar baghal bi mihnat-i shabha-i hijr
'ashiq-o-diwana budam ishtiyaqam dad ajr

My beloved is next to me, without the ordeal of the nights of separation from him.
I was a mad lover, [but] I got the reward of my passionate desire.[49]

Jahanara ends her treatise on 27 Ramazan 1050 H/18 January 1641, with more praise of her master, to whom she dedicates the text. She also has an evaluation of it as a valuable guide for the seekers (*salikan*) of the path of righteousness. "Each word in it is [like] a priceless pearl, each sentence a necklace of pearls that decorates the ear and the neck of the seekers of the path to righteousness."[50] In sum, Jahanara presents her initiation into

---

[49] Ibid., pp. 109–10. It is worth recalling that Jahanara was also a poet; scholars mention other verses in addition to the ones included in *Munis al-Arwah* and *Sahibiya*. See Rahman, "Taimuri Shahzadiyon", pp. 338–56. The author mentions an elegy of Shah Jahan cited from a certain Munshi Shail Chand's Urdu work.

[50] Ibid., p. 110: "*har harfi azan gauharist bi-baha. har fiqra azan hast 'iqd-i lulu-i zinat bakhsh-i-yi gush o gardan-i salikan-i rahi huda.*"

the Qadiri order not simply as a result of Dara Shukoh's influence but as emerging from her own spiritual development. We may however also consider here some additional factors for this transformation. Women seem to have been given special place in the Qadiri Sufi order. Among the existing Mughal popular Sufi *tazkiras* it is perhaps only in Qadiri *tazkiras*, such as the *Akhbar al-Akhyar* by Shaikh 'Abd al-Haqq Dehlavi, that we have a significant, albeit brief, portion describing female saints. By contrast, in other hagiographical accounts written by the Chishtis during Mughal times there is little on past Indian, let alone contemporary, women saints. We know that there were prominent female Qadiri Sufis in this period: the sister of the most prominent Qadiri Sufi of Jahanara's times, Miyan Mir, was also an important Sufi. In his *tazkira* of Miyan Mir, *Sakinat al-Auliya'*, Dara Shukoh devotes an important part of the book to her spiritual accomplishments.[51] Another factor that may have drawn Jahanara to the Qadiri saints was their renown in poetry and Persian epistolography. Mulla Shah was a noted poet. Dehlavi's account of his own family at the end of the *Akhbar al-Akhyar* furnishes a specimen of elevated prose studded with high-quality verses, and the author mentions his father and uncle as accomplished poets too.[52]

Continuing as a Chishti

However, despite her initiation into the Qadiri order, it is notable that Jahanara continued to present herself as a *murid* of Khwaja Mu'in al-Din. In an appendix to the *Munis al-Arwah*, she describes her visit to the khwaja's tomb at Ajmer in 1643, about three years after her Qadiri initiation. When she arrived at the tomb, she offered supererogatory prayers every day, and one night she also celebrated *milad* (the birth ceremony of the Prophet). Out of extreme reverence for the saint, she would not use a bed nor

---

[51] Dara Shukoh, *Sakinat al-Auliya'*, pp. 153–6.
[52] Dehlavi, *Akhbar al-Akhyar*, pp. 300–4 for women saints; pp. 304–29 for the author's own and his family's accounts.

would she stretch her legs in the direction of his tomb nor even turn her back towards it. Because of the grace of he whom she calls the master preceptor (*pir-i dastgir*), she writes that she experienced a variety of spiritual states during this visit.

> One-fourth of the day remained when I went to the holy shrine. I rubbed my pale face with the dust of that threshold and went barefoot from the outer door to the dome, kissing the ground. Entering the dome, I circumambulated "the illuminated tomb of my own *pir*" seven times. I swept the ground with my eyelashes and made the fragrant dust of that place the collyrium of my eyes. I felt myself in such a state of mental delight that it cannot be described in writing. Because of extreme delight, I became bewildered and I did not know what to say or what to do. In short, I rubbed the perfume and "covered the grave with a canopy of roses which I had carried on my own head." Then I moved to the marble mosque built by my father where I performed prayers. I returned again to the dome and recited from Qur'an the *suras* of Ya-Sin and Fatiha for his soul. I stayed there until the time of the evening prayer and lit the candle in his name and broke my fast with the water of the spring. I saw a strange evening there which was better than the morning. However, my sincerity and love did not allow me to return home from such a sacred place full of grace, which was a corner of tranquillity. What could I have done? The beloved has put a string (of love) around my neck, he takes me wherever he likes.[53] If I could have, I would have remained forever in that mausoleum which was a wonderful centre of tranquillity, for I am a lover of this place and I would also have been honoured and blessed with circumambulating it. The next morning, which was Friday, I set out for Agra with my father.[54]

In addition, she had a specially prepared copy of her *Munis al-Arwah*, which she gifted to the custodians of the tomb so that it might remain there in perpetuity. Jahanara expresses the hope that her master will accept it and continue to grant his "attentive-

---

[53] Jahanara, *Munis al-Arwah*, p. 122: "*rishta-i dar gardanam afganda dust / miburad har ja ki khatir khwah-i ust.*"
[54] Ibid., pp. 120–2.

ness" (*tawajjuh*) towards her. She concludes this passage with the following verse:

*Muʿin al-Din-i-ma fani-st dar haqq
az an baqi shuda dar zat-i mutlaq*

Our Muʿin al-Din is annihilated in Truth.
He thus became eternal in God.

Notable in particular are the last lines of this appendix where she combines in herself the *muridi* of Khwaja Muʿin al-Din who lived centuries earlier, and of Mulla Shah Badakhshi who lived in her own time. She expects that with the grace-filled attention of the two, her own illusory existence (*hasti-yi mauhumi*) will become eternal (*hasti-yi bi-zawal*). The reader may infer at work here a heightened sense of her spiritual achievements, as well as a reflection of the enviable power stemming from the royal household.

Jahanara does not describe the nuances of her relationship in later years with the Qadiri saint Mulla Shah Badakhshi. From imperial chronicles we know, however, that she paid two further visits to Kashmir, one in 1645–6, and the second between 1651 and 1652. During the first visit the emperor stayed in Kashmir for five months, and during the second for over two months. We know that Mulla Shah met Shah Jahan and also composed and presented a poem in his praise. Obviously, during these two visits Jahanara very likely met Mulla Shah, though there is no record of it. And yet, despite her Qadiri affiliation, when she died in 1681 she identified herself only as a *"murid-i Khwajagan-i Chisht"*. Was this because she disapproved of Mulla Shah once he welcomed Aurangzeb's ascension and presented verses praising the new emperor? We know that Jahanara continued to enjoy an important position in Aurangzeb's time: Aurangzeb is said to have conferred on her the title of Badshah Begum, *Sahibat al-Zamani*, even though she was no longer active in politics. On ceremonial occasions, such as the distribution of gifts and conferment of titles, she was treated as the most senior member of the royal family.⁵⁵ All the same, it is difficult not to speculate that there might have been an alteration in her relations with Mulla Shah once her probably favourite brother Dara Shukoh had been killed by her less favourite brother Aurangzeb and the latter welcomed as emperor by Mulla Shah – an alteration she hinted at by her self-description at the end of her life.

In sum, Jahanara possessed real political power which was recognised even by European traders and important chieftains of the Mughal domain. She had considerable agency of her own which was approved of even by Aurangzeb – who was usually distrustful, especially in the matter of his complaints against Dara Shukoh's interference and her response. This was despite her demonstrated affection for and alliance with Dara Shukoh. We noted evidence of this in particular in her intervention during the war of succession, making a plea for Dara Shukoh's superior claims compared to those of his other brothers. When Shah Jahan was constrained to rescind power, she preferred to be diplomatic and stay silent. We do not know Jahanara's position on the father–son dispute, but European sources record that she was able to secure a *mu'afi nama* – a letter from Shah Jahan forgiving Aurangzeb. But she decided to stay with her father when Aurangzeb confined him alongside his two wives – Akbarabadi Mahal and Fatehpuri Mahal – and a considerable number of attendants. Aurangzeb showed grace in allowing her to do so. Over the last moments of Shah Jahan's life she remained in constant contact with Aurangzeb and planned their father's burial according to her wishes. After Shah Jahan's death she was completely reconciled with Aurangzeb and, in turn, Aurangzeb allowed her to retain all her *jagirs* and properties. She was given the highest honour during ceremonial occasions. She then moved to an appropriately appointed mansion in Delhi where she passed away in 1681. When she died she was considered the richest princess of her time. Aurangzeb did not,

⁵⁵ Khan, *Ma'asir-i 'Alamgiri*, p. 131; Khan, *Mir'at al-'Alam*, Vol. 2, pp. 410–11, for Mulla Shah Badakhshi's verses in praise of Aurangzeb.

however, allow her will to be fully implemented on the pretext of *shar'ia* law.⁵⁶

On the matter of imposition of the very unpopular *jizya* by Aurangzeb, Manucci's report of the efforts of Jahanara to plead with her brother against it suggests she maintained her earlier position in political matters, even after she had reconciled with Aurangzeb. Manucci says:

> It was during the years 1678 and 1679 that Aurangzeb decided to impose a new tribute upon all Hindus. All the high-placed and important men at the court opposed themselves to this measure . . . But all was in vain, and the king stood firm . . . Begum Sahib, eldest sister of the king, a very generous princess, wanted to make a fresh appeal. With this intent she paid her brother a visit and entreated most humbly that he would not go farther with this affair, and to touch him more deeply she brought forward a comparison. "Just think sire," said she, "that the lands of Hindustan are like a vast ocean; your majesty and all the members of our royal family are like ships navigating its waters and ploughing through its waves. Where is there any sovereign prince who would desire to load with imposts the sea on which he sails? Who has ever seen the physician pay the patient? From this I conclude, with your majesty's permission, that if the sick man has to pay the physician who cures him; if the ships and sailors must always try to render the seas favourable and pacific towards them in order to navigate with success and happily arrive at port; in the same way your majesty ought to appease and soften the ocean of your subjects. For in what way can you expect them to pay taxes if you overburden them and provoke their waves by this unaccustomed demand? Abandon, then, sire, this purpose, lest there be a rebellion in this kingdom. Let your majesty reflect that violent

---

⁵⁶ It is reported that Jahanara had left behind a sum of 3 crore rupees, which she had willed to be distributed to the attendants of the Chishti shrines. But as per the rule of *shari'a*, Aurangzeb distributed only one-third of it to them. He seems however to have been impressed by her spiritual accomplishments. The attributes of God, *al-Hayyu wa'l Qaiyum*, and the metre and some words in the verse, i.e. *ghariban, bas-ast*, used in an epitaph at his grave, even if installed later, resemble markedly those at Jahanara's grave.

winds usually raise and disturb the seas, swell high their waves, and transform the whole into a terrifying tempest. By its violence everything is swept to the shore, and the poor and persecuted people are ruined." When she had finished this harangue, and impressed on him the force of this comparison, she attempted to throw herself at his feet and, as it were, pay him the adoration and homage of a subject to her sovereign. Coming from a sister, this was a thing still more to be prized. But the prince, stiff and unmoved in his ideas, at once dismissed her . . .[57]

In matters of piety she repeatedly mentions her brother Dara Shukoh's influence: he, as we noted, had advised her to read specific Sufic texts and be initiated into the Qadiri order via Mulla Shah Badakhshi. But all the evidence also suggests she had a will of her own and asserted a certain independence in her thinking. She decided for herself who her *pir* would be, choosing the *pir* inspired by her own vision of the Prophet himself. She also asserted that Sufic perfection was not the sole preserve of men.

Jahanara's Sufi practice and writings offer a personal understanding of Sufism and comprise a statement of her distinct place in it. As a confident woman writer she presents her story, poetry, and Sufi experiences alongside her accounts of the order and the place of the male *pir*. With her writings and by asserting the truth of the doctrine of *wahdat al-wujud* she conveys her social and political motives in narrative and poetry. In the two texts she left behind, Jahanara also articulates her personal spiritual and imperial authority. Her historical and authorial selves are fused by her constant use of "I": we get a personalised view of the intellectual and spiritual journey of a royal woman whose participation in and negotiations with the existing imperial milieu not only richly informs her life but presents a lens through which we can examine the lives of other royal women. We will see below some evidence of it in whatever we know of her sister Roshanara's Sufi endeavours through the letters she received from Shaikh Saif al-Din, the

[57] Manucci, *Storia do Mogor*, Vol. 3, Part IV, pp. 274–5.

son and representative of her *pir* Shaikh Muhammad Ma'sum Sirhindi.

Roshanara Begum: An Introduction

Just as Dara Shukoh excited the jealousy of his brothers, Jahanara became the envy of other female members of the royal household, including her sisters. Here I discuss the spiritual careers of Roshanara, or Roshanrai, and her niece Zeb-un-nisa', on whom there is information. Zeb-un-nisa' would look up to Jahanara's achievements and say she devoutly aspired to be like her aunt. Roshanara, born in 1618, was close to Aurangzeb and throughout her life worked as a virtual agent for him; she disliked Dara Shukoh and may have been jealous of her sister Jahanara's high position. Contemporary European observers claimed that after Aurangzeb came to power she pleaded forcefully for Dara Shukoh's execution and celebrated his killing by giving a feast.[58] She sought to realise two aims, the first of which was to attain a central position of power in court politics. Notable are terms like "most precious pearl of the ocean of the empire (*durra-i fakhira-i bahr-i saltanat*)" used for her by Muhammad Kazim. Kazim also mentions her close relationship with Aurangzeb as "a sincere, true, and strong ally and devotee of the king of the world and caliph of the time [Aurangzeb] (*sidq-i ikhlas-o-'aqidat wa rusukh-i yakjihati-o-iradat be khidmat-i Khadiv-i Jahan wa Khalifa-i zaman*)".[59] Bernier gives an account of her spectacular procession.[60] We know she was also granted a special mansion as her quarters. During the fifth regnal year of Aurangzeb, when the emperor recovered from a serious ailment, she organised in her mansion (*haram-kada-i quds*) a magnificent celebration, and at the emperor's command all (*jami'*) the nobility and high officials attended the ceremony

---

[58] Bernier, *Travels in the Mogul Empire*, p. 100; Manucci, *Storia do Mogor*, Vol. 1, pp. 255 and 356.

[59] Kazim, *'Alamgirnama*, pp. 368, 752–3, for instance.

[60] Bernier, *Travels in the Mogul Empire*, pp. 351–2 and 372–3.

and presented their obeisance and greetings to her. In turn she granted precious robes (*khal'at*) to about fity high nobles of high status (*'umdaha*).[61] She could not, however, acquire more than a modicum of power in state matters and Aurangzeb did not treat her as Shah Jahan had treated Jahanara. Shrewd and mistrusting of everyone as he was, Aurangzeb was not one for sharing power with his family. Roshanara thus turned her attentions to piety and spiritual attainment. Here too she sought to create the impression of harbouring the same lofty ambitions for spiritual status as Jahanara. However, she displayed no interest in the Qadiri or Chishti orders and may have avoided them precisely because of Dara Shukoh and Jahanara's association with them. Moreover, her temperament would have placed her very far from a Chishti or Qadiri sensibility, orientation, and mode of thinking. Instead, she turned to the Mujaddidi–Naqshbandi shaikhs, who shared her hatred and enmity for Dara Shukoh and who were close to her favourite brother Aurangzeb.

Aurangzeb, even if probably not formally a disciple of any Naqshbandi shaikh, had close relations with the Naqshbandi order. Bakhtawar Khan says Muhammad Ma'sum visited the court several times at the explicit request of Aurangzeb, and that Muhammad Ma'sum's sons enjoyed high positions (*mu'azzaz-o-muqarrab*). He seems to have encouraged the presence of at least one member of the Sirhindi family at the court at all times. It is also noted that Aurangzeb strongly encouraged his sons and daughters to take spiritual instruction from the Mujaddidi–Naqshbandis and to be formally initiated into the order.[62] Roshanara, who revered and supported Aurangzeb, must also have been influenced to some degree by him in her choice of this Sufi order. However, we must be careful with this kind of characterisation by association, for it is equally important to consider her actions, beliefs, and com-

---

[61] Kazim, *'Alamgirnama*, pp. 752–3. See also A'zam, *Maktubat-i Khwaja*, Letter 77, pp. 185–6, for her *haveli* and its *baraka*.

[62] See Chapter 8 on the Naqshbandis, below.

mitments as an imperial woman of the court – as we saw above in relation to Jahanara – as being at the same time the genuine result of her assertive will and agency. Jahanara was not interested in Chishti and Qadiri Sufism merely because it reflected her allegiance to Dara Shukoh, an important male member of the royal family; and Roshanara too cannot be supposed to have been interested in Naqshbandi Sufism solely on account of Aurangzeb's interest in the order. Like Jahanara, she was a highly educated and politically astute individual who was likely drawn to Naqshbandi Sufism for her own reasons.

Letters from Shaikh Saif al-Din to Roshanara Begum

Several letters were addressed to Roshanara by a very prominent member of the Mujaddidi–Naqshbandi family, Shaikh Muhammad Saif al-Din, the son of the reigning spiritual preceptor of the order at that time, Shaikh Muhammad Ma'sum, the son and successor of Shaikh Ahmad Sirhindi.[63] Shaikh Ma'sum was Roshanara's main guide. Shaikh Saif al-Din was appointed by his father as the delegate from the order whose function it was to take members of the royal family under his spiritual guidance and secure his own footing in the royal court and administration. Often in the letters he uses the expression *hazrat-i ishan-i ma* ("he who is our lord") to refer to his father, Muhammad Ma'sum, or to his grandfather, Shaikh Ahmad Sirhindi, and at times to them both.

These letters, comprising responses composed by Shaikh Saif al-Din, provide answers to questions that the princess had posed to him through their correspondence. The kinds of questions she asked pertained to her own spiritual experiences and observations, which demonstrate that Roshanara, like her sister, had lofty aims and great ambition. In his answers Shaikh Saif al-Din provides affirmation and praise for her achievements and indicates that

---

[63] A'zam, *Maktubat-i Khwaja*.

she has attained the most elevated stage of Sufi enlightenment. In addition, in these letters he projects the spiritual accomplishments of his own family and order, and there is a good deal of polemics as well when he warns her of the deficiencies in other orders, especially those such as the Chishti and the Qadiri that propound the *wahdat al-wujud* doctrine. This was because, in his understanding, they mistook illusion for reality.

The letters are not dated but, based on the content and progression of topics, it is reasonable to assume that the order in which they appear in the *maktubat* (and are discussed here) is roughly chronologically correct. The correspondence between Roshanara and Saif al-Din continued over a period of eight or nine years. The letters reveal two aspects to their relationship. On the one hand we see a stylised and formal exchange between a Sufi master and his disciple (even though the shaikh here is very young; born in 1645 and writing between 1662 and 1671, he would at best have been in his early twenties). At the same time the letters demonstrate a two-sided collaboration wherein Roshanara's enlightenment helps her to acquire status, and in the process Saif al-Din's family grows in renown and political reckoning. One may note the exalted terms in which Roshanara's position is assessed:

> The sky prostrates before that part of the earth where there are but one or two people who sit together for the sake of God. Several seekers of God who are close to each other sit together for some time and this leads to a great blessing (*barakat-i 'azima*). It is because of the great kindness of God that this fortune has been bestowed upon you [i.e. you are in a position to sit with my disciples, etc.] . . . It is also a wondrous event that your edifying discussions (*suhbat*) have had such a great effect and influence that others now benefit from your knowledge and enlightenment as well. This was clear from yesterday's letter. Be thankful to God, for as the Qur'an says, "If you are thankful, you will be even more blessed" . . . It is due to the extraordinary grace of God that you have earned these perfections without your physical presence before a master (*ghayibana kasb-i in kamalat*), so much so that others now are learning from you as well. This is very rare among

rulers. This kind of grace has not been witnessed before our time, especially among royal women. It is even rare among dervishes. It is all due to your love and commitment to your shaikh.[64]

Here, we may say that Roshanara is certified a position to which Jahanara did not even aspire and, as a matter of fact, the shaikh elevates her to the sort of spiritual status which Dara Shukoh claimed.[65] Shaikh Saif al-Din also states: "Regarding what you [Roshanara] had written about others in the order being absorbed in silent prayer (*zikr-i dil*), you should tell them it is the work of one of the first organs of mystical understanding, *latifa-i ruh*. To arrive at the more refined, truer stage of true unity of attributes, training in *latifa-i akhfa*, the sixth spiritual organ, is required [a practice specific to Naqshbandi Sufism]."[66] The letter contains a discussion of the unity of one's own attributes (*sifat-i khud*) with the attributes of God (*sifat-i haqq*). This state is *wahdat al-wujud*; however, there is a very subtle distinction (*daqiqa*) to be drawn between two very similar states: either Roshanara has come to a stage where she sees her own state as God (the unity of existence: *mu'tabar bar wahdat-i wujud*), or she has come to a stage where she sees her own state as a reflection (*partaw*) of God, which is slightly less than the first. The difference is very subtle.[67]

---

[64] *Maktubat-i Saif*, Letter 7, p. 90.

[65] Dara Shukoh, *Sakinat al-Auliya*, pp. 9–10. Badakhshani cites the following original Persian in the Introduction: *"Allah ta'ala azanja ki fazl-i u shamil-i mulk o malikat ast wa sa'ilan ra mujib wa taliban ra qarib, sawal-i in 'ajiz ra ijabat farmud. Ruz-i panjshanba dar man be bisto-panj-salagi dar khwab budam ki hatifi awaz dad char bar be-takrar guft ki anchi be-hich yaki az badshahan-i ru-i zamin muyassar nashuda, an Khuda'i ta'ala be-tu dad"* (Since God's grace is with the state and country, and He is inclined to respond to everyone who approaches Him with his entreaties, He listened to this humble person's prayer. On one Thursday [thus], when I was twenty-five years old, I heard in my dream a voice from heaven, repeating four times, that "God has bestowed upon you what has never been available to any king on this earth").

[66] *Maktubat-i Saif*, Letter 9, p. 92.

[67] Ibid., Letter 9, pp. 91–2.

Once Roshanara writes that she has attained the stage of *latifa-i akhfa*, Saif al-Din tells her she has seen a mirror of her own self and should remain standing there facing the mirror. He ends the letter by saying she is now far enough along on the Sufi path to instruct other women in the harem. Significant in this connection are also the last lines of yet another letter in which the shaikh highlights in particular the distinguishing and glorious features of his own family and order which set them apart. The letter reads as follows:

> The special authority [*wilayat*] given to the Prophet and his companions disappeared for 1000 years, then returned in the Naqshbandiyya order with our own masters, my grandfather, and father; before that, people only knew about *fana'*, *baqa'*, and *tauhid* – but now they understand how to go beyond these stages as well . . . The founder of our order attained that highest stage of authority, not known since the time of the Prophet and his companions. What remained after that time was only *wilayat-i sughra*, that is, *fana'* and *baqa'*. These were fully manifested. With my grandfather, this riddle was solved because he understood that this authority was only the *beginning* of the journey. After the next stage, *wilayat-i 'ulya* [belonging to angels, the "higher authority"], there follows the perfection of prophethood; and after that – the *haqiqat-i Qur'an* and *haqiqat-i Muhammadi*. At this stage, the Sufi practitioner will know the meaning behind the *huruf-i muqatta'at* [the letters at the beginnings of some Qur'anic *suras*], and will understand what it is to be God's *beloved*, not just God's *lover*. It is the Naqshbandiyya that understands this: it gathered the seeds from Bukhara and Samarqand and sowed them in India, that substance which is rooted in the soil of Mecca and Medina (*ki maya'-ash az khak-i Yasrib-o-Batha ast*). For years, the water of God irrigated this field, and crops grew – the crops of gnosis (*ma'rifat*) and love (*mahabbat*). The Naqshbandiya has acquired all these perfections, and all the other masters and shaikhs, the *imams* of the time, *khalifas*, the *qutbs* and *abdals* – they are but shadows. I pray that I, Saif al-Din, should be among these perfect ones in the life hereafter.[68]

---

[68] Ibid., Letter 10.

He then instructs Roshanara to read out his letter in the company of women in the royal harem so that they too may become aware of the perfections of such masters, and that their belief may become strengthened: "And tell them [also] about *fana'-i qalb*; be vigilant, and careful about the conditions of your disciples, especially your sister, Khair-un-nisa', who [all due to your guidance] appears to be on the correct path."[69]

Saif al-Din praises her by saying that even some of the great Sufi shaikhs who completed the forty-day seclusion (*chilla*) and were dutiful in their practices (such as the *zikr-i jahr*, the spoken-aloud recitation practised by Chishtis as opposed to the Naqshbandis, who preferred *zikr-i khafi*, silent recitation) had not acquired such a high position as had Roshanara. Of course, her achievements are all explained by her association with the Mujaddidi–Naqshbandi order. What she has accomplished, he also ascribes to her association with the "Ahmadiya Ma'sumiyya" part of the order, and to her conscious dissociation from the Qadiriya and Chishtiya. The spread of the practice of *zikr-i qalbi* was, says Saif al-Din, due to the lifelong work of his father and grandfather (Ahmad Sirhindi), as this practice was rare among earlier Sufis.[70] To put in perspective Roshanara's great achievement, Saif al-Din says that even one as exalted as Shaikh Auhad al-Din Kirmani (d. 1238), who spent sixty years absorbed in prayer day and night, had only at the end of those six decades experienced a vision of true reality. As Kirmani had put it:

> Sixty years of struggle led to only a single night of beholding the face of fortune; for so many years and months I have roamed the skies, have completed seclusions (*chillas*), and yet have not attained even this much, that in the midst of the bazaar, I am with my friend as if in seclusion, which indicates *zikr-i dawam*, perpetual litanies, or the other stages like *fana'-i qalb*, *fana'-i jazba* and *fana'-i nafs*, which is higher than *fana'-i zikr* by several degrees.[71]

[69] Ibid., Letter 24, pp. 113–14.
[70] Ibid., Letter 7, p. 88.
[71] Ibid.

Here too Shaikh Saif al-Din seems to reiterate that her position is on par with what Dara Shukoh claimed he had achieved.[72] Further, there is an obvious reflection on the Qadiriya order – the one that Jahanara had chosen. Saif al-Din says even the Naqshbandi Sufis who were not immediately connected to his father and grandfather had not attained the same status. They began with practices of breath control (*habs-i dam*), prayers of negation and affirmation (*zikr-i nafy-o-isbat*), and then, after many years, some had possibly arrived at the stage of movement of the heart (*harakat-i qalb*). The Qadiris too begin with prayers of negation and affirmation, and after years might attain a higher stage such as *zikr-i qalb*; but the practice of concentrated attention (*tariqa-i tawajjuh*) was exclusive to Mujaddidi saints and shaikhs. It was claimed that Qadiri Sufis and others had come to them for assistance, beginning with instruction in the name of God's essence (*ism-i zat*) which comprises all the other names (*asma'*). After extensive and intense exercises (*riyazat-i shaqqa*), if God were very kind to them, they might perhaps for a single moment (*turfat al-'ayn*) experience pure inspired vision (*ilqa'*). Saif al-Din writes: "This is my own order, the Ahmadiya, which collects in itself all other orders, and is higher than any other order in its claims on reality and in its status. Whoever comes into this order is blessed with the favours of God. And you [Roshanara] are blessed too; I offer you my congratulations on joining this order, the best of all orders."[73]

This epistolary exchange between shaikh and royal disciple includes other dimensions. In response to a question posed by Roshanara about annihilation of the self, or *fana'-i nafs*, Saif al-Din says:

> Know that contingent essence (*zat-i mumkin*) is nonexistence (*'adam*). There are two stages of existence: contingent (*imkan*), which is really nonexistence, and absolute (*wujub*), true existence. All the attributes

---

[72] *Sakinat al-Auliya*, p. 10, for Dara Shukoh's unusually high claims of spiritual accomplishment.
[73] *Maktubat-i Saif*, Letter 7, p. 89.

(*sifat*) of perfection that are found in existence (*sam', basar, hayat, kalam, iradat*, etc.) are all borrowed from that high stage of absolute existence, *wujub*. All the attributes, which in themselves are nothing, are mere reflections of absolute existence. Similarly, contingent knowledge (*'ilm-i mumkin*) is but a reflection of divine, absolute knowledge. If one thinks he has acquired independent attributes that are shared with the special attributes of God, of the Necessary Existence (*wajib al-wujub*), that person is deceived, for this is but an illusion, and indeed it is a betrayal of sacred trust (*khiyanat al-amanat*). When God decides to bestow special grace upon a person, that person acquires mystical understanding (*ma'rifat*) such that he is able to forget his own self and be attentive to and perfectly aware of true reality, the roots of reality (*asl*). In this state, he considers his own essence (*zat*) to be nonexistent, to be a mere stone without perception or movement (*bi-hiss-o-harakat*). As Maulana Rumi says, "When you recognise yourself in that which is first (*nakhust*), you start attributing yourself to that majesty (*hazrat*); and whoever knows that they are a mere shadow (*zill*), then it is all the same whether you live or die." Try to understand this stage of meditation that I am teaching you and think about it in this way: consider your own attributes to be completely nothing, and attribute everything to the absolute root of reality. In the stage of annihilation of attraction [to God] (*fana'-i jazba*), even if the disciple is completely engrossed, human attributes (*sifat-i bashari*) still exist; but because of the overpowering nature of that attraction (*ghalba-i jazba*), he cannot appreciate the attributes as being his own. In contrast, in the state of true annihilation (*fana'-i haqiqi*), human attributes are completely erased and there is no trace left of human existence (*wujud-i bashari*). Praise be to God that you have understood the annihilation of the heart (*fana'-i qalb*) and the annihilation in the state of attraction to God without guidance. I hope you will make this a regular part of your practice.[74]

Roshanara has thus already experienced that vision, the result of what the Mujaddidis termed "seclusion in a public gathering (*khalwat dar anjuman*)" – for, after all, as a royal figure she had to be physically present at courtly gatherings, and yet she could

[74] Ibid., Letter 7, pp. 89–90.

discharge her duties while carrying within herself this rare enlightenment. Saif al-Din refers to *zikr-i qalb* – recitation from the heart as distinct from mere articulation. This is perfected only after many periods of practising breath control (*ba'd az muddat-ha … habs-i dam*). Saif al-Din then refers again to the shortcomings of the rival Qadiri and Chishti orders. On annihilation of the self (*fana'-i nafs*) he again cites Rumi: "Everyone who remains far from his roots (*asl-i khwish*] / Seeks the time of union (*wasl-i khwish*) with those origins."[75]

Having answered her questions and confirming she has already attained significant levels of mystical understanding, Saif al-Din goes on to tell Roshanara that if she remains in doubt, they could meet and discuss matters in person. Earlier, he had instructed the princess in contemplative practice (*muraqaba*); when performing as taught, she perceived a ray of light and thought it a reflection of some aspect of the divine; she also felt permeated with heat from this appearance of the Divine Name (*az zuhur-i ism-i ilahi*). Association with this Name, he explains, is called either *fana'* or *baqa'*, and he instructs her further in the practice of prayer in seclusion (*i'tikaf*).

> Many dervishes, having attained *fana'* and *baqa'*, become completely lost, bewildered by their own existence (*wujud*). As it says in the Qur'an, "Look into your own selves." When you repeat "*La ilaha illa llah*", it implies that all aims (*maqasid*) are now denied, except God. The second implication is that one's own attributes all refer to the one root, God. When some shaikhs attain these two stages of perfection, they begin with the stage of *wilayat-i kubra*, which is given to prophets, and also companions of prophets – saints.[76]

Here, Saif al-Din again gives the princess a brief history of his own order and its achievements, ostensibly with the purpose of explaining to her the significance of what she had experienced:

[75] Ibid., Letter 8, p. 90.
[76] Ibid., Letter 10, pp. 92–3.

After the time of the prophets, for a thousand years this authority was hidden – that is, until it re-emerged among saints in the community of my grandfather Ahmad Sirhindi, and father Ma'sum. After God solves all the riddles of this stage for saints like them, they progress to *wilayat-i 'ulya*, the higher authority reserved for angels. After that, the next stage is the perfection of the prophets, which is a different matter. I hope you, Roshanara, may be blessed with all the stages of spiritual perfection.[77]

He then suggests that what Roshanara has written to him shows that she has acquired *wilayat-i 'ulya*, normally a condition of being reserved for angels:

Earlier, you wrote saying that during your practice of meditation (*dar 'ayn-i muraqaba*) you saw light three times at your right, as though from a luminous lamp. Then something came into your heart (*khatir*). You thought this might be the light of the Divine Attributes (*nur-i sifat-i ilahi*). And you also wrote that you felt a pervading heat, like the warmth of a hammam. I gave thanks to God and am so happy to know you have experienced these things. This light is indeed the manifestation of the Divine Name (*ism-i ilahi*), which is the guide for seekers (*murabbi-yi salik*). The two stages of *fana'* and *baqa'* mark the merging of the seeker with that Divine Name (*luhuq be-'ayn*).

It was all the more extraordinary that the princess had managed to attain all this on the very first night that she engaged in meditative seclusion (*i'tikaf*). However, the shaikh claims some of credit redounds to him as well, because her meditation was rendered more fruitful by the attention (*tawajjuh*) he had devoted on her, to the point that he was aware of her experiences even before receiving her letter: "Indeed, I was *with you* [in spirit, though not in body] when it happened. The blessing (*barakat*) came to me, and I understood that I was sharing it with you. Words fail to describe the nature of the prayers and the extent of my attentive meditations that I performed for you. I hope, after some time, that the effects of this spiritual connection will continue to make

[77] Ibid.

themselves known."⁷⁸ Besides taking some credit for her vision through his tutoring and guidance, Saif al-Din elaborates on the difficult duties of the Sufi who has accomplished the *wilayat-i 'ulya*, i.e. the stage of the spiritual authority of angels. When one is at this stage, he writes, the essence of a saintly person, previously veiled, is unveiled and becomes manifest. Since the angels themselves are infallible, they are safe from all sins and can benefit fully from the grace of this elevated stage. Further, as a true Naqshbandi, he insists that access to the highest stages of enlightenment gives one a correct understanding of the *shari'a*.

> Be vigilant upon this point; you might attain all the stages and states that are possible in this world, but if you lack rectitude and integrity (*istiqamat*) you will be destroyed and find only illusion, not true spiritual power. But if perfect integrity is yours, then do not worry; and if you experience spiritual states as well, that is wonderful. You must be attentive to these states (*ahwal*) and do not pay so much attention to your disciples (*muridan-i shuma*); you should be always aware of the path that you are treading and keep seeking to go further.⁷⁹

Since angels are infallible, the Sufi should also be free from all sin (*gunah*) and should adhere perfectly to *shari'a*, for without this there can be only deception (*istidraj*). "If you are simply carrying out the *shari'a* and do not feel ecstatic passion (*wajd*), that is alright; however, combining perfect integrity (*istiqamat*) with *shari'a* is best."⁸⁰ What is of the greatest significance here is, however, that Roshanara is now considered a *murshid* herself and other women in the royal household are described as her disciples. The young shaikh then writes a long letter to highlight the highest spiritual stages that the princess has attained.

> You wrote that in your waking state you find your eyes fatigued and you yourself tired. You find your attributes separated from your own

---
[78] Ibid., Letter 11, pp. 93–4.
[79] Ibid., Letter 12, pp. 94–5.
[80] Ibid.

self. You see them as a reflection of the divine attributes. This is correct and true and is the authentic (*mu'tabar*) meaning of *fana'*, that in the waking state one should see oneself as nothing . . . Finding one's own attributes to be mere reflections of divine attributes is a sign of epiphany. *Fana'* of the *latifa-i ruh* [a high state in the Naqshbandi tradition] is acquired only after the manifestation of divine attributes. You have understood this. You have also written about your own capacities and abilities that God has granted you, and about a group in the harem that finds your teachings helpful.

As usual, Saif al-Din cannot resist taking a dig at the Chishtis, here described as those "who believe in *wahdat-i wujud* [but] cannot distinguish between shadow and root reality and consider the shadow to exactly coincide with reality (*'ayn-i asl*)." Previously, figures such as Ibn al-'Arabi, Mansur al-Hallaj, and Bayazid Bistami are mentioned competitively or somewhat dismissively in relation to the "understanding of our teacher [Ma'sum]". This teacher has apparently attained a stage higher than *wahdat-i wujud*, because "those who are imprisoned in *wahdat-i wujud* are deprived of the perfections which are given to humans at a further stage." The superior stage attained by Ma'sum in turn comes from his father and master, Ahmad Sirhindi, to whom the *tauhid-i wujudi* had been first divulged, but who then passed beyond that stage. It is suggested that the princess too has been able to follow in their footsteps.

> From that narrow lane of *tauhid* you've come out and are now on the broad path of truth to reality. Many Sufis have trodden this path of the hidden (*ghayb al-ghayb*) without the help of the perfect master, but it is difficult to find the straight path . . . I am delighted to hear about all the benefit that others are deriving from your wisdom, especially the spiritual exercises of Hafiza Fatima [another woman in the harem], who also sees herself as a reflection of *fana'* and cannot see her own self. It is obvious that the reflection of *fana'* is reflected from your own heart. Be attentive, stay engaged.[81]

[81] Ibid., Letter 46, pp. 134–6.

Roshanara is thus not simply a Sufi like her sister Jahanara; rather, she has the position of a Mujaddidi–Naqshbandi *khalifa*, entrusted with the task of guiding others in the royal harem. Of significance here is another letter in reply to the princess' query concerning what the shaikh identifies as the "cleansing of the four elements", and the manifestation of the lights of the Ka'ba.

> You said that a state descended upon you; reading this was a great pleasure. Grace and the manifestation of light are associated with specific places like Sirhind, the house of righteous guidance. You also have a share in this because of your connections to our order. What you had written about the cleansing of the four elements (*taswiyat-i 'anasir-i arba'*) and that you saw a light; it is possible that this was the light of true reality of the Ka'ba that was reflected in yourself. Your heart became illuminated by a beam, even if by reflection. This is a great blessing. Remain constantly engaged in *zikr* (litanies) and *fikr* (thought and meditation). I will help you and regard myself as your assistant from afar.[82]

There is another interesting letter which sheds light in some measure on non-religious matters not found in political chronicles, but which also reads like a perfect corollary of the above. The reference is to a special mansion Aurangzeb had granted the princess beyond the fortress walls, and her intention to transfer her residence there. It runs as follows:

> Your noble letter arrived at a most fortunate moment. I hear of your moving to a new mansion (*haveli*) and wish you a successful and blessed move. I am very happy [to hear this]. As my grandfather knew, each piece of land has its own grace (*faiz*) and special attributes; for each piece of land is connected with a different stage – *fana', baqa',* etc. – and each good place of living has its own visions and experiences that it can afford. My grandfather said that when he went to Lahore, and arrived at someone's mansion, he was graced with the knowledge of *fana'*. He has written of this in his letters. Then he

[82] Ibid., Letter 62, pp. 157–8.

moved to a different lodging and there experienced knowledge of *baqa'*. He would describe the illumination (*anwar*) of his own and his neighbours' houses, would notice the realities and actualities of those stations and villages as he beheld them. Some realities were about true belief, some about infidelity; this kind of discovery (*kashf, inkishaf*) was my grandfather's specialty, and is rare, not found readily in our own time. Be thankful to God that you have also realised something new upon your move; seek more from God, ask more from him of this capacity.[83]

The case of Roshanara thus shows how the Naqshbandis of Sirhind, who had had no access to the court earlier, had now even gained access to the royal household. Her version of Islamic piety also contested the correctness of the truth that Jahanara had experienced and emphasised as a member of the Qadiri order. To Jahanara, *wahdat al-wujud*, as we have seen above, was not a mere shadow, it was Reality itself. Her Qadiri shaikh, Mulla Shah, was in her understanding the chief (*pishwa*) of all other investigators (*muhaqqiqan*) of spiritual matters, the imam of the monotheists (*muwahhidan*) of the entire universe, the sole head of all the noble saints. Her master's speech was in her view divinely inspired, and he claimed he had found God and could facilitate the true seeker's access to Him. All this to Roshanara and her Naqshbandi teachers was mere deception.

Roshanara died at a relatively young age, while in her fifties, in 1671. Some European cloak-and-dagger accounts suggest Aurangzeb had her killed because she had illicit sexual relations with young men; Manucci, for example, claims that "angered at the misconduct of his sister, Aurangzeb shortened her life by poison . . . [and] she experienced herself his cruelty, dying swollen out like a hogshead, and leaving behind her the name of great lasciviousness."[84] In light of the letter of condolence that Saif al-

---

[83] Ibid., Letter 77, pp. 185–6. The mansion mentioned here could be Roshanara Bagh in Delhi today, north-west of the walled city and beyond the Kashmiri Gate area, where the princess is buried, but which is now in ruins.

[84] Manucci, *Storia do Mogor*, Vol. 2, p. 190. Cf. Bernier, *Travels*, pp. 132–3,

Din wrote to Aurangzeb, this seems more than a little unlikely. In the letter he describes a vision of glad tidings (*basharat*) that one of his highly respected disciples experienced, wherein he saw the Prophet Muhammad himself bestowing upon Roshanara nothing less than the *wilayat-i kubra*, her "final certificate" of spiritual authority. In the last stages of her life, he says, she was especially blessed with God's grace because she had great affection for others and had rendered such great service to the dervishes. He trusts therefore that God has forgiven all her mortal sins.[85]

Unlike Jahanara, Roshanara did not leave us her own writings, and no access is possible to her voice, not even in a stylised form. Reading between the lines of third-party accounts, however, we catch glimpses of a remarkable, assured, and canny woman. The questions and clarifications she asked of her Sufi guide did not pertain to simple requests for instructions and teachings, but to *her own* spiritual experiences and observations, which demonstrate that she, like her sister, had lofty aims and great ambition. According to the Naqshbandi tradition at least, she attained the utmost stage of Sufi enlightenment that humans can possibly hope to achieve, and this she earned *through correspondence,* without her physical presence before a master. She projects herself not simply as an accomplished Sufi but also as a teacher and guide for women inside the royal household. Shaikh Saif al-Din, her master, simply verified her claims, stating: "This was very rare among rulers," or again, "This kind of grace has not been witnessed before our time, especially among royal women. It is rare even among dervishes." Through her uncommon experience of "seclusion in public gatherings"

---

where there is a story of her illicit love affairs; a variant version is found in Tavernier, *Travels in India*, Vol. 1, pp. 299–300.

[85] Ibid., Letter 35, p. 124. It is also of significance to note some terms and titles used for her by Bakhtawar Khan, such as "a queen with angelic manners and qualities (*malika-i malaki sifat-o-khasa'il*)", "a sanctified queen (*malika-i taqaddus ihtijab*)", and a "queen with sacred virtues (*malika-i qudsi shama'il*)". See Khan, *Mir'at al-'Alam*, Vol. 1, pp. 152, 187, and 212.

(*khalwat dar anjuman*), the implication is that she competed in her spirituality not simply with Jahanara but with her brother Dara Shukoh. This is suggested by a verse:

Az birun darmiyan-i bazaram
waz darun khalwatast ba yaram

Externally I am in the midst of the bazaar.
In my interior I am secluded with my beloved.

In general, the contrasting images of Jahanara and Roshanara we have inherited owe a great deal to the writings of seventeenth-century European writers who drew upon the story of two sisters supporting rival candidates in the succession struggle of the 1650s. These writers were more favourably disposed to Jahanara, with whom they had greater contact in view of her interest in trade, than with the more aloof Roshanara. Typical of this is Bernier, who says Roshanara was "less beautiful than her sister, neither was she so remarkable for understanding," adding that "she amassed but little wealth, and took but an inconsiderable part in public affairs."[86] However, even the European images of Roshanara are rare, and one of the most common which rather improbably depicts her in a sari comes a half-century after her death in François Valentijn's *Oud en Nieuw Oost-Indiën*, published in the 1720s.[87] On the other hand it is clear that many oral legends concerning the two sisters circulated in the sort of bazaar gossip that European travellers were apt to pick up and report in seventeenth-century

---

[86] Bernier, *Travels in the Mogul Empire*, p. 14. The French version in Tinguely, ed., *Un Libertin dans l'Inde Moghole*, p. 52, is slightly different.

[87] Valentijn, *Oud en Nieuw Oost Indiën*, Book 4, Part 2, pp. 246–7, where the sari is described as "her wash-cloth". This dress is unlikely in view of her close association with the Naqshbandi shaikhs, who would have disapproved of other peoples' social and cultural customs and practices (*rusum-i biganagan*). Another common print is by Jakob van der Schley, from the *Histoire Générale des Voyages* (1751–2), which depicts her in a more generic Mughal female costume.

Delhi, such as the role of highly placed Mughal ladies in facilitating the Maratha leader Shivaji's escape from prison in 1666.[88] A piquant variant may be found in later narratives in the Maratha world, claiming that Roshanara was deeply in love with Shivaji, whose masculinity is thus portrayed as irresistible even to his enemies. Versions of this story with Roshanara as Aurangzeb's daughter can be found in Hindi literature as late as the 1920s.[89] This would hardly have been pleasing to a princess who strove to attain such a high level of mystical accomplishment in the Mujaddidi–Naqshbandi order, whether for purely spiritual or partly political motivations.

Zeb-un-nisa' (1639–1701): An Introduction

This brings us to the third member of our royal triptych. Zeb-un-nisa' was the oldest daughter of Aurangzeb, born in February 1639 to Begum Dilras Bano, daughter of a major Mughal noble, Shah Nawaz Safawi. Her first tutor was Hafiza Maryam, the mother of 'Inayat Allah Khan, an important noble of his time. At a very young age she memorised the Qur'an, for which she received from her father a reward of 30,000 gold coins. She also received the highest level of education in Arabic and Persian from some of the best scholars of her time, and "in writing various kinds of hand, such as *nasta'liq*, *naskh*, and *shikasta* correctly, she had full competence."[90] Among her other tutors was the famed seventeenth-century poet Sa'id Ashraf Mazandarani (d. 1704), a grandson of the noted Iranian scholar Mulla Taqi Majlisi (d. 1670). Ashraf Mazandarani visited Aurangzeb's court around the beginning

---

[88] For the standard narrative on this episode, see Sarkar, *Shivaji and His Times*, pp. 157–67.

[89] See Gupta, "(Im)possible Love", pp. 195–221, for a discussion of Kalicharan Sharma's *Shivaji va Roshanara*. Stories of falling in love with Shivaji are also associated with Princess Zeb-un-nisa', the veracity of which Jadunath Sarkar, as we saw above, questions. Cf. Sarkar, "Zeb-un-Nisa's Love Affairs".

[90] Shibli Nu'mani, "Zeb-un-nisa", Vol. 5, pp.100–11.

of his reign. The emperor appointed him a tutor for the princess, who was then twenty years old.[91] She continued to consult Mazandarani for her writings, both in prose and poetry, for about fourteen years, until in 1672 he returned to Iran.[92]

Aurangzeb apparently held Zeb-un-nisa' in high esteem. She was his little lamb, for wherever he went, she was sure to go; she appeared to act practically as a primary consultant for the emperor. Until about 1680 we find no mention of her opposition to Aurangzeb's political and religious measures. She did not, however, agree to be initiated into her father's favourite Mujaddidi–Naqshbandi order, even though she corresponded and had a dialogue with them, though, as we will see below, on some delicate and tense literary matters. In 1091 H (1680–1) she lost Aurangzeb's confidence in the wake of her younger brother Prince Muhammad Akbar's rebellion against the emperor. The prince was assigned the task of leading an expedition against the rebel Rathor Rajputs. Reportedly "misled" by the Rajputs, he turned against the emperor and sent him a letter reminding him of the contribution of the Rajputs to the establishment of Mughal power, and their importance for the Mughal state. It appears that Zeb-un-nisa' too did not approve of Aurangzeb's measures against the Rajputs. She was in correspondence with her rebel brother and was suspected to have added her voice in his support. As a result the emperor not only stopped her stipend, he also had her imprisoned in Salimgarh fort in Delhi, where she died in May 1701. According to a report, when Aurangzeb heard of her death he broke down weeping and ordered a tomb to be built over her grave.[93] Saqi Musta'id Khan sums up Zeb-un-Nisa's achievements:

[91] Bilgrami, *Sarw-i Azad*, under the entry on Mulla Ashraf Mazandarani.
[92] Ibid., p. 117; Khwushgu, *Safina-i Khwushgu*, p. 20; idem, *Natayij al-Afkar*, p. 55, cited in Ansari, *Farsi Adab*, p. 12. Mazandarani later returned to India, became associated with Prince 'Azim al-Shan in Bihar, and died in Munger (near Patna). Differing dates such as 1704, 1709, or even later – after 1711 – are given as the date of his death. See Mazandarani, *Diwan-i Ash'ar*, Editor's Introduction.
[93] Shibli Nu'mani suggests she was soon forgiven by the emperor; he says

She appreciated the value of learning and skill; and all her heart was set on the collection, copying and reading of books and she turned her kind attention to improving the lot of scholars and gifted men. The result was that she collected a library the like of which no man had seen; and large numbers of theologians, scholars, pious men, poets, scribes and calligraphers by this means came to enjoy the bounty of this lady hidden in the grandeur of the harem: for example, Mulla Safi al-Din Ardabili (or Qazwini) by her order took up his residence in Kashmir and engaged in making a translation [into Persian] of Razi's *Tafsir al-Kabir*, the "Great Commentary on the Quran", which came to be entitled *Zeb al-Tafasir*, "The ornament of commentaries [on the Qur'an]". Other tracts and books have [also] been composed in her honoured name. She died in her father's lifetime, in the 46th year of his reign in 1701.[94]

She is also reported to have asked Ardabili to go on the hajj pilgrimage, generously funded his trip, and guided him to write an account of his travels and experiences of his visits to Mecca and Medina. The result was a treatise with details of his journey called *Anis al-Hujjaj*, the first of its kind written in Persian in India.[95]

Zeb-un-nisa' was in contact with the Sufi shaikhs of her time, albeit not as a disciple. We have seen that Aurangzeb not only encouraged the Mujaddidi–Naqshbandi family's representative at

---

that in 1683, when Ruh-Allah Khan's mother Hamida Bano Begum died, the emperor sent condolences through her, and in the same year all the formalities of the wedding of Prince Kam Baksh were performed at her palace. He writes that all the important nobles of the court, at the emperor's instance, walked to the princess' palace. But Shibli provides no references for these incidents. Cf. Shibli Nu'mani, "Zeb-un-nisa".

[94] Khan, *Ma'asir-i 'Alamgiri*, pp. 322–3. See also Bakhtawar Khan's *Mir'at al-'Alam*, pp. 152 and 393. Bakhtawar Khan sums up his account with the phrase: "the dignity of that fine person [lit. large tree] of the garden of the virtues is much more majestic than that of all other children [of the king]. May it grow further every day (*qadr-i raf'at-i an mahin-i dauha-i hadiqa-i hasanat az sa'iri farzandan be-darja-i a'la ast. Ummid ki har ruz afzun-tar bad*)!"

[95] For a description of it, see Nadwi, "Anis-ul-Hujjaj", pp. 5–24; Qaisar, "From Port to Port", pp. 331–49, and Khan, "A Hajj Pilgrim's Travelogue", pp. 7–12.

the court, he also wanted his sons and daughters to be tutored by them. We can safely assume he would also have wished Zeb-un-nisa', being his favourite daughter, to be initiated into this order. However, we have no evidence – as we do in the case of Roshanara – of her acceptance of the emperor's wish. There are, however, three letters of Mujaddidi–Naqshbandi saints to her. One of these is written by Shaikh Muhammad Naqshband (d. 1703), son of Shaikh Muhammad Ma'sum, the chief spiritual master of the order and the third *qaiyum*. He wrote her a letter after his hajj in 1684.[96] The other two letters are by his cousin Shaikh 'Abd al-Ahad "Wahdat", son of Shaikh Muhammad Sa'id (d. 1661), who was the third son of Shaikh Ahmad Sirhindi. 'Abd al-Ahad was a poet of Persian with Wahdat as his pen name; he also composed poetry in Hindavi under the pen name Gul.[97] After his own hajj in 1095 H, he wrote letters to Zeb-un-nisa', when she was imprisoned, consoling her on her final days in this world, and also perhaps persuading her to seek the emperor's forgiveness.

Shaikh Muhammad Naqshband's letter is short and concerns routine matters, while 'Abd al-Ahad's letters, also on the insignificance of this worldly life, are very poetic and of high literary stature. The letters are titled, "Letter concerning pain and grief (*dar bayan-i dard-o-gham*)" and "Letter concerning Sadness and Grief (*dar bayan-i huzn-o-gham*)".[98] It is not unreasonable to speculate here that Aurangzeb allowed these Naqshbandi Sufis to interact with Zeb-un-nisa' even while she was under arrest, perhaps in the hope that she might reconsider her views.

Zeb-un-nisa' displays a sense of refinement in her correspondence and dialogue with the Sufi shaikhs. She received a conventional

[96] Muhammad, *Wasilat al-Qubul*, Letter 72, pp. 88–9.
[97] Kashmiri, *Gulshan-i Wahdat*, pp. 51–3 and 55–9. Ghulam Mustafa Khan reproduced these letters as "Some Unpublished Letters to Zebunnisa", pp. 22–9. See also Chapter 8 on the Naqshbandis for Shaikh 'Abd al-Ahad Wahdat as a poet in both Persian and Hindavi.
[98] See the appendix to this chapter for these letters.

letter from Shaikh Muhammad Naqshband, but Shaikh 'Abd al-Ahad's letters are important in that even though their themes are religious, the letters are in a highly literate language, interspersed with verses, one of them ending with selections from Rumi's *Masnawi*. The letters include some poems of noted Persian poets and some of his own. The shaikh obviously knew that for her attention he needed to write his letters in exalted and poetic language. The letters of other writers and scholars of her time that were addressed to her were also of the same high quality.[99] Zeb-un-nisa' herself wrote elegant prose, as we see from a collection of her writings entitled *Zeb al-Munsha'at*, reportedly compiled by Mirza Muhammad Khalil.[100]

Was Zeb-un-nisa' also an accomplished poet, and were some or all the verses in the well-known *Diwan-i Makhfi* actually composed by her? These are questions on which historians and litterateurs remain divided.[101] One reason for their doubts is the view that only later *tazkira* writers – like Lachhmi Narayan Shafiq, the author of *Gul-i Ra'na*, and Bhagwandas Hindi Lakhnawi, the author of *Hadiqa-i Hindi* – are apparently the first Mughal Indian scholars to include her as a poet in their *tazkiras*, which they compiled no earlier than some fifty years after her death.[102] Interesting here

---

[99] See Khalil, *Ruq'at-i Mirza*, fls 103a–104a, 104b–105b, 109a–109b, 112a–113a, 116b,122b–123a, for letters on daily routine and exchange of gifts. For a description of this manuscript, see Rieu, *Catalogue of the Persian Manuscripts*, Vol. 2, p. 826.

[100] Sarkhwush, *Kalimat al-Shu'ara'*, p. 33; Sandilawi, *Makhzan*, cited in Shibli, *Maqalat-i Shibli*, Vol. 5, p. 105. The catalogue of the Anjuman-e Taraqqi-ye Urdu, pp. 10–11, mentions the same collection as *Zeb al-Ma'ani*.

[101] Jadunath Sarkar's "Zeb-un-nisa's Love Affairs" began casting the first doubts, which have continued in both English and Urdu writings on the princess until the beginning of the present century. Sharma, "Forbidden Love", considers her an "accomplished poet". He remains more non-committal, though, in his *Mughal Arcadia*, pp. 31 and 172.

[102] Shafiq, *Gul-i Ra'na*; Lakhnawi, *Hadiqa-i Hindi*, pp. 280–1. Bhagwandas gives the wrong year, 1107 H, for the princess' death. Qasemi corrects it in his notes, though he too mars it with a typo, 1131 H instead of 1113 H.

are also Shibli's observations and several other references.¹⁰³ Shibli says Ghulam 'Ali Azad's *Yad-i Baiza* cites only two verses by her. He also cites Ahmad 'Ali Sandilawi's *Makhzan al-Ghara'ib*, which too is a later *tazkira* integrating information from several earlier compilations. Shibli quotes Sandilawi: "The *Diwan* of Zeb-un-nisa's verses [itself] hasn't passed by my eyes. But a selection of it I have seen in a *tazkira*, though this is not reliable. The reason is that this *tazkira* also attributes to her several other known verses of the master poets (*ustadan*)." The same *tazkira*, Shibli adds, retails an anecdote of a notebook (*bayaz*) having fallen into a tank (*hauz*) from the hands of an attendant named Iradat Fahm. He concludes that there is no denying Zeb-un-nisa' was a poet, but believes her poetry was largely lost, and it may have been because of this unfortunate accident. We will note below some verses from a poem in which Mazandarani describes the same incident. Significantly, Siraj al-Din 'Ali Khan Arzu under his account of 'Aqil Khan Razi also mentions a full ghazal by her, with that of 'Aqil Khan Razi written in response (*jawab*).¹⁰⁴

Shibli also notes that Zeb-un-nisa' was so steeped in poetry that poetry figures even in the routine business of her life. By way of illustration he cites the following two interesting incidents: Ni'mat Khan 'Ali sent to Zeb-un-nisa' a crest jewel (*kulghi*) for sale. The princess purchased it but took some time paying its price. The poet then sent her the following verses as a tongue-in-cheek reminder to pay up:

Qasemi also doubts the published *diwan's* attribution to her in his notes (*ta'liqat* [footnotes]), no. 161, p. 331. For a discussion of Shafiq's *Gul-i Ra'na*, see Sharma, "Forbidden Love", p. 771.

¹⁰³ Shibli, *Maqalat-i Shibli*, Vol. 5, pp.106–8.

¹⁰⁴ Arzu, *Majma' al-Nafa'is*, fls 23b, 36b, and 180: "*in ghazal dar jawab-i ghazal-i Zeb-un-nisa' ki sabiyya-i Aurangzeb Badshah gufta, wa Begum shagird-i Mulla Muhammad Sa'id Ashraf Mazandarani bud.*" Arzu gives the first verse (*matla'*) of the *ghazal* as follows: "*Garchi man Laili asasam, dil chu majnun binawa-st / sar be-sahra mi zadam lekin haya zanjir-i pa-st.*" The *ghazal* is available in the Nawal Kishore Lucknow edition (1929) of the *Diwan-i Makhfi*, p. 23.

Ay bandagi-at sa'adat-i akhtar-i man
dar khidmat-i tu 'iyan shuda jauhar-i man
Gar jigha kharidanist pas ku zar-i man
war nist kharidani bezan bar sar-i man

O, you to be enslaved by whom is my good fortune,
My quality became evident in your service.
If the crest-jewel is worth buying, then where is its price?
Or if you refuse the purchase, then hit my head with it.

Pleased at the witticism, the princess apparently gave him 5000 rupees and returned the crest-jewel. Being a generous patron of architecture, she later built a big pavilion all made of mica, and the same Ni'mat Khan 'Ali wrote a short poem in its praise, three couplets of which (including a chronogram) are as follows:

Furughash gar chunin darad jahan tab
kasi shab ra nakhwahad did dar khwab
Chu 'ajiz gasht nutqam az sanayash
shudam juya-i tarikh-i binayash
Pa-yi Tarikh-i an gufta zamana
burad zang-i dilam a'ina khana

Its shine keeps the world so bright,
that no one would see night even in a dream.
As I could not find words to praise it,
I looked for a chronogram for this construction.
Time then announced its chronogram:
"The mirror-house [that] frees the heart of rust".[105]

There are also some stray but significant contemporary references which need to be considered to evaluate the differing opinions of her as a patron and poet. Amongst them are the phrases and words that Ashraf Mazandarani (d. 1704) used in his poems and the *qasidas* that he wrote in praise, despite his widely known dislike of Hindustan. Note the following, for instance:

---

[105] Shibli Nu'mani, *Maqalat-i Shibli*, Vol. 5, pp.106–8.

*Ay khusrau-i pisha / khirad-pisha-i ki dar 'ahdat
bas ki kar-i hunar rawad bala
Mi shawad dar libas-i dukhtar-i raz
sad falatun-i khum-nashin paida.*

O wise one by profession, in your reign,
the work of art has scaled great heights.
A hundred Platos have come up,
sitting in the pitcher, all clothed in wine.[106]

Ashraf also invokes the names of great Persian poets of yore, Hafiz of Shiraz and Khwaja Nasir, to suggest the elevated level of the princess' assembly.

*Mahram az ahl-i fazl Khwaja Nasir
Khwaja Hafiz ze jumla-i shu'ara'*

[You are] an intimate of Khwaja Nasir and Khwaja Hafiz,
poets, who among all poets were endowed with excellence.[107]

In order to serve the princess appropriately, Mazandarani makes it clear that the intellectuals employed by her need to balance various aspects of their activity, from poetry to medicine.

*Gashta kaifiyat-i mutala'-i'am
maghz-i andisha ra nishat afza,
Chun tal-'i 'ashiqan be-yak suyam
jam' gardida daftar-i shu'ra'*

---

[106] Mazandarani, *Diwan-i Ash'ar-i Ashraf Mazandarani*, pp. 91–4 (especially p. 93), from the poem, *Dar talab-i rukhsat az janab-i 'ulya Zeb-un-nisa' Begum*. For Mazandarani's Indian career, see Dale, "A Safavid Poet", pp.197–212; and Sharma, *Mughal Arcadia*, pp. 172–6. My reading of the first line here is different from that of the editor Muhammad Hasan Saiyidan. He reads *Ay khirad-pisha-i* as meaning "O wise person", while I also read *Ay Khusrau-i pisha* basing myself on the Khuda Bakhsh Library Patna manuscript. This reading is supported by the fact that the word "Khusrau" goes better with the word *'ahdat* meaning "reign" in the same line. See Khuda Bakhsh Oriental Public Library, Patna, MS. 4249, ff. 23b and 24b.

[107] *Diwan-i Ash'ar-i Ashraf Mazandarani*, p. 93.

Kuh Tur-i be-janib-i digar
az tasanif-i Bu 'Ali Sina
Tarf-i az qit 'ha-i-i ustadan
hama yaquti-yi tamam ajza'
Gah be-rasm-i nukta pardazan
garm fikr-i qasida-o-insha',
Gah be Qanun-i danish anduzan
fikri-yi hall-i mushkilat-i Shifa.

The state of my studies is a source,
of joy for the essence of thought.
Like the lovers' star, on one side,
I have collected together volumes of poets.
A sacred pile like Mount Sinai,
on the other side, of the books of Avicenna,
On the one side, the master poets' verses,
all shining like ruby stones.
Sometimes like the scholars of a fine idea,
I am engaged in composing a poem and elegant prose.
Sometimes busy with [Avicenna's] *Qanun*,
Or engrossed with the difficulties of his *Shifa*.[108]

Mazandarani does not stint on adjectives for his patron the princess, as we see from the following verse ending with a play on the meaning of her name.

Be hasab shah-i kishwar-i danish
be nasab shahzada-i 'ulya'
partaw-i dudman-i Timuri
zinat-i ruzgar zib-i nisa'

In accomplishment, ruler of the domain of knowledge,
And in lineage a lofty princess.
Illumined ray of the family of Timur,
the decoration of Time, the ornament of women.

Or again, we find the following address: "O Qibla! your court

---

[108] Ibid., p. 92.

is adorned by the gathering of poets (*qibla-gaha! be-dargah-i tu ki hast / majma '-i sha'irān-i bazm-ara')*.[109] Among other occasional poems is one in which the poet complains of one of the assistants, whom the princess has assigned to help him work in her library (*Dar shikwa-i yak-i az 'amala-i kitabkhana be khidmat-i shahzada*). This poem begins:

> *Qadr-i danishwar shinasa nur-i chashm-i 'alama*
> *ay ki hargiz qudrat-i ham-chashmi-at jawza' na-dasht*
> *Az sukhan-ha-i tu gasht awaza-i danish buland*
> *warna dar daur-i falatun in qadar ghaugha na-dasht*
> *Dar funun-i danish az insha'-o-shi'r-o-nahw-o-sarf*
> *harchi pursidam zaban-i khwus-bayanash la nadasht*

> O you who admire the wise, O you, light of the world's eye.
> Not even Gemini dared become your rival.
> Because of your poetry, wisdom was much celebrated.
> Not even in the time of Plato was it so acclaimed.
> In the wise arts – letters, poetry, and all sorts of grammar,
> For the questions I had, she had a ready response.[110]

Mazandarani adds glowing tributes to her even on the smallest of matters, comparing her to great women of the past, such as the Prophet's wife Khadija, Bilqis (the Queen of Sheba), and other such. Note how he describes her intellectual accomplishments, even in the context of a rather banal eulogising poem:

> You know every person's ability,
> you appreciate everyone's value.
> Your imagination in the spring of understanding,
> decorates the garden of ideas.
> Bravo! You know the secrets of ideas,
> And you grasp their nuances.
> To take the tome of wisdom to the extreme,
> becomes easy if you are the patron.

[109] Ibid., pp. 93 and 94.
[110] Ibid., pp. 132 and 134.

> When you write the book of your wisdom, it reads like Plato's book,
> and yet you have not borrowed from it.
> With your nuanced and elegant prose,
> you dig out the meanings of a rose garden from the rocks.[111]

Again, there are several interesting hints in the 29-verse poem captioned "Seeking an excuse for the Royal Notebook's falling into water (*Dar ma'zirat dar ab uftada-i Bayaz-i Badshahi*)" that Ashraf Mazandarani wrote, narrating the tale of how – because of her attendant's negligence – a notebook with the writings of Zeb-un-nisa' fell into a tank:

> Plato is entranced in the wine-jar remembering your wisdom,
> like one intoxicated yet yearning to drink still more.
> From your decorated platter you have scattered pearls,
> like the pearl of your words, aglow as it is fallen in the water.
> That special royal notebook filled on all sides,
> with your select words in place of shining silvery dust,
> which, alas, fell yesterday from Iradat Fahm's hand,
> that moon-like notebook, like a shining fish in the water.
> First I thought it was the reflection of its bright neck,
> But on a closer look, saw the book lying there.
> Its leaves looked like the petals of a rose,
> while it lay in the water, they lost their glow,
> The ocean of shining verses has thrown up a tempest,
> the boat [of her book] faces whirling waves,
> as if the canal's waters have run over
> and the garden of her verse has been ruined.
> The washed off folios, with the vignette (*shamsa*) on the front,
> or perhaps a wet muslin has fallen over the sun.[112]

---

[111] Ibid., pp. 182 and 185. The original verse runs: "*Khadija 'ismata Biqlis shana / Jhadd-i har kas shinasa qadr dana/ khayal-at dar bahar-i nuqta-dani / chaman paira-i gulzar-i ma'ani/ zihe dana-i asrar-i ma'ani / ada fahm-i rumuz-i nukta dani / rasandan daftar-i danish ba-payan / murabbi gar tu bashi bashad asan/ nawisi gar kitab-i danish-i khwud / khurad bar fikr-i Aflatun tawarud/ be-kah-i mu-shigafiha-i insha' / bar ari ma'ani-yi gulshan ze khara.*"

[112] *Diwan-i Ash'ar-i Ashraf Mazandarani*, pp. 130–2: "*Dar khum aflatun ze yad-i danishat sar-khwush buwad / hamchu makhmuri ki dar fikr-i sharab*

The introduction written by a noted seventeenth-century poet and prose writer, Mulla Reza'i Rashid, to a lost album (*muraqqa'*) of Zeb-un-nisa', available in the Khuda Bakhsh Oriental Public Library, also illustrates the princess' special interest in poetry and generous patronage to scholars and poets.[113] In addition, the following hemistich included in Shaikh 'Abd al-Ahad Wahdat's 1694 letter to her furnishes yet another piece of evidence to suggest that she was not just one of the most literate princesses of her time but also considered a poet: "If you are a poet, one hemistich is like a tome for you (*Tu gar sha'ir-i misra'-i daftari-st*)."[114] We may also note the following verses of an elegy which Mazandarani's disciple Champat Rai wrote at his master's instance following her death and sent him for improvement and correction (*islah*). Champat also mentions her pen name in this verse.

Rakht-i hasti bast chun Zeb-un-nisa' Begum ze dahr
zin gham-o-zari jahan chun dida-i a'ma shuda
In ki tasir-i kalamash dar mizaj-i ruzgar
ruh-bakhsh-o-jan faza tar az dam-i 'Isa shuda
Bud az shirin kalami khusraw-i mulk-i sukhan
Ta ze 'alam raft zeb az kishwar-i ma'ani shuda

---

uftada ast / An murassa' khwan guhar rizi ki ta shud jalwagar / durr-i alfazat ki bas ba ab-o-tab uftada ast/ An bayaz-i khasa-i shahi ki bar atraf-i an / ja-i afshan nutqha-i intikhab uftada ast / Dush az dast-i Iradat Fahm khakam dar dahan / chun bayaz-i sina-i mahi dar-ab uftada ast/ Awwalan 'aks-i bayaz-i gardanash kardam guman / nik chun kardam nazar didam kitab uftada ast/ Hast ba auraq-i an guya khawas-i barg-i gul / ta darab uftada ast az ab-o-tab uftada ast, / Bahr-i shi'r-i abdarash baz tufan karda ast / kashti-ash dar char mauj-i inqilab uftada ast / Guiya az sar badar rafta-st ab-i jadwalash / kin-chunin gulzar-i ash'arash kharab uftada ast/ Shusta auraq ast pish-i shamsa-i sar-lauh-i u / ya magar dastar-i tar dar aftab uftada ast.

[113] For details on this album, Rahman, "Taimuri Shazadiyon", pp. 431–40. He also mentions Mahfuzul Haq of Presidency College, Calcutta, publishing a reproduction of this album in an Urdu monthly, *Shama'* (Agra), December 1925.

[114] See the appendix below for this letter.

*Khwish ra andar takhallus garchi makhfi miniwisht
dar hunar lekin zyada shuhra-i giti shuda
Sal-i tarikh-i wafatash ra chun pursidam ze 'aql
az rah-i hasrat be-guft ah az jahan makhfi shuda*

> When Zeb-un-nisa' Begum took her life's trappings from this world,
> the world turned blind crying in grief.
> The impact of her poetry on her time was
> more soul-stirring and life-giving than Jesus' breath.
> She ruled the world of poetry because of her sweet verse,
> when she left, beauty deserted the domain of ideas.
> She wrote her pen name as Makhfi [literally: hidden],
> Though her skill gave her great fame in the world.
> When I asked Wisdom for a chronogram of her death,
> it sighed and said: "She became hidden (*makhfi*) from the world."[115]

The fact that this contemporary Champat Rai clearly mentions her pen name as "Makhfi" and even uses it for the chronogram of her death: "She became hidden (*makhfi*) from the world"

---

[115] See Khuda Bakhsh Oriental Public Library, Patna, MS. H.L. No. 2512, fls 60b–61a, Champat Rai "Ashna", *Mufid al-Insha'*, which includes his letters and also a large number of the letters of his father Meghraj or Sukhraj, written on behalf of various Mughal nobles. Champat compiled these letters on the advice of Mazandarani, who characterised them as *sada-o-purkar* (plain and useful). Champat also sent his *ghazals* to Mazandarani for correction (see fls 92b–93a). Compiled in 1112 H/1701 at Rangpur, the opening folio of the text is missing, and the chronogram which begins: *"Dar khitta-i Rangpur-i ma'mur / k'anast nishat-bakhsh-i janha"*, is given in the last verse as *"Tarikh-i tamamiash khirad guft /gardid zahi matin insha."* Nurul Hasan Ansari notes Champat Rai's elegy cited above, but does not comment on it; in his account of the princess he is mostly interested in giving tales and legends about her life and poetry. Cf. Ansari, *Farsi Adab*, pp. 312–20 (see also pp. 399–401 for Champat Rai). Ansari's view of the poet Makhfi who resided in Shahjahanabad, and several of whose *ghazals* he says are included in the Nawal Kishore edition of the *Diwan-i Makhfi*, seems to be based on Mahfuzul Haq's article published in *Ma'arif,* May 1927. For an early English translation of fifty of her *ghazals*, see Lal and Westbrook, *The Diwan of Zeb-un-Nissa*. Also see Sarkar, *Studies in Mughal India*, pp. 79–90; Shibli Nu'mani, "Zeb-un-nisa".

(1113 H), provides additional evidence against those who, following Sarkar, might continue to cast doubt on whether this Mughal princess – who dared to oppose her formidable father, Aurangzeb, and paid a heavy political price for it – was indeed an accomplished poet.

To conclude then, here are a handful of the verses of "Makhfi". The first of these uses well-known tropes regarding the Muslim and the idolater (or Brahmin), already familiar to us from at least the late-sixteenth century.

> I am not a Muslim but an idolater,
> I bow before the image of my Love and worship it.
> I am not a Brahmin,
> My sacred thread I cast away.
> For round my neck I wear
> Plaited hair instead.

A second verse focuses instead on ideas of exile, or imprisonment, appropriate enough for Zeb-un-nisa'.

> Long is your exile, Makhfi, and long your yearning,
> Long you should wait, your heart within you burning.
> Looking thus forward to your home returning,
> But now what home have you, Unfortunate one![116]

A final melancholy *ghazal* draws on somewhat the same mood.

> *Shud tahi khumkhana o hangama-i mai bar shikast*
> *Man darin daur-i musalsal zahr ashamam hanuz*
> *Dil ze dastam raft o sauda-i jununam dar sar-ast*
> *Talkhi-yi kamam ba kam o talib-i kamam hanuz*

> The wine cellar became empty, the turmoil of wine ceased.
> In this enchained circle, a drinker of poison I remain.
> The heart escaped me, my mad melancholy is at its peak,
> My bitter desires were fulfilled, [yet] a seeker of my desires I remain.[117]

---

[116] Slightly different translations of these verses may be found in Lal and Westbrook, *The Diwan of Zeb-un-Nissa*, pp. 18 and 22.

[117] *Diwan-i Makhfi*, p. 6.

Conclusion

This chapter has been concerned with the contrasting profiles of three Mughal royal women across two generations and two reigns in the seventeenth century. All three were brought up in a time when the Mughals had long given up the peripatetic Central Asian milieu in which someone like Gulbadan Begum, Humayun's sister, was brought up, and which influenced her narrative text, the *Humayun Nama*. They were all given an extended education in Arabic and Persian, though it is not certain whether any of them was extensively exposed to Turkish, which was usually considered a more "masculine" language by the seventeenth century in India. In the course of this education, all of them were undoubtedly exposed to a variety of secular and religious influences within the broad framework of the Sunni Islam which dominated the Mughal court (despite the presence there of appreciable numbers of Shi'is, some closely related to the royal household, such as Yamin al-Daula Asaf Khan and later Shayista Khan).

Despite this common upbringing and context, the personal and religious trajectories of Jahanara, Roshanara, and Zeb-un-nisa' diverged considerably, proving that, for elite women in Mughal India, family was not necessarily destiny. Jahanara chose an orientation that took her to the Chishti Sufi order, already strongly preferred by her great-grandfather Akbar in the second half of the sixteenth century, and then added to it through dealings with a Qadiri Sufi master, perhaps under the influence of her brother Dara Shukoh. She maintained a strong public profile, was considered an excellent manager of financial and political affairs, and showed considerable interest in commerce, following in the footsteps of her father Shah Jahan. In contrast, her younger sister Roshanara showed far less inclination to play a public role, even though she is believed to have been a key political player during the succession struggle of the 1650s and thereafter. I have also striven to show her close connections with the Mujaddidi–Naqshbandi order, whose presence in the court was undoubtedly encouraged by Aurangzeb, and who tried to exercise an influence on the feminine part of the Mughal household through the mediation of Roshanara. Two decades into Aurangzeb's reign, the Naqshbandis had gained a substantial foothold in the court, even though it was still a contested one. This may explain their efforts to maintain dealings with the third of the princesses whose career is addressed here, Aurangzeb's daughter Zeb-un-nisa'. However, this princess appears far more inclined to literary patronage than to the encouragement of the Mujaddidi brand of Islamic "revival", as it was then being practised both in the court and beyond. And yet this literary common ground could still be shared between her and figures such as the Naqshbandi Shaikh 'Abd al-Ahad "Wahdat". However, the extended period when she was obliged to retire from public life (after supporting her rebellious brother) reduced the role she might have played in the Mughal court of the late-seventeenth century. While addressing the questions of the "agency" of these princesses within the heavy constraints posed by the nature of our sources, I have also hoped to show how important it is to understand the feminine dimension of the relationship between politics, religion, and Sufism in the "high" Mughal period.

If we attempt an overview of Aurangzeb's relationships with these three women, a complex and intriguing picture seems to emerge and has a bearing on both our understanding of this emperor's psychobiography as well as the nature of relations between the Mughals and the Sufis. We have earlier in this book examined almost exclusively the lives and ideas and relationships of Mughal *men* and Sufi *men*. This chapter emphasises the need to move beyond this male-centric perspective. First, it suggests that women often played a significant role in this world dominated by men, and not always entirely behind the scenes. They advised emperors, arbitrated in conflicts, negotiated between opposing parties, and mediated a relationship between the temporal and sacred order. While some, like Roshanara, only affirmed the will of the emperor, others questioned the wisdom of the emperor's judgments, sometimes persuading him to rethink his decisions.

In relation to Jahanara, it is clear that Aurangzeb continued to respect and honour her through his reign despite her greater closeness earlier to his main rival Dara Shukoh. Allaying the apprehensions of a highly alert and constantly suspicious man such as Aurangzeb, who felt he was beset by enemies within his own household and who ruthlessly quelled any sign of rebellion – regardless of whether the incipient rebel was male or female – seems in retrospect little short of extraordinary, and Jahanara seems to have been among the very few to have succeeded in stilling the emperor's prickliness.

In a different sense and in her own way Zeb-un-nisa' too seems a remarkable and attractive person. It is intriguing that the trajectory of her life in relation to Aurangzeb is the reverse of Jahanara's: like her *'amma* (paternal aunt), she sided with an enemy within their own family: where Jahanara had shown a definite bias for Dara, Zeb-un-nisa' showed a clear partiality for Aurangzeb's rebellious son. And yet while Jahanara retained Aurangzeb's respect despite being only his sister, his daughter Zeb-un-nisa' paid the severest price: she was imprisoned and died a prisoner even though she was, apparently, her father's favourite daughter. Aurangzeb's grief at her death, and the evidence of remorse he seems to have felt by having a tomb constructed for her, are an ironically poignant reminder of the sadism often noted in this emperor's personality.

Second, this chapter shows how important theological dialogues were in the lives of these women, in the constitution of their individual selves, and in mediating the relationship between Sufic orders and the court. Very rarely do we find explorations of *pir–murid* relations between male Sufi preceptors and Mughal women. Partly, this is because of the relative paucity of evidence, but partly the reason for such erasure is the earlier pervasiveness of male-centric frames. In this sense, these three princesses break the gendered monotony to provide us fascinating evidence which goes against the general grain. From their memoirs and epistolary writings we are enabled glimpses into differing ideals of womanly piety. At one level we see the ideal woman as submissive not merely within the masculine ethos of ruling men, but also, if she is to manage to live a full and unhindered life, as properly subordinate within a spiritual ethos. In this realm – seen by the dominant males who control the royal woman's every move and existence as reassuringly disconnected from her sexuality – she is expected to be guided by one specific figure with impeccably saintly credentials and a respected lineage of long immersion in godliness. It may not be stretching the point to argue that male Sufi practice played a powerful role in the subordination, domestication, and submission of women to men within the royal household. Women were expected to experience sublimation within a world of spirituality even as that world repressed female sexuality. We might see here a world of Sufi spirituality in which the desexualised woman is constrained, even compelled, to discover an alternative method of ecstasy. The interactions of Roshanara with her spiritual guide, even more clearly than those of Jahanara and Zeb-un-nisa', show how intricately certain Sufi orders could weave a web around royals. To those unpredisposed to the attractions and comforts of religion, hers can seem a story of the usefulness of a powerful *murid* by her *pir* for ends that go well beyond matters of the spirit – here specifically to gain access to power for his own Sufi order in Aurangzeb's court, which he accomplishes in part by disparaging hints aimed against rival Sufi orders that might threaten his own foothold in the royal court.

At another level, the texts I have explored reveal the evidence of a more complex relationship between royal women and their spiritual mentors. Turning our gaze from Roshanara to Jahanara, we find a woman asserting her agency, keen to define her own way of relating to the different spiritual orders and choose the individual she will accept as her master. She consults Dara Shukoh but takes all the decisions herself and not always in accordance with her brother's wish. She claims to be the agent of her own enlightenment despite the fact that within her world such enlightenment is not even considered possible without the mediation of a spiritual master. She chooses to accept the guidance of Mulla Shah of the Qadiri order but never breaks her ties with the

Chishtis. As in the sphere of politics, she demonstrates a capacity to converse with those with differing ideals and negotiate seemingly conflicting positions.

Third, the chapter shows that these women were neither mentally secluded within the harem nor insulated from the world nor devoid of literary training and education. They were all literary figures, respected for their learning. They wrote poetry, patronised poets, built libraries, and helped create a literary culture around the court. If immersion in poetry and literary pursuits were ways of containing women within spaces that were unthreatening for ruling men, they were equally the link between the feminine royal interior with the wider male world outside. In this sense, in supporting their literary training, it seems possible to argue that Aurangzeb was unknowingly subverting his own desire to seclude royal females from the world of men.

One could argue about the limits of feminine actions and assertions within the masculine world of that time; but equally one could turn the argument around to underline the significance of these engagements within the limits of that age. A more deferential and traditional view of women's lives in the courts of Muslim rulers, specially in relation to their sexuality and spirituality, has long been the norm in history writing. A normalised idea of discretion and a thick purdah of supposed respect for the woman's privacy have helped curtain off from historical analysis the everyday as well as apocalyptic problems and difficulties that these women faced, living as they did lives comprehensively dictated by male rulers. This norm has been questioned, defied, and set aside by feminist historians and scholars within the broad area of gender studies. It seems to me that the time has come for students of an older generation, such as myself, schooled as we have long been to defer to the wisdom of our elders, to break free and attempt an understanding of women's lives along different lines. Because, I believe, in the process we will arrive at a more compelling and fuller understanding of the relations between the Mughals, "their" women, and the world of Sufi spirituality.

Appendix: The Mujaddidi–Naqshbandi Shaikhs' Letters to Zeb-un-nisa'

1. Letter from Shaikh Muhammad Naqshband (d. 1703), after his return from the hajj in 1095 H/1684.

After praise and prayers, compliments, and greetings: [This letter] is presented to Her Royal Highness, who modestly sits behind the veils of chastity and purity, grandeur and greatness. It has been some time since there has been any news of the fortunate state of the Fatima of our time. In any case, I keep praying for you, for your progress through the spiritual stages and the longevity of your life, and I await acceptance [of my prayers] from the court (*dargah*) of God who answers petitions (*Mujib al-da'wat*):

> *Mi-tawanad ki dihad ashk-i mara husn-i qabul*
> *An ki dur sakhta ast qatra-i barani ra*

> I hope He will accept my tears,
> He who created a pearl from a drop of rain.

Lady of the World [Your Highness], this world is the field where the next world is cultivated; everything that is sown here is reaped there. In short, today is the time of action, for tomorrow everything is in the hands of God. A few months ago, after the pilgrimage [to the holy place of] the Saiyid of Prophets [Muhammad], may they be blessed and honoured, and prayer and circumambulation of the Ka'ba and [prayers in the] Mina valley, I arrived in the victorious [Mughal] army camp and enjoyed a variety of favours from the Religion-Protecting Emperor [Aurangzeb], May God make him victorious. I am writing these few words and am dispatching someone special from my own retinue, Haji Mansur, so that [I] become gladdened by reports of the well-being of your pious self (*zat-i qudsi sifat*) as soon as possible. [I] hope to be honoured by receiving your reply.

Two Letters from Shaikh 'Abd al-Ahad Wahdat (d. 1713)

2a. Letter 44 from the Gulshan-i Wahdat, *in praise of pain and grief.*

... What do I write, and what do I say, and what do I indicate? If I speak of Him, I am speechless; and if I speak of something other than Him, it is also inappropriate and untrue. Alas! One is impossible, the other is exceedingly troublesome. But to speak of Him, although it may be incomplete, is better than speaking of something other than Him. However, everything that is most complete the seeker should desire; even though this world is a prison, so long as you are imprisoned in it, there should remain a connecting thread with that desire for Him.

> *Che 'aish ast budan giriftar-i u*
> *Khush an murgh ku rah be-damash burad*

> What a wonderful life it is, to be imprisoned by Him.
> Happy is the bird guided to the net.

How wonderful is captivity, for those worldly people who are held captive by it; how wonderful is prison, that even those who sit in rose gardens desire it!

> *Shakh-i gul murgh-i qafas gasht be-murghan-i chaman*
> *Ta be-wasf-i gul-i ru-i tu gushudim nafas*

> The rose-stalk was a caged bird for the birds in the flower-garden,
> Until we began to describe your rose-face.

How can they not be in search of that restless, turbulent [state], such that rest in it is restlessness, and repose in it is turbulence? But "Whoever does not taste [it] does not know [it]."

> *Yak-i be barg-i khazan guft zard(-i) ru ze che-i*
> *beguft ta ke na dani bahar ma'zur-i*

Layla ze zulf-i mushk-bu har kas ke dida mu be mu
Danad ke zanjir az che ru dar gardan-i Majnun bud

Someone asked the autumn leaf: "Why is your complexion yellow?"
It replied, "Since you do not know spring, you are excused."
Of Layla: anyone who has seen the hair from [her] musk-scented tresses
Knows why there were chains around Majnun's neck.

They sing this song because of the worth [of it] which they know so well:

Har tira shab-i ke ba tu-am uftad raz
Ham az taraf-i sham kunad subh aghaz
Ba in hama gar 'iwaz-i dehand-am na deham
Kutah shab-i chenin be-sad 'umr-i deraz

Every dark night when I am with you, the secret is encountered.
Dawn begins to break even from the West.
Nevertheless: if they traded me, I would not give
the brief night [that passes] in this way, for a hundred long lifetimes.

Amada gashta-am digar imshab nazara ra
peywand [karda]-am jigar-i para-para ra

I am prepared, once more, tonight for a spectacle:
For I've stitched together my shredded liver.

I have said, still say, and will go on saying that if there were no wares of pain and disappointment in this prison-house, and if all its easts and wests were not worth even a single lane, and if the seeds of tears did not come into hand in this field, all would have been [only] a complete worthless mirage, and a ruined tavern, without colour and scent.

Harki burda ganj, az-in wirana burd

Anyone who plundered this world [thinking it a treasure] has plundered a wasteland.

For this reason, it is said that the Messenger of God – Peace Be Upon Him – was always in [mournful] thought and was always sad.

Bas kunam gar in sukhan afzun shawad
Khwud jigar chi bud ki khara khun shawad

I should stop; for if I speak further,
Not just the liver, even a stone will bleed.

Tu gar shaʿir-i misraʿ-i daftar-i-st.

If you are a poet, one hemistich is a tome.

Besides, you do not give this pained one anything of worth; and you do not count [me] among those who are capable and worthy, but the *hadith-i qudsi*, "Greatness is mine [God's] alone", testifies against that [assessment of yours]. For this pained one, the common generosity which is expressed in silver and gold is not appropriate for winning over my heart; I am a Sufi vagrant in search of God; I belong to a group that wishes you well; and if you want this group to keep praying to God for your welfare, perhaps this [generosity] is not appropriate.

Ma sabuk-ruhan harifan-i giran-jani na-im
Hamchu bu-yi gul nasim-i mi-kunad taskhir ma

We who are light-spirited are not so wearied with life,
To overpower us, who are like the rose's scent, a little breeze is enough.

Our speech is a sign and glad tidings [for you]. O you of high lineage, you of exalted worth, I swear by God and God's honour, that the day when I tied myself to keep prayers for Your Majesty with a firm thread, from that day it [my attachment] has not been slack and will not slacken. However, do not be misguided by [whether] the others have heard of it or not. Now in these days that ʿAbida Banu has informed me of your kindness and courage, what can be written and what can I tell you of how much I have prayed for you, your high station, and your well-being! May God – the high and praiseworthy – advance your desire, passion, and taste [until they are] perfect and magnificent, in this world and the next. Amen.

Ta bud guftagu sukhan-am na-tamam bud
Nazam be khamushi ki sukhan ra tamam kard

While I was speaking, my speech was incomplete;
I am proud of my silence, for it completed my speech.

2b. Letter 47 from the Gulshan-i Wahdat concerning sadness and grief:

In the name of God, compassionate and merciful.

Ay khuda dard-i ma-ra darman makun
Dardmandan ra ze bi-dardan makun

O God do not cure my pain!
Do not turn those who suffer into those who have no pain.

Dear Lady, on this path, there is nothing more fruitful than grief and sadness, and no worthier wares than burning and melting [with grief].

Mata'-i k-az-in rah guzar mi-burand
Lab-i khushk o chashman-i tar mi-burand

The wares they take from this street are
Parched lips and wet eyes.

There is a precious *hadith*, "If someone was weeping from sadness in the [Muslim] community, God would have mercy upon that community in its weeping, and whomever God wants to grant good things, he places a mourner in his heart." In other words, if someone sad weeps in the community, of course God – Praise be to Him – shows mercy to that whole community due to that person's lament; and whomever God – Praise be to Him – blesses and favours, He instills the practice of mourning in his heart. Someone has said it well:

Mughanni berau nauha-gar ra beyar
figan zakhm o nishtar-i ra beyar

Go away, musician, bring the mourner;
throw out the plectrum and bring the lancet.

Thus, it has been reported about Muhammad, Lord of the World (Peace Be Upon Him), that He was always in [mournful] thought and was connected with grief. The spiritual master of this worthless one [myself] has spoken a subtle point on this subject: if there were any wares and drink in this world free from grief, they would not be worth a single grain.

One day, this poor person [the writer] was attending to the illuminated grave of Muhammad, Lord of the World (Peace Be Upon Him), and at that moment a piece of paper fell upon my knees from the World of the Beyond. When I opened it, he [Muhammad] had written: "Do not be happy; verily God does not like those who are [unduly] happy; upon you [will necessarily be enjoined] grief; for verily God loves the hearts that grieve. In other words, do not be happy, because God, May He be Praised, loves every grieving heart."

I said to myself: the kindling has been set ablaze; after that, there is no concern for relief, and madness poured into my head. Now, there is no place for anyone conscious. The house was inhabited for a long time, now it must be ruined; for a long time, we have [been infatuated with] wisdom and learning, [but] after this, madness must show itself; a lifetime was spent in the tulip garden of well-being; now it must be the time for travelling through the valley of love.

Hamsaya-i afsurda-dilan chand tawan bud
Ay sukhtagan khana-i parwana kuja shud?

For a time, be a neighbour to those whose hearts are dejected;
O you who have burned [with grief], where is the house of the moth?

Guzashta-st anki chun afsurda-i chand
dilam buda be-khwab-o-khwurd khursand

The time has passed when, like those dejected,
my heart was content with [mere] food and sleep

Kanun jan-am malul az kar-i hasti-st
harif-i 'ishq ra aghaz-i masti-st

Now my soul is tired of the task of life in this world.
For a competitor in love, now intoxication has begun.

From that day until now I have been staying in this desert of grief and have made it my homeland; I dread the company of those who do not grieve and who are happy.

Be bulbulan-i chaman bi-ghaman nawa sanjid
Nawa-i murgh-i qafas mi-kunad asir mara

Those who are free from grief sing in tune with the nightingales of the garden;
The song of the captive bird captivates me.

True, there is nothing in love except melting (*gudakhtan*); there is this burning (*sukhtan*), not artificial contrivance (*sakhtan*); on this road, there is rest in restlessness and success in failure, there is harmony in burning, and [one is endowed with spiritual] secrets in melting [with pain]. There is relief in being wounded, honour in being humbled [as a slave of God]. There is freedom in captivity, liberation in being bound. Grief here is the source of joy, and sadness of separation is the source of communion with God.

Gharaz az 'ishq-i tu-am chashni-yi dard-o-gham ast
w-ar-na zir-i falak asbab-i tana'um chi kam ast

The aim of love for you is to get the taste of pain and grief;
Otherwise there is indeed no lack of means of prosperity in this world.

In sum, the Friend [God] keeps demanding wretchedness; as much as you can, let the desire for Him precede all your own desires, and hold fast the reins [of your own desire]. Two guests will not fit in one house. You are the cloud over your sun; give up yourself up and then start travelling. And if you cannot do it, beat your own head and don't consider yourself to be a lover.

Nazukan ra safar-i 'ishq haram ast haram

For the delicate, the path of love is prohibited and out of bounds.

He who said [this] has said it beautifully:

Agar dari dil-i dar sina-i tang
Majal-i gham dar-u farsang farsang
sala-i 'ishq dar-deh w-ar-na zinhar
sar-i ku-ye firagh az dast mag(u)zar

If you have a heart in your narrow chest,
there is a vast field for grief to run free.
Accept the call of love, otherwise beware:
Don't leave the lane of repose.

O you who know nothing: why do they demand all this burning and melting of you, and why do they ask from you all this pain and suffering? They want to completely steal you from yourself, and turning the Qibla of attention from every [other] direction, [and try] to make you pay attention to their own Majesty. How wonderful is this good fortune and success!

An ra ki sultan-i khwud kushad dani chi bashad abru?

Do you know what happens to the honour of he who kills his own Sultan?

[God said:] Whoever kills himself, I will pay him the compensation. O you of few means sitting high, if you want to be bountiful and successful, be restless for a few breaths in search of that, and if you wish your heart to become a watchful scout, be a tyrant for a few moments in the crucible of toil. Verily the spectacle of the tyranny of the Beloved is difficult, when worlds are set aside, and the Friend confronts you; but it is a wonderful position. Wise men say that healthy constitutions without the bitterness of medicine, and the enjoyment of honey without the sting of bees, is worthless. As someone said of a pearl:

> *Ta ham-chu hina suda na gardi be tah-i sang*
> *Hargiz be kaf-i pa-i nigari na rasi*
> *Ta khak-i tu-ra kuza na sazand kulalan*
> *Hargiz be lab-i bada-gusari na rasi*

> Until like henna you are not ground beneath a stone,
> You'll never reach the sole of the foot of a beauty;
> Until your dust is not made into a clay pot by potters,
> You will never touch the lips of the wine-drinker.

Dear Lady, kings distinguish those who are given audience with them with robes of honour and noble presents at their time of leaving; and they guide those who are high of ambition and lofty of nature; it must be remembered also that when Adam first stepped down from the heavens upon this earth, he had no provisions for the road except for weeping and lamenting, and had no wares except for this priceless jewel as means for the road. Happy is the person who, his whole life beginning to end, does not stray outside this valley, and is distinguished by the light of divine presence and eternal happiness.

> *Yad dari be-waqt-i zadan-i tu*
> *hama khandan budand o tu giryan*
> *an-chunan zi ki waqt-i murdan-i tu*
> *hama giryan buwand-o-tu khandan*

> Remember: at the time of your birth,
> All were smiling and laughing, and you were crying.
> Live now in such a way, that at the time of your death,
> All be weeping and you be smiling and laughing.

O my dear, one must not appoint far-sighted reason as counsellor in this matter, and one must not make a friend of outward planning (*tadbir-i zahiri*) upon the road to madness [spiritual intoxication]. For it was well said:

> *Dil andar zulf-i Layla band-o-kar az 'ishq-i Majnun kun*
> *Ki 'ashiq ra ziyan darad maqalat-i khiradmandi*

Bind your heart with Layla's hair, act with the passion of Majnun;
For the lover is ill served by wise discourses.

The path of reason and the path of passion and madness are separate. Reason wants roses and gardens, passion demands flaming fire. Reason is bound by [considerations of] shame and [good] fame; passion is beyond this station.

Masnawi

Shad bash ay 'ishq-i khush sauda-i ma
Ay tabib-i jumla 'illat-ha-i ma
Ay dawa-i nakhwat-o-namus-i ma
ay tu Aflatun-o-Jalinus-i ma

Be happy, O happy mad passion of mine!
O doctor of ours, [healer of] all diseases!
O medicine for our pride and honour,
O you, our Plato and Galen!

Z-in khirad bigana mi-bayad shudan
chang dar diwanegi bayad zadan
azmudam 'aql-i dur-andish ra
ba'd az-in diwana sazam khwish ra

One must distance oneself from wisdom;
One must beat the drum with madness.
I have tested far-sighted reason;
And then, I have made myself mad.

'Aql guyad jubba-o-dastar ku
'ishq guyad khana-i khammar ku
'aql hasti mi-kunad k-in dar-khur-ast
'ishq masti mi-kunad k-in dar-khur-ast

Reason says, "Where is the tunic and turban?"
Passion says, "Where is the wine-seller's house?"
Reason [merely] exists, this is proper;
Passion [exists in] drunken ecstasy, this is proper.

'Aql mi-guyad parishani makun
'ishq mi-khandad ki nadani makun
'aql mi-guyad ke in asudegi-st
'ishq mi-guyad ki in aludegi-st

Reason says, "Do not be disturbed!"
Passion laughs [at Reason and replies], "Don't be ignorant!"
Reason says, "This is repose."
Passion says [in reply], "This is contamination."

'Ishq ra guyi ki dar qur'an naguft
'ishq ra dar ganj-i ma auha nahuft
Rabb(i) ari-ni az zaban-i 'ishq bud
li ma'a -llah az zaban-i 'ishq bud

You could say Passion is whatever is not said in the Qur'an;
[Rather] passion is hidden in the revealed treasure [Qur'an]
"O Lord, show me," came from the tongue of passion [Qur'an 2: 260]
"For me, there is [a time] with God," came from the tongue of passion (*hadith*).

'Ishq nab(u)wad pisha-i har bu'l-hawas
'ishq ra ham 'ashiqan danand wa bas

Passion must not be the occupation of everyone with desire;
Only [true] lovers know passion, and nobody else.

More than this would grieve listeners, and this terrifying tale truly will destroy repose.

Dar nayabad hal-i pukhta hich kham
Pas sukhan kutah bayad wa's-salam

No raw person can understand the state of the mature;
Speech must now be brief; and so, farewell.

8

The Naqshbandi Shaikhs of Sirhind in Aurangzeb's Empire and Its Aftermath

Introduction

AS HAS BEEN MADE apparent earlier in this book, the Mughals had a long-standing relationship with the Naqshbandi shaikhs (or khwajas). They were invited by Babur (d. 1530) to participate in the celebration of his victories. His son and successor Humayun (d. 1556) also had close connections with them despite his fascination with the Shattari saints in India, for which he was chastised by his eastern Mughal kinsman Mirza Haidar Dughlat (d. 1551). Two great-grandsons of Khwaja 'Ubaid-Allah Ahrar (d. 1490), the noted fifteenth-century Naqshbandi shaikh, are reported to have been associated with Humayun's administration. Similarly, Akbar (d. 1605) had close relations with members of this order during the early years of his reign. A great-grandson of Khwaja Ahrar accompanied the emperor's aunt Gulbadan Begum as a leader of the holy pilgrimage in 1578. Gradually, for political and pragmatic reasons, Akbar then drifted away from them.[1] Also notable is the fact that Akbar extended generous patronage to a major Naqshbandi saint, Khwaja Kha-

---

[1] See Alam, "Sufi Shaikhs", Chapter 2 above; see also Foltz, *Mughal India and Central Asia*, Chapter 5, on the Naqshbandiya and the Mughals, pp. 93–105.

wand Mahmud (d. 1642), a direct descendant from his mother's side of Baha al-Din Naqshband (d. 1389), the eponymous founder of the order; Khwaja Khawand had migrated from Central Asia and settled in Kashmir.[2] Jahangir tried to persuade this saint to settle in Agra, and Shah Jahan sent him a huge monetary gift at his coronation.[3] The chronicler Lahori mentions the grant of a few villages (*mauza'i chand be-tariq-i suyurghal*) for the khwaja and his sons and the family, and rich cash awards on the days of celebrations of the weighing and other ceremonies.[4] In addition, the saint's son, Khwaja Qasim, carried a letter from Sa'd Allah Khan, the noted *wazir* of Shah Jahan, to the Uzbek leader Nazr Muhammad Khan.[5]

The Mughals also honoured them sometimes for political, administrative, and diplomatic reasons. Several Mawarannahri–Naqshbandis, including the Dehbidi and the Juybari khwajas, were associated with the Mughal court. Jahangir as a prince had a close association with several descendants of Khwaja Ahrar, and while some of them lost their positions after he ascended the throne, the emperor still had a close connection with more than one Dehbidi shaikh.[6] Lahori discusses at some length the diplomatic dimension of Khwaja 'Abd al-Rahim's appointment by the Uzbek ruler Imam Quli Khan as an ambassador to the Mughal court, even as he is identified as a noble and high-statured progeny and a learned member of the sublime Naqshbandi community.[7] Muhammad Salih Kamboh notes there were three Dehbidi khwajas

---

[2] For details of this Kashmir branch of the Naqshbandi order, see Damrel, "Forgotten Grace". See also Ahmad, *Hazrat Khwaja Naqshband*, pp. 358–407; Rizvi, *A History of Sufism*, Vol. 2, pp. 181–5.

[3] Kamboh, *Shah Jahan Nama*, Vol. 3, p. 284; Khafi Khan, Muhammad Hashim, *Muntakhab al-Lubab*, Vol. 1, p. 549.

[4] Lahori, *Badshahnama*, Vol. I, pp. 332–3.

[5] Zaidi, ed., *Maktubat-i Sa'ad Allah Khan*, p. 74, Letter No. 35. See also the editor's notes, pp. 112–13.

[6] Foltz, *Mughal India*, pp. 96–7.

[7] Lahori, *Badshahnama*, Vol. I, pp. 231–7.

in Shah Jahan's service – Khwaja Hasan, Khwaja Hashim, and Khwaja Muhammad Sharif – and all three held *mansab*s of 600 *zat* and 100 *sawar*. In addition, Kamboh mentions one 'Abd al-Rahman Naqshbandi who held a *mansab* of 800 *zat* and 200 *sawar*.[8] Khwaja 'Abd al-Rahman's daughter was married to Prince Sulaiman Shukoh. During the Balkh and Badakhshan campaigns of the Mughals, a Ju'ibari Naqshbandi Taiyib Khwaja, son of Khwaja Husain, is reported to have been received by Shah Jahan with honour. He was granted a *khil'at* and 1000 *muhr*s (gold coins).[9] Lahori in his *Badshahnama* notes many more Naqshbandis in Mughal service as well as in the service of Central Asian rulers visiting the court, some of them coming initially as representatives of the Uzbek rulers; later we notice them listed as Mughal officials. Notable among these were Khwaja Qasim Hisari Naqshbandi, who held a *mansab* of 600/100. In the same rank, according to Kamboh, were two Dehbedi khwajas, Muhammad Sharif and Hasan. Lahori also notes several other Naqshbandis with higher *mansabs*: Latif Khan Naqshbandi and 'Abd al-Wahhab Dehbedi both held 1000 *zat*, with 400 *sawar* for the former, and 200 for the latter. There was yet another Dehbidi, Rahmat-Allah, with a rank of 800/200, and Khwaja Nur-Allah who held a rank of 500/50. Khwaja 'Abd al-Rahman Naqshbandi held a rank of 700/150. He was perhaps the same 'Abd al-Rahman who, in Kamboh's mention, was promoted to 800/200. Amongst the Juybari branch of the Transoxanian Naqshbandis, we have several other names, such as Khwaja Baqa, Khwaja Ishaq Dehbedi, Khwaja 'Abd-Allah Naqshbandi, Khwaja Zain al-Din Naqshbandi, Khwaja Muhammad Raza, and more who are noticed without names as *khwajazadagan*, from Balkh and different parts of Transoxania. Several of them were favoured by the emperor with substantial cash awards.[10]

[8] Ibid., pp. 371–8.
[9] Kamboh, *Shah Jahan Nama*, Vol. 2, p. 423.
[10] Lahori, *Badshahnama*, Vol. 1, pp. 185, 310; Vol. 2, pp. 216, 223, 232, 252, 265, 316, 386, 471, 478, 577, 582, 609, 612, 637, 645, 683, 736, 741,

The Sirhindi Shaikhs and the Mughals

It was Khwaja Baqi-Billah (d. 1603) who established the Naqshbandi order as an important Sufi *silsila* in Mughal North India, which thrived and flourished as the Mujaddidi–Naqshbandi order later under the leadership of his disciple, Shaikh Ahmad Sirhindi (d. 1624), and his descendants.[11] We need to be careful when reading certain obviously exaggerated accounts in the Mujaddidi hagiography of Mujaddidi–Naqshbandi shaikhs' relations with the Mughals. Muhammad Ihsan, the author of *Rauzat al-Qaiyumiya*, for instance, tells us that nearly all the Mughal rulers barring Akbar were wholly subservient to Mujaddidi saints. Jahangir, he continues, initially put Shaikh Ahmad Sirhindi in prison but after a year released him and gave him the option of either staying back at the court or returning to his homeland. In the time of Shah Jahan, when Sirhindi's son Shaikh Muhammad Ma'sum, who inherited from his father the high stature of *qaiyumiyat* and was the master of the family, nearly all the princes and princesses became initiated into the Naqshbandi–Mujaddidi order. In return the shaikh decided to bestow the throne upon Aurangzeb; meanwhile, on noticing the great power of the saints, Dara Shukoh decided to get affiliated with the *silsila*, but he was snubbed and told that the decision to bestow power on Aurangzeb had already been taken. And in Aurangzeb's own time the emperor's son Muhammad A'zam, and sisters Roshanara and Gauharara, became Shaikh Ma'sum's disciples. As a matter of fact, if we were to believe Muhammad Ihsan, a very large part of the Muslim world – including Turkey, Syria, Yemen, Kashgar, Balkh, and Badakhshan – had also recognised Shaikh Ma'sum's greatness. He would have us believe that there was scarcely a project pertaining to the running of the state which did not follow the dictates of this shaikh.[12]

744, 746, 752. See also Foltz, pp. 101–2, for 'Abd al-Karim, 'Abd al-Rahim, and Taiyib Khwaja Juibari and Shah Jahan.

[11] See Chapter 2 in this volume.

[12] Ihsan, *Rauzat al-Qaiyumiya*, Vol. 1 on Shaikh Ahmad Sirhindi, the

Rauzat al-Qaiyumiya's exaggerated hagiography notwithstanding, the Mughals, Aurangzeb in particular, had close connections with the Mujaddidi family. Bakhtawar Khan is one of several who mention Aurangzeb's generous patronage to them. Bakhtawar Khan records repeated visits by several of them to the court to benefit from imperial generosity (*muqarrar ba mulazamat i aqdas rasidah mashmul i 'awatif shud*); he says they all commanded high respect from the emperor (*nizd-i hazrat zill-i illahi be ghayat mu'azzaz and*). He specifically mentions several of Shaikh Ahmad Sirhindi's sons, Shaikh Muhammad Sa'id (d. 1661), Shaikh Muhammad Yahya (d. 1684), and Shaikh Muhammad Ma'sum (d. 1669), and the last-named's sons Shaikh Sibghat-Allah (d. 1710), Shaikh Muhammad Ashraf (d. 1707), Shaikh Muhammad Siddiq (d. 1718), Shaikh Muhammad Naqshband (d. 1703), Shaikh 'Ubaid-Allah (d. 1672), and Shaikh Saif al Din (d. 1685).[13] He

---

first *qaiyum*; Vol. 2 on Shaikh Muhammad Ma'sum, the second *qaiyum*; Vol. 3 on Shaikh Muhammad Naqshband, the third *qaiyum*; and Vol. 4 on Shaikh Muhammad Zubair, the fourth *qaiyum*. The author was the son of Shaikh Ma'sum's great-grandson Shaikh Hasan Ahmad Sirhindi (d. 1736). His exaggeration apart, we have evidence of connections with Central Asia right from Shaikh Ahmad Sirhindi's time (Shaikh Muhammad Ma'sum's letters to Shaikh Habib-Allah Bukhari [d. 1698] and Muhammad Murad Shami), and also evidence of correspondence with some scholars of Hijaz, and rulers of the Islamic world. See, for instance, Shaikh Muhammad Sa'id's letter to the ruler of Yemen: Naqshbandi, *Maktubat-i Sa'idiya*, Letter 87, pp. 149–50. By the eighteenth century, however, the Mujaddidi–Naqshbandi order had reached a large part of the Islamic world. Gaborieau, *et al.*, eds, *Naqshbandis*, Sections 3–7, pp. 289–715; Barbir, "All in the Family", pp. 327–55; Foley, "The Naqshbandiyya–Khalidiyya Islamic Sainthood", pp. 521–54; Weismann, *The Naqshbandiyya*, chapters 5–8 in particular; Baghdadi, *Al-Hadiqat*; al-Muradi, *Silk al-Durar*; Akimushkin, "A Rare Seventeenth Century Hagiography", pp. 62–7; Yaycioglu, "Guiding Tradition", pp. 1542–1603; Fusfeld, "Naqshbandi Sufism"; Mu'tamadi, *Maulana Khalid Naqshbandi*. The first part of the book is a biography of Maulana Khalid; in the second part the author translates his Arabic treatise and Kurdish letters and documents. Ziad, "From Yarkand to Sindh", pp. 125–68.

[13] Khan, *Mirat al-'Alam*, Vol. 2, pp. 412–14. There is however evidence of

also records the presence of Shaikh Muhammad Saʿid and Shaikh Muhammad Maʿsum at the imperial camp at the time of Aurangzeb's expeditions against Dara Shukoh in 1658, a few months after his accession to the throne, and the emperor's grant to them of 300 *ashrafis*.[14] Before he left for the hajj, Shaikh Maʿsum, according to a Mujaddidi *tazkira*, had predicted the Mughal throne for Aurangzeb.[15]

Of particular interest for our purposes here are the letters of several eminent members of the family, and also the scattered evidence from the contemporary political chronicles and other sources of the time. We know that almost all the eminent members of Shaikh Ahmad Sirhindi's family, Shaikh Muhammad Saʿid, Shaikh Muhammad Maʿsum, amongst his sons, and amongst his grandsons Shaikh ʿUbaid-Allah, Shaikh Saif al-Din, Shaikh Muhammad Naqshband, and Shaikh ʿAbd al-Ahad "Wahdat" (d. 1714) left to us collections of letters, like their progenitor Shaikh Ahmad Sirhindi.

Historians have noted some of these collections and discussed the relationships between the Mughal emperors and the Mujaddidi–Naqshbandis. Of them Saiyid Athar Abbas Rizvi alone has noted the activities and writings of Sirhindi's grandsons in the

---

the presence of other Sirhindi shaikhs at the imperial camp. See, for instance, for Shaikh Sibghat-Allah and Muhammad Ashraf: Maʿsumi, *Maqamat-i Maʿsumi*, Vol. 3, Persian text, pp. 273–4 and 327; Vol. 2, translation, pp. 375 and 429. Maʿsumi was a close member of the family. His father Mir Fazl-Allah (d. 1706) was Shaikh Ahmad Sirhindi's grandson, his mother was Shaikh Maʿsum's daughter. The book provides important details on the Sirhindi family. Maʿsumi also reports this interesting remark by Princess Gauharara Begum: "my brother earned the kingdom of India strangely at a very cheap price (*ʿajab arzan kharida and*). He granted to the shaikhs an offering (*niyaz*) of only 12,00 rupees before their travel [for *hajj*]." Maʿsumi, *Maqamat-i Maʿsumi*, p. 207.

[14] Khan, *Mirʾat al-ʿAlam*, Vol. 1, pp. 122–3.

[15] Maʿsumi, *Maqamat-i Maʿsumi*, Vol. 3, Persian text, p. 207, Vol. 2, translation, p. 272.

context of his discussion of the Naqshbandi order, a discussion which he extends up to the early-nineteenth century. Rizvi notes at length the letters addressed to the emperor, Aurangzeb.[16] Yohanan Friedmann has an essay on Aurangzeb's relations with Sirhindi's two sons, Shaikh Muhammad Sa'id and Shaikh Muhammad Ma'sum.[17] But the chief concern of both these scholars has been the influence these shaikhs exerted on Aurangzeb's politics. This perspective – i.e. Naqshbandi shaikhs determining to a large extent the course of Mughal politics – was earlier developed by several historians, including K.A. Nizami, I.H. Qureshi, and Aziz Ahmad. They illustrated this view by pointing to Aurangzeb's departure in this domain from the legacy of Akbar and Jahangir.[18]

In this final chapter I will examine a few of these letters and contextualise some of them in the social milieux within which they were written – though it must be conceded at the outset that there is no way of infallibly ascertaining their correct chronological order. Furthermore, my purpose is not to discuss the presence or absence of the political influence of the Naqshbandi shaikhs. In fact, I maintain, as I have done earlier, that before we can even raise such a question we must examine the core of the relationship between the shaikhs and the rulers, in particular Aurangzeb – for these are relationships which seem to me to be spiritual and intellectual before – and if at all – they become political. I argue that Aurangzeb's politics developed irrespective of these influences and owed much more to his own "absolutist" tendencies, as well as to his efforts to build coalitions – temporary or permanent – which

---

[16] Rizvi, *A History of Sufism*, Vol. 2, pp. 482–91.

[17] Friedmann, "The Naqshbandis and Aurangzeb", pp. 209–20.

[18] Nizami, "Naqshbandi Influence on Mughal Rulers", pp. 41–52. Ahmad, *Studies in Islamic Culture*, pp. 182–90; Qureshi, *Muslim Civilization*, pp. 27–271. Friedmann maintains the Naqshbandi Sufis did not play any political role whatsoever and were simply Sufis. Friedmann, *Shaykh Ahmad Sirhindi*, p. 106. This view has been questioned and critiqued. See Ikram, *Rud-e Kausar*, pp. 277–92. See also Alam, "Maulana Azad and the Memory of India's Islamic Past".

bore obvious marks of his own earlier pious training and temperament. When taking decisions, Aurangzeb hardly looked to any of the existing shaikhs or nobles for advice or instruction. In fact, if the question of influence even arises, we have to look conversely at how keenly Aurangzeb asserted *his* influence over the course of state affairs, as well as on the saints and scholars of his time. My effort here is therefore to show the nature of the relationship of the Naqshbandi shaikhs with Aurangzeb in its spiritual and intellectual dimensions.

Sufism and *Shari'a* in the Sirhindi Shaikhs' Tradition

While Shaikh Ahmad Sirhindi may or may not have succeeded in influencing the Mughal emperors, he was certainly a great father – loving, affectionate, even if a disciplinarian; he trained and tutored his sons, and despite projecting his own image with unprecedented success, promoted high spiritual positions for his sons, creating through them a formidable world for his order. Many of his sons and grandsons became prominent shaikhs and carried forward his mission with the zeal and fervour shown by his example. His oldest son, Khwaja Muhammad Sadiq (d. 1616), was given a *khilafat* at an early stage, while for his second son, Shaikh Muhammad Ma'sum, whom he wanted as his successor, there came into being miraculous stories connected with his birth and childhood. It was reported that when Ma'sum was born, Sirhindi saw a vision of the Prophet, together with a large number of his companions and Sufis of the past, on a visit to Sirhind to congratulate him on Ma'sum's birth. The Prophet is reputed to have declared, "This son of yours will be the best of his time among the Sufis in spiritual accomplishments and nearness to God . . . and you will also now be accorded a high position, word of which he will later spread through the world." Shaikh Ma'sum's mother too had a vision at his birth and is reported to have said, "I had an unusual experience at the time of his birth. I saw a light illuminating the entire world from the east to the west and a large number of angels and prophets visiting our house to congratulate me."[19] Later Ma'sum trained one of his own sons, Shaikh Muhammad Naqshband, to succeed him. Shaikh Ahmad Sirhindi's third son was also among the eminent scholars of his time, as is reflected in his learned letters.

In their writings these Sufis do not simply show elaborate and convincing arguments to legitimise their distinctive Mujaddidi–Naqshbandi positions, i.e. *wahdat al-shuhud*, *zikr-i khafi*, and so on. Ahmad Sirhindi argued his doctrinal and practical positions in a very forceful and eloquent way, and, as we know, did not contest the title of "renovator of Islam for the second Islamic millennium (beginning in 1592 CE)", which was bestowed on him by the famous Islamic scholar of the time 'Abd al-Hakim Sialkoti. This title in fact subsequently became eponymous with the name and identity of the order itself. In his writings, Sirhindi comes out as a great Sufi with an uncompromising focus on *shari'a* as well. His sons and several others of the family carried on this legacy of the order equally powerfully. We may note here some details, in quotes and in paraphrases, from a long letter by Shaikh Muhammad Ma'sum to a Mughal official, Mirza 'Ubaid Allah Beg,[20] who seems to know good Arabic too, as appears from a large number of *hadiths* and Qur'anic verses cited in the letter without Persian translations:

> Makhduma (O Master)! It is commonly said that the way of the Sufi is not to infringe upon the affairs of the creatures of God nor to treat anyone badly. This is not true and contains much that is evil . . . I don't know the people who believe this to be the way of the Sufi. Which Sufis do they mean? Our *pirs*, the Naqshbandi shaikhs, follow *sunna* (the path of the Prophet), refrain from *bid'a*

---

[19] Ihsan, *Rauzat al-Qaiyumiya*, Vol. 2, p. 2.
[20] 'Ubaid-Allah Beg, who was close to Dara Shukoh, seems thus a strong advocate of both *wahdat al-wujud* and *sulh-i kull*, as we can also understand from the tone of this letter: Ma'sumi, *Maqamat-i Ma'sumi*, Vol. 3, Persian text, pp. 456–7.

(innovation), enjoining what is right, and forbidding what is wrong (*al-amr bi'l ma'ruf wa'n nahy 'ani'l munkar*. Qur'an 3: 104). They hate (*bughz*) the others and fight against them (*jihad*) for the sake of Allah and His Prophet. These are the established parts of the Faith (*wajibat-o-fara'iz-i din*).[21]

He adds that even within the Naqshbandi tradition a master like the great Khwaja Baha al-Din differed with his *pir* Amir Kulal and obtained the opinion of the *'ulama* of his time in support of his position; and that Sufi texts too go over the details of what are good and bad acts. He then asks:

> What else is this, if not [the Islamic] *al-amr bi'l ma'ruf wa'n nahy 'ani'l munkar*? Is it infringement (*ta'arruz*) or non-infringement (*'adm-i ta'arruz*)? Do those who advocate non-infringement in the religious affairs of others believe in rewards and punishments in the life hereafter? Why should they not correct the wrongs that others do? If they don't, they obviously deny the life hereafter. Don't we warn a blind person if we see him approach a well or if we notice a poisonous snake in his path? Had God wanted non-infringement, why would He have sent the prophets with *shari'a* and punished people who did not follow it? How can Islam claim to be [the final] religion, having annulled all other earlier religions? If non-infringement were correct practice, then the Prophet of Islam would not have waged *jihad* against infidels. Weren't infidels his enemies and God's?

He cites Qur'anic verses, *hadiths*, and the sayings of past Sufis such as 'Abd al-Qadir Gilani, Muhyi al-Din Ibn al-'Arabi, and Shaikh Mu'in al-Din of Ajmer. He selects in particular the verses that highlight differences between the pious and the misguided, those targeted by divine wrath: "O ye who believe! Take not My enemies and yours as friends" (60: 1); "O ye who believe! Turn not (for friendship) to people on whom is the wrath of Allah" (60: 13); "O Prophet! Strive hard against the unbelievers and the hypocrites and be firm against them" (66: 9). He also cites in this section a

[21] Ma'sum, *Maktubat-i Ma'sumiya*, Vol. I, Letter 29, pp. 110–38, in particular p. 111, for the passage in quotes; Urdu translation, Vol. 3, Letter 29, pp. 86–121.

saying of Shaikh Junaid Baghdadi, who is generally mentioned in Sufi writings as their undisputed chief (*saiyid al-ta'ifa*). Baghdadi states: "My act is strictly in line with the Qur'an and *hadiths*, and the person who does not remember the Qur'an by heart and writes down no *hadith* will not [deserve to] be a legitimate leader who can be followed in the Sufi tradition." He then adds that to advocates of the doctrine of *wahdat al-wujud* – who say " 'all creatures mirror and manifest Divinity and that since they have no other position save their being the manifestation of Divinity, we should be friendly to them all and regard none as evil' – our response is [simply this] that there is unequivocal Qur'anic proof for unalloyed hostility against infidels." He goes on: "Whatever be their position, we are not concerned with *fass* (Ibn al-'Arabi's *Fusus al-Hikam*). Our concern is the *nass* (the Qur'an and *hadith*)." Here he engages in a long discourse against the *wujudi* Sufis of his time, projecting them as lax in acting on the *shari'a*. He highlights the position and practice of past *wujudis*, including his own grandfather Shaikh 'Abd al-Ahad, his predecessors Shaikh 'Abd al-Quddus Gangohi, and above all Ibn al-'Arabi, asserting that even they would not have approved of the practice of the *wujudis* of his time.[22] He concludes his discussion with 'Abd al-Rahman Jami's verses from his *Silsilat al-Zahab*; Jami, he says, was also a *wahdat al-wujudi*. The citation begins as follows: "*Tark-i azar kardan ay khwaja/ daftar-i kufr rast dibacha* (To adopt a position of harming none, Khwaja / is [indeed] the prologue of a tome of unbelief)."[23]

The writer of the letter then alludes to how such an understanding of Sufism reflects existing Mughal politics:

> It is strange that a group of those who have adopted the way of *sulh-i kull* and doing no harm to others (*kam azari wa sulh-i kull*)

[22] This seems to echo Khwaja Baqi-Billah's judgment, challenging his contemporary Chishtis' views of their own forebears. See Chapter 2 above.
[23] Ma'sum, *Maktubat-i Ma'sumiya*, Vol. 1, pp.110–38, esp. pp. 116–17 and 117–20.

are good to the unbelievers, the Jews, the jogis, the brahmans, the heathens, the renegades, the Armenians, to all others except those who follow the path of the Prophet, the people of *sunna-wa-jama'a*, the righteous group that will get salvation in the life hereafter (*firqa-i najiya*) . . . This group is in alliance (*sulh*) with the others, and are bent upon hurt and harm (*azar, iza, takhrib*) to Muslims. It is indeed a strange *sulh-i kull* that implies hostility to the Muhammadis and friendship with other peoples, in flagrant violation of the Qur'an's plea for hatred and enmity (*mahall-i ghalzat be-nusus-i Qur'ani*) against them.

To Shaikh Ma'sum these Sufis and those who endorsed their position were the same as their non-Muslim allies and friends. "*Al-kufr millatun wahida* (unbelief in all forms springs from the same creed)," he quotes, and then cites Qur'anic verses which define the hallmarks of a Muslim: "Ye are the best of peoples, evolved for mankind, enjoining what is right, forbidding what is wrong" (3: 110), ". . . that enjoin good and forbid evil; and observe the limits set by Allah" (9: 112).[24]

The Shaikh here seems to be critiquing Dara Shukoh's position in particular. We know Dara Shukoh was the most ardent advocate of such an approach to non-Muslims, and towards Hindus in particular. He wrote several texts in support of his understanding of their beliefs, and, as we have seen, translated certain Hindu religious scriptures. His broad position was that there was common ground for many spiritual positions in Islam and Hinduism. Maulana Azad tells us that he, Dara,

> bowed to the Hindu dervishes with the same supplications and sincerity as he did to Muslim Sufis . . . Who can deny the truth that if in the world of *sahib-i hal* (i.e Sufi) too there can be a distinction between infidelity and Islam, where will the difference be between the blind and the seeing? The moth looks for the candle. It yearns not simply for the candle of *haram*, for if it does so, its desire to burn is not complete ('*ashiq ham az Islam kharabast-o-ham az kufr /*

---

[24] Ibid., Vol. I, pp.110–38, esp. p. 121.

parwana chiragh-i haram-o-dair nadanad) (The lover is spoilt both by Islam and infidelity / the moth knows not if the lamp it craves is in Haram or a temple).[25]

In the letter earlier quoted, Shaikh Ma'sum too joins issue with those who invoke Qur'anic verses such as: "O, ye who believe! Guard your own souls: if ye follow (right) guidance, no hurt can come to you from those who stray."[26] He says the term right guidance (*ihtida*) here includes pious acts, enjoining the just, and forbidding evil – the three distinctive marks of a Muslim. This does not mean that a Muslim can be indifferent to the evil acts of unbelievers. Rather this phrase is a kind of consolation for him; it means that if Muslims are pious and perform their assigned tasks dutifully, no matter what the result, the persistence of unbelievers in unbelief cannot hurt the pious Muslim.[27] Then follows a long discussion on *shari'a*, a return to the question of enjoining good and forbidding evil, and the virtues of *jihad*, i.e. struggle and sacrifice to destroy infidelity and promote the right path, in support of which he adduces a remarkably large number of *hadiths*, several also with polemical overtones.[28]

In several other letters Shaikh Ma'sum reiterates the above position. In particular, one letter focuses attention on the nature of relations that the shaikh recommends a Muslim should have with a non-Muslim.[29] This letter is in response to a query from a certain Shaikh Durvesh Muhammad Barki of Jalandhar, apparently Shaikh Ma'sum's disciple (*murid*), regarding the meaning of the Qur'anic verse, "Let not believers take for protectors unbelievers rather than believers: if any of them do that, there will be no help

---

[25] Azad, *Sufi Sarmad Shahid*, p. 20. See also the chapter entitled "In Search of a Sacred King" within the same volume.

[26] Qur'an, 5: 105.

[27] Ma'sum, *Maktubat-i Ma'sumiya*, Vol. I, p. 122.

[28] Ibid., pp.110–38; also esp., pp. 125–38.

[29] Ma'sum, *Maktubat-i Ma'sumiya*, Vol. III, Letter 55, pp. 86–92; see also ibid., Urdu translation, Vol. 3, Letter 55, pp. 105–11.

from Allah: except by way of precaution, that ye guard yourselves from them."[30] Shaikh Ma'sum here reproduces what the noted Islamic scholar Fakhr al-Din Razi says about this verse in *Tafsir-i Kabir* (or *Mafatih al-Ghayb*), his commentary on the Qur'an.[31] He writes that the verse, according to Razi, concerns the forbidding of contacts with unbelievers, and he cites several other similar verses, such as "take not into your intimacy those outside your ranks",[32] and "take not the Jews and the Christians for your allies and protectors".[33] We should note the categories of Muslim/non-Muslim relationship with which Razi begins his commentary of this verse: there could be three possible cases of this relationship, he says – first, a Muslim's approval of what unbelievers believe, and therefore his or her desire to be close to them; second, a Muslim may merely pretend to have good relations, the aim being to maintain a conflict-free social order; and third, something in between these two, i.e. good relations in response to good behaviour among unbelievers, and an effort at close relations. The first, Razi says, is forbidden; the second is allowed; in the third case the Muslim is cautioned vigilance – because good conduct among unbelievers' and close relations with them may convince Muslims of the goodness within the religions of unbelievers.

Shaikh Ma'sum links Razi's commentary to the conditions that prevailed in Mughal India:

> Most false Sufis and renegades these days (*sufiya-i kham wa malahida-i in waqt*) have no hesitation allying with and befriending unbelievers and claim that the way of the devout (*faqir*) is to be bad to no one. Glory be to God! The head of all the prophets and the chief of all the *faqirs* and the *walis*, who took pride in his being a *faqir* (*al-faqr fakhri*), was commanded by God and chose to be harsh to unbelievers and hypocrites and fought against unbelievers; they [on the other

---

[30] Qur'an, 3: 28.

[31] For this important text, see Lagarde, *Les secrets de l'invisible*; see also Nadvi, *Imam Razi*.

[32] Qur'an, 3: 118.

[33] Qur'an, 5: 51.

hand] having gone astray, have chosen a way in total disregard of the Prophet's preferred path. Strange *faqirs* are they (*'ajab fuqara and*)!

The letter also disapproves of the employment of non-Muslims in state service. In support of this position he again cites from Razi, this time two reports from the era of 'Umar, the second Pious Caliph. 'Umar refused to employ a Christian as his secretary (*katib*) despite his having been recommended by one of the Caliph's officials as a man who possessed an uncommonly strong memory and was the best scribe available (*la yu'raf aqwa hifzan wa la ahsan khattan minhu*). 'Umar also reprimanded Abu Musa Ash'ari, one of his major officials and companion of the Prophet, when he employed a Christian as his secretary. He quoted a Qur'anic verse and affirmed his position, saying: "I will not bestow honour on a person for whom God has contempt (*la ukrimu-hum iz ahanahum-Allah*) . . . [and] will not come near a person from whom God Himself has kept away (*wa la udni-him iz ab'ada-hum-Allah ta'ala*)."[34]

The Sirhindi Shaikhs' Self-Image

Shaikh Ahmad Sirhindi also claimed to be the *qaiyum* of his time, and another aspect of this was unprecedented as well: while the title "Mujaddid" (Renewer) for the second millennium was meant exclusively for him, he allowed *qaiyumiyat* (the position of *qaiyum*) to be inherited by his son.[35] What then was this key concept? *Qaiyumiyat*, as Shaikh Ma'sum elaborates it, is an essential part

---

[34] Ma'sum, *Maktubat-i Ma'sumiya*, Vol. III, Letter 55, pp. 86–92, esp. pp. 91–2; ibid., Urdu translation, Vol. 3, Letter 55, pp. 105–11, esp. pp. 110–11. See also below for a treatise by Shaikh Ma'sum's son Shaikh 'Ubaid-Allah on non-Muslim employment.

[35] According to reports it was Mulla 'Abd al-Hakim Sialkoti, a major seventeenth-century scholar, who called Shaikh Ahmad "Mujaddid-i Alf-i Sani", and there is an interesting discussion on the question of Sirhindi's claim to *qaiyumiyat* among some modern scholars, centred however only around Muhammad Ihsan's *Rauzat al-Qaiyumiya*. Ikram, *Rud-e Kausar*, pp. 292–308.

(or *zat*) of God, and thereby the *qaiyum* is not simply a deputy or *khalifa* of God, but rather one who sustains the manifestations of all the attributes of God in the world. He is the person who ensures the continuity and stability of this world. Since *qaiyumiyat* is an attribute of God, the human carrier of it effectively takes on a function of God. This position, he says, was bestowed upon human beings after hundreds or thousands of years of existence.[36] A *qaiyum* is he who deputises for God in this world, and all categories of Sufis, including those who have an elevated status such as Abdal, Aqtab, Afrad, and Autad, are thus under him; he virtually becomes the destination of the whole world. The world exists because of him, and no one attains *qaiyumiyat* without accessing the *zat* of God (*isalat*) – which Shaikh Ma'sum suggests he himself had acquired, mediated through his father.

And like his father, Ma'sum made extraordinary claims for himself. He says when he was still young, some fourteen years old, he submitted to his father: "I find a light in my own self illuminating the world, absorbing each and every particle, like the rays of the sun, and I feel that if that light disappears, the world will grow dark." When he reported this experience to his father, the response he says was that he was destined to be the *qutb* (pole) of his time, and to be so would be an aspect of his *qaiyumiyat*.[37] He also remarks elsewhere that his father Ahmad Sirhindi was made of the clay left over from the creation of the Prophet, and that he himself was made from the clay left over from the creation of his father. The clear implication is Ma'sum's belief that he alone has inherited his father's mantle, and indeed there is no doubt that he was accepted as the second *qaiyum*.[38] He asserts that there has been none amongst Sufis who has come anywhere close to the achievements of Ahmad Sirhindi, and that if any Sufi thinks

---

[36] Ibid., Vol. 1, Letter 86, pp. 223–5, and Letter 203, pp. 279–82. I have briefly summarised the contents of these two letters.

[37] Ibid., Letter 86, pp. 223–5.

[38] Ibid., Letter 192; Ma'sumi, *Maqamat-i Ma'sumi*, Vol. 3, Persian text, p. 78.

or pretends otherwise, his belief resembles a mouse dreaming of being a camel.

Shaikh Ma'sum's position is elaborated in *Hasanat al-Haramayn*, in which he is reported to have said that, one day, at the time of the morning prayer, a little before sunrise, he saw himself surrounded by a large number of human beings and angels, all prostrate before him. He was utterly astonished but soon discovered it was actually the Ka'ba which had enclosed and embraced him, and therefore he had seen them prostrate before the Ka'ba as if prostrate before him. It was noted by the person who reported this incident that those familiar with the secrets of Shaikh Ma'sum's high position, and of the depths of the ocean of the gnosis of his father Shaikh Ahmad Sirhindi, would know that this same experience had transpired with the father as well. At all the places that Shaikh Ma'sum visited during his hajj pilgrimage in Hijaz, he shows himself being warmly welcomed by all the souls of the Companions of the time of the Prophet, in particular Ayesha, Fatima, Hasan, 'Usman (the third Pious Caliph), Ibrahim (the minor son of the Prophet), as well as others.[39]

It does not stop here, for Shaikh Ma'sum once also had a vision of a large number of angels descending on Sirhind, and it appears they had all arrived because, finding him closest to Allah, they wanted a close view of his divine "belovedness" (*mahbubiyat*).[40] And thus had it come to pass that the town of Sirhind too had come to enjoy a very special status, of which we are told by both Shaikh Ma'sum and his father Shaikh Ahmad. According to them, the town of Sirhind contained in itself the sublime and sacred light which arose from the Ka'ba, and which made Sirhind the envy of all the places in Hind, not to speak of Central Asia (*wilayat*).[41] In Sirhind the earth of Hind mingled with the water of *wilayat*, and its earth was mixed with that of the blessed city

---

[39] 'Ubaid-Allah, *Hasanat al-Haramayn*.

[40] Ma'sumi, *Maqamat-i Ma'sumi*, Vol. 3, Persian text, p. 110; ibid., Vol. 2, Urdu translation, p. 135.

[41] Hisari, *Maktubat i Imam Rabbani*, Vol. 2, Letter 22, pp. 37–8.

of the Prophet, Medina, and illumined with rays from the light of the Ka'ba.[42]

There is no dearth of material with similar stories and assertions. It was reported, for example, that several members of the family as well as Shaikh Ma'sum's disciples visualised him as most resembling the Prophet Muhammad – he stood as distinct among humans as the Prophet had done in the assembly of all the other prophets.[43] There is, again, a report in the *Hasanat al-Haramayn* to the effect that he had the vision wherein the lights which emanated from his own person were so dazzling that he thought he was the Ka'aba incarnate.[44] The compiler of the *Maqamat-i Ma'sumi* reports another account from his father:

> One day Shaikh Ma'sum visited the grave of his grandfather Shaikh 'Abd al-Ahad, who was an eminent saint of the Chishti–Sabiri order. While returning from his visit to his grave, he suddenly raised his head from contemplation and told him [the compiler's father]: "I noticed that my grandfather had come out of his grave and was entreating me [to give him] the spiritual grace I had inherited from God, which was like an ocean with unfathomable depth (*bahr-i bi-payan*), nourishing the whole world, [and so] he wanted just a drop of it, because he [being my grandfather, and so close to me] deserved it the most."

Thereafter Shaikh Ma'sum gave him the requested drop; his grandfather Shaikh 'Abd al-Ahad then thanked him and happily returned to his own grave. The compiler adds that Shaikh Ma'sum not only possessed all the perfections of *wilayat*, he even had the accomplishments of prophethood which had been inherited by his father Shaikh Ahmad Sirhindi a thousand years after the death of the Prophet, and thereafter by Shaikh Ma'sum.[45] We could go on in the same vein *ad nauseam* with such claims to world-beating sublimity by the Mujaddidi shaikhs.

[42] Ma'sum, *Maktubat-i Ma'sumiya*, Vol. 1, Letter 80; Vol. 3, Letter 81; see also Vol. 3, Letters 48, 142, and 239.
[43] Ma'sumi, *Maqamat-i Ma'sumi*, Vol. 3, Persian text, p. 111.
[44] Ibid., p. 116.
[45] Ibid., p. 192.

It is in light of this self-image that we must also consider both Ahmad Sirhindi's portrayal of Akbar, and his son Muhammad Ma'sum's portrayal of Dara Shukoh, including that prince's defeat by Aurangzeb in the War of Succession. Dara Shukoh is anathematised in terms stronger even than is Akbar. Notable here is a vision of Shaikh Muhammad Ma'sum, reported in *Hasanat al-Haramayn*, that he had in Medina before his return to India:

> When it came time for the departure from Medina, the Khwaja [Muhammad Ma'sum] came to the grave [*muwajaha*] of the Prophet to seek his guidance on whether it would be appropriate for him to return to India or stay on there. He was given a clear hint of permission to leave. At this same time he recalled the emperor's eldest son [Prince Dara Shukoh], the enemy of the *shari'a* and *shari'a*-following people – in particular people associated with the Naqshbandi *silsila* and the family of Mujaddid-i Alf-i Sani, since he was constantly attempting to harm them . . . [and] in this matter he [again] supplicated the Prophet. The shaikh reports that he felt that the Prophet came before him with a naked sword in his hand and hinted at the execution of Dara. And it happened just as the Prophet had hinted. Indeed, a few years earlier, Shaikh Muhammad Ma'sum had forecast this turn of events to Aurangzeb in Sirhind at the shrine of Mujaddid-i Alf-i Sani. And it happened just as it had been predicted. This was a *karamat* of Khwaja Muhammad Ma'sum and a miracle of the Prophet as well.[46]

These claims had an obvious bearing on Shaikh Ahmad Sirhindi's mission – social, religious, or political – and that of his immediate successors. The complement to this was Sirhindi's attack on policies which sustained a culture that differed from his own. He targeted Akbar, declaring him a heretic. To seek legitimacy for such assertions he projected his own position. If by commissioning *Tarikh-Alfi* Akbar's intention was to project and interpret a history of the past thousand years of Islam, Sirhindi's intention as renewer and renovator of the faith was to show the

---

[46] Mujaddidi, *Hasanat al-Haramayn*, pp. 203–4; Ma'sumi, *Maqamat-i Ma'sumi*, Vol. 3, Persian text, pp. 207–8.

way of Islam for the future thousand years; in fact if in earlier times there may have been one "renewer" of the tradition of the Prophet for every century, he considered himself the renewer for the entire millennium ahead. Whether he got this idea from Akbar's court or from his own mind is moot.[47]

Aurangzeb, given his adherence to an orthodox Sunni position, would not have welcomed the Akbari idea of millenarianism. He was also hostile to some other millenarian movements of his time: he took drastic steps against the Da'udi Tayyibi, Nizari Isma'ili, and Imam Shahi sects. While Akbar had welcomed the Da'udi Da'i of his time, Aurangzeb executed his grandson Qutb Khan.[48] We may only speculate whether he would have favoured Shaikh Ahmad Sirhindi's claim since there is no direct evidence either way.[49]

---

[47] Azfar Moin says "Akbar was declared to be the Renewer of the Second Millennium", and suggests Sirhindi's millenarianism has a connection with Akbar's claim. He cites in support of Akbar's millenarianism a passage from a recent Iranian edition of *Tarikh-i Alfi*. But the passage in this edition appears to be disjointed, out of context, and very likely interpolated. See Moin, *Millennial Sovereign*, pp. 132–6.

[48] Sheikh, "Aurangzeb as Seen from Gujarat", pp. 557–81. Related to Sirhindi's claim of millenarian leadership and Aurangzeb, Safar Ahmad Ma'sumi mentions an interesting conversation between the emperor and Shaikh Muhammad Naqshband. Aurangzeb asked the shaikh: "While your grandfather's being the Mujaddid of this millennium is disputed, people call me so too. What is the truth in this matter?" The shaikh replied: "My grandfather received this sublime title (*khitab-i mustatab*) from God. There is no harm, if you too have been divinely inspired so (*gar shuma ham mulham be-in ma'ni gardida*)." The emperor, writes Ma'sumi, felt very ashamed (*khajalat bi hisab*) and bowed his head (*chihra . . . sar be gariban andakht*): Ma'sumi, *Maqamat-i Ma'sumi*, Vol. 3, p. 303.

[49] In connection with Shaikh Ahmad Sirhindi's self-image are many inflated titles his descendants were given by senior members of the family, or those with which they are remembered by their devotees in their own time and after: 'Urwat al-wusqa for Shaikh Ma'sum; Khazin al-Rahmat for Shaikh Muhammad Sa'id; Hujjat-Allah for Muhammad Naqshband; Muhtasib-i Ummat, given by Shaikh Ma'sum for his son Saif al-Din; Murawwij al-Shari'a

Even at the risk of simplifying somewhat, it can be said that Aurangzeb was primarily a *shari'a*-observing man and a *fiqh*-oriented Muslim. He commissioned the well-known text *Fatawa-i 'Alamgiri* and was very close to the Gujarati scholars 'Abd al-Qawi and Qazi 'Abd al-Wahhab.[50] This was perhaps reason enough for his close association with the Mujaddidi shaikhs, who in their outlook maintained an equilibrium between *shari'a* and *tasawwuf*.

The Sirhindi Shaikhs and the Court

The Mujaddidis in India, like the Naqshbandis in Central Asia, seem to have endeavoured to gain proximity to kings and royal families, very likely because in their understanding it was through rulers that one could ensure enforcement of the *shari'a*. But this involved complex strategising. Shaikh Ahmad Sirhindi tried getting close to Jahangir; for his son Shaikh Ma'sum there is not much evidence showing a direct connection to Shah Jahan (r. 1628–58). For the Mujaddidi tradition we have already noted a pronounced resentment against Dara Shukoh, whose influence on Shah Jahan was very strong. Nevertheless, Shaikh Muhammad Ma'sum is reported to have mentioned Shah Jahan favourably a couple of times. Indian Muslims, according to him, would be in Shah Jahan's debt until the Day of Judgment for what he had done to restore the dignity and symbols and practices of Islam, such as cow slaughter and the construction of mosques, which had earlier been abandoned. Shaikh Muhammad Ma'sum also says the emperor had, after his ascension, circumcised him in person.[51] He speaks with fondness of Shah Jahan's love for mangoes and is

---

for Shaikh Ma'sum's other son Muhammad 'Ubaid-Allah; and Dalil-Allah for Muhammad Sa'id's son 'Abd al-Ahad 'Wahdat' (d. 1714).

[50] See also Larocque, "Mahamat Prannath and the Pranami Movement", pp. 342–78; Sharma, Society and Culture in Northern India".

[51] Ma'sumi, *Maqamat-i Ma'sumi*, Vol. 3 Persian text, p.199; ibid., Vol. 2, Urdu translation, p. 261.

delighted to confirm his own tastes conformed with those of the emperor.[52]

Yet, for all these self-aggrandising aperçus, there does not seem to have been any real involvement of this shaikh in Shah Jahan's court. At celebrations of the birth of the Prophet he is reported to have once visited the court for a discussion on the practice of *salam*, a practice he did not approve. It seems he was on this occasion so disgusted at what transpired that he vowed never to return to the court. Shah Jahan's noted minister Shaikh Sa'ad-Allah Khan appears not to have been drawn to the shaikh either, and in fact criticised him in the presence of the emperor. According to a Mujaddidi report, Sa'ad-Allah fell under a curse because of his antipathy to the shaikh and the Sirhindi family, and the curse caused him to suffer from a serious colic pain. Once, as he lay in pain, he entreated the shaikh's forgiveness and asked his help for a cure, which the shaikh refused, whereupon the minister died some days later.[53] In this context, it is noteworthy that Sa'ad-Allah showed scepticism rather than reverence for Shaikh Ahmad Sirhindi. Having read Sirhindi's letters he is reported to have sarcastically remarked that their composition showed a matchless scribe (*munshi-yi bi-nazir*) – a conspicuously left-handed compliment which appears not to have endeared him to Shaikh Ahmad Sirhindi's followers.[54]

Shaikh Ma'sum's popularity was greater however in some circles outside the court. One of his close disciples, Mulla Musa Bhattikoti (d. 1711), is reported to have spoken of accompanying his master on a trip to Shah Jahan's Delhi. When they arrived there, he noticed that despite the fact that the emperor harboured

[52] Ibid., p. 200, Vol. 2, Urdu translation, p. 262.

[53] Ma'sumi, *Maqamat-i Ma'sumi*, Vol. 3, Persian text; ibid., Vol. 2, Urdu translation, pp. 272–3. Because of these circumstances it is interesting to note that Shaikh Ma'sum cited his father's advice to never visit a royal court – which could have been an alibi for his failure to become influential in court.

[54] Ibid., p. 59, Vol. 2, Urdu translation, p. 64.

a misinformed view of the shaikh, the latter was able to draw thousands of people to his assembly. Later, says the same disciple, during the reign of Aurangzeb the shaikh's guidance took a totally different shape, so much so that the emperor, his son, other relatives, and several nobles all became his disciples.[55] Shaikh Ahmad Sirhindi's descendant and successor is thus not simply portrayed as a great scholar like him, but as also a great fighter for his mission. We have strong statements on this in the writings of another of Sirhindi's sons, Shaikh Muhammad Sa'id.[56] To a considerable measure, Sirhindi's descendants very strategically and cleverly seemed to give up the earlier claim attributed to Khwaja 'Ubaid-Allah Ahrar of their wielding a position even higher than that of the king (a claim discussed earlier). At the same time, they left no stone unturned in their efforts to find favour with the royal family and the Mughal court; they might even be said to have besieged the Mughal elite. We can assume that Turani Sunnis, as noted earlier, had a natural inclination to be close to them, despite the fact that Sirhindi's line did not succeed exclusively, there being two other important Naqshbandi centres in Mughal India, one in Kashmir and another in Aurangabad.[57] We can also assume that they did not have it easy when trying to access the court in Jahangir and Shah Jahan's reigns. But, as we saw above and will see in greater detail below, they did develop strong ties with the court of Aurangzeb.

The adding of Sirhindi's title, "Mujaddidi", to their order's name echoes the case of Khwaja 'Ubaid-Allah Ahrar, whose name too was made part of the name of an order. However, Sirhindi and his descendants were careful not to make overt political claims

---

[55] Ma'sumi, *Maqamat-i Ma'sumi*, Vol. 3, Persian text; ibid., Vol. 2, Urdu translation, p. 598.

[56] Naqshbandi, *Maktubat-i Sa'idiya*, Letters 30, 31, 64 and 69, pp. 57–74, 120–1, and 129–31, for instance.

[57] Damrel, "Forgotten Grace", for Kashmir; Digby, "The Naqshbandis in the Deccan", pp. 167–207; see also Digby, *Sufis and Soldiers in Awrangzeb's Deccan*; Green, *Indian Sufism*.

like those made by Khwaja 'Ubaid-Allah Ahrar.[58] They agreed to remain subservient to rulers who recognised them, even though their claims to spiritual and religious accomplishment were unprecedented. A drive to achieve control over court and king was, however, integral to the Mujaddidi tradition. It went hand in hand with their aggrandising and stature-raising efforts, these in turn complemented by blandishments against those who resisted them as well as proclamations declaring such opponents abhorrent and beyond the pale of Islam.

Aurangzeb, as a prince and later as emperor, appears to have been very close to the Sirhindi family. The evidence of this comes not simply from Naqshbandi traditions – which include several letters by contemporary shaikhs and hagiographical accounts – but also from political chronicles and *tazkiras*. The Naqshbandi tradition remembers the emperor as a disciple of Shaikh Muhammad Ma'sum. He and his brother Shaikh Muhammad Sa'id wrote several letters to Aurangzeb similar to those they wrote to their disciples. For instance, in one of these letters Shaikh Ma'sum elaborates upon why certain litanies and prayers are necessary for those affiliated to the Naqshbandi order. In the same letter he also defines at length the distinctive features of the order.[59] The heading of a letter Shaikh Sa'id wrote to Aurangzeb is significant: "*dar nisbat-i muhabbat wa faza'il-i tariqa-i naqshbandiyya wa dar ma'ni-ye muridi wa muradi wa ahadis dar fazilat i ba'z i a'mal*" (On the attachment with, and virtues of, the Naqshbandi order; and an explication of the meaning of seeking and being sought after; and some sayings of the Prophet on the virtues of certain [pious] acts).[60] This clearly indicates Aurangzeb's close spiritual connection with the order, almost that of a master (*murad*, i.e. *pir*) with his disciple (*murid*).

In another letter he refers to the arrival of an order (*nishan*) from Prince Aurangzeb, and in response expresses his appreciation

---

[58] See Chapter 2 above.
[59] Naqshbandi, *Maktubat-i Sa'idiya*, Letter 37, pp. 91–2.
[60] Ibid., Letter 46, pp. 102–5.

of Aurangzeb's concern for religious matters and fear of punishment and expectation of reward in the life hereafter. He cites several *hadiths* in this letter regarding pious practices and prayers and insists on Aurangzeb's support for the *shari'a*-following *'ulama*. The letter ends with a request to the prince to include among his confidants a member of the family – his nephew, Shaikh Muhyi al-Din, who has just left to join Aurangzeb.[61] In yet another letter Shaikh Sa'id portrays the current predicament of the *shari'a* in the Mughal domains and hopes the prince will reinforce the *shari'a* because he is, as he calls him, *Muhyi-i qawa'im-i din-i qawim* (one who strengthens the pillars of the true religion). He sent this letter with his son, Muhammad Lutf-Allah, whom he describes as a confidant of the prince (*mahram-i sudda-i'ulya*).[62] Around 1655–6, when Aurangzeb was engaged in the War of Succession, Shaikh Muhammad Ma'sum, Shaikh Muhammad Sa'id, and their younger brother Shaikh Muhammad Yahya, set out for the hajj, the details of which Muhammad Sa'id writes, on behalf of his own self and his brothers', on his way from Sironj.[63] When the prince learnt of their departure he apparently sent one of his servants, Kamil Beg, to accompany them to the Hijaz.[64]

We have seen above the hesitation of Shaikh Ma'sum to return to India from the Hijaz in the late 1650s and his request to the Prophet to determine whether it was advisable for him to do so. Here we note the letter that Shaikh Sa'id wrote to the emperor after their return to Sirhind, stating that they are safely returned

---

[61] Ibid., Letter 45, pp. 99–101.

[62] Ibid., Letter 65, p. 121. It is significant that this term for the prince, *Muhyi-i qawa'im-i din*, reminds us of the name and title *Muhyi al-Din* (Reviver of the Faith) which Aurangzeb acquired after he ascended the throne. In Letter 37, pp. 91–2, and Letter 84, pp. 144–5, he addresses him as *Muhyi al-Sunna wa al-Islam* (restorer of the traditions of the Prophet and Islam) and *Muhyi-i Anwar al-Sunnat al-Baiza* (restorer of the Prophet's luminous tradition).

[63] Ibid., Letter 84, pp. 144–5.

[64] Ibid., Letter 37, p. 92.

and well settled at home, and busy praying for the stability of the emperor and his empire:

> Thanks be to God that with the rising of the sun of guidance, the darkness of infidelity and misbelief has disappeared, and heresy and bad innovations have been completely uprooted, and the standards of justice are raised to the highest horizon . . . besides this, if you are well disposed and care for rearing the faith – and thus from this concern for the faith – it would be to your glory if you issued orders to leaders devoted to the service of Islam prohibiting open violations of the law, including drinking (*muskirat*). And also orders regarding the rehabilitation of old mosques and abandoned madrasas and welfare of the *'ulama* and reverence for the pious that would promote the pillars of the glorious *shari'at* and give strength (*tamkin*) to the empire.[65]

We can see by implication from the content and tone of this letter how close the shaikh was to the emperor. Not long after Aurangzeb's assumption of power, however, the shaikh fell sick and in 1659 the emperor invited him to the court for medical treatment. The shaikh wrote to his brother, Shaikh Muhammad Ma'sum, about the facilities made available to him there, and noted in particular the generous treatment meted out to him at the court: ". . . and I am amazed that for the last four days the emperor has made particular arrangements; he himself supervised the preparation of food for me (*Badshah 'ajib takid-o-ihtimam mi farmayad, khwud tabikh taiyar sakhta mi farastad*)." Initially, the letters suggest he hoped to recover within a few days; then they take on a more pessimistic tone, with a premonition of death, before he in fact passed away in 1661. The emperor had made special arrangements for the shaikh's treatment by a European physician while in Delhi.[66]

An earlier letter refers in explicit terms to another missive that Prince Aurangzeb had sent him, informing him of his victory

---

[65] Ibid., pp. 91–2.
[66] Ibid., Letters 99 and 100, pp. 215–16.

in a battle.⁶⁷ Earlier, having received intelligence of the Golconda ruler's violation of an agreement with the Mughals, and of Aurangzeb's expedition against him, the shaikh had written to the prince to be ruthless with enemies of the empire and assured him of a special prayer (*khatm-i khwajagan*) for his victory. The letter is replete with a large number of *hadiths* projecting the Companions of the Prophet as guiding lights of the truth. The Shi'is are here stated to be outside the orbit of Islam (*az jirga-i Islam kharij*), and therefore *jihad* against them is deemed obligatory.⁶⁸

Shaikh Saif al-Din (d. 1685) and Aurangzeb

Customarily, Shaikh Ma'sum would depute from among his disciples special representatives for the guidance of selected regions. Seeing Aurangzeb and his court as an important part of such domains for his disciples, he naturally paid special attention to selecting his representative there, choosing one of his favourite sons, Shaikh Muhammad Saif al-Din, to train and tutor the emperor and members of the royal family. Muhammad Baqir of Lahore (d. 1109 / 1697–8) was the other such representative, very likely sent to assist Saif al-Din, but also to serve independently during his absence from the court.

Shaikh Muhammad Saif al-Din was perhaps the closest to Aurangzeb among Shaikh Ahmad Sirhindi's grandsons. He represented his father, the *pir* of the emperor, and served as a special envoy of the Mujaddidi order at the court to advise and supervise the emperor's training in Naqshbandi practices and report on progress to his own father. From Shaikh Saif al-Din we have several letters which indicate the emperor's formal initiation into the order and his spiritual achievements. As regards his initiation into the order, he speaks of it in particular in two of his letters,

---

⁶⁷ Ibid., Letter 40, pp. 94–5.
⁶⁸ Ibid., Letters 66 and 82, pp. 122–6 and 141–3.

one addressed to Muhammad Baqir of Lahore – an important member of the Naqshbandi Mujaddidi *silsila* – and another addressed to Sufi Sa'd-Allah Kabuli – who was also an important member of the order and reputedly close to the emperor. He writes to Kabuli that the emperor was initiated into the Naqshbandi order by his father Shaikh Muhammad Ma'sum, stayed in Sirhind for some time, and had three meetings with him until leaving for Agra on hearing the news of Shah Jahan's death (*Badshah be-dukhul-i tariqa-i 'aliya musharraf gashta bisyar muta'assir gasht, sih suhbat ba Hazrat-i Ishan dasht. Chun Shah Jahan wafat yaft be-jihat-i zarur mutawajjih-i Akbarabad gasht*).[69] He mentions favours that he himself had earned from the emperor, and that he had advised Prince Muhammad A'zam to become a *murid* in the Naqshbandi order, and that his persuasion had succeeded. The emperor had been pleased to join the order and at his son having joined the same order; he was in fact attentive to his son's closeness to the shaikhs. Prince Mu'azzam too is mentioned as being close to Shaikh Saif al-Din: on occasion he sought explanations of spiritual matters from the shaikh, to which the shaikh responded generously.[70] At court, as a representative of his father, the shaikh initiated a number of Aurangzeb's kin and senior nobles, including an important religious figure, Muhammad Muhsin of Delhi, and another who was the religious leader of the Fatehpuri mosque, into the Mujaddidi–Naqshbandi order. In response to one of his son's letters, his father Shaikh Ma'sum writes back appreciating what he has accomplished at court and towards ennobling the spiritual practices of the emperor. When Saif al-Din showed the emperor Shaikh Ma'sum's letter, it is reported that the emperor was elated and wrote back to him, but this letter of the emperor has not unfortunately become available. We can, however, note Shaikh Ma'sum's response to this missing letter. He shows happiness over

---

[69] A'zam, *Maktubat-i Khwaja Muhammad Saif al-Din* (henceforth A'zam, *Maktubat-i Saif*), pp.114–16, and Letter 83 to Sa'd-Allah Kabuli, pp. 193–4.
[70] Ibid., Letter 52, p. 143.

the fact that his son Saif al-Din is so close to the emperor, says he is happy at the way Saif al-Din has influenced the emperor's decisions; he appreciates the son for "enjoining what is right, and forbidding what is wrong (*al-amr bi'l ma'ruf va'n nahy 'ani'l munkar*)". It is also reported that during his stay at court in 1678 Saif al-Din was among the witnesses of the wedding (*nikah*) of Muhammad A'zam in the presence of Qazi 'Abd al-Wahhab, Mir Saiyid Muhammad Qanauji, and Mullah 'Iwaz Wajih.[71]

Shaikh Ma'sum took a special interest in training the emperor, so besides Shaikh Saif al-Din he also especially deputed a couple of his other *khalifas* for this purpose. In a couple of letters the emperor, while reporting his own experience, is also curious about their meanings and implications. The shaikh in response, Saif al-Din reports, described and explained the significance of his experience in terms of what in Naqshbandi tradition is referred to as solitude in company (*khalwat dar anjuman*). "After praising God, having noticed what the emperor's experiences had been, he states that the effects of Naqshbandi spirituality on the emperor have been so extraordinary that divinity and spiritual sublimity were present in him, even more so in moments of forgetfulness, and on occasions when he is busy with the people (*istila-i nisbat wa huzuri-yi u ta'ala, bar nahji ghalaba namuda ast ki dar amakin-i ghaflat wa hangami ikhtilat bishtar jalwa mifarmayad*)." This is one of the greatest favours that God has bestowed on him. He then relates a story from 'Abd al-Rahman Jami's *Nafahat al-Uns*; a certain person visited Khwaja Baha al-Din Naqshband and asked him if "in your *tariqa* there is [the practice of] *zikr, saut*, and *sama*?" He replied that there was not; then he was asked, "what is the foundation of your *tariqa*?" The khwaja replied, "it is *khalwat*

---

[71] Khan, *Ma'asir-i 'Alamgiri*, p. 78. His name here is given in the text as Shaikh Saif-Allah Sirhindi. Musta'id Khan also reports that on 13 Muharram 1079 (1668), the emperor visited Shaikh Saif al-Din and had a long conversation with him and thus elevated his stature among his other family members (*be-tazkira-i kalimat-i ifadat asar suhbat dashata wa shaikh-i mazkur ra dar aqranash be-ikram bardashta*), p. 84.

dar anjuman (solitude in company), in appearance with people, in actuality with Allah." Saif al-Din then elaborates on the Sufi term *huzur* (divine presence), describing the distinction between *huzur* in the case of a novice and in the case of an accomplished seeker:

> ... *nisbat* in the case of the novice is not so strong, because he is not able to maintain his spirituality in the midst of worldly activities. But when an accomplished seeker is blessed with the same *huzur*, he acquires perfect stability to maintain that status, and in fact it increases in those circumstances. This *huzur* comes from within [God becomes present] ... You should be grateful to Allah for this great boon that he has bestowed upon you (*shukr-i in ni'mat-i 'uzma baja biyarand*).[72]

In Saif al-Din's estimation the emperor had risen to the level of a *muntahi* – a Sufi who has arrived at the highest stage of mysticism.

Saif al-Din reiterates the same expressions but in largely different ways in his other letters. In one of them he congratulates Aurangzeb on having almost reached an important Sufi stage of *lata'if*, namely *latifa-i akhfa*, which meant great proximity to the sacred steps of his master (*murshid*), namely Shaikh Ma'sum, and thus nearing the steps of the Prophet Himself. In another letter, which is very brief and in Arabic, he focuses on the emperor's attention to his responsibilities in the affairs of his subjects.[73] The emperor appears also to have shown some concern over sartorial choices, including the legality of wearing royal robes. Saif al-Din tells him elegant and decent robes are permissible and fine (*mahmud*) if worn with good intent, whereas to give up such apparel merely to gain popularity as a dervish or ascetic is *mazmum* (damnable).[74] One letter shows the curiosity of the emperor to ascertain the whereabouts or welfare of several other members of the Mujaddidi order.[75]

---

[72] A'zam, *Maktubat-i Saif*, Letter 39, pp. 128–9.
[73] Ibid., Letter 161, pp. 255–6; Letter 165, pp. 260–1.
[74] Ibid., Letter 59, p. 153.
[75] Ibid., Letter 69, p. 169.

THE NAQSHBANDI SHAIKHS 361

Besides the emperor and Prince Muhammad A'zam we have – as discussed in the preceding chapter – evidence of Princess Roshanara's (d. 1671) closeness to Shaikh Saif al-Din. Several letters contain instructions for her and elaborate on the virtues of the Naqshbandi order.[76] A letter that Saif al-Din wrote to the emperor condoling her death is notable: it says a pious man who does not wish to divulge his identity saw the Prophet assure him in his waking state that, "since the late Begum was in much service of the dervishes, she was blessed by God because of it."[77]

Shaikh Saif al-Din was so overjoyed by the spiritual state of the emperor that he reiterated this frequently in his reports to Shaikh Ma'sum. The father's response to his son's excitement is of interest: "All that you have written of the emperor I have noted, and praised Allah on that account. Such an experience is rare (*'anqa*) when among rulers." In another letter he calls it a special *latifa* which brings one closer to the Prophet; in yet another response he says it is a *ghara'ib-i ruzgar* (wonder of the time) for such a thing to have happened to the emperor.[78]

An anecdote shows Shaikh Saif al-Din's power at the time. He was very likely the person mentioned as a scion of the *pir* of the Naqshbandi order (*yaki az pirzadaha-i silsila-i Naqshbandiya*) who, according to Chishti tradition, together with the public censor (*muhtasib*) interfered in a *sama'* programme (musical

---

[76] Ibid., Letters 7, 34, and 46; pp. 87, 124, and 134, for instance.

[77] For details, see Chapter 7 in this volume. According to *Maqamat-i Ma'asumi* (Vol. 3, pp. 256–7) and *Rauzat al-Qaiyumiya* (Vol. II, pp. 281 and 284), the tomb over the grave of Shaikh Muhammad Ma'sum was erected by Roshanara. She paid for the land on which the shrine was built. The land belonged to one of the sons of the deceased shaikh – acccording to Maqamat Shaikh Saif al-Din, as well as Rauzat Shaikh 'Ubaid-Allah. She also built a mosque near the tomb. Over a lakh of rupees were spent on building the tomb, and 4000 rupees on the mosque. Later in the same tomb were buried eight members of Shaikh Ma'sum's family, including sons and grandsons, by the time of the compilation of the *Rauzat*. See also Parihar, *History and Architectural Remains of Sirhind*, pp.125 and 168.

[78] Ma'sum, *Maktubat-i Ma'sumiya*, Letters 220 and 242, pp. 265–6 and 287.

séance) held at Shaikh Qutb al-Din Bakhtiyar Kaki's shrine in Mehrauli (near Delhi). The séance was being conducted under the leadership of Saiyid Gharib-Allah, a *khalifa* of Shaikh Da'ud Gangohi, an important Chishti–Sabiri shaikh in Shaikh 'Abd al-Quddus Gangohi's line. This shaikh visited Delhi annually on the occasion of Bakhtiyar Kaki's *'urs* ritual, had reportedly met Shah Jahan, and was close to Dara Shukoh. The Naqshbandi *pirzada* and the *muhtasib* objected to the arrangement of the *sama'* and threatened to arrive at the shrine to stop it, which they in fact then did. Saiyid Gharib-Allah was ordered to leave Delhi immediately. The saiyid reacted to the order combatively along the lines of a vision in which Bakhtiyar Kaki himself advised him to violently oppose this interference in the celebrations. The report goes that when the saiyid heard of the approach towards the *sama'* party of the Naqshbandi *pirzada* and the *muhtasib*, and finding panic within his disciples and other participants in the *sama'*, he sought Bakhtiyar Kaki's advice. Thereupon he saw the saint's grave splitting down the middle and Bakhtiyar Kaki himself emerging therefrom in red (fire-coloured) robes, reciting this verse:

Gulgun libas kard-o-sawar-i samand shud
Yaran hazar kunid ki atish buland shud

Attired in red-coloured apparel, he [the beloved] is riding a rapid steed.
Beware, O friends, for the fire has risen high!

Saiyid Gharib-Allah took this to mean that Shaikh Kaki wanted him and his followers to resist. Totally entranced and inspired with Kaki's message, the shaikh stood up to dance (*halash digargun gasht wa be-raqs-o-tawajud dar-amad*), the *sama'* continued, and the *qawwals* sang so beautifully that even the *pirzada* and the *muhtasib* were deeply moved (*asar-i riqqat dar girift*):

Az asar-i yakjihati gasht mast
ham but-o-ham butgar-o-ham butparast

The passionate love left them all inebriated,
the idol, the idol-maker, and the idol-worshipper.

Saiyid Gharib-Allah had to leave Delhi nevertheless. But even as he left the city he declared that the emperor – upon whose instance the *pirzada* and the *muhtasib* had acquired such an excess of power – too would be forced out of Delhi, never to return. And it came to pass that within a short time Aurangzeb left for the Deccan (in 1681), where he eventually died, and after a time (*ba'd chand muddat*) the Naqshbandi *pirzada* also died (in 1685) – or so the Chishti version would have it.[79]

Another of Shaikh Ma'sum's sons, Muhammad 'Ubaid-Allah (d. 1672), who had the title *Murawwij al-Shari'a* (propagator of the *shari'a*), was also very close to the emperor. Besides *Hasanat al-Haramayn* – the account of his father's spiritual experiences in Mecca and Medina which, as noted above, he compiled in Arabic – there is a collection of his letters known as *Khazinat al-Ma'arif*. Most of these letters are addressed to the emperor and concern his religious tutoring and instruction (*nasihat*). In one of his letters he mentions a treatise entitled *Dar 'adam-i ta'mil i kuffar* (Concerning the Prohibition on Employing Infidels) which, he says, he sent to the emperor for consideration.[80] His recommendation to the emperor of such a text is reminiscent of his father Shaikh Ma'sum's views on shunning infidels when deciding on personnel to induct into state service (in the shaikh's letter discussed earlier). The son also mentions, in one of his letters to his brother, Shaikh Muhammad Parsa, the vision that their father

---

[79] 'Ali, *Sawati' al-Anwar*, f. 444. Earlier a similar incident is also reported to have taken place, when Mulla 'Abd al-Qawi, Aurangzeb's noted Gujarati cleric associate, had a discussion with Shaikh Da'ud Gangohi. The mulla was convinced of Gangohi's position both with the evidence he gave from a Bukhari *hadith* and the demonstration of the spiritual impact of the *sama'* itself. The mulla was totally nonplussed, lost whatever knowledge he possessed, and regained it after he sought the shaikh's forgiveness. Cf. Quddusi, *Iqtibas al-Anwar*, pp. 834–6.

[80] Hadi, *Khazinat al-Ma'arif*, Letter 95, p. 122. For Sirhindi shaikhs' discussion of the question of non-Muslim employment, see also Ihsan, *Rauzat al-Qaiyumiya*, Vol. 2, pp. 201–2.

Shaikh Ma'sum had in Medina just before his return from there.[81] The vision, as outlined above, was of the Prophet's appearance, sword in hand, advising elimination of the enemy Dara Shukoh. We also know how unusually kind Aurangzeb was to Muhammad 'Ubaid-Allah when he was taken ill, asking him to arrive in Delhi for his treatment. But Muhammad 'Ubaid-Allah was unhappy away from his home town, as he says in a letter to his brother Shaikh Muhammad Naqshband, who succeeded Shaikh Ma'sum as the third *qaiyum* and prime leader of the family.[82]

Shaikh Muhammad Naqshband (d. 1703), the Third *Qaiyum*, and Aurangzeb

Shaikh Muhammad Ma'sum died in 1669.[83] He left behind six sons, and a large number of spiritual deputies (*khalifa*s) and disciples spread over nearly the entirety of northern India and beyond to the frontiers in Afghanistan and Mawarannahr. We have noted what has appeared of significance in the careers of two of his sons. The other four were, first, Shaikh Sibghat-Allah (d. 1710); second, Shaikh Muhammad Naqshband (d. 1703), who succeeded his father; third, Shaikh Muhammad Ashraf (d. 1707) who, along with Sirhindi's other grandson Shaikh 'Abd al-Latif (d. 1699), lived mostly in the imperial camp; and finally, his sixth and youngest son Muhammad Siddiq (d. 1719), reportedly the *pir* of the early-eighteenth-century Mughal emperor Farrukh Siyar (r. 1712–19).

---

[81] Ibid., Letter 141, p. 156.

[82] Ibid., Letter 129, pp.145–6.

[83] While the noted Persian poet Nasir 'Ali Sirhindi wrote an elegy for him, two chronograms – *"rafta ze 'alam Imam-i Ma'sum"* and *"Qiblat al-Abdal"* – are also attributed to Aurangzeb, who is said to have composed them extempore (*barjasta*) as he heard the news of his death. Ma'sumi, *Maqamat-i Ma'sumi*, Vol. 3, p. 251. Bakhtawar Khan also mentions the first chronogram, but not that it was composed by Aurangzeb. Khan, *Mir'at al-'Alam*, Vol. 2, p. 413.

It seems Shaikh Naqshband's succession was not acceptable to the entire family, and one of the reasons given is that his nomination by his father was not properly witnessed. His cousin, Muhammad Farrukh (d. 1709), Shaikh Muhammad Saʻid's eldest son, was reportedly among his most open critics. Another of Shaikh Saʻid's sons, Shaikh ʻAbd al-Ahad "Wahdat", however, supported Muhammad Naqshband, accompanying him in 1678 on his first hajj pilgrimage as the third *qaiyum*. Wahdat came to be so close to him that, after his death in 1703, Wahdat's disciple Muhammad Murad Kashmiri, the compiler of his letters *Gulshan-i Wahdat*, sought him out to ask if he, Wahdat, had succeeded as the fourth *qaiyum*. Wahdat, in all humility, responded in the negative, though he did not in his humility find it necessary to mention Muhammad Naqshband's son Muhammad Zubair, who in fact succeeded as the fourth *qaiyum*.[84]

Saif al-Din, who was also among the first to support Shaikh Muhammad Naqshband's claim to *qaiyumiyat*, continued to serve as the principal representative of the order in Aurangzeb's court, so we must presume Muhammad Naqshband allowed him to stay there and act independently, this being done as a kind of compromise within the family. Another of Shaikh Naqshband's brothers, Muhammad ʻUbaid-Allah, we have already seen as close

---

[84] Cf. Kashmiri, *Gulshan-i Wahdat*, a collection of Shaikh ʻAbd al-Ahad Wahdat's letters, Letter 87, pp. 141–2. The collection also contains at the end (*tatimma-i maktubat*) some letters of Wahdat's elder brother Shaikh Muhammad Farrukh, and his two sons Shaikh Abu Hanifa and Shaikh Taqi. Muhammad Farrukh was a notable scholar and teacher of his time. He wrote a commentary on Mulla ʻAbd al-Hakim's *Khayali*, a commentary on *Al-ʻAqaʼid al-Nasafi*, the noted book on Sunni dogmatics. Aurangzeb is also reported to have attended his class on *Sahih Bukhari*, the most authentic *hadith* collection. Maʻsumi, *Maqamat-i Maʻsumi*, Vol. 3, p. 155. See also Quddusi, *Iqtibas al-Anwar*, p. 899. Barasvi also joined Shaikh Farrukh's class and calls him a second ʻAbd al-Hakim Siyalkoti of his time. For the difference and dispute in the Sirhindi family, see Sirhindi, *Rauzat al-Qaiyumiya*, Vol. 3, pp. 25–57. Muhammad Farrukh's third son, ʻAli Raza, chose the Chishti–Qadri *silsila*. Maʻsumi, *Maqamat-i Maʻsumi*, Vol. 4, *taʻliqat-o-tauzihat*, pp. 207–8.

to the emperor. Shaikh Saif al-Din died in 1685, 'Ubaid-Allah having preceded him in 1672. From the mid-1680s the family's contact with the emperor, then, was in the main through Shaikh Muhammad Naqshband.

There are from the pen of Shaikh Muhammad Naqshband a large number of letters.[85] They contain information regarding three treatises that he wrote on different theological themes – on *tauba* (repentance); on descriptions of the attributes of God; and on the *Risala-i Gunah-i Kabira-o-Saghira* – a treatise on considerable and inconsiderable sins.[86] His letters say that these *risala*s were also destined for the eyes of the emperor, and he gives passages from the treatises in one such letter. The second set of letters date from the period in which Aurangzeb had already moved to the Deccan and state that he, Shaikh Muhammad, will soon visit the imperial camp there, more specifically that, being keen to meet the emperor in person, he plans to go to Mecca for the hajj and will meet the encamped emperor en route. Shaikh Muhammad also writes to the Shahzadi Begum – Princess Zeb-un-nisa' – from the camp about his intent to proceed for the hajj.[87] In one of these letters, No. 71, which ends with his compliments to the emperor, he adds compliments on behalf of his sons Abu al-'Ala, Muhammad 'Umar, Muhammad Kazim, and his nephew Muhammad Parsa, indicating thereby that the emperor is already adequately acquainted with his family.[88] He writes to one of his associates, Haji Habib-Allah, reporting his arrival at the royal camp:

> As I left with the intention of *haramayn sharifayn*, I received an imperial *farman* with the special signature of the emperor expressing his desire that I visit him. And so I'm here, enjoying many hospitalities and courtesies, and he is not willing to allow me to leave the camp. He called his son Muhammad Kam Bakhsh and handed him over to me, saying that, "In the company of the sages (*buzurgs*) of this

[85] Muhammad, *Wasilat al-Qubul ila Allah-i wa al-Rasul*.
[86] Ibid., Letter 19, pp. 25, 27, and Letter 38, p. 51.
[87] Ibid., Letter 58, p. 71; Letter 72, pp. 88–9.
[88] Ibid., Letter 71, pp. 87–8.

tariqa I have benefited, and you too must benefit from them, and remain in their service (*khidmat-i ishan mashghul shawid*)." In line with this command, then, I became engaged with the prince, and he was delighted. He came to me the following day as well, following his father's command. And later, he came into my presence on his own, several times.

The shaikh was accompanied at the camp by his three sons. He stayed quite long time at the camp, and says in one of his letters, "I am still in Sholapur for a few days because of my own needs, while the emperor has moved, but I will join him after a few days." In another letter he mentions yet another hajj trip, en route to which he would stay at the imperial camp, but this time, because of news of disturbance on the sea routes (on account of European piracy in the Arabian Sea), he returned to Delhi and eventually planned to go on the hajj overland.[89] After returning to Shahjahanabad and Sirhind he sought the emperor's advice on the best route to take. Around the same time, in 1697, Shaikh Wahdat and Shaikh Muhammad Farrukh took the sea route, and being stranded in Mokha performed the hajj a year later, in 1698.[90]

The Shaikh in the *Waqa'i'* of Ni'mat Khan 'Ali

Testimony of the emperor's intimacy with Shaikh Naqshband that comes not from Naqshbandi accounts is to be found in an account of a "great saint's dream" that Ni'mat Khan 'Ali, a well-known poet-satirist and writer associated with the Mughal court, describes and caricatures in the context of his *waqa'i'* regarding the siege of Golconda.[91] In this dream a saint saw his grandfather, identified by 'Ali as the founder of the order to which the saint belonged, forecasting the fall of the citadel of Golconda. 'Ali describes this

---

[89] Ibid., Letter 124, p. 139.
[90] Kashmiri, *Gulshan-i Wahdat* (*Tatimma*), Letter 114 of Shaikh Muhammad Farrukh, p. 164.
[91] Kaicker, *The King and the People*, pp. 108–16.

alongside a discussion in the imperial camp in which the chief qazi, 'Abd-Allah, and some nobles advocate lifting the siege, since believers on both sides are dying; they argue that the fight was thus against the faith, for those on the side of Abu al-Hasan, the ruler of Golconda, were as much Muslim as they were themselves (*Abu al-Hasan wa lashkariyanash hama musalman-and wa . . . ba'zi az in janib niz muslim-and, har ruz be-qatl mirasand. Natija inki jidal mukhalif-i shar'i mubin ast wa qital munafi-yi din-i matin*). The emperor declined the advice and the qazi was transferred. The saint and his grandfather here were none other than Shaikh Muhammad Naqshband and Shaikh Ahmad Sirhindi. Here is the incident, in 'Ali's own words – it begins by establishing the significance of the Naqshbandis:

> As the news spread, the chief of the great saints (*masha'ikh-i kibar*) once had a dream regarding the situation. The shaikh is a man of countless miracles. He is awake while sleeping and dreaming while awake. His grandfather, who is the founder of the mystic order of the saints of established piety and the spiritual guide of the emperor (*sar-i halqa-i silsila-i iradat-i sajjada nashin-i musallam al-wilayat, pir-o-murshid-i hazrat-i pir-o-murshid*), had said, "I went to heaven and had an audience with God." He asked, "How are your sons?" I said that they were grateful for their life and good fortune. He gave me a studded turban-jewel and, bidding me good-bye, said, "Go and guide the people who are going astray." Now a generation has passed. The hereditary jewel, which is God-given and like a cock's crest, is exhibited at intervals, and at the time of visitation such a huge crowd assembles that in the thick of the multitude a few heads are lost like bubbles under men's feet.

The anecdote now turns to the circumstances of the siege in the Deccan.

> In short, the saint with his turban-jewel appeared in a dream to his best and most virtuous successor and said, "O my son, you take for yourself alone the food and sweets of offerings and do not send me my share." "O grandfather," replied the shaikh, "Sweets and food are not to be had much these days because of the general distress (*parishani-yi*

khass-o-'amm). Disciples are so constrained in this campaign that they no longer offer bread and butter (lit. sweets and bread) to the dead. I myself am fed up with these men. On the other hand His Majesty is engaged in so energetic a struggle to conquer the fort that he has stitched with his own hand one of the bags brought to fill the trench – and that too after having performed his ablutions. Yet the fort has neither fallen into our hands nor been blown up. People are helpless. Direct your blessing to the conquest of the fort, and then you shall have abundant sweets (*tawajjuhi dar maftuh shudan-i qil'a kun, an zaman halwa bisyar khwahi yaft*). Great heavens! It is well known that sweets are given after a reconciliation, but it is a miracle of the saint that he desires them at a time of war (*subhan-Allah ki halwa dar ashti bashad, pas in hama az karamat-i an buzurgwar ast ki dar jang mi khwahad*)."

The grandfather asked, "O son, do you speak truly that the emperor stitched the bag with his own hands?" The shaikh confirmed his statement with an oath. Thereupon the exalted saint said, "Awake at once and convey this good news to the emperor that we shall take the fort and hand it over to him [the emperor], we will take over everyone inside the fort, sparing neither friend nor foe. But the bag stitched by the auspicious hands of His Majesty must not be filled with dust and thrown down to be trampled underfoot. Rather, it must be filled with gold and given to my son (*bayad ki az zar pur karda be-farzandam dihad*)."

So it would appear that the travails of the Mughal army besieging the fort were now over, given the miraculous power of this saint and his order. The account continues:

Since the venerable saint has promised the conquest of the fort in a few days, no worry remains. The shaikh is himself eager to fulfil his vow. He is enquiring to the best of his capacity from the well-informed how big the bag is. With this dream, distracted hearts were composed and strict orders for attack given (*takid bar yurish raft*). The prediction of the shaikh might be on the instigation of a noble, though the shaikh is himself a saint and a noble. It is reported of him that even in his early years he had vouchsafed revelations and miracles. Many "true" dreams are reported of him. One of these has been put into verse by a disciple. I happened to see it in a notebook and added to the sanctity of the dream with this incident (*in waqiʻa ra be-an waqiʻa musharraf sakht*).

> The shaikh saw the Devil in a dream,
> The robber of faith and piety.
> With his heart pure like a mirror,
> He recognised the Devil immediately.
> He took him to task with a reproach,
> And struck a blow on his head.
> And catching him by the beard, he said,
> "From the court of God, you were cursed and turned."
> "O you who mislead mankind,
>   with the ring of mischief in your neck."
> "All your worship and prayer is meant to deceive
>   and seduce people."
> When the shaikh struck the second blow,
> He was awakened by his own slap.
> And as he came out of his sweet sleep,
> He saw in his hand his own beard.
> "It was a struggle with the devil of the self,"
>   the shaikh thought, and left his beard with a hearty laugh.
> Who but an infidel would not believe the story?
> What if this is not miracle absolute?

The writer then concludes rather ambiguously: "The leader of the spies and the chief of intelligence posted for espionage in the bazars and streets goes from door to door and visits every lane and picks up news from everywhere."[92]

---

[92] ʻAli, *Waqaʼiʻ-i Niʻmat Khan ʻAli*, pp. 8–12. I have quoted from N.H. Ansari's abridged translation with some additions and modifications, and to give a flavour of ʻAli's wit and satire have also added some sentences and phrases from the original. Ansari, *Chronicles of the Seige of Golkonda Fort*, pp. 8–10. For ʻAli and his changing attitude to Aurangzeb, see Irfan, "Aurangzeb ki hajw se madh tak", pp. 430–52. See also Kaicker, *The King and the People*, pp. 108–16.

Because this incident is in a source not associated with the literature generated by the Naqshbandi–Mujaddidi, it is an important confirmation of our conclusions drawn earlier. Ni'mat Khan 'Ali is evidently annoyed at the emperor not taking the advice of the qazi and the nobles while being egged on by the Naqshbandi–Mujaddidi shaikh. We also learn of course that Shaikh Muhammad Naqshband retains proximity with the emperor even when camped.

The Mujaddidis in Mughal Society

But the Mujaddidi–Naqshbandis' role was more complex and varied perhaps than meets the eye. For instance, Shaikh Muhammad Naqshband's son Muhammad 'Umar was, after the death of his first wife, eventually married to the daughter of the last ruler of Golconda, Sultan Abu al-Hasan. Saqi Musta'id Khan says, "Abu al-Hasan Haidarabadi had three daughters. The first of them, according to the imperial order, was married to Sikandar of Bijapur. The second to Muhammad 'Umar, son of Shaikh Muhammad Naqshband, chief of the shaikhs of Sirhind. While the third one was the wife of 'Inayat Khan the son of Jumdat al-Mulk Asad Khan."[93] Muhammad 'Umar is effectively equated here with the prince of Bijapur and the son of the most prominent Mughal noble. Curiously the Naqshbandi shaikh, who had consistently damned Shi'is as outside the pale of Islam's community (*kharij-i jirga-i islam*), was here the only Sunni out of the three marrying an ostensibly Shi'i woman. It is difficult to discern the conditions under which this unlikely matrimonial alliance was forged. In the event, this second wife of Muhammad 'Umar also predeceased him.[94]

We have seen that a reasonably large number of the members of this family were engaged in Sufi disciplines, and in establishing and consolidating their relations with important political elites, the

---

[93] Khan, *Ma'asir-i 'Alamgiri*, p. 312.
[94] Muhammad, *Wasilat al-Qubul*, Vol. 2, Letter 52, p. 93.

emperor included. The major figures apart, there were quite a few on whose stature as theologians we have references. Shaikh Ahmad Sirhindi made every effort to make sure that good, if not the best, religious scholars and theologians of the time should emerge from his own family. In particular, there was Shaikh Muhammad Saʿid's son, Shaikh Muhammad Farrukh, whose repute suggested he was among the most learned scholars of *hadith* of his time: the legend goes – even if it is from family hagiographic accounts – that even Aurangzeb took lessons in the ninth-century *hadith* compilation of *Sahih al-Bukhari* from him.[95] Thus, letters are not all that we possess, there is evidence of their other intellectual engagements in diverse other sources as well.

The writings of at least one of the descendants of Shaikh Ahmad Sirhindi, again a son of Shaikh Muhammad Saʿid, namely Shaikh ʿAbd al-Ahad "Wahdat" (d. 1714), are also of note. More than twenty treatises are attributed to him on varying themes of theology and *tasawwuf*. Some of these are on highly nuanced topics in Muslim jurisprudence: his *Asrar al-Jumaʿ* (Secrets of Friday) deals with the virtues of Friday and his *Risala Nafi al-Ishara fiʾ al-Salat* (Treatise on Raising the Index Finger in Prayers) discusses the significance of raising the index finger while reciting the *tashahhud* in prayer. Both works are in Arabic. The other notable treatises are *Sabil al-Rishad* (Path of Righteousness), dealing with different aspects of *tasawwuf*, *Burhan-i Jail* (Great Evidence), and *Badaʾiʿ al-Shariʿa* (Wonders of Islamic Law). There are, in addition, several texts elaborating on the specific principles of the Naqshbandi–Mujaddidi order, as well as polemical treatises defending and debating issues in the writings of Shaikh Ahmad Sirhindi. ʿAbd al-Ahad also wrote a biography in Arabic of Shaikh Ahmad Sirhindi, entitled *al-Jannat al-Samaniya* (Eight Heavens), summarising

[95] Interestingly, Muhammad Murad Kashmiri, compiler of the *Gulshan-i Wahdat*, mentions him as *ʿallama-i ʿasr* (the most learned scholar of the age). *Sahih al-Bukhari* is seen by Sunni Muslims as the most authentic collection of *hadith*. Maʿsumi, *Maqamat-i Maʿsumi*, Vol. 3, pp. 405–7, mentions him as *qudwat al-ʿulama, maulavi-yi manavi*.

the accounts of the shaikh in the two major seventeenth-century Persian hagiographies – Muhammad Hashim Kishmi's *Zubdat al-Maqamat* and Shaikh Badr al-Din Sirhindi's *Hazarat al-Quds*.[96] The editor of a recent edition of an Arabic variant, who introduces it, says that when Shaikh 'Abd al-Ahad visited the *Haramayn Sharifayn* in the company of his cousin Shaikh Muhammad Naqshband, the *'ulama* and the people of Arabia expressed their eagerness to know of the life and conditions of Mujaddid-i Alf-i Sani. They demanded that he write a book with an account of his life, spiritual knowledge, and accomplishments, since books on Sirhindi's life, such as *Zubdat al-Maqamat* and *Hazarat al-Quds*, were in Persian. In response to their demands Wahdat wrote a book in Arabic which, besides summarising the two major Persian hagiographies, included additional useful information.

Shaikh 'Abd al-Ahad was another who compiled a treatise in Arabic on his father's visit to Medina, a trip he made with Shaikh Muhammad Ma'sum as well as other sons and nephews in 1657–8. This account, the *Lata'if al-Madina*, was (as outlined in the preface) also composed in response to the demands of people in Medina and so is in Arabic. It draws on his own observations and is addressed to those in Medina who were followers of the Naqshbandi order. This was in line with his cousin Shaikh Muhammad 'Ubaid-Allah's account, *Hasanat al-Haramayn*, of his father's travels and spiritual experiences in Mecca and Medina. The latter text too was originally written in Arabic, being later translated into Persian for an Indian audience by Badr al-Din Sirhindi's son, Muhammad Shakir.[97] Amongst his other works,

---

[96] Siddiqui, *Al-Jannat al-Samaniya*. The last chapter (*al-jannat al-samina*, eighth heaven) is dedicated to a refutation of the criticism of Shaikh Ahmad Sirhindi's views (*radd al-shubhat al-warida 'ala kalamihi al-sharif*), pp. 73–95.

[97] Mujaddidi, *Lata'if al-Madina*; Musa-za'i, *Hasanat al Haramayn*. I will discuss the significance of these Arabic texts later, together with an analysis and discussion of another important comprehensive account of Shaikh Ma'sum – *Nata'ij al-Haramayn* by Muhammad Amin Badakhshi – and of an important *khalifa* of Shaikh Ahmad Sirhindi, Muhammad Adam Binori.

the versatile Wahdat wrote a tract on a verse from Rumi's *Masnawi*.[98]

From this wealth of detail we can glean the nature and extent of the closeness between the families of Shaikh Ahmad Sirhindi and Aurangzeb. Several members of the Mughal nobility, male and female, are reported to have been in correspondence with the Sirhindi family.[99]

Whether the Sirhindi shaikhs influenced the politics of the court is not, as I said earlier, my chief concern, but it is undeniable that on many routine matters, such as the appointment and dismissal of officials, their say apparently carried weight. In a letter to Shaikh Ma'sum, Shaikh Saif al-Din repeats an instruction that Ma'sum had given him when leaving for the court – that the purpose of gaining proximity to the emperor's ear was to end injustice.[100] However, when it came to the emperor's major policy decisions – however greatly they may have been in line with Sunni orthodoxy – it is difficult to account for them in terms of the influence of these saints. All that seems possible is to note the

---

This text is in three volumes and remains unpublished. A copy of it is in the British Library, and other copies are held in collections in Pakistan.

[98] Kishan Chand Ikhlas notes that Nawab Shukr-Allah Khan – who was also a poet with the *takhallus* "Khaksar", was an important noble and also son-in-law of 'Aqil Khan Razi, himself a major Persian and Hindavi poet. He wrote a commentary on Rumi's *Masnawi* with Shaikh Sirhindi (*be-ittifaq-i Hazrat Shaikh Sirhindi ki jami'-i jami' 'ulum budand*). Ikhlas, *Hamesha Bahar*, pp. 69–70.

[99] Such letters include those from Shaikh Muhammad Ma'sum addressed to Mir Mu'in al-Din, Nawab Mukarram Khan, Tarbiyat Khan, Ja'far Khan Jumdat al-Mulki, Ziya al-Din Husain, Mirza Lutf-Allah Khan; and amongst noblewomen to Begum Jiyo (whose real name is reported to have been Farzana Begum, and who was the wife of Ja'far Khan 'Umdat al-Mulk), and Janan Begum (daughter of Khan-i Khanan). See also Ma'sum, *Maktubat-i Ma'sumiya*, Vol. 1, Letters 23 and 54 to Janan Begum; Letter 176, pp. 337–8, to Lutf-Allah Khan; Letter 207, p. 386, to 'Abd al-Latif Lashkar Khani; ibid., Vol. 2, Urdu translation, Letter 100, pp. 176–7, to Amir Khan; Letter 124, pp. 237–8, to Himmat Khan; Vol. 3, Urdu translation, Letter 71, p. 135.

[100] A'zam, *Maktubat-i Saif*, Letter 4, pp. 82–3.

opinions they expressed on Hindus, and on Shi'is in particular. Shaikh Ma'sum in continuity with what his father Shaikh Ahmad Sirhindi had said, discusses the nature of the relationship that a Muslim should have with a Hindu and is absolutely clear that under no circumstances can a non-Muslim be taken into confidence. To provide evidence for this as Islamic he does not simply cite and interpret Qur'anic verses, he also invokes incidents from the history of Islam, from the time of the Prophet and 'Umar the second Caliph. All this he does to argue his point that a non-Muslim should never be employed by a Muslim state, not even if he be more competent than Muslims available for the purpose. The shaikh notes that only weaker Sufis say there is no harm in befriending infidels – on the grounds that in a life of devotion (*faqiri*) there should be no place for enmity. However, he asks what this *faqiri* really means. Is it higher than that of the Prophet Himself, who took pride in his own *faqiri*? And does the Qur'an not command him to fight against infidels (*kuffar*) and hypocrites (*munafiqin*) with great force (*jahid i'l-kuffar wa'l-munafiqin w' aghluz 'alaihim*)? How strange the *faqirs* of our times, he says, who can commend departures from the path of the Prophet.[101]

In like vein, Shaikh Muhammad Sa'id in his letters to Prince Aurangzeb, written when he was engaged in battles against the Deccan sultans, declares that Shi'is are outside the bounds of Islam (*az jirga-i islam kharij and*). The struggle and fight against them he characterises as being *muhimmat-i islam* (important tasks of Islam), more important even than regular prayers.[102]

The *risala* that Shaikh 'Ubaid-Allah sent to the emperor has been noted earlier; it was probably sent sometime in the late 1660s and speaks of the prohibition on the employment of infidels. And yet we know for certain that at no stage in the entire period of Aurangzeb's reign were Shi'is or Hindus actually excluded from state service; it has in fact been noted that several eminent

---

[101] Ma'sum, *Maktubat-i Ma'sumiya*, Urdu translation, Vol. 3, Letter 55, pp. 105–11.
[102] Naqshbandi, *Maktubat-i Sa'idiya*, Letter 66, pp. 122–4.

nobles in the emperor's court were Hindus and Shi'is even until he breathed his last.¹⁰³

The Controversy Around Shaikh Ahmad Sirhindi's Doctrine and Its Defence

While the Sirhindi shaikhs were close to the emperor and several nobles, and enjoyed an eminent position in society, their Sufi religious views were not acceptable to a very significant segment of Sunni religious scholarship. There were problems, as I have shown, that the family encountered with reference to the *shari'a* – Shaikh Ahmad Sirhindi's Sufi establishment was obviously not generally palatable to all. There were rival orders and theologians interested in examining the veracity of the high claims made by members of the family. At the same time, Mughal society saw a large number of forcefully argued treatises, some defending the shaikh in relation to the *shari'a* and others opposing his views. Several historians have noted the existence of this controversy, with some of them seeing the controversy as evidence of Sirhindi not enjoying much of a reputation as a great Sufi of the Mughal period.¹⁰⁴ In recent years Iqbal Mujaddidi, who has written extensively on the Mujaddidi–Naqshbandi order in Urdu, has painstakingly collected some of the defences.¹⁰⁵

Among the earliest of these is a defence of Sirhindi's controversial claim of the *haqiqat-i Ka'ba* being greater (*afzal*) than the *haqiqat-i Muhammadiya*. The defence was penned by Mulla Muhammad Amin Badakhshi, a disciple of one of Shaikh Sirhindi's eminent *khalifas*, Adam Binori. Adam Binori had been sent on the hajj (and virtually exiled) on the orders of Shah Jahan when the emperor grew worried at his popularity and the large numbers of his disciples. In the Hijaz, when Binori began

---

¹⁰³ Ali, *The Mughal Nobility under Aurangzeb*, pp. 7–37, 95–135, and 175–7; idem, *Mughal India*, pp. 262–304.

¹⁰⁴ Cf. Friedmann, *Shaykh Ahmad Sirhindi*, pp. 94–102.

¹⁰⁵ Mujaddidi, "Hazrat Mujaddid Alf-i Sani", Vol. 2, pp. 791–811. The article was first published in a journal, *Nur-e Islam*, (Sharqpur), Special Issue on Hazrat Mujaddid-e Alf-e Sani, from which I have sketched this account.

preaching the doctrine of Shaikh Sirhindi, controversy arose on, among other things, the matter of the *afzaliyat* (superiority) of the Ka'ba, which Amin Badakhshi tried to address in his epistle titled *al-Mufazala bain al-Insan wa'l-Ka'ba* (1658). The penning of this epistle points to a key dimension of the controversy surrounding Sirhindi's claims and his defence, which had acquired a somewhat pan-Islamic dimension, and was discussed, disputed, and defended in the Hijaz as well. This is confirmed by sources from within the Hijaz.

A good part of this effort at defence came from Sirhindi's sons, grandsons, and network of disciples. In 1683 his eminent grandson Shaikh Muhammad Naqshband – the third *qaiyum* – penned one such defence. This was the year in which Sirhindi's opponents reportedly obtained an imperial order stopping the teaching of Sirhindi's letters. This then caused a surge in the number of treatises written in Sirhindi's defence, their number rising – if we are to believe Kamal al-Din Muhammad Ihsan (author of the *Rawzat al-Qaiyumiya*) – to 180; and of this number 72 were written by the sons and grandsons of Shaikh Sirhindi alone.[106] Another aspect of the controversy centred around the translation of the shaikh's letters into Arabic, which Shaikh Muhammad Beg Uzbeki Burhanpuri (b. 1632), in a treatise also written in 1683, claimed were incorrectly translated and thus propagated errors about the shaikh's teachings.

The controversy over Shaikh Ahmad Sirhindi's claims was to continue for many more years, gaining among his defenders important eighteenth-century *'ulama* such as Shah Wali-Allah Dehlavi, and writings in favour and against continue to be produced to this day.[107]

---

[106] Ibid., esp. p. 797. These defending treatises included texts by Shaikh Saif al-Din Sirhindi, son of Shaikh Muhammad Ma'sum Sirhindi, Shaikh 'Abd al-Ahad Wahdat, Shaikh Muhammad Ashraf, Shaikh Muhammad Sibghat-Allah, all Sirhindi's grandsons, Shaikh Muhammad Yahya, his son, and Shaikh 'Abd al-Latif's grandson through Sirhindi's daughter Khadija.

[107] Ibid., esp. pp. 805–11. Part of this controversy was also reflected, as we saw briefly, in eighteenth-century politics.

Aurangzeb did take heed of some of these problems and took action to solve them while remaining close to the family. In fact he even sought the Sirhindi family's forgiveness for the trouble caused to them by the outcries against them. There is in this context a letter of Shaikh Wahdat (of the *Gulshan-i Wahdat*), which is addressed to the compiler of the collection, Muhammad Murad Kashmiri. It describes the summoning of Shaikh 'Abd al-Ahad to the court by Aurangzeb in response to the Sirhindi family's opponents questioning some passages in Sirhindi's writings:

> You may have heard that I had come to the *Dar al-Khilafat* and had not intended to see the emperor. But something happened which was destined to happen, as a result of which the emperor summoned me to come to the court [and when I arrived] he showed great kindness. During these days, some people, jealous of the *Tariqa-i Ahmadiya*, had approached the emperor stating that there are several issues in the *maktubat* of Shaikh Ahmad Sirhindi written against the *shari'a*, [and] while all his disciples and *khalifas* believe that these are correct, the issues are blasphemous and heretical (*mujib-i ilhad wa zandaqa*). Some of the letters which discuss "secrets" [of the religion] are like the inexplicable words of the Qur'an [*mutashabihat*] and require interpretation.

He then adds to his explanation of the controversy.

> Since these issues were beyond the comprehension of the stupid, and since they had raised the question, people were initially taken in and this led to disorder (*tawahhush*). However, friends and respected members [of the order and the family] refuted them. Great commotion ensued, and they also approached and pressed upon the people of the court of justice, and time and again brought the matter to the notice of the emperor. Then the emperor summoned me to his private chambers to reply to their objections and explain those passages by my grandfather. I replied then that it was impossible that there could be anything offensive to the *shari'a* in the writings of my grandfather, even if it seemed apparently so. In the terse and nuanced discourse of the Sufis we often encounter some things that persons such as us, who are short of understanding, do not understand. And

it is not appropriate to bring such matters to the public for discussion and disputation. Whatever part of the speech or writing of our sages we understand should be accepted, and that which is beyond our comprehension, and appears to be contrary to the *shari'a* – the knowledge of this should be handed over to Allah. We should never think, and we should never suggest, that such discourses are against the illumined *shari'a*. Therefore, I should be excused from being present to discuss the truth or meaning of such matters.

Apparently, this spirited defence of Shaikh Ahmad Sirhindi and his infallible wisdom was deemed adequate by Aurangzeb. Wahdat thus concludes his account:

Thanks be to God that the Emperor is [now] satisfied and has withdrawn [himself] beyond the limit of such controversial conversation. He sent some of his nobles to me to ask for forgiveness (*uzr khwahi*), stating that: "God forbid (*na'uz-billah*), I did not intend it to be a case and judgment, [and] even if there was a qazi present, he was only there to resolve certain questions. Since you did not come, I would not insist on troubling you to come now. If any questions still arise, I will write to you." This was how it transpired from the month of Ramazan until today, which is the second of Shawwal. Since then there has been no discussion, and the enemies are crestfallen (*mu'anidan ham para pashiman shudand*). If there is any report to you contrary to what I have written, do not trust it. Allah has bestowed greatness on the Ahmadi *tariqa* even if the enemies [lit. the idol worshippers] do not like it. For a few days I will remain here, and then will leave for Sirhind. Give my *salam* to your father and friends especially 'Abd al-Mu'min. And my special *du'a* for Muhammad Yusuf.[108]

Again, as regards chronology, we know that the disturbances mentioned in this letter occurred after the death of Shaikh Ma'sum, very likely during the 1670s. We have also seen above that later, during the Golconda siege in the 1680s, Shaikh Muhammad Naqshband, the third *qaiyum*, served as adviser and was virtually *pir* of the imperial camp.

[108] Kashmiri, *Gulshan-i Wahdat,* Letter 5, pp. 17–18.

The Sirhindi Shaikhs and Their Followers in Early-Eighteenth-Century Delhi

In 1707 when Aurangzeb died and his sons were mobilising coalitions to fight for the throne, the general impression was that Prince Muhammad A'zam – whom the emperor had kept close to himself in the Deccan and who was considered abler and more equipped – would win the throne. According to the Mujaddidi–Naqshbandi tradition, however, Prince Muhammad Mu'azzam, who then held charge of the Jamrud *thana* in the north-western frontier, was the one blessed to succeed to the throne by the fourth *qaiyum*, Shaikh Muhammad Zubair (d. 1739), who had assumed the Sirhindi family mantle after the death of his father Muhammad Naqshband (d. 1703). In 1707, coincidentally, Shaikh Zubair had gone off to Kabul at the invitation of his disciples, and while there met Prince Muhammad Mu'azzam, to whom he predicted his victory, and thereafter, on his return to Hindustan, joined his retinue. Shaikh Zubair is also said to have crowned the prince at Lahore. When Muhammad Mu'azzam arrived in Sirhind, Shaikh Zubair's brother, Shaikh Muhammad Sibghat-Allah, tied a turban on the prince's head. Prediction of the victory, we are told – albeit by hagiographers – converted Prince Muhammad A'zam's near victory into defeat at the Battle of Jaju near Agra; on account of Shaikh Zubair's influence (*tawajjuh*: literally, attentiveness) a strong dust storm was raised which blinded the eyes of soldiers in A'zam's army.[109] Prince Mu'azzam, as we know, ascended the throne as Bahadur Shah, and in his retinue were some members of the Sirhindi family.[110]

The new emperor, however, soon deviated from the right path of *sunna wa jama'a*, ordered the name of 'Ali, the Prophet's

---

[109] Ihsan, *Rauzat al-Qaiyumiya*, Urdu translation, Vol. 4, pp. 56–64. For Shaikh Muhammad Zubair, see Rizvi, *A History of Sufism*, Vol. 2, pp. 244–5.

[110] Ma'sumi, *Maqamat-i Ma'sumi*, Vol. 3, p. 282, for the author's presence in Sambhar in 1122 (1710), during the emperor's campaigns against the Rajputs.

cousin and son-in-law, and the fourth Righteous Caliph, to be mentioned as "The Prophet's Successor" (*wasi-yi Rasul-Allah*) in Lahore in the Friday sermon (*khutba*) in 1712, and thus earned the curse of the shaikh.[111]

If we are to believe Ihsan, Farrukh Siyar also received blessings from the Mujaddidis for suppressing the Sikhs. Their claims stretch on into the period when Mughal rule was weakening: the coming to power of Muhammad Shah in 1719 was apparently because of Shaikh Muhammad Zubair's blessings. The shaikh suggested the change in his name from Roshan Akhtar to Muhammad Shah and sent him his turban. In his time, the shaikh lived in Delhi in considerable luxury, and this was despite his problems with several of the emperor's favourites.[112] The shaikh also reportedly intervened in and fanned the celebrated Delhi shoe-makers' riot. His magnificent prescience included his forecast of Nadir Shah's invasion in the late 1730s.[113]

Around the early-eighteenth century Delhi finally appears to have emerged as the true centre of the Mujaddidi shaikhs. After the death of Shaikh Muhammad Naqshband in Sirhind, Shaikh Zubair migrated from Sirhind and lived in Delhi. Shaikh 'Abd al-Ahad "Wahdat", his cousin, also chose to live in Delhi; and several other members of the Sirhindi family were constrained to leave Sirhind after the raids of Sikhs on the town.[114] Their presence became more noticeable in Delhi amongst the reputed scholars and

[111] Ihsan, *Rauzat al-Qaiyumiya*, Urdu translation, Vol. 4, pp. 84–90. For Koki Jiyo, see 'Abd al-Ghafur, Hafiz Khidmatgar Khan, and Roshan al-Daula, see Irvine, *Later Mughals*, pp. 263–90; Chandra, *Parties and Politics*.

[112] These favourites included Koki Jiyo, 'Abd al-Ghafur, Hafiz Khidmatgar Khan, and Roshan al-Daula.

[113] Ihsan, *Rauzat al-Qaiyumiya*, pp. 147–55. For the shoe-makers' riot, see Alam, Introduction in *Crisis of Empire*; Kaicker, *The King and the People*.

[114] Ihsan, *Rauzat al-Qaiyumiya*, pp. 81–4. Initially, before the Sikh raids in Sirhind, the reason seems to have been Shaikh Zubair's unpopularity with his own family members. Besides the family dispute, the Sikh raids in Sirhind were also a reason for Shaikh 'Abd al-Ahad's decision to move to Delhi. Some of 'Abd al-Ahad's disciples also thought, as we saw above, that

poets of the city. Of those in the family that were in evidence, the most important name to emerge was that of Wahdat, popularly known in Delhi literary circles as Miyan Shah Gul. In almost all *tazkiras* of Persian poetry he is mentioned as a significant poet; his *divan* included *qasidas,* ghazals, *ruba'is*, and other important verse forms. In his ghazals we have a delicate combination of Sufism and literary aesthetics. Eighteenth-century *tazkira* writers speak highly of his poetry. Khwushgu says even though he was rarely free from spiritual and mystic engagements, he was a master poet of many fresh and colourful ideas. Ikhlas' view is less sympathetic: he says it was only occasionally that he penned miraculous verses, and his *divan* was relatively short.[115]

Wahdat's disciples included the noted eighteenth-century poet Shaikh Sa'd-Allah "Gulshan" (Rose Garden), who called himself so because, it is reported, his *murshid* (preceptor) was none other than Gul.[116] Gulshan was also the master and tutor of Khwaja Muhammad Nasir 'Andalib, the author of *Nala-i 'Andalib*. 'Andalib, as we have seen, was not simply a great poet, he was also the father of one of the most representative poets of the time, Khwaja Mir Dard (1720–85).

While we can legitimately speculate that Shaikh 'Abd al-Ahad's high literary stature would have been a major factor in these great poets' attraction to him, it is significant that they and several others remained associated with the Sirhindi Mujaddidi lineage even after his death in 1714. Mirza Mubarak-Allah Iradat Khan "Wazih" (d. 1717), a poet and the author of *Tarikh-i Iradat Khan*, a well-known account of the early-eighteenth century, was also associated with the Naqshbandi order.[117] Several other names from

---

he would succeed Shaikh Muhammad Naqshband as the fourth *qaiyum*. Kashmiri, *Gulshan-i Wahdat*, Letter 87, pp. 141–2.

[115] Khwushgu, *Safina-i Khwushgu*, p. 69; Ikhlas, *Hamesha Bahar*, p. 238.

[116] Khwushgu, *Safina-i Khwushgu*, p. 165.

[117] He was a *murid* of a certain Mir Sanjar Mashhadi Naqshbandi (d. 1693) and a disciple of Mir Muhammad Zaman Rasikh Sirhindi. See Editor's Introduction in Mehr, *Tarikh-i Iradat Khan*.

the 1710s, 1720s, and 1730s, can be added to the list. In 1739, when Shaikh Muhammad Zubair died, Delhi saw the compilation of a most notable Sufi literary text, namely *Nala-i 'Andalib* by Khwaja Nasir 'Andalib (d. 1759). In this text the Sufi poet and scholar 'Andalib chose to write down in Persian various discourses and stories from the world of Islam and Muslims. These had been originally narrated and shared in Hindi as a pious act to commemorate the demise of his *murshid*, Shaikh Muhammad Zubair.

'Andalib explains the reason for the title of his book. He says he called it *Nala-i 'Andalib* (The Wailings of the Nightingale) because of its resonance with his master Sa'd-Allah's title Gulshan, and Gulshan's own master's title Gul (rose) – he being popularly known as Miyan Gul or Shah Gul. 'Andalib says he was thus fortunate in having heard many stories of the *gul* and *bulbul* (the rose and the nightingale), the significance of which he intended to develop in his text. He also suggests that because of the beauty of the story and because of the fact that everything described there shows the reader in true form what he describes in the text, it could just as well have been called *Fanus-i khayal* (The Chandelier of Imagination) or *A'ina-i Jamal* (The Mirror of Beauty) or *Muraqqa'-i Taswir* (The Album of Pictures) or *Afsun-i Taskhir* (The Magical Spell / Incantation of Conquest) or even in Arabic *Ahsan al-Qisas* (The Best of Tales / Stories) or in Persian *Afsana-i Jananan* (The Fable / Story of the Beloved) or in Hindi *Prem Kahani* (Love Story) and *Chetavani* (Warning). At the end of the preface are cited several verses by Khwaja Mir Dard and Bedar, including a *qit'a* by Khwaja Mir Dard, the last line of which is a chronogram, "*Nala-i Andalib-i Gulshan-i ma-st*" (1135 H, 1740/1).[118]

'Andalib was also the founder a new branch of the Mujaddidi order known as Tariqa-i Muhammadiya, which continued for the most part with the Mujaddidi emphasis on *sunna*, *shari'a*, and their exclusionary and uncompromising attitude to non-

[118] 'Andalib, *Nala-i 'Andalib*, pp. 3–5. For 'Andalib, Dard, and Bedar, see Jalibi, *Tarikh-i Urdu Adab*, Vol. 2, pp. 723–3 and 900–30. See also Rizvi, *A History of Sufism*, Vol. 2, pp. 245, 372–3, and 456–7.

Muslims, though it allowed some accommodation in matters of *sama'* (music) and Shi'is, and a certain flexibility in questions relating to *wahdat al-wujud*.[119] No illustrious shaikh remained in Delhi to claim the position of *qaiyum* in the Sirhindi family after Shaikh Zubair. Over the eighteenth century the Mujaddidi order's popularity continued, however, under Mirza Mazhar Jan-i Janan (d. 1781), and Shaikh Ghulam 'Ali (d. 1824).[120]

We also see members of the Sirhindi family, such as In'am-Allah Khan Yaqin (d. 1756), through whom the Mujaddidi version of Islam continued its firm footing in Delhi's literary circle. Yaqin was Shaikh 'Abd al-Ahad's grandson. His father was Nawab Azhar al-Din Mubarak Jang Bahadur, a notable Mughal official of Muhammad Shah's period who rose to a higher position (*bisyar be jah-o-maknat*) in the 1750s as an associate of 'Imad al-Mulk Ghazi al-Din Khan (d. 1800), a key figure in Mughal politics under Ahmad Shah (r. 1748–54), 'Alamgir II (r. 1754–9), and Shah Jahan II (r. 1759). His mother was the daughter of a prominent 'Alamgiri noble, Hamid al-Din Khan. Yaqin died young. He was tutored and trained in Urdu poetry by Mirza Mazhar Jan-i Janan. Yaqin's name figures prominently among the three major poets, along with Mazhar and Hatim, who started a new style in Urdu poetry, in reaction to what is commonly known in the history of Urdu poetry as *iham-gu'i* (ambiguity).[121]

Benefiting from the patronage they enjoyed from Aurangzeb, his successors, and the Mughal nobles, the Sirhindi Naqshbandi shaikhs were thus able to exercise a considerable influence on Delhi's elite literate society too. An apt recollection can be found in Mir Dard's playful verse, in which the pen-names of four noted

---

[119] 'Andalib, *Nala-i 'Andalib*, pp. 209–10, 310–22, 337–9, 512–50, and 795–7, for references to Hindu rituals, beliefs, and *wahdat al-wujudi* Sufis; Vol. 2, pp. 665–75 for reference to Shi'i beliefs, for instance.

[120] Rizvi, *A History of Sufism*, Vol. 2, pp. 245–9. Weismann, *The Naqshbandiyya*, pp. 63-7.

[121] Mushafi, *Tazkira-i Hindi*, p. 275, cited by Jalibi, *Tarikh-i Adab-i Urdu*, Vol. 2, Part 1, p. 372. See also Qasim, *Majmu'a-i Naghz*, Part 2, p. 355.

Naqshbandi–Mujaddidi Sufis – i.e. Mir Dard himself, his father Nasir 'Andalib, another Naqshbandi Mujaddidi Shaikh Sa'd Allah Gulshan (who was a disciple of Shaikh Muhammad Zubair), and finally Shaikh Ahmad Sirhindi's grandson Shaikh 'Abd al-Ahad Wahdat – are given:

> *Dard az bas 'andalib-i gulshan-i wahdat shuda-st*
> *jalwa-i ru-i gul-i u ra ghazal-khwan mi kunad.*[122]
> Dard has become the nightingale of the garden of Oneness.
> The splendour of a rose's appearance makes him sing ghazals.

Summing up

With Aurangzeb's support and patronage, the family of Shaikh Ahmad Sirhindi acquired a very prominent position at the court; and then beyond the court under his son Shaikh Muhammad Ma'sum and grandson Shaikh Muhammad Naqshband. Their distinguished position continued in the early-eighteenth century and their proximity to the rulers – despite the fact that they no longer had the same institutional presence in the shape of a regular representative at the court – was not in doubt. On the other hand their presence outside the court gradually grew more pronounced. The new branch of the Naqshbandi–Mujaddidi order that emerged meant that Mujaddidis and members of the new branch commanded high status in Delhi's elite literary circles. There is also some evidence of their penetration into sections of Awadh society, a significant part of which had hitherto been the cradle of the Chishti–Sabiri tradition. The Mujaddidi–Naqshbandi order was introduced there by Saiyid Shah 'Alam-Allah (d. 1684), great-grandfather of the famed early-nineteenth-century revivalist and jihadist Saiyid Ahmad Shahid. Shah 'Alam-Allah met and became the *murid* and *khalifa* of Sirhindi's noted disciple

---

[122] Jalibi, *Tarikh-e Urdu Adab,* Vol. 2, p. 723, citing Khwaja Mir Dard, *Ah-i Sard,* Matba' al-Ansar, 1308 H/1890. The words *gulshan, wahdat,* and *gul* allude here to Sa'ad-Allah Gulshan, 'Abd al-Ahad Wahdat, and his Hindavi pen-name Gul.

Shaikh Adam Binori in Lahore in the later years of Shah Jahan's reign. He established a Mujaddidi Sufi centre near his hometown in Rai Bareli, in the neighbourhood of Lucknow, defended and enthusiastically propagated his master's brand of Sufism, and challenged the entrenched position of the Chishti–Sabiris in Awadh. Later, when Binori migrated to the Hijaz, he came close to the Sirhindi family, and one of his grandsons became a *khalifa* of Shaikh Muhammad Ma'sum's son Shaikh Muhammad Siddiq.[123]

It is clear that Aurangzeb's patronage helped build up the Naqshbandis in India after they had passed time in the political wilderness.[124] Significant here is the response of Shah Kalim-Allah Shahjahanabadi (d. 1729), the great Chishti saint of his time in Delhi, to a complaint he received from his disciple Shaikh Nizam al-Din Aurangabadi (d.1730), whom he had deputed to represent and propagate his teachings in the Deccan (Aurangabad) to Mughal nobles in the imperial camp. Shaikh Nizam's complaint was that the Mughals under Prince Muhammad A'zam had resisted his efforts to gain access to the nobles. As an example he said about two or three hundred men under the prince prevented him and his disciples from performing the *zikr-i jahr* (loud litanies, peculiar to the Chishti order) in the Jami' mosque. In reply, Shah Kalim-Allah advised him to maintain caution, not to express his anger over the denial; it was advisable (*mauzu', khub, be-sawab aqrab*) for him to conduct the silent litanies and meditation (*zikr-i khafi wa muraqaba*) preferred by Naqshbandis in the prime hours of the day, and in the morning and early evening (*ruzi tamam . . . wa dar tarfai al-nihar*). For, Shah Kalim-Allah said, while the Naqshbandis disputed the legitimacy of the Chishti practice of loud litanies, it behoved Chishtis not to question the sublimity of rituals preferred

---

[123] al-Hasani, *Tazkira-i Hazrat Saiyid Shah*, pp. 38–40, 42–3, 65, 70, 73, 81, 87, 120–3, and 145–6.

[124] This does not mean that Aurangzeb had no connection whatsoever with the Chishtis. There is some evidence of Aurangzeb's relations with and visits to the Chishti shrine of Ajmer, and he is buried in a Chishti shrine. See Moini, "The City of Ajmer"; Rice and Sen, "Visiting Ajmer Sharif".

by other orders. Kalim-Allah was thus suggesting that his plaintive deputy adhere to what was politic.

Kalim-Allah also gave another reason for his advice. Shaikh Nizam had been connected with the Naqshbandi order and thus had the authority to conduct their rituals as well *(shuma tariqa-i Naqshbandiya niz darind, ihmal-i u chira rawa mi darid khususan mardum-i Turaniha ra hamin az silsila-i Naqshbandiya musharraf mi sakhta bashand)*. While characterising some of the Mughals who had misbehaved with Shaikh Nizam as nothing less than "Pharaonic" (*Fir'auniyan*) in their comportment, the underlying reason for Shah Kalim-Allah's advice in favour of discretion to ensure the success of his mission was undoubtedly the unprecedented power of the Naqshbandi order under Aurangzeb.[125] He says:

> The Emperor of Hindustan is a descendant of Amir Timur, who was a devout follower of Khwaja Baha al-Din Naqshband (*iradat-i tamam dasht*). The Emperor thus [too] is very close to the Naqshbandi order ... The Turanis, each and every one of them, are connected with the Naqshbandi order and it is for this reason that the order is so widespread today (*imruz tariqa-i Naqshbandiya ... bisyar sha'i' ast*). They are familiar with only the Naqshbandi rituals and practice, they have no value for any other *silsila*.[126]

The great Chishti shaikh's response – and meagre consolation – from Delhi to his eminent disciple Shaikh Nizam al-Din in the Deccan, reveals his avowed helplessness in winning over Mughal nobles to Chishti Sufi doctrines and practices.

Shah Kalim-Allah Shahjahanabadi does not choose here to recall his own Chishti order's close connections with the earlier Mughals. Not much mention is made of the relations of Akbar, Jahangir, Shah Jahan, Dara Shukoh, and Jahanara with Chishti and Qadiri saints. True, the emperor Muhammad Shah had differences with Shaikh Zubair on some serious matters. But the Mughal

[125] Shahjahanabadi, *Maktubat-i Kalimi*, Letter 6, pp. 13–15; Letter 7, p. 16.
[126] Ibid., Letter 7, p. 14; Letter 72, p. 67.

emperor of the day did not have Akbar or Shah Jahan's power to change the Mughal royal house's spiritual orientation. Shah Kalim-Allah's mission to revive the power of his order was thus to try winning over the commoner class of people. He explained to Shaikh Nizam that his aim of overtures to state officials (*ahl-i duwal*) was not so that they would scale high spiritual stages or become true Chishtis or fall into trances during *sama'* and *raqs* assemblies. Instead, "The real purpose is that because of their entrance (*dukhul*) in the [Chishti] order, it will acquire an enhanced value in the eyes of people in general, and they will then be attracted to join it." The strategy was to gain the support of non-Turanis and other such – of people not necessarily associated with the state. The idea of success had now shifted, and the shift shows by implication the power of the Naqshbandis in the court and beyond it.[127]

---

[127] For the Chishtis in Delhi in the eighteenth century under Shah Kalim-Allah and his disciples, such as Shaikh Fakhr al-Din, son of Shaikh Nizam al-Din (d. 1785), see Rizvi, *A History of Sufism*, Vol. 2, pp. 296–308; and Nizami, *Tarikh-i Masha'ikh-i Chisht*, Vol. 5, pp. 105–50 and 185–249. Nizami writes (p. 224) that Shaikh Fakhr al-Din reinstated the Chishti order in the royal palace too.

Conclusion

For a dynasty extinguished over a century and a half ago, the Mughals continue to play an important part in South Asia's everyday life. We regularly encounter traces of the monuments they built – from Lahore, Delhi, and Agra, all the way to Dhaka, Cuttack, and Aurangabad. The literature they patronised is still read and sometimes sung, and the heritage of their administrative institutions, even if modified by British intervention, persists in attenuated shapes in the post-Independence states of the region. The Mughals are still at the heart of several discussions and disputes integral to cultural politics today, whether because of Bollywood films about them or controversies arising out of political efforts to efface them. For such reasons it is obvious that every serious reader of South Asia's history must come to terms with the Mughals and their heritage, and acknowledge that proper understanding is an alternative to clichés about a virtuous Akbar and a villainous Aurangzeb.

One of the key problems with popular representations of the Mughals is people neglecting the fact that, since this dynasty flourished between the sixteenth and eighteenth centuries, it existed at a time very different from our own. Mughal preoccupations and mentalities were in several respects quite obviously not ours. As historians we must see the differences and try to read our sources accordingly to understand their nature, carefully weighing questions of both distance and proximity.

Let us take a few examples. The legendary and immortal Khwaja Khizr (or "Green Prophet"), considered to be the regular guide of Sufis in their search for truth, figured significantly even in royal Mughal life. The Mughals revered him and believed in his presence and powers. In his memoirs, Jahangir says he visited the house of Asaf Khan on 30 January 1617 to celebrate the special feast in the name of Khwaja Khizr (*jashn-i Khwaja Khizr*, also called Khizri).[1] Later, in 1654, during their visit to Ajmer, Shah Jahan and his son Dara Shukoh are reported to have had a vision of Khwaja Khizr in the neighbourhood of the shrine of Shaikh Muʿin al-Din Chishti.[2] In another text, by ʿAbd al-Sattar ibn Qasim Lahori, Jahangir is reported to have looked for some perspicacious Sufis to interpret a dream he saw early in his reign. The emperor stated that in this dream he saw a huge crowd in the city of Lahore, collected near a tall tower at the shores of a turbulent river. On top of the tower stood a powerful angelic man – whom he could not see clearly because he was behind a thin cloud – holding two green ropes with iron hooks fixed at their lower ends, dangling from his right and left sides. Those from the crowd on the ground caught in the hooks were thrown into the river, where a big amphibious creature caught them and carried them off into deeper water, even as they writhed and lamented piteously. It struck Jahangir that the two sides of the river were heaven and hell. He saw his father and late brothers on the right side, that is to say in heaven, whereupon he beseeched the angelic man to take him to them. But the man declined his request because, he said, he had not yet been ordered to do so. Jahangir then withdrew his request, believing this a vision of the Angel of Death (*malak al-maut*). Next evening, ʿAbd al-Sattar reports, as the emperor related the dream over his usual nocturnal meeting, he was congratulated by some of the religious men present for having had the vision and was told that it simply meant he would live a long life. Far from being satisfied with their response, Jahangir found it inadequate and lamented that in his own time there remained no devout man (*khuda-parast, khuda-shinas, asrar-dan*) equal to Shaikh Jalal Thanesari, Shaikh Nizam Amethi, Shaikh

---

[1] See Jahangir, *Toozuk-i Jahangeeree*, p. 173.
[2] See Beach and Koch, *King of the World*, Plate 42, for an illustration.

Nizam Narnauli, or Shaikh Salim Chishti, who had lived in his father's time and would have provided a cogent interpretation of his dream.³

It seems that for the Mughal ruler his dream life was as important as his waking one – a notable difference between life in Mughal times and ours. And this then should make us remember that both Khwaja Khizr and dream interpretation had close connections with Sufism (or *tasawwuf*), which in Mughal India was not simply the path of belonging to the world beyond. Rather, as the princess Jahanara pointed out, Sufism was very considerably this-worldly as well, and regarded as a source of stability and strength for the everyday affairs of the human world. Sufism was seen to organise the warp and weft of Muslim life, including life and politics at the court and in the royal household during the Mughal era. But approaches to *tasawwuf*, as I tried to show in the Introduction, did not remain the same in post-Mughal times.

The central purpose of this book has been to examine how Sufis impacted this-worldly life in Mughal India. It has shown the complex and varied relationship between Mughal rulers, nobles, and royal households with Sufi shaikhs in order to understand both how this relationship shaped Mughal politics and how politics in turn influenced Sufi discourses. The Sufis I have chosen to focus on belonged in the main to three dominant *silsilas*: the Naqshbandi–Mujaddidis, who were centred around a more conservative or orthodox understanding of *shari'a* and *sunna*; and the Chishti–Sabiris and Qadiris who were committed to a more accommodating and eclectic approach to spirituality. Historians have generally discussed the question of the Mughal–Sufi equation with reference to the Naqshbandi order, and devoted particular attention to Shaikh Ahmad Sirhindi (d. 1624), the founder of the Mujaddidi branch of that order – as well as to his disciples and his ideology – revolving around the extent and nature of their

---

³ Lahori, *Majalis-i Jahangiri*, pp. 26–8.

influence on seventeenth-century Mughal Indian politics. There is no denying the importance of this debate, as I have suggested in the preceding pages. But it is also my contention that we would be in a better position to re-evaluate such questions if we did not limit discussion to the Naqshbandi shaikhs.

For this reason I began the book with a review of the careers, politics, and ideology of some of the Chishti–Sabiri Sufis who occupied a prominent position in the social and cultural life of Indian Muslims in the early-sixteenth century, when the Mughals began their conquest of northern India and progressively consolidated power. We saw that while the worldview of the Naqshbandis, who had just come from Central Asia, did not fit too well with the emerging Mughal vision of power, the dynasty found a strong basis of support for itself in the Chishti ideology. As a consequence the Chishtis held the edge at the time of Akbar in the second half of the sixteenth century.

Notwithstanding claims in the Naqshbandi shaikhs' hagiographical accounts, they enjoyed no distinct position at the court, nor among the Mughal Indian nobility (*umara*) – let alone the status of royal *pirs* – even in the time of Jahangir and Shah Jahan. During the time of Aurangzeb (r. 1658–1707), however, they came to be far more firmly installed in the court and royal household. Here I refer to the principal Indian branch of the *silsila*, which was begun by Khwaja Baqi-Billah (d. 1603), being strengthened and expanded under the leadership of his disciple Shaikh Ahmad Sirhindi, who is generally remembered in South Asian Islamic literature as "Mujaddid-i Alf-i Sani" (Renewer of Islam in the Second Millennium). Nevertheless, throughout the seventeenth century and even later, Sirhindi's high spiritual position did not go unchallenged. A significant group of orthodox Sunni divines disputed the validity of his views on some critical religious issues. Despite this opposition, the Sirhindi Naqshbandis continued in their endeavour to gain the status that the Ahrari Naqshbandis had once enjoyed in Central Asia. Undeterred by the relative indifference of kings and nobles, they continued to expand and fortify their position in society. On the other hand, Naqshbandis from other branches – such as Khwaja Khawand Mahmud in Kashmir, the Dehbedis and Juibaris, and much later Baba Shah Musafir in Aurangabad – did enjoy patronage from the Mughal court and became close with certain nobles.

The Chishtis, who were close to the court during the period, for their part supported the Mughals in various aspects of their politics, particularly their policy of *sulh-i kull* (Peace towards All). This policy fitted well with the Mughal notion of building a wide base of support with many distinct constituents. For example, from the middle of the sixteenth century they depended heavily on Iranian support and adopted Persian as their preferred language. They usually tried not to exacerbate sectarian differences or conflicts with the Hindus, building on a pragmatic tradition partly inherited from foregoing Delhi sultans. In my earlier work I have remarked on an anecdote concerning how, in the early-thirteenth century, Sultan Shams al-Din Iltutmish, in response to a delegation of the *'ulama* who asked him to deal with vanquished Hindus uncompromisingly in accordance with the *shari'a*, replied that Muslim presence in India was still like salt in a dish, that is, rather minimal. The observation can be said to have been applicable virtually unchanged under the Mughals.

This book has gone in some depth into the views of an eminent seventeenth-century Chishti shaikh, 'Abd al-Rahman Chishti, whose interventions were ambitious and wide-ranging. A principal point of contention between Sunnis and Shi'is was the question of 'Ali's position, and his succession to the *khilafat* following the death of the Prophet. Shaikh 'Abd al-Rahman's views on him were close to what the Mughals would have preferred, that is, Chishti claimed the need to differentiate two fundamental features of the prophethood of the Prophet Muhammad: *wilayat* and *nubuwwat*. Muhammad was a *nabi*, the messenger of God, but also a *wali*, that is a friend of God. 'Abd al-Rahman thus proposed that while Abu Bakr, the first legitimate successor according to the Sunnis, was the first *khalifa* (deputy, successor) of Muhammad in his role as the *nabi*, ʿAli was the first to succeed him as a *wali*. He approvingly cited the *hadith* in which the Prophet addressed ʿAli and said: "You are for me as Harun was for Musa. The only difference is that there will not be a prophet after me." He also invoked several opinions of past Sunni scholars in support of the Shiʿi view of the existence of a promised Mahdi. Such a reading of the past facilitated conditions that could diminish the conflict between Sunnis and Shiʿis. Time and again, ʿAbd al-Rahman came up with creative solutions that were both plausible and offered something to both sides in a dispute, even while maintaining his own inherited identity in the complex religious, social, and political space of Mughal India. It seems to me that he thus tried most imaginatively to construct bridges between various groups of Hindus and Muslims and their beliefs and ideologies. Since he viewed the beliefs of Hindus and Muslims as multi-stranded, it was also possible for him to point to convergences across specific strands.

In ʿAbd al-Rahman Chishti's understanding, real Sufis were those who were accepting of all who said the *kalima* and turned their face towards Allah. He also argued that the Sufi *mazhab* was not strictly confined to the traditional schools of jurisprudence. True Sufis, in his conception, were above distinctions between the schools of jurisprudence and concerned only with proper conduct – which to him was the true *shariʿa*. Rather than seeking to fulfil their own desires, Sufis should seek out interactions with a variety of God's creatures within a balanced Islamic approach. ʿAbd al-Rahman sought support for his position by quoting verses from Rumi's *masnawi* and following Rumi even further, claiming he was at one with all seventy-two Muslim sects. In the prevailing circumstances of Mughal India, this was an intriguing representation of Sunni Islam.

ʿAbd al-Rahman Chishti's stand also gained support from another Sufi *silsila*, the Qadiris. In the Mughal prince Dara Shukoh's life and writings we have an excellent manifestation of their ideas and worldview. I have therefore discussed Dara Shukoh's views with special reference to his translation of a Hindu text, the *Yoga-vasistha*, which comprises a conversation between Vasistha Muni and the god Rama. Dara Shukoh read this text not simply as a book on Vedanta but saw Rama as an ideal king through whom he visualised his own future.

The Mughals thus continued to search for ideals of kingship far beyond the *shari'a*. The Nasirean conception of ethics was taken as a model by the early Mughals, and Jahangir even showed interest in European norms of kingship.[4] It has been suggested that prince Murad Bakhsh showed interest in the administration under the Sassanian ruler Khusrau-Anushirwan (r. 531–79) and commissioned a Persian translation, *Tauqi'at-i Kisrawi*, by Jalal al-Din Tabataba'i of an earlier Arabic version of a relevant Pahlawi text.[5] The Mughals were certainly keen to understand norms of governance in other cultures. But few of them went as far as Dara Shukoh, who showed persistent interest in Indic theories of kingship and how they might serve as a model to be followed in Mughal India. His effort was quite unprecedented. Not even Akbar went so far as to see the Mahabharata as a model for Mughal political governance; he was curious about it, and made an effort to understand it, but not to follow it.[6] Dara Shukoh's interest in Rama's career was moreover because he wished to show that a man of God, as he saw his own self, could also be an ideal ruler. Dara Shukoh's Qadiri connections thus enabled him to see in the Hindu world many important things that could be appropriated to draw Hindus closer to the world of Mughal Islam. He thus writes that his translation of the Upanishads was inspired by his close spiritual association with his *pir* Mulla Shah Badakhshi.[7]

---

[4] Alam and Subrahmanyam, "Mediterranean Exemplars", pp. 105–29.

[5] Manuscripts may be found in the Staatsbibliothek zu Berlin and the Bodleian Library, Oxford (Ethé-Bodleian 1470). Several lithograph versions from the nineteenth century, printed in Kolkata and Lucknow, also exist.

[6] In this my understanding differs from that of Truschke, *Culture of Encounters*.

[7] Dara Shukoh, *Sirr-i Akbar*, Preface.

I have also tried to show in this book a significant feature of the Qadiri order's involvement in Mughal politics through an examination of the princess Jahanara's interest in Qadiri Sufism. In turn, through the career of another princess, Roshanara, I have shown the Naqshbandi–Mujaddidi Sufis' evolving stand with regard to women, perhaps because the princess held such a high position in the royal household under Aurangzeb. Yet another Mughal princess, Zeb-un-Nisa' – an accomplished poet in her own right – also had, I argue, her own distinct conception of the relationship between the worlds of court, politics, and Sufis.

All in all, my effort through the preceding chapters has been to highlight some notable features of Mughal politics by studying a wide range of sources, court chronicles, and narrative works on the one hand, and Sufi texts on the other. In this I have tried to carry throughout my conviction that Sufism cannot be studied simply as an esoteric doctrine, but that it must be comprehended as a social force deeply connected with the everyday as well as with political life.

A number of excellent studies of Sufis in Mughal India have appeared over the years, but the complexity, variety, and nuances of relations between Mughal political elites and Sufis have not seen close critical attention. The compartmentalisation of academic disciplines, and the distance between historians on the one hand and scholars of religion on the other, have perhaps been reasons for this gap in the existing literature. Historians of Mughal India have traditionally worked within a paradigm that champions political and fiscal history over other possibilities. As a consequence, over the last century they have not paid much attention to *tasawwuf* and its entwinement with Mughal politics. This book is an attempt to address the absence in the hope that future historians will pay more attention to many texts which their predecessors have too often set aside as hagiographical accounts not worthy of examination alongside "secular" political chronicles, memoirs, travel accounts, and epistolary collections. We are still very far from the time when the last word will have been said about the relationship between the Mughals and the Sufis of their time.

Bibliography

A'zam, Muhammad, *Maktubat-i Khwaja Muhammad Saif al-Din*, compiled by Muhammad A'zam (son of Khwaja Saif al-Din), ed. with an Introduction by Ghulam Mustafa Khan, available online at Marfat.com.

'Abbasi, Mustafa ibn Khaliqabad, *Darya-i Asmar: Tarjuma-i Kathasaritsagar*, ed. Tara Chand and Amir Hasan Abidi, Aligarh, 1954, rpntd New Delhi, 1997.

Abidi, S.A.H., "Diwan-i Hafiz: Nuskha-i Shahan-i Mughaliya", *Qand-e-Parsi* 11 (Zamistan 1375 / December 1996–March 1997).

Abu al-Fazl, *A'in-i Akbari*, ed. Syed Ahmad Khan, rpntd Aligarh, 2005; English translation by H.S. Jarrett, ed. Jadunath Sarkar, rpntd Delhi, 2008.

Abu al-Fazl, *Akbarnama*, ed. Agha Ahmad Ali and Abdur Rahim, Calcutta: Bibliotheca Indica, 1873.

Abu al-Fazl, *Akbarnama*, trans. H. Beveridge, rpntd Delhi: Low Price Publications, 2002.

Abu al-Fazl, *Akbarnama*, Vol. I, ed. Agha Ahmad 'Ali and 'Abdur Rahim, Calcutta: Asiatic Society, 1877; English trans. H. Beveridge, Delhi: Low Price Publications, rpntd 2002.

Abu al-Hasan, *Minhaj al-Salikin, Tarjuma-i Jogbasisht* [of Dara Shukoh], Lucknow: Nawal Kishor, 1898; rpntd Patna: Khuda Bakhsh Oriental Public Library, 1992.

Addas, Claude, *The Quest for the Red Sulphur: The Life of Ibn Arabi*, Cambridge: The Islamic Text Society, 1993.

Ahmad, Aziz, *Studies in Islamic Culture in the Indian Environment*, Oxford: Oxford University Press, 1964.

Ahmad, Shamsuddin, *Hazrat Khwaja Naqshband aur Tariqat-i Naqshbandiya* (in Urdu), Srinagar: Gulshan Publishers, 2001.

Ahmad, Zubaid, *The Contribution of India to Arabic Literature from Ancient Times to the Indian Mutiny of 1857*, Allahabad: Dikshit Press, 1946; rpntd Lahore: Sh. Muhammad Ashraf, 1967.

Aiyar, K. Narayanaswami, trans., *Laghu Yogavasishtha*, 1st edn, Madras: Thomson, 1896; rpntd Madras: Adyar Library and Research Centre, 1971.

Akimushkin, O.F., "A Rare Seventeenth Century Hagiography of the Naqshbandiyya-Mujaddiyya", *Manuscripta Orientalia: International Journal for Oriental Manuscript Research, Institute of Oriental Studies*, St Petersburg, Vol. 7, Issue 1, March 2001.

Alam, Absar, *Mujaddid-i Alf-i Sani ki Ihya-i Tahrik-i Islam aur Salatin-i Mughaliya* (Mujaddidi Alf-i Sani's Movement for the Renovation of Islam and the Mughal Kings), Lahore: Hira Publications, 1989.

Alam, Muzaffar, *Crisis of Empire in Mughal North India: Awadh and the Punjab*, 1986; rpntd Delhi: Oxford University Press, 2013.

Alam, Muzaffar, "Maulana Azad and the Memory of India's Islamic Past", paper presented at the Maulana Azad Institute, Kolkata, July 2012.

Alam, Muzaffar, "Mughal Philology and Rumi's *Mathnawi*", in Sheldon Pollock, Benjamin Elman, and Ku-ming Kevin Chang, eds, *World Philology*, Cambridge, MA: Harvard University Press, 2015.

Alam, Muzaffar, "The Debate Within: A Sufi Critique of Religious Law, *Tasawwuf*, and Politics in Mughal India", in Rosalind O'Hanlon and David Washbrook, eds, *Religious Cultures in Early Modern India: New Perspectives*, London, 2011; revised version above, Chapter 3.

Alam, Muzaffar, *The Languages of Political Islam*, Ranikhet: Permanent Black, and Chicago: University of Chicago Press, 2004.

Alam, Muzaffar, "The Mughals, the Sufi Shaikhs, and the Formation of the Akbari Dispensation", *Modern Asian Studies* 43, No. 1 (2009).

Alam, Muzaffar, and Sanjay Subrahmanyam, *Indo-Persian Travels in the Age of Discoveries, 1400–1800*, Cambridge: Cambridge University Press, 2007.

Alam, Muzaffar, and Sanjay Subrahmanyam, "Mediterranean Exemplars: Jesuit Political Lessons for a Mughal Emperor", in Lucio Biasiori and Giuseppe Marcocci, ed., *Machiavelli, Islam and the East: Reorienting the Foundations of Modern Political Thought*, London: Palgrave Macmillan, 2018.

Alam, Muzaffar, and Sanjay Subrahmanyam, *Writing the Mughal World*, Ranikhet: Permanent Black, and New York: Columbia University Press, 2011.

Alam, Muzaffar, Françoise Nalini Delvoye, and Marc Gaborieau, eds, *The Making of Indo–Persian Culture: Indian and French Studies,* Delhi: Manohar, 2000.

Alavi, Seema, *Muslim Cosmopolitanism in the Age of Empire*, Cambridge MA: Harvard University Press, 2015.

Algar, Hamid, "A Brief History of the Naqshbandi Order", in Marc Gaborieau, Alexandre Popovic, and Thierry Zarcone, eds, *Naqshbandis: Historical Developments and Present Situation of a Muslim Mystical Order*, Istanbul-Paris: Institut Français d'Etudes Anatoliennes d'Istanbul, 1990.

Algar, Hamid, "Political Aspects of Naqshbandi History", in Marc Gaborieau, Alexandre Popovic, and Thierry Zarcone, eds, *Naqshbandis: Historical Developments and Present Situation of a Muslim Mystical Order*, Istanbul-Paris: Institut Français d'Etudes Anatoliennes d'Istanbul, 1990.

Algar, Hamid, "The Naqshbandi Order: A Preliminary Survey of Its History and Significance", *Studia Islamica*, Vol. 44 (1976).

Ali, M. Athar, *Mughal India: Studies in Polity, Ideas, Society*, Delhi: Oxford University Press, 2006.

Ali, M. Athar, *The Mughal Nobility under Aurangzeb,* revised edition, Delhi: Oxford University Press, 1987.

'Ali, Muhammad Akram bin Shaikh Muhammad, *Sawati' al-Anwar,* British Library, India Office manuscripts, Ethé 654 (I.O. Islamic 2705).

'Ali, Ni'mat Khan-i, *Waqa'i'-i Ni'mat Khan-i 'Ali,* Lucknow: Nawalkishor, 1928.

Amin, Shahid, *Conquest and Community: The Afterlife of Warrior Saint Ghazi Miyan*, Chicago: University of Chicago Press, 2015.

Amin, Shahid, "On Retelling the Muslim Conquest of India", in Partha Chatterjee and Anjan Ghosh, eds, *History and the Present*, New Delhi: Permanent Black, 2002.

Amin, Shahid, "Un Saint Guerrier: Sur la conquete de l'inde du Nord par les Turcs au XI siècle", *Annales: Histoire, Sciences Sociales* 60, No. 2 (March–April 2005).

Amma, Visweswari. *Udayana and His Philosophy*, Delhi, 1985.

'Andalib, Khwaja Muhammad Nasir, *Nala-i' Andalib,* Bhopal: Matba'e Shahjahani, Vol. 1, 1308 H/1891, Vol. 2, 1310 H/1893.

Ansari, Muhammad Abdul Haq, *Sufism and Shari'ah: A Study of Shaykh Ahmad Sirhindi's Efforts to Reform Sufism*, Leicester: The Islamic Foundation, 1986.
Ansari, N.H., *Chronicles of the Siege of Golkonda Fort (An Abridged Translation of the Waqa'i' of Ni'mat Khan-i 'Ali)*, Delhi: Idarah-i Adabiyat-i Delli, 1975.
Ansari, Nurul Hasan, *Farsi adab be-'ahd-e Aurangzeb*, Delhi: Indo-Persian Society, 1969.
Ansari, Nurul Hasan, "*Lata'if al-Lughat*', in M.H. Siddiqi, ed., *The Growth of Indo-Persian Literature in Gujarat*, Baroda: Department of Persian, Arabic & Urdu, University of Baroda, 1985.
Aquil, Raziuddin, *Sufism, Culture and Politics: Afghans and Islam in Medieval North India*, Delhi: Oxford University Press, 2007.
Arzu, Siraj al-Din 'Ali Khan, *Majma' al-Nafayis*, Khuda Bakhsh Oriental Public Library, Patna, Ms. H.L. No. 237, fls 23b, 36b, and 180.
Aslam, Muhammad, *Muslim Conduct of State*, Islamabad: University of Islamabad Press, 1974.
'Attar, Farid al-Din, *Asrar-nama*, ed. Muhammad Riza Shafi'i Kadkani, Tehran, 2009.
'Attar, Farid al-Din, *Musibat-nama*, ed. Nurani Visal, Tehran, 1994.'
'Attar, Farid al-Din, *Ushtur-nama*, ed. Mahdi Muhaqqiqi, Tehran, 1961.
Azad, Abul Kalam, *Sufi Sarmad Shahid*, rpntd from Khwaja Hasan Nizami's journal *Nizamul Mashaikh*, Hyderabad: Abul Kalam Research Institute, 1986.
Azmi, Shoaib, "Hikayat-i az Hafiz-i Shiraz dar Sahna-i Razm wa Bazm-i Timuriyan", *Qand-e-Parsi* 16 (Zamistan 1380 / December 2001–March 2002).
Babur, Zahir al-Din Muhammad, *Baburnama*, English translation by A.S. Beveridge, Delhi: Oriental Reprints, 1970.
Babur, Zahir al-Din Muhammad, *Baburnama*, English translation by Wheeler M. Thackston, New York: Modern Library, 2002.
Bada'uni, 'Abd al-Qadir, *Muntakhab al-Tawarikh*, ed. Tofigh H. Sobhani, Tehran: Asar wa Mafakhir-i Farhangi, 3 vols, 1379-80 Sh. / 2000–1, Vol. 2.
Bada'uni, 'Abd al-Qadir, *Muntakhab al-Tawarikh*, ed. Kabiruddin Ahmad, Ahmad 'Ali, and W.N. Lees, Calcutta: Bibliotheca Indica, 1869, Vol. III.

Bada'uni, 'Abd al-Qadir, *Najat al-Rashid*, Lahore: Idara-i Tahqiqat-i Pakistan, Danishgah-i Panjab, 1972.

Baghdadi, Muhammad ibn Sulaiman, *Al-Hadiqat al-Nadiya fi al-Tariqat al-Naqshbandiya,* Urdu translation by Sultan Ahmad Afghani, revised by Shahzad Mujaddidi Saifi, Lahore: Dar al-Ikhlas, 2000.

Baljon, J.M.S., *Religion and Thought of Shah Wali-Allah Dihlawi, 1703–1762,* Leiden: E.J. Brill, 1986.

Balkhi (al-), Abu-Zaid Ahmed bin Sahl, *Kitab al-Bada'a wa al-Tarikh*, ed. Marie-Clement Huart, Paris, 1901.

Baqi-Billah, Khwaja Muhammad, *Kulliyat-i Baqi-Billah*, ed. Abul Hasan Zaid Faruqi and Burhan Ahmad Faruqi, Lahore: Din Muhammad and Sons, n.d.

Barbir, Karl A., "All in the Family: The Muradis of Damascus", in Heath W. Lowry and Ralph Hattox, eds, *Congress on the Social and Economic History of Turkey,* Princeton, 1983.

Bashir, Aamir, "*Shari'at* and *Tariqat*: A Study of the Deobandi Understanding and Practice of *Tasawwuf*", Unpublished M.A. dissertation, International Islamic University, Malaysia, 2010.

Beach, Milo C., and Ebba Koch, *King of the World: The Padshanama, an Imperial Mughal Manuscript from the Manuscript Library, Windsor Castle*, London: Thames and Hudson, 1997.

Berkey, Jonathan P., *Popular Preaching and Religious Authority in the Medieval Islamic Near East*, Seattle, WA: University of Washington, 2001.

Bernier, François, *Travels in the Mogul Empire, 1656–1668*, revsd edn, based on Irving Brock's translation, by Archibald Constable, London: Oxford University Press, 1916; repntd Delhi: Chand, 1972.

Bhagavata Purana, Persian translation attributed to Faizi Fayyazi, MSIO Islamic 1544 and IO Islamic 452, Asian and African Collection (formerly Oriental and India Office Collections), British Library, London.

Bhattacarya, France, "Hari the Prophet: An Islamic View of a Hindu God in Saiyid Sultan's *Nabi Vansa*", in Perween Hasan and Mufakharul Islam, eds, *Essays in Memory of Mumtazur Rahman Tarafdar*, Dhaka, 1999.

Bhavishya Purana, with Hindi translation by Shri Ram Sharma, Bareilly, UP, in two volumes, 1967–8.

Bilgrami, Mir 'Abd al-Wahid, *Haqa'iq-i Hindi*, trans. S.A.A. Rizvi, Kashi: Nagari Pracharini Sabha, 2014 V.S. / 1957.
Bilgrami, Mir 'Abd al-Wahid, *Sab' Sanabil*, Urdu translation by Muhammad Khalil Barakati, Bheondi, Maharashtra: Rizwi Kitabghar, 1981.
Bilgrami, Mir Ghulam 'Ali Azad, *Ma'asir al-Kiram*, ed. Maulavi 'Abdul Haq, Hyderabad, 1913.
Binbaş, Ilker Evrim, *Intellectual Networks in Timurid Iran: Sharaf al-Din Yazdi and the Islamicate Republic of Letters*, Cambridge: Cambridge University Press, 2016.
Binbaş, Ilker Evrim, "Sharf al-Din Ali Yazdi (*ca.* 770s–858 / *ca.* 1370s–1445): Prophecy, Politics, and Historiography in Late Medieval Islamic History", PhD thesis, University of Chicago, 2009.
Bladel, Kevin van, "The Astrological Current in the Formation of Islamic Historiography", unpublished paper presented at the University of Chicago, 10 February 2010.
Bokhari, Afshan, "Between Patron and Piety: Jahan Ara Begum's Sufi Affiliations and Articulations", in John J. Curry and Erik S. Ohlander, eds, *Sufism and Society: Arrangements of the Mystical in the Muslim World, 1200–1800 C.E.*, London and New York: Routledge, 2011.
Bokhari, Afshan, "Imperial Transgressions and Spiritual Investitures: A Begam's 'Ascension' in Seventeenth-Century Mughal India", *Journal of Persianate Studies*, Vol. 4, 2011.
Bokhari, Afshan, "Masculine Modes of Female Subjectivity: The Case of Jahanara Begam", in Anshu Malhotra and Siobhan Lambert-Hurley, eds, *Speaking of the Self: Gender, Performance and Autobiography in South Asia*, Durham: Duke University Press, 2015.
Bonazzoli, Giorgio, "Composition of the Puranas", *Purana*, Vol. 25 (2), 1983.
Bonazzoli, Giorgio, "Remarks on the Nature of the Puranas", *Purana*, Vol. 25 (1), 1983.
Buehler, Arthur F., "The Naqshbandiyya in Timurid India: The Central Asian Legacy", *Journal of Islamic Studies*, Vol. 7, No. 2 (1996).
Chanda, Avik, *Dara Shukoh: The Man Who Would be King*, Delhi: HarperCollins, 2019.
Chandra, Satish, *Parties and Politics at the Mughal Court 1707–1740*, rpntd Delhi: Oxford University Press, 2004.

Chekhovich, O.D., *Samarqand Documents*, Moscow, 1974.

Chishti, 'Abd al-Rahman, *Mir'at al-Asrar* (Urdu translation), trans. Wahid Baksh Sayyal Chishti Sabri, Lahore: Ziya al-Qur'an, 1993.

Chishti, 'Abd al-Rahman, *Mir'at al-Asrar*, MS. Or. 216, Asian and African Collections (formerly Oriental and India Office Collections), British Library, London.

Chishti, 'Abd al-Rahman, *Mir'at al-Makhluqat*, MS. Or. 1883, Asian and African Collections (formerly Oriental and India Office Collections), British Library, London.

Chishti, 'Abd al-Rahman, *Mir'at-i Madari*, British Museum, Add. Mss. 16,858.

Chishti, 'Abd al-Rahman, *Mir'at-i Madariya*, Aligarh Muslim University, Subhanallah MS 297/46.

Chishti, 'Abd al-Rahman, *Mir'at-i Mas'udi*, British Museum, Or. Mss. 1837.

Chishti, 'Abd al-Rahman, *Mir'at-i Mas'udi* (Urdu translation), trans. Muhammad Abd al-Ghani Shah Qadiri, as *Saulat-i Mas'udi*, Lucknow: Matba'-i 'Alavi, 1869.

Chittick, William C., *Imaginal Worlds: Ibn 'Arabi and the Problem of Religious Diversity*, Albany, 1994.

Chodkiewicz, Michel, *An Ocean Without Shore: Ibn 'Arabi, the Book and the Law*, trans. David Streight, Albany, NY: State University of New York Press, 1993.

Clooney, Francis X., "Evil, Divine Omnipotence and Human Freedom: Vedanta's Theology of Karma", *The Journal of Religion*, Vol. 69(4), 1989.

Corbin, Henry, *Creative Imagination in the Sufism of Ibn 'Arabi*, trans. Ralph Mannheim, Princeton, NJ: Princeton University Press, 1969.

Crollius, A. Ary Roest, "Reflections on the Majma'-al-Bahrayn of Dara Shukoh", in Christian W. Troll, ed., *Islam in India: Studies and Commentaries*, Delhi: Vikas, 1982.

Currie, P.M., *The Shrine and Cult of Mu'in al-Din Chishti of Ajmer*, Delhi: Oxford University Press, 1989.

Dahnhardt, Thomas, *Changes and Continuity in Indian Sufism: A Naqshbandi–Mujaddidi Branch in the Hindu Environment*, 2nd imp., New Delhi: D.K. Printworld Ltd, 2007.

Dale, Stephen F., "A Safavid Poet in the Heart of Darkness: The Indian Poems of Ashraf Mazandarani", *Iranian Studies*, Vol. 36, No. 2, 2003.

Dale, Stephen F., *The Garden of the Eight Paradises: Babur and the Culture of Empire in Central Asia, Afghanistan and India, 1483–1530*, Leiden: Brill, 2004.

Dale, Stephen F., "The Legacy of the Timurids", *Journal of the Royal Asiatic Society*, 3rd Series, Vol. 8, No. 1 (1998).

Dale, Stephen F., and Alam Payind, "The Ahrari Waqf in Kabul in the Year 1546 and the Mughul Naqshbandiyyah", *Journal of the American Oriental Society*, Vol. 119, No. 2 (1999).

Damrel, David W., "Forgotten Grace: Khwaja Khawand Mahmud Naqshbandi in Central Asia and Mughal India", Unpublished Ph.D. Dissertation, Department of Religion, Duke University, 1991.

Damrel, David W., "The 'Naqshbandi Reaction' Reconsidered", in David Gilmartin and Bruce Lawrence, eds, *Beyond Turk and Hindu: Rethinking Religious Identities in Islamicate South Asia*, Gainesville: University Press of Florida, 2000.

Dar, Bashir Ahmad, *A Study in Iqbal's Philosophy*, Lahore: Sh. M. Ashraf, 1944.

Dara Shukoh, *Hasanat al-'Arifin*, ed. S. Makhdum Amin, Tehran: Tahqiqat wa Intisharat-i Wessman, 1973.

Dara Shukoh, *Jugbashist*, ed. Tara Chand and S.A.H. Abidi, Aligarh: Aligarh Muslim University, 1968.

Dara Shukoh, *Majma 'ul-Bahrain*, ed. M. Mahfuz-ul-Haq, Calcutta, 1929.

Dara Shukoh, *Safinat al-Auliya'*, Lucknow: Nawal Kishor, 1872.

Dara Shukoh, *Sakinat al-Auliya'*, ed. Tara Chand and S.M. Riza Jalali Naini, Tehran: Elmi, 1953.

Dara Shukoh, *Sakinat al-Auliya'*, with Urdu translation by Maqbul Beg Badakhshani, Lahore: Packages Limited, 1971.

Dara Shukoh, *Sirr-i Akbar (Sirr-ul-Asrar)*, ed. Tara Chand and S.M. Riza Jalali Naini, Tehran: Taban, 1957.

Dasgupta, S.N., *A History of Indian Philosophy*, Cambridge: Cambridge University Press, 1922.

de Jong, Frederick, and Bernd Radke, eds, *Islamic Mysticism Contested: Thirteen Centuries of Controversies and Polemics*, Leiden: Brill, 1999.

Dehlavi, Shaikh 'Abd al-Haqq Muhaddis, *Maraj al-Bahrain*, Persian text edited with Urdu translation by Sana-ul Haqq Siddiqi, Karachi: Muhammad Ala, III/H 2/5, Nazimabad, 1968.

Dehlavi, Amir Hasan Sijzi, *Fawa'id al-Fu'ad*, Lucknow, 1885; translated by Bruce Lawrence, New York, 1992.

Dehlavi, Shah Ghulam 'Ali, *Makatib-i Sharifa*, Urdu translation by Muhammad Nazir Ranjha, Kandiyan: Khanqah-e Sirajiyya Naqshbandiyya Mujaddidiyya, 2009.

Dehlavi, Shaikh 'Abd al-Haqq Muhaddis, *Akhbar al-Akhyar*, Deoband: Kutubkhana Rahimiya, n.d.

Diagne, Souleyman Bachir, *Islam and Open Society: Fidelity and Movement in the Philosophy of Muhammad Iqbal*, trans. Melissa McMahon, Oxford: African Books Collective, 2010.

Digby, Simon, "'Abd al-Quddus Gangohi (1456–1537 CE): The Personality and Attitudes of a Medieval Indian Sufi", *Medieval India: A Miscellany*, 3 (1973).

Digby, Simon, "Dreams and Reminiscences of Dattu Sarvani, a Sixteenth Century Indo-Afghan Soldier" (in 2 parts), *The Indian Economic and Social History Review*, Vol. 2 (1965).

Digby, Simon, "Mas'udi", *Encyclopedia of Islam*, New Series, Leiden, Vol. VI, 1991.

Digby, Simon, *Sufis and Soldiers in Awrangzeb's Deccan: Malfuzat-i Naqshbandiyya by Baba Shah Mahmud*, Delhi: Oxford University Press, 2001.

Digby, Simon, "The Naqshbandis in the Deccan in the Late Seventeenth Century and Early Eighteenth Century AD: Baba Palangposh, Baba Musafir and their Adherents", in Marc Gaborieau, *et al.*, eds, *Naqshbandis: Historical Development and Present Situation of a Muslim Mystical Order*, Istanbul-Paris: Institut Français d'Etudes Anatoliennes d'Istanbul, 1990.

Digby, Simon, "The Sufi Shaikh and the Sultan: A Conflict of Claims to Authority", *Iran* 28 (1990).

D'Onofrio, Svevo, "A Persian Commentary to the Upanishads: Dara Shikoh's *Sirr-i Akbar*", in D. Hermann and F. Speziale, eds, *Muslim Cultures in the Indo-Iranian World during the Early-Modern and Modern Periods*, Berlin: Schwarz, 2010.

Doniger, Wendy, *Dreams, Illusions and Other Realities*, Chicago: University of Chicago Press, 1984.
Dughlat, Mirza Haidar, *A History of the Moghuls of Central Asia, Being the The Tarihk-i Rashidi of Mirza Haidar Dughlat*, trans. E. Denison Ross, London: Curzon Press; New York: Barnes and Noble, rpntd 1972.
Dughlat, Mirza Haidar, *Tarikh-i Rashidi*, Persian text edited by Wheeler M. Thackston, Cambridge, MA: Harvard University Press, 1996.
Elias, Jamal J., *The Throne Carrier of God: The Life and Thought of 'Ala ad-Dawla as-Simnani*, Albany, NY: State University of New York Press, 1995.
Ernst, Carl, "Fayzi's Illuminationist Interpretation of Vedanta: *The Shariq al-Ma'rifa*", in Firoozeh Papan-Matin, ed., *The Indo-Persianate World*, special issue of *Comparative Studies of South Asia, Africa and the Middle East*, 30, No. 3 (2010).
Ernst, Carl W., "Muslim Studies of Hinduism? A Reconsideration of Arabic and Persian Translations of Indian Languages", *Iranian Studies*, Vol. 36, No. 2, (June 2003).
Ernst, Carl, "The Khuldabad–Burhanpur Axis and Local Sufism in the Deccan", in Anna Dallapiccola and Stephanie Lallemant, eds, *Islam and Indian Regions*, Stuttgart: Franz Steiner Verlag, 1993.
Ernst, Carl, and Bruce Lawrence, *Sufi Martyrs of Love: Chishti Sufism in South Asia and Beyond*, New York: Palgrave Macmillan, 2002.
Ethe, Carl Hermann, *Catalogue of Persian Manuscripts in the Library of the India Office*, Oxford, 1903.
Falasch, Ute, "Badi al-Din Shah Madar to Qazi Shihab al-Din Daulatabadi: An Epistle", in Søren Christian Lassen and Hugh van Skyhawk, eds, *Sufi Traditions and New Departures: Recent Scholarship on Continuity and Change in South Asian Sufism*, Islamabad: Taxila Institute of Asian Civilizations, Quaid-i-Azam University, 2008.
Falasch, Ute, "Badi' al-Din", in Kate Fleet, *et al.*, eds, *Encyclopedia of Islam,* 3rd edn, Leiden: Brill, 2009.
Falasch, Ute, *Heiligkeit und Mobilität: Die Madariyya Sufibruderschaft und ihr Gründer Badi' al-Din Shah Madar in Indien, 15.–19. Jahrhundert*, Berlin: Lit Verlag, 2015.
Falasch, Ute, "Islamic Mystic Tradition in India: The Madari Sufi Brotherhood", in Imtiaz Ahmad and Helmut Reifeld, eds, *Lived Islam in*

South Asia: Adaptation, Accommodation, and Conflict, Delhi: Social Science Press, 2004.

Fani Kashmiri, *Diwan-i Fani*, Srinagar: Matba' Mahbub-Shahi, n.d.

Fani Kashmiri, *Masnawiyat-i Fani*, ed. S.A.H. Abidi, Srinagar: Jammu and Kashmir Academy of Arts, Culture, and Languages, 1964.

Farman, Muhammad, *Iqbal aur Tasawwuf*, Lahore: Bazm-i Iqbal, 1958.

Farooqi, Naimur Rahman, *Medieval India: Essays on Sufism, Diplomacy, and History*, Allahabad: Laburnum Press, 2006.

Faroqhi, Suraiya, *The Ottoman and Mughal Empires: Social History in the Early Modern World*, London: I.B. Tauris, 2019.

Faruqi, Abu al-Hasan Zaid, *Hazrat Mujaddid aur unke Naqidin* (The Mujaddid and His Critics), Delhi: Shah Abu al-Khair Academy, 1977.

Faruqi, Burhan Ahmad, *The Mujaddid's Conception of Tauhid*, Lahore: Sh. Muhammad Ashraf, 1940.

Faruqui, Munis D., "Dara Shukoh, *Vedanta*, and Imperial Succession in Mughal India", in Vasudha Dalmia and Munis D. Faruqui, eds, *Religious Interactions in Mughal India*, Delhi: Oxford University Press, 2014.

Faruqui, Munis D., "The Forgotten Prince: Mirza Hakim and the Formation of the Mughal Empire in India", *Journal of the Economic and Social History of the Orient*, Vol. 48, No. 4 (2005).

Faruqui, Munis D., *The Princes of the Mughal Empire, 1504–1719*, Cambridge: Cambridge University Press, 2012.

Felek, Ozen and Alexander D. Knysh, *Dreams and Visions in Islamic Societies*, Albany, NY: SUNY Press, 2012.

Findiriski, Abu al-Qasim, *Muntakhab-i Jug Basisht* (Selections from the *Yoga-vasistha*), ed. Fathullah Mojtabai, Tehran: Iranian Institute of Philosophy, 2006.

Firishta, Muhammad Qasim Hindu Shah Astrabadi, *Tarikh-i Firishta*, ed. Mohammad Reza Ansari, Vol. 1, Tehran, 2009.

Firishta, Muhammad Qasim, *Tarikh-i Firishta*, Vol. I, Puna: Dar al-Imarah, 1247 AH/1832, Urdu trans., 'Abdul Hay Khwaja Deoband: Maktaba-i Millat, 1983.

Fleischer, Cornell, "Ancient Wisdom and New Sciences: Prophecies at the Ottoman Court in the Fifteenth and Early Sixteenth Centuries", in Massumeh Farhad and Serpil Bagci, eds, *Falnama: The Book of Omens*, Washington, DC: Arthur M. Sackler Gallery, Smithsonian Institute, 2009.

Foley, Sean, "The Naqshbandiyya-Khalidiyya Islamic Sainthood, and Religion in Modern Times", *Journal of World History*, Vol. 19, No. 4, 2008.

Foltz, Richard C., *Mughal India and Central Asia*, Karachi: Oxford University Press, 1998.

Friedmann, Yohanan, "The Naqshbandis and Aurangzeb: A Reconsideration", in Marc Gaborieau, *et al.*, eds, *Naqshbandis: Historical Development and Present Situation of a Muslim Mystical Order*, Istanbul-Paris: Institut Français d'Etudes Anatoliennes d'Istanbul, 1990.

Friedmann, Yohanan, *Shaykh Ahmad Sirhindi: An Outline of His Thought and a Study of His Image in the Eyes of Posterity*, Montreal: McGill University, 1971.

Friedmann, Yohanan, *Shaykh Ahmad Sirhindi: An Outline of His Thought and a Study of His Image in the Eyes of Posterity*, rpntd Delhi: Oxford University Press, 2000.

Fusfeld, Warren, "Naqshbandi Sufism and Reformist Islam", *Journal of Asian and African Studies*, Vol. 18, Nos 3–4, July–October,1983.

Gaborieau, Marc, "Criticising the Sufis: The Debate in Early-Nineteenth Century India", in Frederick de Jong and Bernd Radke, eds, *Islamic Mysticism Contested: Thirteen Centuries of Controversies and Polemics*, Leiden: Brill, 1999.

Gaborieau, Marc, *Le Mahdi incompris: Sayyid Ahmad Barelvi (1786–1831) et le millénarisme en Inde*, Paris: CNRS Editions, 2010.

Gaborieau, Marc, "Sufism in the First Wahhabi Manifesto: *Siratu'l Mustaqim* by Isma'il Shahid and 'Abdul Hayy", in Muzaffar Alam, Françoise Nalini Delvoye, and Marc Gaborieau, eds, *The Making of Indo–Persian Culture: Indian and French Studies*, Delhi: Manohar, 2000.

Gaborieau, Marc, Alexandre Popovic, and Thierry Zarcone, eds, *Naqshbandis: Historical Development and Present Situation of a Muslim Mystical Order*, Istanbul-Paris: Institut Français d'Etudes Anatoliennes d'Istanbul, 1990.

Gandhi, Supriya, "Mughal Self-Fashioning, Indic Self-Realization: Dara

Shikoh and Persian Textual Cultures in Early Modern South Asia", Ph.D. Dissertation, Harvard University, 2011.

Gandhi, Supriya, *The Emperor Who Never Was: Dara Shukoh in Mughal India*, Cambridge, MS: Belknap Press of Harvard University Press, 2020.

Gandhi, Supriya, "The Prince and the *Muvahhid*: Dara Shikoh and Mughal Engagements with *Vedanta*", in Vasudha Dalmia and Munis Faruqui, eds, *Religious Interactions in Mughal India*, Delhi: Oxford University Press, 2014.

Ghorab (al-), Mahmoud, "Muhyiddin Ibn al-'Arabi Amidst Religious (*adyan*) and Schools of Thought (*madhabib*)", in Stephen Hirtenstein and Michael Tiernan, eds, *Muhyiddin Ibn 'Arabi: A Commemorative Volume*, Shaftesbury: Element Books Limited, 1993.

Ghose, Rajarshi, "Politics of Faith: Karamat Ali Jaunpuri and Islamic Revivalist Movements in British India, *c.* 1800–73", Ph.D. Dissertation, University of Chicago, 2012.

Godlas, Alan, "Sufism", in Andrew Rippin, ed., *The Blackwell Companion to the Qur'an*, London, 2006.

Grafton, Anthony (with April Shelford and Nancy Siraisi), *New Worlds, Ancient Texts: The Power of Tradition and the Shock of Discovery*, Cambridge, Mass., 1992.

Green, Nile, *Indian Sufism Since the Seventeenth Century: Saints, Books, and Empires in Mughal Deccan*, London: Routledge, 2006.

Green, Nile, *Sufism: A Global History*, Chichester: Wiley-Blackwell, 2012.

Green, Nile, "The Religious and Cultural Role of Dreams and Visions in Islam", *Journal of the Royal Society*, 3 (2003).

Gross, Jo-Ann, "Economic Status of a Timurid Sufi Shaikh: A Matter of Conflict or Perception", *Iranian Studies*, Vol. 21 (1988).

Gross, Jo-Ann, "Multiple Roles and Perceptions of a Sufi Shaikh: Symbolic Statements of Political and Religious Authority", in Marc Gaborieau, Alexandre Popovic, and Thierry Zarcone, eds, *Naqshbandis: Historical Developments and Present Situation of a Muslim Mystical Order*, Istanbul-Paris: Institut Français d'Etudes Anatoliennes d'Istanbul, 1990.

Gupta, Charu, "(Im)possible Love and Sexual Pleasure in Late-Colonial North India", *Modern Asian Studies*, Vol. 36, No. 1, 2002.

Habib, Irfan, "The Family of Nur Jahan during Jahangir's Reign", *Medieval India: A Miscellany*, Vol. I, 1969.

Habib, Irfan, "The Political Role of Shaikh Ahmad Sirhindi and Shah Waliullah", *Enquiry*, Vol. 5 (1961).

Habib, Mohammad, "Chishti Mystic Records of the Sultanate Period", *Medieval India Quarterly*, Vol. 1, No. 2, 1950.

Hadi, Muhammad, compiler, *Khazinat al-Ma'arif*, ed. Ghulam Mustafa Khan, Karachi: 'Abdul Ghaffar Memon, 1973.

Haider, Mansura, "Agrarian System in Uzbek Khanates of Central Asia", *Turcica*, Vol. 7, 1974.

Haider, Mansura, "Urban Classes in the Uzbek Khanates, XVI–XVII Centuries", in Graciela de la Lama, ed., *Central Asia: Papers Presented at the 30th International Congress of Human Sciences in Asia and North Africa*, Mexico City: El Colegio de Mexico, 1976.

Hali, Altaf Husain, *Hali's Musaddas: The Flow and Ebb of Islam*, trans. Christopher Shackle and Javed Majeed, Delhi: Oxford University Press, 1997.

Hanneder, Jurgen, *Studies on the Moksopaya*, Wiesbaden: Abhandlungen fur die Kunde des Morgenlandes, 2006.

Haq, Mushirul, *Muslim Politics in Modern India, 1857–1947*, Meerut: Meenakshi Prakashan, 1970.

Haravi, Amir Hasan, *Masnawi-ha-i 'Irfani*, ed. Sayyid Muhammad Turabi, Tehran, 1992.

Harbans Purana, IO Islamic 1777, Asian and African Collections (formerly Oriental and India Office Collections), British Library, London.

Haroon, Sana, "Reformism and Orthodox Practice in Early Nineteenth-Century Muslim North India", *Journal of the Royal Asiatic Society*, Vol. 21, No. 3, 2011.

Hasan, S. Nurul, "The Theory of the Nur Jahan 'Junta' – A Critical Examination", *Proceedings of the Indian History Congress*, Vol. 21, 1958.

Hasani (al-), Muhammad, *Tazkira-i Hazrat Saiyid Shah 'Alam-Allah Hasani Rai Barelwi*, Lucknow: Maktaba-i Islam, 1970.

Hasrat, Bikrama Jit, *Dara Shikuh: Life and Works*, 2nd edn, Delhi: Munshiram Manoharlal, 1982.

Hasrat, Bikrama Jit, *Dara Shikuh: Life and Works*, Calcutta, 1953.

Hazra, R.C., *Studies in the Upapuranas, vol. I, Saura and Vaisnava Upapuranas*, Calcutta, 1958.

Herman, A.L., "Indian Theodicy: Samkara and Ramanuja on Brahmasutra II.1.32–36", *Philosophy East and West*, Vol. 21(3), 1971.

Hisari, Shah 'Abd al-Haq Chakar, *Maktubat i Imam Rabbani,* Kanpur: Nawal Kishor, 1906.

Hujwiri, Ali ibn Usman, *alias* Data Ganj-bakhsh, *Kashf al-Mahjub*, ed. Muhammad Shafi, Lahore: Nawa'i Waqt, 1968.

Husaini (al-), Saiyid Nafis, *Saiyid Ahmad Shahid se Haji Imdad-Allah ke ruhani rishte*, Lahore: Saiyid Ahmad Shahid Academy, 2003.

Ibn 'Arabi, Muhyi al-Din, *Al-Futuhat al-Makkiya*, ed. 'Othman Yahya, revised by Ibrahim Madkour, Cairo and Paris, 1972.

Ibn Rukun, Shaikh Badhan (*alias* Miyan Khan ibn Qiwam al-Mulk Jaunpuri), *Maktubat-i Quddusiya*, Delhi: Matba' Ahmadi, 1287 AH./1870.

Ihsan, Muhammad, Abu al-Faiz Kamal al-Din Muhammad Ihsan Mujaddidi Sirhindi, *Rauzat al-Qaiyumiya*, original Persian compilation *c.* 1730s, completed *c.* 1786 (?) Urdu translation, Lahore: Maktaba-e Nabaviya, 2002, 4 volumes.

Ikhlas, Kishan Chand, *Hamesha Bahar,* edited with notes and an introduction by Zubair Ahmad Qamar, New Delhi: Sajida Zubairi Publications, 2003.

Ikram, Muhammad, *Rud-e Kausar* (Urdu) rpntd 1967, Delhi: Adabi Dunya, n.d.

Ingram, Brannon, *Revival from Below: The Deoband Movement and Global Islam*, Berkeley: University of California Press, 2018.

Iqbal, Muhammad, *Kulliyat-i Iqbal* (Urdu), Lahore: Shaikh Ghulam Ali and Sons, 1973.

Iqbal, Muhammad, *Payam-i Mashriq,* trans. Ahmad Javed, Islamabad: Alhambra Publishing, 2000.

Iqbal, Muhammad, "The Doctrine of Absolute Unity as Expounded by Abdul Karim al-Jilani", *Indian Antiquary*, September 1900.

Irfan, 'Abdur Rabb, "Aurangzeb ki hajw se madh tak: Ni'mat Khan-i 'Ali ka Zahni safar", *Ma'arif,* June 1990.

Irvine, William, *The Later Mughals*, edited and augmented with the History of Nadir Shah's Invasion by Jadunath Sarkar, Vol. 2, Calcutta: M.C. Sarkar & Sons, 1922.

Isfahani, Fazl-Allah ibn Ruzbihani, *Suluk al-Muluk,* ed. Muhammad 'Ali Muvahhid, Tehran: Intisharat-i Khwarizmi, 1362 Shamsi/1983.

Isfahani, Fazl-Allah ibn Ruzbihani, *Mihman-nama-i Bukhara*, ed. Manuchehr Satudeh, Tehran: Bungah-i Tarjuma wa Nashr-i Kitab, 1341 Shamsi/1962.

Islam, Riazul, *Sufism in South Asia: Impact on Fourteenth Century Muslim Society*, Karachi, 2002.

Jacobi, Herman, *Jaina Sutras Part 2: Translation of the Uttaradhyanasutra and Sutrakitanga*, Oxford: Oxford University Press, 1895, rpntd Delhi, 1989.

Jaffery, Nausheen, *Jahan Ara Begum: A Biographical Study 1614–1681*, Delhi: Idarah-i Adabiyat-i Delli, 2011.

Jahanara, *Munis al-Arwah*, ed. Qamar Jahan Begam, Karachi: S.M. Hamid 'Ali, 1992.

Jahanara, *Risala-i Sahibiya*, ed. Muhammad Aslam, *Journal of the Research Society of Pakistan*, Vol. 16, No. 4, 1979 (cited as *Sahibiya*).

Jahangir, Nur al-din, *Toozuk-i-Jahangeeree (Tuzak-i Jahangiri)*, ed. and printed at his Private Press by Syud Ahmud (Saiyid Ahmad Khan), Ally Gurh (Aligarh), 1864.

Jahangir, Nur al-Din, *Tuzuk-i Jahangiri*, rpntd Aligarh: Sir Syed Academy, Aligarh Muslim University, 2007.

Jalibi, Jamil, *Tarikh-i Adab-i Urdu* [18th century], Vol. 2, Part 1, 5th reprint, Delhi: Educational Publishing House, 1993.

Jalibi, Jamil, *Tarikh-i Urdu Adab*, Vol. 2, Part 2, Delhi: Educational Publishing House, 1997.

Jami, 'Abd al-Rahman, *Tariqa-i Khwajagan*, ed. 'Abd al-Hayy Habibib, Kabul: Intishrat-i Anjuman-i Jami, 1962.

Jami, *Naqd al-Nusus fi Sharh Naqsh al-Fusus*, ed. William C. Chittick, Tehran: Mu'asses Pazhohish-i Hikmat wa Falsafa-i Iran, 1991.

Jayasi, Malik Muhammad, *Kanhavat*, ed. Parameshwarilal Gupta, Banaras, 1971.

Johnson, Kathryn Virginia, "The Unerring Balance: A Study of the Theory of Sanctity (*wilayah*) of 'Abd al-Wahhab al-Sha'rani", PhD thesis, Harvard University, 1985.

Kachru, Sonam, "Of Forgetting and the Obscure Place of Dreams: How the Book of Dreaming Entered Kashmirian Historiography", paper presented at the 41st Annual Conference on South Asia, Madison, WI, October, 2012.

Kaicker, Abhishek, *The King and the People: Sovereignty and Popular Politics in Mughal Delhi*, New York: Oxford University Press, 2020.

Kamal, Razi Ahmad, *Masha'ikh-e Chishtiya Sabiriya*, New Delhi: Maktaba Jamia, 1997.

Kamboh, Muhammad Salih, *Shah Jahan Nama*, ed. Ghulam Yazdani, rev. Waheed Qureshi, Lahore: Majlis-e Taraqqi-ye Adab, rpntd 1972, 3 volumes.

Karamustafa, Ahmet T., *Sufism, the Formative Period*, Edinburgh: Edinburgh University Press, 2007.

Kashani, 'Izz al-Din Mahmud bin 'Ali, *Misbah al-Hidaya wa Miftaha al-Kifaya*, ed. 'Iffat Karbasi and Muhammad Riza Barzgar Khaliqi, Tehran, 2008.

Kashifi (-al), Fakhr al-Din 'Ali ibn Husain Wa'iz, *Rashhat 'Ain al-Hayat*, ed. 'Ali Asghar Mu'iniyan, Tehran: Bunyad-i Nikukari-i Nuriyani, 1977.

Kashmiri, Muhammad Murad, *Gulshan-i Wahdat* (Letters of Shaikh 'Abd al-Ahad Wahdat Sirhindi), compiled by Muhammad Murad Kashmiri, ed. 'Abdullah Jan Faruqi, revised by Ghulam Mustafa Khan, Karachi: Idara-e Mujaddidiya, 1966.

Kazim, Muhammad, *'Alamgirnama,* ed. Maulawi Khadim Husain and Maulawi 'Abd al-Hayy, gen. ed. W. Nassau Lees, Calcutta: Asiatic Society,1868.

Khafi Khan, Muhammad Hashim, *Muntakhab al-Lubab*, Vol. 1, ed. K.D. Ahmad and Wolseley Haig, Calcutta: Bibliotheca Indica, 1869; English translation, section dealing with Aurangzeb's reign, ed. S. Moinul Haq, Karachi: Pakistan Historical Society; and ed. A.J. Syed, Bombay: Popular Prakashan, 1977.

Khafipour, Hani, ed., *The Empires of the Near East and India: Source Studies of the Safavids, Ottomans, and Mughal Literate Communities*, New York: Columbia University Press, 2019.

Khalil, Mirza Muhammad, *Ruq'at-i Mirza Muhammad Khalil,* British Library, Additional Ms. 16,819, fls. 103a-104a, 104b-105b, 109a-109b, 112a-113a, 116b,122b-123a.

Khan, Abul Fath Qabil, *Adab-i 'Alamgiri* of Abul Fath Qabil Khan, ed. Abdul Ghafur Chaudhari, Lahore: Idara-i Tahqiqat-i Pakistan, University of Panjab, 1971.

Khan, Alim Ashraf, *Shaikh 'Abd al-Haqq Muhaddis Dehlavi: Hayat wa 'Ilmi Khidmat*, Delhi: Islamic Wonders Bureau, 2001.

Khan, Bakhtawar, *Mir'at al-'Alam*, ed. Sajida Alvi, Lahore: Majlis-e Taraqi-ye Adab, 2 vols.

Khan, Ghulam Mustafa, "Some Unpublished Letters to Zebunnisa", *Sind University Arts Research* (Hyderabad), Vol. 4, 1964–5.

Khan, Iftikhar A., "A Hajj Pilgrim's Travelogue and Manual: The Sea Traveler 1676-1677", *Journal of the Pakistan Historical Society*, Vol. 60, No. 1, 2012.

Khan, Iqtidar Alam, "Shaikh Abdul Quddus Gangohi's Relations with Political Authorities: A Reapparaisal", *Medieval India: A Miscellany*, Vol. 4.

Khan, Iqtidar Alam, "The Nobility Under Akbar and the Development of His Religious Policy, 1560–1580", *Journal of the Royal Asiatic Society*, 1968, Parts 1–2.

Khan, Iqtidar Alam, *The Political Biography of a Mughal Noble: Mun'im Khan Khan-i-Khanan, 1497–1575*, Delhi: Orient Longman, 1973.

Khan, Samsam al-Daula Shahnawaz, *Ma'asir al-Umara*, Vol. II, Calcutta: Bibliotheca Indica, 1891.

Khan, Saqi Musta'id, *Ma'asir-i 'Alamgiri* , ed. Agha Ahmad 'Ali, Calcutta: Asiatic Society of Bengal, 1871; English translation by J.N. Sarkar, Calcutta: Asiatic Soceity of Bengal, 1947.

Khan, Syed Ahmad, *Asar al-Sanadid*, ed. Khaliq Anjum, 2 vols, rpntd New Delhi: National Council for Promotion of Urdu Language, 2003.

Khan, Syed Ahmad, *Maqalat-i Sir Sayyid*, ed. Muhammad Isma'il Panipati, Lahore, Majlis-i Taraqqi-i Adab, 1962.

Khan, Zain, *Tabaqat-i Baburi*, trans. Syed Hasan Askari, Delhi: Idarah-i Adabiyat-i Dilli, 1982.

Khatoon, Rehana, "'Abd al-Latif 'Abbasi Gujarati aur Masnawi-i Maulana-i Rum", Unpublished Paper presented to a seminar of Haryana Academy, Chandigarh, 2007.

Khwandamir, *Habib al-Siyar*, Tehran: Khayyam, 1352 Shamsi/1973, Vol. 4.

Khwushgu, Bindraban Das, *Natayij al-Afkar*, in Nurul Hasan Ansari, *Farsi adab be-'ahd-e Aurangzeb*, Delhi: Indo-Persian Society, 1969.

Khwushgu, Bindraban Das, *Safina-i Khwushgu*, ed. S. Shah Md. Ataur Rahman, Patna: Institute of Studies and Research in Arabic and Persian, 1959.

Kidwai, Riaz-ur-Rahman, *Biographical Sketch of Kidwais of Avadh, with Special Reference to Barabanki Families,* Aligarh: Kitab Ghar, 1987.

Kinra, Rajeev, "Infantilizing Baba Dara: The Cultural Memory of Dara Shekuh and the Mughal Public Sphere", *Journal of Persianate Studies* 2 (2009).

Kinra, Rajeev, "Revisiting the History and Historiography of Mughal Pluralism", *ReOrient*, Vol. 5, No. 2, Spring 2020.

Kinra, Rajeev, *Writing Self, Writing Empire: Chandar Bhan Brahman and the Cultural World of the Indo-Persian State Secretary,* Berkeley: University of California Press, 2015.

Knysh, Alexander, "Ibn 'Arabi in the Later Islamic Tradition", in Stephen Hirtenstein and Michael Tiernan, eds, *Muhyiddin Ibn 'Arabi: A Commemorative Volume*, Shaftesbury: Element Books Limited, 1993.

Koch, Ebba, *Mughal Art and Imperial Ideology: Collected Essays*, Delhi: Oxford University Press, 2001.

Kugle, Scott, "'Abd al-Haqq Dihlawi, an Accidental Revivalist: Knowledge and Power in the Passage from Delhi to Makka", *Journal of Islamic Studies* 19, No. 2 (2008).

Kugle, Scott, "Heaven's Witness: The Uses and Abuses of Muhammad Ghawth's Mystical Ascension", *Journal of Islamic Studies* 14, No. 1 (2003).

Kugle, Scott, *Rebel Between Spirit and Law: Ahmad Zarruq, Sainthood, and Authority in Islam,* Bloomington and Indianapolis: Indiana University Press, 2006.

Kugle, Scott, "Usuli Sufis: Ahmad Zarruq and His South Asian Followers", in Eric Geoffroy, ed., *Une voie soufie dans le monde: La Shadhiliyya,* Paris: Maisonneuve et Larose, 2005.

Kulabi, Tawakkul Beg, *Ahwal-i Shahi* (*Ahwal-i Mulla Shah Badakhshi*), British Library, Persian Collection, Ms. Or. 3203.

Kumar, Sunil, "Assertion of Authority: A Study of the Discursive Statements of Two Sultans of Delhi", in M. Alam, F.N. Delvoye, and M. Gaborieau, eds, *The Making of Indo-Persian Culture: Indian and French Studies*, Delhi: Manohar, 2000.

Lacrosse, Joachim, "Some Remarks about a Meeting between Socrates and an Indian (Aristoxenus 53)", *Archiv fur Geschichte der Philosophiei*, Vol. 89(3), 2007.

Lagarde, Michel, *Les secrets de l'invisible : Essai sur le Grand Commentaire de Fakhr al-Dîn al-Râzî*, Beirut, Albouraq, 2008.

Lahori, Abd al-Hamid, *Badshahnama*, Vol. 1, ed. Kabiruddin Ahmad and 'Abdur Rahim, Calcutta, 1867–8.

Lahori, Abd al-Sattar bin Qasim, *Majalis-i Jahangiri*, ed. Arif Naushahi and Mo'een Nizami, Tehran: Miras-i Maktub, 2006.

Lakhnawi, Bhagwandas Hindi, *Hadiqa-i Hindi* (*Chaman-i Charum*), ed. Sharif Husain Qasemi, Delhi: National Mission for Manuscripts, 2015.

Lal, Magan, and Jessie Duncan Westbrook, *The Diwan of Zeb-un-Nissa: The First Fifty Ghazals*, New York: E.P. Dutton, 1913.

Lal, Ruby, *Domesticity and Power in the Early Mughal World*, Cambridge: Cambridge University Press, 2005.

Lal, Ruby, *Empress: The Astonishing Reign of Nur Jahan*, New York, W.W. Norton, 2018.

Larocque, Brendan, "Mahamat Prannath and the Pranami Movement: Hinduism and Islam in a Seventeenth-Century Mercantile Sect", in Vasudha Dalmia and Munis D. Faruqui, eds, *Religious Interactions in Mughal India*, Delhi: Oxford University Press, 2014.

Lawrence, Bruce B., "An Indo-Persian Perspective on the Significance of Early Sufi Masters", in Leonard Lewisohn, ed., *Classical Persian Sufism from its Origins to Rumi*, London: Khanqahi Nimatullahi Publications, 1993.

Lawrence, Bruce, "Biography and the 17th Century Qadiriya of North India", in Anna Dallapiccola and Stephanie Lallemant, eds, *Islam and Indian Regions*, Stuttgart: Franz Steiner Verlag, 1993.

Lawrence, Bruce, "Veiled Opposition to Sufis in Muslim Asia", in Frederick de Jong and Bernd Radke, eds, *Islamic Mysticism Contested: Thirteen Centuries of Controversies and Polemics*, Leiden: Brill, 1999.

Lawrence, Bruce B., ed., *The Rose and the Rock: Mystical and Rational Elements in the Intellectual History of South Asian Islam*, Durham: Duke University Press, 1979.

Lawrence, Bruce B., and Carl W. Ernst, *Sufi Martyrs of Love: Chishti*

Sufism in South Asia and Beyond, New York: Palgrave Macmillan, 2002.

Lefèvre, Corinne, "Pouvoir et noblesse dans l'Empire moghol: Perspectives du règne de Jahangir (1605–1627)", *Annales Histoire, Sciences Sociales* 62, No. 6 (2007).

Lefèvre, Corinne, "Recovering a Missing Voice from Mughal India: The Imperial Discourse of Jahangir (r. 1605–27) in His Memoirs," *Journal of the Economic and Social History of the Orient*, 50, No. 4 (2007).

Lewisohn, L., and C. Shackle, eds, *'Attar and the Persian Sufi Tradition: The Art of Spiritual Flight*, London: I.B. Tauris, 2007.

Livingstone, David, *Adam's Ancestors: Race, Religion and the Politics of Human Origins*, Baltimore, 2008.

Ma'sum, Shaikh Muhammad, *Maktubat-i Ma'sumiya*, 3 volumes, rpntd, Karachi: Lala Asrar Muhammad Khan, 370 Garden West, 1976, Vol. I; Urdu translation by Saiyed Zawwar Husain, Karachi: Zawwar Academy, 1979.

Ma'sumi, Mir Safar Ahmad, *Maqamat-i Ma'sumi*, Persian text edited and translated into Urdu with an Introduction and Notes by Muhammad Iqbal Mujaddidi, Lahore: Ziyaul Qur'an, 2004.

Madani, Husain Ahmad, *Naqsh-e Hayat*, rpntd Delhi: Al-Jami'at Book Depot, 2011.

Maghribi, Ahmad Zarruq, "Qawa'id al-Tariqa fi al-Jama' bain al-Shari 'a wa al-Haqiqa", Summary in Abd al-Haqq Muhaddis Dehlavi, ed., *Maraj al-Bahrain*, Urdu trans. Sana ul-Haqq, Nazimabad, 1968.

Mahabharata, Persian translation, Introduction by Abu al-Fazl, ed. S.M. Riza Jalali Naini and N.S. Shukla, trans. Mir Ghiyas al-Din 'Ali Qazvini, Vol. 1, Tehran, 1979.

Malik, Rahim Rizazadeh, ed., *Dabistan-i Mazahib*, Tehran: Tabistan, 2 vols, 1362 Sh. / 1983.

Manucci, Niccolao, *Mogul India, or Storia do Mogor*, transl. William Irvine, 4 vols., London: John Murray, 1907–8.

Manz, Beatrice Forbes "Women in Timurid Dynastic Politics", in Guity Nashat and Lois Beck, eds, *Women in Iran: From the Rise of Islam to 1800*, Chicago: University of Illinois Press, 2003.

Markham, C.R., ed., *Narrative of the Embassy of Ruy González de Clavijo to the Court of Timour at Samarcand, A.D. 1403–6, Translated with*

Notes, a Preface, and an Introductory Life of Timour Beg, London: Hakluyt Society, 1859.

Matilal, B.K., "Samkara's Theodicy", *Journal of Indian Philosophy*, Vol. 20(4), 1992.

Mayaram, Shail, *Against History, Against State*, New York: Columbia University Press, 2003.

Mayaram, Shail, "The Mughal State Formation: The Mewati Counterperspective", *Indian Economic and Social History Review*, 34, No. 2 (1997).

Mazandarani, Ashraf, *Diwan-i Ashʻar-i Ashraf Mazandarani*, ed. Muhammad Hasan Saiyidan, Tehran: Majmuʻa-i Intisharat-i Adabi wa Tarikhi Mauqufat-i Mahmud Afshar Yazdi, 1373 *Sh.*/1994.

Meerathi, ʻAshiq Ilahi, *Tazkirat al-Khalil*, rpntd Karachi: Maktabat al-Shaikh, Bahadurabad, n.d.

Meerathi, ʻAshiq Ilahi, *Tazkirat al-Rashid*, rpntd Saharanpur: Isha'at-ul-ʻUlum, 1977.

Mehr, Ghulam Rasul, ed., *Tarikh-i Iradat Khan*, Lahore: Idara-e Tahqiqat-e Pakistan, 1981.

Metcalf, Barbara Daly, *Islamic Revival in British India: Deoband, 1860–1900*, Princeton: Princeton University Press, 1982.

Mikkelson, Jane, "The Way of Tradition and the Path of Innovation: Aurangzeb and Dara Shukuh's Struggle for the Mughal Throne", in Hani Khafipour, ed., *The Empires of the Near East and India: Source Studies of the Safavid, Ottoman, and Mughal Literate Communities*, New York: Columbia University Press, 2019.

Minkowski, Christopher, "King David in Oudh: A Bible Story in Sanskrit and the Just King at an Afghan Court", Inaugural Lecture for the Boden Professorship, University of Oxford, 7 March 2006.

Mir Khwand, *Tarikh-i Rauzat al-Safa'*, introduction by ʻAbbas Parwiz, Tehran, 1959; English translation by E. Rehatsek, ed. F.F. Arbuthnot, rpntd Delhi, 1982.

Moin, A. Azfar, *The Millennial Sovereign: Sacred Kingship and Sainthood in Islam*, New York: Columbia University Press, 2012.

Moin, Azfar, "The Millennial and Saintly Sovereignty of Emperor Shahjahan According to a Court Poet", in Hani Khafipour, ed., *The Empires of the Near East and India: Source Studies of the Safavids, Ottomans, and Mughal Literate Communities*, New York: Columbia University Press, 2019.

Moini, Syed Liaquat Hussain, "The City of Ajmer in Last Years of Aurangzeb's Reign 1678–1707", Unpublished M.Phil. Dissertation, Aligarh Muslim University, 1978.

Mojtabai, Fathullah, "*Muntakhab-i Jug Basasht*; or, Selections from the *Yoga-Vasistha* Attributed to Mir Abu'l-Qasim Findiriski", PhD Dissertation, Harvard University, 1976.

Montgomery, James A., *Aramaic Incantation Texts from Nippur*, Philadelphia: University of Pennsylvania, 1913.

Moosvi, Shireen, *People, Taxation and Trade in Mughal India*, Delhi: Oxford University Press, 2008.

Morris, James Winston, 'Ibn 'Arabi and His Interpreters, Part II: Influences and Interpretations", *Journal of the American Oriental Society*, Vol. 107, No. 1 (1987).

Mu'tamadi, Mahindukht, *Maulana Khalid Naqshbandi wa Pairuwan-i Tariqat-i U*, Tehran: Pazhang, 1368/1989.

Muhammad, 'Imad al-Din, *Wasilat al-Qubul ila-llah-i wa'l-Rasul* (Letters of Shaikh Muhammad Naqshband Sirhindi), compiled by 'Imad al-Din Muhammad, ed. Ghulam Mustafa Khan, Hyderabad: Sindh University, 1963.

Mujaddidi, Muhammad Iqbal, "Hazrat Mujaddid Alf-i Sani ke defa' mein likhi janey wali kitaben", in idem, *Tazkira-e Ulama-o-Mashaikh-e Pakistan-o-Hind*, Vol. 2, Lahore: Progressive Books, 2013.

Mujaddidi, Muhammad Iqbal, ed., *Lata'if al-Madina*, facsimile edition, with an introduction and summary in Urdu, Lahore: Hauza-i Naqshbandiya, 2004.

Mujaddidi, Muhammad Iqbal, ed., *Hasanat al-Haramayn*, edited with Urdu translation and annotations, Dera Ismail Khan: Maktaba Sirajiya Khanaqah-i Ahmadiya Sa'idiya, Musa-za'i Sharif, 1981.

Muqtadir, Khan Bahadur 'Abdul, ed., *Catalogue of Arabic & Persian Manuscripts in Khuda Bakhsh Oriental Public Library*, Patna, Vol. XIV, rpntd Patna, 1970.

Muradabadi, Shah Fazle Rahman Ganj, *Manmohan ki Batein*, rpntd Patna: Khuda Bakhsh Oriental Public Library, 1990.

Muradi (-al), Muhammad Khalil bin 'Ali, *Silk al-Durar fi a'yan al-qarn al-sani al-'ashar*, Beirut: Dar al-Kutub al-'ilmiyya, 1997, 4 volumes.

Mushafi, Ghulam Hamadani, *Tazkira-i Hindi*, ed. 'Abd al Haq, Aurangabad: Anjuman Taraqqi-ye Urdu, 1933.

Muttaqi (al-), 'Ala al-Din 'Ali, *Kanz al-'Ummal fi Sunan al-Aqwal wa al-Af'al*, ed. Shaykh Bakri Hayyani and Shaykh Safwat al-Saqa, Beirut, 2004.

Nadwi, Abdus Salam, *Imam Razi* (Urdu), Azamgarh: Darul Musannefin Shibli Academy, rpntd, 2015

Nadwi, Shah Mu'inuddin, "Anis-ul-Hujjaj: Hindustan ka Farsi Zaban ka Pahla Nayab Safar-nama", *Ma'arif*, Vol. 93, No. 1.

Naim, C.M., "The Maulana who Loved Krishna", *Economic and Political Weekly*, Vol. 48, No. 17, 27 April 2013.

Nair, Shankar, "Sufism as Medium and Method of Translation: Mughal Translations of Hindu Texts Reconsidered", *Studies in Religion/ Sciences Religieuses*, 43, No. 3 (September 2014).

Nair, Shankar, *Translating Wisdom: Hindu–Muslim Intellectual Interactions in Early Modern South Asia*, Oakland: University of California Press, 2020.

Naqshbandi, Abdul Majid Ahmad Saifi Mujaddid, ed., *Maktubat-i Sa'idiya*, Lahore: Maktaba Hakim Saifi, Rabi' i, 1385 H/1965.

Narhari, H.G., "Samkara and Vyasa on the Theory of Karma", *Bulletin of the Deccan College Research Institute*, 17, 1955.

Nishapuri, Shaikh Farid al-Din 'Attar, *Tazkirat al- Auliya*, ed. Muhammad Istelami, Tehran: Intisharat-i Zavvar, 1366 sh. / 1987.

Nizami, K.A., *Akbar and Religion*, Delhi: Idarah-i-Adabiyat-i-Delli, 1989.

Nizami, K.A., *Hayat-i Shaikh 'Abd al-Haqq Muhaddis Dehlavi*, Delhi: Nadvat al-Musannifin, 1964.

Nizami, K.A., "Naqshbandi Influence on Mughal Rulers and Politics", *Islamic Culture*, Vol. 39, 1965.

Nizami, K.A., "Shattari Saints and Their Attitude Towards the State", *Medieval India Quarterly*, Vol. 1, No. 2 (1950).

Nizami, K.A., *Tarikh-i Masha'ikh-i-Chisht*, Delhi: Nadvat al-Musannifin, 1953.

Nizami, K.A., *Tarikh-e Masha'ikh-i Chisht*, Vol. 5, Delhi: Idarah-i Adabiyat-i Dilli, 1984.

Nizami, Moin Ahmad, *Reform and Renewal in South Asian Islam: The Chishti-Sabiris in 18th–19th Century North India*, Delhi: Oxford University Press, 2017.

Nu'mani, Shibli, *Al-Kalam*, rpntd Azamgarh: Darul Musannefin, Shibli Academy.

Nu'mani, Shibli, *'Ilm al-Kalam*, rpntd Azamgarh: Darul Musannefin, Shibli Academy.

Nu'mani, Shibli, *Sawanih-i Maulana Rum*, Delhi: Daftar-i Urdu-i Mu'alla, Shahjahani Press, n.d., rpntd Azamagarh: Darul Musannefin Shibli Academy.

Nu'mani, Shibli, "Zeb-un-nisa", in *Maqalat-i Shibli*, Vol. 5, rpntd, Azamgarh: Darul Musannefin Shibli Academy, 1955.

Obrock, Luther, "History at the End of History: *Srivara's Jainatarangini*", *Indian Economic and Social History Review*, 50, No. 2 (2013).

Orsini, Francesca, "Inflected Katha: Sufis and Krishna Bhaktas in Awadh", in Munis D. Faruqui and Vasudha Dalmia, ed., *Religious Interactions in Mughal India,* Delhi: Oxford University Press, 2014.

Osella, Filippo, and Caroline Osella, eds, *Islamic Reform in South Asia*, Cambridge: Cambridge University Press, 2013.

Pagani, Samuela, "The Meaning of the *Ikhtilaf al-Madhahib* in 'Abd al-Wahhab al-Sha'rani's *al-Mizan al-Kubra*", *Islamic Law and Society* 11, No. 2 (2004).

Pagden, Anthony, *The Fall of Natural Man: The American Indians and the Origins of Comparative Ethnology*, Cambridge, 1982.

Panasikara, Vasudeva Sharma, ed., *Laghuyogavasistha: Text with Sanskrit Commentary, Vasistha-Candrika*, Delhi: Motilal Banarsidass, 1937.

Panipati, Nizam al-Din, *Jug Basisht, Dar Falsafah wa 'irfan-i Hind*, ed. Saiyid Muhammad Riza Jalali Naini and N.S. Shukla, Tehran: Eqbal, 1981.

Panipati, Qazi Sana-Allah, *Tafsir-i Mazhari*, Urdu translation by Abd al-Dayim al-Jalali, Delhi, 1961.

Parihar, Subhash, *History and Architectural Remains of Sirhind: The Greatest Mughal City on Delhi–Lahore Highway*, New Delhi: Aryan Books International, 2006.

Parsa, Khwaja Muhammad, *Qudsiyya (Kalimat-i Baha al-din Naqshband)*, ed. Ahmad Taheri Iraqi, Tehran: Kitabkhana-i Tahuri, 1356 Shamsi/1975.

Paul, Jurgen, "Forming a Faction: The Himayat System of Khwaja Ahrar", *International Journal of Middle Eastern Studies*, Vol. 23 (1991).

Prasad, Beni, *History of Jahangir*, 3rd edn, Allahabad: Indian Press, 1940.

Qaisar, A.J., "From Port to Port: Life on Indian Ships in the Sixteenth and Seventeenth Centuries", in Ashin Das Gupta and M.N. Pearson,

eds, *India and the Indian Ocean, 1500–1800*, rpntd Delhi: Oxford University Press, 1999.
Qalandr, Hamid, *Khair al-Majalis*, ed. K.A. Nizami, Aligarh: Aligarh Muslim University, 1959.
Qanungo, Kalika-Ranjan, *Dara Shukoh*, 2nd edn, Calcutta: Sarkar, 1952.
Qasemi, S.H., "Sharh-ha-'i-i Diwan-i Hafiz dar Hind", *Qand-e-Parsi* 11 (Zamistan 1375 / December 1996–March 1997).
Qasim, Qudrat-Allah, *Majmu'a-i Naghz*, ed. Hafiz Mahmud Sherani, Part 2, Delhi: Taraqqi-ye Urdu Board, rpntd, n.d.
Quddusi, Muhammad Akram Barsavi, *Iqtibas al-Anwar*, Urdu translation by Wahid Bakhsh Sayal Chishti Sabiri, Lahore: Bazm-e Ittihadul Muslimin, 1409 H/1988.
Qureshi, I.H., *Muslim Civilization in India and Pakistan*, Lahore, 1961,
Qureshi, Ishtiaq Husain, *The Muslim Community of the Indo-Pakistan Subcontinent, c. 610–1947: A Brief Historical Analysis*, rpntd Karachi: Ma'aref, 1977.
Qushairi, Abu al-Qasim, *Risala al-Qushairi*, Persian translation by Abu 'Ali Hasan ibn Ahmad Usmani, ed. Badi al-Zaman Farozanfar, Tehran: Bungah-i Tarjuma wa Nashr-i Kitab, 1345sh. / 1966.
Qutb-i Jahani, Sufi Sharif, *Atwar fi Hall al-Asrar*, MS Or. 1883, Asian and African Collections (formerly Oriental and India Office Collections), British Library, London; also included in idem, *Majmu'a-i Rasa'il*, Lucknow: Nawal Kishor, 1885.
Radtke, Bernd, "Ijtihad and neo-Sufism", *Asiatische Studien* 48 (1994).
Rahman, Fazlur, *Islam*, 2nd edition, Chicago: Chicago University Press, 1979.
Rahman, Fazlur, ed., *Selected Letters of Shaikh Ahmad Sirhindi*, Lahore: Iqbal Academy Pakistan, 1968.
Rahman, Jamilur, "Falgiri-i Padshahan-i Timuri Hind az Diwan-i Hafiz", *Qand-e-Parsi* 16 (Zamistan 1380 / December 2001–March 2002).
Rahman, Mufti 'Azizur, *Tazkira-e Masha'ikh-e Deoband*, Bijnor: Madani Dar-ul-Talifat, n.d.
Rahman, Sabahuddin 'Abdur, "Taimuri Shahzadiyon ka 'Ilmi Zauq, I", *Ma'arif*, May 1942.
Rahman, Sabahuddin 'Abdur, "Taimuri Shazadiyon ka 'Ilmi Zauq II", *Ma'arif*, June 1942.
Rahman, Sabahuddin 'Abdur, *Bazm-i Sufiya*, Azamgarh: Darul Musannefin, Shibli Academy, 1949.

Randles, W.G.L., "'Peuples sauvages' et 'états despotiques': La pertinence, au XVIe siècle, de la grille aristotélicienne pour classer les nouvelles sociétés révélées par les Découvertes au Brésil, en Afrique et en Asie", *Mare Liberun*, No. 3, 1991.

Razi, 'Aqil Khan, *Waqi'at-i 'Alamgiri*, ed. Zafar Hasan, Aligarh: Aligarh Historical Institute, 1945.

Razi, Najm al-Din, *Mirsad al-'Ibad ila al-Mabda' wa al-Ma'ad*, ed. Muhammad Amin Riyahi, Tehran, 1973.

Rice, Yael, and Dwaipayan Sen, "Visiting Ajmer Sharif: Artistic and Religious Patronage at the Court of Aurangzeb", Paper presented at the Annual South Asia Conference, University of Wisconsin, Madison, 2013.

Richards, John F., "The Formulation of Imperial Authority under Akbar and Jahangir", in Muzaffar Alam and Sanjay Subrahmanyam, eds, *The Mughal State, 1526–1750*, Delhi: Oxford University Press, 1998.

Rieu, Charles, *Catalogue of the Persian Manuscripts in the British Museum*, London, 1883.

Rieu, Charles, *Catalogue of the Persian Manuscripts in the British Museum*, Vol. 2, rpntd, London: Trustees of the British Museum, 1966.

Rizvi, Mujeeb, "Hasrat ki bhi Qabul ho Mathura mein Haziri", in idem, *Pichhe Phirat Kahat Kabir Kabir*, Delhi: Dilli Kitab Ghar, 2009.

Rizvi, S. Athar Abbas, *A History of Sufism in India*, Delhi: Munshiram Manoharlal, 1978–2002.

Rizvi, S.A.A., *Muslim Revivalist Movements in Northern India in the Sixteenth and Seventeenth Centuries*, Agra, 1966.

Rizvi, S.A.A., *Shah 'Abd al-'Aziz: Puritanism, Sectarian Polemics and Jihad*, Delhi, 1982.

Rizvi, S.A.A., "Sixteenth Century Naqshbandiyya Leadership in India", in Marc Gaborieau, Alexandre Popovic, and Thierry Zarcone, eds, *Naqshbandis: Historical Development and Present Situation of a Muslim Mystical Order*, Istanbul-Paris: Institut Francais d"Etudes Anatoliennes d"Istanbul, 1990).

Rizvi, Saiyid Athar Abbas, *Shah Wali-Allah and His Times*, Canberra: Ma'rifat Publishing House, 1980.

Robinson, Francis, "Islamic Reform and Modernities in South Asia", in Filippo Osella and Caroline Osella, eds, *Islamic Reform in South Asia*, Cambridge: Cambridge University Press, 2013.

Rocher, Ludo, *The Puranas*, Vol. II, Fasc. 3 in Jan Gonda, ed., *A History of Indian Literature*, Wiesbaden, 1986.

Rocher, Ludo, "Reflections on One Hundred and Fifty Years of Purana Studies', *Purana*, Vol. 25(I), 1983.

Rosenthal, Franz, *The Technique and Approach of Muslim Scholarship*, Analecta Orientalia Series, Vol. 24, Rome: Pontificium Institutum Biblicum, 1947.

Roy, Asim, *The Islamic Syncretistic Tradition in Bengal*, Princeton, 1983.

Sadiq, Muhammad, *Tabaqat-i Shahjahani*, British Library, India Office Ms. 705, fls. 17a–18a. (The *Tabaqas Nahum* [ninth] and *Dahum* [tenth] were edited and published in 1991 and 1993 by Professor Muhammad Aslam Khan of the Department of Persian, Delhi University.)

Sadriniya, Baqir, *Farhang-i Masurat-i Mutun-i 'Irfani*, Tehran, 2009.

Safina-i Bahr al-Muhit, MS. Orient Fol. 248, Staatsbibiothek zu Berlin.

Sahir, 'Abdul 'Aziz, *Mihrab-e Tahqiq*, Karachi: Idarah-i Yadgar-i Ghalib, 2012.

Sakhawi (al-), Shams al-Din Muhammad ibn 'Abd al-Rahman, *Al-Ajwibat al-Murdiyya*, ed. Muhammad Ishaq Muhammad Ibrahim, Riyadh, 1997.

Sandilawi, Ahmad 'Ali, *Makhzan al-Ghara'ib*, cited in Shibli, *Maqalat-i Shibli*, Vol. 5, rpntd, Azamgarh: Darul Musannefin Shibli Academy, 1955.

Sanyal, Usha, *Devotional Islam and Politics in British India: Ahmad Riza Khan Barelwi and His Movement, 1870–1920*, Delhi: Oxford University Press,1996.

Saraswati, Dayanand, *Satyarth Prakash*, English translation *Light of Truth* by Shri Durga Prasad, rpntd New Delhi, 1970.

Sarkar, Jadunath, *Shivaji and His Times*, 2nd edn, London: Longmans, Green and Co, 1920.

Sarkar, Jadunath, "Zeb-un-Nissa's Love Affairs", *Modern Review*, January 1916; rpntd in idem, *Studies in Mughal India*, London: Longmans, Green and Co, 1920.

Sarkhwush, Muhammad Afzal, *Kalimat al-Shu'ara'*, ed. Sadiq Ali Dilawari, Lahore: Shaikh Mubarak Ali Tajir-e Kutub, 1942.

Schimmel, Annemarie, *Gabriel's Wing: A Study into the Religious Ideas of Sir Muhammad Iqbal*, Lahore: Iqbal Academy, 1989.

Schimmel, Annemarie, "Some Notes on the Cultural Activity of the First Uzbek Rulers", *Journal of Pakistan Historical Society*, Vol. 8, No. 3 (1960).

Shaʿrani (al-), ʿAbd al-Wahhab, *Al-Mizan al-Kubra*', ed. al-Shaikh Abd al-Waris Muhammad Ali, Beirut: Dar al-Kutub al-ʿIlmiya, 1998.

Shaʿrani (al-), ʿAbd al-Wahhab, *Al-Tabaqat al-Kubra*', ed. Khalil al-Mansur, Beirut: Dar al-Kutb al-'Ilmiya, 1997.

Shah Ismaʿil Shahid Dehlavi, *ʿAbaqat*, with an Introduction by Saiyid Muhammad Yusuf Banori, Karachi: al-Majlis al-ʿIlmi, 1380 AH/ 1960–1 CE; Urdu translation by Saiyid Munazir Ahsan Gilani, with an Introduction by Ziauddin Shakeb, Lahore: Idara-e Islamiyat, n.d.

Shah Ismaʿil Shahid Dehlavi, *Sirat-i Mustaqim* (Urdu translation), rpntd Deoband: Kutubkhana Ashrafiya Rashid Company, n.d.

Shah Ismaʿil Shahid Dehlavi, *Taqwiyat al-Iman maʿ Tazkir al-Ikhwan*, rpntd Deoband: Faisal Publications, 1999.

Shah Rafiʿ al-Din Dehlavi, *Majmuʿa-i Rasaʾil*, ed. ʿAbdul Hamid Khan Sawati, 2 vols, Gujranwala: Madrasa Nusrat ul-ʿUlum, Vol. 1, 1964; Vol. 2, 1993.

Shahjahanabadi, Shah Kalim-Allah, *Maktubat-i Kalimi*, Delhi: Matbaʿ Yusufi, 1301 H/1883.

Shahnawaz Khan, Samsam al-Daula, *Maʾasir al-Umara*, Calcutta: Biblioteca Indica, 1891.

Shaikh Rukn al-Din, *Lataʾif-i Quddusi*, Delhi: Matbaʿ Mujtabaʾi, 1311 AH/1894.

Shaked, Shaul, "Some Iranian Themes in Islamic Literature", in Philippe Gignoux, ed., *Recurrent Patterns in Iranian Religions: From Mazdaism to Sufism*, Paris: Association pour l'avancement des Études Iraniennes, 1992.

Sharh-i Masnawi-i Maulana Rum maʾ dibacha-i ʿAbd al-Latif, MS No. F. 1785, Nawwab Muzammilullah Library, Aligarh.

Sharma, Sandhiya, "Society and Culture in Northern India in the Reeti Poetry", Ph.D. Dissertation, Jawaharlal Nehru University, New Delhi, 2000.

Sharma, Sunil, "Forbidden Love, Persianate Style: Reading Tales of Iranian Poets and Mughal Patrons", *Iranian Studies*, Vol. 42, No. 5, 2009.

Sharma, Sunil, *Mughal Arcadia: Persian Literature in an Indian Court*, Cambridge: Harvard University Press, 2017.

Shattari, Muhammad Ghaus, *Gulzar-i Abrar*, Urdu translation: *Azkar-i Abrar*, by Fazl Muhammad Jeori, Lahore: Islamic Book Foundation, rpntd 1395 H/1975.

Shaw, Robert Barkley, "The History of Khwajas of Eastern Turkistan", ed. N. Elias, *Journal of the Asiatic Society of Bengal*, Vol. 66, Part 1 (1899).

Shea, David, and Anthony Troyer, *Dabistan, or School of Manners*, London: Allen and Co., 3 vols, 1843.

Sheikh, Samira, "Aurangzeb as Seen from Gujarat: Shi'i and Millenarian Challenges to Mughal Sovereignty", *Journal of the Royal Asiatic Society*, Third Series, Vol. 28, No. 3, 2018.

Sidarus, Adel, "A Western Mirror for Princes for an Eastern Potentate: The Adab al-saltanat by Jerome Xavier SJ for the Mogul Emperor", *Journal of Eastern Christian Studies* 63, nos 1–2 (2011).

Siddiqui, Mazheruddin, "A Historical View of Iqbal's Ideas on *Tasawwuf*", *Islamic Studies* (Islamabad), Vol. 5, No. 4, 1966.

Siddiqui, Muhammad Badr-ul-Islam, ed., *Al-Jannat al-Samaniya* (Eight Heavens), Jhelum: Khanaqah-e Sultaniya, 2007.

Simnani, 'Ala al-Daula, *Al-'Urwa li ahl al-Khalwa wa al-Jalwa*, ed. Najib Mayel Haravi, Tehran: Intisharat-i Maula, 1362 sh. / 1983.

Simnani, 'Ala al-Daula, *Chihl Majlis*, compiled Amir Iqbal Sistani, ed. 'Abd al-Rafi' Haqiqat, Tehran: Shirkat-i Mu'allifan wa Mutarjiman-i Iran, 1358 sh. / 1979.

Simnani, 'Ala al-Daula, "Mala Budda Minh fi al-Din", *Fasl* 6 in *Musannafat-i Farsi*, ed. Mayel Heravi. Tehran: Shirkat-i Isharat-i 'Ilmi wa Farhangi, 1369 sh. / 1991.

Simnani, Jahangir Ashraf, *Lata'if-i Ashrafi*, compiled Nizam Yamani, Urdu translation 'Abd-ul-Haqq and 'Abd-us-Sattar, 4 vols, Ambedkar Nagar: Danish Book Depot, 1997–2007.

Sirhindi, Shaikh Ahmad, *Maktubat-i Imam Rabbani*, ed. 'Aziz al-Din Dehlavi, Delhi, 1873.

Sirhindi, Shaikh Ahmad, *Maktubat-i Imam-i Rabbani*, Kanpur: Nawal-Kishor, 1906.

Sirhindi, Shaykh Ahmad, *Risala dar Kawa'if-i Shi'a*, Persian text edited with a translation by Ghulam Mustafa Khan, Rampur, India: Hashmat Ali Khan, Mahalla Thana Pakhar, 1965.

Sirhindi, Shaykh Ahmad, *Risala Radd-i Shi'a*, Aligarh: Aligarh Muslim University Manuscripts, *Farsiya Mazhab wa Taswwuf*, No. 202, *shamil* no. 201.

Sirhindi, Shaykh Ahmad, *Risala-i Mabda' wa Ma'ad*, edited with Urdu translation by Saiyid Zawwar Husain Naqshbandi Mujaddidi, Karachi: Idara-i Mujaddidiya, Nazimabad, 1968.

Sirhindi, Shaykh Ahmad, *Risala-i Radd-i Rawafiz*, Urdu translation by Ghulam Mustafa Mujaddidi, in Shaykh Ahmad Sirhindi, *Rasa'il-i Mujaddid-i Alf-i Sani*, New Delhi: Arshad Brothers, 2005.

Slaje, Walter, "Liberation from Intentionality and Involvement: On the Concept of *Jivanmukti* in the Moksopaya", *Journal of Indian Philosophy* 28 (2000).

Slaje, Walter, *Vom Moksopaya-Sastra zum Yogavasistha-Maharamayana: Philologische Untersuchungen zur Entwicklung- und Uberlieferungsgeschichte eines indischen Lehrwerks mit Anspruch auf Heilsrelevanz*, Vienna: Österreichischen Akademie der Wissenschaften, 1994.

Somadeva, *Tales from the Kathasaritsagara*, ed. and transl. Arshiya Sattar, New Delhi, 1994.

Somadeva, *The Ocean of Story, Being a Translation of Somadeva's Katha Sarit Sagara*, ed. N.M. Penzer, translated by C.H. Tawney, London, 1924–8.

Subrahmanyam, Sanjay, "A Note on the Kabul Kingdom Under Muhammad Hakim Mirza (1554–85)", in *La Transmission du savoir dans le monde musulman peripherique, Lettre d'information*, No. 14 (1994).

Surur, Taha 'Abd al-Baqi, *Al-Tasawwuf al-Islami wa al-Imam al-Sha'rani*, Cairo: Dar-i-Nuhzat-i-Misr, 1952.

Szuppe, Maria, "Status, Knowledge, and Politics: Women in Sixteenth-Century Safavid Iran", in Guity Nashat and Lois Beck, eds, *Women in Iran: From the Rise of Islam to 1800*.

Tabari (al-), Muhammad bin Jarir, *Jami' al-Bayan 'an Ta'wil Ay al-Qur'an*, ed. 'Abd-Allah bin 'Abd al-Muhsin al-Turki, Riyadh, 2003.

Tabari (al-), Muhammad bin Jarir, *Tarikh al-Rusul wa al-Muluk*, ed. Muhammad Abu al-Fazl Ibrahim, Cairo, 1960.

Tarafdar, M.R., *Husain Shahi Bengal, AD 1494-1538: A Socio-Political Study*, Dhaka, 1965.

Tareen, SherAli K., *Defending Muhammad in Modernity*, Ranikhet: Permanent Black 2020, and Notre Dame: University of Notre Dame Press, 2020.

Tattavi, Qazi Ahmad, and Asaf Khan Qazwini, *Tarikh-i Alfi*, ed. Ghulam Riza Tabatab'i Majd, Tehran: Intisharat-i 'Ilmi wa Farhangi, 1382 sh. / 2003.

Tavakoli-Targhi, Mohamed, "Contested Memories of Pre-Islamic Iran", *The Medieval History Journal*, Vol. 2(2), 1999.

Tavakoli-Targhi, Mohamed, "Orientalism's Genesis Amnesia", *Comparative Studies of South Asia, Africa, and the Middle East*, Vol. 16(1), 1996.

Tavernier, Jean-Baptiste, *Travels in India*, ed. and trans. V. Ball and W. Crooke, 2nd edn, 2 vols, London: Oxford University Press, 1925.

ter Haar J.G.J., *Follower and Heir of the Prophet: Shaikh Ahmad Sirhindi as a Mystic*, Leiden: Het Oosters Instituut, 1992.

Thackston, Wheeler M., *Tarikh-i Rashidi*, Cambridge, MA: Harvard University Press, 1996.

Thanawi, Ashraf 'Ali, *al-Tanbih al-Tarabi fi Tanzih Ibn al-'Arabi*, Thana Bhawan: Ashraf al-Matabi', 1346 AH / 1927.

Thanawi, Ashraf 'Ali, *Haqq al-Sama'*, Kanpur: Matba' Razzaqi, 1327 AH / 1909.

Thanawi, Ashraf 'Ali, *Hikayat-i Auliya*, Karachi: Dar-ul-Isha'at, n.d.

Thanawi, Ashraf 'Ali, *Imdad al-Fatawa*, ed. Mufti Muhammad Shafi', Karachi: Maktaba Darul 'Ulum, 2010.

Thanawi, Ashraf 'Ali, *Karamat-e Imdadiya*, Kanpur: Matba' Nizami, n.d.

Thomi, Peter, "The Yogavasistha in Its Longer and Shorter Version", *Journal of Indian Philosophy* 11 (1983).

Tinguely, Frédéric, ed., *Un Libertin dans l'Inde Moghole: Les Voyages de François Bernier (1656–1669)*, Paris: Editions Chandeigne, 2008.

Truschke, Audrey, *Culture of Encounters: Sanskrit at the Mughal Court*, New York: Columbia University Press, 2016.

'Ubaid-Allah, Muhammad, *Hasanat al-Haramayn* (Arabic) translated into Persian by Muhammad Shakir ibn Badr al-Din Sirhindi, edited with an Introduction by Muhammad Iqbal Mujaddidi, Dera Ismail Khan: Maktaba-i Sirajjiya Khanaqah-i Ahmadiya Sa'idiya, Musa-za'i Sharif, 1981.

'Ubaid-Allah, Mujaddidi Muhammad Iqbal, ed., *Lata'if al-Madina*, facsimile edition, with an introduction and summary in Urdu, Lahore: Hauza-i Naqshbandiya, 2004.

Upadhyaya, Ved Prakash, *Kalki Avatar aur Muhammad Sahib*, Urdu translation by 'Azizul Haq 'Umari, Maunath Bhanjan, n.d.

Urunbaev, Asom, ed., *The Letters of Khwaja 'Ubayd Allah Ahrar and His Associates*, English translation with notes by Jo-Ann Gross, Introductory essays by Jo-Ann Gross and Asom Urunbaev, Leiden: Brill, 2002.

Usmani, Shams Naved, and S. 'Abdullah Tariq, *Agar ab bhi na jage to*, Delhi, 1989.

Valentijn, François, *Oud en Nieuw Oost Indiën*, Book 4, Part 2, Amsterdam: Joannes van Braam, *et al.*, 1726.

Varma, Ved Prakash, "Non-Theism in the Mimamsa Philosophy", in Ved Prakash Varma, ed., *Philosophical Reflections: Essays on Socio-Ethical Philosophy and Philosophy of Religion*, Lucknow, 2005.

Vassie, Roderic, "Persian Interpretations of the Bhagvadgita in the Mughal Period", Ph.D. dissertation, School of Oriental and African Studies, London, 1988.

Venkatesananda, Swami, *Vasistha's Yoga*, Albany, NY: SUNY Press, 1993.

Vettam, Mani, *Puranic Encyclopaedia*, rpntd Delhi, 1998.

Vikor, Knut, "The Shaykh as *Mujtahid*: A Sufi Conception of *Ijtihad*", in Alfonso Carmona Gonzalez, ed., *El Sufismo y las normas del Islam: Papers Presented at the IV International Conference on Islamic Legal Studies: Law and Sufism*, Muricia: Editora Regional de Murcia, 2006.

Walbridge, John. *The Wisdom of the Mystic East: Suhrawardi and Platonic Orientalism*, Albany, 2001.

Wali-Allah, Shah, *Al-Tafhimat al-Ilahiya*, 2 vols, ed. Ghulam Mustafa al-Qasimi, Hyderabad, West Pakistan: Shah Wali-Allah Academy, 1967–1970.

Wali-Allah, Shah, *Anfas al-'Arifin*, Delhi: Matba' Mujtaba'i, 1917.

Wali-Allah, Shah, *Hama'at*, translated into Urdu as *Tasawwuf ki Haqiqat aur uska Falsafa-i Tarikh*, with an Introduction by 'Ubaidullah Sindhi, rpnt. Deoband: Maktaba-i Rahmaniya, 1969.

Wali-Allah, Shah, *Hujjat al-Allah al-Baligha*, Cairo: Dar al-Turas, 1355 AH/1936.

Walker, Paul E., "The Doctrine of Metempsychosis in Islam", in Wael B.

Hallaq and Donald B. Lille, eds, *Islamic Studies Presented to Charles J. Adams*, Leiden, 1991.
Waseem, M., trans. and ed., *On Becoming an Indian Muslim: French Essays on Aspects of Syncretism*, Delhi: Oxford University Press, 2003.
Weismann, Itzchak, *The Naqshbandiyya: Orthodoxy and Activism in a Worldwide Sufi Tradition*, London: Routledge, 2007.
Winter, Michael, *Society and Religion in Early Ottoman Egypt: Studies in the Writings of 'Abd al-Wahhab al-Sha'rani*, New Brunswick and London: Transactions Books, 1982.
Yaycioglu, Ali, "Guiding Tradition and Laws Disciplining Bodies and Souls: Tradition, Science, and Religion in the Age of Ottoman Reform", *Modern Asian Studies*, Vol. 52, No. 5, 2018.
Zaidi, Nazir Hasan, ed., *Maktubat-i Sa'ad Allah Khan*, Lahore: Idara-e Tahqiqat-e Pakistan, Punjab University, 1968.
Zaki, Mohammed, "Mir'atul Makhluqat of Abdur Rehman Chishti", in D. Devahuti, ed., *Bias in Indian Historiography*, Delhi, 1980.
Zarqani (al-), Muhammad ibn 'Abd al-Baqi, *Mukhtasar al-Maqasid al-Hasana fi Bayan al-Ahadis al-Mushtahira 'ala al-Alsina*, ed. Muhammad al-Sabbagh, Beirut, 1982.
Ziad, Waleed, "From Yarkand to Sindh via Kabul: The Rise of Naqshbandi–Mujaddidi Sufi Networks in the Eighteenth and Nineteenth Centuries", in Abbas Amanat and Assef Ashraf, eds, *The Persianate World: Rethinking a Shared Sphere*, Leiden: Brill, 2019.
Ziegler, Norman P., "Rajput Loyalties during the Mughal Period", in John F. Richards, ed., *Kingship and Authority in South Asia*, Delhi: Oxford University Press, 1998.

Index

Aaron (Harun) 139, 154n48, 394
Abaqat 13–15, 17
Abbasids 123, 156
'Abd al-Ahad, Shaikh (father of Ahmad Sirhindi) 341, 348
'Abd al-'Aziz, Shah, of Delhi 16, 16n27, 23, 29
'Abd al-Bari, Khwaja 69, 71
'Abd al-Hakim Sialkoti 339, 345n35, 365n84
'Abd al-Haqq Muhaddis Dehlavi 42–3, 83, 94–5, 97n6, 100n10, 101n15, 102n18, 110, 116n66, 126, 129, 130–1, 133, 149, 267
'Abd al-Hayy Phulati, Shah 16n27, 17n29
'Abd al-Khaliq Ghijduwani, Khwaja 63
'Abd-Allah, Khwaja (son of Baqi-Billah) 100n10
'Abd-Allah ibn 'Abbas 169, 198, 207
'Abd-Allah ibn Mirza Ibrahim ibn Shahrukh, Mirza 57–8, 77
'Abd-Allah of Jaunpur, Saiyid 157
'Abd al-Latif, Shaikh 364, 377n106
'Abd al-Latif 'Abbasi Gujarati 102n18
'Abd al-Qadir Jili (Gilani) Muhyi al-Din, Shaikh 133, 340

'Abd al-Qawi, Mulla 8, 351, 363n79
'Abd al-Quddus Gangohi 49, 50–5, 80–3, 95, 236n38, 341, 362
'Abd al-Rahim, Shaikh (father of Shah Wali-Allah) 10
'Abd al-Rahim, Khwaja 332, 333n10
'Abd al-Rahim Wilayati, Shaikh 19, 40
'Abd al-Rahman Chishti 27, 35, 42–5, 56, 80n82, 93, 94–111, 114–22, 123–7, 128, 137–63, 164–92, 193–216, 393–4
'Abd al-Rahman Qidwa'i 149, 154
'Abd al-Razzaq, Shah, of Awadh 27
'Abd al-Sami', Maulana, of Rampur 20–1
'Abd al-Sattar ibn Qasim Lahori 226n22, 390–1
'Abd al-Shahid, Khwaja 66, 70–1, 73
'Abd al-Wahhab, Qazi 351, 359
'Abd al-Wahid Bilgrami, Mir 27, 79n79, 198–9
abdal ("the Substitutes", a class of Sufis) 117, 289, 346, 364n83
Abhinanda (Abhinandan) 220, 223n16, 224, 226, 239, 243, 244, 249
Abraham (Ibrahim) 99, 102, 154n47, 194

INDEX

Abu al-Fath Chishti, of Awadh 146, 160
Abu al-Fath Qidwa'i 154
Abu al-Fazl 55–6, 60–1, 72, 79–84, 121, 129, 164, 174n25, 203, 226n22, 267
Abu al-Hasan (Sultan of Golconda) 368, 371
Abu al-Hasan Hasri 103
Abu al-Riza, Shaikh 10
Abu Bakr (the first Pious Caliph) 121, 393
Abu Bakr Shibli 100n10, 103
Abu Hanifa 100n10, 103, 104, 112, 125, 140, 156
Abu Sa'id, Sultan 57n17, 58, 72, 77
Abu Tahir al-Kurdi al-Madani, Shaikh 13
adab (moral conduct, manners) 87, 104, 117
Adam (father of the human race) 44, 142, 150, 154, 164, 167–72, 175–9, 183–5, 187–90, 192–3, 195, 197–8, 202–8, 213, 215–16, 328; his children 177–8
Adam Binori, Shaikh 7, 10, 16, 373, 376, 386
Afghanistan 364
Afghans 1, 49, 64, 67, 72n59; and Chishtis 50–4, 83, 92
Agra (Akbarabad) 66, 69, 79, 82, 85, 118, 120, 126, 223n18, 260, 262, 263, 266, 279, 332, 358, 380, 389
ahadiyat 100–1, 198
Ahl-i Hadith 31
Ahl-i sunnat wa jama'at, ahl-i sunna wa jama'a (the Sunni community) 90, 99, 102, 112, 120, 121, 125, 143, 144, 342, 380
Ahmad. *See* Prophet Muhammad
Ahmad 'Abd al-Haqq of Rudauli, Shaikh 51, 95, 97, 166
Ahmad ibn Hanbal 109, 156
Ahmad ibn Jalal al-Din Khwajagi 64–5
Ahmad Khattu, Shaikh 53
Ahmad Mirza, Sultan 58, 60
Ahmad Shah, Emperor (r. 1748–54) 384
Ahmad Shahid, Saiyid 14, 16–20, 22, 29–30, 40, 385
Ahmad Sirhindi, Shaikh 7, 14, 15, 27, 28n52, 38, 42, 48, 49n2, 86, 91–5, 97, 100n10, 101, 103, 110, 111–16, 120n75, 123–6, 161, 208, 286, 290, 294, 296, 304, 334–9, 345–53, 357, 364, 368, 372–9, 385, 391–2
Ahmad Zarruq 43, 110n49
ahrar (free men) 38–9
Ahrar, 'Ubaid-Allah, Khwaja 41, 57–65, 68–71, 73, 75–8, 85, 89, 98, 162, 331–2, 353–4
ahwal (mystical states) 295; and *aqwal* (sayings) 12, 100
A'in-i Akbari 56, 82n84, 129, 164n1, 174n25, 183n41
'Aja'ibat ka Zuhul aur 'Aja'ibat ka Qubul 32–3
ajlaf (the low-born) 134, 151
Ajmer 72, 79, 84, 93, 115n63–4, 117–18, 137, 146–7, 160, 162, 262, 266, 267, 278–80, 340, 386n124, 390

INDEX

Akbar, Emperor 7, 45, 48, 50, 55, 67n48, 102n18, 124, 129, 196, 223, 226, 235, 248, 256–7, 260, 267, 269, 334, 337, 350, 389, 395; and Chishtis 41, 50, 56, 78–84, 93, 117–18, 315, 387–8, 392; and Naqshbandis 50, 70–8, 84–92, 93, 95, 114, 116, 118, 126, 160–1, 331–2, 349; religious innovations of 73, 114, 116

Akbarabad. *See* Agra

Akbarnama 60n28, 61n31, 81, 84n90, 102n18. *See also* Abu al-Fazl

Akhbar al-Akhyar 83, 94, 97n6, 100n10, 101n15, 129, 130–1, 133, 278

Akhi Jamshid Qidwa'i, Qazi 153, 154n48

akhlaq (ethics) 29, 245, 252n75, 256–7

'Ala al-Daula Simnani 88, 101–2, 114, 117, 125, 149

'Ala al-Din 'Attar, Khwaja 69, 72

'Alam-Allah, Saiyid Shah 16, 385–6

'alam (world) 199, 203–4, 228n25, 237; *'alam-i ajsam* (World of Bodies) 12; *'alam-i baqa* (the world of eternity) 225, 227; *'alam-i fani* ("the transient world" i.e. this world) 225, 236; *'alam-i kaun wa makan* (World of Being and Space) 101n11; *'alam-i malakut, 'alam-i malak wa malakut* (World of Angels) 136, 147; *'alam-i misal* (World of Similitudes) 12, 13, 150, 191, 205, 208; *'alam-i nasut* (World of Men) 147

'Alamgir II, Emperor (r. 1754–9) 384

Alanqua 121

'Ali ibn Abi Talib (the Prophet's son-in-law and the fourth Pious Caliph) 4n4, 17, 44, 96, 98, 99, 106, 121, 126, 140, 144, 145, 149, 154, 156, 159, 181, 204, 380, 393–4

'Ali Khawass, Shaikh 108–9

'Ali Sabir, Shaikh 97

Aman-Allah of Sandila, Shaikh 138

Ambala 263

Amir Husaini Haravi 175n27

Amir Khusrau 112–13

Amir Kulal, Shaikh 56, 340

'Andalib, Muhammad Nasir, Khwaja 6, 165, 382–5

Anfas al-'arifin 10n12, 10n13

angels 35, 136n11, 142–3, 159, 168n12, 170, 172, 175, 192, 199, 206, 265, 275, 289, 294–5, 339, 347; *nurani* (made of light) 171; *'unsuri* (elemental) 147, 171, 173

Anis al-Hujjaj 303

Anwar al-Qur'an 178n33, 196–7

Anwar al-Sati'a 21

'aqa'id (religious beliefs) 31, 100, 134

'Aqil Khan Razi 266n20, 306, 374n98

'aql (reason, intellect) 39, 132, 193, 329–30; *wa fikr* (and speculation) 104

Arabia 17, 363, 373

Arabic 16, 31, 84, 178n33, 194, 203, 224n19, 225, 243, 256, 301, 315, 335n12, 339, 360, 363, 372, 373, 377, 383, 395
a'raf (Purgatory) 193
Arjuna 171, 187, 190n51, 201, 244n63, 252–3
Armenian(s) 342
Arzu, Siraj al-Din 'Ali Khan 306
Asar al-Sanadid 17, 29–30
ashraf (those of noble birth) 133
Ashraf 'Ali Thanawi 20, 22–6, 40
Ashraf Jahangir Simnani, Shaikh, Saiyid 105, 117, 129, 137, 148–9, 155n50
Ashraf Mazandarani 301–2, 306–12, 313n115
Asrar-i Khudi 38
'Attar, Farid al-Din 103, 148, 175, 233, 234, 276
Atwar dar Hall-i Asrar 167n9, 224, 228–30, 235
Auhad al-Din Kirmani 35, 290
auliya'. See *wali*
Aurad-i Chishti 155
Aurangabad 353, 386, 389, 393
Aurangzeb, Emperor 39, 45, 120, 122, 218, 261–6, 280–5, 297–306, 314–19, 389; and Chishtis 8, 386n124; and Naqshbandi–Mujaddidis 6, 46, 285–6, 303–4, 315–16, 334–8, 349–51, 353–60, 363–72, 374–5, 378–80, 384–7, 389, 392, 396
avatara (avatar) 184n41, 210, 212, 243
Awadh 16, 27, 51, 95, 98, 121n76, 130, 146, 148, 150, 152, 154n48, 159, 198, 385–6

Awadhi. See Hindi
'Awarif al-Ma'arif 151
Azad, Abu al-Kalam, Maulana 342–3
Azad Bilgrami, Ghulam 'Ali 199n61, 302n91, 306

Baba Lal 219
Baba Shah Musafir 393
Babur, Zahir al-Din Muhammad 50, 57n17, 60, 161; and Chishtis 52, 54–5, 82; and Naqshbandis 55, 61–6, 69–70, 331
Baburnama 60–3, 65–6
Bada'uni, 'Abd al-Qadir 67, 69n51, 70–4, 83, 129–30, 136, 165n2
Badakhshan 74n66, 333–4
Badi' al-Din Madar, Shah. See Madar, Shah Badi' al-Din
Badr al-Din Sirhindi 15, 373
Badshahnama 263n12, 332–3
Baghdad 103, 165
Baha al-Din Naqshband, Shaikh 56–7, 59, 63, 69, 72, 75, 89n101, 97, 332, 340, 359, 387
Bahadur Shah, Sultan of Gujarat 52–3
bai'at (pledging allegiance, initiation) 19; critique of 30
Bairam Khan 67n48, 69, 72
Baisunghar Mirza 62
Bakhtawar Khan 285, 299n85, 303n94, 335, 364n83
Balakot 18n32, 20
Balkh 333–4
Bani Isra'il 139, 152–5
baqa' (subsistence) 225, 227, 237,

239, 277, 289, 293–4, 297–8.
See also *fana'*
Baqi-Billah, Khwaja 10, 41, 85–93, 97, 100–1, 111, 114, 124, 334, 341n22, 392; *Al-Barahin Qati'at al- Zalam al-Anwar al-Sati'a* 21–2
barzakh-i kubra (Great Isthmus) 101n11
Bayazid Bistami 296
Bengal 118, 194
Bernier, François 218n3, 261, 284, 298n84, 300
Bhagavad-Gita, Bhagavadgita, Gita 166, 174n26, 199, 201, 241, 253
Bhagavata-Purana 183, 202
bhang 134, 136, 137
Bharadwaja (Bharadwaj) 227–8, 230, 248, 255
Bhavishya Purana 167, 196
Bhavishyottarapurana (Bhabikh Uttarpuran) 45, 180
bid'a (innovation) 8, 16n27, 17, 22, 30–1, 103, 124, 208, 339
Bihar, 55n13, 151, 302n92
bi-shar' (antinomian) 44, 128
Brahma (Brahm; Hindu deity) 171, 175–7, 179, 183, 190–1, 193–4, 197–8, 213, 245–7, 251
Brahman (Brahm; the Absolute) 231–4, 238
Brahmanical 197, 209, 220, 221. *See also* Hindu
Brahmanism 198. *See also* Hindu
Brahmins, Brahmans (Hindu priestly class) 112, 174n25, 194, 212n85, 242, 342
Braj. *See* Hindi

Brij Mohan Lal Kanpuri 28n52
British 20, 40, 195, 389
Bu 'Ali Qalandar 35
Buddhist 210
Bukhara 59, 64n41, 77, 165, 289

Caliph(s), Caliphate 96, 103, 113, 121, 123, 156, 182, 267, 345, 347, 375, 381
Central Asia, Central Asian 1, 2, 41–2, 48, 50, 57–63, 74n66, 84, 92, 94, 111, 113, 160–2, 257, 315, 332–3, 334n12, 347, 351, 392
Chaghatai 61, 75–6
Champat Rai 312–13
Chandayan 162
Chihil Majlis 21n38, 101n14, 107n37
China 1, 71n54
Chinese 77, 204, 216
Chishti(s), Chishtiya 3, 4n4, 5, 6, 30–1, 41, 55, 69, 78–84, 97–8, 114–15, 129, 161, 267–9, 272, 278–80, 282n56, 285–7, 315, 318–19, 390–1; and Hindus and other religions 27, 44–6, 116, 124–6, 141–3, 161–3, 165–216, 393–4; and Madaris 44, 137–8, 146–8, 153, 159–60, 162; and Naqshbandis 6–10, 40–3, 49, 54, 85–9, 92–4, 110, 114, 123–5, 162–3, 208, 287, 290, 293, 296, 341, 361–3, 385–8; and Nizami Chishtis 97; and Sabiri Chishtis 7–9, 18–19, 22–3, 40, 42–5, 46, 50–6, 94–110, 116–22, 137, 223, 348, 365n84, 391–3

Chishti–Sabiri. *See* Chishti
Christ. *See* Jesus
Christian(s), Christianity 113, 203, 214, 344, 345

de Clavijo, Ruy González 259
Dabistan-i Mazahib 129, 132, 134–7
Daniyal, Prince 73
Dara Shukoh, Prince 7, 27, 45–6, 129, 133–4, 151, 154n48, 164, 165n2, 217–58, 261, 263–75, 278, 281, 283–6, 288, 291, 300, 315, 317, 318, 334, 336, 339n20, 342, 349, 351, 362, 364, 387, 390, 394–5
Dard, Khwaja Mir 6, 382–5
dargah (shrine) 128, 223
Darwesh Muhammad Barki of Jalandhar, Shaikh 343–5
Dasaratha (Dasrat) 228, 242
Dattu Sarvani 52–4
Da'ud Gangohi, Shaikh 362, 363n79
David (Biblical) 154n48, 199
Da'wat-i asma'-i hasana (invocation of the Divine Names) 67, 119n72
Day of Judgment (*qiyamat*) 143–4, 183–4, 237, 351
Dayanand Saraswati 196–7
Deccan 48, 363, 366, 368, 375, 380, 386, 387
Delhi 6, 8, 9, 16, 17, 19, 28n52, 29, 46, 52, 55n13, 67n48, 70, 79, 85–6, 126, 154n48, 165, 195n57, 260, 263, 267, 281, 298n83, 301, 302, 352, 356, 358, 362–4, 367, 380–9

Delhi Sultanate 1, 268, 393
Deobandi(s), Deoband School 19–26; and Chishti–Sabiri 22–3, 26
dervish 9, 58, 60, 72, 81, 83, 88, 148, 151, 288, 293, 299, 342, 360, 361. See also *faqir*
Dev, devata, devta (deity). *See* Hindu
Devil 101–2
dharma 184, 235, 243
Dharmashastras (Hindu law codes) 28
din (faith, religion) 142, 182, 192
Din-i Ilahi 73n64
Diwan-i Makhfi 305, 306n104, 313–14
Divinity 11, 31, 77, 112, 117, 140, 153, 341, 359
Diwan-i Hafiz 26n46, 35, 104n23
doha (Hindi couplet) 8, 10, 162
dream(s) 28, 53–4, 61–2, 139, 254–8, 288n65, 367–70, 390–1
Dughlat, Mirza Haidar 61, 66–9, 331

East India Company 19, 195n57
European(s) 195, 215–16, 256–7, 367, 395; accounts of the Mughals 261, 281, 284, 298, 300–1; in the Mughal Empire 263, 356

Faisla-i Haft Mas'ala 20–2
Faisla-i Wahdat al-Wujud wa Wahdat al-Shuhud 13
faiz (divine bounty, grace) 117, 193, 297
Faizi Fayyazi 80

Fakhr al-Din Dehlavi, Shaikh 6, 388n127
fana' 34, 237, 239, 277, 289–94, 296–7
Faqr 39, 64, 85, 91, 344
faqir ("poor"; dervish, Sufi) 13, 30–1, 246, 344–5, 375
Farghana 61, 161
Farid Bukhari, Shaikh 91, 116n66
Farid al-Din Ganj-i Shakar Mas'ud, Shaikh 105, 267
Farrukh Siyar, Emperor 364, 381
Fatawa-i 'Alamgiri 351
Fatehpur Sikri, Fathpur Sikri, Fathpur 76, 79, 80
fatiha (prayer of blessing) 74; (prayers to seek blessings for the dead) 20–1, 279
fatiha-i kitab-i injil 153–4
Fatima (daughter of the Prophet) 17, 143, 181–4, 320, 347
Fawa'id al-Fu'ad 165
Fazle Rahman Ganj Muradabadi, Shah 28
Fihi ma fihi 38n77
Findiriski, Abu al-Qasim 224–5, 230–9, 244, 248
fiqh (jurisprudence) 42–3, 100, 106, 111–12, 351
Firdausi, Firdausi Suhrawardi (Sufi order) 55n13, 104, 151
Firishta, Muhammad Qasim 51, 165n2
Fusus al-Hikam 24–6, 100, 101n15, 142, 341
Futuhat al-Makkiya 101, 144, 158, 170n17, 204, 205n68, 206. *See also* Ibn 'Arabi

Fuyuz al-Haramain 10n11

Gabriel (Jibril) Archangel 37, 98–9, 135–6
Ganges (Ganga) 53, 54, 192, 199
Gangoh 8, 52
Gauharara, Princess 334, 336
Genesis, Book of 215
Gharib-Allah, Saiyid 362–3
(al-)Ghazali, Abu Hamid 34, 106
(Al-)Ghazali 34
Ghulam 'Ali of Delhi, Shaikh (Shah) 6, 9, 29, 384
Gita. See *Bhagavad-Gita*
Golconda 357, 367–8, 371, 379
Gujarat, Gujarati 52–4, 67n48, 78, 147, 271, 351, 363
Gulbadan Begum 260, 315, 331
Gulshan, Sa'd-Allah 382–3, 385n122
Gulshan-i Wahdat 304n97, 321–30, 365n84, 367n90, 372n95, 378, 379n108, 381n114
Gulzar-i Abrar 129, 131–2
Gwalior 67n48

habs-i dam 162, 291, 293
hadith (pl. *ahadith*) 8, 12, 21, 30, 94, 108–9, 121–2, 126, 140, 144, 169, 172, 181, 198, 205, 207, 214, 229, 271, 323–4, 330, 339–41, 343, 354–5, 357, 363n79, 365n84, 372, 394
Hafiz Shirazi 26n46, 35, 38–9, 104, 149n32, 201, 234, 308
Hajj 17, 73, 90, 263, 303–4, 320, 336, 347, 355, 365–7, 376
Hali, Altaf Husain 36
(al-)Hallaj, Mansur 296
Hama'at 11–12

Hamida Bano Begum 260
Hanafi, Hanafite (school of jurisprudence) 23, 74, 94, 100, 108, 112, 125, 156
Hanbali, Hanbalite (school of jurisprudence) 108, 156
Haqa'iq-i Hindi 27, 79n79, 198–9
haqiqa 12, 90, 111
Haqiqat-i Muhammadi(ya) 101n11, 289, 376
Haqq al-sama' 23
Haramayn Sharifayn 366, 373
Harun. *See* Aaron
Hasan (the Prophet's grandson) 96, 347
Hasan Abdal 271
Hasan Naqshbandi, Khwaja 69–70
Hasan Nizami, Khwaja 36n70, 38
Hasanat al-Haramayn 347–9, 363, 373
Hasrat Mohani 27
Hazarat al-Quds 373
heaven(s) (*falak*, pl. *aflak*; *swarga/surg*) 117, 135, 147, 150, 171, 176, 183, 185, 186, 188, 190, 199, 200, 207, 212, 276, 288n65, 328, 368, 390. *See also* Paradise
Hebrew 154
hell 5, 176, 193, 212, 276, 390
Hijaz 94, 110n49, 126, 334n12, 347, 355, 376–7, 386
himayat (protection) 62
Hind. *See* Hindustan
Hindal, Mirza 67
Hindawi 201–2
Hindi 8, 79, 383; Awadhi 28, 162, 198, 202; Braj 162

Hindu(s): ascetics (*sanyasi*) 134–6; in the Mughal state 74, 122, 282–3, 375–6; learning Persian 51; Muslim interactions with 20, 26–8, 91, 161–3, 342–3, 393–5; pandits 187, 192, 202, 225–6, 241; practices 134–6, 162, 195, 208, 384n119; Sufis 28; Vaishnava 183, 198
Hindu mythology: cosmology and cosmogony 44–5, 164–202, 207–8, 214; demons (*daitya, dait*) and 173, 175, 177, 188; gods (*dev, devata, devta*) and 28, 44, 170, 171–3, 175–8, 185–6, 188, 197, 208, 214, 228, 250–2; heavenly beings (*gandharva, gandharb*) and 176, 228; *raksasa, rakshas* and 175, 243; sages, saints (*rishi, rsi, rikshir*) and 169n15, 174–6, 178, 197, 208–9, 212, 214, 219, 228, 242, 247; *'unsuri devata* and 179, 188
Hindu philosophy. *See* Philosophy, Indic
Hindustan (Hind) 65–6, 69–70, 85, 92, 112–15, 145–8, 159–60, 171, 188, 282, 307, 380, 387
Hriday Ram 27
Hujjat al-Allah al-Baligha 110n46, 124n83
Hujwiri, 'Ali ibn 'Usman (Data Ganj-Bakhsh) 106–7
Humayun, Emperor 68–69, 71, 260, 315; and Chishtis 52–5, 82–3; and Naqshbandis 66–70,

331; and Shattaris 66–7, 93, 119n72, 331
Humayun Nama 260, 315
Husain (the Prophet's grandson) 96, 167, 181–2, 184, 187, 197
Husain Ahmad Madani 20, 40
Husain Balkhi, Shaikh 151
Husain Quli Khan 70–1
Husam al-Din, Shaikh 86
Huzaifa 139
huzur (presence) 359–60; *huzur-i qalb* (the presence of the heart, total devotion) 17

'*ibadat* 31, 90, 102, 251–2
Iblis 169, 175, 194
Ibn 'Arabi, Ibn al-'Arabi 10, 15, 23–6, 35, 37, 88, 89n101, 90, 100–1, 107, 109, 142, 144, 158, 170n17, 193, 204–5, 208, 235, 296, 340–1
Ibn Hazm, Abu Muhammad 'Ali ibn Ahmad ibn Sa'id 107n35
Ibrahim Lodi, Sultan 52, 64, 161
Ibrahim Sharqi, Sultan 155, 158–9
ihsan 11
Ikhlas, Kishan Chand 374n98, 382
Ilah Bakhsh of Lahore, Saiyid 6–8
Ilahdad, Shaikh 86
'*ilm* (knowledge) 130; '*ilm-i din* (religious knowledge) 129–30, 156; '*ilm-i ladunni* (knowledge from the divine) 139; '*ilm-i mu'amala* (pl. '*ulum-i mu'amala*; the science regarding human relationships) 24, 26; '*ilm-i mukashafa* (pl. '*ulum-i mukashafa*; the science concerning miracles and visionary insights) 24, 26; '*ilm-i mumkin* (contingent knowledge) 292
'*Ilm al-Kalam* 34
imam(s) 289; (of schools of jurisprudence) 23, 112, 125; (Shi'i) 96–7, 144, 145, 156
iman (faith) 275
Imdad-Allah, Haji 18–22, 40
Injil (New Testament) 139, 153, 180
al-Insaf fi Bayan-i Sabab al-Ikhtilaf 10
Iqbal, Muhammad 37–41
'Iqd al-Jid fi al-Ijtihad wa al-Taqlid 10
Iran, Iranian 57, 64, 67n48, 70, 122, 161, 224, 257, 260, 301–2, 393
'Iraqi, Fakhr al-Din 39, 200
'Irfan-i Hafiz 26n46
'Isa. *See* Jesus
'*ishq* 37, 39, 79, 326–30
Islamic jurisprudence 8, 10, 12, 23–4, 43, 100, 103, 106–12, 125, 140, 156, 372, 394
Islamic law 3, 21, 27, 94, 106–10, 123–5
Islamic world 36; 107, 109–10, 165; South Asia and the larger, 126, 334n12
Isma'il Shahid, Shah 13–18, 20, 22, 30, 39, 40
Isna 'Ashari (Twelver Shi'i). *See* Shi'a
i'tidal 99, 102, 122
i'tikaf (seclusion) 293–4
Izalat al-Khafa 'an Khilafat al-Khulafa' 10

440 INDEX

Jahanara, Princess 5, 46, 261–84, 286, 288, 291, 297–300, 315–18, 387, 391, 396; and Chishtis 5, 268–9, 278–80, 387; and Qadiris 5, 269–78, 280, 387, 396

Jahangir, Emperor 38, 124, 161, 223–6, 230, 235, 256, 261, 269, 392; and Chishtis 4n4, 118–19, 120n75, 163, 272, 387; and Europeans 256–7, 395; and Hindus 225–6; and Naqshbandis 38, 332, 334, 337, 351, 353; and Qadiris 119–20; and Shattaris 119; and Sufis 4, 118–20, 163, 390–1

Jahangir Ashraf Simnani. *See* Ashraf Jahangir Simnani

Jaimini 211–12

Jaina 210

Jaju, Battle of 380

Jalal al-Din Panipati, Shaikh 97

Jalal al-Din Tabataba'i 395

Jalal al-Din Thanesari, Shaikh 80, 84, 88, 390

Jami, 'Abd al-Rahman 15, 75n69, 89, 101n14, 144–5, 260, 267, 341, 359

(al-)Jannat al-Samaniya 372, 373n96

Jaunpur 130, 148, 150–1, 155, 157, 159

Jawahar al-Tafsir 141

Jayasi, Malik Muhammad 162, 198

Jazba 26, 290, 292

Jeronimo Xavier 256–7

Jesus (Christ, 'Isa) 132, 140, 145, 150, 214, 313

Jew, Jewish 44, 113, 138–40, 152–5, 342, 344

Jibril. *See* Gabriel

jihad 64n41, 340, 343, 357, 385; against the British 19, 40

jinn(s) 141, 143, 168–73, 177, 179–80, 185–90, 192, 195, 203n63, 213, 214

jivanmukti (liberation in life) 221, 248–9

jizya 74, 282

jnana (jnan; knowledge) 219, 221n10, 228n25, 232, 251

jogi. See *yogi*

Judaism 214

Jug Basisht, Jug Bashist. See *Yogavasistha*

Jumman, Saiyid, Shaikh 129, 132, 135–6

Junaid Baghdadi 12, 341

jurist(s) 11, 26, 106–7, 110n49, 123, 158

Ka'ba 205, 297, 320, 347–8, 376–7

Kabul 59n23, 66, 69–70, 74n66, 78, 85, 134, 263, 271, 380

kafir (pl. *kuffar*; unbeliever) 8, 20, 79, 102, 123, 157, 175, 363, 375

kahin (Jewish scholar) 139

Kailash 173, 174, 177, 185–6, 223n18

kalam (Islamic theology, scholasticism) 100, 112

(Al-)Kalam 34

Kalan, Khwaja 66

Kalid-i Masnavi 26n46

Kalim-Allah Shahjahanabadi, Shah 6, 386–8

kalima (the word of the faith) 102, 394
Kalimat al-Haqq (of Ghulam Yahya) 13
Kalimat al-Haqq (of Sir Syed Ahmad Khan) 30
Kaljug (*Kaliyuga*). See *Yuga*
Kalki 183–4, 197n59
Kalki-Purana 183, 201
Kalpi 131, 148, 151, 155
Kamboh, Muhammad Salih 264n17, 332–3
Kamran, Mirza 68
Kanhavat 198
Kanpur 20, 128
karamat. See miracle
Karamat aur Mu'jiza 32–3
kashf, mukashafa (mystical unveiling) 10, 20, 24, 26, 104, 111, 298; critique of 31
Kashf al-Kunuz 201, 224
Kashf al-mahjub 106–7
Kashgar 71, 72, 77, 334
(al-)Kashifi, Fakhr al-Din ibn Husain Wa'iz 57
Kashmir 85–6, 120, 132, 134, 220, 222, 224, 263, 272–4, 280, 303, 332, 353, 393
Kathasaritasagara 172, 222n13
Kaurava(s) 187, 189
khalifa (deputy of a saint) 16, 28, 51, 64, 69, 72, 77, 80, 86, 87, 119, 132–3, 137, 142, 149, 269, 289, 297, 346, 359, 362, 364, 373, 376, 378, 385–6
khalwat dar anjuman 292, 300, 359–60
Khazinat al-Asfiya' 120n75
Khazinat al-Ma'arif 363

Khalid Naqshbandi, Maulana 334n12
Khalil Ahmad Saharanpuri 20–2
khanqah 22, 59, 80, 85, 91, 234
khatm-i khwajagan 357
Khawand Mahmud (Khwaja Nura; 16th c.) 66–9, 71
Khawand Mahmud ('Alavi Husaini) Khwaja (d. 1642) 85, 331–2, 393
khayal 31–2, 229
khilafat (deputyship) of the Prophet 99, 393; of a saint 18, 118
Khirqa 87
Khizr (Khwaja Khizr; Elias) 132, 389–91
khudi 38
Khurasan, Khorasan 59, 63, 77, 113
Khusrau Anushirwan 395
Khusus al-kilam 24
Khwajagi Khwaja 62–3, 71
Khwurd, Khwaja 10
kingship 76, 80, 117, 395; European theories of 256–7, 395; Indic theories of 221–2, 245–56, 257–8, 395; Perso-Islamic theories of 256–7
Krishna (Krsna, Kishan) 27, 28, 167, 171, 186–9, 190n51, 194, 197–9, 201–2, 213, 224, 245, 252–3
ksatriya(s) (*chhatri*) 221n11, 247–8, 253
kufr (unbelief) 22, 79, 90, 111, 341–2
Kulliyat-i Baqi-Billah 86–7, 90–9

Lahore 6, 8, 68, 85, 86, 263, 270–2, 297, 357–8, 380–1, 386, 389, 390
Lamhat 14
Lata'if al-Madina 373
latifa (pl. *lata'if*; subtle spiritual centre) 264, 288–9, 296, 360–1
Lata'if-i Ashrafi 105n27, 129, 149n32
Lata'if-i Quddusi 52–4
Lauh-i Mahfuz (the Preserved Tablet) 185n44
Lodi(s), Lodi dynasty 51–6, 154n48
Lucknow 39, 129, 152–3, 160, 386, 395n5

Mabda' wa Ma'ad 110–12
Madar, Shah Badi' al-Din 12, 35, 44, 115, 123–4, 128–63, 168n11
Madari(s) Madari order 44, 132–6, 138; and Jews 152–5
Madrasa Rahimiya 10
Mahabharata (*Mahabharat*) 171, 174, 179, 187, 189, 190n51, 202, 252, 256, 395; Persian translation of 164n1, 203, 226n22, 234
Mahadeva (Mahadev) 167–88, 197–8, 209, 224, 244n63, 250–2
Mahdi 143–5, 157–8, 394
Mahdism 157
Mahmud Mirza, Sultan 57n17, 62, 72
Mahmud Hasan (Deobandi) 40
Mahmud Kanturi, Qazi 137–8, 140, 150, 154, 156, 160, 168n11

Majma' al-Bahrain 27, 165n2, 236, 242, 250
Majnun and Layla (Layli, Laili) 21, 306, 322, 328–9
Makanpur 130, 133, 135, 138, 152, 158–9
Makhdum-i A'zam 77
Makhfi 261n9, 305–6, 313–14
Makatib-i Sharifa 9n10
Maktubat-i Imam Rabbani 15, 27, 94, 110–12, 208
Maktubat-i Quddusiyya 51n4, 55n10
Maktubat-i Ma'sumiya 339–45, 348, 361, 374–5
Maktubat-i Sa'idiya 334n12, 354, 375
Maktubat-i Saif 287–300, 358, 360–1, 374
malamati 123
malfuz (pl. *malfuzat*) 14, 16n27, 86–7, 89, 137, 165, 167–8
Maliki, Malikite (school of jurisprudence) 108, 144
Malwa 54, 152
Mandu 53
Manjhan, Shah 53
Manmohan ki Baten 28
mansab 72, 333
Mantiq al-Tair 148
Manucci, Niccolao 263n12, 282–3, 284n58, 298
Maqalat-i Sir Sayyid 30–2
Maqamat-i Ma'sumi 335n13, 336n15, 339n20, 346n38, 347n40, 348–9, 350n48, 351n51, 352n53, 353n55, 361n77, 364n83, 365n84, 372n95, 380n110
Maqsad-i Aqsa 145

Maraj al-Bahrain 43, 110n49
ma'rifa, ma'rifat 90, 111–12, 130, 199, 229n26, 236–7, 274–5, 289, 292
marsiya, marsiya-gu'i 39
Maryam Zamani 260
mashrab 105, 121, 156–7, 160, 171
Masnawi 21, 26n46, 33–5, 38n77, 102, 225, 305, 374, 394
Mathura 171n19, 188
Maturidis 112
maulud, milad 21, 22n39, 278
Mawarannahr, Mawarannahri 55–7, 59, 61, 63, 64n41, 69, 74, 76, 83, 89, 92, 332, 364
Mayar, Battle of 19
mazhab (pl. *mazahib*; school of jurisprudence) 42, 94–5, 98–9, 102–5, 107–8, 112, 121, 144, 156–8, 212, 394
Mazhar Jan-i Janan, Mirza 6, 13, 17, 28, 384
Mecca 73, 126, 140, 146, 159, 260, 263, 289, 303, 363, 366, 373
Medina 13, 115n63, 126, 140, 145, 159, 162, 289, 303, 348–9, 363–4, 373
Mina, Shah 129, 153, 160
Minhaj al-Din al-Siraj 121
Mir Khwand 169n15, 170n17, 198
miracle (*karamat, khawariq, karishma*) 10, 13, 20, 24n44, 29, 86, 349, 368–9; critique of 32–3
mi'raj (Ascension) 135–6
Miran Sadr-i Jahan Pihani 91
Mir'at al-Asrar 43, 56, 94, 96–110, 114–23, 149n33, 166, 190–3, 203–8
Mir'at al-Haqa'iq 96n4, 165n5, 199–201
Mir'at al-Makhluqat 44, 96n4, 141, 160, 165–90, 195–203, 208–14
Mir'at al-Wilayat 96n4
Mir'at-i Madariya 43, 96n4, 115, 123–4, 128, 137–63
Mir'at-i Mas'udi 96n4, 115, 120n75, 160
Mirza 'Aziz Koka 91
misaq (pl. *mawasiq*; covenant) 203
(Al-)Mizan al-Kubra 108n39
Miyan Mir 269–70, 272, 278
Moghulistan 61
Moksopaya 220, 222, 233n33
Moses (Musa) 139, 140, 154n47–8, 159, 207, 214, 394; *wilayat* of 139, 159, 194
Mu'awiya 4n4, 121
Mughal(s): and Chishtis 41–5, 49–56, 69, 78–85, 93, 94–5, 116–22, 123–4, 162–3, 267–9, 272, 278–80, 315, 386–8, 390–2; and Hindus (and other non-Muslims) 26–8, 45–6, 74–5, 122, 124, 126–7, 160–1, 164, 215, 226, 282–3, 341–3, 363, 393, 395; and Naqshbandis 42, 46, 48–50, 55–6, 60–78, 84–93, 95, 110–14, 122–3, 160–2, 285–301, 302–5, 315–16, 318, 320–30, 331–45, 351–88, 391–2, 396; and Qadiris 46, 118–19, 267–78, 280–3, 315, 318, 391–3, 395–6; and Shattaris 66–7, 93, 119n72, 331; and Shi'is 74, 121, 160,

315; and Sufis 4–9, 41–3, 46–7, 48–94, 124–7, 389–96
Mughal princesses 46, 260–330, 396
Muhammad. *See* Prophet Muhammad
Muhammad Akbar, Prince 302
Muhammad Amin Badakhshi 373n97, 376–7
Muhammad Ashraf, Shaikh 335–6, 364, 377n106
Muhammad A'zam, Prince 334, 358–9, 361, 380, 386
Muhammad Baqir of Lahore 357–8
Muhammad Beg Uzbeki Burhanpuri, Shaikh 377
Muhammad Da'ud Gangohi, Shaikh 8, 363n79
Muhammad Farrukh, Shaikh 365, 367, 372
Muhammad Ghaus of Gwalior, Shaikh 67
Muhammad Ghausi Shattari 129, 131–2, 133
Muhammad Gujarati, Saiyid 118–19
Muhammad Hakim, Mirza 69–70, 78
Muhammad Ihsan, Kamal al-Din 334, 339, 345n35, 361n77, 363n80, 365n84, 380–1
Muhammad Ishaq Dehbidi, Shaikh 85
Muhammad Kam Bakhsh, Prince 366
Muhammad Kazim (historian) 284–5
Muhammad Lutf-Allah (son of Shaikh Muhammad Sa'id) 355
Muhammad Mahdi ibn Hasan 'Askari (imam) 141, 143–5, 156
Muhammad Ma'sum, Shaikh 10, 120n75, 284–6, 294, 296, 304, 334–65, 373–5, 377n106, 379, 385–6
Muhammad Mu'azzam, Prince (future Bahadur Shah) 358, 380–1
Muhammad Muhsin of Delhi 358
Muhammad Muqtada Amkinagi, Khwaja 86
Muhammad Murad Kashmiri 365, 372n95, 378
Muhammad Naqshband, Shaikh 304–5, 320, 335–6, 339, 350n48–9, 364–7, 377, 379, 381n114
Muhammad Parghari, Maulana 66–8
Muhammad Parsa, Khwaja (deputy of Baha al-Din Naqshband) 89n101, 97
Muhammad Parsa, Shaikh (son of Muhammad Ma'sum) 363, 366
Muhammad Qasim Nanautwi 20
Muhammad Qazi, Maulana 65n42, 77
Muhammad Sadiq (17th c. historian) 64, 65n42, 129, 132–3
Muhammad Sadiq, Khwaja (son of Ahmad Sirhindi) 338
Muhammad Sa'id, Shaikh 335–7, 350n49, 353–7, 365, 372, 375
Muhammad Saif al-Din, Shaikh 283, 286–300, 335–6, 350n49, 357–61, 365–6, 374, 377n106

Muhammad Shah, Emperor 381, 384, 387
Muhammad Sharif, Khwaja 333
Muhammad Sibghat-Allah, Shaikh 335–6, 364, 377n106, 380
Muhammad Siddiq, Shaikh 335, 364, 386
Muhammad 'Ubaid-Allah, Shaikh (son of Muhammad Ma'sum) 335–6, 345n34, 347n39, 350n49, 361n77, 363–6, 373, 375
Muhammad 'Umar (son of Muhammad Naqshband) 366, 371
Muhammad Yahya, Khwaja (son of Khwaja Ahrar) 62–3, 66
Muhammad Yahya, Khwaja (Naqshbandi shaikh during Akbar's reign) 73
Muhammad Yahya, Shaikh (son of Ahmad Sirhindi) 335, 355, 377n106
Muhammad Zubair, Shaikh 6, 334n12, 365, 380–1, 383–5, 387
Muhibb-Allah of Allahabad, Shah 46
muhtasib 361–3
Mu'in al-Din Chishti, Khwaja 8, 79, 83, 84, 97, 115, 117–18, 123, 134, 146, 148, 267–9, 278, 340, 390
Mu'in al-Din, Khwaja (d. 1674; son of Khawand Mahmud) 85
Mu'in, Khwaja (son of Khawand Mahmud 'Khwaja Nura') 69, 71–2
mujaddid (renewer); *mujaddid-i alf-i sani* ("renovator of Islam for the second Islamic millennium") 14–15, 38, 113–14, 339, 345, 349–50, 373, 392
mujtahid 108, 109, 123, 140, 156, 157
Mulla Shah Badakhshi 263, 267, 269–70, 272, 280, 283, 395
Mumtaz Mahal 262
Munafiq 182, 375
Munir Marghinani, Maulana 61
Munis al-Arwah 5, 261, 266–9, 278–80
Muntakhab al-Tawarikh 67n48, 69n51, 129–30, 165n2
Muntakhab-i Jug Basisht 224, 230–5
muqtada (guide, leader) 61, 116
Murad Bakhsh, Prince 395
muraqaba 40, 293–4, 386
murid (Sufi aspirant) 38, 51, 79, 87, 91, 117, 120n75, 133, 148n29, 268–9, 278, 280, 295, 318, 343, 354, 358, 382n117, 385
murshid (Sufi master) 17, 38, 56, 120, 236, 265, 268–9, 271–3, 275, 295, 360, 368, 382, 383
Musa. *See* Moses
Musa Bhattikoti, Mulla 352–3
Musaddas-i Hali 36
Muslim law. *See* Islamic law
Muslim modernist(s) 29–40; critique of Sufism 17–18, 20–6, 28–41
Mutahhar, Qazi 150–1
Muzaffarnagar 18, 22

nabi (prophet) 8, 98, 115, 181n37, 393–4

Nadir Shah 381
Nafahat al-Uns 267, 359
nafs (soul, carnal soul, ego) 14, 32, 64–5, 103, 229, 236–7, 290–1, 293
Na'im-Allah Bahraichi 28
Najat al-Rashid 129–30
Najm al-Din Kubra 139, 145
Najm al-Din Razi 35
Nala-i 'Andalib 165, 382–4
namaz 17, 134
Namiqa dar bayan mas'ala-i tasawwur-i shaikh 30
Naqshbandi(s), Naqshbandiyya 3, 6, 10, 30, 48, 83, 84, 87, 92–3, 94, 97–8, 111, 122, 215, 331, 393; Ahrari 73, 78, 91, 93, 392; and Chishtis 6–7, 9–10, 40–1, 43, 45, 54, 86–90, 95, 110, 111, 114–15, 123–5, 153, 160–3, 208; and Hindus and other religions 26–8, 90–1, 111–12, 341–4, 375, 384; Central Asian 50, 55–66, 68–78, 83, 84–6, 89, 160, 162, 331–3, 351; Dehbidi 332–3, 393; Ju'ibari 76, 332–3, 393; Naqshbandi–Mujaddidi(s) 6, 9, 13, 15, 17, 22, 29, 33, 41–2, 46–7, 48–50, 85–95, 111–14, 118, 120n75, 285–301, 302–5, 315–16, 318, 320–30, 331–88, 391–3, 396; and *shari'a* 43, 57–9, 90–1, 111–14, 295, 338–45, 349, 351, 355–63, 373, 383–4, 391
Narada (Narad Muni) 185–8, 194, 246
Nasir 'Ali Sirhindi 364n83
Nasir al-Din Chiragh, Shaikh 267

Nasirean ethics 395
Nata'ij al-Haramayn 373n97
Nazr Muhammad Khan 332
New World (America) 215–16
Ni'mat-Allah Qadiri, Saiyid 118
Ni'mat-Allah Wali, Shah 142, 233
Ni'mat Khan 'Ali 306–7, 367–71
nisba, nisbat (spiritual connection) 12–13, 19, 359–60
Nizam al-Din of Amethi, Shaikh 121n76, 390
Nizam al-Din Auliya 55n13, 79, 89, 100, 105, 117, 124, 154n48, 165, 267
Nizam al-Din Aurangabadi, Shaikh 386–8
Nizam al-Din Narnauli, Shaikh 391
Nizam al-Din Thanesari, Shaikh 87–8
Nizam Panipati 45, 167n9, 218, 220, 223–4, 225–30, 234, 235, 239, 242–9
nubuwwat 43
Nur al-Din Muhammad 69, 72
Nur Jahan, Queen 226, 260–1
Nur Muhammad Jhanjhanvi, Shaikh (Miyanji) 18, 19, 40
Nusus al-mulhama fi madh al-a'imma 144
Nyayakusumanjali 211

Ottoman Empire 57, 109–10

Padmavat 162, 198
Pahlawi 395
Panchatantra 234
Pandava(s) 187, 189, 190n51
Panipat, Battle of (1526) 52, 64
Paradise 5, 135–6, 193

Parvati 172–8, 180, 182–5, 250
Payam-i Mashriq 37–8
Persia 203. *See also* Iran
Persian: language 96, 161, 393, 395; Hindus learning 51; Indian poets of 26, 96, 261, 278, 301–14, 364n83, 374n98, 381–3; poets and poetry 35, 38, 104, 148, 225–6, 233–5, 238–9, 301–14, 382–5; translations into 45–6, 79n79, 164, 167, 172–4, 187, 196, 201–3, 217–58
Persianate 51, 202, 235, 242, 244, 245, 256, 264
Philosophy, Greek 112, 203, 204; Hellenistic 11; Platonic 39; Roman 203
Philosophy, Indic 208–14, 217–19, 244; Charvaka 211–12; Mimamsa 211–12; Nyaya 211; Vedanta, Vedantic 39, 212, 220, 240, 395
Philosophy, Islamic 39–40, 212n85
Phul (or Bahlul) Shaikh 66–7
pir (Sufi master) 2, 19, 22n39, 49, 53–7, 86, 87, 318, 339, 357, 361, 364, 368 ; royal 80, 82, 84, 100, 111, 131, 148, 392
pir-o-murid, piri-muridi 4, 5, 18, 56, 87, 148n29, 267, 317, 354; critique of 30–31
Pir Shattari, Shaikh 120
Plato 212–13, 308, 310–11, 329
Prabodhacandrodaya (Praboda Chand Uday) 241n54
Prophet(s) 8, 27n30, 28, 32, 44, 94, 101, 132, 141–3, 154n48, 168–9, 179, 181, 194, 214, 293–4, 339, 389, 394; Biblico-Islamic 99, 107, 115, 139, 150, 159, 167, 194, 205, 214, 340, 348
Prophet Muhammad 10n11, 11–12, 17, 18n33, 21, 30, 31, 36n70, 37, 43–4, 58, 75, 85, 89, 90, 96, 98–101, 106, 108–9, 111, 115n63–4, 123–4, 131–2, 135–7, 140, 143–50, 154n48, 156–9, 167, 169, 170, 172, 178, 180, 182, 194, 196–201, 205–7, 225, 231, 267–8, 273–4, 278, 283, 289, 299, 310, 320, 338–40, 342, 344–50, 352, 354, 355, 360, 364, 375, 380–1, 393–4; as Ahmad 139–40, 145–6, 200; and his descendants 96, 123, 137, 144–5, 181–4; as Mahamat 178–80; and his parents 178–9
Punjab 51, 70, 78, 80, 85
Purana(s) 44–5, 167–8, 172, 173n23, 174, 179, 183, 195–7, 202, 209, 241
Pythagoras 212n85

Qadir Shah 151–2
Qadiri(s), Qadiriyya 3, 6, 27, 30, 31n57, 37, 40, 46, 83, 94, 119–20, 217, 267–78, 280–1, 283, 285–7, 290–1, 293, 298, 315, 318, 387, 391, 394–6
qaiyum, qaiyumiyat 6, 10, 304, 334–5, 345–6, 364–5, 377, 379–82, 384
(Al-)Qaiyum (God) 15
Qandahar, Kandahar 68

Qasim Hisari Naqshbandi, Khwaja 332–3
(Al-)Qaul al-Jamil 30
Qawaʻid al-Tasawwuf 43
qazi (judge) 8–9, 61, 154n48, 368, 371, 379
Qidwaʼis 152–5
qiyam 21
Qiyamat 31n57, 183–4, 193, 205, 237. *See also* Day of Judgment, Resurrection
Qiyam al-Din, Shaikh 152
Qunawi, Sadr al-Din 15, 34, 203–4
Qurʼan 28, 29, 30, 111, 122, 140–3, 154, 169, 172, 175n28, 176n29–30, 178, 180, 190n51, 195, 198, 204n65–7, 206, 214, 231, 265, 271, 276n47, 279, 287, 289, 293, 301, 330, 339–45, 375, 378; exegesis of 121, 179, 196–7, 303
Qushairi, Abu al-Qasim 106
qutb (pl. *aqtab*; "the Pole") 97, 117, 118, 129, 140, 159, 289, 346
Qutb al-Din Bakhtiyar Kaki 55n13, 97, 105, 267, 362
Qutb-i ʻAlam, Shaikh 54
Qutb-i Jahani, Sufi (Shaikh Sufi Sharif) 167n9, 201, 223–4, 228–30, 231–2, 235–6, 244, 248, 254

Radd al-ishrak 16
Rauzat al-Safa 141, 169, 170n17
Rae Bareli (Awadh) 16, 386
Rafiʻ al-Din, Shah 13
Rafizi 113, 157

Rah-i sunnat dar radd-i bidʻat 30–1
Rahman ("the Merciful"; a name of God) 27
Rahat Husain Gopalpuri, Maulana Sayyid 178n33
Rai Pithora 115
Rajput, Rajputs 1, 51, 74, 115, 248, 257, 260, 302, 380n110
Rama (Ram, Ramachandra, Ram Chand) 27, 28, 171, 220, 227–30, 236–7, 239, 242, 246, 248, 250–6, 258, 395
Ramayana 220, 234, 235
Ramchandraji Fatehgarhi 28n52
Ranjit Singh 18n32
Rashhat ʻAin al-Hayat 57, 59n23, 77
Rashid Ahmad Gangohi 20, 22n39, 24n44
Rauzat al-Qaiyumiya 334–5, 338–9, 345n35, 361n77, 363n80, 365n84, 377, 380–1
Razi, Fakhr al-Din 303, 344–5
Resurrection (*qiyamat, baʻs*) 35, 204–5, 237
Risala al-Qushairi 106
Risala dar Kawaʼif-i Shiʻa 113n59
Risala-i Iman-i Mahmudi 137
Risala-i Sahibiya 269–78
Risala-i Radd-i Rawafiz 110n48, 112–13
Risala-i Walidiya 65
rishi, rsi (sage). *See* Hindu
Roshanara (Roshan Rai) Princess 46, 261, 262, 283–301, 304, 315–16, 318, 334, 361n77, 396
Rudauli 51, 56, 95, 166
Rukn al-Din, Shaikh 52n6

Rumi, Maulana Jalal al-Din 21, 26n46, 33–8, 41, 102, 107, 225, 233, 292–3, 305, 374, 394
Rushdnama 55, 236

Sab' Sanabil 79n79
Sa'd-Allah of Kantur, Shaikh 148
Sa'd-Allah Khan 4n4, 332, 352
Sa'd al-Din Hamawi 35, 145, 203
sadr 73, 130; *sadr al-sudur* 91
Sadr al-Din al-Qunawi 15, 34, 203
Safavi, Safavid(s) 63, 64n41, 65, 68, 161, 234, 260
Safi al-Din Ardabili (Qazwini) Mulla 303
Safinat al-Auliya' 129, 133–4
Saharanpur 18–19
sajda (prostration) 129
Sakinat al-Auliya' 240n50, 254n80, 278, 288n65, 291n72
Salar Mas'ud Ghazi 115, 120n75, 163
salik 12, 100, 105, 109, 111, 277, 294
Salim Chishti, Shaikh 80, 93, 391
Salima Sultan Begum 69, 72
saltanat 248–9, 256
sama' 4, 8, 11, 20–1, 23, 34, 89, 96, 100, 111, 114, 359, 361–2, 363n79, 384, 388
samadiyat 131, 147–9
Samarqand, Samarkand 57, 59, 61–5, 70–1, 73, 74n66, 77, 259, 289
Sambhal 86, 183
samsara 249
Sana'-Allah Panipati 36n70, 168n12
Sanskrit 44, 154n48, 166, 172, 202, 235; translations into Persian 45–6, 164, 167, 172–4, 196, 201–3, 217–58
Saqi Musta'id Khan 302–3, 359, 371
Sassanian 395
Sat'at 14
Satyartha Prakash 197
Sawanih-i Maulana Rum 33n65, 34
Sawati' al-anwar 7n7, 9n9, 51n3, 56n15, 80, 83n86, 84n91, 361–3
Shafi'i, Abu 'Abd-Allah, Imam 103, 140
Shafi'i, Shafi'ite (school of jurisprudence) 108, 145
Shah Isma'il Safavi 63–5
Shah Jahan, Emperor 4, 46, 99, 132, 233n35, 261–2, 264, 269, 270, 274, 277n49, 281, 285, 315; and Chishtis 118, 120–2, 390; and Naqshbandis 332–4, 351–3, 358, 362, 376, 386, 392; and Qadiris 280; and Sufis 4n4, 387–8
Shah Jahan II, Emperor (r. 1759) 384
Shah Rukh, Mirza (16th c.) 74n66
Shah Tahmasp 68, 260
Shahabad 51–2
Shahrukh Mirza (r. 1405–47) 259
Shaibani Khan 63–4
Shaikh al-Islam 61, 63
Shams al-Din Turk Panipati, Shaikh 97
Shankaracharya (Shankaracharj) 183n41, 210
Sharaf al-Din Husain, Khwaja (Mirza) 71–3, 81

Sharaf al-Din Yahya Maneri, Shaikh 55n13, 104, 117
(al-)Sha'rani, 'Abd al-Wahhab 107–9, 110n46, 126
Sharh-i Adab al-Muridin 104, 117
shari'a, shari'at (religious law) 8, 16–17, 21, 22n39, 23–6, 42–3, 55, 57–9, 90–1, 104–9, 111–14, 124, 131, 133, 142, 170, 173, 177, 180, 182, 186, 198, 252n75, 256, 264–5, 272, 282n56, 295, 338–51, 355–6, 363, 372, 376–9, 383–4, 391, 393–5
Sharqi (dynasty) 130, 155–9
Shattari, Shattaris, Shattariyya 66–7, 87, 93, 119n72, 120, 129, 131–3, 331
Shawahid al-Nubuwwa 144–5
Sher Shah Lodi 53–4, 67, 69
Shibli Nu'mani 21n38, 33–6, 266n20, 301n90, 302n93, 306, 307n105, 313n115
Shihab al-Din Qidwa'i, Qazi 152–5
Shihab al-Din Daulatabadi, Qazi 128n1, 130–1, 150
Shihab al-Din Ghuri 115
Shi'a, Shi'ism, Shi'i 63, 64n41, 74, 112–13, 126, 161, 208, 234, 315, 384; heterodox 63; Isma'ili 350; and Sunni 10, 99, 121, 126, 141–5, 160, 357, 371, 375–6, 393–4; Twelver (*Isna 'Ashari*) 97, 144
shirk 16n28, 22
Shiva 169n15, 173n23, 187, 194
Shivaji 263, 301

shloka (*ashlok*) 27, 174, 186, 211–12
shuhud (perception) 88
shuhudi, shuhudiyat. See *wahdat al-shuhud*
sifat (attribute) 8, 277, 288, 291–2, 294
Sikandar, Prince of Bijapur 371
Sikandar Lodi, Sultan 51
Sikhs 18n32m 29, 381
silsila (spiritual lineage) 5, 6, 9, 18, 34, 36–7, 56, 57, 63n39, 75, 79, 83, 92, 95, 97–8, 131, 133, 146, 148, 153, 160, 267, 273, 334, 341, 349, 358, 361, 365, 368, 387, 391–2, 394; critique of 30
Silsilat al-Zahab 341
Sirat al-Mustaqim 14, 16–17
sirat-i mustaqim (the Straight Path) 99–102, 141, 146, 157
Sirhind 46, 297, 347, 349, 367, 379, 380, 381
Sirhindi Naqshbandis. See Naqshbandi–Mujaddidi *under* Naqshbandi
Sirr-i Akbar 236, 241n56, 252n74, 395n7
Solomon 154n48
South Asian Islam and Muslim 22, 29, 37, 41–2, 94, 114, 118, 124, 127, 193, 389, 392
Sufi(s), Sufism: antinomian and unorthodox 44, 128, 134–7, 157, 162; cosmology and cosmogony 100n11, 101, 198–201, 203–8; Hindu scriptures and 167–202, 208–16; and Hindus and other religions 26–8, 44–5, 55,

124–6, 134, 141–3, 152–5, 161–3, 165–256, 393; and jurisprudence 42, 43, 95, 98, 99–100, 102–4, 106–10, 112, 125; and *shariʻa* 42, 43, 106–10, 111–14, 391, 394
Sufi, Shaikh 121n76
Sufi Badhani, Shaikh 8
Sufi Saʻd-Allah Kabuli 358
Suhrawardi(s), Suhrawardiyya 55n13, 86-7, 94
Suhrawardi, Shihab al-Din 213n85
Sulaiman Nadwi, Saiyid 36, 39
Sulaiman Shukoh, Prince 333
Sulaimanacaritra 154n48
sulh-i kull 26, 45, 116, 121, 124, 126, 156, 160, 339n20, 341–2, 393
Sultan, Sayyid 194
Sultan Khwaja (Khwaja Abd al-ʻAzim) 73
suluk (treading the Sufi path) 157, 236, 237, 239
Suluk al-Muluk (of Fazl-Allah ibn Ruzbihani Isfahani) 64n41
sunna, *sunnat* (Tradition of the Prophet) 8, 16–17, 22n39, 30–1, 43, 75, 89–90, 102–3, 111, 124, 339, 355n62, 383, 391
Sunni 2, 20, 54, 75, 125, 129, 315, 353, 374; and Shiʻi 10, 99, 112–13, 121, 126, 141–5, 160, 208, 357, 371, 375–6, 384, 393–4
Surat (port) 262–3
Suta and Saunaka (Sut and Saunak) 174, 179, 184–5, 187–8

Syed Ahmad Khan 29–33, 35
Syria 44, 139, 159, 334

taʻassub (bigotry) 103, 121, 145, 168
taʻayyun-i awwal (first differentiation) 101n11
Tabaqat-i Nasiri 121
Tabaqat-i Shahjahani 65n42, 83n87, 129, 132–3
(Al-)Tafhimat al-Ilahiya 13
Tafsir al-Kabir 303, 344
Tafsir-i Zahidi 172, 198
Tahzib al-Akhlaq (journal) 32n59
Taj al-Din Sambhali, Shaikh 86–7
tajalli (pl. *tajalliyat*; epiphany) 14, 89, 238–9
tajrid 132, 229, 236
tanasukh 209–10, 212
tanazzulat 11, 12, 14
(al-)Tanbih al-Tarabi fi Tanzih Ibn al-ʻArabi 23–6
taqlid 103
taqwa 29, 139
Taqwiyat al-Iman 16–17
Tardi Beg 54, 82
Tarikh-i Alfi 116n67, 349, 350n47
Tarikh-i Firishta 51n4, 165n2
Tarikh-i Hukama 204
Tarikh-i Iradat Khan 382
tariqa 5, 12, 21, 90, 131, 165, 359, 367, 387
Tariqa-i Ahmadiya 378–9
Tariqa-i Muhammadiya (of Saiyid Ahmad Shahid) 14, 17
Tariqa-i Muhammadiya (of Muhammad Nasir ʻAndalib) 383–4
tasarruf (control) 57, 115

tasawwuf 4, 10–11, 13–14, 16n27, 17–18, 20, 24, 26, 28, 31–43, 50, 55, 79, 86, 90–1, 94, 98, 101, 103, 106, 111, 114, 120, 125, 128, 147, 225–6, 351, 372, 391, 396
tasawwur-i shaikh, critique of 17, 30
Tashkent 58–60
tauhid 15, 16n28, 34, 39, 88, 111, 114, 171, 199, 201, 251, 275n46, 289, 296
Tauqi'at-i Kisrawi 395
tawajjuh 291, 294, 369, 380
Taiyib Khwaja Ju'ibari 333–4
Tazkir al-Ikhwan 16
tazkira (biographical dictionary) 7, 43, 52, 54, 56–7, 60, 80, 82–4, 86, 94, 97–8, 106, 128–9, 132–3, 137, 147, 181, 217, 267–8, 278, 305–6, 336, 354, 382
Tazkirat al-Auliya 103
tazkiya-i nafs (purification of the soul) 20
Thana Bhawan 22
Thanesar 51n3, 80, 84
time 205–7, 211–15, cyclical 184, 190–3, 197; linear 184; Islamic 214; Hindu 214; pre-Adamite 193, 215
Timur 2, 56, 121, 132, 259, 273–4, 309, 387
Timurid(s) (of Central Asia) 63, 70, 76, 259–60; and Naqshbandis 50, 56–65, 68–70, 76–7, 92, 160, 387; queens and princesses 259–60
Torah, Taurah (Old Testament) 139, 180

transmigration of the soul 184, 209–10, 212, 243, 249
Transoxiana, Transoxianan. *See* Mawarannahr
Turan and Turani(s) 1, 122, 353, 387–8. *See also* Central Asia
Turkestan 58, 59, 77
Turkish 315

'Ubaid-Allah, Khwaja (son of Baqi-Billah) 100n10
'Ubaid Allah Beg, Mirza 339–43
Udayanacharya (Udayana) 211–12
'*ulama* 1, 26, 29, 51, 143, 144, 150, 208, 340, 355–6, 373, 377, 393; and Sufis 20–2, 45, 63, 88, 106, 109, 120, 122–3, 155–8, 160; Twelver Shi'i 144; *zahir* 143, 156–7
'Umar (the second Pious Caliph) 113, 345, 375
'Umar Shaikh Mirza 60
Umayyad(s) 123, 156, 182
umma, ummat 98, 143, 157, 350
Upanishads 27, 235, 241n56, 252n74, 395
Urdu 166, 196–7, 376; language, poets and poetry 38, 384–5; translations into 16, 239
'*urs* 8, 20–1, 44, 133, 362
'*Urwat al-Wusqa* 101
(Al-)'Urwa li ahl al-Khalwa wa al-Jalwa 101n14
'Usman (the third Pious Caliph) 347
'Usman, Shaikh (of Bayana) 118
Uttarakhanda 168, 202
Uwais Qarani 148n29, 149, 268
Uwaisi(s) 12, 17, 148–50, 268–9

INDEX

Uzbek, Uzbeks 63, 64n41, 76–7, 122, 161, 332–3

Valmiki (Balmik) 227, 230, 233n33, 248, 255
Varnashrama-dharma 184
Vasistha, Vasishtha (Bashist, Bashisht Muni, Vasista) 167–8, 171, 173–4, 179, 184–6, 197, 219–22, 227–30, 232, 236, 239, 250–4, 395
*Veda*s *(Bed)* 28, 178–80, 186, 188, 190, 194–5, 201; *Atharva Veda (Atharban Bed)* 141, 178–9, 182; *Rg Veda (Rig Bed)* 141, 178–9; *Sama Veda (Siyam Bed)* 141, 178–9; *Yajur Veda (Jajar Bed)* 141, 178–9
Vishnu (Bishan) 177–8, 183, 194
Visvamitra 242, 245–8
Vyasa (Vyas, Byas, Biyas) 171, 174, 179, 180, 186–8, 201, 209–10, 212, 246

wahdat 100–1, 117, 132, 199, 232
Wahdat (Shah Gul), Shaikh 'Abd al-Ahad 10n12, 304–5, 312, 316, 321–30, 336, 350n49, 365, 367, 372–3, 377n106, 378–9, 381–2, 384–5
wahdat al-shuhud (Unity of Perception) 4, 11, 13–15, 38, 41, 101, 153, 339
wahdat al-wujud, wahdat-i wujud (Unity of Being) 4, 10, 11, 13–15, 23, 26, 34, 38, 41, 79, 89n101, 96, 98, 100, 132, 151, 153, 156, 162, 199, 239, 283, 287–8, 296, 298, 339n20, 341, 384

Wahhabi(s), Wahhabism 17, 22, 31
wahidiyat (Oneness) 100–1, 199
wajib al-wujub 204, 292
wajd, wijdan (ecstatic passion, trance) 8, 26, 34, 86, 90, 277, 295
Waqi'at 'Ammat al-Wurud 32
wali (pl. *auliya*'; saint) 11, 24, 26, 98, 106, 108, 115, 121, 344, 393–4
Wali-Allah, Shah 9–16, 18, 20, 26, 29, 30, 36n70, 40, 42, 110n46, 113n59, 124n83, 377
Waqa'i'-i Ni'mat Khan 'Ali 367–71
Wazih, Mirza Mubarak-Allah Iradat Khan 382
wilayat (sainthood; authority) 43, 84, 91, 98, 117, 139, 145, 155, 159, 160, 289, 347, 348, 368; and *nubuwwat* (prophethood) 98, 393; *wilayat-i kubra* 293, 299; *wilayat-i Muhammadiya* 144; *wilayat-i Musawi* 139; *wilayat-i sughra* 289; *wilayat-i 'ulya* 289, 293–5
Wilayat (Central Asia) 347
wujud (being, existence) 10n12, 13–15, 88–9, 100n11, 153, 175, 237, 292–3
wujudi. See *wahdat al-wujud*

Yaqin, In'am-Allah Khan 384
Yamuna 51, 52, 199
Yarkand 77
Yemen 334–5
Yoga *(Jog)* 194, 219, 244n63, 252
Yogasastra 241

454 INDEX

Yogavasistha, Yoga Vasistha 27, 166–7, 201, 217–58; *Atwar dar Hall-i Asrar* of Qutb-i Jahani 228–30, 236–7; *Jugbashist* of Dara Shukoh 217–19, 239–58, 395; *Jug Basisht* of Nizam Panipati 225–8; *Laghu Yogavasistha* 220–1, 223–4, 226, 233n33, 239, 249; *Minhaj al-Salikin* (Urdu translation of Dara Shukoh's version) 239; *Muntakhab-i Jug Basisht* of Findiriski, 230–5, 237–9; translations into Persian 45–6, 217–19, 223–58
Yogavasistha-sara 223n18, 224, 229
yogi (jogi) 44, 112, 134–7, 151, 176, 342
Yuga (era) 167, 169–70, 183, 188, 191–7, 208, 243: *Dwapara-yuga* (*Dwapar Jug*) 170–1, 173, 179, 191–2, 197; *Kali-yuga* (*Kaljug*) 170, 172, 178, 180, 182–4, 188–9, 191–3; *Satya-yuga* (*Satjug*) 170–1, 173, 179, 191; *Treta-yuga* (*Treta, Tratya*) 170–1, 173, 179, 191
Yunus Khan 61

Zabur (Psalms) 180

zahir (apparent, manifest, outward) 23, 98, 104, 133, 138
Zahiri (school of jurisprudence) 107
Zain al-'Abidin, king of Kashmir 222
Zain al-Din, Maulana 69
zamin-bosi (kissing the ground) 100
zandaqa (heresy, deviance) 90, 111, 208, 378
zat (essence) 8, 11, 292, 346; *zat-i ahad, zat-i haqq* (divine essence) 12, 175, 236; *zat-i mutlaq* (Absolute Essence) 100n11, 274, 280; *zat-i mumkin* (contingent essence) 291; *zat-i wajib al-wujub* (essence of the Necessary Being) 204
zauq (taste, delight) 26, 86, 90
Zeb al-Munsha'at (*Zeb al-Ma'ani*) 305
Zeb al-Tafasir 303
Zeb-un-nisa', Princess 46, 261, 284, 301–18, 320–30, 366, 396
zikr, 288, 290–1, 293, 297, 339, 359, 386; *jahr*, 290, 386; *khafi*, 290, 339, 386
Zubdat al-Maqamat 373

www.ingramcontent.com/pod-product-compliance
Ingram Content Group UK Ltd.
Pitfield, Milton Keynes, MK11 3LW, UK
UKHW041921140426
5217IPUK00014B/252